DATA

MODELING MADE SIMPLE

with CA ERwin Data Modeler r8

first edition

DATA

MODELING MADE SIMPLE

with CA ERwin Data Modeler r8

first edition

Donna Burbank

Steve Hoberman

Technical Editor: Neil Buchwalter

Technics Publications

New Jersey

Published by:

Technics Publications, LLC
966 Woodmere Drive
Westfield, NJ 07090 U.S.A.
www.technicspub.com

Edited by Carol Lehn

Cover design by Mark Brye

Cartoons by Abby Denson, www.abbycomix.com

This book is printed on recycled acid-free paper.

ISBN, print ed. 978-1-9355040-9-2
First Printing 2011
Printed in the United States of America
Library of Congress Control Number: 2011932777

Contents at a Glance

Contents

My love for drawing began in kindergarten, where I created my first works of art using crayons and construction paper. There is no denying that every picture told a story. I chronicled my summer vacations, trips to the beach, and fun times playing in the yard through these pieces of paper that my mother hung on the refrigerator door.

As my school years passed, my artistic talents were called upon in a variety of ways. There were display boards and collages I assembled for history and health classes. The success of my science fair projects depended heavily on the visual presentation. In each of these cases, and many others, I was challenged to tell a story through pictures.

Fast forward to today. I find myself in a profession where I tell stories about data using pictures; what the data modeling community knows as Entity Relationship Diagrams. As a database designer, I call upon the creative, artistic side of my brain to help me succeed in telling those stories. It is not surprising that many successful data architects come from a background in the fine arts. Data modeling is a unique blend of technical skills and creativity.

Information Technology is an ever changing art form. Like the colors of the crayons in a Crayola 64 box that have changed over the years to match current styles and trends, IT development tools and methods have changed to meet the needs of new technologies. As a data professional, I recognize the need to keep my toolset and knowledge current to support these new technologies.

With CA ERwin r8, CA Technologies has enabled a new world for data artists like me with this modeling platform. This release includes functionality enhancements and additions that cultivate the data model artist within me. Whether I chose to color in the lines or dare to venture outside of the lines, CA ERwin r8 allows me to paint the picture of my data in almost any way I desire.

Never invest in any idea you can't illustrate with a crayon.
-- Peter Lynch, author and famous Wall Street investor

Data Modeling Made Simple with CA ERwin Data Modeler r8 is an excellent resource for the ERwin community. The data modeling community is a diverse collection of data professionals with many perspectives of data modeling and different levels of skill and experience. Steve Hoberman and Donna Burbank guide newbie modelers through the basics of data modeling and CA ERwin r8. Through the liberal use of illustrations, the inexperienced data modeler is graphically walked through the components of data models and how to create them in CA ERwin r8.

As an experienced data modeler, Steve and Donna give me a handbook for effectively using the new and enhanced features of this release to bring my art form to life. The book delves into advanced modeling topics and techniques by continuing the liberal use of illustrations. It speaks to the importance of a defined data modeling architecture with soundly modeled data to assist the enterprise in understanding of the value of data. It guides me in applying the finishing touches to my data designs.

My life has changed since my kindergarten days. Gone are the times when I struggled to understand when to use the raw sienna and burnt orange crayons. In my life today, there are many new options, including inch worm, jazzberry jam, mango tango, and wild blue yonder crayons. I look for resources like this book to better understand the complexities of my work and how to effectively use CA ERwin r8. This book will uncover the hidden artist within you and guide your hand as you paint your data world.

Tom Bilcze
President, CA Technologies Modeling Global User Community

Acknowledgements

From Donna

I'd like to thank a number of individuals who were instrumental in bringing this book to light. Above all, Steve, who is a consummate professional. This is our second book together, and it is yet again a pleasure to work with someone as dedicated, intelligent, and forthright—he is a true gem in the industry. Thanks also to Tom Bilcze, for his dedication to the ERwin community, and for the best use of a crayon analogy I have seen to date. Appreciation to Neil, for the weekend metadata discussions. Thanks to Kathy Savard, for answering my persistent questions and for continually working to make the documentation better. Kudos to Pijus Das for being the only one able to answer a final, gnawing technical question. And thanks primarily to my family and friends, for their patience in my absence for the past months, and for acting interested when I bring up relational database theory during dinner conversations. And thanks to Jake, for the mango sorbet.

From Steve

Donna, it was great to work with you again on our second book. Thank you for being such a dedicated team player; you are skilled at 'smooshing' content, and you mow the lawn really well. Thanks to all of the people who volunteer for our data management user groups, such as DAMA – you all help to advance our industry and keep us connected. Thanks Carol, for the superb editing job, Mark for the dynamite cover, and Abby for the great cartoons. Thanks to my family for tolerating my responses to "Dad, can you play with me?", "Honey, it's after midnight", and "Your dinner is getting cold", with "Just five more minutes on the computer and I'll be right there."

Read me first!

Welcome to **Data Modeling Made Simple with CA ERwin Data Modeler r8**. For many of you, this is your first introduction to data modeling. For others, it might be a refresher, or a guideline on how to use the CA ERwin Data Modeler tool. Whatever your reason for picking up this book, we hope you find it a valuable tool to demystify the terminology and techniques that exist around data modeling in general and the CA ERwin toolset in particular. The goals of this book are to equip you with a practical working knowledge of data modeling concepts and best practices, and how to apply these principles with CA ERwin Data Modeler r8. You'll build many CA ERwin data models along the way, mastering first the fundamentals, and later in the book, the more advanced features of CA ERwin Data Modeler.

This book combines real-world experience and best practices with down to earth advice, humor, and even cartoons to help you master the following ten objectives:

1. Understand the basics of data modeling and relational theory, and how to apply these skills using CA ERwin Data Modeler
2. Read a data model of any size and complexity with the same confidence as reading a book
3. Understand the difference between conceptual, logical, and physical models, and how to effectively build these models using CA ERwin's Data Modelers Design Layer Architecture
4. Apply techniques to turn a logical data model into an efficient physical design, and vice-versa, through forward and reverse engineering for both 'top down' and bottom-up design
5. Learn how to create reusable domains, naming standards, UDPs, and model templates in CA ERwin Data Modeler to reduce modeling time, improve data quality, and increase enterprise consistency
6. Share data model information with various audiences using model formatting and layout techniques, reporting, and metadata exchange
7. Use the new workspace customization features in CA ERwin Data Modeler r8 to create a workflow suited to your own individual needs
8. Leverage the new Bulk Editing features in CA ERwin Data Modeler r8 for mass metadata updates, as well as import/export with Microsoft Excel
9. Compare and merge model changes using CA ERwin Data Modelers Complete Compare features
10. Optimize the organization and layout of your data models through the use of Subject Areas, Diagrams, Display Themes, and more

Section I provides an overview of data modeling: what it is and why it is needed. The basic features of CA ERwin Data Modeler are introduced with a simple, easy-to-follow example. Section II introduces the basic building blocks of a data model, including entities, relationships, keys, and more. How-to examples using CA ERwin Data Modeler are provided for each of these building blocks, as well as 'real world' scenarios for context. Section III covers the creation of reusable standards, and their importance in the organization. From standard data modeling constructs such as domains, to CA ERwin-specific features such as UDPs, this section covers step-by-step examples of how to create these standards in CA ERwin Data Modeling, from creation, to template building, to sharing standards with end users through reporting and queries. Section IV discusses conceptual, logical, and physical data models, and provides a comprehensive case study using CA ERwin Data Modeler to show the interrelationships between these models using CA ERwin's Design Layer Architecture. Real world examples are provided from requirements gathering, to working with business sponsors, to the hands-on, nitty-gritty details of building conceptual, logical, and physical data models with CA ERwin Data Modeler r8.

Throughout Section IV, we'll walk you through an example of creating a conceptual, logical, and physical model for a fictitious company called Baker Cakes. Baker Cakes is a family-run business whose main stakeholder is Bob Baker, the owner/operator of Baker Cakes. Bob is in charge of making most decisions, from database design to icing color selection. In our example, we're building a new application for Baker Cakes, who is looking to build a new application to manage their data. They currently have a small, home-grown application built in Microsoft Access, but it's not giving them the information they need. They'd like to start from scratch and build a new system. They would also like to improve their reporting—with the current system it's difficult for them to get basic sales revenue results. Sounds like a challenge? Read Section IV and find out how we solve Baker Cakes' business problem with the help of data models.

If you don't have a copy of CA ERwin Data Modeler available, you can download a free Community Edition at www.erwin.com to get started with your learning process. Answers to exercises as well as sample files and templates can be found at www.erwin.com/datamodelingmadesimple and will be referenced in the book.

Data modeling is more than a job or a career - it is a mindset, an invaluable process, a healthy addiction, a way of life. Remember to Keep It Simple, and enjoy the ride!

Donna Steve

SECTION I
Overview

Section I provides an overview of data modeling: what it is, and why it is needed. The basic features of CA ERwin Data Modeler are introduced with a simple, easy-to-follow example.

Chapter 1 introduces the concept of a data model using a map analogy, and explains how the data model is such a powerful wayfinding tool for multiple audiences at three different levels of detail (conceptual, logical, and physical). Chapter 2 explains the benefits and high level features of a data modeling tool, and Chapter 3 provides an overview of the key features of CA ERwin Data Modeler, along with a step-by-step example of creating your first data model.

CHAPTER 1
Data Model Overview

How do I get there?
Maps, blueprints, data models
Please show me the way

I gave the steering wheel a heavy tap with my hands as I realized that once again, I was completely lost. It was about an hour before dawn, I was driving in France, and an important business meeting awaited me. I spotted a gas station up ahead that appeared to be open. I parked, went inside, and showed the attendant the address of my destination.

I don't speak French and the attendant didn't speak English. The attendant did, however, recognize the name of the company I needed to visit. Wanting to help and unable to communicate verbally, the attendant took out a pen and paper. He drew lines for streets, circles for roundabouts along with numbers for exit paths, and rectangles for his gas station and my destination, MFoods. The picture he drew resembled that which appears in Figure 1.1.

Figure 1.1 Simplification of Geographic Landscape

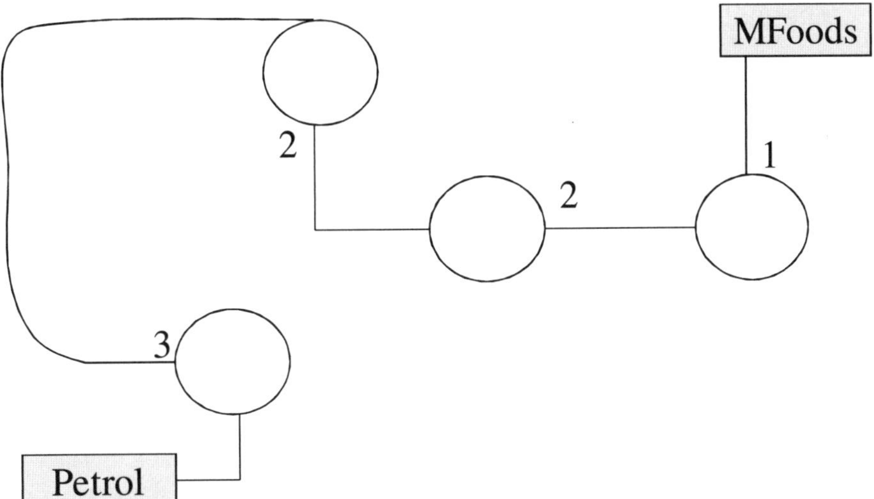

With this custom-made map, which contained only the information that was relevant to me, I arrived at my address without making a single wrong turn. This map was a model of the actual roads I needed to travel.

A map simplifies a complex *geographic* landscape in the same way that a data model simplifies a complex *information* landscape. This chapter explains the data model and its role as an invaluable wayfinding tool.

Wayfinding

If the term 'data model' does not excite you or your business users, try the term 'wayfinding' instead. Wayfinding encompasses all of the techniques and tools used by people and animals to find their way from one site to another. If travelers navigate by the stars, for example, the stars are their wayfinding tools. Maps and compasses are also wayfinding tools.

All models are wayfinding tools. A model is a set of symbols and text used to make a complex concept easier to grasp. The world around us is full of obstacles that can overwhelm our senses and make it very challenging to focus only on the relevant information needed to make intelligent decisions. A map helps a visitor navigate a city. An organization chart helps an employee understand reporting relationships. A blueprint helps an architect communicate building plans. The map, organization chart, and blueprint are all types of models that represent a filtered, simplified view of something complex, with the goal of improving a wayfinding experience by helping people understand part of the real world.

It would probably have taken me hours of trial and error to reach my destination in France, whereas that simple map the gas station attendant drew provided me with an almost instantaneous broad understanding of how to reach my destination. A model makes use of standard symbols that allow one to grasp the content quickly. In the map he drew for me, the attendant used lines to symbolize streets and circles to symbolize roundabouts. His skillful use of those symbols helped me visualize the streets and roundabouts.

A Data Model Represents an Information Landscape

When I was in college, the term 'information overload' was used to mean our brains had reached the maximum number of words spoken by the professor, appearing on her flipcharts, and in the page of notes in front of me. It was time for a stroll around campus, a game of tennis, or a couple of quarters in Space Invaders to get my mind recharged and ready for more. Today however, it seems that we are creating and receiving more and more information, and taking fewer and fewer breaks. I have heard it quoted several times that the amount of information in the world is increasing by over 60% per year! I shudder to myself, wondering what very small portion of all of this information we really, truly understand.

Luckily, there is a tool that can help simplify all of this information - the data model. A data model is a wayfinding tool for both business and IT professionals, which uses a set of symbols and text to precisely explain a subset of real information to improve communication within the organization and thereby lead to a more flexible and stable application environment. A line represents a motorway on a map of France. A box with the word 'Customer' within it represents the concept of a real customer such as Bob,

IBM, or Walmart on a data model. In other words, a map simplifies a complex *geographic* landscape in the same way that a data model simplifies a complex *information* landscape. In many cases, the complexities in the actual data can make those roundabouts in France look ridiculously simple.

Our broad definition of a data model as a set of symbols and text which precisely explain a subset of real information encompasses models in many different forms. Data models can look like the box and line drawings (Entity-Relationship Models) which are the subject of this book, or they can take other forms, such as Unified Modeling Language (UML) Class Diagrams, spreadsheets, or State Transition Diagrams. All of these models are wayfinding tools designed with the single purpose of simplifying complex information in our real world.

Modeling Business Cards

Business cards contain a wealth of data about people and the companies for which they work. In this book, I illustrate many data modeling concepts by using business cards as the basis for a model. I opened the drawer in my nightstand (a scary proposition, as it had not been cleaned since the mid-1980s) and grabbed a handful of business cards. I chose my current business card, a business card from an internet business that we tried to start years ago when dot-com was hot, a business card from a magician who performed at one of our parties, and a business card from one of our favorite restaurants. I changed the names and contact information, and reproduced them here, in Figure 1.2.

Figure 1.2 Four Business Cards from Steve's Nightstand

findsonline.com

Internet Auction Experts

Steve@findsonline.com
Jenn@findsonline.com

Steve and Jenn
(973) 555-1212

What information do you see on these business cards?

Assuming our objective with this exercise is to understand the information on the business cards, with an end goal of building a successful contact management application, let's begin by listing some of this information:

Steve Hoberman & Associates, LLC
BILL SMITH
Jon Smith
212-555-1212
MAGIC FOR ALL OCCASIONS
Steve and Jenn
58 Church Avenue
FINE FRESH SEAFOOD
President

We quickly realize that even though we are dealing with only four business cards, listing all the data would do little to aid our understanding. Now, imagine that instead of limiting ourselves to just these four cards, we looked through all the cards in my nightstand—or worse yet, every business card that has ever been received! We would become overloaded with data quickly.

A data model groups data together to make them easier to understand. For example, we would examine the following set of data and realize that they fit in a group (or spreadsheet column heading) called **Company Name**:

Steve Hoberman & Associates, LLC
The Amazing Rolando
findsonline.com
Raritan River Club

Another spreadsheet column heading could be **Phone Number**. Table 1.1 captures this subset of the business card information in the form of a spreadsheet.

Table 1.1 Subset of Business Card Information in a Spreadsheet Format

	Company	Phone number
Business card 1	Steve Hoberman & Associates, LLC	212-555-1212
Business card 2	findsonline.com	973-555-1212
Business card 3	The Amazing Rolando	732-555-1212
Business card 4	Raritan River Club	(908)333-1212 (908)555-1212 554-1212

Taking this exercise a step further, we can organize the data on the cards into the following groups:

- Person name
- Person title
- Company name
- Email address
- Web address
- Mailing address
- Phone number
- Logo (the image on the card)
- Specialties (such as “MAGIC FOR ALL OCCASIONS”)

So, are we finished? Is this listing of groups a data model? Not yet. We are still missing a key ingredient: the interactions or relationships between these groups. For example, what is the interaction between **Company Name** and **Phone Number**? Can a **Company** have more than one **Phone Number**? Can a **Phone Number** belong to more than one **Company**? Can a **Company** exist without a **Phone Number**? These questions, and others, need to be asked and answered during the process of building the data model.

In order to build any wayfinding tool, one must get lost enough times to know the right path. For example, the first person who builds a map of a region must have taken quite a bit of time and made quite a few wrong turns before completing the map. The process of building a map is both challenging and time-consuming.

The same is true for the process of completing a data model. There is the ‘data model’ and then there is ‘data modeling’. Data modeling is the process of building a data model. More specifically, data modeling is the set of techniques and activities that enable us to capture the structure and operations of an organization, as well as the proposed information solution that will enable the organization to achieve its goals. The process requires many skills, such as listening ability, courage to ask lots of questions, and even patience. The data modeler needs to speak with individuals from many different departments with varying levels of technical and business experiences and skills. The data modeler not only needs to understand these individuals’ views of their world, but also be able to demonstrate this understanding through feedback during the conversation, and also as a final artifact in the form of the model. At the beginning of a project, it is rare that you, as the data modeler, are handed all of the information you need to complete the model. It will require reading through lots of documentation and asking hundreds of business questions.

Catering for Difference Audiences and Purposes

As we mentioned in the previous section, a data modeler needs to work with individuals from many different departments with varying levels of technical and business experiences and skills. When you are speaking to a businessperson, for example, you will use your data model as a communication mechanism to document and define the business rules around the data they need to run their business. A conversation with a database administrator (DBA), on the other hand, is likely to focus on database performance or storage considerations. To speak to these different audiences and generate the information appropriate to each, there are various levels of data models: Conceptual, Logical, and Physical[1].

- **Conceptual**. The audience for a conceptual data model (CDM) is a businessperson, and the goal of the CDM is to communicate core business concepts and their definitions. Think of the CDM as a 'bird's eye view' of an organization's data assets. The CDM contains a very broad view containing only the basic and critical concepts for a given scope, and typically fits on a single piece of paper. Here, basic means that the business concept is usually mentioned a hundred times a day in normal conversation. Critical means that without this business concept, the department, company, or industry would be greatly changed. Some concepts are common to all organizations, such as **Customer**, **Product**, and **Employee**. Other concepts are very industry or department specific, such as **Policy** for the insurance industry or **Trade** for the brokerage industry.
- **Logical**. A logical data model (LDM) represents a detailed business solution. It is how the modeler captures the business requirements without complicating the model with implementation concerns such as software and hardware. The LDM is more detailed than the CDM and typically contains a larger number of objects.
- **Physical**. The audience for the Physical Data Model (PDM) is typically a database administrator or technical database professional. The PDM is the 'incarnation' or 'instantiation' of the LDM and represents a detailed technology solution. It is optimized for a specific context (such as specific software or hardware). A physical data model is the logical data model modified with performance-enhancing techniques for the specific environment in which the data will be created, maintained, and accessed.

[1] Although conceptual, logical, and physical model levels are fairly standard across the data management field, there are other model levels, and other opinions on the subject. For a more robust discussion of data modeling levels, we refer you to the book, Data Modeling for the Business, by Steve Hoberman, Donna Burbank, and Chris Bradley.

Key Points

- Wayfinding encompasses all of the techniques and tools used by people and animals to find their way from one site to another.
- A data model is a wayfinding tool for both business and IT professionals, which uses a set of symbols and text to precisely explain a subset of real information to improve communication within the organization, and thereby lead to a more flexible and stable application environment.
- A data modeling tool provides an automated, graphical way to easily understand information stored in databases.
- Data models come in many different forms. The most common and globally-understood form is a spreadsheet.
- The data model format that is the subject of this book, entity-relationship modeling, is similar to the spreadsheet, yet is type-based, contains interactions, and is extensible.
- Data modeling is the process of building the data model. This process requires many non-technical skills, such as listening ability, courage to ask lots of questions, and patience.
- Data models are created for specific audiences and purposes using data modeling levels (conceptual, logical, physical).

CHAPTER 2
Data Model Tools Overview

Data is Complex
Diverse, Widespread and Siloed
Help Make It Simple

In our example from Chapter 1, we were in a small town in France, where a pencil and paper were enough to draw a simple wayfinding map using symbols and pictures to get the point across. Now imagine if we visited a client in Beijing—a sprawling, metropolitan city that moves at a rapid pace. There is no time to stop at a gas station and have a conversation with the attendant in order to ask directions. With cars and bicycles zipping past us, we need to make a decision quickly regarding which road to take. Unfortunately, the road signs are of little help, since we never studied Chinese in school!

Luckily, the rental car had come equipped with a Global Positioning System (GPS). I had never used one before but, given our predicament, I decided to turn it on. Immediately, we were shown a graphical layout of the roads and were able to pinpoint where we were. A quick press of a button translated the directions from Mandarin to English and a helpful voice calmly gave us step-by-step directions to help us find our destination. After this experience, I was immediately hooked. I would never use a paper map again. First on my list to purchase when I returned home was a GPS for my own vehicle.

There are many similarities between navigating geographic landscapes and navigating information landscapes. Increasing volumes of information, and businesses that run at a breakneck pace can be overwhelming for today's data management professional. Not only are data volumes increasing, but information exists on a variety of platforms in diverse formats. A database administrator in a typical organization can often be responsible for running databases in several 'languages': DB2, Oracle, Microsoft SQL Server, Teradata, etc. And each of these 'languages' can be as different as English from Chinese. Manual processes, such as pencil and paper, or even spreadsheets or drawing tools, are not enough to handle these information volumes in multiple formats and languages. This is where a data modeling tool like CA ERwin Data Modeler comes in. Like a GPS, it is able to translate multiple database languages into an easily understood, graphical format. In an automated way, it provides the roadmap for your information landscape. And, like the GPS, once most data management professionals use a data modeling tool to automate their database maintenance and creation, they'll never go back to manual processes again.

Data modeling tools provide a number of efficiencies that we will discuss next, such as automation, reuse, and error checking, which ultimately reduce the time and money spent on the development and maintenance of software systems. In addition, automation and reuse not only save on costs but increase the quality of information, as common definitions are reused across projects, ensuring consistency. The error-checking features in data modeling tools improve the overall quality of data structures and database design.

Data Modeling Tool Benefits

VISUAL SIMPLICITY

The common element the map and the GPS share in our previous examples is the ability to take a complex environment and display it using a simple, graphical image. In the case of a data modeling tool, it's not roads we need to decipher, but complex data structures that, without a data model, would require technical code to manage and understand. The visual simplicity of data modeling tools is a main factor in their growth in popularity since their introduction in the late 1980s[2]. Consider how difficult it would be to surf the internet without the graphical World Wide Web. Computer-to-computer internet connectivity was available before the graphical web pages we've grown to expect existed, but the Internet did not become popular until people were able to navigate using user-friendly graphics and web addresses.

[2] The ERwin data modeling tool was first launched in 1989. The tool celebrated its 20th anniversary in 2009.

Without getting into the details of data modeling (we'll do that in later chapters), the following examples will give you a general sense of the intuitive, graphical nature of a data model. Compare the Data Definition Language (DDL), which is text-based code that tells the database the structures to create, in Figure 2.1 with the graphical data model in Figure 2.2.

Figure 2.1 Data Definition Language (DDL)

```
CREATE TABLE Account
(
customer_id      char(18) NOT NULL ,
account_id       char(18) NOT NULL
)
go
ALTER TABLE Account
ADD CONSTRAINT XPKAccount PRIMARY KEY CLUSTERED (customer_id
ASC,account_id ASC)
go
CREATE TABLE Customer
(
customer_id      char(18) NOT NULL ,
first_name       char(18) NULL ,
last_name       char(18) NULL
)
go
ALTER TABLE Customer
ADD CONSTRAINT XPKCustomer PRIMARY KEY CLUSTERED (customer_id ASC)
Go
...more
```

Figure 2.2 Graphical Data Model

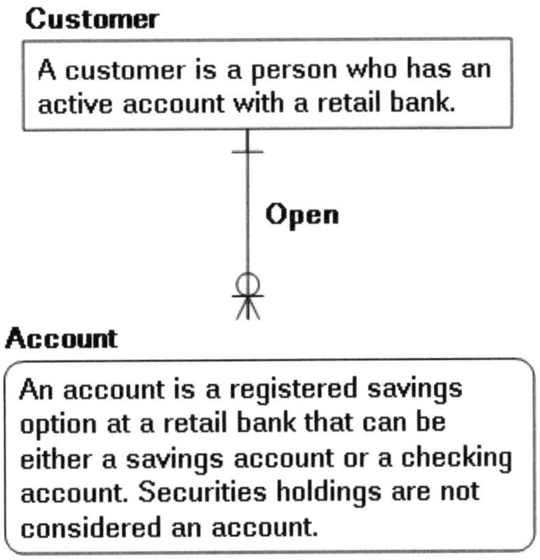

Customer

A customer is a person who has an active account with a retail bank.

Open

Account

An account is a registered savings option at a retail bank that can be either a savings account or a checking account. Securities holdings are not considered an account.

Even without understanding data modeling, you should get a general sense of what the model in Figure 2.2 is trying to express. In a basic sense, we understand that we're talking about customers opening an account at a bank. Figure 2.1 is certainly more difficult to decipher, although it may be useful for a more technical audience.

AUTOMATION

Another benefit of using a data model is automation. Instead of manually writing code to generate data structures, a data modeling tool allows you to generate this code automatically from a graphical design. Software designers use a similar paradigm with visual integrated development environments (IDEs), which allow designers to build their software graphically with reusable buttons, dialog boxes, etc. generate code 'behind the scenes' with little manual effort. Think of a data modeling tool as a 'data IDE', where physical data structures can be generated using visual graphics without having to manually type code, or data definition language (DDL).

The other challenge of coding DDL manually is that each database platform has its own language or 'flavor'. While there are some industry-wide standards such as ODBC (Open Database Connectivity), the majority of major database vendors have customized this standard to create their unique competitive differentiators. Since the average organization has a number of different DBMS systems in house, the database professional would need to learn a different 'language' for each DBMS. Like the GPS that is easily able to translate the visual map into multiple languages, a data modeling tool can generate multiple database 'languages' from the same visual diagram.

REUSE

This basic tenet of "Design once, reuse many times" is a key aspect of the value of data modeling tools. A single visual diagram can be used across the organization to store core information assets such as 'customer', 'product', and 'vendor'. When a new project is built to manage customer information, the developers can reuse the definitions that have already been built in the data modeling tool, saving time and money, and creating objects and definitions that are standardized across the organization.

It's not just database information that can be shared and reused across the organization. A robust data modeling tool can also export definitions to other tools and technologies such as UML (for application development), XML (for web-based application development), or Excel spreadsheets and web-based reports for business users, for example. With this flexibility, a data modeling tool can become a single source of reference for core information assets.

GOVERNANCE AND AUDITS

Using a central, automated data modeling tool also facilitates data governance and auditing. A data modeling tool can easily track who is using information assets and when they have updated them. For example, auditing may require a business to define how a field is calculated and derived on a financial report, or where sensitive patient information is used in a health care organization. A data modeling tool tracks the interrelationships between data elements, and provides the 'where used' analysis that is required for information audits. With the expansion of government regulations such as Sarbanes-Oxley, Basel II, or HIPAA, automated data management tools are becoming the industry standard, as the need to audit and manage information becomes more closely regulated. Can you imagine an accounting department of a major organization using manual, paper receipts, instead of automated systems? Think of a data modeling tool as the 'accounting system' for data.

ERROR-CHECKING AND VALIDATION

Automation also provides the benefit of error-checking, in addition to the benefits of efficiency, reuse, and governance mentioned previously. A data modeling tool can provide valuable validation tools to enforce naming standards, ensure that definitions are provided, and even whether the basic rules of database design have been enforced.

As in many aspects of modern life, we have moved beyond manual processes and require the sophistication of automated tools to assist with the volume and complexity of the information in a typical organization.

Data Modeling Tool Features

With the growth in popularity of data modeling, there have emerged an increasing number of data modeling tool options on the market. As with any good or service, however, there is a wide range of options available, and it is important to choose 'the right tool for the right job'. A professional organization should choose an enterprise-class modeling tool. Just as a major organization wouldn't run its accounting department using a simple spreadsheet, the same organization shouldn't use a simple drawing tool for its data management initiatives.

While the exhaustive list of features required in an enterprise modeling tool are beyond the scope of this book, some of the main differentiators that you should look for in an enterprise data modeling tool include the following:

- **Metadata capture**. Many simple drawing or modeling tools only create a visual picture and lack the feature of storing metadata. In general terms, metadata is text that describes what a user needs to see. Metadata is important because it aids in clarifying and finding the actual data. A robust modeling tool should have a place to store metadata definitions for both business and technical information.
- **DDL creation**. A core value proposition of data modeling is the time savings and consistency created from automated data definition language (DDL) creation. Many drawing or high-level architecture tools don't have DDL generation capabilities, or the level of detail provided in the DDL that is created is very generic. Make sure that the tool you choose supports the DBMSs used by your organization, and that the level of detail provided meets your needs.

- **Information sharing with other tools and technologies**. While a main use case of data modeling is for database creation, there are many other tools and technologies that can benefit from the definitions defined in the data modeling tool. A robust data modeling tool should have information sharing capabilities with a wide range of other technologies, as well as reporting capabilities for the non-technical audience.
- **Versioning and audit trails**. To support governance, an enterprise data modeling tool should support versioning and audit capabilities. Make sure that this versioning occurs at the object-level, not the file level. That is, make sure that you can track the history of an individual data element (i.e. who changed the definition of customer and when).
- **Design layers**. Data models are created for multiple audiences, and an enterprise data modeling tool should accommodate different display options and notations for business-level models and technical models. These different views should be linked so that, for example, you can generate a technical model from a business-level design. As we discussed in Chapter 1, these layers are commonly referred to as conceptual, logical, and physical models.
- **Repository-based model management**. In order to share information across the organization in a consistent and efficient manner, data (or metadata) needs to be stored in a common repository. Think of a repository as simply a common storage container that manages the versioning, change management, and data standards that are built across multiple models in the organization. A single designer may be able to get away without a repository-based management system, but once a team grows to two or more resources accessing model information, it is necessary to have a common 'brain' to manage and share information.
- **Intuitive graphics and layout features**. A data model is your communication mechanism to share valuable information about your organization's data and the business rules that govern that data. Particularly when working with a business audience, the look-and-feel of the model and the ease of reading the diagram are critical. You shouldn't have to use a drawing or presentation tool to build models for a business audience—make sure the tool you choose has a wide array of font, style, layout, and formatting options.
- **Easy to use**. This last item, ease of use, can't be stressed enough. While it is important to have a robust set of features to meet your needs, if the tool is difficult to work with, you will be continually frustrated, and your productivity (and sanity!) will suffer. Make sure that the tool you choose has an intuitive way of performing the basic features you'll need in your daily job. Most data modeling tools have a trial download that you can use to give the product a test run before you make your purchasing decision—take advantage of that.

Key Points

- A data modeling tool helps manage the vast and complex data environments found in the modern organization.
- A data modeling tool adds value to the business through cost reduction and improved data quality by providing visual simplicity, automation, reuse, governance, and error-checking.
- An enterprise data modeling tool should support features such as: metadata capture, data definition language (DDL) creation, information sharing with other tools and technologies, versioning and audit trails, design layers, repository-based model management, intuitive graphics and layout features, and easy to use.

CHAPTER 3
CA ERwin Data Modeler Overview

Go – Give it a Try
Data Modeling with ERwin
Keeping it Simple

CA ERwin Data Modeler has a long history within the data modeling community, and has evolved to include a wealth of features and functions to support the data management professional. It's beyond the scope of an introductory book to cover all of the features of the tool. In this book, we'll provide an overview of the main features of the product that are important to the typical data management professional. We'll outline them in this chapter, and indicate where we'll take a deeper look at each feature later in the book. In this chapter, we'll walk you through a simple example of creating your first data model with CA ERwin Data Modeler, so you'll be familiar with the basic features before we go into greater detail.

Key Features

The following paragraphs outline some of the key features and functions of CA ERwin Data Modeler.

DATABASE REVERSE ENGINEERING AND DISCOVERY

A key challenge that many organizations face today is simply understanding what data they have. With data volumes continuing to grow, combined with a legacy of information silos within departments, often a first task within a data management effort is to create an inventory of existing data assets. CA ERwin Data Modeler helps build an inventory of data assets by extracting the undocumented information contained within databases and database scripts in a process called reverse engineering. See Chapter 19 for more information about database reverse engineering and discovery.

DATABASE FORWARD ENGINEERING AND DESIGN GENERATION

While creating an inventory through reverse engineering can be seen as a 'bottom-up' approach, a key benefit of creating data models is in using a 'top down' approach by creating or modifying designs in the data model, and using the data model to generate data structures for you, a process called forward engineering. In using a data model design for database creation, you get the benefit of reuse and error reduction across the organization, as multiple stakeholders can share, view, and verify the database structures before they are implemented. Design can also happen at the business level, where business rules and requirements are documented in the data model, and then carried forward in the technical implementation. We'll discuss this mix of business and technical requirements definition in the next section on Design Layer Architecture.

See Chapter 19 for more information about database forward engineering and design generation.

DESIGN LAYER ARCHITECTURE

Recall from the Chapter 1 that we defined several levels of data models:

- **Conceptual:** defines a high-level, thumbnail view of core business concepts:
- **Logical:** captures business requirements and describes detailed business rules.
- **Physical:** describes a physical database environment and optimizes that environment for performance and quality.

CA ERwin Data Modeler's Design Layer Architecture was designed to help modelers manage and synchronize these three distinct modeling layers, shown in Figure 3.1.

Figure 3.1 Data Modeling Design Layers

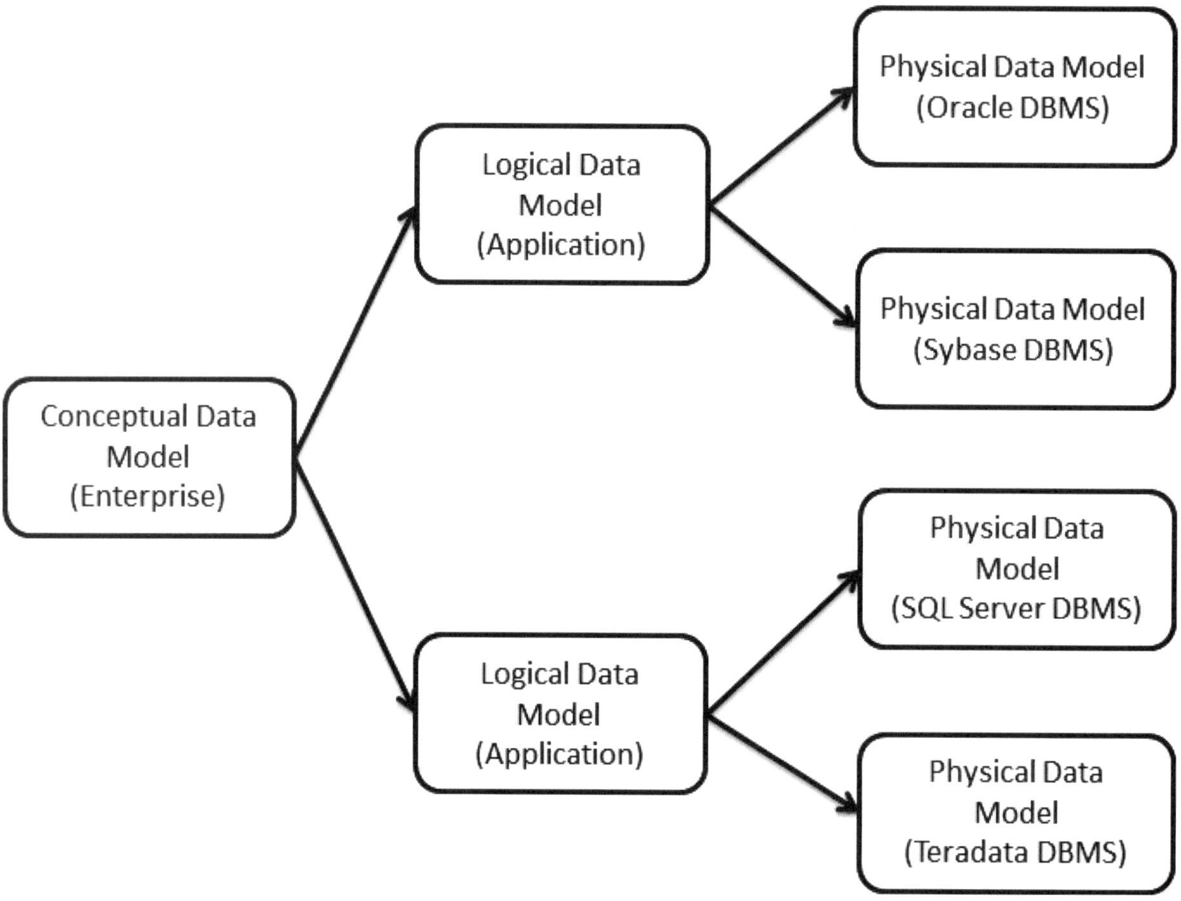

For example, a conceptual data model may show the core business concepts and their definitions, as shown in Figure 3.2. The following examples are taken from the eMovies model that we'll discuss later in the chapter.

Figure 3.2 Conceptual Data Model

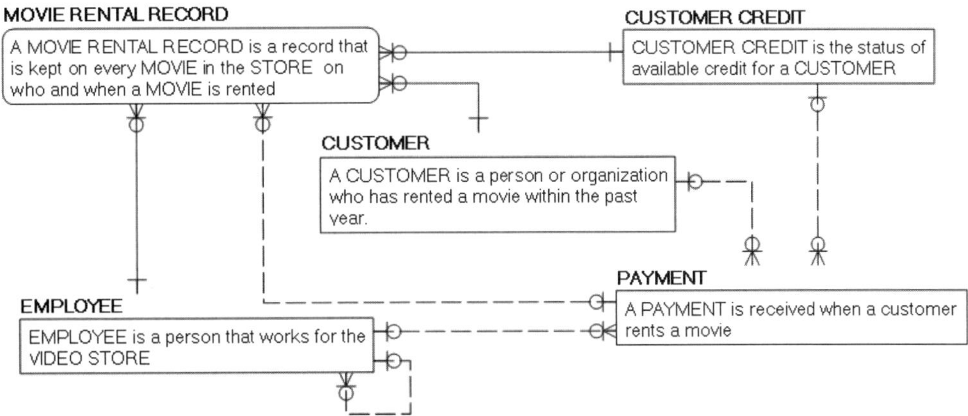

A logical data model is still focused on the business, but shows more detailed business rules (via relationships) and foreign key constraints, as seen in Figure 3.3.

Figure 3.3 Logical Data Model

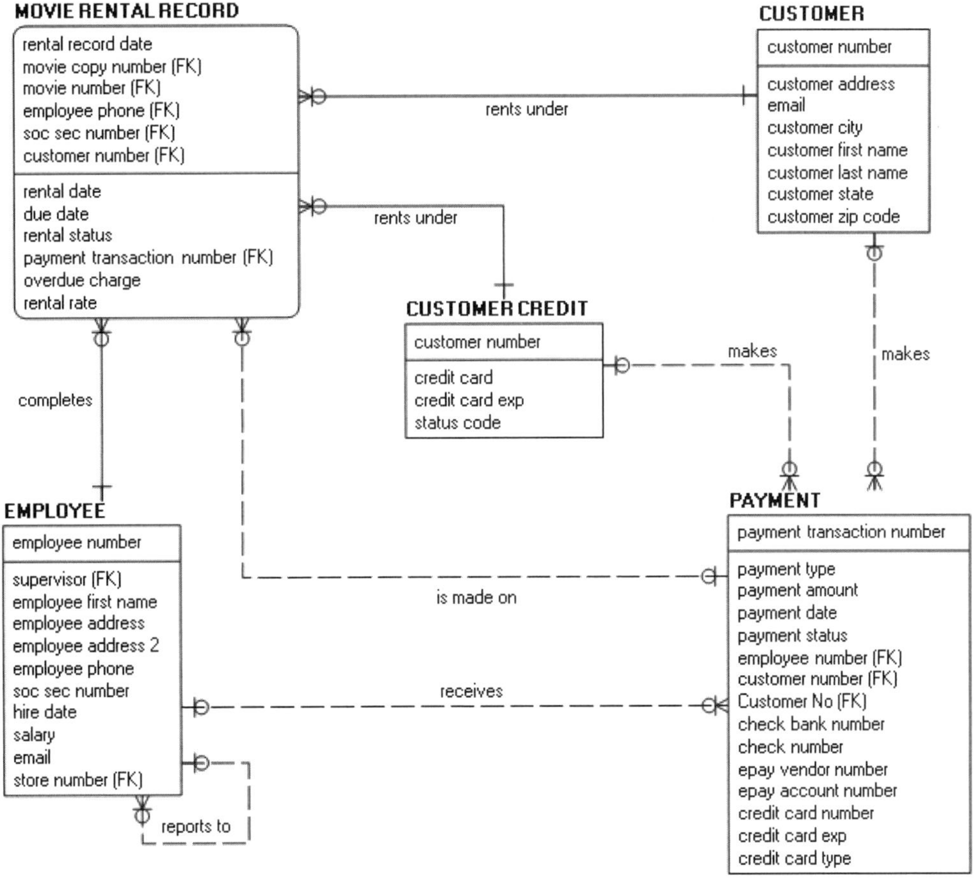

A physical data model describes a physical database implementation on a particular platform, as shown in Figure 3.4.

Figure 3.4 Physical Data Model

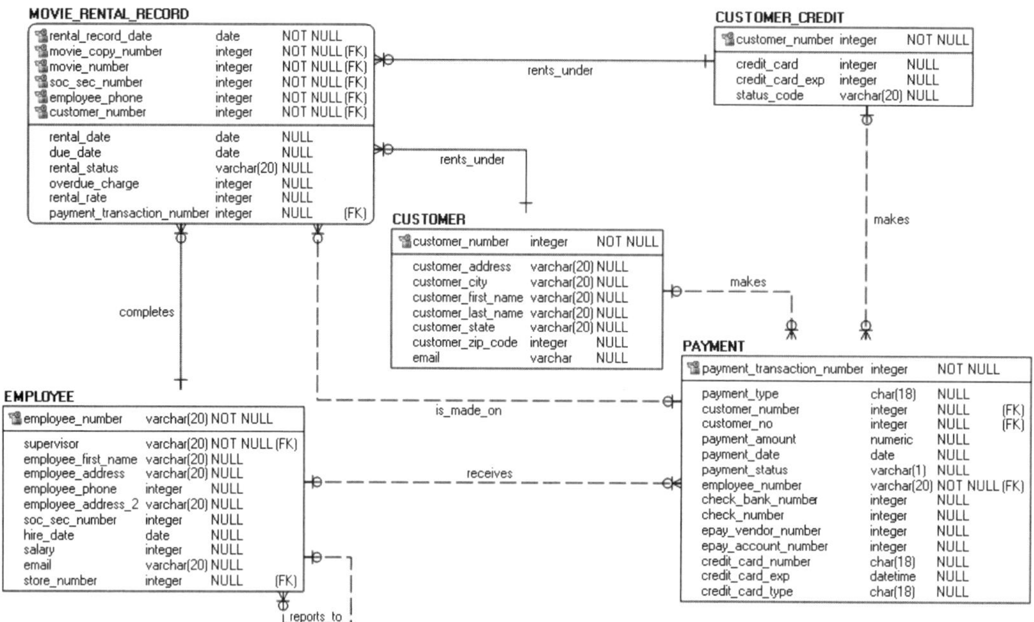

We will go into more detail on how to create and manage design layers in Section IV.

REUSABLE DESIGN STANDARDS

A large part of the benefit achieved in using data models are the quality improvements and increases in efficiency that come from reusing common design standards across the organization. CA ERwin Data Modeler has a number of ways to create and share reusable standards including naming standards, data type standards, model templates, and more. Section II discusses reusable design standards in more detail.

COMPLETE COMPARE

Managing change and creating consistency are dual challenges for today's data management professional. As there are more and more data sources across the organization, keeping these sources in synch is increasingly difficult. This is where CA ERwin Data Modeler's Complete Compare comes in. Complete Compare automates bidirectional synchronization of models, scripts, and databases, compares one item with the other, displays any differences and permits bidirectional update. If model changes are targeted for a database, CA ERwin Data Modeler can automatically generate a script to make these changes (known as an ALTER script). Chapter 19 discusses Complete Compare in more detail.

DIAGRAMMING AND VISUALIZATION

Data models provide a simple, graphic display to visualize complex database structures in an intuitive way. CA ERwin Data Modeler has a number of features to help make your models more visually appealing. Font, color, and layout features are as robust as you'll find in the majority of drawing tools on the market today, so you can create custom displays for different audiences and requirements. Diagrams in CA ERwin Data Modeler provide a way of organizing the various layouts and displays that you create. We'll cover the diagramming and visualization features of CA ERwin Data Modeler in more detail in Chapter 8.

LARGE MODEL MANAGEMENT

CA ERwin Data Modeler provides a number of ways to help you manage large enterprise models. Subject areas provide a logical grouping of data objects, so that you can organize information by organization, subject, role, technology, etc. In addition, advanced features such as auto-layout, on-demand user interface components, and 'bird's-eye' navigation allow you to easily visualize large models. Chapter 9 covers the features that assist with large model management in more detail.

REPORTING AND PUBLICATION

Often, you'll want to share the information in your models through reports. Every copy of CA ERwin Data Modeler is bundled with a copy of SAP Business Objects' Crystal Reports Developer Edition. Users can use out-of-the-box reports, or create their own. A generic ODBC interface is available for those who use other reporting tools. We'll cover reporting in Chapter 16.

PERSONALIZATION AND CUSTOMIZATION

CA ERwin Data Modeler provides a completely customizable solution so that you can personalize your environment to suit your company's individual needs—making your job easier and more efficient. From fully customizable data definition language (DDL) templates on the back-end to custom display themes and reporting on the front-end, CA ERwin Data Modeler allows you to create a work environment suited to your needs. Some specific functionality includes:

- **Display Themes:** Display Themes allow you to create reusable formatting themes for reuse among teams and projects—adding a common look and feel to cross-model efforts. You can customize colors, fonts, backgrounds, borders, etc.
- **User-Defined Properties (UDPs):** give the flexibility to add custom properties to model objects, such as data stewards, document attachments, and more.
- **Macro Language:** provides triggers and stored procedures you can tailor to your business needs.

We'll cover ways to customize your modeling environment in Chapters 8 and 9.

INTEGRATION AND METADATA EXCHANGE WITH OTHER TOOLS

It's easy to integrate CA ERwin Data Modeler with other projects and tools with metadata import or export from a wide variety of sources, including BI tools, MDM hubs, other data modeling tools, Extract, Transform, Load (ETL) tools and Unified

Modeling Language (UML) tools. The metadata exchange capabilities in CA ERwin Data Modeler are described in more detail in Chapter 16.

Starting with a Sample Model – the eMovies Model

Let's start by working with the sample model provided with the installation of CA ERwin Data Modeler, called eMovies. This model is built around a fictitious movie rental company, and provides a good 'real-world' example of the implementation of model design layers, diagrams, subject areas, and many other features that we've discussed already or will introduce in future sections. If you don't have a copy of CA ERwin Data Modeler available, you can download a free Community Edition at www.erwin.com to get started with your learning process. Don't worry if you don't know how to data model yet. Open up the product, walk through the sample model provided, and experiment with building some test models of your own.

To launch CA ERwin Data Modeler from the Windows Programs menu, select **CA|ERwin|ERwin Data Modeler r8|ERwin Data Modeler**, shown in Figure 3.5. Note that this is the default path suggested at installation—your administrator may have changed this configuration.

Figure 3.5 Launching CA ERwin Data Modeler

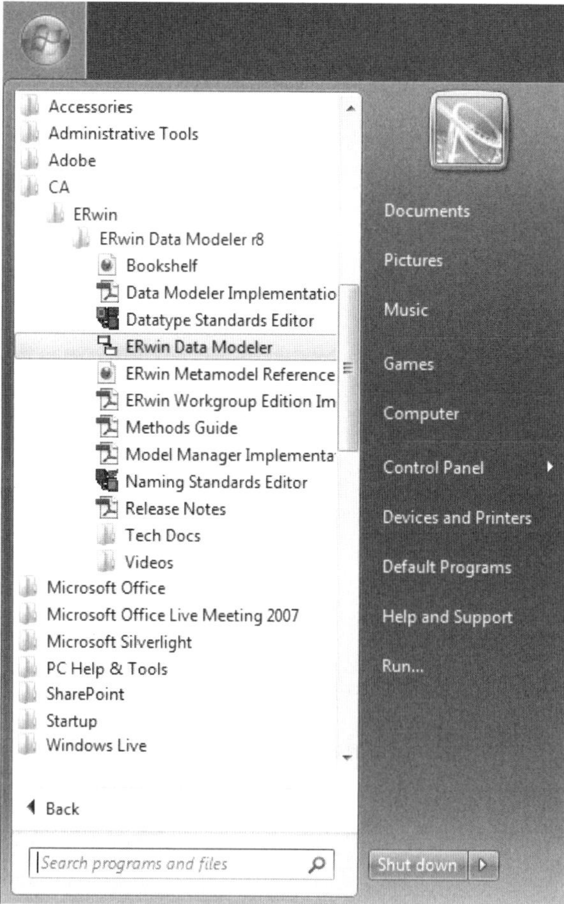

The CA ERwin Data Modeler workspace will appear, as shown in Figure 3.6.

Figure 3.6 CA ERwin Data Modeler Workspace

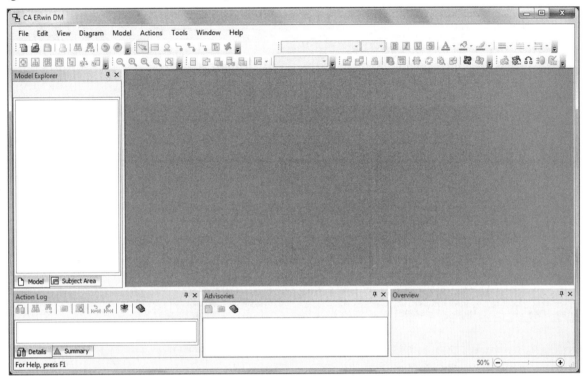

The workspace is initially empty. Since a blank page can be intimidating, let's open the sample **eMovies** file so that we'll have something concrete to work with. Select **File|Open** and the **Open File** dialog will appear. Select the **eMovies** model, as shown in Figure 3.7. The default location for the sample model is found in the **`C:\Program Files\CA\CA ERwin Data Modeler r8\BackupFiles\Samples\Standard`** directory with the file name **`eMovies.erwin`**.[3] The **eMovies** model appears[4], as shown in Figure 3.8, showing several of the main features of the CA ERwin Data Modeler Workspace highlighted with circled letters, A-I. Let's walk through some of the main features of the CA ERwin Data Modeler environment using the **eMovies** example.

[3] Note that the eMovies file is read-only by default, so that you don't overwrite the standard example. If you'd like to customize the eMovies file, it's best to save and rename it as a separate file. We'll walk through how to do this in Chapter 8. Also note that your directory structure might be slightly different, depending on the operating system you're using. For example, when running a 64-bit OS, you may see **`C:\Program Files (x86)`**... indicating that CA ERwin is running as a 32-bit application.

[4] You'll notice that throughout the book, our examples are shown in black-and white, without shadows, while the defaults in CA ERwin Data Modeler have colors, shadows, and shading. For ease of reading in a printed book, we've changed these color schemes. If you would like to follow-along using the same look-and-feel and model properties as the examples, you can download the **`madesimple.erwin_tmpl`** file from the www.erwin.com/datamodelingmadesimple web site. We'll discuss how to use templates in Chapter 15.

Figure 3.7 Opening the eMovies Sample Model

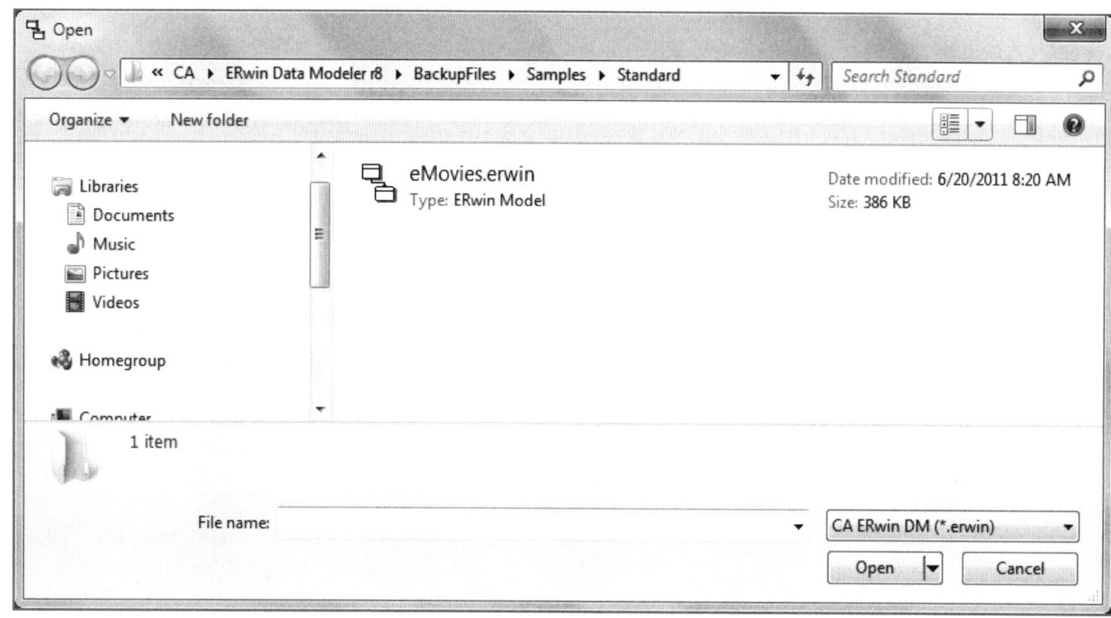

Figure 3.8 The CA ERwin Data Modeler Workspace

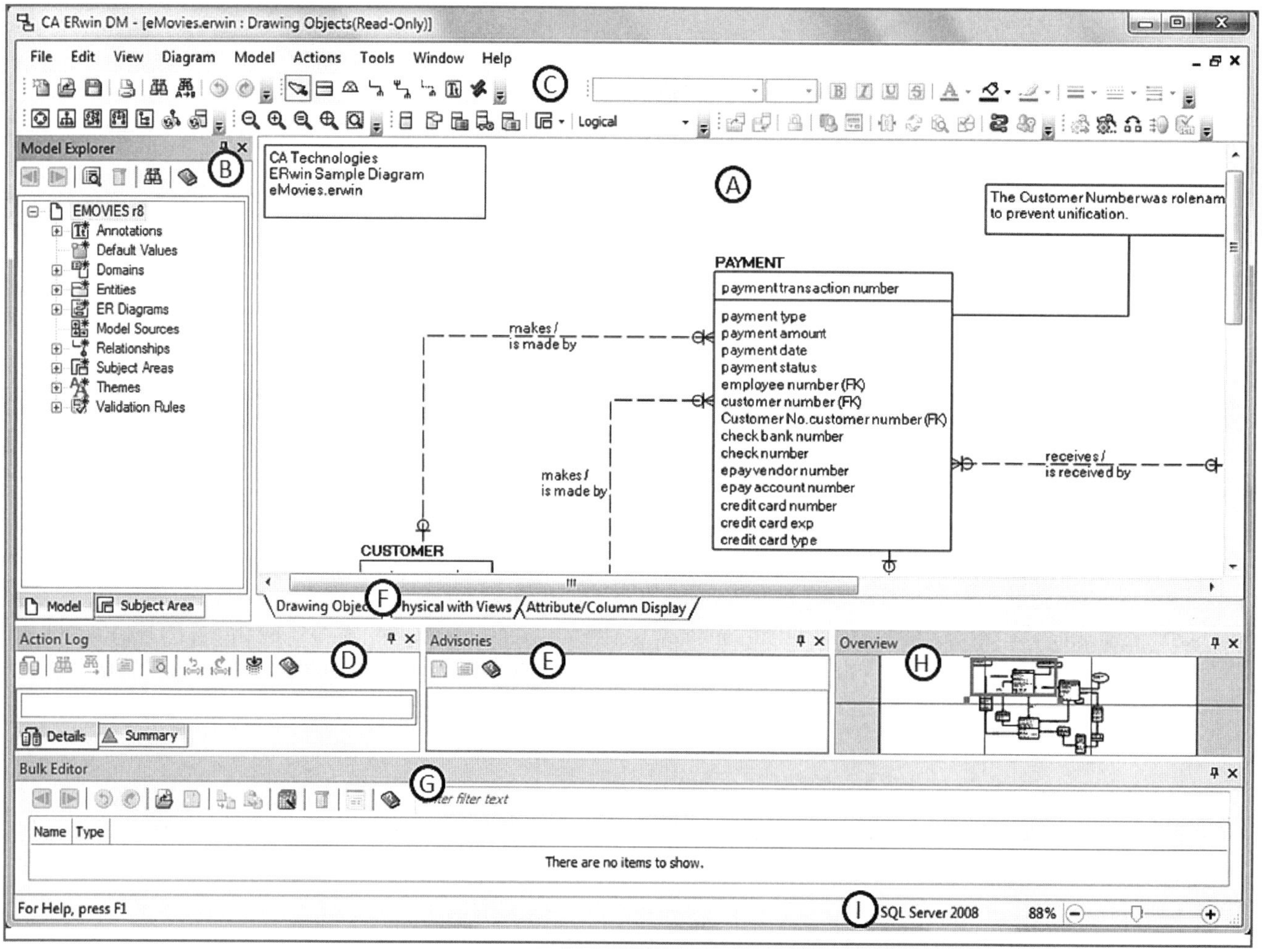

A- Diagram Window: This pane is the main 'drawing palette' where you'll create your graphical models. You'll spend much of your time here working with CA ERwin Data Modeler.

B- Model Explorer: As an alternative to the graphical display in the diagram window, the Modeler Explorer provides a tree-based view from which you can easily add, delete, edit, view, navigate, and organize model objects.

C- Toolbars: There are a number of toolbars that help you quickly perform frequent tasks. Depending on your preferences, the toolbars may be shown or hidden, and toolbar buttons can be hidden or shown. All of the toolbars are dockable so that you can drag them to any location in the workplace and they dock along the edge of the window or let them float freely in the window if you prefer. There are eleven total toolbars including: Standard, Toolbox, Formatting, Layout, Zoom, Display, Mart, Database, Alignment, Drawing, and Transformations. Detailed descriptions of the toolbars and their functionality can be found in Appendix A. Customization of toolbars is covered in Chapter 9.

D- Action Log Pane: The Action Log is a powerful feature in CA ERwin Data Modeler, and goes beyond the standard undo/redo functionality found in many tools. It provides a real-time log of actions you perform, and allows you to selectively choose which items from the log stack you want to undo. We'll go into more detail regarding the Action Log and its features in Chapter 9.

E- Advisories Pane: The Advisories Pane displays messages associated with actions you perform when working with your model. Each message on this pane shows you when a change or edit you make to a property is valid and alerts you when the action you have taken violates a modeling rule. When you receive an alert, you can immediately correct your action instead of searching for the transaction at a later time.

F- Diagram Tabs: As we discussed in the last chapter, Diagrams provide a way to create custom display formats for various audiences or purposes. Within each diagram, you can define display options for diagrams and diagram objects. For example, you might want to display objects and their definitions for a business user, and show all of the technical details to a DBA for the same model or subject area. You'll see that the **<model>** view of the eMovies model has three default diagrams: **Drawing Objects**, **Physical with Views**, and **Attribute/Column Display**, as shown in Figure 3.9. Switch between these tabs to get a good feel for what Diagrams can do. We'll cover diagrams in more detail in Chapter 8.

Figure 3.9 Diagram Tabs in eMovies Model

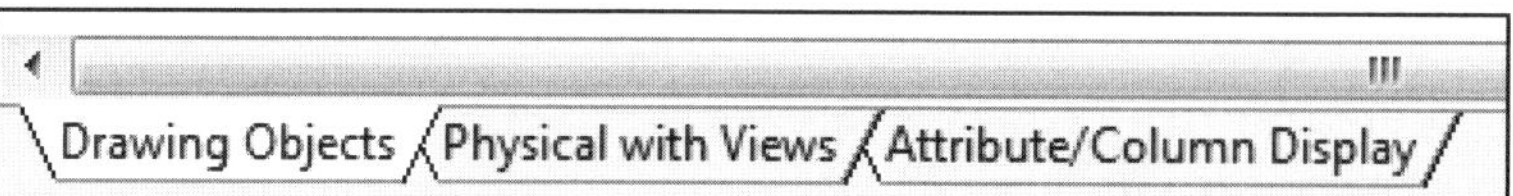

G- Bulk Editor Pane: The Bulk Editor is a powerful new feature in CA ERwin Data Modeler r8 that allows you to update a large number of objects and their properties at the same time in 'bulk', using a spreadsheet-style approach. It also allows for export to Excel, queries, and reporting using a wizard-driven interface. Note: The Bulk Editor is not shown by default in CA ERwin Data Modeler. Select **View|Windows|Bulk Editor Pane** to make it visible in the Workspace.

Users familiar with previous versions of CA ERwin Data Modeler (r7.3 and earlier), can think of the Bulk Editor as the evolution of the Data Browser, which was removed in the r8 release. As one user put it, "The Bulk Editor is Data Browser on steroids". The Bulk Editor is covered in more detail in Chapter 16.

H- Overview Pane: The Overview Pane, shown in Figure 3.10, provides 'bird's-eye' navigation for large models, with the ability to easily zoom in on specific areas of the diagram. Give this a try for yourself. To navigate to a particular area of the model, click on the rectangle in the Overview Pane and drag it to the particular area of the diagram you'd like to focus on. Notice that the diagram in the diagram window moves to match the direction of the rectangle.

Figure 3.10 Navigating with the Overview Pane

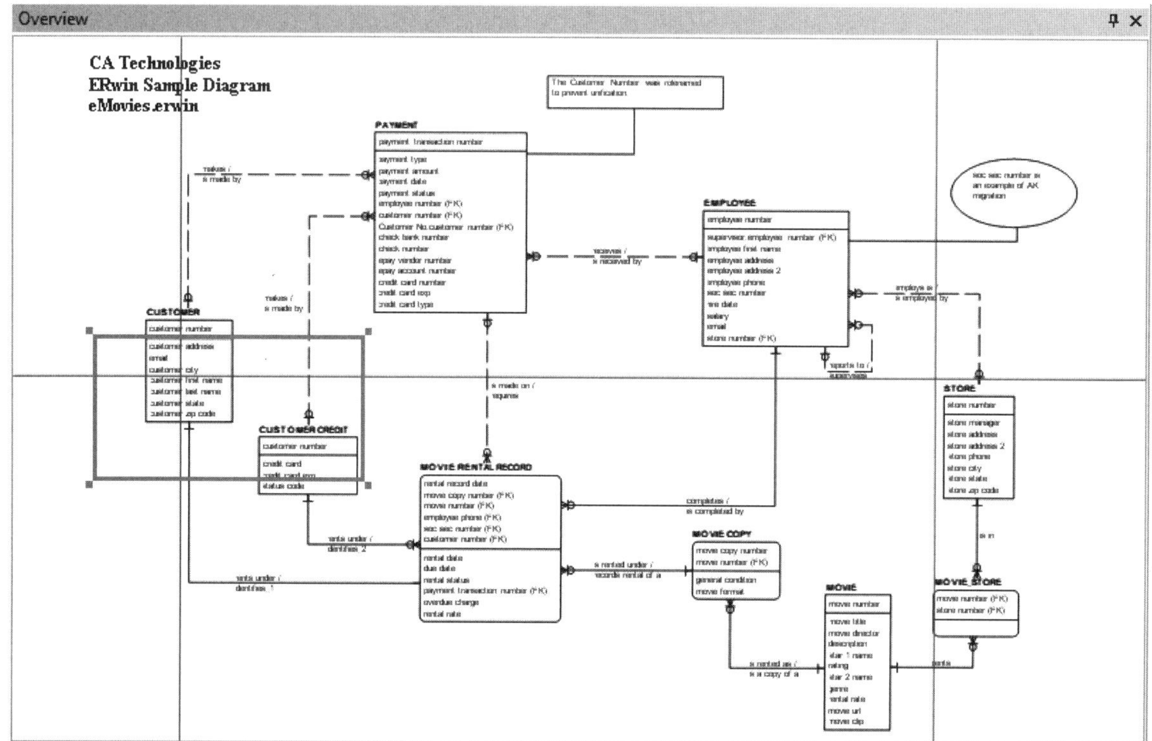

To zoom in on a particular area of the model, click on one of the corners of the rectangle, and drag inwards (i.e. making the rectangle smaller). To zoom out, do just the opposite, clicking on the corner and dragging outwards. The easiest way to understand this is to give it a try and see for yourself.

I- Status Bar: The left-hand side of the Status Bar provides a description for the selected button, menu option, or task that you are performing. On the right-hand side, it identifies the selected target server and zoom level, and lets you change the zoom level on a diagram. You can easily increase or decrease the viewing size of the diagram you are working on by using the **Zoom Percentage** drop-down, the **-/+** buttons, or the slider bar. The right-hand side of the Status Bar is shown in Figure 3.11.

Figure 3.11 Right Side of the CA ERwin Data Modeler Status Bar

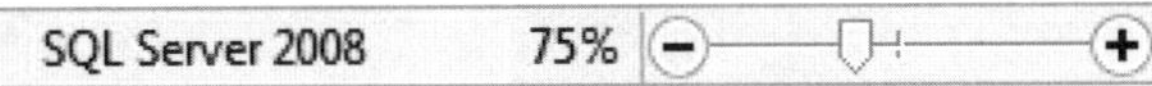

Navigating the eMovies Model

Now that you have a basic understanding of the CA ERwin Data Modeler environment, take a look at the graphical model itself in the diagram window. The **eMovies** model is a logical/physical model and opens by default to the logical in the **<model>** view, which shows all objects in the model, as seen in Figure 3.8. For this example, let's 'zoom in' on a particular area of the business, and focus on just the **Accounting** Subject Area. To switch Subject Areas, click on the **Subject Area** tab in the Model Explorer, and select **Accounting** from the drop-down menu at the top, shown in Figure 3.12.

Figure 3.12 Switching Subject Areas via the Model Explorer

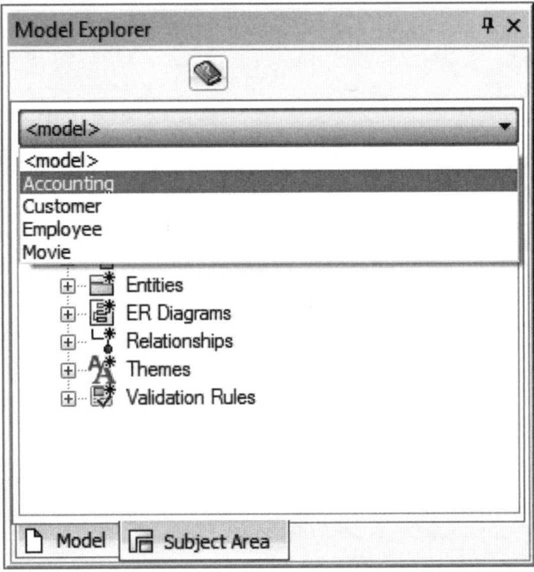

You'll now see just the objects relating to **Accounting** in the diagram window shown in Figure 3.13. Figure 3.13 also provides an overview of the main components of the physical data model, and references the chapter where we describe this object in more detail, for easy reference.

Figure 3.13 Basic Components of the Logical Data Model

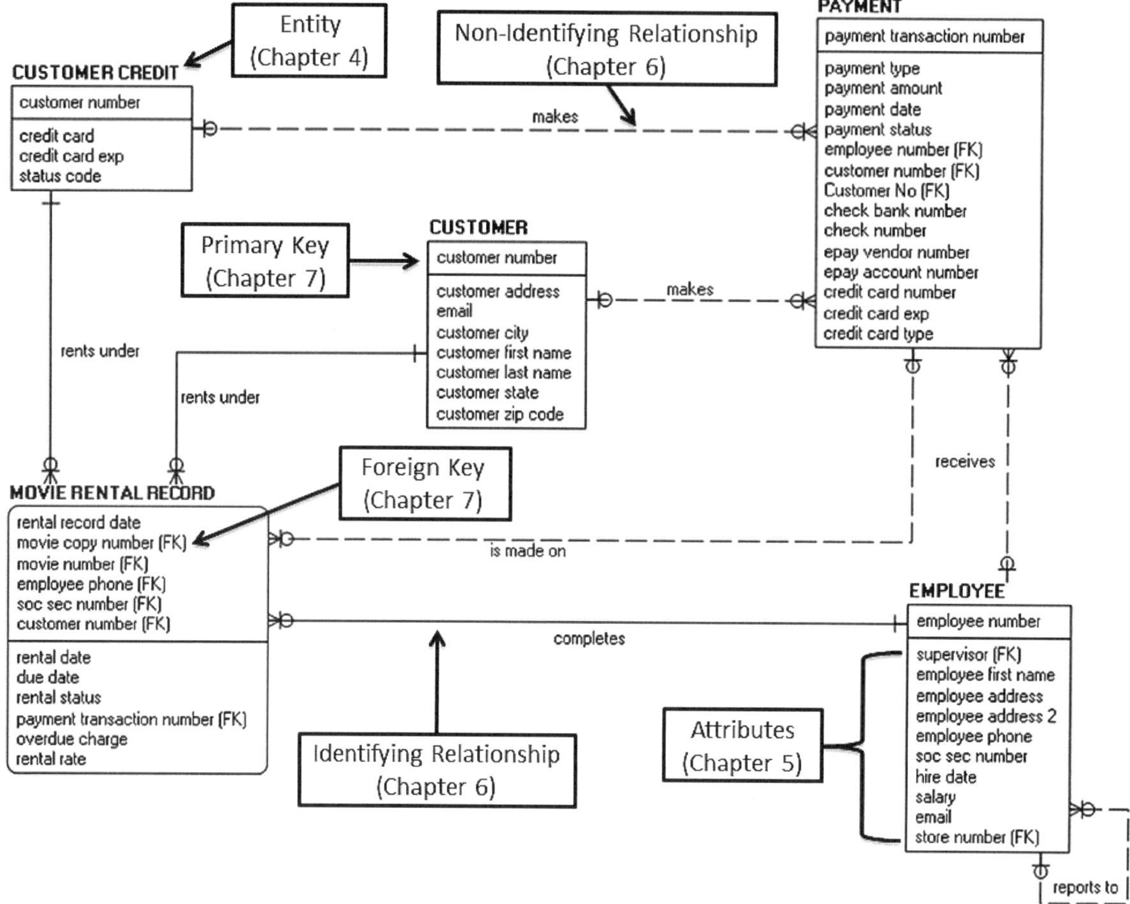

Note that the currently-selected Subject Area is also shown in the title bar of CA ERwin Data Modeler, along with the name of the model and current diagram, as shown in Figure 3.14. The asterisk * that appears after the diagram name indicates a change has been made in the model that has not yet been saved.

Figure 3.14 CA ERwin Data Modeler Title Bar

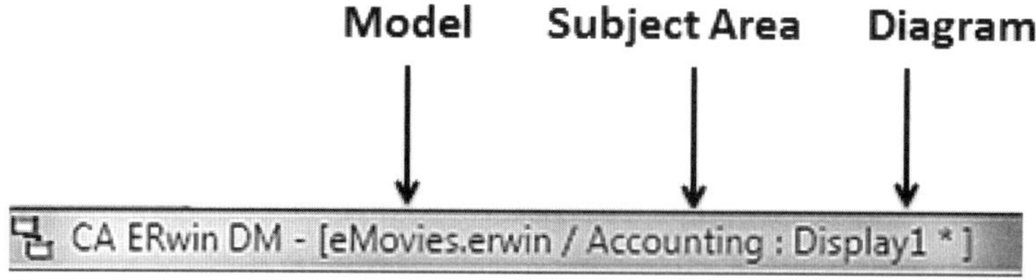

To see the physical model, use the Design Layer Indicator to toggle from logical to physical, as shown in Figure 3.15.

Figure 3.15 Toggling from Logical to Physical Models

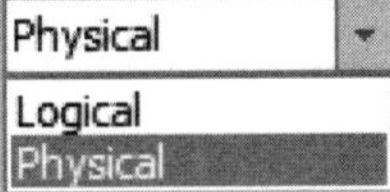

The physical **eMovies** model is shown in Figure 3.16. Once again, we've defined the main object types in the physical data model, and where you can find more information about them.

Figure 3.16 Basic Components of the Physical Data Model

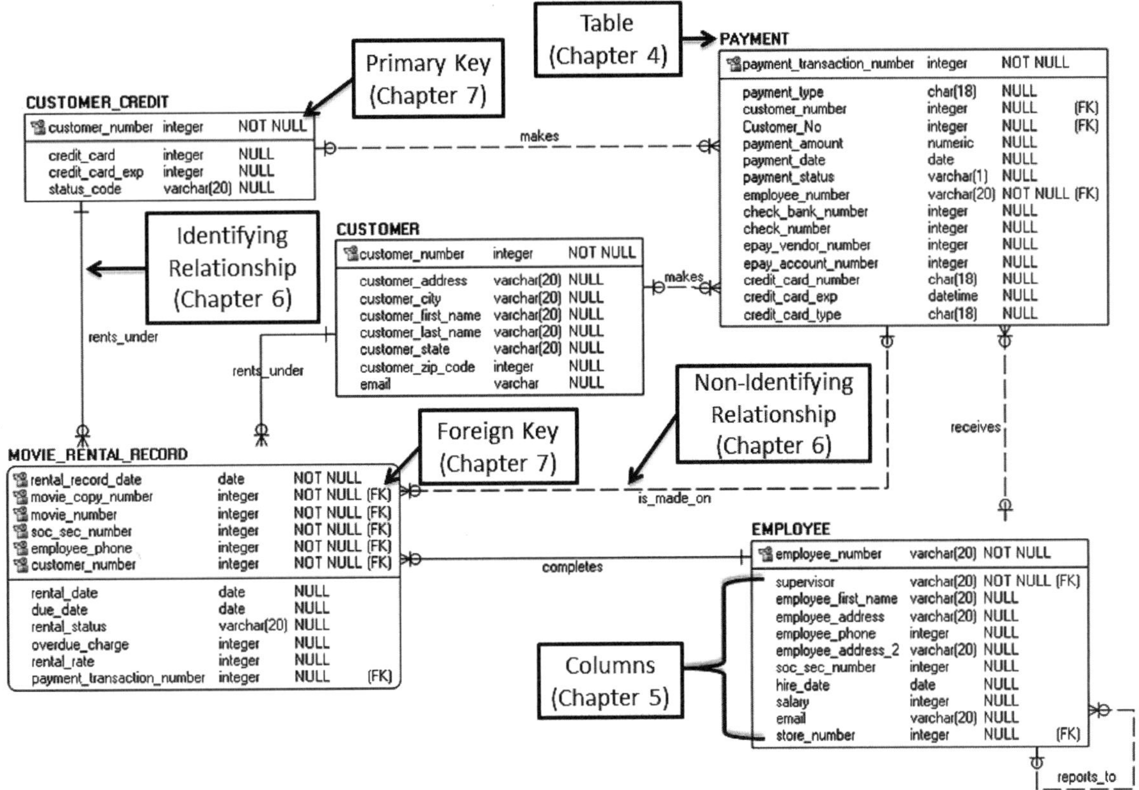

You might have noticed that your default model looks slightly different from the one in this book, particularly the 'lines' in the model. In this book, we'll be using the IE (Information Engineering) notation, which is commonly known as the 'Crows Feet' notation. The default notation in CA ERwin Data Modeler is IDEF1X Notation, as shown in 3.17.

To change the notation used in your Model, simply select **Model|Model Properties** to invoke the Model Properties Editor dialog, shown in Figure 3.18. In this dialog, you can change the notation style of your model, as well as several other key properties[5].

---

[5] Remember, if you'd like your models to match the book, in this case using the IE Notation, you can download the **madesimple.erwin_tmpl** file from the www.erwin.com/datamodelingmadesimple web site. We'll discuss how to use templates in Chapter 15.

Figure 3.17 Data Modeling using IDEF1X Notation

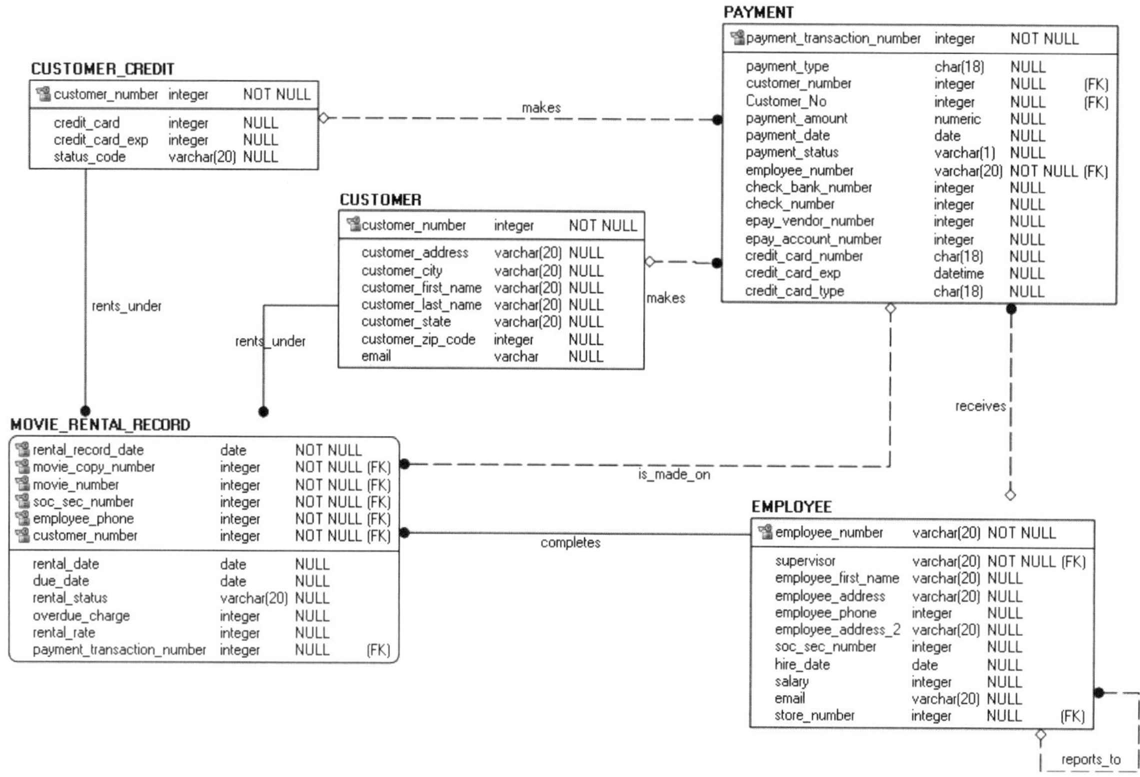

Figure 3.18 Changing Modeling Notation in the Model Properties Editor

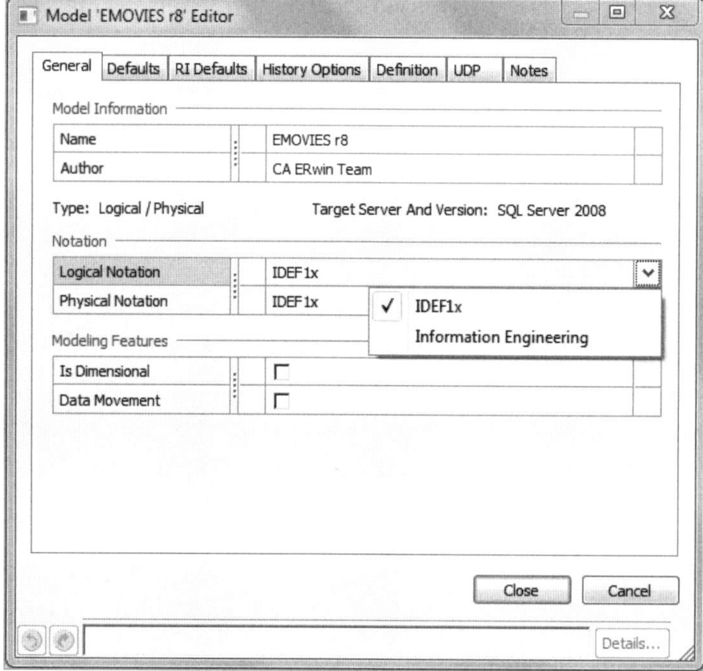

Since much of the power of a data model is in its visual and graphical nature, you'll most likely spend a great deal of your time in the diagram window building your model. But you can also manage your model in a non-graphical way via the Model Explorer, shown in Figure 3.19 (using the physical model). There is a great deal of non-graphical descriptive information about a model, also known as metadata, that is stored with each model and can be easily managed via the Model Explorer. In the Model Explorer, you'll see a list of the logical or physical model objects that can be created and edited. You'll notice that some items, such as entities, appear on the diagram as well, while others, such as Validation Rules, work 'behind the scenes', supporting the rules and processes behind the graphical model.

Figure 3.19 Model Explorer for a Physical Data Model

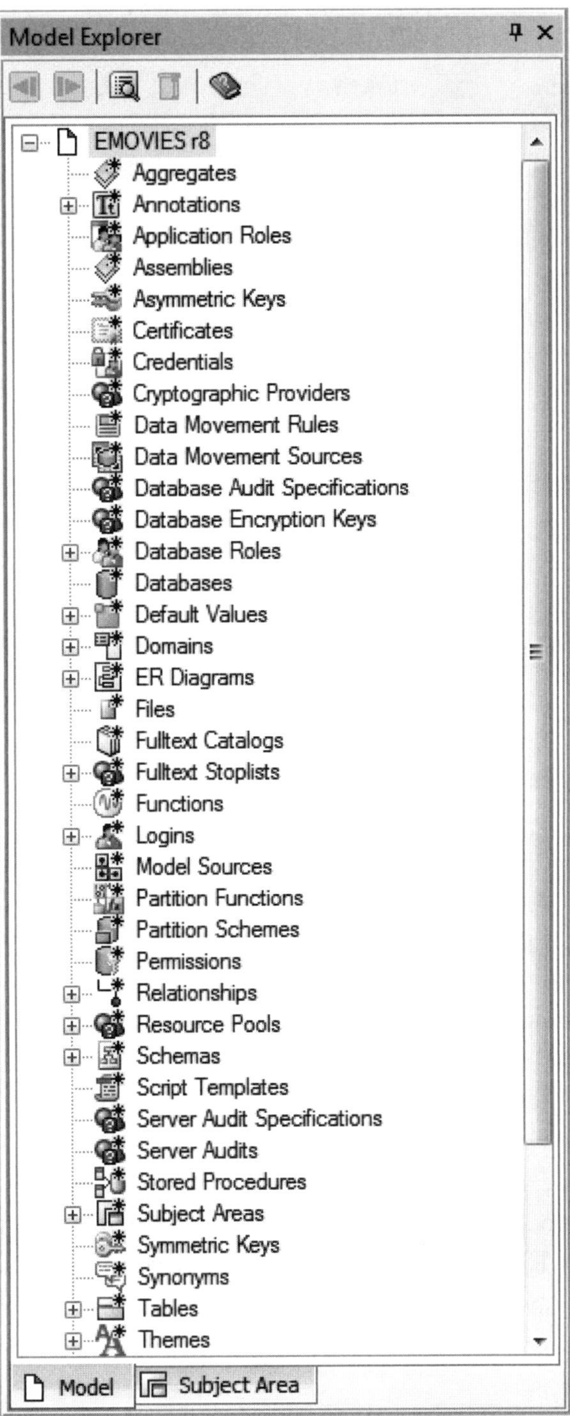

Creating a Model

Now that we've gotten more comfortable with the CA ERwin Data Modeler environment by working with the **eMovies** model, let's create our own model. Select **File|New** from the **Main Menu**, and the **Create Model** dialog appears, as shown in Figure 3.20.

Figure 3.20 Create Model Dialog

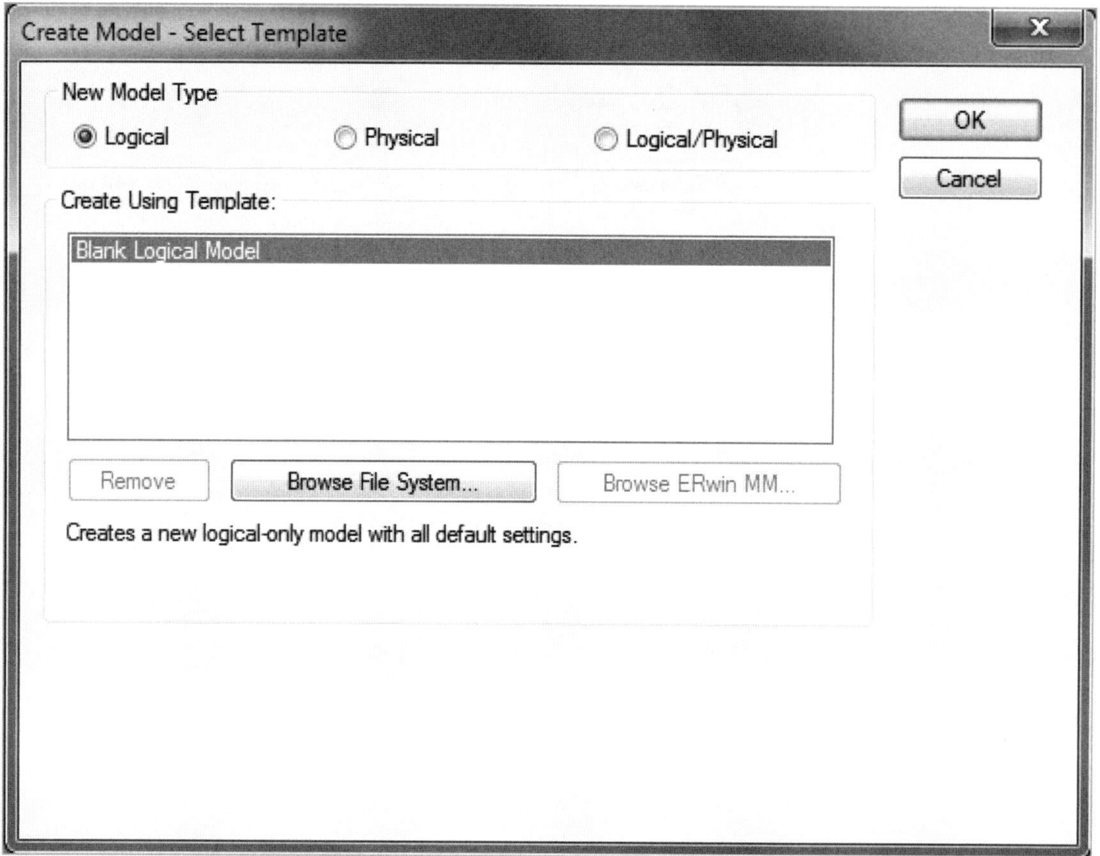

You'll see that your first choice is to select the type of model: **Logical**, **Physical**, or **Logical/Physical**. We'll go into detail about the various types of models and how they interact in Section IV, so don't worry about that for now. For now, simply think of the logical model as the business view of your data, and the physical model the technical view. To give us an opportunity to see how both model types work, select **Logical/Physical** as the **New Model Type**, as shown in Figure 3.21. You'll notice that when you switch to the **Logical/Physical** type, a new selection option is shown for the **Target Database**. Since a physical model is designed to generate data definition language (DDL) for a specific database platform, you'll need to select which database you're using so that CA ERwin Data Modeler can customize the syntax for that specific environment. For this example, use the default selection of SQL Server 2008. The drop-down menu will show you a list of all of the database options available to you.

Figure 3.21 Creating a Logical/Physical Model

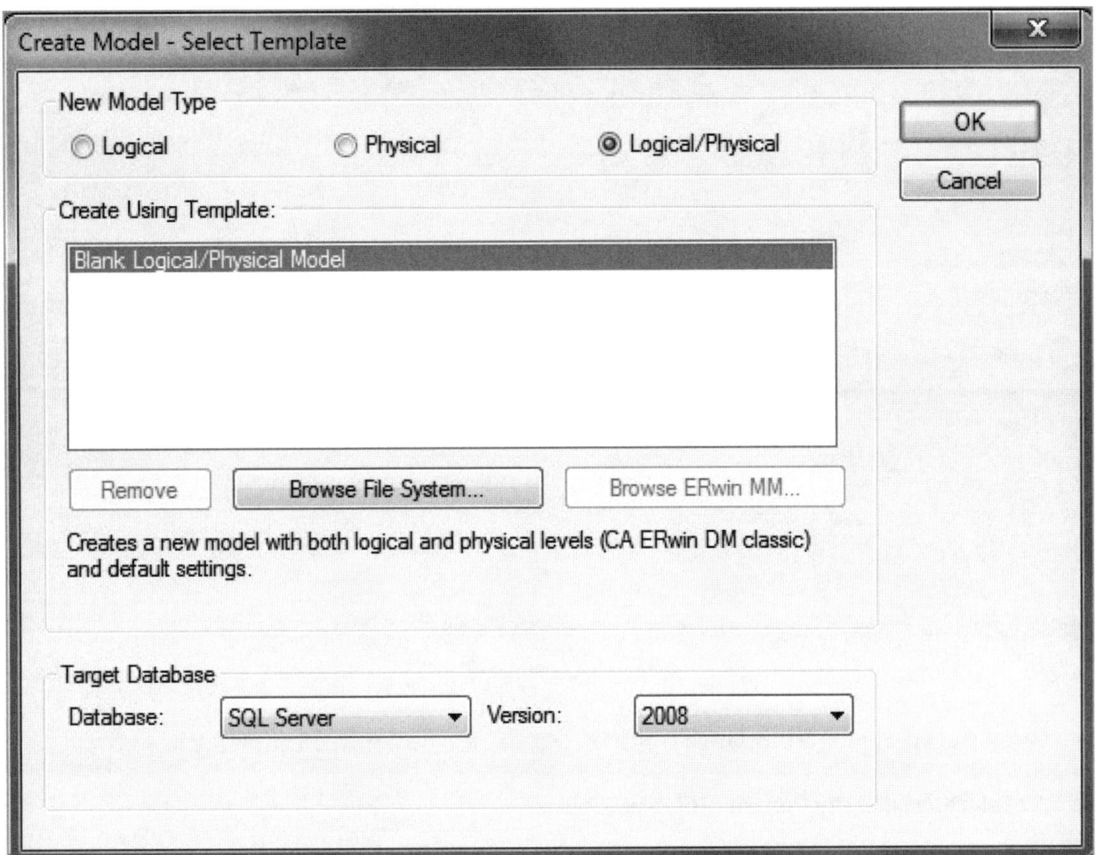

The final choice you'll need to make is to choose a Template for your model. CA ERwin Data Modeler makes extensive use of templates throughout the application to allow you to save custom settings, standardize the look-and-feel and set default properties for your model. We'll explain Templates and how to create your own custom Templates in more detail in Chapter 15. For now, select the default choice of **Blank Logical/Physical** model. A blank model will be created, as shown in Figure 3.22. You may notice that this model and workspace look a bit different than yours. We'll discuss how to personalize your Workspace and Diagram settings in Chapter 9.

We now have a blank slate to begin creating our first data model. We haven't covered the basics of data modeling yet--we'll do that in Section II, so for now, just experiment based on the knowledge you have already. Let's think back to our business card example in Chapter 1. We defined some basic data objects that related to our business cards, such as **Business Card** and **Contact**. Let's put these objects onto your data model.

Figure 3.22 Blank Logical/Physical Model

Select the **Entity** object from the Toolbox Toolbar, shown in Figure 3.23.

Figure 3.23 Selecting an Entity from the Toolbox Toolbar

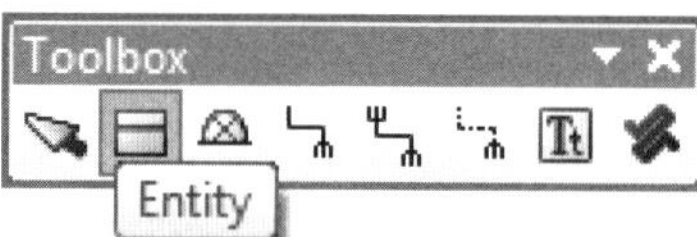

Next, click on the diagram window, and an entity will be created with the default name of **E/1**, as shown in Figure 3.24. Note: If you want to drop multiple entities consecutively, hold the **`Ctrl`** key down as you select and drop the objects from the toolbar. This is known as multi-drop mode.

Figure 3.24 Creating an Entity with Default Name

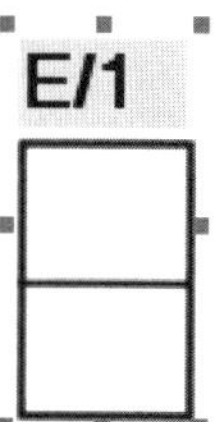

We'll want to name this entity **Business Card**. You'll see that the name is already highlighted and in edit mode, so you can simply start typing after you drop the entity. If for some reason you exit edit mode (by moving to a different area of the diagram or pressing the **`ESC`** key), you can always return to edit mode by highlighting the entity and pressing the **F2** key. After you're finished typing the name, press ENTER and your entity should now look like Figure 3.25.

Figure 3.25 Naming an Entity

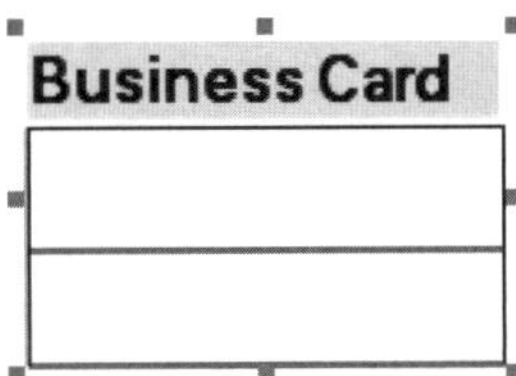

After naming the entity, the next thing we'll want to do is to add attributes for this object. Without going into the detail that we'll cover in Section II, think of attributes as the descriptors for your object. What things do we want to use to describe our **Business Card**? One piece of information we listed was **Person Name**. Press the TAB key to enter the attribute edit mode, as shown in Figure 3.26.

Figure 3.26 Creating an Attribute

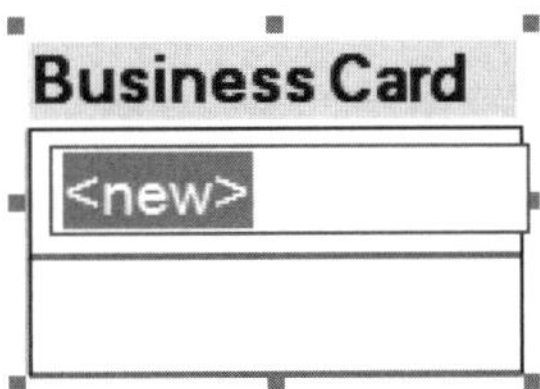

Simply type the name of the attribute, just as you did in the entity name. After you type **Person Name**, press ENTER, and you'll see a prompt to enter a second attribute, indicated by **<new>**, as show in Figure 3.27.

Figure 3.27 Naming an Attribute

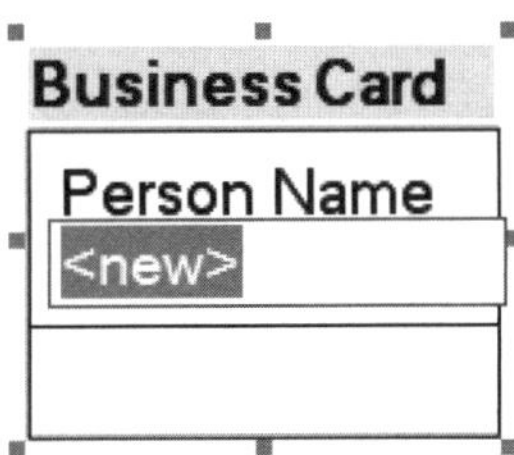

We'll just add one for now, so hit ESC to bypass this, and your entity should look similar to Figure 3.28.

Figure 3.28 Entity with a Single Attribute

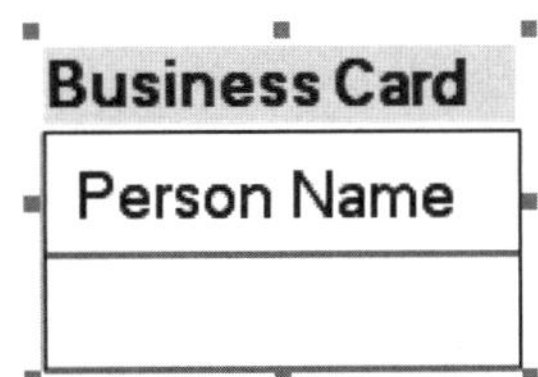

You'll notice that there is a line below the **Person Name** attribute. Attributes 'above the line' within an entity are called primary keys—they are the attributes that uniquely identify an object (more on this in Chapter 7). For now, we'll use **Person Name** as our primary key, and we'll want to add some other attributes about our business card. Press the TAB key to move to the 'below the line' section, as shown in Figure 3.29.

Figure 3.29 Creating a Non-Primary Key Attribute

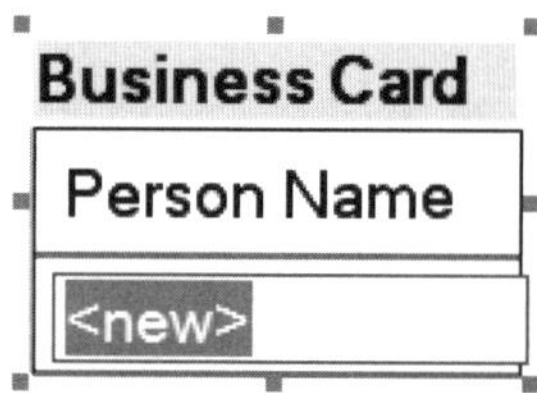

Enter two more attributes: **Person Title**, and **Company Name**. Press the ENTER key after you are finished creating the first attribute to move into edit mode for the second attribute. Note: Hitting the ESC key or moving your cursor to another area of the diagram with your mouse removes you from edit mode when you are finished adding attributes. When you are finished, your model should look like Figure 3.30.

Figure 3.30 Entity with Attributes Defined

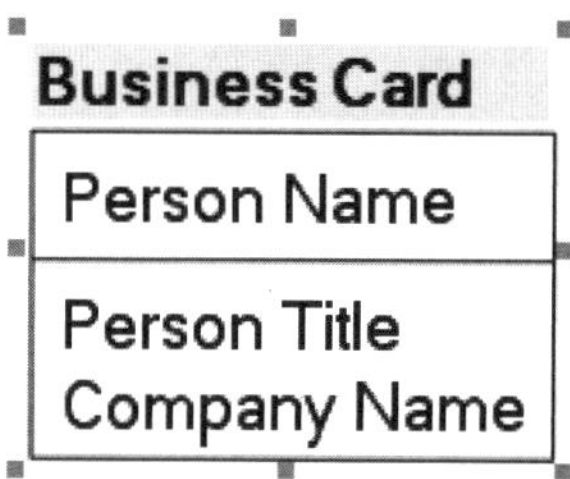

Using the navigation keys is a simple way to quickly enter basic information about model objects, such as the name. But to enter more detailed information, you'll want to use the property editors. Right-click on the **Business Card** entity and the context menu shown in Figure 3.31 appears. You'll see a list of the property editors you can invoke: Entity Properties, Attribute Properties, and Key Group Properties.

Figure 3.31 Context Menu to Invoke Property Editors for an Entity

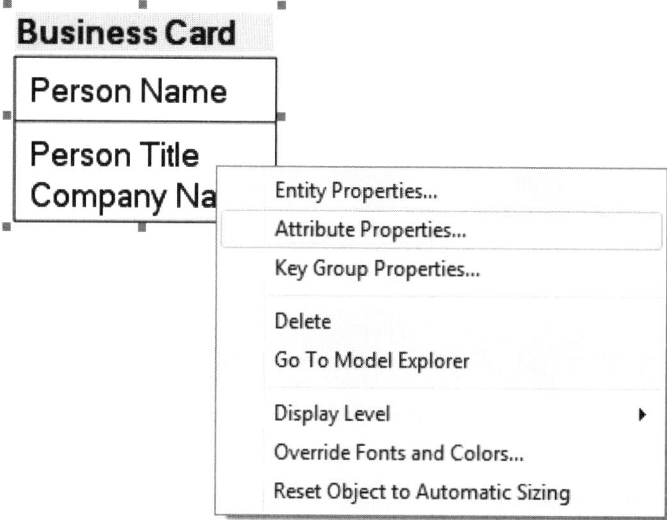

Select the **Attribute Properties** menu item and the Attributes Properties Editor appears, as shown in Figure 3.32. Note that if the default size for a column is too narrow, some of the text may be hidden. You can easily resize the field lengths by selecting the field divider line and dragging to the desired size so that all text is displayed.

Figure 3.32 Attribute Properties Editor

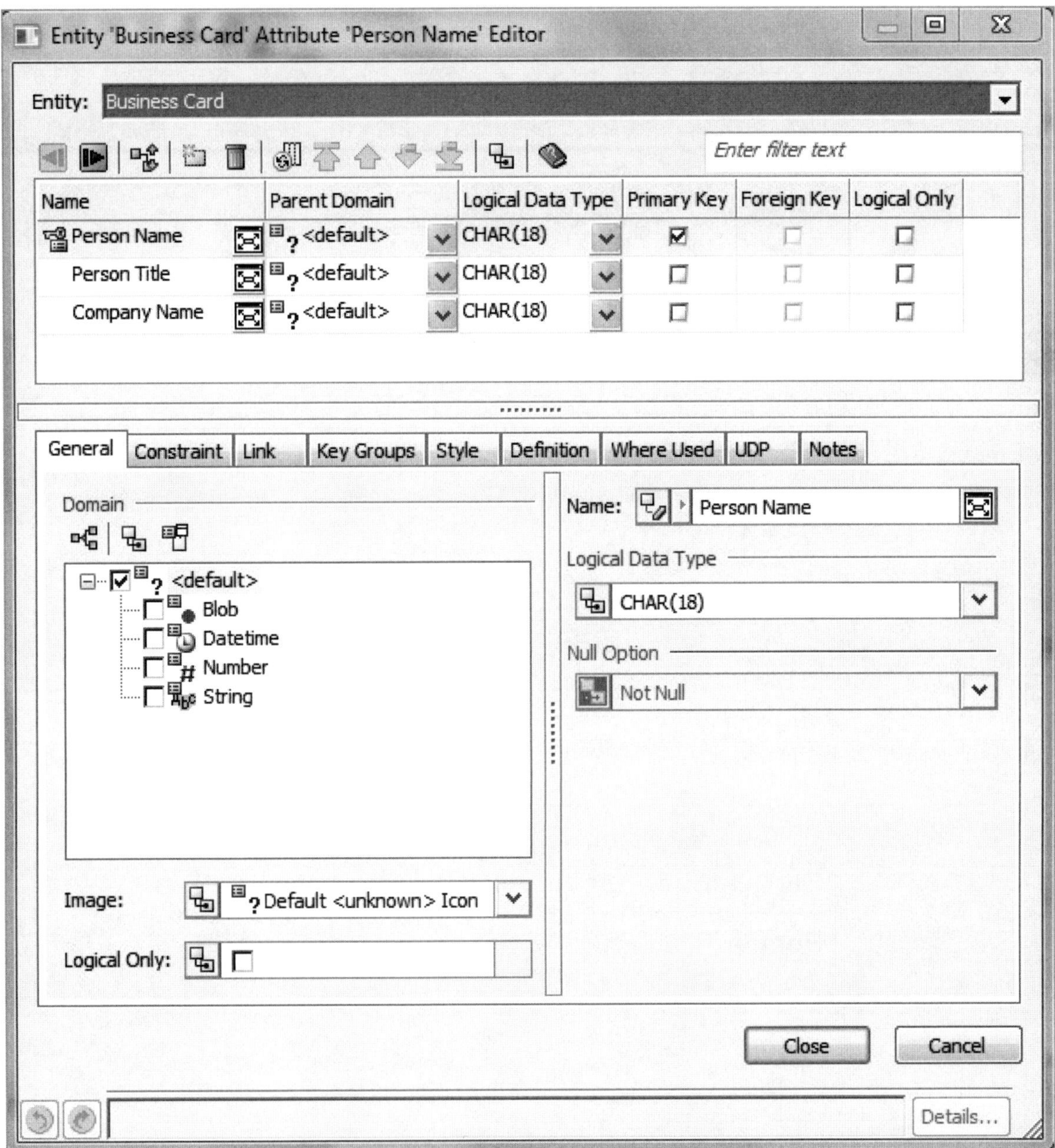

We'll go through the details of this property editor in Chapter 5, so don't worry about the specifics for now. Just browse through the various tabs and options to get a sense of the type of information you can define.

Note that you can also open the Attribute Properties Editor by double-clicking on a particular attribute. The Attribute Properties Editor will open with that attribute highlighted. If we double-click on the entity instead, the Entity Properties Editor will open, where we can enter information such as the name and description of the entity, shown in Figure 3.33. Give this a try.

Figure 3.33 Entity Properties Editor

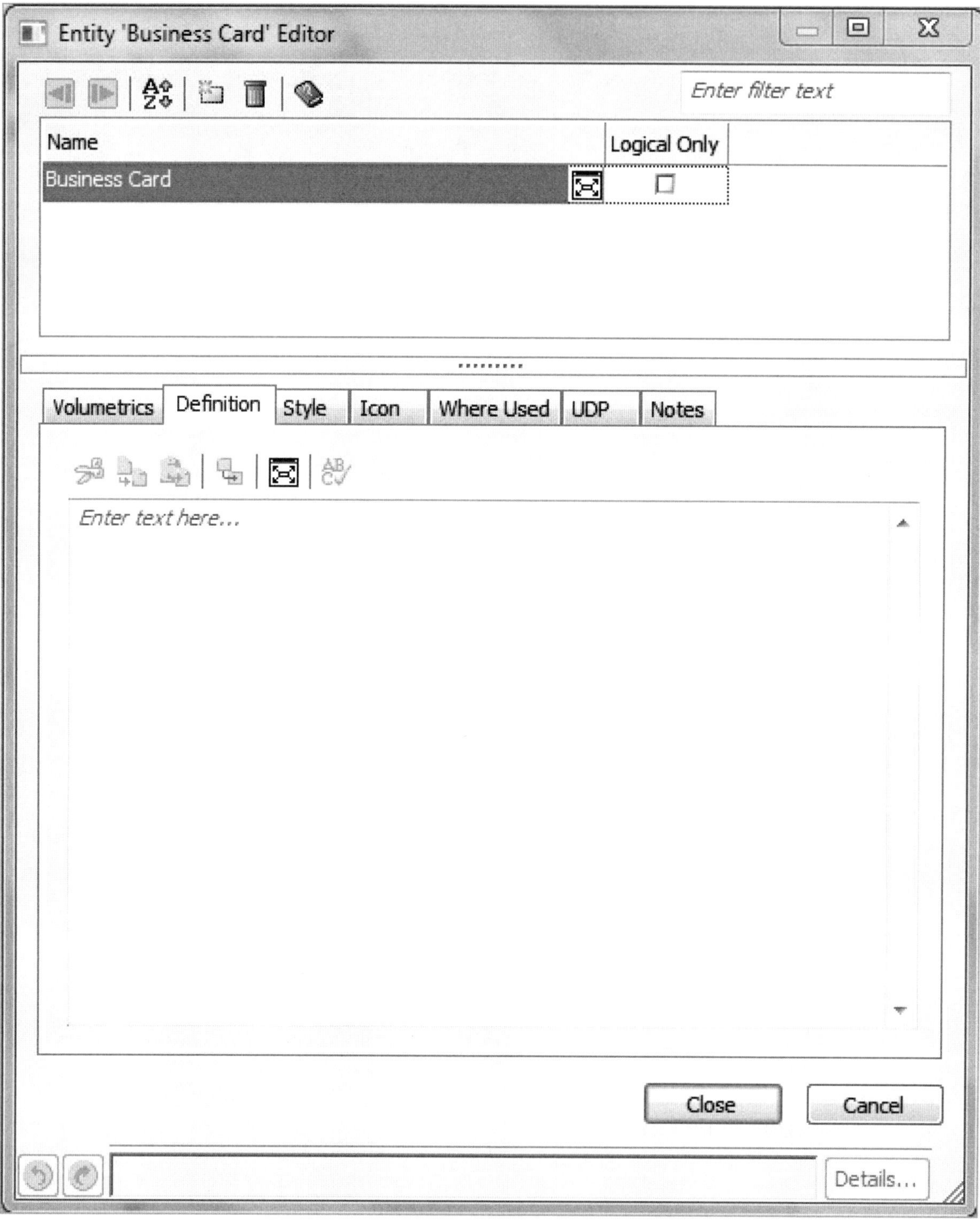

It can take a while to get used to the navigation and keystroke functions, so here are some tips to refer to as you are creating and editing entities and attributes:

- The TAB key moves you through the sections of an entity. To try this, select an entity, and press the TAB key multiple times—you will be moved from the name field, to the primary key section, to the non-primary key section.
- The ENTER key creates a new entry within a section. For example, you can create multiple attributes within a section by using the ENTER key to create a new attribute.
- Hold the CTRL key while selecting and dropping objects from the **Toolbox Toolbar** to enter multi-drop mode. This allows you to create multiple objects without re-selecting the object from the toolbar.
- The first click on an entity selects the entity. The second click places you into edit mode for the entity name. A double-click opens the property editor for the object.
- Hitting the ESC key removes you from edit mode.

Now that we know how to create entities and their attributes, let's define a second entity called **Contact** with the attributes **Contact Id** and **Email Address** as the primary key attributes, as shown in Figure 3.34. We won't walk you through this step-by-step—you should have the hang of it now.

Figure 3.34 Adding the Contact Entity

Business Card
Person Name
Person Title
Company Name

Contact
Contact Id
Email Address

An important process in building a data model is defining the relationships between data objects. (We'll cover relationships in more detail in Chapter 6.) In a data model, relationships are shown as lines. To create a relationship between **Business Card** and **Contact**, first select the **Identifying Relationship** object from the Toolbox Toolbar, as shown in Figure 3.35.

Figure 3.35 Selecting an Identifying Relationship from the Toolbox Toolbar

Next, click on **Business Card** to define it as the parent entity, then **Contact** to define it as the child. Your model should look similar to Figure 3.36.

Figure 3.36 Creating a Relationship Between Two Entities

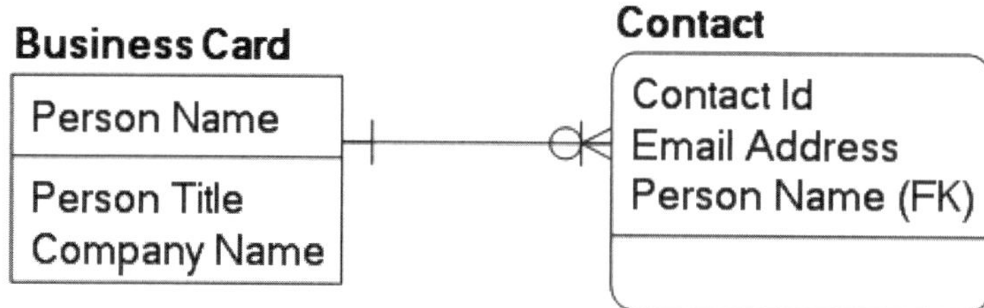

You'll notice that a new attribute was created in the **Contact** entity with (FK) written next to it. This is called a foreign key, and is automatically created by CA ERwin Data Model for certain relationship types. We'll cover foreign keys in Chapter 7.

Congratulations! You've created your first data model. You won't win any data modeling awards with this model you've created, but don't worry--we'll walk through the basics of data modeling throughout this book and show you how to make this model better. For now, it's enough to get a sense of the CA ERwin Data Modeler landscape and how to use the tool. You'll be a pro soon enough, and then you can tape your data models to your wall, like a true data architect.

Now that we've created a simple logical model, let's switch to the physical model and explore that model type. To switch model types, use the **Design Layer Indicator** on the Toolbox Toolbar, as shown in Figure 3.37.

Figure 3.37 Switching Design Layers from Logical to Physical

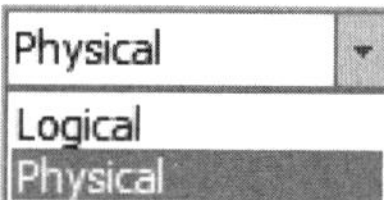

The physical model will look similar to Figure 3.38.

Figure 3.38 Physical Data Model

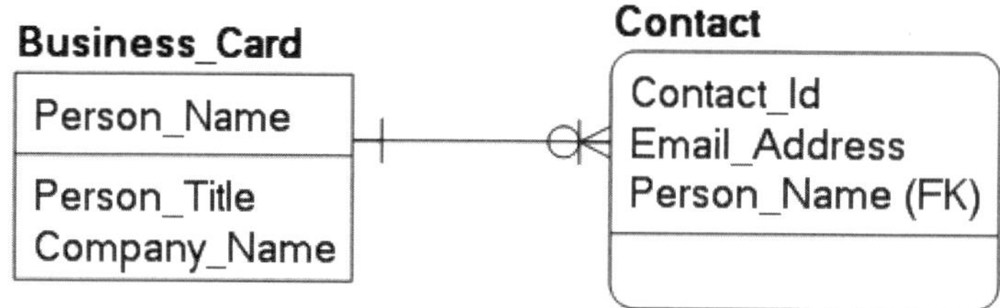

You'll notice that the model looks very similar to the logical, but the names have changed slightly, using underscores instead of spaces. We'll discuss how to control logical and physical naming conventions in Chapter 12. In our simple model, the logical and physical models look much the same, but as you get deeper into physical database design, there will be many more properties and design decisions that you will need to set that will cause the models to diverge. We will cover physical data models in more detail in Chapter 19.

To get a sense of the different types of properties that can be defined in the physical data model, right-click on the **Business Card** table (entities in the physical model are called tables), and you will see a list of the numerous property editors that can be invoked. Figure 3.39 shows a list of the property editors for a physical table. You'll also notice that the Model Explorer contains a larger number of objects than for the logical model, with information specific to the selected database platform (Refer to Figure 3.19).

Figure 3.39 Property Editors for Physical Models

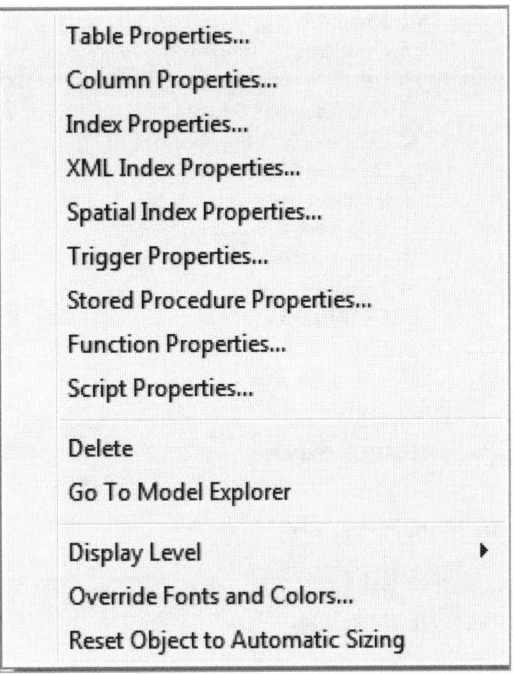

Before we go any further, let's name our model. Take a look at the Model Explorer in Figure 3.40 and you'll notice that the default model name is **Model_1**.

We'll want to change this to something more user-friendly. One easy way to change the model name is to simply select the model name in the Explorer Tree, then click to enter edit mode. Once in edit mode, type the name of your model. In this case, let's call our model **Business Card Model**, as shown in Figure 3.41. You can also name a model in the Model Properties Editor dialog (refer to Figure 3.18 to see this dialog). The advantage of using the Model Properties Editor is that you can set other model properties there at the same time, such as owner, description, etc.

Figure 3.40 Default Model Name in Model Explorer

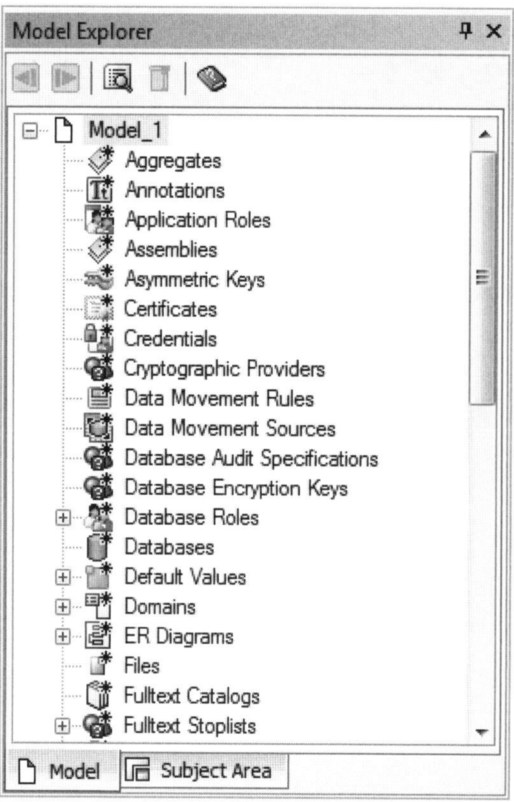

Figure 3.41 Naming a Model in the Model Explorer

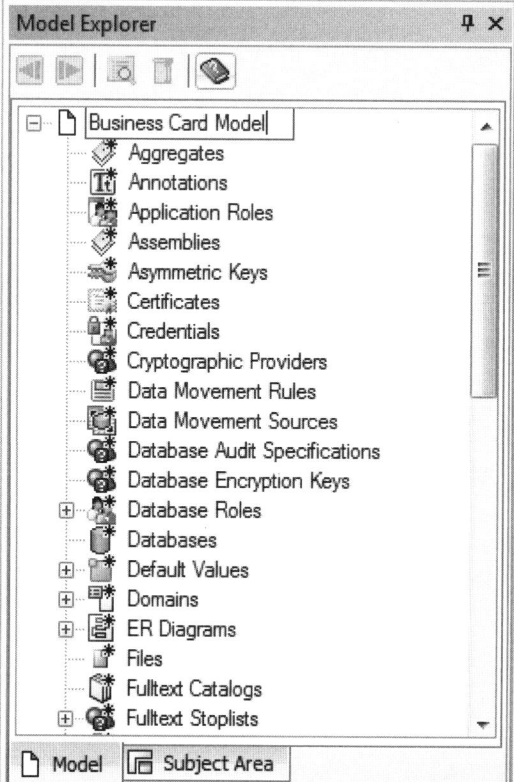

Saving Your Model

After you've made changes to a model or created a new model, you'll want to save on a regular basis to make sure your changes are maintained. Note that most organizations with modeling teams use CA ERwin Data Modeler Workgroup Edition[6] to help manage change, including conflict resolution and audit trails, and store models in a centralized model repository. This book, however, will focus primarily on a stand-alone, file-based approach to saving a model using CA ERwin Data Modeler Standard Edition.

To save the model we just created, simply select **File|Save** or choose the **Save** button from the Standard Toolbar. The **Save As** dialog will appear, as shown in Figure 3.42, and you can choose a directory to store your model. (Note: You can change the default directory for saving models using the **Tools|Options** menu.) In this example, we'll store our model in the **`My Models`** directory. Give your model the file name **`Business Card Example.erwin`**.

Figure 3.42 Saving a Data Model

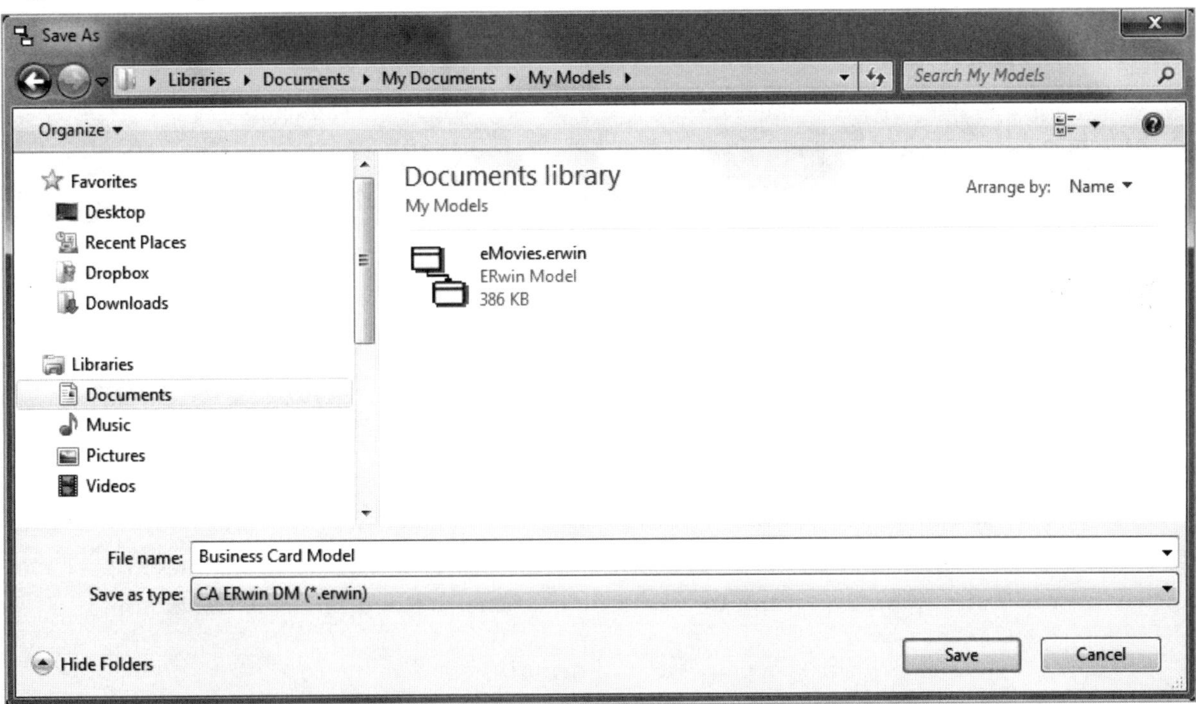

Note that the default file extension is **`.erwin`**. Invoke the drop-down menu for the **Save as type** field, and you will see that there are other file formats that can be selected, as shown in Figure 3.43.

---

[6] In versions prior to CA ERwin Data Modeler r8, the Workgroup Edition was called Model Manager. In r8, the functionality of Model Manager is now included in the CA ERwin Data Modeler Workgroup Edition.

Figure 3.43 Saving an ERwin Model as an Alternate File Type

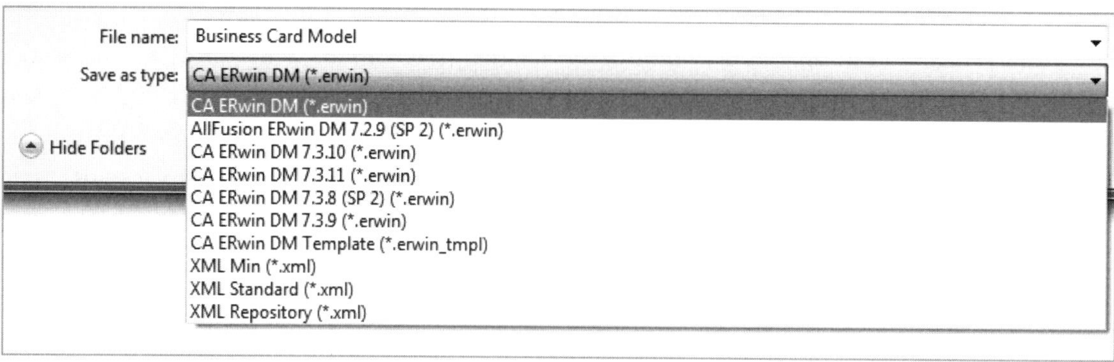

These multiple file types enable you to share your models more easily with other tools, as well as previous versions. Table 3.1 provides a list of the file types supported for saving, with a brief description of each. In addition, you will see file types for specific CA ERwin Data Modeler versions. Note that CA ERwin Data Modeler is backward compatible only, i.e. you can save a model as an earlier version, but you cannot open a model, for example, created in r7.0 in r4.1.4.

Table 3.1 File Types Supported for Saving

File Extension	Description
.erwin	**.erwin** is the supported file type for CA ERwin Data Modeler version 7.0 and later.
.erwin_tmpl	**.erwin_tmpl** is an ERwin Template file. See Chapter 15 for a full discussion of Templates. Note: Templates in v4.1.4 are supported with the **.ert** file format.
.XML	You can use **.XML** format to export model data to applications that support **XML**. XML format replaces the text-based **.ERX** format used in earlier versions of this product. XML format provides structured markup of model metadata according to elements that are defined in the XML Schema. There are three types of **.XML** Formats: • **XML Standard Files:** The Standard XML format does not expand macros or names. This file can be imported back into CA ERwin Data Modeler. • **XML Standard with Min Info Files:** Only saves the minimum amount of information needed by CA ERwin Data Modeler to reopen the model. Properties that are derived from other properties or that are read-only are not saved. • **XML Repository Format Files:** The Repository format expands names, macros, and physical names. Derived properties are exported. A file saved in this format cannot be opened with CA ERwin Data Modeler.

You have created and saved your first data model. Now you'll probably want to close your model and take a well-deserved break. Select **File|Close** and you will see the Universal File Close Dialog appear, as shown in Figure 3.44. Note that the Universal File Close Dialog only appears if there are unsaved changes in your model, so you may have to edit your model slightly after saving (e.g. move the placement of an entity) to get this dialog to appear in this example. Remember that an asterisk (*) appears in the title bar when there are unsaved changes to the model.

Figure 3.44 Universal File Close Dialog

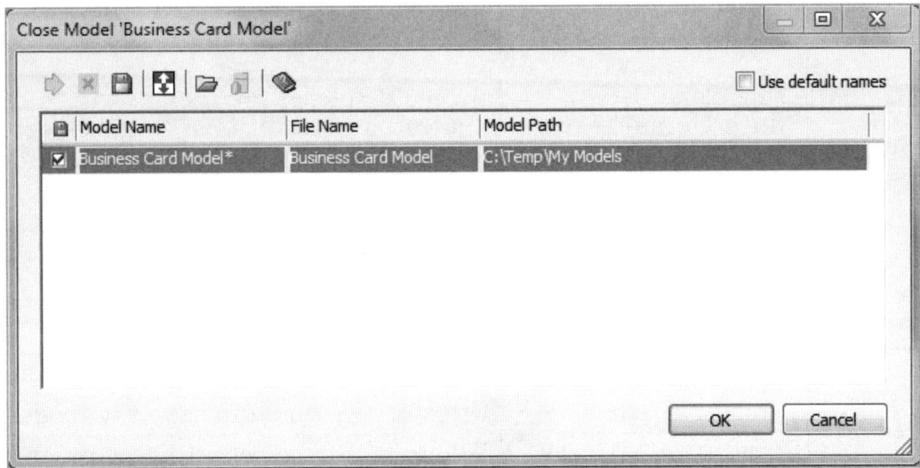

The Universal File Close Dialog contains a number of options, outlined in Table 3.2.

In our example, since we've already saved our model, you can uncheck the **Save** option and simple select **OK** to close the dialog.

This book is only the beginning of your learning process with CA ERwin Data Modeler. Join the online community and keep your learning process going at www.erwin.com. There is a dedicated page for this book at www.erwin.com/datamodelingmadesimple where you can find sample models, answers to exercises, and more. The **Business Card Example.erwin** file is located on this page, so you can compare your work with the model we put together.

Table 3.2 Universal File Close Dialog Options

Icon	Option	Description
	Mark/Unmark selected model for activation	Specifies whether to activate the model. Note: This option is not available unless you are exiting the application and are closing multiple open models after performing a Complete Compare operation. We'll cover Complete Compare in Chapter 19.
	Mark/Unmark selected models for closing	Specifies whether to close the selected model.
	Mark/Unmark selected models for saving	Indicates whether to save the selected model when there are unsaved changes.
	Invert	With the invert feature, selected rows become unselected and unselected rows become selected.
	Browse for a directory path	Opens the **Save As** dialog so you can select a directory in which to save the model.
	Browse for a Mart path	Allows you to select a library in which to save the model on the mart. If the **Save** check box was not selected, it is set automatically for you. Note: This option is not available unless you are connected to the mart. Available in CA ERwin Data Modeler Workgroup Edition only.
	Mark/Unmark Selected Model(s) for Saving	Save the selected model. By default, this check box is selected when there are unsaved changes. Clear the check box to close the model without saving the changes.
Model Name Business Card Model*	Model Name	Lists the name of the open model(s).
File Name Business Card Model	File Name	Lists the file name of the open model(s). This field is the same as the **Model Name** when the **Use Default Name** check box is selected.
Model Path C:\Temp\My Models	Model Path	Shows the path of each open model.
Use default names	Use Default Names	Specifies to use the model name as the file name, if the file name has not been set.

Key Points

- CA ERwin Data Modeler's Design Layer Architecture allows you to create business-driven designs with a 'top down' approach or create a technical data inventory with a 'bottom up' approach.
- Reusable standards in CA ERwin Data Modeler help increase data quality and efficiency.
- Complete Compare helps manage change across multiple models.
- CA ERwin Data Modeler provides a number of ways to customize your modeling environment.
- A great way to get started with CA ERwin Data Modeler is to begin with the sample eMovies model.
- The CA ERwin Data Modeler Workspace has a number of features to help you build and manage your models, including the: Diagram Window, Model Explorer, Toolbars, Action Log Pane, Advisories Pane, Diagram Tabs, Bulk Editor Pane, Overview Pane, and Status Bar.
- The online community at www.erwin.com is a great way to learn more about data modeling in general and CA ERwin Data Modeling in particular.

SECTION II
Components

Now that that you'd have a general overview of data modeling, and understand a bit how the CA ERwin Data Modeler interface operates, this section will provide more detail on the basic fundamentals and building blocks of data modeling. We'll cover entities in Chapter 4, data elements in Chapter 5, relationships in Chapter 6, and keys in Chapter 7. In addition, in Chapter 8 we will provide tips on how to optimize the layout and organizations of your data models. In Chapter 9 we will discuss personalizing the CA ERwin Data Modeler workspace.

CHAPTER 4
Entities

Concepts of interest
Who, What, When, Where, Why, and How
Entities abound

As I walked around the room to see if any students had questions, I noticed someone in the last row had already finished the exercise. I walked over to where she was sitting and looking over her shoulder, noticed only a handful of boxes on the page. The large box in the center contained the word 'Manufacturing'. I asked her for her definition of 'Manufacturing'. "Manufacturing is the production process of how we turn raw materials into finished goods. All the manufacturing steps are in this box."

The data model boxes (also known as 'entities'), however, are not designed to represent or contain processes. Instead, they represent the concepts that are used *by* the processes. The Manufacturing entity on her model was eventually transformed into several other entities, including **Raw Material**, **Finished Goods**, **Machinery**, and **Production Schedule**.

This chapter defines the concept of an entity and discusses the different categories (Who, What, When, Where, Why, and How) of entities. Entity instances are also defined. The three different levels of entities, conceptual, logical, and physical, are also explained, as well as the concepts of a weak versus a strong entity. We'll conclude the chapter with an example of how to create entities in CA ERwin Data Modeler.

Entity Explanation

An entity represents a collection of information about something that the business deems important and worthy of capture. A noun or noun phrase identifies a specific entity. It fits into one of several categories - who, what, when, where, why, or how. Table 4.1 contains a definition of each of these entity categories along with examples.

Entity instances are the occurrences or values of a particular entity. Think of a spreadsheet as being an entity, with the column headings representing the pieces of information about the entity. Each spreadsheet row containing the actual values represents an entity instance. The entity **Customer** may have multiple customer instances with names Bob, Joe, Jane, and so forth. The entity **Account** can have instances of Bob's checking account, Bob's savings account, Joe's brokerage account, and so on.

Table 4.1 Definitions and Examples of Entity Categories

Category	Definition	Examples
Who	Person or organization of interest to the enterprise. That is, "*Who* is important to the business?" Often a 'who' is associated with a role such as Customer or Vendor.	Employee, Patient, Gambler, Suspect, Customer, Vendor, Student, Passenger, Competitor
What	Product or service of interest to the enterprise. It often refers to what the organization makes that keeps it in business. That is, "*What* is important to the business?"	Product, Service, Raw Material, Finished Good, Course, Song, Photograph
When	Calendar or time interval of interest to the enterprise. That is, "*When* is the business in operation?"	Time, Date, Month, Quarter, Year, Calendar, Semester, Fiscal Period, Minute
Where	Location of interest to the enterprise. Location can refer to actual places as well as electronic places. That is, "*Where* is business conducted?"	Mailing Address, Distribution Point, Website URL, IP Address
Why	Event or transaction of interest to the enterprise. These events keep the business afloat. That is, "*Why* is the business in business?"	Order, Return, Complaint, Withdrawal, Deposit, Compliment, Inquiry, Trade, Claim
How	Documentation of the event of interest to the enterprise. Documents record the events, such as a Purchase Order recording an Order event. That is, "*How* does the business stay in business?"	Invoice, Contract, Agreement, Account, Purchase Order, Speeding Ticket

The column headings in a spreadsheet can be considered 'metadata'. They describe what the data is, and put context around the information. If you had a spreadsheet with no headings (or metadata), it would be very difficult to understand what the data in the rows meant. Data modeling and CA ERwin deal with these column headings, or the metadata. A relational database is obviously more complicated, but this is a close enough example to show the point.

The spreadsheet example in Figure 4.1 could be considered a simple 'data model' showing a **Customer** entity and the information that is important to describing a customer: name, country, etc. In a data model, these descriptors are called, 'attributes', and we go into more detail about these in Chapter 5.

Figure 4.1 How a Spreadsheet Relates to a Data Model

Customer Name	Company	Country	Year Purchased
Hans Kleigel	Komputers R Us	Germany	1970
Mary Jones	Big Bank Co	USA	1999
Proful Bishwal	Global Software	India	2005
Ming Lee	My Favorite Store	China	2008
Giovanni Petra	IL Mio Caro	Italy	2000

If we were to show the same information in a traditional entity-relationship model, it would be shown as in Figure 4.2.

Figure 4.2 Spreadsheet Data Shown as a Data Model

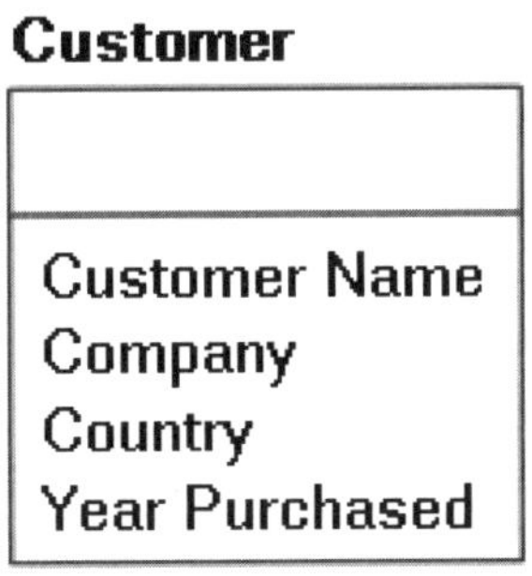

Entity Types

The beauty of data modeling is that you can take the same information and show it at different levels of detail, depending on the audience. The previous chapter introduced the three levels of detail: conceptual, logical, and physical. Entities are components of all three levels.

For an entity to exist at a conceptual level, it must be both basic and critical to the business. What is basic and critical depends very much on the concept of scope. At a universal level, there are certain concepts common to all companies, such as **Customer**, **Product**, and **Employee**. Making the scope slightly narrower, a given industry may have certain unique concepts. **Phone Number**, for example, will be a valid concept for a telecommunications company, but perhaps not for other industries, such as manufacturing. Each company may have concepts that are unique to its business or its way of doing business. For example, **Complaint** could be a concept for a consumer affairs department. **Person** and **Company** could be valid concepts in our business card example.

Entities at a logical level represent the business at a more detailed level than at the conceptual level. In general, a concept represents many logical model entities.

Examining the concept **Address** in more detail could produce a large number of logical entities, including **Email Address**, **Web Address**, and **Mailing Address**.

At a physical level, the entities correspond to database tables. The rigor applied to the logical model is reversed, at times, to make applications perform well or to manage space more efficiently. **Web Address** and **Email Address** could be logical entities that translate directly into physical tables. However, if there is a reporting requirement to view all virtual address information, we may decide to combine both **Web Address** and **Email Address** into the same physical entity. With very large volumes of data, we might also decide to break up **Email Address** into several physical entities, each of a more manageable size. So at times, one logical entity can break down into several physical tables, and even more frequently, one physical table can be created from many logical entities (we'll discuss this in more detail in Chapter 19).

An entity is shown as a rectangle with its name inside. Figure 4.3 contains several entities from a sample ice cream store.

Figure 4.3 Sample Entities

Ice Cream Flavor

Ice Cream Size

Ice Cream Order

Notice that there are two types of rectangles: those with straight corners, such as **Ice Cream Flavor** and **Ice Cream Size**, and those with rounded edges, such as **Ice Cream Order**. Without introducing technical data modeling jargon, it is enough to know that the rectangles with straight right angle corners are strong and those with rounded corners are weak.

Strong entities, also called independent entities stand on their own. They represent one occurrence of a person, place, or thing independent of any other entities. In order to find the information about a particular **Customer**, for example, its **Customer Identifier** could be used to retrieve it from the database. "This is Bob, Customer Identifier 123." An **Ice Cream Flavor** of 'Chocolate' might be retrieved with 'C'. An **Ice Cream Size** of '2 Scoops' might be retrieved with simply the number '2'.

Weak entities need to rely on at least one other entity. This means you *cannot* retrieve an entity instance without referring to an entity instance from another entity. Another name for a weak entity is a dependent entity, because its existence is dependent upon the existence of one or more other entities. For example, **Ice Cream Order** might be retrieved by an **Ice Cream Flavor** or **Ice Cream Size**, *in combination with* something within **Ice Cream Order** such as a **Sequence Number**.

A data model is a communication tool. Distinguishing strong from weak entities (or independent from dependent entities) on the model helps us understand the relationships and dependencies between entities. For example, a developer reading a data model showing that **Ice Cream Order** is a weak entity that depends on **Ice Cream Flavor**, would develop the application program to ensure that an ice cream flavor is present before orders for it are placed. That is, 'Chocolate' must be available as a flavor in the software system before an order for chocolate ice cream may be placed.

Let's start here by creating a data model in CA ERwin Data Modeler, using the entities we just described: **Ice Cream Flavor**, **Ice Cream Size**, and **Ice Cream Order**. The first two, remember, are strong entities.

Creating Entities

Let's start by creating the **Ice Cream Flavor** entity. Open a new logical model and select the **Entity** icon from the Toolbox Toolbar, as shown in Figure 4.4. If you are unfamiliar with how to create a new model, refer to Chapter 3.

Figure 4.4 Creating an Entity from the Toolbox Toolbar

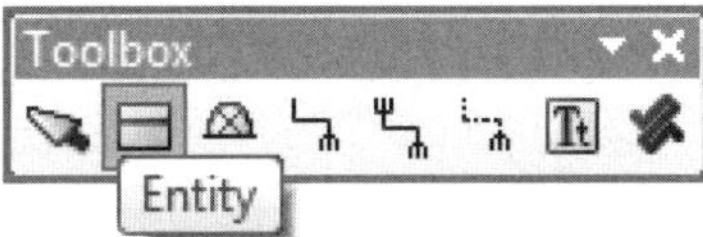

Then, simply click anywhere on the blank diagram workspace to create the new entity. You will notice that this new entity is given a default name of **E/1**, as shown in Figure 4.5. We'll want to change this to **Ice Cream Flavor**.

Figure 4.5 New Entity with Default Naming

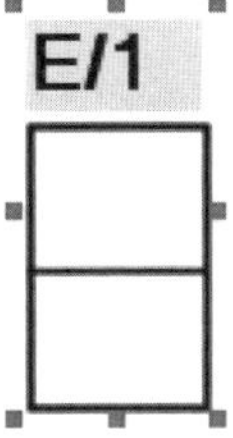

The name field is automatically highlighted and ready for data entry after dropping a new entity onto the workspace. Simply type the name of the new entity: 'Ice Cream Flavor', and your entity should look similar to the one in Figure 4.6.

Figure 4.6 Ice Cream Flavor Entity

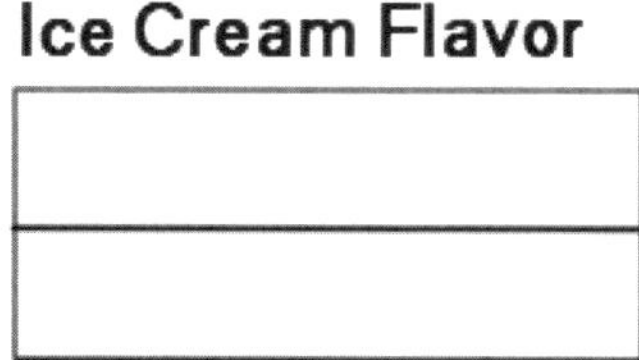

You might be wondering why there is a dividing line in the entity box. We'll explain this more in Chapter 5 when we discuss attributes of an entity, but for now you might want to show only the entity itself, without attributes. Recall our discussion of focusing information for your audience using varying displays? In this case, we want to display our model information at the entity level only. One easy way to change the focus is to click on the **Entity Display Level** icon in the Display Toolbar, as shown in Figure 4.7. Note that you may receive an information dialog asking "After setting the default display style for the diagram, do you want to remove any existing overrides on objects in the diagram?" We'll discuss the concepts of display theme inheritance in Chapter 8, so simply select **No** to move forward for now. A simple way of thinking of this option is that **Yes** will force the change onto all objects on the diagram, and **No** will leave in place any custom changes you've made to individual diagram objects (i.e. perhaps you want one entity shown with the definition display level, and all others with attribute display level).

Figure 4.7 Switching to Entity Display Level

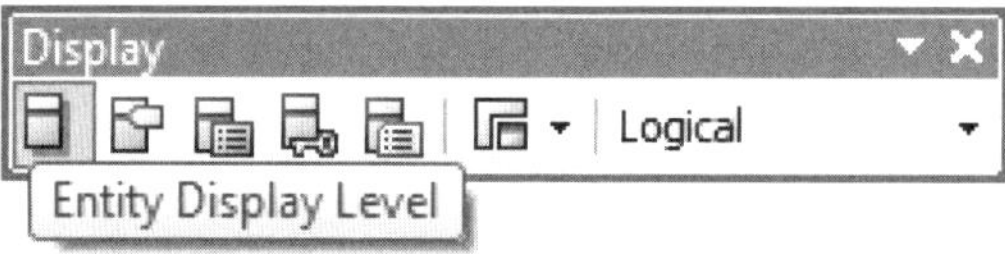

This will show the entity only, without those distracting lines, as shown in Figure 4.8. This is a nice presentation for business users, who normally want to see only a high-level model.

Figure 4.8 Ice Cream Flavor Entity using Entity Display Level

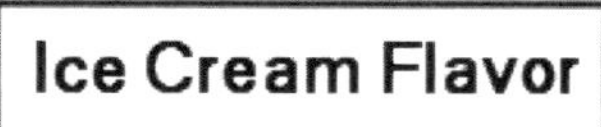

Now create two additional entities: **Ice Cream Size**, and **Ice Cream Order**. (Note: A handy tip for creating multiple entities at once is to hold down the **CTRL** key as you select the icon entity from the toolbar and drop the objects onto the diagram. This will enable 'multi-drop' functionality.) The result should look something like Figure 4.9. If you need to move an entity after dropping it, select the entity using the left mouse button, and hold the button down while you drag the mouse to move the entity to the desired location, and then release the mouse. For handy ways to layout and align entities automatically, refer to Chapter 8.

Figure 4.9 Ice Cream Entities

This looks similar to our list of entities in Figure 4.3, but recall that **Ice Cream Order** is a dependent entity, and therefore should have rounded corners. You can't have an order without knowing the flavor and size that the customer wants. So how do we indicate this?

This might have been confusing to you as you were creating the entities—there was no selection box for 'independent' vs. 'dependent' entity. So how do you flag **Ice Cream Order** as 'dependent'? The answer lies in the definition of a dependent entity. A dependent entity only exists in its *relationship to other entities*, in this case **Ice Cream Flavor** and **Ice Cream Size**. You'll have to create an identifying relationship between these entities and **Ice Cream Order** to indicate its dependent status. We'll discuss this in more detail when we describe relationships in Chapter 6. For now, we'll simply show you that after creating a relationship between **Ice Cream Flavor** and **Ice Cream Order**, the box for **Ice Cream Order** becomes rounded. Figure 4.10 shows what the model looks like with **Ice Cream Order** as a dependent entity.

Figure 4.10 Showing a Dependent Entity

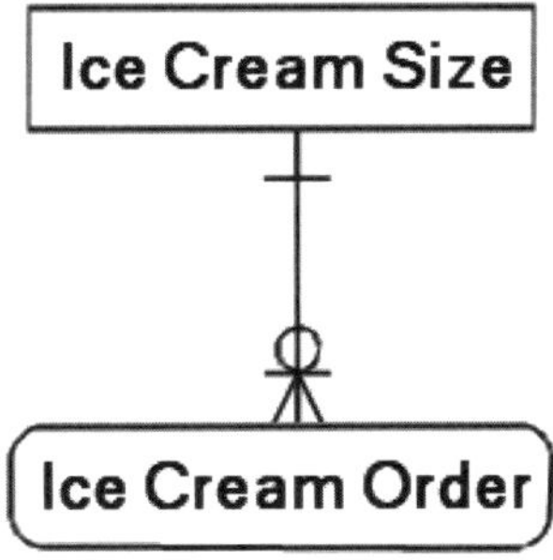

So, in other words, you don't *create* a dependent entity. You *make an entity dependent* by describing its relationship with other entities. Stay tuned until Chapter 6, where you'll learn more about relationships.

Creating Entity Definitions

As we've discussed, a key driver for creating a data model is communication. An important part of this communication, especially when defining requirements and objectives with business people, is to arrive at a clear definition for core business terms and concepts. Creating clear definitions and arriving at consensus is an important stage in data model creation. Skipping this stage can cause dangerous consequences down the road.

Let's go back to our ice cream example. In the previous section, we created three entities: **Ice Cream Flavor**, **Ice Cream Size**, and **Ice Cream Order**. Let's enter a definition for our **Ice Cream Size** entity. Begin by highlighting the entity and right-clicking to show the entity menu. From this menu, select **Entity Properties**, as shown in Figure 4.11. You will see the Entity Properties Editor, as shown in Figure 4.12.

Figure 4.11 Invoking the Entity Properties Editor

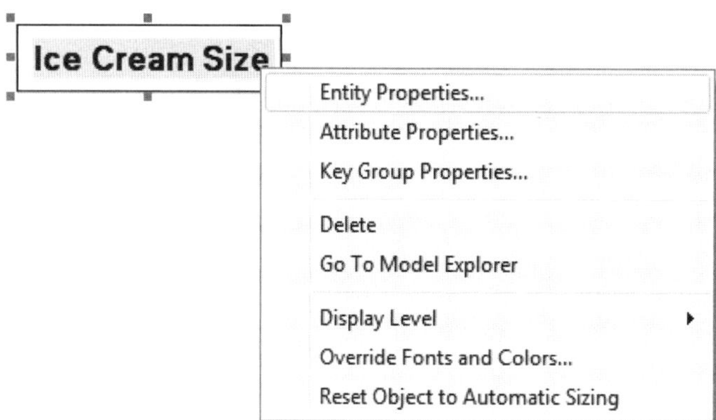

Figure 4.12 Entity Properties Editor

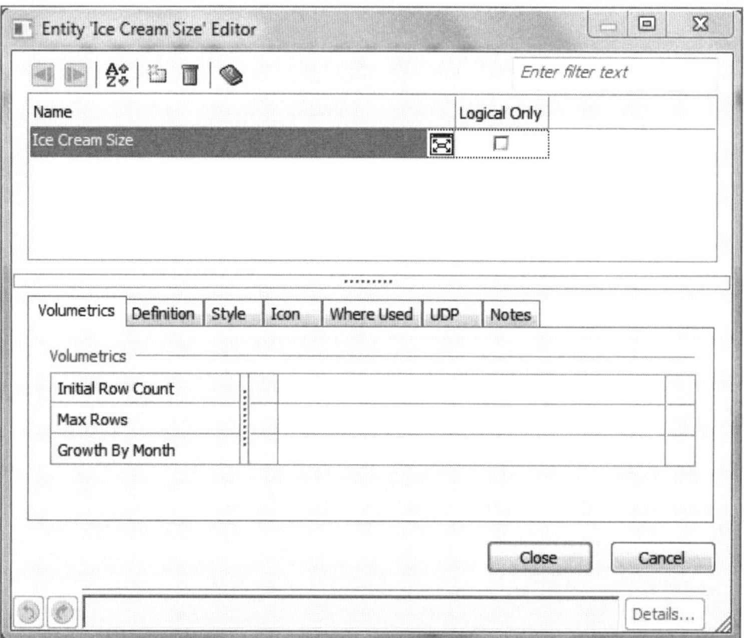

To enter the definition, simply move to the **Definition** tab and type the definition into the dialog box, as shown in Figure 4.13.

Figure 4.13 Entering a Definition in the Entity Properties Editor

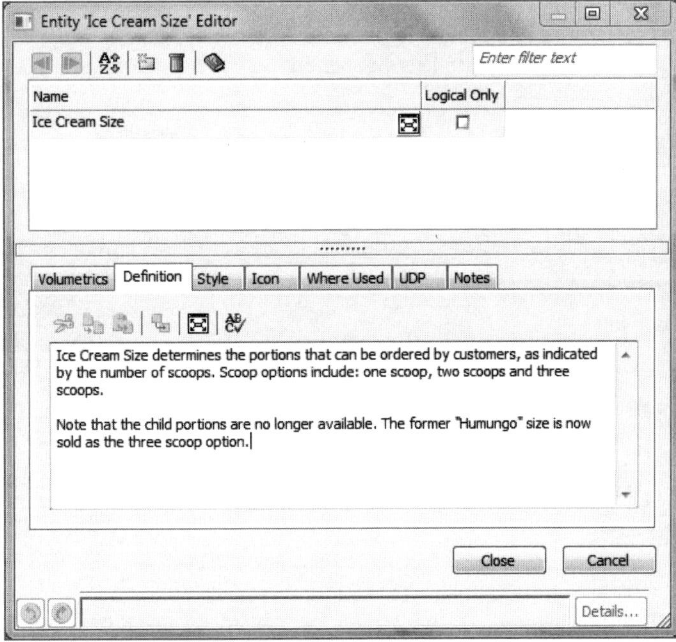

Before we make this definition final, we'll want to make sure that we've spelled everything correctly using the **Spell Check** option, as shown in Figure 4.14.

Figure 4.14 Invoking Spell Check

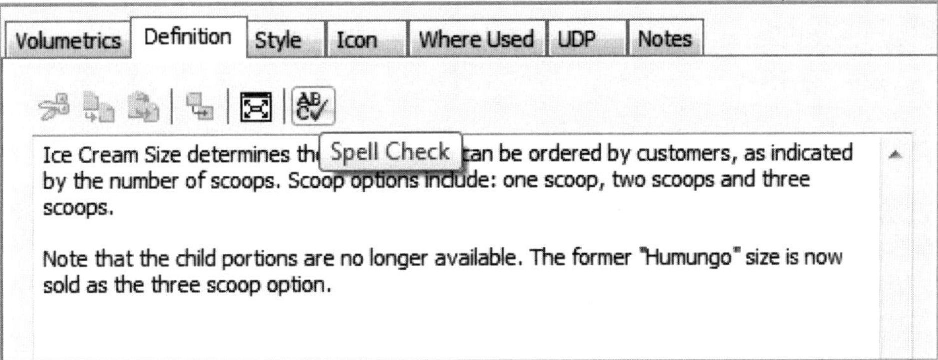

When you invoke **Spell Check**, you'll see that it catches our word "Humungo", as shown in Figure 4.15. We'll select **Ignore** for now, but we may want to consider creating a customized dictionary to contain these special words used by our company. Now that we've finished entering our definition, select **Close** to exit the Entity Properties Editor.

Figure 4.15 Using Spell Check to Correct Errors

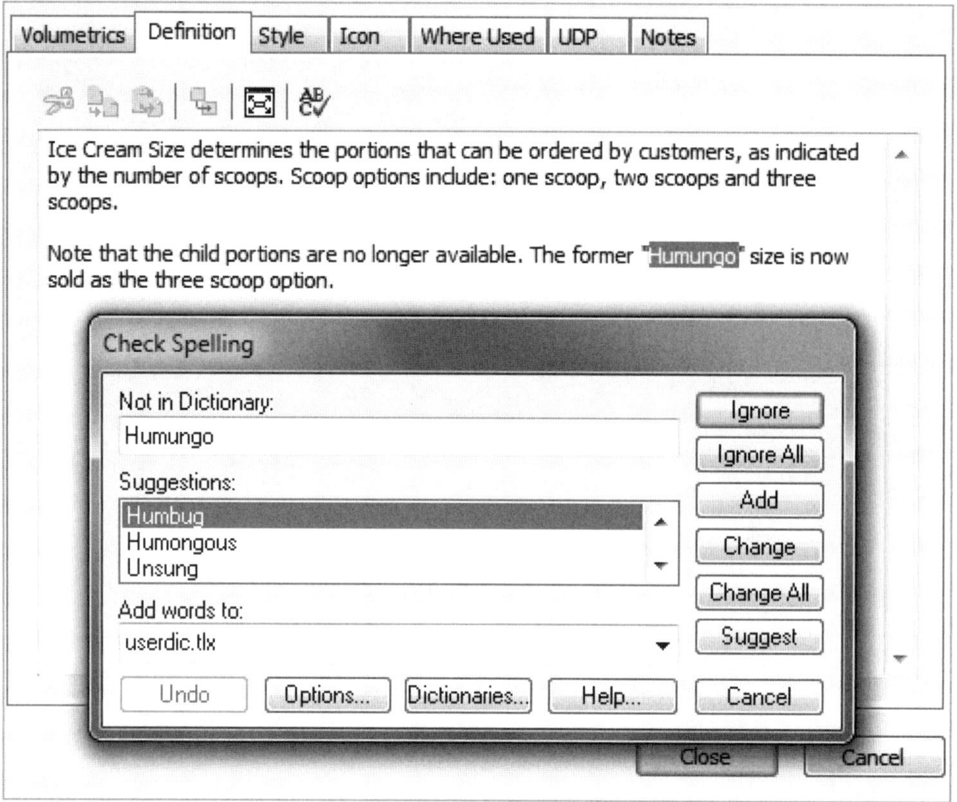

Next, we'll want to show this definition on the model, so that business users can easily read them and check them for accuracy. Last time we used the Display Toolbar to change the display level for our diagram. This time, let's use the menu bar. Select the **View|Display Level|Definition** menu to show the entity and its definition on the model, as shown in Figure 4.16.

Figure 4.16 Selecting the Definition Display Level

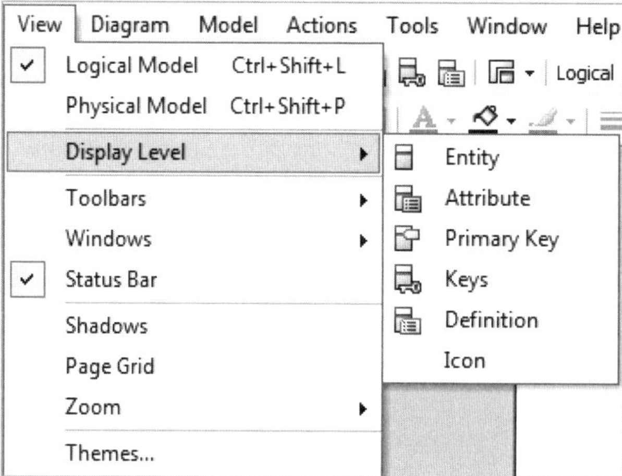

The result will look like Figure 4.17.

Figure 4.17 Entity using Definition Display Level

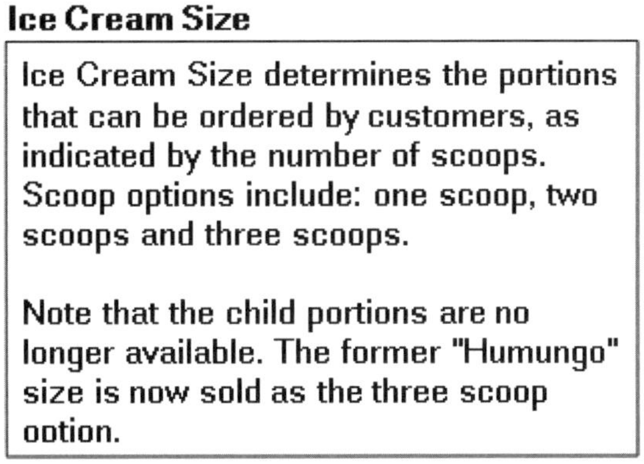

Ice Cream Size

Ice Cream Size determines the portions that can be ordered by customers, as indicated by the number of scoops. Scoop options include: one scoop, two scoops and three scoops.

Note that the child portions are no longer available. The former "Humungo" size is now sold as the three scoop option.

Note that you may have to resize the entity to see the entire definition. You can resize entities by selecting the entity and dragging the corners of the 'box'.

Now that you've learned how to create an entity and its definition, in the next chapter we'll discuss how to add even more descriptive detail to our entity using data elements. If you'd like an example of this simple model we created, the `Ice Cream Example.erwin` file is located on www.erwin.com/datamodelingmadesimple, so you can compare your work with the model we put together.

Key Points

- An entity represents a collection of information about something that the business deems important and worthy of capture. An entity fits into one of several categories - who, what, when, where, why, or how.
- A noun or noun phrase identifies a specific entity.
- Entity instances are the occurrences or values of a particular entity.
- An entity can exist at the conceptual, logical, or physical level of detail.
- An entity can be strong or weak, also known as independent or dependent.
- In CA ERwin Data Modeler, entities can be shown at different levels of detail, depending on the audience.
- It is important to create clear definitions for each entity.
- Use the Spell Check feature in CA ERwin Data Modeler when you are creating definitions.

CHAPTER 5
Data Elements

Spreadsheets have columns
Just like data elements
Models all around

Data elements add descriptive 'flavor' to the entities in your data model. For example, if we have a **Customer** data entity, what information is needed to track or describe customers: name, age, gender, etc? This chapter defines the concept of a data element and the three different levels at which a data element can exist: conceptual, logical, and physical. Domains and the different types of domains are also discussed. We'll conclude the chapter with hands-on examples of how to work with elements and domains in CA ERwin Data Modeler.

Data Element Explanation

A data element is a property of importance to the business whose values contribute to identifying, describing, or measuring instances of an entity. For example, the data element **Claim Number** identifies each claim. The data element **Student Last Name** lists the surname for each student. The data element **Gross Sales Amount** measures the monetary value of a transaction.

Returning to our spreadsheet analogy, the column headings on a spreadsheet are data elements. The cells beneath each column heading are the values for that column heading. Data elements can be thought of as the column headings in a spreadsheet, the fields on a form, or the labels on a report. Figure 5.1 shows an example using a spreadsheet. In this example, **Customer Name**, **Company**, **Country**, and **Year Purchased** are data elements.

Figure 5.1 Data Elements in a Spreadsheet

Customer Name	Company	Country	Year Purchased
Hans Kleigel	Komputers R Us	Germany	1970
Mary Jones	Big Bank Co	USA	1999
Proful Bishwal	Global Software	India	2005
Ming Lee	My Favorite Store	China	2008
Giovanni Petra	IL Mio Caro	Italy	2000

Data Element Types

As with entities, data elements can exist at conceptual, logical, and physical levels. A data element at the conceptual level must be a concept both basic and critical to the business. We do not usually think of data elements as business concepts, but depending on the business need, they can be. When I worked for a telecommunications company, **Telephone Number** was a data element that was so important to the business that it was represented on a number of conceptual data models.

A data element on a logical data model represents a business property, and is called an attribute. Each data element shown contributes to the business solution and is independent of any technology, including software and hardware. For example, **Ice Cream Flavor Name** is a logical data element because it has business significance, regardless of whether records are kept in a paper file or within the fastest database on the market.

A data element on a physical data model represents a database column. The logical attribute **Ice Cream Flavor Name** might be represented as the physical column **ICE_CRM_FLVR_NAM**.

We use the term *data element* throughout the text as a general term. However, we would recommend using the term that is most comfortable for your audience. For example, a business analyst might prefer the term 'attribute' or 'label', while a database administrator might prefer the term 'column' or 'field'. In CA ERwin Data Modeler, data elements at the logical level are called attributes and at the physical level they are called columns.

Domain Explanation

The complete set of all possible values that a data element may have is called a domain. A domain is a set of validation criteria that can be applied to more than one data element. For example, the domain **Date**, which contains all possible valid dates, can be assigned to any of these data elements:

- Employee Hire Date
- Order Entry Date
- Claim Submit Date
- Course Start Date

A data element may never contain values outside of its assigned domain. The domain values are defined by specifying the actual list of values or a set of rules. **Employee Gender Code**, for example, may be limited to the domain of (*female*, *male*).

Employee Hire Date may initially be assigned the rule that its domain contain only valid dates, for example. Therefore, this may include values such as:

- February 15th, 2005
- 25 January 1910
- 20030410
- March 10th, 2050

Because **Employee Hire Date** is limited to valid dates, it does not include February 30th, for example. We can restrict a domain with additional rules. For example, by restricting the **Employee Hire Date** domain to dates earlier than today's date, we would eliminate March 10th, 2050. By restricting **Employee Hire Date** to YYYYMMDD (that is, year, month, and day concatenated), we would eliminate all the examples given except for 20030410. Another way of refining this set of values is to restrict the domain of **Employee Hire Date** to dates that fall on a Monday, Tuesday, Wednesday, Thursday, or Friday (that is, the typical workweek).

In our example of the business card, **Contact Name** may contain thousands or millions of values. The values from our four sample cards in Figure 1.2 would be

- Steve Hoberman
- Steve
- Jenn
- Bill Smith
- Jon Smith

This name domain may need a bit of refining. It may be necessary to clarify whether a valid domain value is composed of both a first and last name, such as 'Steve Hoberman', or just a first name, such as 'Steve'. Could this domain contain company names such as 'IBM', as well? Could this domain contain numbers instead of just letters, such as the name R2D2 from the movie Star Wars? Could this domain contain special characters, such as the name O(+>? O(+>, representing "The Artist Formerly Known as Prince" (the musician Prince changed his name to this unpronounceable "Love Symbol" in 1993).

There are three different types of domains:

- **Format.** Format domains specify the standard types of data one can have in a database. For example, Integer, Character(30), and Date are all format domains. The format domain for **Ice Cream Size** might be Character(15), meaning a particular **Ice Cream Size** can contain any sequence of characters and be at most 15 characters in length.
- **List.** List domains are similar to a drop-down list. They contain a finite set of values from which to choose. List domains are refinements of format domains. The format domain for **Order Status Code** might be Character(10). This

domain can be further defined through a list domain of possible values {Open, Shipped, Closed, Returned}. The list domain for **Ice Cream Size** would be {one scoop, two scoops, three scoops}.

- **Range.** Range domains allow all values that are between a minimum and maximum value. For example, **Order Delivery Date** must be between Today's Date and three months in the future. As with list domains, range domains are a refined version of a format domain.

Domains are very useful for a number of reasons:

- Improves data quality by checking against a domain before inserting data. This is the primary reason for having a domain. By limiting the possible values of a data element, the chances of bad data getting into the database are reduced. For example, if every data element that represents money is assigned the Amount domain, consisting of all decimal numbers up to 15 digits in length including two digits after the decimal point, then there is a good chance that each of these data elements actually do contain currency. Gross Sales Amount, which is assigned the amount domain, would not allow the value 'R2D2' to be added.
- The data model communicates even more. When we display domains on a data model, the data model communicates that a particular data element has the properties of a particular domain, and therefore the data model becomes a more comprehensive communication tool. We learn, for example, that Gross Sales Amount, Net Sales Amount, and List Price Amount all share the Amount domain and therefore, share properties such that their valid values are limited to currency.
- Greater efficiency and consistency in building new models and maintaining existing models. When a data modeler embarks on a project, she can use a standard set of domains, thereby saving time by not reinventing the wheel. Any new data element that ends in Amount, for example, would be associated with the standard Amount domain, saving analysis and design time.

We will cover domains in CA ERwin Data Modeler briefly in this chapter, and in more detail in Chapter 10.

EXERCISE: Assigning Domains

What is the most appropriate domain for each of the three data elements below?

- Email Address
- Gross Sales Amount
- Country Code

For our answers to this exercise, visit www.erwin.com/datamodelingmadesimple.

Creating Data Elements

Now that we understand what data elements are, let's add some data elements to our model in CA ERwin Data Modeler (If you don't have the `Ice Cream Example.erwin` model from the last section, you can download it from www.erwin.com/datamodelingmadesimple). In the last section, we created a logical entity called **Ice Cream Size**. We created this entity and added a business definition, but we did not describe the detailed values that further define **Ice Cream Size**. For example, are there names associated with each size (e.g. small, medium, or large, or kiddie, regular, whopper)? Are there a certain number of scoops associated with each name? Do certain regions offer some sizes, but not others? Are certain sizes only sold during certain times of the year? Let's add some data elements, or 'attributes' since we're talking about a logical data model, to our **Ice Cream Size** entity.

Let's continue using the model we created in the last chapter. Using this model, select the **Ice Cream Size** entity and right-click to generate the context menu for the entity. Then select the **Attribute Properties** option, as shown in Figure 5.2.

Figure 5.2 Invoking the Attribute Properties Editor

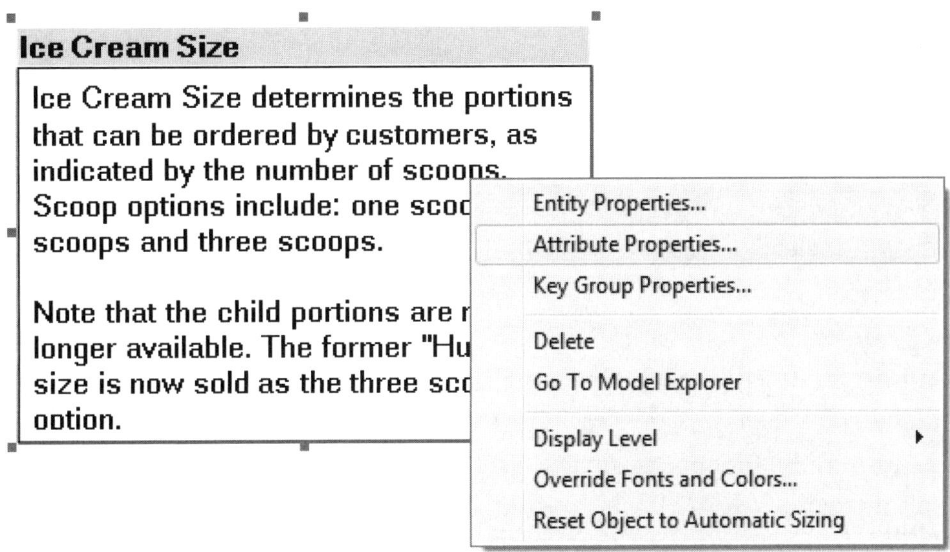

The Attribute Properties Editor appears, as shown in Figure 5.3.

Figure 5.3 Attribute Properties Editor

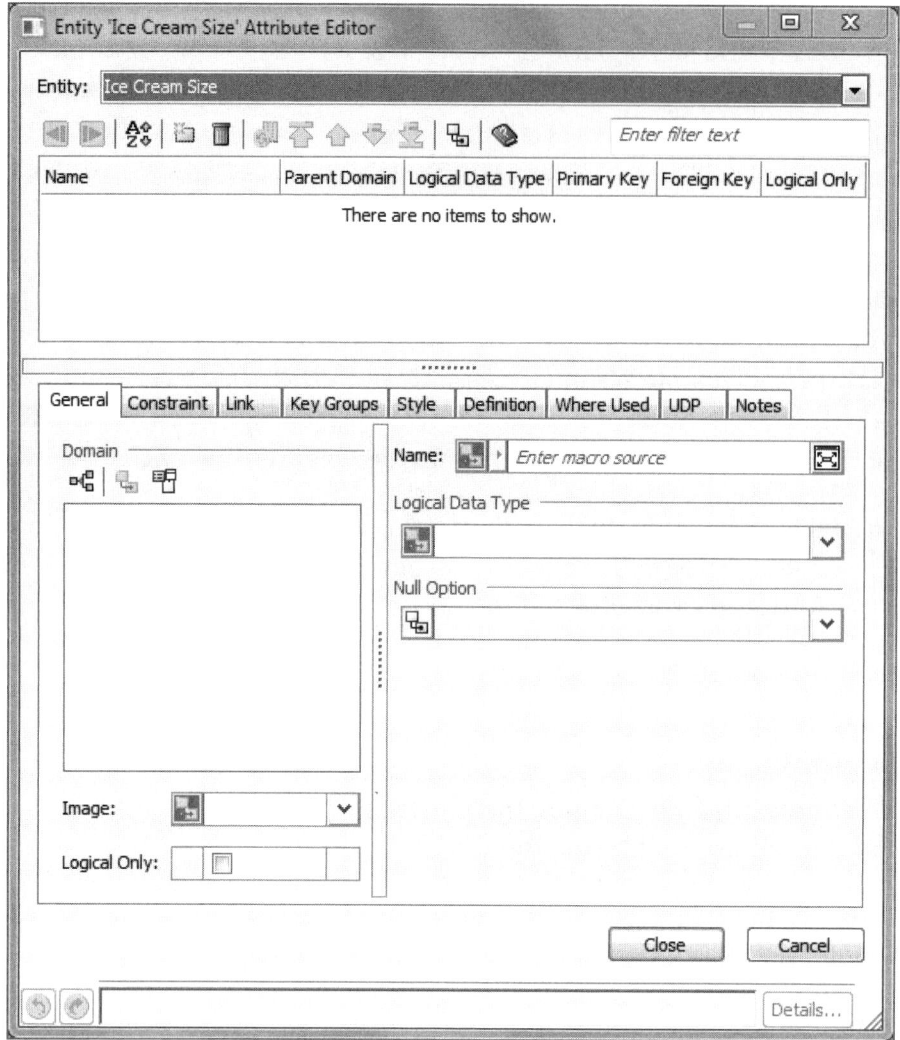

Let's add an attribute called **Ice Cream Size Name** that lists the names used for the ice cream sizes. In North America, for example, the sizes include: Kiddie, Small, Medium, Large, and WhopperMunga. Select the **New** button, and a new attribute with the default name **<default>** is created, as shown in Figure 5.4.

Figure 5.4 Creating a New Attribute

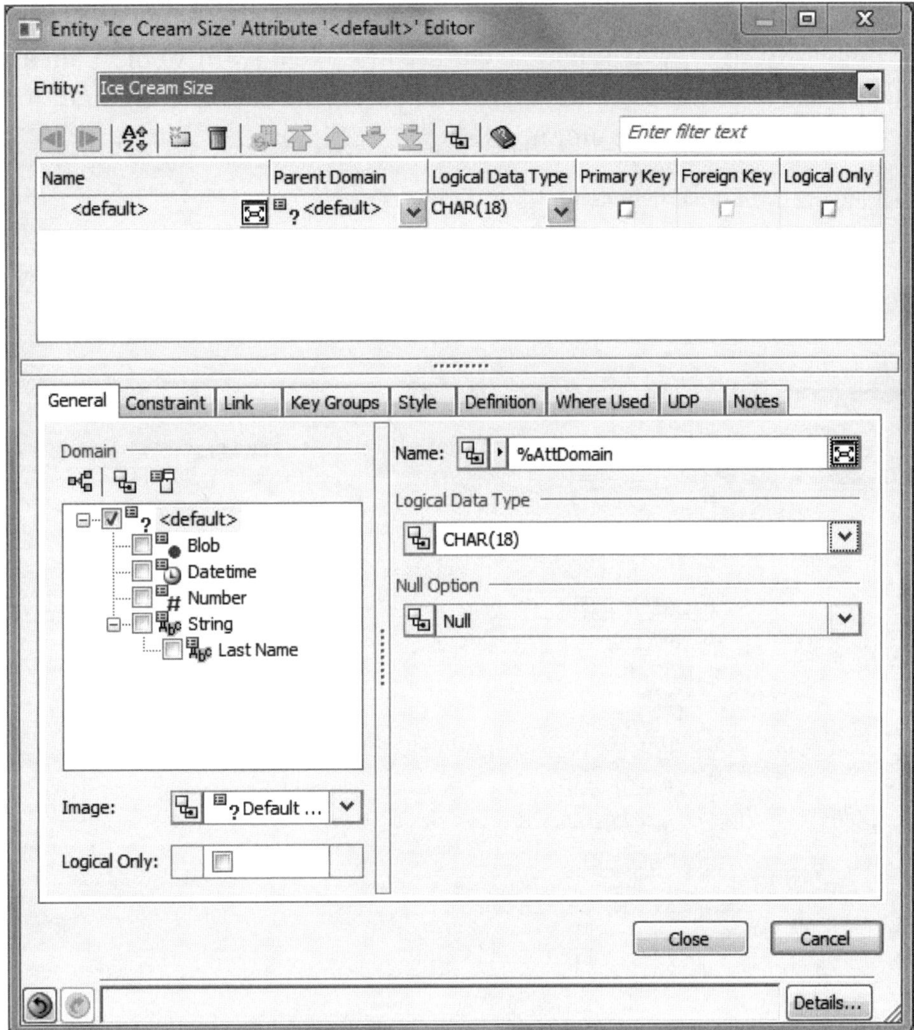

Change this default name by simply highlighting the **Name** field and typing **Ice Cream Size Name**, as shown in Figure 5.5.

Figure 5.5 Naming an Attribute

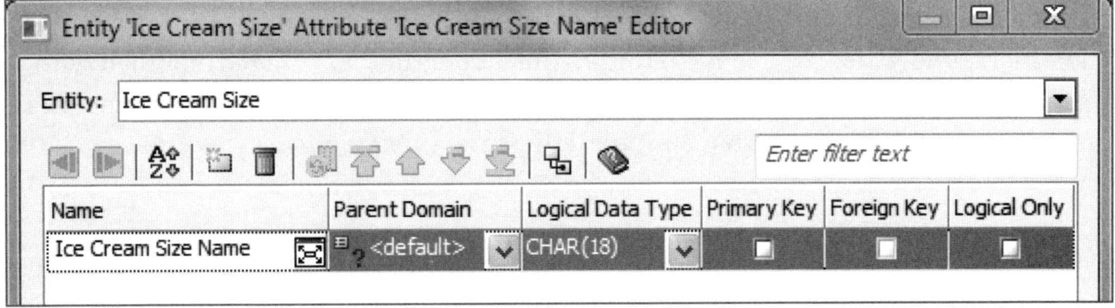

We'll also want to define what type of information is stored in this attribute. For example, would the information be a number, a string, a date, etc? You'll see that the default for the **Logical Data Type** is CHAR(18), meaning that 18 characters can be stored in this field. That should be fine for our existing ice cream names, but there is discussion within management about potentially adding a new flavor next month called “SuperBigWhopperMunga”, which has 20 characters. We’ll want to plan ahead, and this name wouldn’t fit in our existing data type. One option would be to change this field to a text field by using the drop-down menu, as shown in Figure 5.6.

Figure 5.6 Changing the Data Type of an Attribute

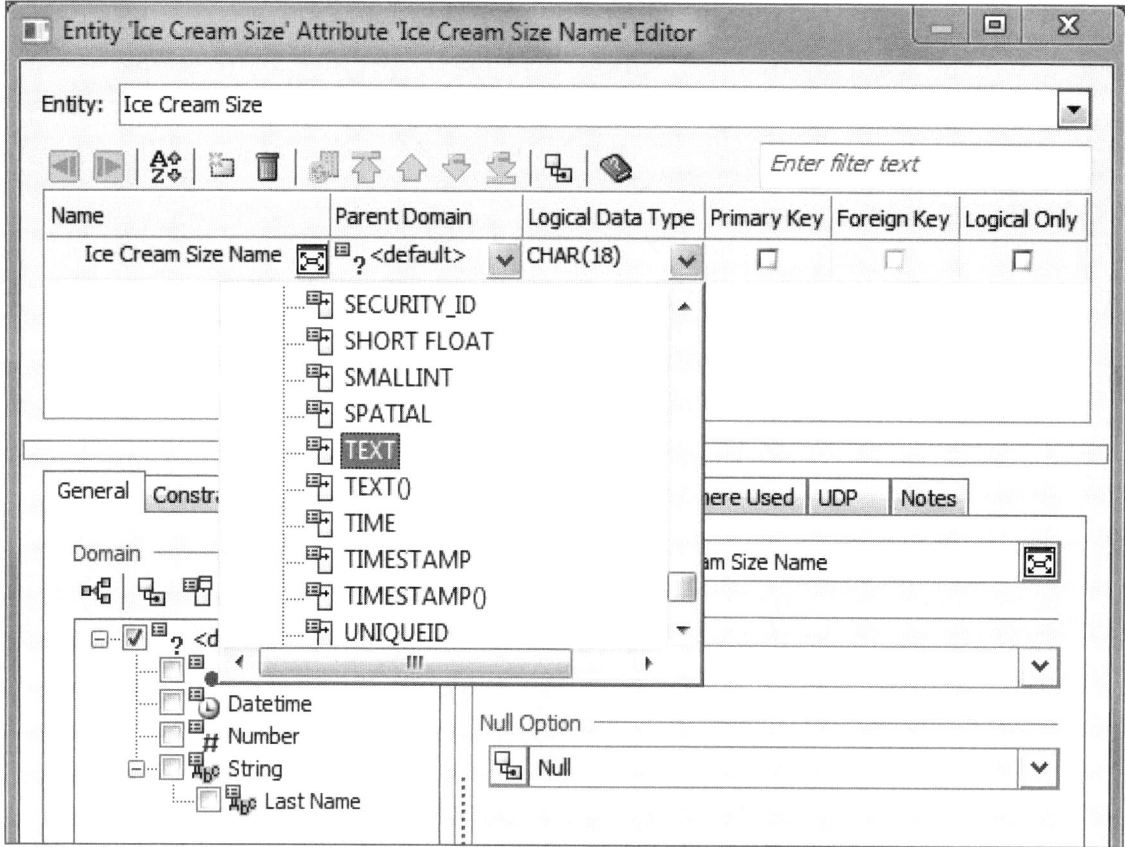

Remember from earlier in the chapter, however, that a domain is a recommended way to create common formats for data elements such as attributes. Instead of “reinventing the wheel” and creating a custom data type for this attribute, let’s see if there are any pre-defined domains that we can use instead. Use the drop-down menu for the **Parent Domain** field, and you’ll see the list of pre-defined domains that comes installed with CA ERwin Data Modeler, as shown in Figure 5.7. The domain **String** looks like a promising option, since our **Ice Cream Size Name** attribute is a text string.

Figure 5.7 Selecting a Domain for an Attribute

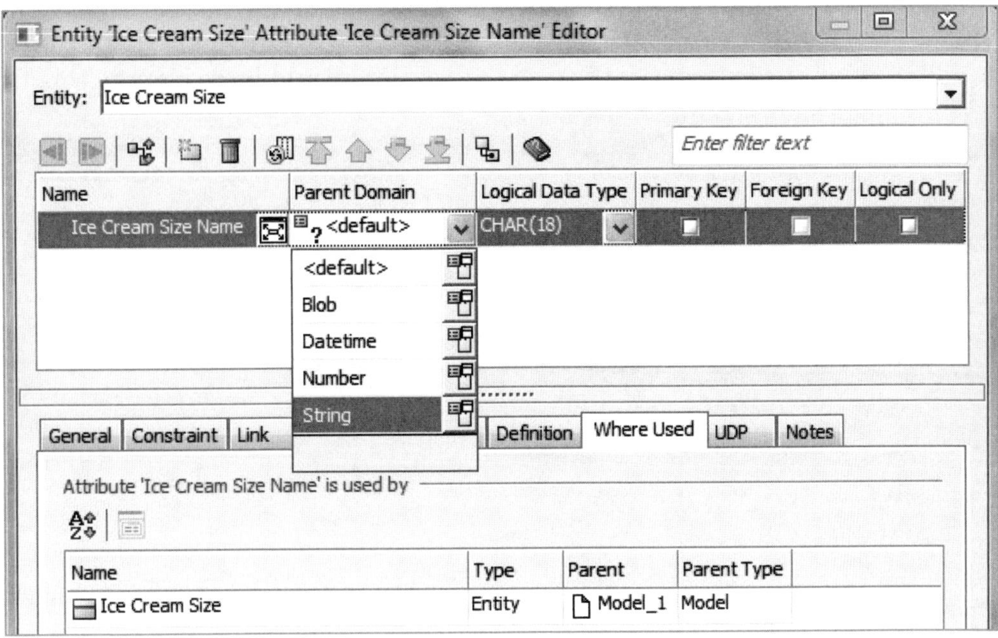

But we're not exactly sure of the length of this new **String** domain, or anything else about it. To find out if this domain would suit our needs, click on the **Domain Dictionary** button, shown in Figure 5.8.

Figure 5.8 Invoking the Domain Dictionary Button

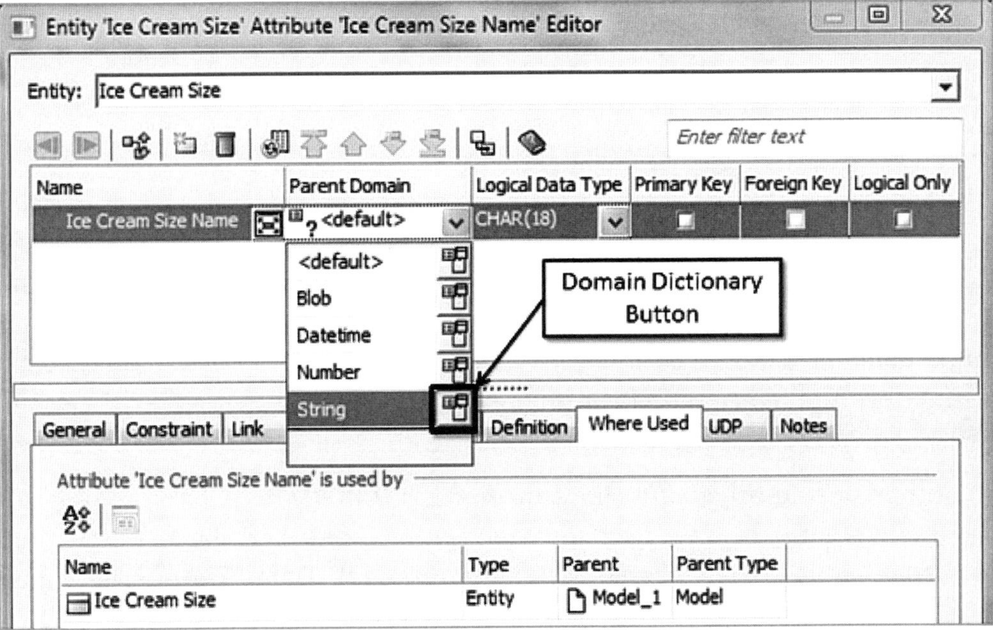

The Domain Dictionary, shown in Figure 5.9, shows you detailed information about this domain. Notice that the **Logical Data Type** for the **String** domain is **VARCHAR(20)**, which means that 20 characters can fit in this field—perfect to hold our new **SuperBigWhopperMunga** flavor. (Note: For more information on the difference between **CHAR** and **VARCHAR** data types, refer to the Glossary at the end of the book.)

Figure 5.9 Domain Dictionary

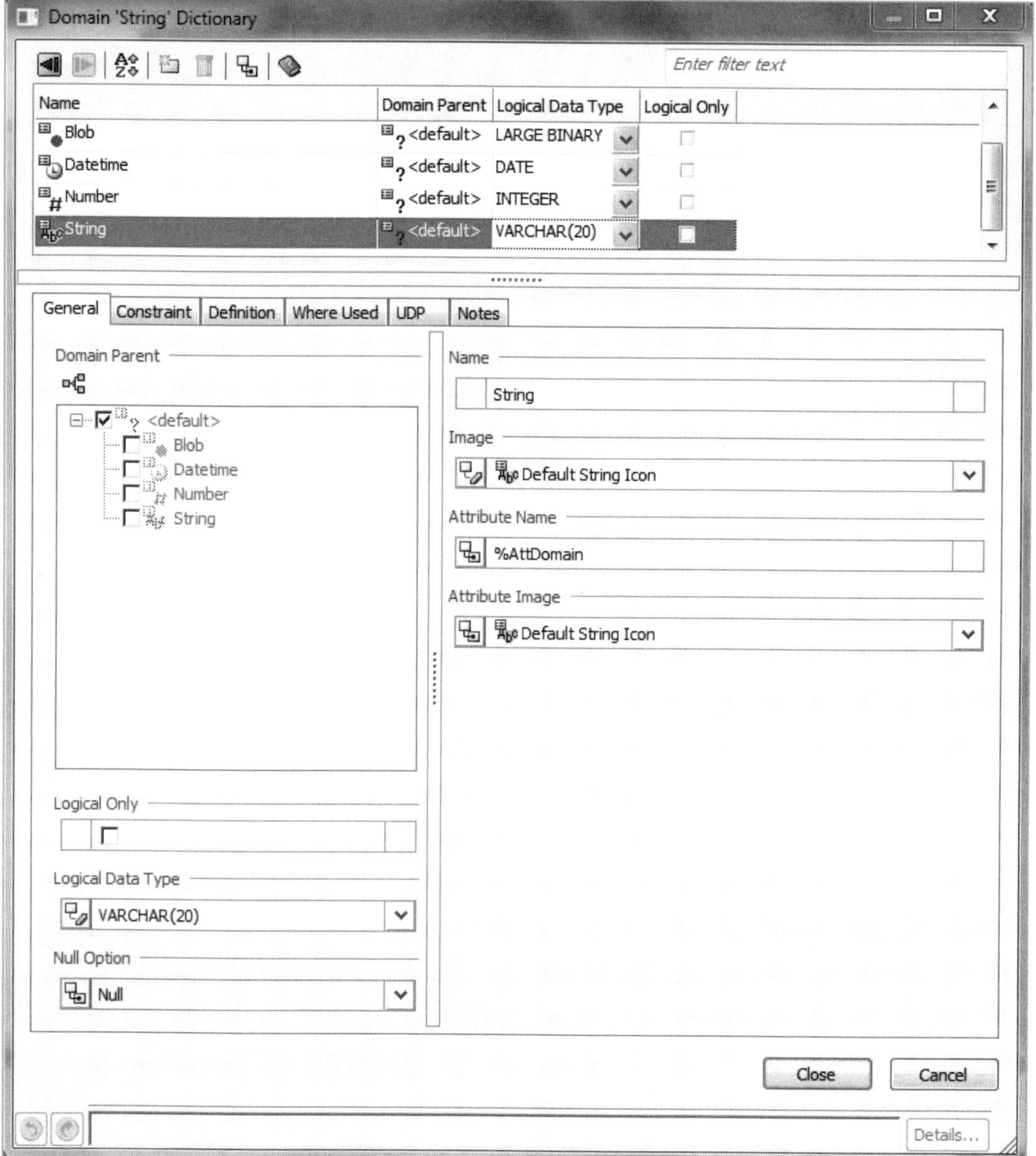

We'll go into more detail about the Domain Dictionary in Chapter 10—we'll just concern ourselves with the data type for now. Select **Close** and the **String** domain will be shown in Figure 5.10. Notice that the **Logical Data Type** has changed to **VARCHAR(20)**, which is the data type of the **String** domain we selected. In a real-world scenario, we most likely would want to create a specific domain for name fields, perhaps even adding valid values. We'll go into more detail on how to create custom domains in Chapter 10.

Figure 5.10 Attribute using a Predefined Domain

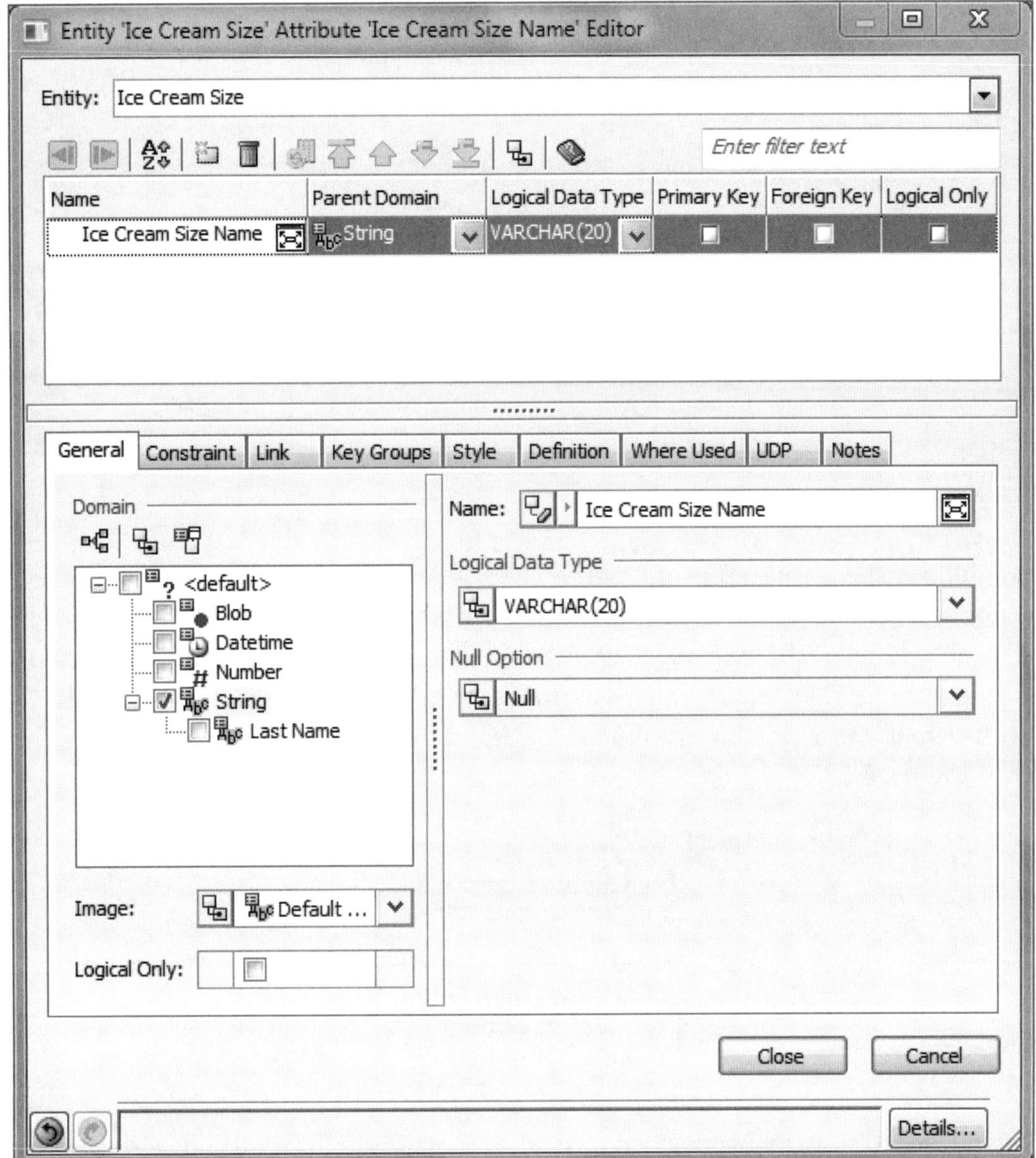

Another key property that you'll want to set for this attribute is the **Null Option**, which is key to data quality and data entry validation. The simplest way to think of the null option is that it indicates whether a data value is required for this attribute. But to wax philosophical for a moment, in actuality NULL is a special concept in relational theory that is neither equal to nor unequal to any value in any data type. It is not zero, an empty string, or false, but undefined or having no value. Another way to view NULL is to consider it a state, not a value, i.e. the state of having no value (similar to a Zen Koan).

In this case, the name of the ice cream size is important to include, so we'll want to make sure that the **Ice Cream Size Name** field is not left undefined when data is entered. Set the **Null Option** field to **Not Null**, as shown in Figure 5.11.

Figure 5.11 Defining the Null Option for an Attribute

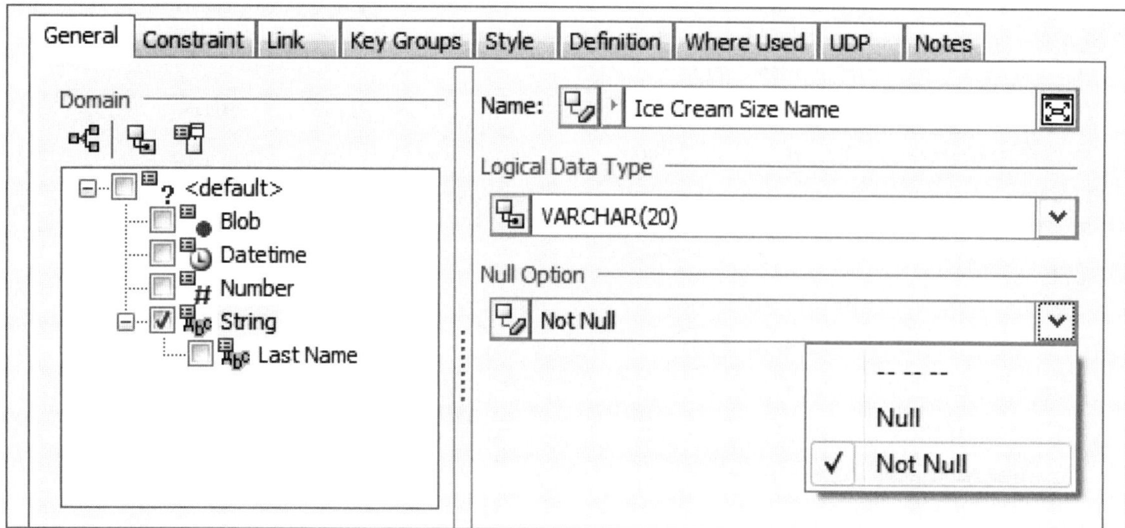

You can follow the same steps to enter the other attributes we discussed, such as number of scoops, season offered, etc. We won't go through each of the steps to show this—you should have the hang of it by now. Create two additional attributes: **Number of Scoops** (integer, Not Null) and **Season Offered** (VARCHAR(20), Not Null). When you are finished entering the attributes for **Ice Cream Size**, your model should look similar to Figure 5.12.

Figure 5.12 Attributes for the Ice Cream Size Entity

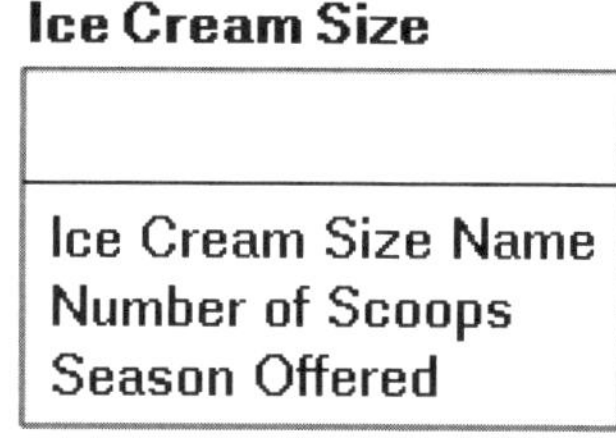

If you don't see the attributes on your model, you might have to change the Display Level to show attributes from the Display Toolbar shown in Figure 5.13.

Figure 5.13 Selecting the Attribute Display Level

You should now have an understanding of how to create attributes and define key properties, such as name, data type, and nullability in CA ERwin Data Modeler. We also covered the importance of domains, and how you can select pre-defined domains for your attributes. We'll talk more about elements in Chapter 7, when we discuss the concept of keys, which are a special type of element used to uniquely identify an entity, and in Chapters 18 and 19 when we discuss logical and physical data modeling. Domains will be covered in more detail in Chapter 10. If you'd like an example of the model we updated in this chapter, the modified **Ice Cream Example_Chapter5.erwin** file is located on www.erwin.com/datamodelingmadesimple.

In the next chapter, we'll discuss relationships between entities.

Key Points

- A data element is a property of importance to the business whose values contribute to identifying, describing, or measuring instances of an entity.
- A domain is a set of validation criteria that can be applied to more than one data element.
- There are different types of domains, including format, list, and range domains.
- In CA ERwin Data Modeler, the Attribute Properties Editor allows you to easily define a number of properties for an attribute, including name, data type, null option, and domain.
- There are predefined domains in CA ERwin Data Modeler that you can use, and you can also create your own using these as a guide.

CHAPTER 6
Relationships

Rules all around us
Relationships tell the tale
Connecting the dots

The relationships between data entities are as important as the definitions of entities and elements that we've discussed in the previous chapters, and are key to understanding business requirements. This chapter defines rules and relationships and the three different levels at which relationships can exist: conceptual, logical, and physical. Data rules are distinguished from action rules. Cardinality and labels are explained so that you can read any data model as easily as reading a book. Other types of relationships, such as recursive relationships and subtyping, are discussed as well. Hands-on examples of how to create the various relationship types in CA ERwin Data Modeler are included.

Relationship Explanation

In its most general sense, a rule is an instruction about how to behave in a specific situation. The following are examples of rules that you are familiar with:

- Your room must be cleaned before you can go outside and play.
- If you get three strikes, you are out and it is the next batter's turn.
- The speed limit is 55 mph.

Rules are visually captured on our data model through relationships. A relationship is displayed as a line connecting two entities. It captures the rules between these two entities. If the two entities are **Employee** and **Department**, the relationship may capture the rules "Each Employee must work for one Department" and "Each Department may contain many Employees."

Relationship Types

A rule can be either a data rule or an action rule. Data rules are instructions on *how* data relate to one another. Action rules are instructions on *what to do* when data elements contain certain values. Let's talk about data rules first.

There are two types of data rules - structural and referential integrity (RI) data rules. Structural rules (also known as cardinality rules) define the quantity of each entity instance that can participate in a relationship.

For example:

- Each product can appear on one or many order lines.
- Each order line must contain one and only one product.
- Each student must have a unique student number.

RI rules focus on ensuring valid values:

- An order line cannot exist without a valid product.
- A claim cannot exist without a valid policy.
- A student cannot exist without a valid student number.

When we define a structural rule, we get the corresponding RI rule for free. For example, if we define this structural rule on our data model, "Each order line must contain one and only one product", it is automatically assumed and included that "An order line cannot exist without a valid product."

Action rules on the other hand, are instructions on *what to do* when data elements contain certain values:

- Freshman students can register for at most 18 credits a semester.
- A policy must have at least three claims against it to be considered high-risk.
- Take 10% off of an order if the order contains more than five products.

In our data models, we can represent the data and enforce data rules, but we cannot enforce action rules on a data model. A student data model can capture the level of student, such as Freshman or Senior, as well as the number of credits each student is taking each semester, but cannot enforce that a freshman student register for no more than 18 credits a semester.

Returning to our ice cream example, I eventually ordered a double scoop of ice cream in a cone - one scoop of Chocolate and one scoop of Banana. Many relationships can describe the process of placing this order, such as:

- An ice cream container can be either a cone or cup.
- Each ice cream container can contain many scoops of ice cream.
- Each ice cream scoop must reside in an ice cream container (or our hands would get really sticky holding that scoop of banana ice cream).
- Each ice cream flavor can be chosen for one or many ice cream containers.
- Each ice cream container can contain many flavors.

The three levels of granularity that apply to entities and data elements, also apply to the relationships that connect entities. Conceptual relationships are high level rules that connect key concepts. Logical relationships are more specific and enforce the rules between the logical entities. Physical relationships are also specific rules and apply to the physical entities that the relationship connects. These physical relationships eventually become database constraints, which ensure that data adheres to the rules. So, in our ice cream example, "Each ice cream container can contain many scoops of ice cream", can be a conceptual relationship. This high-level rule can be broken down into more detailed, logical relationships, such as defining the rule on the different types of containers: "An ice cream container can be either a cone or cup." This logical relationship then translates into the physical relationship "An ice cream container must be of one ice cream container type, whose values are 'cone' or 'cup' or 'not applicable'.

Cardinality

Cardinality defines the number of instances of each entity that can participate in a relationship. It is represented by the symbols that appear on both ends of a relationship line. It is through cardinality that the data rules are specified and enforced. Without cardinality, the most we can say about a relationship is that two entities are connected in some way through a rule. For example, **Person** and **Company** have some kind of relationship, but we don't know much more than this.

The domain of values to choose from to represent cardinality on a relationship is limited to three values: zero, one, or many. *Many* (some people read it as *more*), means any number greater than one. Each side of a relationship can have any combination of zero, one, or many. Specifying zero or one allows us to capture whether or not an entity instance is required in a relationship. Specifying one or many allows us to capture 'how many' of a particular instance participates in a given relationship.

Because we have only three cardinality symbols, we can't specify an exact number (other than through documentation), as in "A car has four tires." We can only say, "A car has many tires." A data model represents something in the real world. In capturing this something, there is always a tradeoff between refinement and simplicity. The greater the variety of symbols we show on a model, the more we can communicate. But more symbols also means greater complexity. Data modeling (using the IE notation in this book) forfeits a certain amount of refinement for simplicity. The advantage is we can explain very complex ideas with a simple set of symbols.

Each of the cardinality symbols is illustrated in the following example of **Ice Cream Flavor** and **Ice Cream Scoop**. An ice cream flavor is a selection choice for an ice cream scoop. An ice cream scoop must be one of the available ice cream flavors. Formalizing the rules between flavor and scoop, we have:

- Each **Ice Cream Flavor** can be the selection choice for one or many **Ice Cream Scoops**.
- Each **Ice Cream Scoop** must contain one **Ice Cream Flavor**.

Figure 6.1 captures these business rules.

Figure 6.1 Ice Cream Flavor and Ice Cream Scoop, Take 1

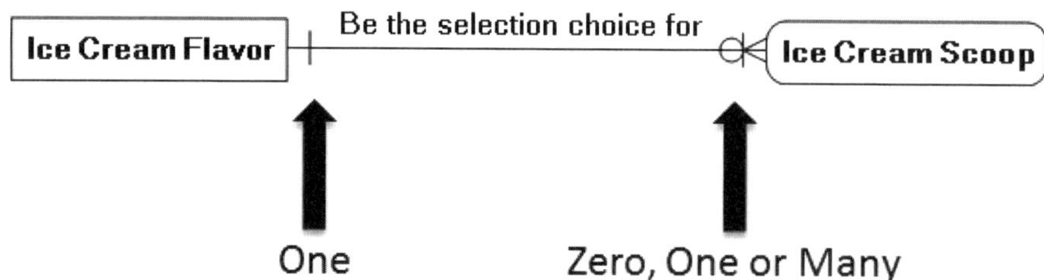

The small vertical line means 'one'. The circle means 'zero'. The triangle with a line through the middle means 'many'. Some people call the 'many' symbol a *crow's foot* (because it looks like a crow's foot!). Another way to decipher these cardinality markers is to think of how a small child would answer the question "how many scoops?" If the answer is "one", they'd hold up one finger. In a data model, this would be shown as follows: Think of that as an index finger showing 'one' scoop. If the answer is more than one scoop, they hold up several fingers. Think of the following as several fingers sticking up: What this notation is saying is that an ice cream flavor can be the selection choice for 1 or more scoops, and it *must* be assigned to at least one scoop. If it's not a requirement that a flavor be assigned to a scoop, you can put a '0' instead of a '1' next to the crow's foot , which is what we used in the example in Figure 6.1.

Having a zero in the cardinality means we can use optional-sounding words such as 'may' or 'can' when reading the relationship. Without the zero, we use mandatory-sounding terms such as 'must' or 'have to'.

So instead of being redundant and saying:

- Each **Ice Cream Flavor** can be the selection choice for *zero*, one or many **Ice Cream Scoop**s.

We take out the word 'zero' because it can be expressed using the word 'can', which implies the zero:

- Each **Ice Cream Flavor** *can* be the selection choice for one or many **Ice Cream Scoop**s.

Relationship lines are frequently labeled to clarify the relationship and express the rule that the relationship represents. Thus, the label "Be the selection choice for" on the line in this example, helps in reading the relationship and understanding the rule. Labels are generally placed and read 'clockwise' on the model diagram. A relationship has a parent and child. The parent entity appears on the 'one' side of the relationship, and the child appears on the "many" side of the relationship. When I read a relationship, I always start with the entity on the one side of the relationship first. "Each **Ice Cream Flavor** can be the selection choice for one or many **Ice Cream Scoop**s." It's then followed by reading the relationship from the many side: "Each **Ice Cream Scoop** must contain one **Ice Cream Flavor**." In truth, it doesn't matter which side you start from, as long as you are consistent.

I also always use the word 'each' in reading a relationship, starting with the parent side. The reason for the word 'each' is that you want to specify, on average how many instances of one entity relate to a different entity instance. 'Each' is a more user-friendly term to me than 'A'.

Let's change the cardinality slightly and see how this impacts the resulting business rule. Assume that because of the rough economy, this ice cream shop decides to allow consumers to select more than one flavor in a scoop. Figure 6.2 contains the updated cardinality.

Figure 6.2 Ice Cream Flavor and Ice Cream Scoop, Take 2

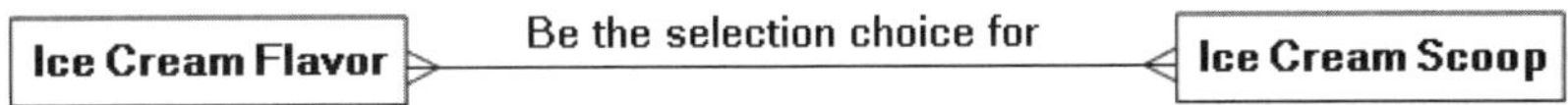

This is known as a many-to-many relationship, in contrast to the previous example, which was a one-to-many relationship. The business rules here are read as follows:

- Each **Ice Cream Flavor** must be the selection choice for many **Ice Cream Scoops**.
- Each **Ice Cream Scoop** must contain many **Ice Cream Flavors**.

Make sure the labels on relationship lines are as descriptive as possible. Here are some examples of good label names:

- contain
- work for
- own
- initiate
- categorize
- apply to

Always avoid the following words as label names, as they provide no additional information to the reader (you can use these words in combination with other words to make a meaningful label name; just avoid using these words by themselves):

- has
- have
- associate
- participate
- relate
- be

For example, replace the relationship sentence:

- A **Person** is *associated* with one **Company**.

With:

- A **Person** is *employed* by one **Company**.

Many modelers capture labels on both sides of the relationship line, instead of just one side, as shown in this chapter. In weighing simplicity versus precision, I chose simplicity. The other label can be inferred from the label that appears on the model. For example, I assumed the label 'contain' in Figure 6.2 and read the rule from **Ice Cream Scoop** to **Ice Cream Flavor** this way: "Each **Ice Cream Scoop** must contain one **Ice Cream Flavor**."

Identifying vs. Non-Identifying Relationships

Recall our discussion in Chapter 4, where we outlined the difference between Independent (Strong) and Dependent (Weak) entities. A dependent entity exists only in its relationship to other entities. A classic example of a dependent entity is an **Order**. An **Order** is a distinct entity that is tracked within the organization; a retail store may, for example, track how many orders were taken in a particular month. To retrieve an order, however, you need additional information, such as what **Product** was ordered, and which **Customer** ordered the product. This is where an identifying relationship comes in. An identifying relationship is represented by a solid line. In Figure 6.3, we see the business rules that create **Order** as a dependent entity.

Figure 6.3 Example of an Identifying Relationship

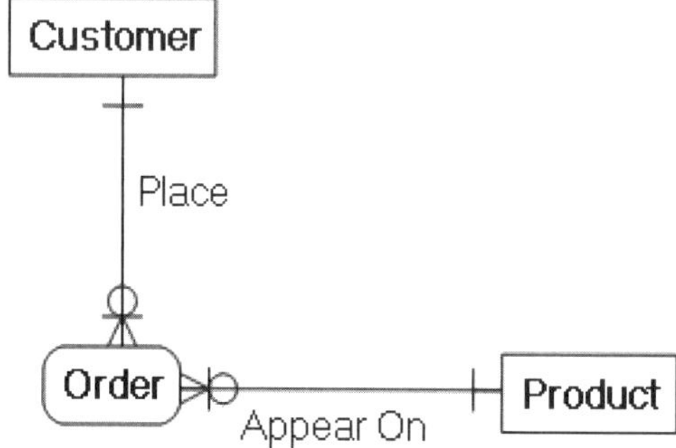

Reading the model in Figure 6.3 gives us the following rules:

- Each **Customer** may place one or more **Orders**.
- Each **Product** may appear on one or more **Orders**.

A non-identifying relationship is represented by a dashed line. With non-identifying relationships, each entity can be retrieved independently, and does not require information from the other entity. For example, we might keep track of the **Location** each **Customer** visits, shown in Figure 6.4.

Figure 6.4 Example of a Non-Identifying Relationship

A common usage of non-identifying relationships is for lookup tables. For example, you might have a table containing all of the location codes with a relationship to customer indicating the location he or she has visited.

Creating Relationships

We've learned a lot of terms and concepts around relationships in this chapter. To help make sense of these, let's put them into action with CA ERwin Data Modeler.

Let's implement the following business rule using relationships:

- Each **Customer** may own one or more **Accounts.**

First create two entities on a logical model: **Customer** and **Account**, using the **Entity Display** level setting (For assistance with creating a logical model, refer to Chapter 3. For help with how to create entities and set the display level, refer to Chapter 4). Your model should look similar to Figure 6.5.

Figure 6.5 Customer and Account Entities

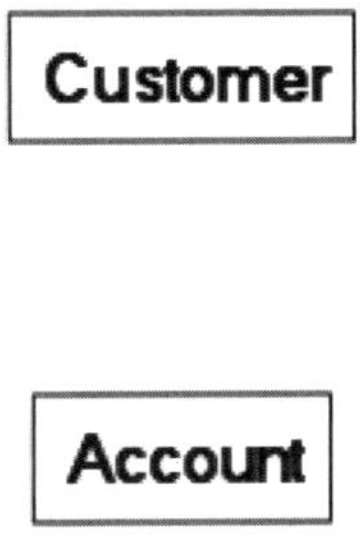

Customer

Account

Next, we'll need to create the relationship that implements the business rule. On the Toolbox Toolbar, shown in Figure 6.6, you will see three types of relationship lines:

- Identifying Relationship
- Many-to-Many Relationship
- Non-Identifying Relationship

Figure 6.6 Relationship Lines on the Toolbox Toolbar

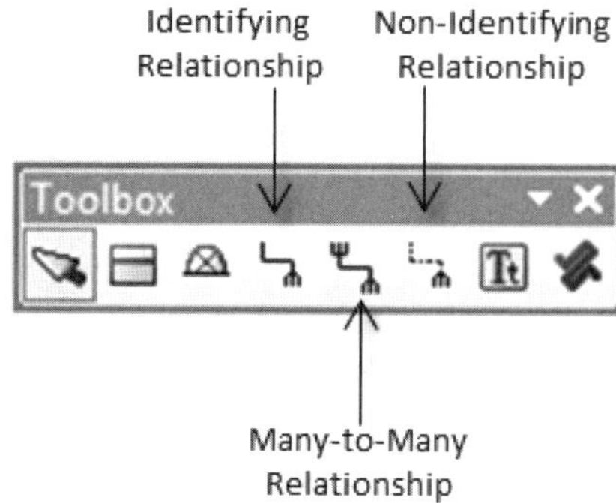

In this case, we have an Identifying Relationship. The business rule assumption in this case is that an **Account** cannot be retrieved without **Customer** information. Select the **Identifying Relationship** button, then click on the parent entity followed by the child entity. In this case, the parent entity is **Customer**. The result should look similar to Figure 6.7.

Figure 6.7 Identifying Relationship between Customer and Account

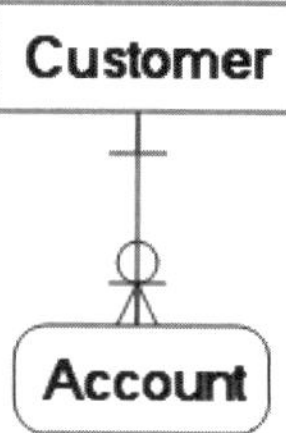

Notice that the **Account** entity now has rounded corners, indicating that it is a dependent or weak entity.

Next, we will add the verb phrase to complete the business rule sentence. A person may '**own**' one or more accounts. To add a verb phrase, highlight the relationship line, right click to invoke the context menu, and select **Properties**, as shown in Figure 6.8.

Figure 6.8 Invoking the Relationship Properties Editor

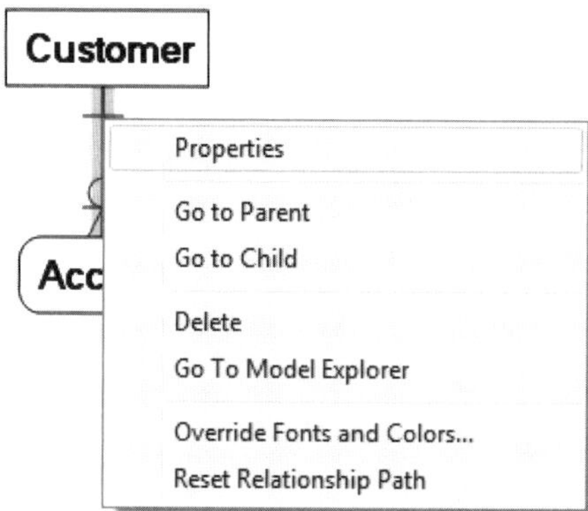

The Relationship Properties Editor appears, as shown in Figure 6.9. Note that double-clicking on the relationship line will also invoke the Relationship Properties Editor.

Figure 6.9 Relationship Properties Editor

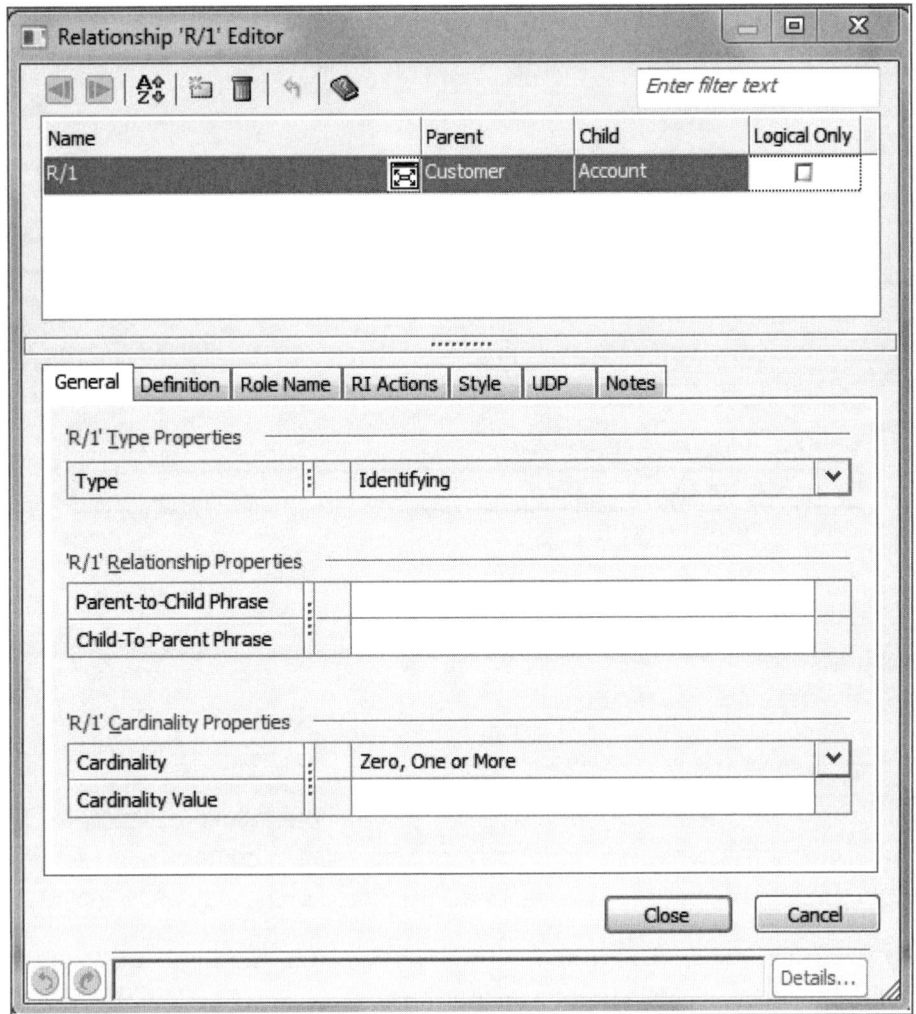

In the Relationship Properties Editor, you can set a number of properties, including name, cardinality, definition, etc. Notice that the name automatically created for this relationship is '**R/1**'. When you add a relationship, the relationship is labeled *R/n*, where *R* stands for relationship, and *n* is a unique number starting at 1. Each number is assigned only once per model, even if a relationship is later deleted.

We recommend consistently using a present tense verb as the verb phrase, because a present tense verb makes it easy to convert the boxes and lines into a sentence. To add our verb phrase from the parent **Customer** to the child **Account**, type '**own**' in the **Parent-to-Child Phrase** field, as shown in Figure 6.10.

Figure 6.10 Adding a Verb Phrase in the Relationship Editor

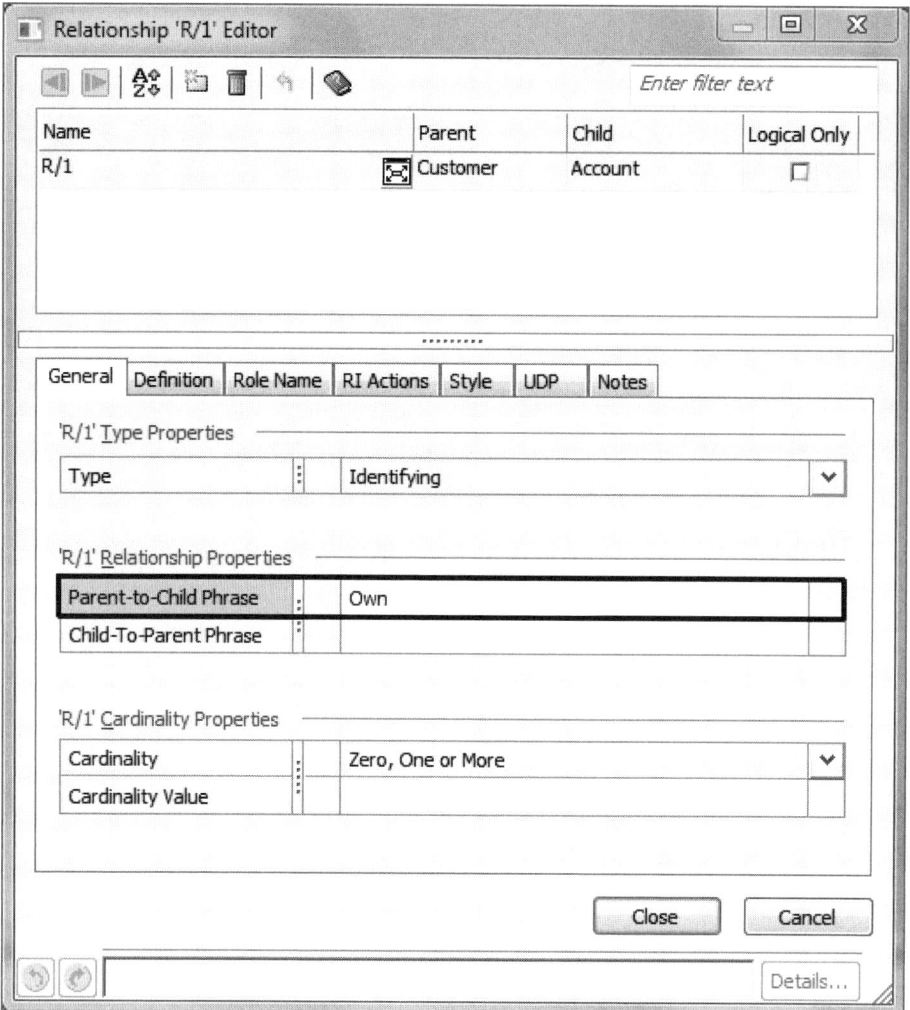

Select **Close** to return to the diagram. You will notice that the diagram looks exactly the same as it did in Figure 6.7. What happened? By default, relationship names are not shown on the diagram, so we'll have to change that setting. Select a blank area on your diagram and right-click to invoke the Diagram Context Menu, shown in Figure 6.11.

Figure 6.11 Invoking the Diagram Context Menu

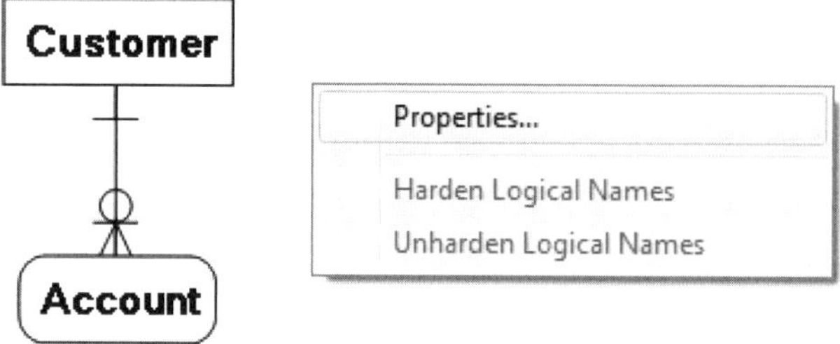

Select **Properties,** and the Diagram Properties Editor will appear, as shown in Figure 6.12.

Figure 6.12 Diagram Properties Editor

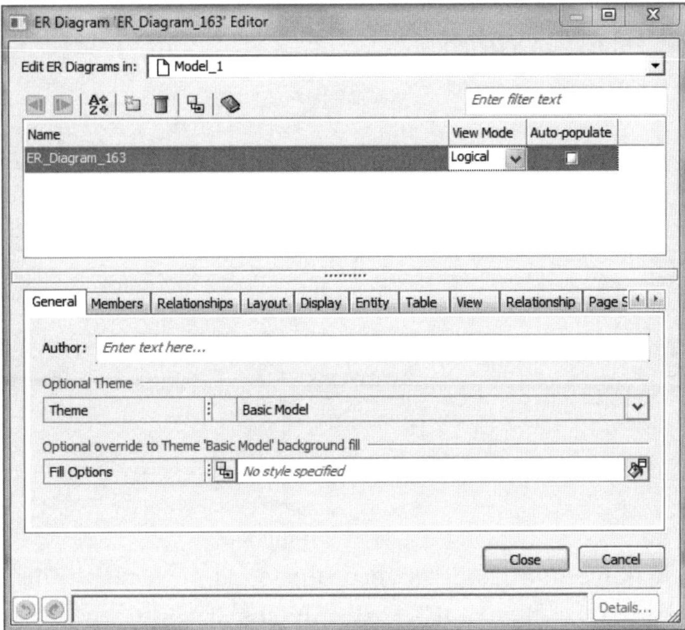

Go to the **Display** tab and select the **Display Parent-to-Child Verb Phrase** box, as shown in Figure 6.13.

Figure 6.13 Setting Property to Show Verb Phrases on a Diagram

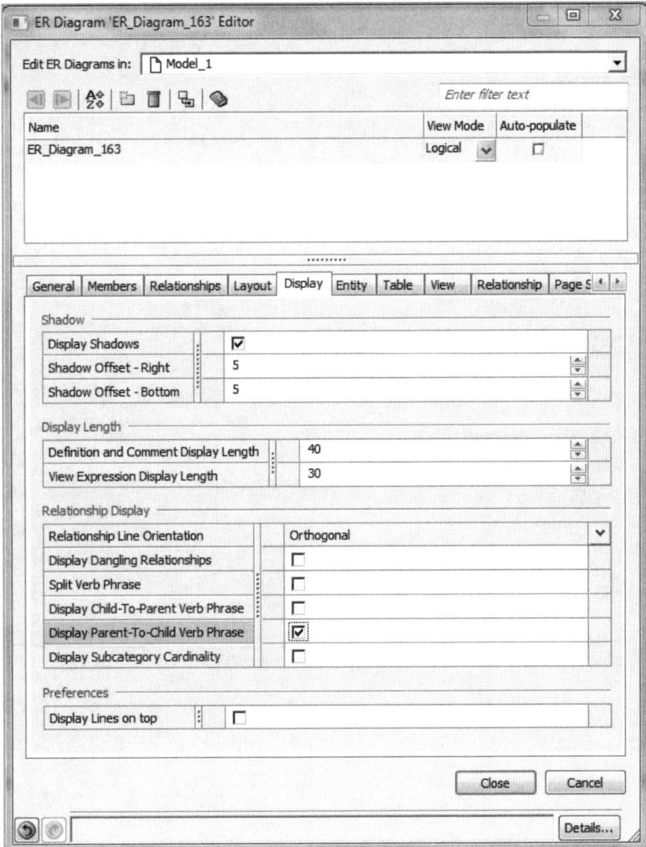

Select **Close** to return to the diagram. The result should look similar to Figure 6.14.

Figure 6.14 Showing Verb Phrases on a Diagram

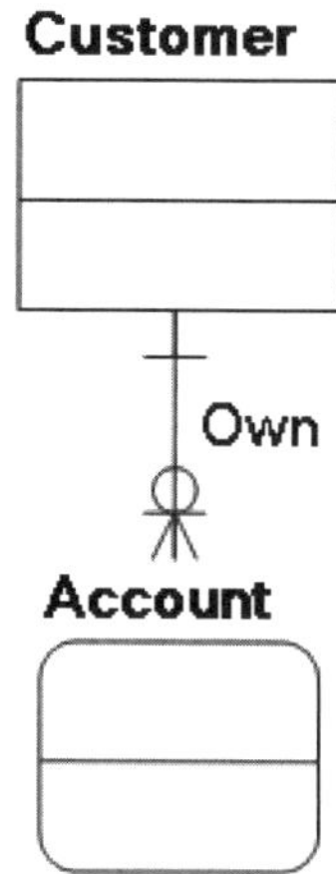

Note that the default placement for the verb phrase is across the line. To move it to the 'clockwise' position shown in Figure 6.14, simply select the verb phrase text and drag it to the right. Let's read this model to see if we have implemented our business rule correctly. It reads "Each **Customer** may own one or more **Accounts**", which matches our business rule.

Figure 6.15 Changing the Cardinality of a Relationship

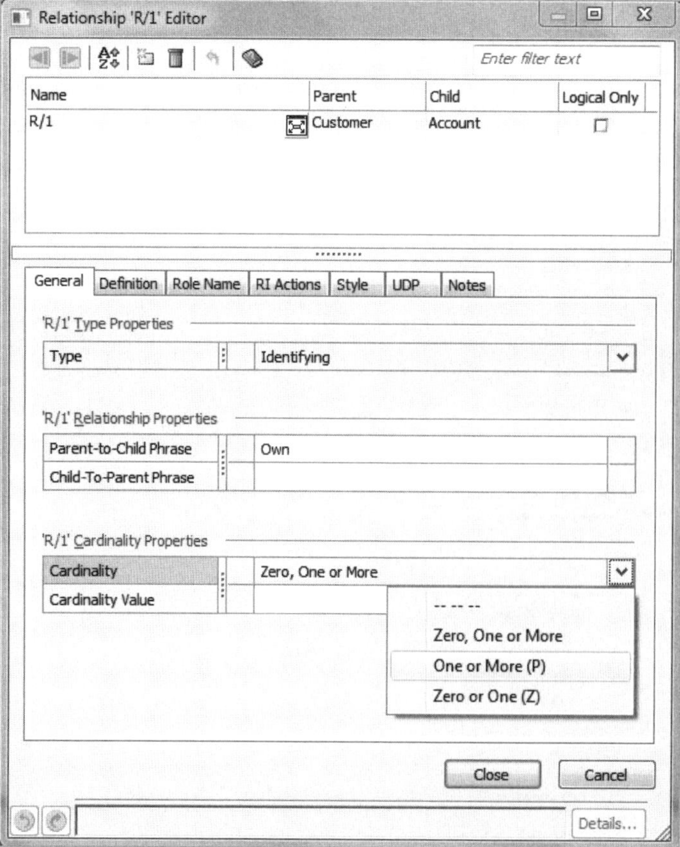

In this case, we did not need to change the cardinality or RI rules—the defaults worked well for us. But what if the business rule changes? For example, after we discussed this model and the associated business rules with our sponsor, they clarified that each customer *must* have one or more account. That's key to the definition of customer—they must have an account with the company. To implement this, we'll need to change the cardinality. Open the Relationship Properties Editor, and you will see that the default cardinality, is **Zero, One or More**. Change this to **One or More** by using the drop-down menu, as shown in Figure 6.15 on the facing page.

After clicking **Close**, you will be returned to the modified model, which should look similar to Figure 6.16. The business rule now correctly reads: "Each customer *must* own one or more accounts."

Figure 6.16 Identifying Relationship with Cardinality of One or More

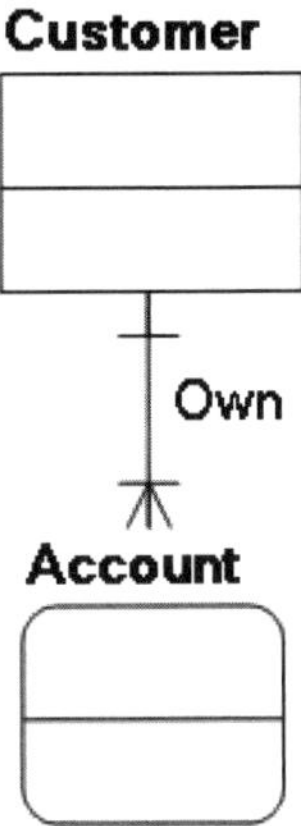

Now let's move to our second business rule:

- Each **Company** must own an office in one or more **Locations.**

The first step is to create two entities on our logical model: **Company** and **Location** (for help with how to create entities, refer to Chapter 4). The next step is to define whether this is an independent or dependent relationship. In this case, we have a lookup table with location codes, which exist independently from our company information--so we have an independent relationship. This time, we'll select the **Non-Identifying Relationship** button from the toolbar, as shown in Figure 6.17.

Figure 6.17 Selecting a Non-Identifying Relationship from the Toolbox Toolbar

Using this relationship type creates the model shown in Figure 6.18.

Figure 6.18 Independent Relationship between Company and Location

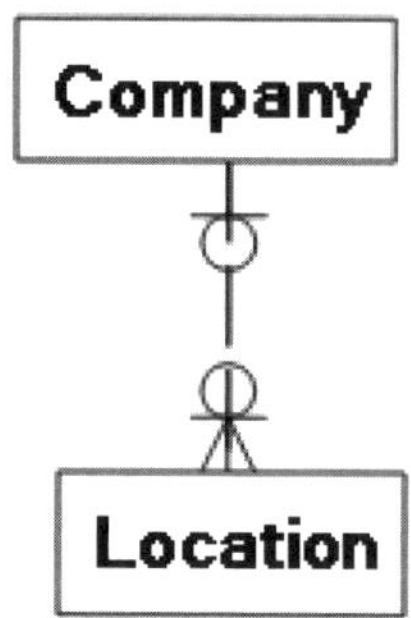

Figure 6.19 Changing Verb Phrase and Cardinality of a Relationship

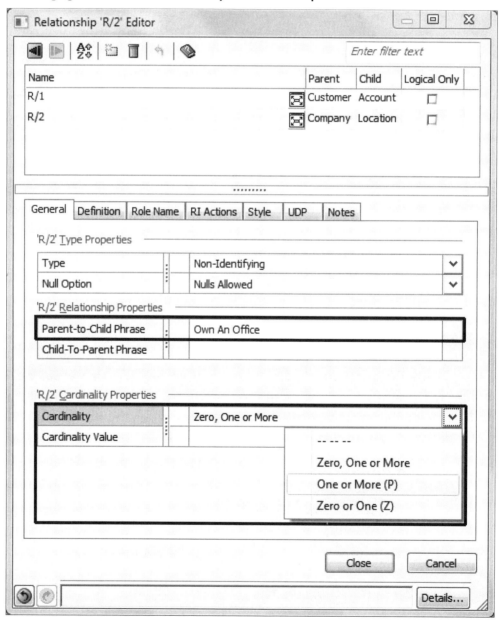

Notice that the relationship line is now dashed, indicating an independent relationship. Also notice that the cardinality contains zero on both ends of the relationship, i.e. the relationship is optional on both sides. Recall that for the dependent relationship, the relationship to the parent was mandatory. Speaking of cardinality, let's read the business rule for this model to see if we have our cardinality correct. It currently reads: "Each **Company** may have one or more **Locations**." We'll need this to be mandatory: "Each **Company** *must* have one or more **Locations**." And to make the rule read correctly, we'll need to add the correct verb phrase. The company must *own an office* in one or more locations. This is an important distinction. For example, it's not enough to have a P.O. Box or mailing address in the location; the company must have a physical office. Let's make both of these changes at once in the Relationship Properties Editor, as shown in Figure 6.19 on the facing page.

The model will now look similar to Figure 6.20. Note that if the verb phrase in your diagram crosses the relationship line, simply highlight the verb phrase and drag it to the 'clockwise' location where it's more readable.

Figure 6.20 Independent Relationship with Verb Phrase and Mandatory Setting

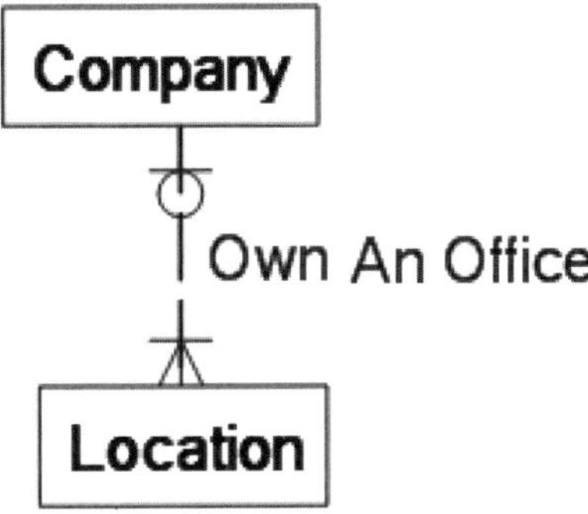

And the business rule will correctly read:

- Each **Company** must own an office in one or more **Locations**.

By now, you should feel comfortable creating and modifying relationships and their properties. For a detailed list of the properties on the **General** tab of the Relationship Properties Editor, refer to Figure 6.21 and Table 6.1.

Figure 6.21 General Tab of Relationship Properties Editor

General | Definition | Role Name | RI Actions | Style | UDP | Notes

'R/1' Type Properties

Type	Identifying

'R/1' Relationship Properties

Parent-to-Child Phrase	
Child-To-Parent Phrase	

'R/1' Cardinality Properties

Cardinality	Zero, One or More
Cardinality Value	

Table 6.1 Field Descriptions for General Tab of Relationship Properties Editor

Field	Description
Type	The **Type** field allows you to change the type of relationship between Identifying and Non-Identifying via a drop-down menu.
Parent-to-Child Phrase	The **Parent-to-Child Phrase** is the verb phrase that exists from the parent to the child. It is the 'verb' in the sentence in which the parent entity is the subject and the child entity is the object. E.g. In the sentence "Each Customer may ***place*** one or more Orders.", 'place' is the **Parent-to-Child Phrase**. Note: The parent entity is the object you click on first when creating a relationship.
Child-To-Parent Phrase	The **Child-To-Parent Phrase** is the verb phrase that exists from the child to the parent. It is the 'verb' in the sentence in which the child entity is the subject and the parent entity is the object. E.g. In the sentence "Each Order may ***be placed by*** one or more Customers.", 'place' is the **Child-To-Parent Phrase**.
Cardinality	The **Cardinality** field allows you to define whether a relationship's cardinality is either. • **Zero, One or More:** Each parent table is connected to zero, one, or more instances of the child table. • **One or More:** Each parent table is connected to one or more instances of the child table. • **Zero or One:** Each parent table is connected to zero or one instance of the child table. • **Exactly (——):** If a relationship is defined by an exact number of instances, see the **Cardinality Value** field below.
Cardinality Value	The **Cardinality Value** specifies the exact number of child entity instances that each parent entity is connected to (integer values only). Note that once you set a **Cardinality Value**, the **Cardinality** field will automatically be set to '———'. This value applies primarily to the logical model. Since the relational notation does not have a clear indicator for the exact number of instances, standard relational database platforms are not able to account for this.

Recursion

A recursive relationship is a rule that exists between instances of the same entity. A one-to-many recursive relationship describes a hierarchy, whereas a many-to-many relationship describes a network. In a hierarchy, an entity instance has at most one parent. In a network, an entity instance can have more than one parent. Let's illustrate both types of recursive relationships using **Employee**. See Figure 6.22 for a one-to-many recursive example and Figure 6.23 for a many-to-many example.

Figure 6.22 An Employee may work for one Manager

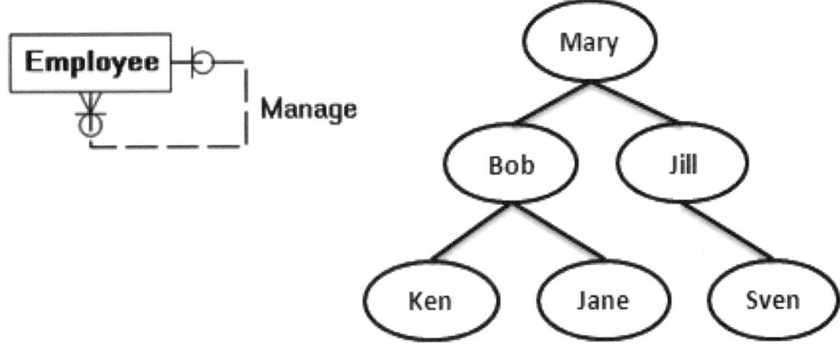

Each Employee may manage one or many Employees.
Each Employee may be managed by one Employee.

Figure 6.23 An Employee must work for many Managers

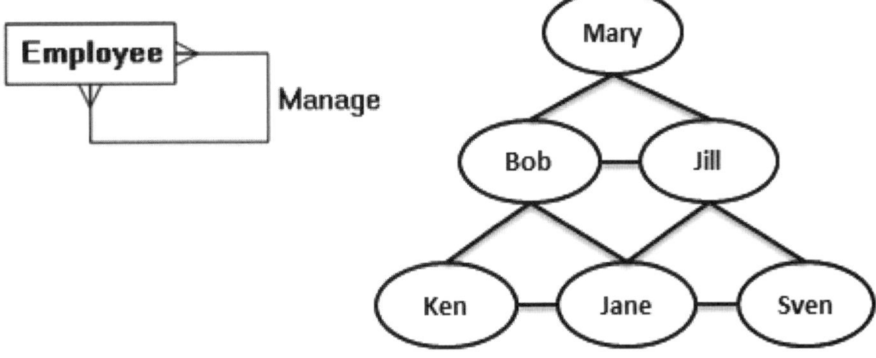

Each Employee must manage many Employees.
Each Employee must be managed by many Employees.

Using sample values such as 'Bob' and 'Jill' and sketching a hierarchy or network can help understand, and therefore validate, cardinality. In Figure 6.22, for example, where the one-to-many captures a hierarchy, each employee has at most one manager. Yet in Figure 6.23, where the many-to-many captures a network, each employee must have many managers, such as Jane working for Bob, Jill, Ken, and Sven. (I would definitely update my resume if I were Jane.)

It is interesting to note that in Figure 6.22, there is optionality on both sides of the relationship. In this example, it implies we can have an **Employee** who has no boss (such as Mary) and an **Employee** who is not a manager (such as Ken, Jane, and Sven).

Data modelers have a love-hate relationship with recursion. On the one hand, recursion makes modeling a complex business idea very easy and leads to a very flexible modeling structure. We can have any number of levels in the organization hierarchy in Figure 6.22, for example. On the other hand, some consider using recursion to be taking the easy way out of a difficult modeling situation. There are many rules that can be obscured by recursion. For example, where is the Regional Management Level in Figure 6.23? It is hidden somewhere in the recursive relationship. Those in favor of recursion argue that you may not be aware of all the rules and that recursion protects you from having an incomplete model. The recursion adds a level of flexibility that ensures that any rules not previously considered are also handled by the model. It is therefore wise to consider recursion on a case-by-case basis, weighing obscurity against flexibility.

Creating a Recursive Relationship

Let's create a recursive relationship in CA ERwin Data Modeler. In this example, we have an organizational unit that reports to another organizational unit. The formal business rule is as follows:

- Each Organizational Unit reports to an Organizational Unit.

First we create an entity called organizational unit, as shown in Figure 6.24.

Figure 6.24 Organizational Unit Entity

Organizational Unit

That was easy enough. The next step is to choose the relationship type. Do we have an independent or dependent entity? Recursive relationships are by nature independent. In other words, you can't have the existence of an object depend on itself. In fact, if we try to do this in ERwin, we get the following error message, shown in Figure 6.25.

Figure 6.25 Error Message for Attempting to Create Identifying Recursive Relationship

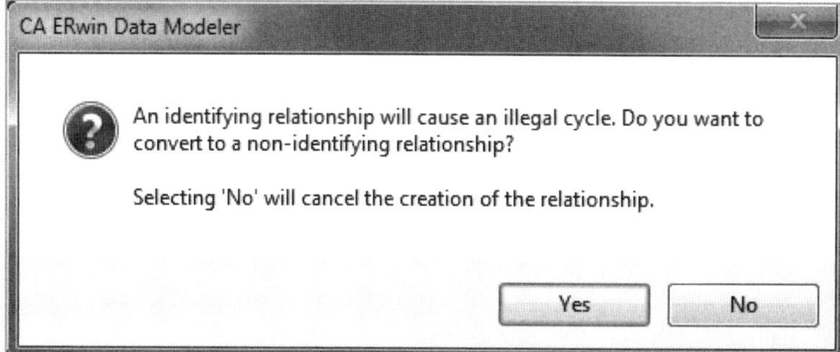

To form the recursive relationship then, select the **Non-Identifying Relationship** button from the Toolbox Toolbar. You'll then need to select the parent (i.e. **Organizational**

Unit) and then the child (i.e. **Organizational Unit**). In essence, you're clicking on the **Organizational Unit** entity twice in a row. The result will look similar to Figure 6.26.

Figure 6.26 Recursive Relationship in CA ERwin Data Modeler

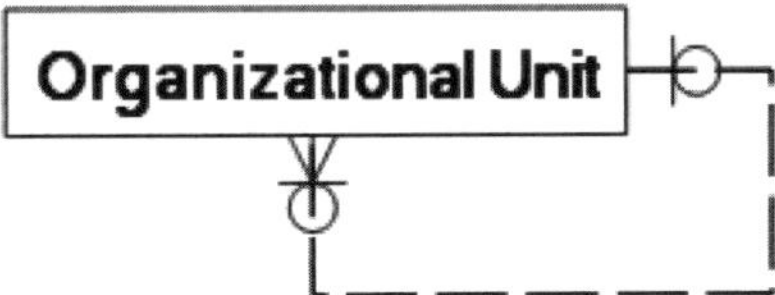

Subtyping

Subtyping groups the common data elements and relationships of entities while retaining what is unique within each entity. Subtyping is an excellent way of communicating that certain concepts are very similar.

In our ice cream example, we are told that an ice cream cone and ice cream cup can each contain many scoops of ice cream, as illustrated in Figure 6.27.

Figure 6.27 Ice Cream Example Before Subtyping

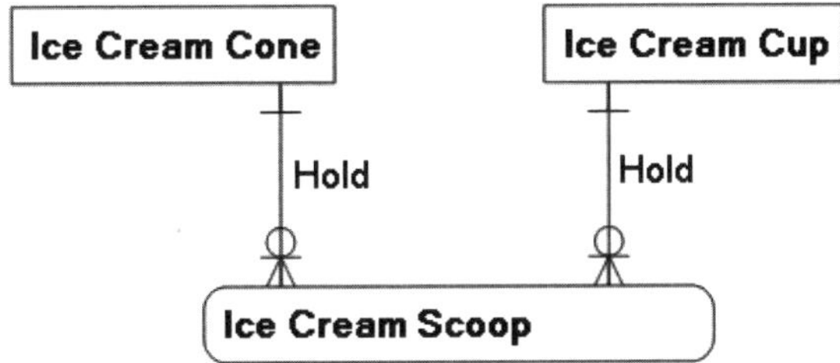

- Each **Ice Cream Cone** can hold one or many **Ice Cream Scoops**.
- Each **Ice Cream Scoop** must be held in one **Ice Cream Cone**.
- Each **Ice Cream Cup** can hold one or many **Ice Cream Scoops**.
- Each **Ice Cream Scoop** must be held in one **Ice Cream Cup**.

You can see that **Ice Cream Cone** and **Ice Cream Cup** serve the same purpose, which is to hold the ice cream. Rather than repeat the relationship to **Ice Cream Scoop** twice, we can introduce subtyping, as shown in Figure 6.28.

Figure 6.28 Ice Cream Example After Subtyping

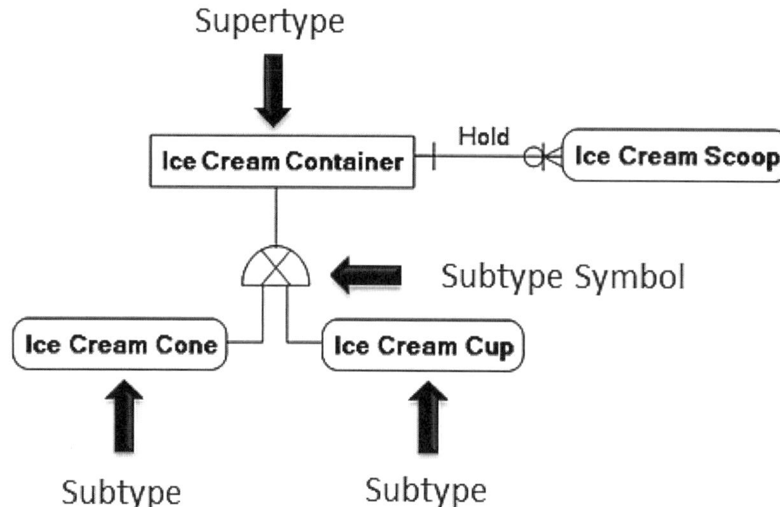

- Each **Ice Cream Container** can hold one or many **Ice Cream Scoops**.
- Each **Ice Cream Scoop** must be held in one **Ice Cream Container**.
- Each **Ice Cream Container** can be either an **Ice Cream Cone** or an **Ice Cream S**coop.
- Each **Ice Cream Cone** is an **Ice Cream Container**.
- Each **Ice Cream Cup** is an **Ice Cream Container**.

The subtyping relationship implies that all of the properties from the supertype are inherited by the subtype. Therefore, there is an implied relationship from **Ice Cream Cone** to **Ice Cream Scoop,** as well as **Ice Cream Cup** to **Ice Cream Scoop**. Not only does subtyping reduce redundancy on a data model, it makes it easier to communicate similarities across what otherwise would appear to be distinct and separate concepts.

Creating a Subtype

Let's create a subtype relationship in CA ERwin Data Modeler. In this example, we're working with an automobile dealer. They sell both cars and trucks, but refer to both by the general term 'vehicle'.

We begin by converting this fact into a business rule that reads as follows:

- Each **Vehicle** can be either a **Car** or a **Truck**

This represents a supertype of **Vehicle** with two subtypes: **Car** and **Truck**. First we'll create three entities: **Vehicle**, **Car**, and **Truck**.

Although the layout of these entities doesn't change the underlying rules, the general convention is to place the supertype (**Vehicle**) on top, with the subtypes spaced evenly below, as is shown in Figure 6.29.

Figure 6.29 Vehicle Entities

To create the subtype relationship between these entities, first select the **Sub-category** button on the Toolbox Toolbar, shown in Figure 6.30.

Figure 6.30 Selecting the Sub-category Button on the Toolbox Toolbar

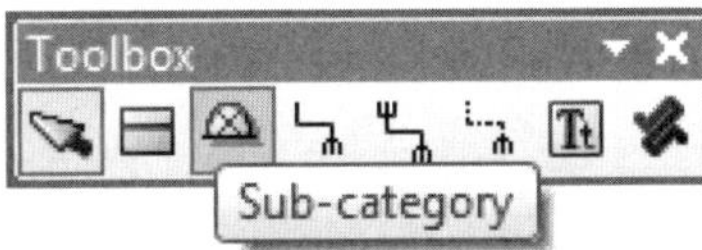

Next, select the supertype, **Vehicle**, then select the first subtype, **Car**. The result will look similar to Figure 6.31.

Figure 6.31 Creating First Portion of the Sub-Category Relationship

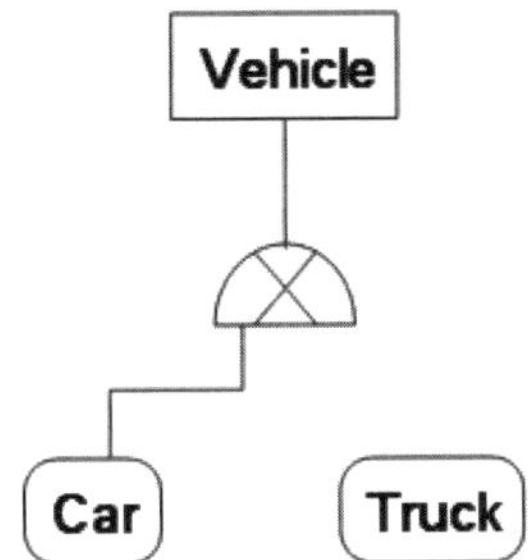

We're halfway there! To complete the subtype relationship, select the **Sub-category** button again. Then click on the subtype symbol ⦻ followed by the **Truck** entity. This will complete the subtype relationship, as shown in Figure 6.32. (Remember, you might want to use multi-drop mode by holding the `Ctrl` key down as you select and drop the subtype relationships from the toolbar).

Figure 6.32 Subtype Relationship

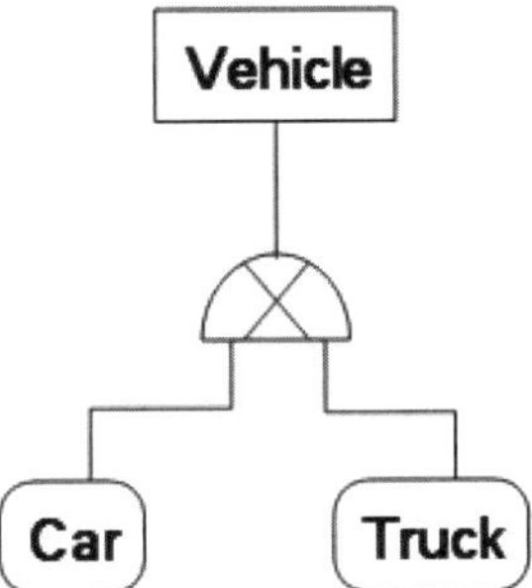

We'll go into more detail about Subtype relationships in Chapter 18. For now, just familiarize yourself with the general concept. For examples of the relationships we created in this chapter, you can download the **Chapter6_Examples.erwin** file from www.erwin.com/datamodelingmadesimple.

EXERCISE: Reading a Model

Practice reading the relationships in this model.
See www.erwin.com/datamodelingmadesimple for our answers.

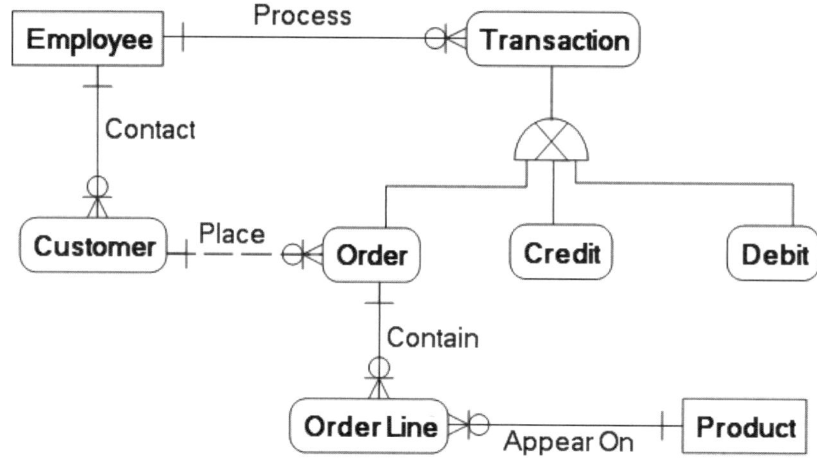

Key Points

- A rule is visually captured on a data model by a line connecting two entities, called a relationship.
- Data rules are instructions on *how* data relate to one another. Action rules are instructions on *what to do* when data elements contain certain values.
- Cardinality is represented by the symbols on both ends of a relationship that define the number of instances of each entity that can participate in the relationship. The three simple choices are zero, one, or many.
- Labels are the verbs that appear alongside the relationship lines. Labels should be as descriptive as possible to retain data model precision, and are generally placed to the right of the relationship line to read 'clockwise'.
- A recursive relationship is a rule that exists between instances of the same entity.
- Subtyping groups the common properties of entities while retaining what is unique within each entity.

CHAPTER 7
Keys

More than one John Doe
Which is the right Customer?
Recall by the key

There is a lot of data out there, but how do you sift through it all to find what you're looking for? That's where keys come in. Keys allow us to efficiently retrieve data, as well as navigate from one physical table to another. This chapter defines keys and distinguishes between the terms candidate, primary, and alternate keys. Surrogate keys and foreign keys and their importance are also explained. Examples of how to leverage keys in CA ERwin Data Modeler are included.

Key Explanation

Data elements identify, describe, or measure the entity instances in which they reside. There is often a need to find specific entity instances using one or more data elements. Those data element(s) that allow us to find specific entity instances are known as keys. The Library of Congress assigns an ISBN (International Standard Book Number) to every book. When the ISBN for this book, 9781935504092, is entered into many search engines and database systems, the book entity instance **Data Modeling Made Simple with CA ERwin Data Modeler r8** will be returned (try it!). A particular **Tax Identifier** can help us find an organization. The key **Account Code** can help us find a particular account.

Candidate Key

A candidate key is one or more data elements that uniquely identify an entity instance. Sometimes a single data element identifies an entity instance, such as ISBN for a book, or **Account Code** for an account. Sometimes it takes more than one data element to uniquely identify an entity instance. For example, both a **Promotion Code** and **Promotion Start Date** are necessary to identify a promotion. When more than one data element makes up a key, we use the term 'composite key'. So **Promotion Code** and **Promotion Start Date** together are a composite candidate key for a promotion.

A candidate key has three main characteristics:

- **Unique**. There cannot be duplicate values in the data in a candidate key and it cannot be empty (also known as 'nullable'). Therefore, the number of distinct values of a candidate key must be equal to the number of distinct entity instances. If the entity Book has ISBN as its candidate key, and if there are 500 book instances, there will also be 500 unique ISBNs.

- **Non-volatile**. A candidate key value on an entity instance should never change. Since a candidate key is used to find a unique entity instance, you would be unable to find that instance if you were still trying to use the value before it was changed. Changing a candidate key would also mean changing it in every other entity in which it appears with the original valuc.
- **Minimal**. A candidate key should contain only those data elements that are needed to uniquely identify an entity instance. If four data elements are listed as the composite candidate key for an entity, but only three are really needed for uniqueness, then only those three should make up the candidate key.

Figure 7.1 contains a data model before candidate keys have been identified.

Figure 7.1 Data Model Before Candidate Keys Have Been Identified

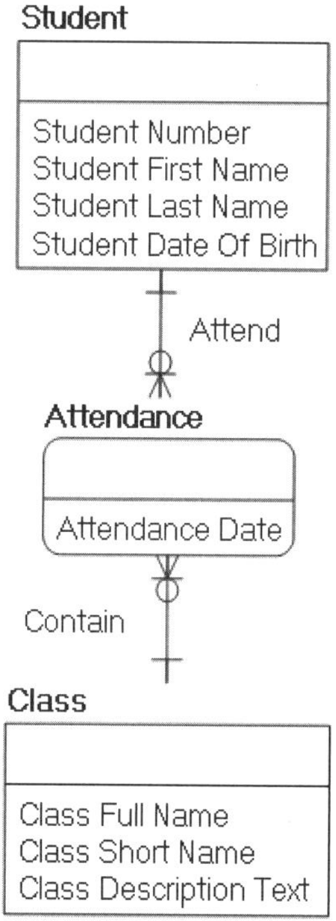

- Each **Student** may attend one or many **Classes**.
- Each **Class** may contain one or many **Students**.

Note that we have a many-to-many relationship between **Student** and **Class** that was replaced by the entity **Attendance** (an associative entity) and two one-to-many relationships (more on this in our normalization section in Chapter 18). In reading a many-to-many relationship, it is helpful to ignore the entity in the middle (**Attendance**, in this example) and just read the labels between the entities on either side. For example, each **Student** may attend one or many **Classes** and each **Class** may contain one or many **Students**. Table 7.1 contains sample values for each of these entities.

Table 7.1 Sample values for Figure 7.1

Student

Student Number	Student First Name	Student Last Name	Student Date Of Birth
SM385932	Steve	Martin	1/25/1958
EM584926	Eddie	Murphy	3/15/1971
HW742615	Henry	Winkler	2/14/1984
MM481526	Mickey	Mouse	5/10/1982
DD857111	Donald	Duck	5/10/1982
MM573483	Minnie	Mouse	4/1/1986
LR731511	Lone	Ranger	10/21/1949
EM876253	Eddie	Murphy	7/1/1992

Attendance

Attendance Date
5/10/2009
6/10/2009
7/10/2009

Class

Class Full Name	Class Short Name	Class Description Text
Data Modeling Fundamentals	Data Modeling 101	An introductory class covering basic data modeling concepts and principles.
Advanced Data Modeling	Data Modeling 301	A fast-paced class covering techniques such as advanced normalization and ragged hierarchies.
Tennis Basics	Tennis One	For those new to the game of tennis, learn the key aspects of the game.
Juggling		Learn how to keep three balls in the air at once!

Based on our definition of a candidate key and a candidate key's characteristics of being unique, non-volatile, and minimal, what would you choose as the candidate keys for each of these entities?

For Student, **Student Number** appears to be a valid candidate key. There are eight students and eight distinct values for **Student Number**. So unlike **Student First Name** and **Student Last Name**, which can contain duplicates like Eddie Murphy, **Student Number** appears to be unique. **Student Date Of Birth** can also contain duplicates such as '5/10/1982', which is the **Student Date Of Birth** for both Mickey Mouse and Donald Duck. However, the combination of **Student First Name**, **Student Last Name**, and **Student Date Of Birth** may make a valid candidate key.

For **Attendance**, we are currently missing a candidate key. Although the **Attendance Date** is unique in our sample data, we will probably need to know which student attended which class on this particular date.

For **Class**, on first glance, it appears that any of its data elements are unique and would therefore qualify as a candidate key. However, Juggling does not have a **Class Short Name**. So because **Class Short Name** can be empty, we cannot consider it a candidate key. Also, one of the characteristics of a candidate key is that it is non-volatile. I know based on my teaching experience that class descriptions can change. Therefore, **Class Description Text** also needs to be ruled out as a candidate key, leaving **Class Full Name** as the best option for a candidate key.

Primary and Alternate Keys

Even though an entity may contain more than one candidate key, we can only select one candidate key to be the primary key for an entity. A primary key is a candidate key that has been chosen to be *the* unique identifier for an entity. An alternate key is a candidate key that although unique, was not chosen as the primary key, but still can be used to find specific entity instances.

We have only one candidate key in the **Class** entity, so **Class Full Name** becomes our primary key. We have to make a choice, however, in **Student**, because we have two candidate keys. Which **Student** candidate key would you choose as the primary key?

In selecting one candidate key over another as the primary key, consider succinctness and security. Succinctness means if there are several candidate keys, choose the one with the fewest data elements or shortest in length. In terms of security, it is possible that one or more data elements within a candidate key will contain sensitive data whose viewing should be restricted. We want to avoid having sensitive data in our entity's primary key because the primary key can propagate as a foreign key and therefore spread this sensitive data throughout our database.

Considering succinctness and security in our example, I would choose **Student Number** over the composite **Student First Name**, **Student Last Name**, and **Student Date Of Birth**. It is more succinct and contains less sensitive data.

Figure 7.2 shows our data model updated with primary and alternate keys. Primary keys are shown above the line in an entity box. Alternate keys are indicated by the (AK) designator listed after the attribute. We'll describe these designators in more detail further on in this chapter.

Attendance now has as its primary key **Student Number** and **Class Full Name**, which appear to make a valid primary key. 'FK' stands for 'Foreign Key', which will be discussed shortly.

Figure 7.2 Data Model Updated with Primary and Alternate Keys

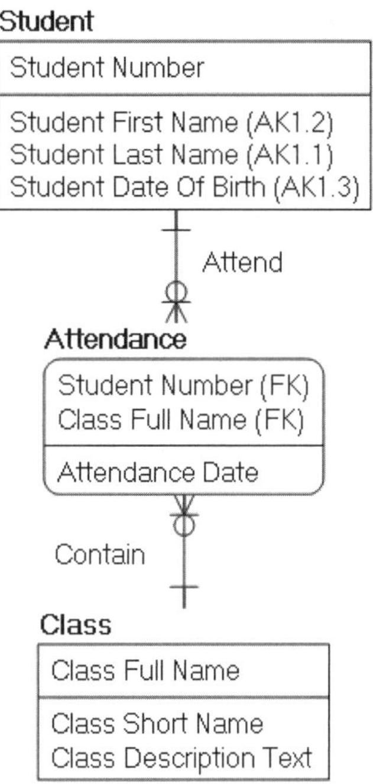

To summarize, a candidate key consists of one or more data elements that uniquely identify an entity instance. The candidate key that is selected as the best way to identify each unique record in the entity becomes the primary key. The other candidate keys become alternate keys. Keys containing more than one data element are known as composite keys.

Surrogate Key

A surrogate key is a primary key that substitutes for a natural key, which is what the business sees as the unique identifier for an entity. It has no embedded intelligence and is used by IT (and not the business) for integration or performance reasons.

Surrogate keys are useful for integration, which is an effort to create a single, consistent version of the data. Applications such as data warehouses often house data from more than one application or system. Surrogate keys enable us to bring together information about the same entity instance that is identified differently in each source system. If the same concept, such as **Student** or **Class**, exists in more than one system, there is a good chance some amount of integration will be necessary. For example, Robert Jones in system XYZ and Renee Jane in system ABC might both be identified in their respective systems as RJ. But if we tried to bring them together using RJ to link them, the data would be incorrect – we'd have Robert and Renee identified as the same person. Instead, a different, non-overlapping, surrogate key could be assigned to each of them. Similarly, if Robert Jones is identified as RJ in system XYZ and BJ in system DEF, the information about him could be consolidated under a single surrogate key value. The fact that they're the same would need to be determined through a separate effort.

Surrogate keys are also efficient. You've seen that a primary key may be composed of one or more attributes of the entity. A single surrogate key is more efficient to use than having to specify three or four (or five or six) attributes to locate the single record you're looking for.

When using a surrogate key, always make an effort to determine the natural key and then define an alternate key on this natural key. For example, assuming a surrogate key is a more efficient primary key than **Class Full Name**, we can create the surrogate key **Class Id** for **Class** and define an alternate key on **Class Full Name**, as shown in Figure 7.3. Table 7.2 contains the values in **Class**.

Figure 7.3 Data Model Updated with Surrogate Key

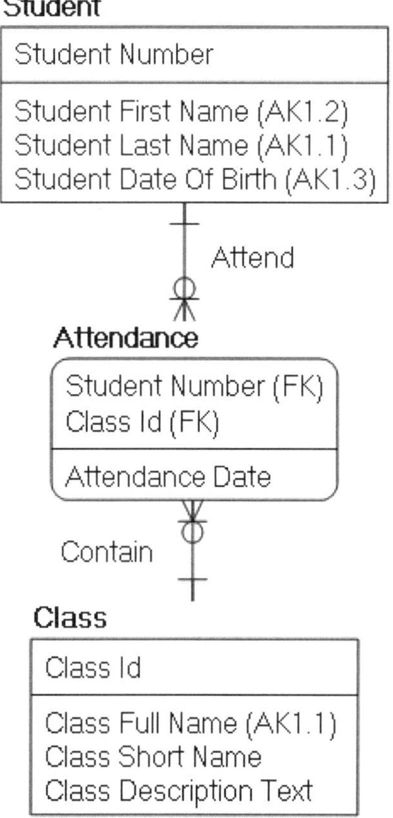

Table 7.2 Class Values Updated with Surrogate Key

Class Id	Class Full Name	Class Short Name	Class Description Text
1	Data Modeling Fundamentals	Data Modeling 101	An introductory class covering basic data modeling concepts and principles.
2	Advanced Data Modeling	Data Modeling 301	A face-paced class covering techniques such as advanced normalization and ragged hierarchies.
3	Tennis Basics	Tennis One	For those new to the game of tennis, learn the key aspects of the game.
4	Juggling		Learn how to keep three balls in the air at once!

In this example, we're using **Class Full Name** as a candidate key, but in the real world, it's never a good idea to use a name as a key because names can change.

Foreign Key

A foreign key is a data element that provides a link to another entity. A foreign key allows a database management system to navigate from one entity to another. For example, we need to know who owns an account, so we would want to include the identifier of the customer to whom it belongs in the entity. The **Customer Id** in **Account** is the primary key of that **Customer** in the **Customer** entity. Using this foreign key back to **Customer** enables the database management system to navigate from a particular account or accounts, to the customer or customers that own each account. Likewise, the database can navigate from a particular customer or customers, to find all of their accounts.

A foreign key is automatically created when we define a relationship between two entities. When a relationship is created between two entities, the entity on the 'many' side of the relationship (the child entity) inherits the primary key from the entity on the 'one' side of the relationship (the parent entity).

In Figure 7.3, there are two foreign keys in the **Attendance** entity. The **Student Number** foreign key points back to a particular student in the **Student** entity. The **Class Id** foreign key points back to a particular **Class** in the **Class** entity. Table 7.3 contains a few **Attendance** entity instances.

Table 7.3 Attendance Entity Instances

Student Number	Class Id	Attendance Date
SM385932	1	5/10/2009
EM584926	1	5/10/2009
EM584926	2	6/10/2009
MM481526	2	6/10/2009
MM573483	2	6/10/2009
LR731511	3	7/10/2009

By looking at these values and recalling the sample values from Tables 7.1 and 7.2, we learn that Steve Martin and Eddie Murphy both attended the Data Modeling Fundamentals class on 5/10/2009. Eddie Murphy also attended the Advanced Data Modeling Class with Mickey and Minnie Mouse on 6/10/2009. Lone Ranger took Tennis Basics (by himself as usual) on 7/10/2009.

Creating Keys

Now that you have a basic understanding of keys and their various types and uses, let's create some keys using CA ERwin Data Modeler. First, start by creating the logical model we used in Figure 7.3, which has entities, attributes and relationships, but no keys. This will build on the skills you've developed in Chapters 3-6, so you might want to refer back to those sections if you have difficulty. Your finished model should look like the one in Figure 7.4.

Figure 7.4 Sample Data Model with No Keys

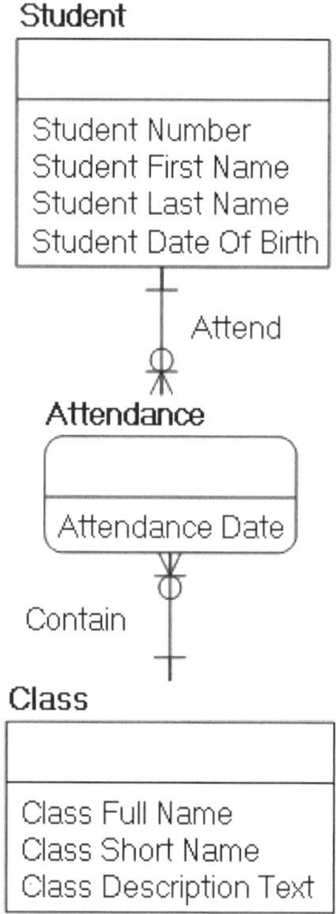

Now let's add the primary and alternate keys to this model. The top portion of the boxes are looking awfully empty, aren't they? Let's fill that area 'above the line' by creating our primary keys for the model. Remember that for the **Student** entity, we selected the attribute **Student Number** as our primary key. Let's define this now in the model. To begin, open the Attribute Properties Editor, shown in Figure 7.5. If you have difficulty with this, refer to Chapter 5, where we introduced attributes.

Figure 7.5 Attribute Properties Editor

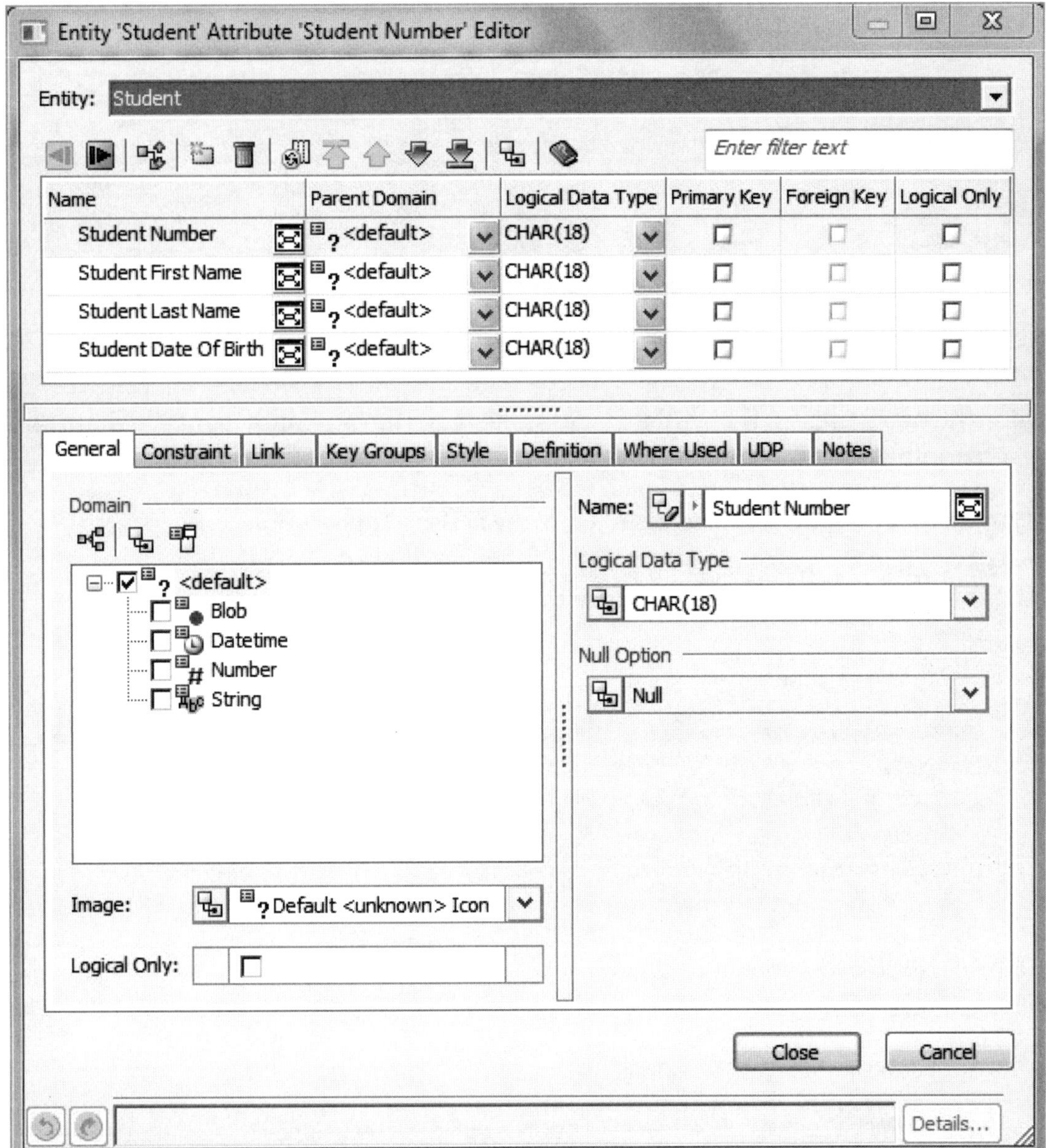

The first thing you may notice is that the order of our attributes is different from that on the diagram. The default setting for the Attribute Properties Editor is to list the attributes alphabetically. In this case, we'd like to view our attributes in the same order in which they are listed on our diagram. To change the way in which the attributes are listed, select the **Sort Items** button, as shown in Figure 7.6.

Figure 7.6 Selecting the Sort Items Button to Change Attribute Order

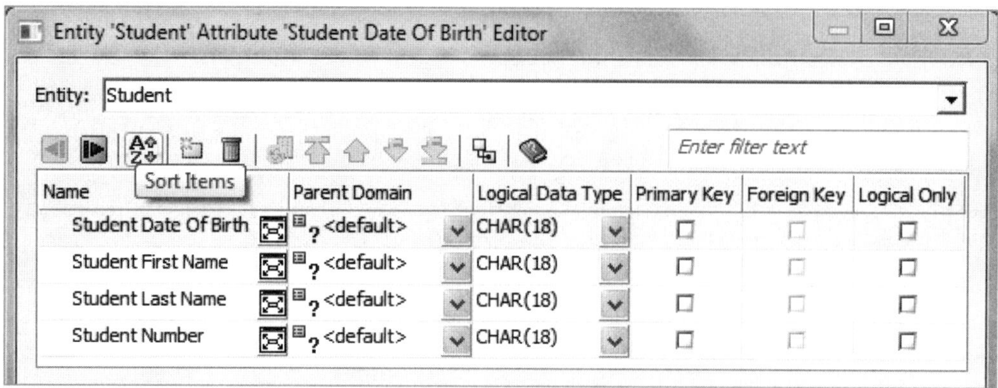

To order the attributes in the editor in the same way they are shown on the diagram, select **Attribute Order** from the drop-down menu, as shown in Figure 7.7.

Figure 7.7 Changing the Attribute Properties Editor Listing to Show Attribute Order

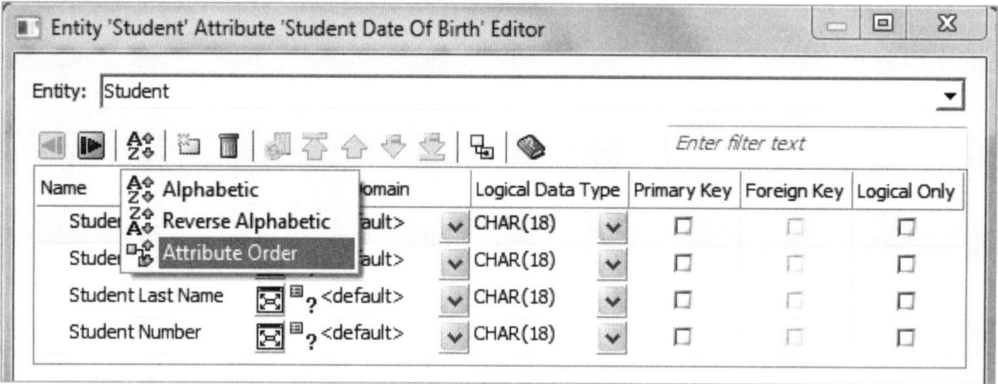

Now our attributes are shown in the order in which we entered them on the diagram, as shown in Figure 7.8.

Figure 7.8 Attributes Shown in Attribute Order

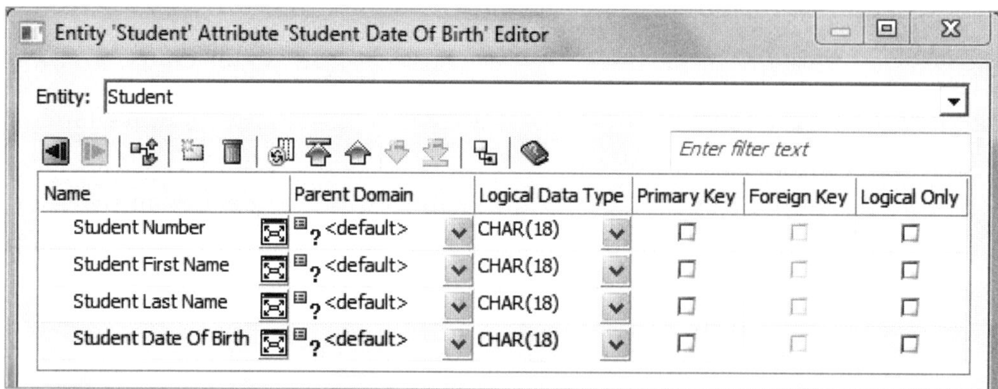

Now let's define **Student Number** as our primary key. You'll notice that there is a checkbox to the right of the attribute name labeled **Primary Key**. Select this checkbox, shown in Figure 7.9.

Figure 7.9 Defining a Primary Key

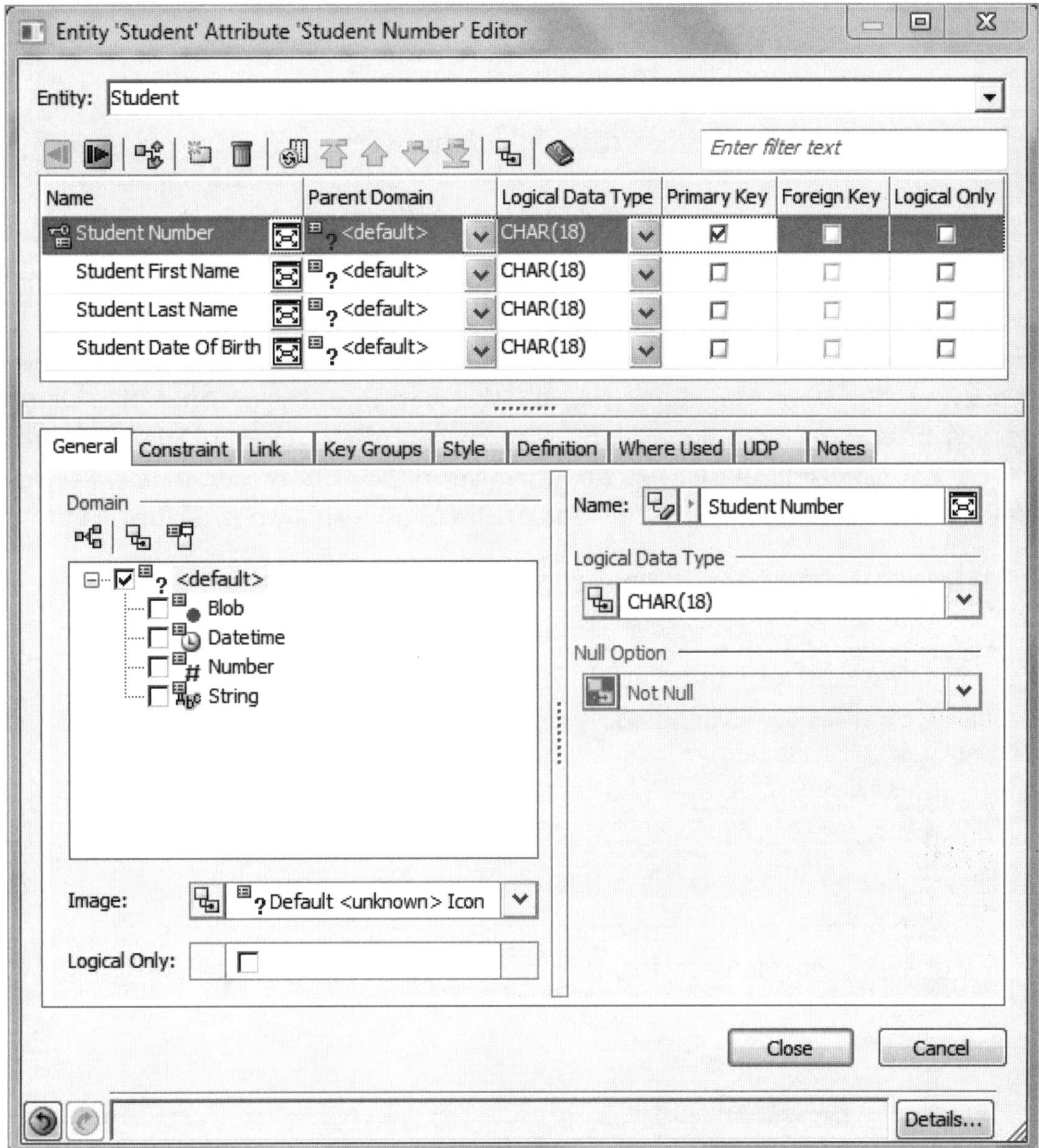

Notice that a key symbol appears next to **Student Number**, indicating that this is the primary key. If we had selected multiple attributes to create a composite primary key, the key symbol would have appeared next to those attributes—we're not limited to a single attribute, although that was the approach we chose in this example.

When you close the dialog by clicking the **Close** button, you'll be returned to the model and can now see that **Student Number** appears 'above the line' in the entity box, as shown in Figure 7.10.

Figure 7.10 Showing the Primary Key 'Above the Line'

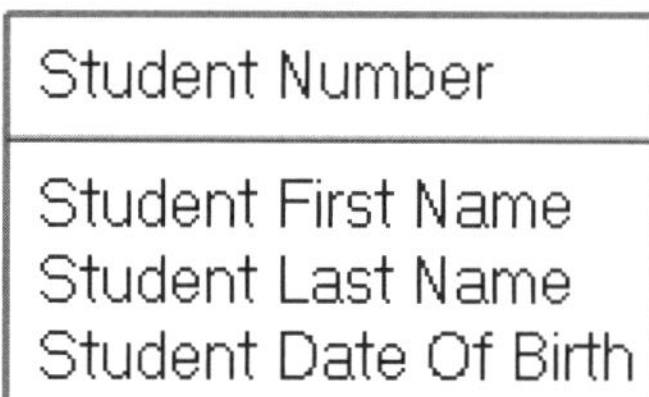

Showing primary keys 'above the line' is a common and traditional way of displaying primary keys in a data model. But perhaps you want to make the point even more clearly by displaying the graphical key icon that we saw in the attributes dialog. You can easily change the display to include the key icon by opening the Diagram Properties Editor (by selecting a blank area on your diagram and right-clicking—see Chapter 6 for more information on this), moving to the **Entity** tab, and selecting the **Display Logical Primary Key (PK) Designator** checkbox, as shown in Figure 7.11.

Figure 7.11 Showing the Primary Key Designator via the Diagram Properties Editor

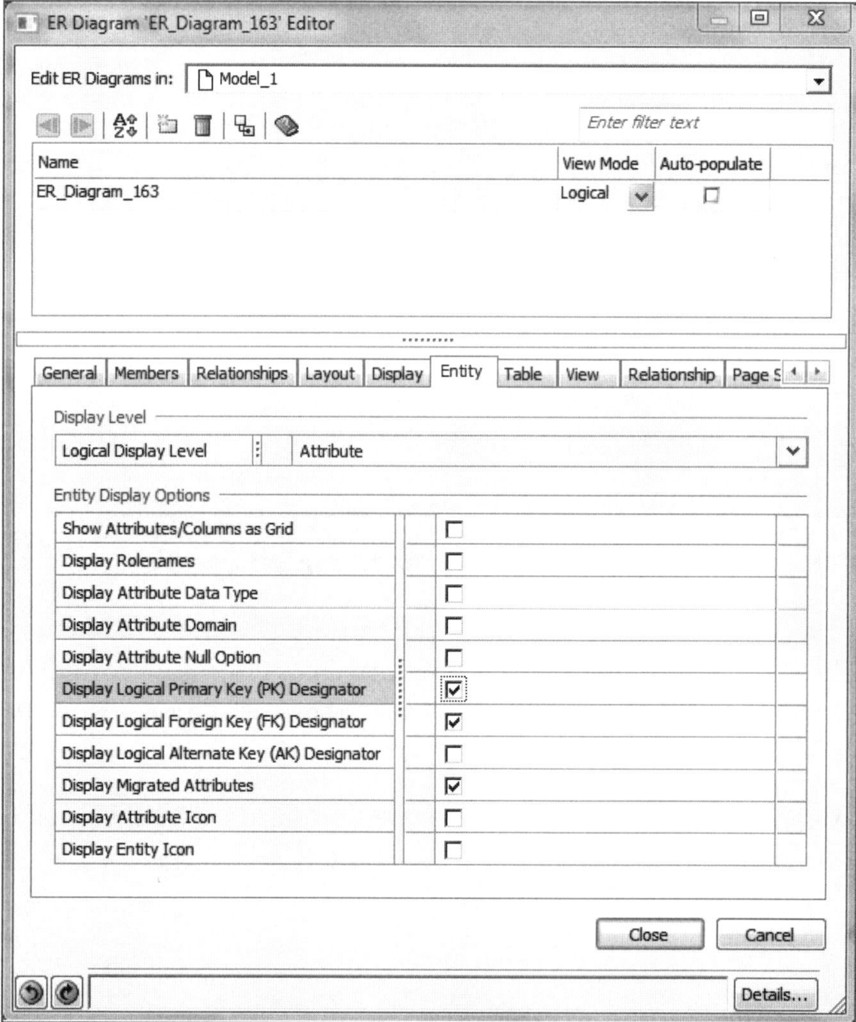

Your model will now show the graphic next to the primary key, as shown in Figure 7.12. There are many ways to display information in CA ERwin Data Modeler—remember to be flexible and use the display that will resonate with your particular audience.

Figure 7.12 Primary Key Designator as Shown by a Key Icon

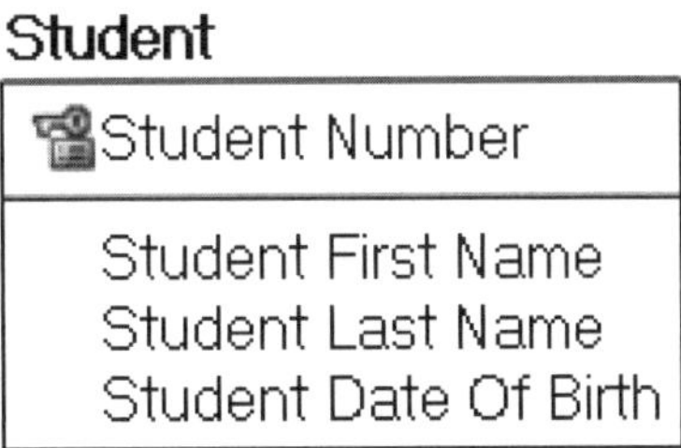

Let's take a step back and see what our model looks like as a whole, shown in Figure 7.13.

Figure 7.13 Our Model So Far

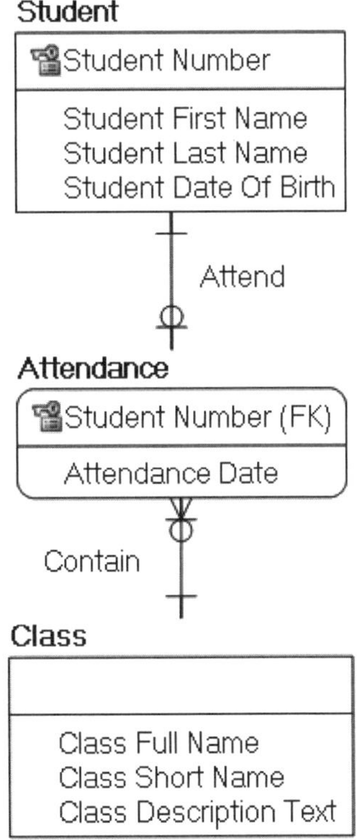

It's looking pretty nice—take time to pat yourself on the back. But wait—what is that key designator doing in the **Attendance** entity? We didn't put that there!

The (FK) indicator gives us a clue here, highlighted in Figure 7.14.

Figure 7.14 Foreign Key Indicator

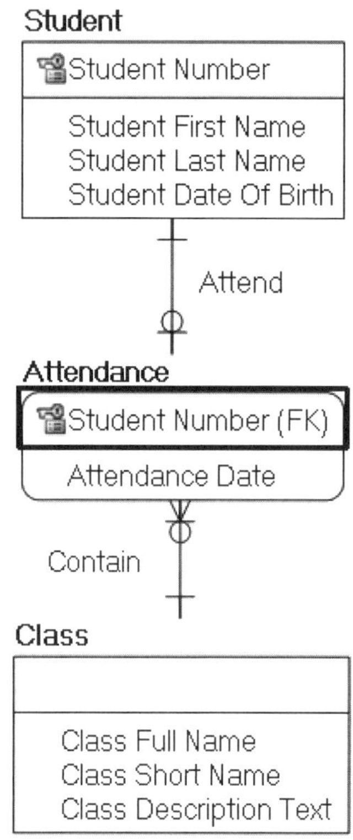

Remember that a foreign key is automatically created when we define a relationship between two entities, and that the entity on the 'many' side of the relationship inherits the primary key from the 'one' side. In this case, **Attendance** inherits the key from the **Student** entity, which is **Student Number**. To distinguish this from a primary key, the (FK) designator is listed. This designator can be switched off through the Diagram Properties Editor, but we recommend that you show it for clarity. CA ERwin Data Modeler sets showing the (FK) designator on the diagram as the default behavior.

Remember that for the **Class** entity, there was not a good attribute to choose as a natural primary key. **Class Full Name** was one option, but wasn't strong enough. So we decided to create a surrogate key called **Class Id** to act as a more efficient primary key. How do we create a surrogate key in CA ERwin Data Modeler?

CA ERwin Data Modeler does not make a distinction between natural primary keys and surrogate primary keys. This is a design decision that you need to analyze based on your unique business and performance needs.[7] All we need to do to create a surrogate key is to create a new attribute called **Class Id** in the **Class** entity and designate it as the primary key. You've learned all of these steps already, so we won't show them again. If you have difficulty, refer back to previous sections to refresh your memory.

---

[7] The decision to use natural keys vs. surrogate keys is a hotly debated topic in the industry. We will not take sides in this book, but will attempt to point out some of the pros and cons of each approach.

When you are finished, your model should look like the one in Figure 7.15.

Figure 7.15 Model with Both Surrogate and Natural Keys

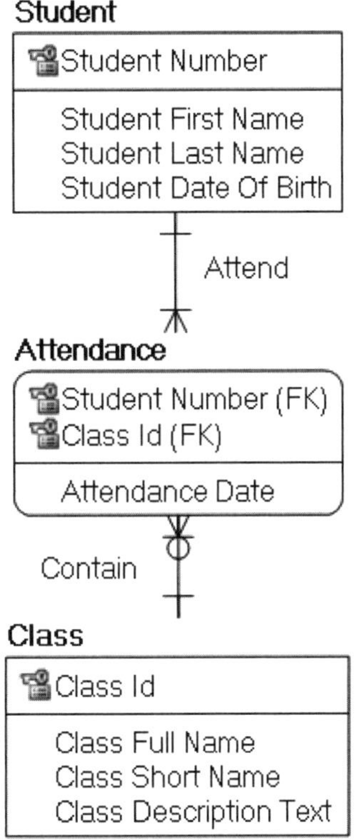

Note that a foreign key called **Class Id** was created in the **Attendance** entity. **Attendance** now has two foreign keys: **Student Number** and **Class Id**. These two foreign keys indicate that to uniquely identify a student's attendance for a particular class, you need both a student number and a class id.

Remember from our earlier discussion that an alternate key is used to denote any combination of attributes which does, in fact, uniquely identify each instance of the entity, but is not chosen as the primary key. In our example, the alternate key for the Student entity was the composite **Student First Name**, **Student Last Name**, and **Student Date of Birth**. Let's create this composite alternate key in CA ERwin Data Modeler.

In the Attribute Properties Editor, select the **Key Groups** tab, shown in Figure 7.16.

Figure 7.16 Selecting the Key Groups Tab to Add an Alternate Key

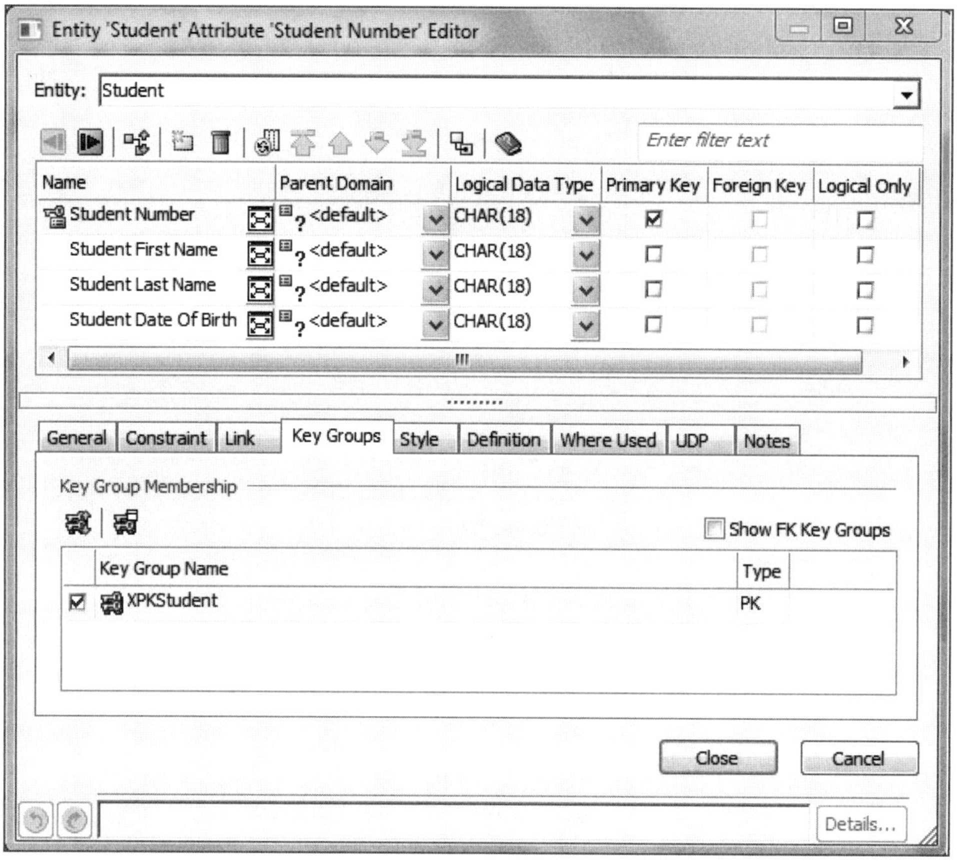

You'll see that there is an existing Key Group that was created when we identified **Student Number** as the primary key. This key group is called 'XPKStudent', indicating that it is the Primary Key (PK) for the **Student** entity. To find out more information about this Key Group, such as which attributes make up this key, select the **Key Group Editor** button from the toolbar, as shown in Figure 7.17.

Figure 7.17 Invoking the Key Group Editor

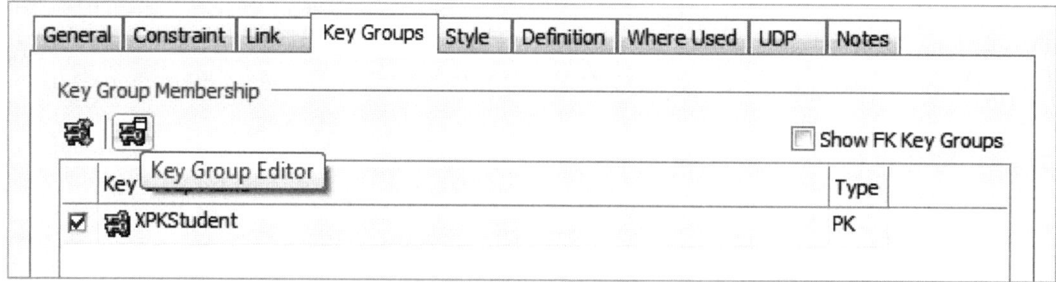

The Key Group Editor, shown in Figure 7.18, shows that this key group has a single member, in this case **Student Number**, as indicated by the check box to the left of the attribute.

Figure 7.18 Key Group Editor

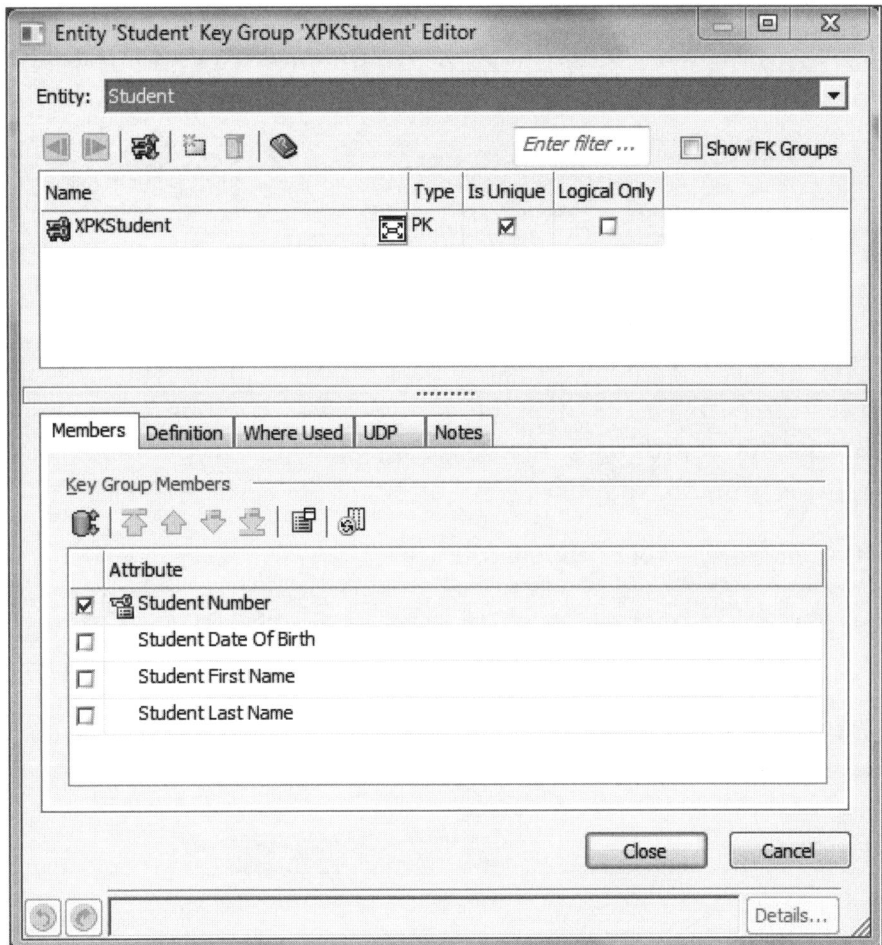

To add an alternate key group, click the **New** button, as shown in Figure 7.19.

Figure 7.19 Adding a New Key Group

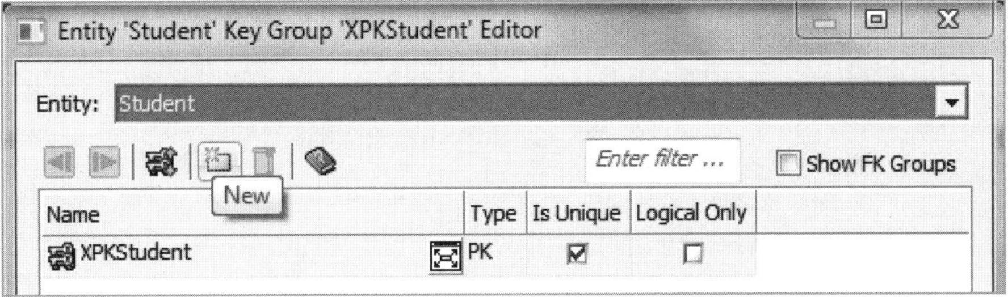

Select **New Alternate Key (Unique)** from the drop down menu that appears, as shown in Figure 7.20. You may be curious about the **Inversion Entry** selection. While we will not be covering inversion entries in this example, a simple explanation is that Inversion Entries are groups of attributes that are used for searches. Identifying these attributes is helpful for the physical designers when they create the physical data model and resulting database. We'll talk more about this when we discuss indexing and views in Chapter 19.

Figure 7.20 Creating a New Alternate Key

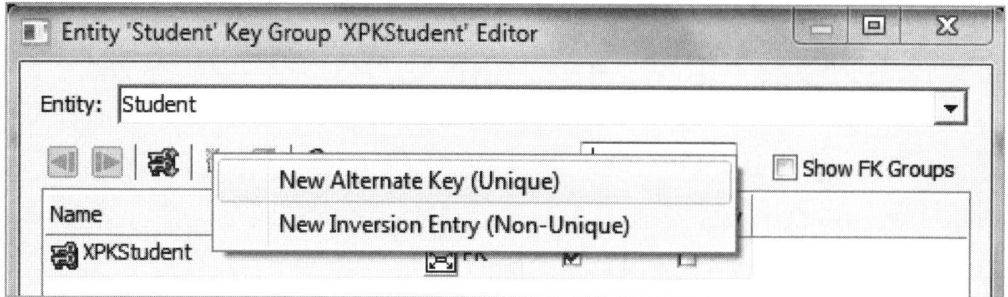

A new entry is created in the Key Group Editor, as shown in Figure 7.21. The default name of the key group is **XAK1Student**, indicating that this is the first alternate key (AK) defined for the **Student** entity. You can change the name of the key group, but let's keep the default for this example. Notice that the **Type** field is set to AK1, indicating that this is an alternate key.

Figure 7.21 Defining the Properties of a New Alternate Key

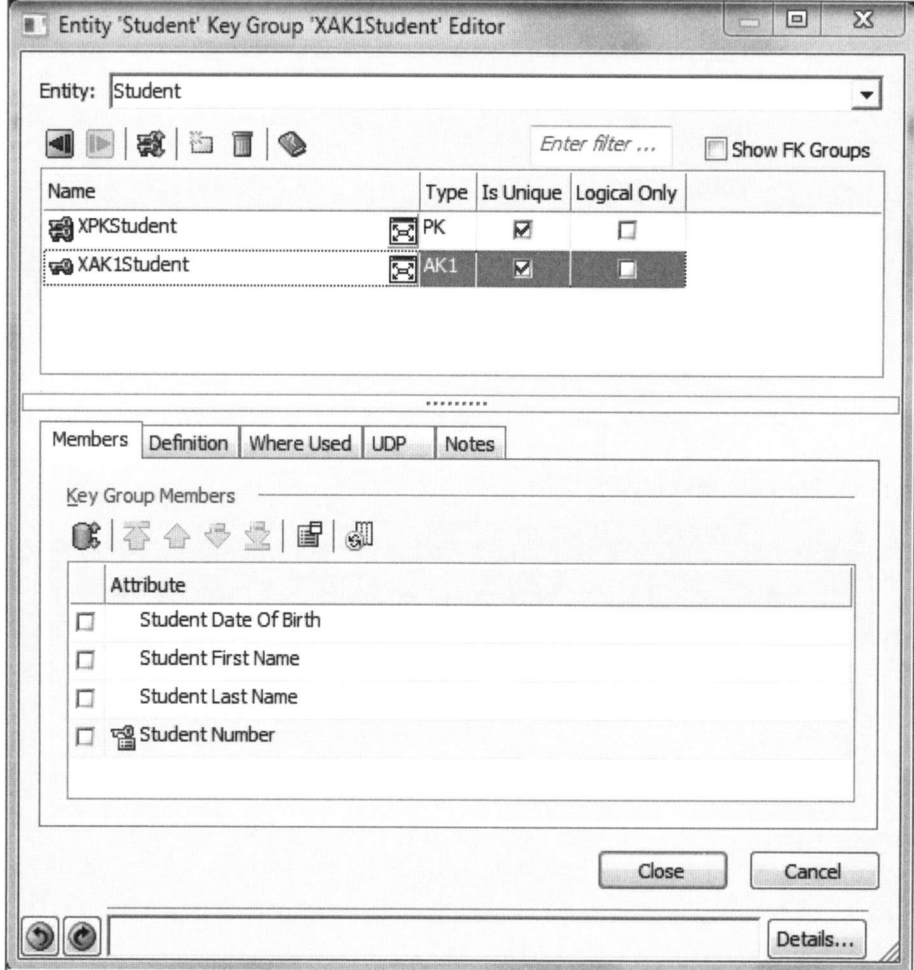

Next we'll want to select the members of this alternate key group. In the **Key Group Members** box, simply select the check box next to the members you want to include in the group. In this case, we'll select: **Student First Name**, **Student Last Name**, and **Student Date of Birth**, as shown in Figure 7.22.

Figure 7.22 Selecting Members of the Alternate Key Group

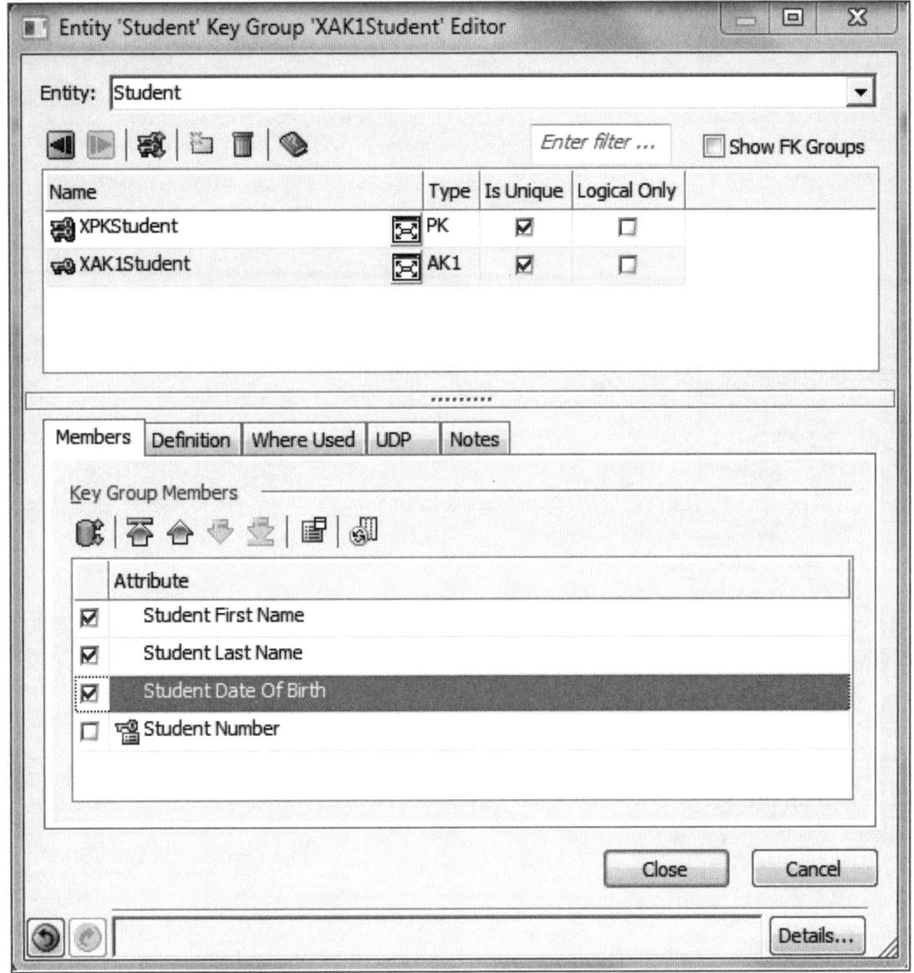

You can also change the order of the attributes within the group. Note that this will not change the order of the attributes in the model itself, but only within the key group. The order of attributes within a key group is important for the physical designs as they create indexes for performance. Indexes will be explained in more detail in Chapter 19. For now, think of indexes as an easy way to search for information. In our example, if we wanted to search for students, we most likely would want to start with their last name, not their first. Make **Student Last Name** the first attribute in the list by using the up arrow, as shown in Figure 7.23.

Figure 7.23 Changing the Order of Attributes within a Key Group

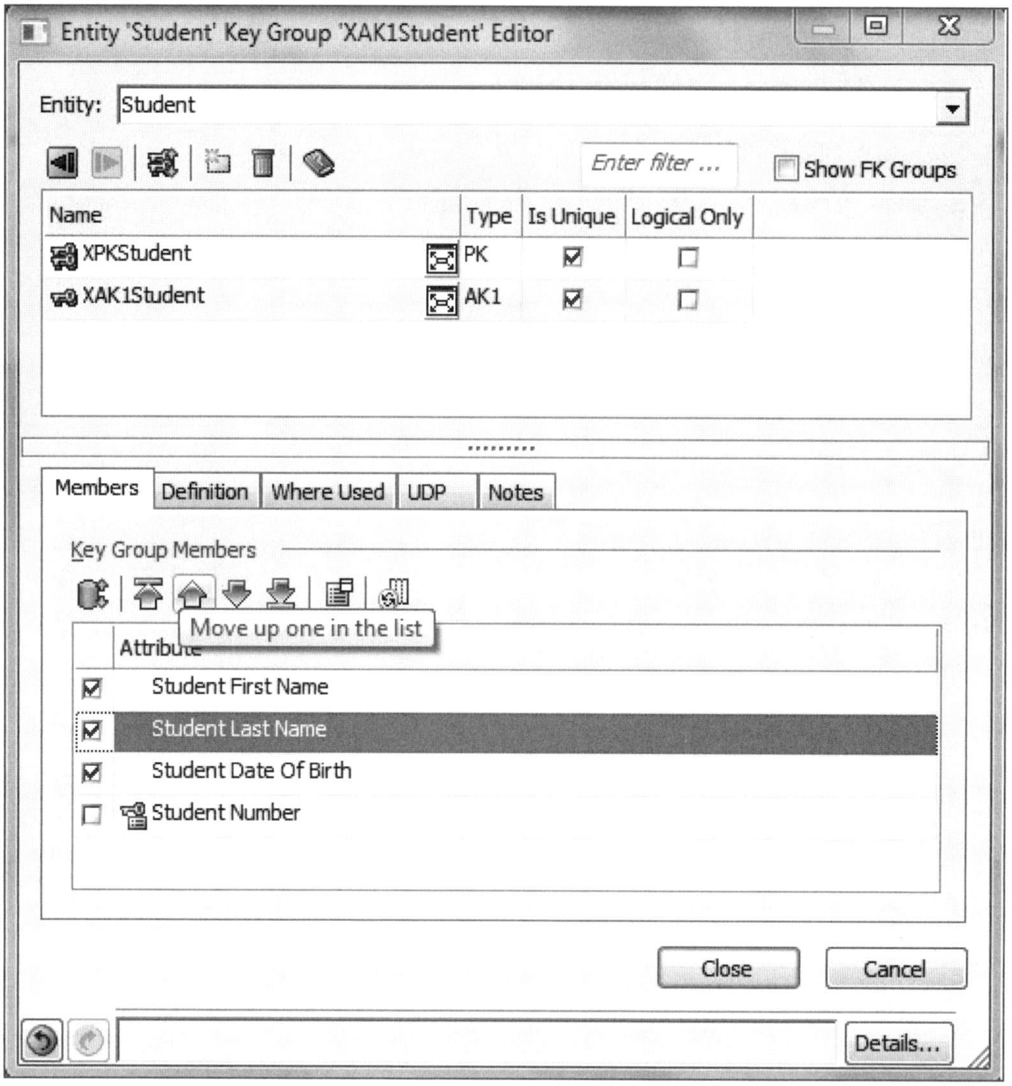

Save your changes by selecting **Close** to return to the Attribute Properties Editor and **Close** again to return to your model. You'll notice that the model looks the same as it did before, in Figure 7.15. To show an alternate key designator on the model, select the **Display Logical Alternate Key (AK) Designator** check box on the **Entity** tab of the Diagram Properties Editor (right-click on a blank area of the diagram to invoke) as shown in Figure 7.24.

Figure 7.24 Showing the Alternate Key Designator via the Diagram Properties Editor

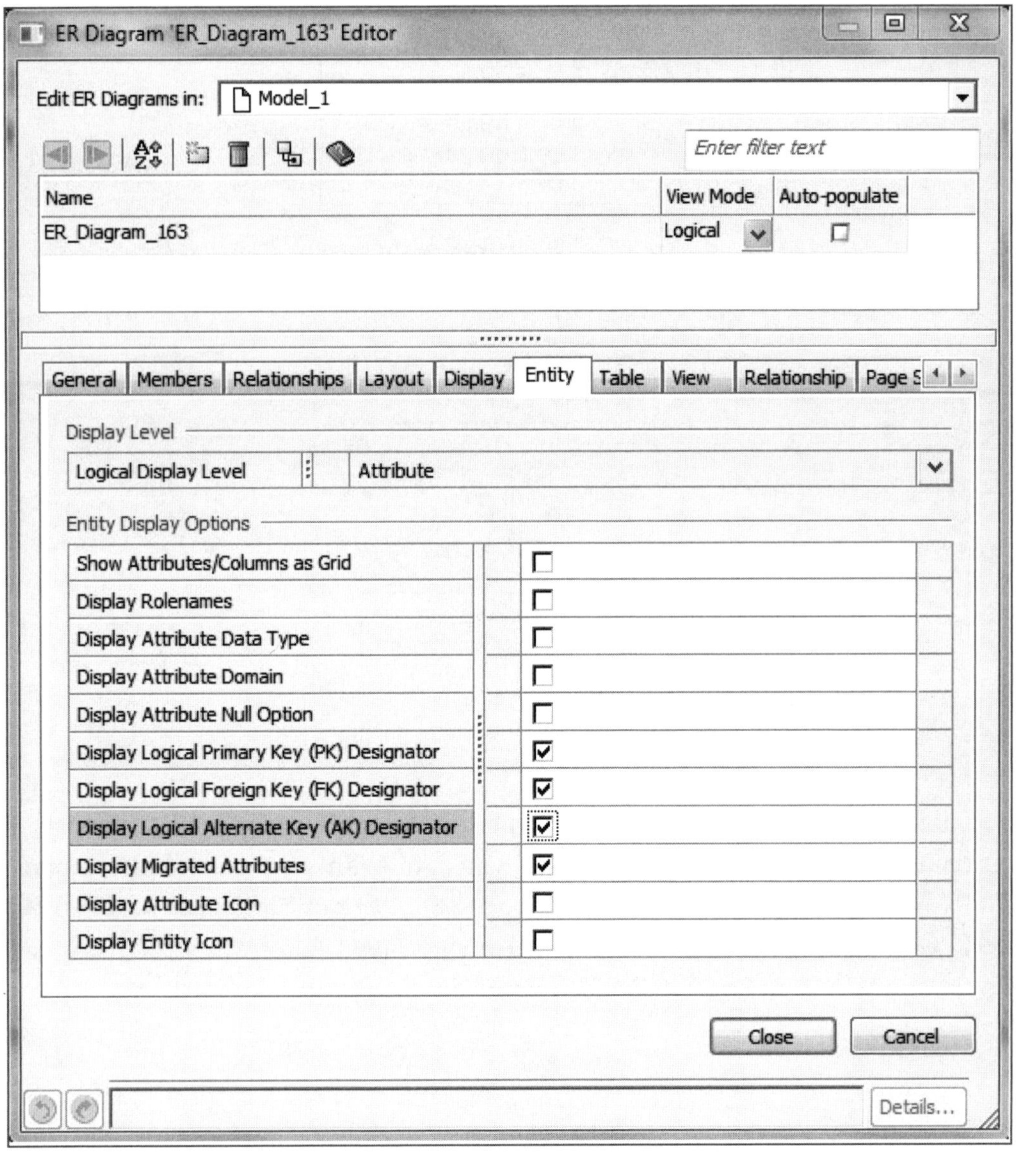

Figure 7.25 shows the diagram with the alternate key designator displayed, which is in the format (AK:X.Y). (AK) indicates that this is an alternate key. 'X' represents the number of the alternate key, which is **1** in this example since this is the only one we've created. 'Y' indicates the order of the attribute within the key group. Notice for example, that although **Student First Name** is the first attribute listed in the **Student** entity, it is the second attribute listed in the alternate key; thus (AK:1.2) is shown on the diagram. Remember that we set **Student Last Name** as the first attribute in the key, which is indicated by (AK1:1).

Figure 7.25 Displaying Alternate Keys (AK) on the Diagram

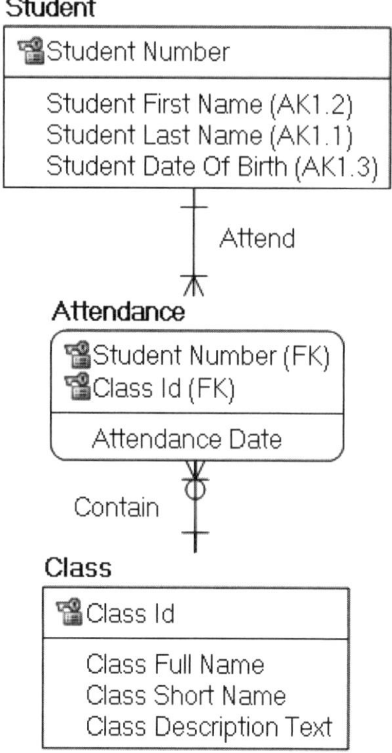

You should now have a good understanding of the various types of keys and their importance and usage in a data model. If you'd like an example of the model we've created, you can download the **Student Attendance.erwin** file from www.erwin.com/datamodelingmadesimple. In the next chapter, we'll cover ways to optimize the organization and layout of your model diagrams.

Key Points

- A key is a data element or set of data elements that helps us find entity instances.
- A candidate key is a set of one or more data elements that uniquely identify an entity instance.
- A candidate key becomes either a primary or alternate key.
- A primary key represents the one or more data elements that uniquely identify an instance of an entity and that is chosen to be *the* unique identifier everyone should use. In contrast, an alternate key also uniquely identifies entity occurrences, but is not chosen as *the* unique key. Primary keys are indicated by (PK) in CA ERwin Data Modeler.
- If a key contains more than one data element, it is known as a composite key.
- A surrogate key is a primary key with no embedded intelligence that is a substitute for a natural key. It is used by IT to facilitate integration and introduce database efficiencies. CA ERwin Data Modeler does not distinguish between surrogate and natural primary keys.
- A foreign key points from one entity instance to another. Foreign keys are not created directly in CA ERwin Data Modeler, but are inferred by the relationships between entities and their primary keys. They are indicated on the model diagram using the (FK) designator.
- Alternate keys can be defined using Key Groups in CA ERwin Data Modeler and are indicated by (AK:X.Y) in CA ERwin Data Modeler. The order of alternate key attributes is important for performance considerations in the physical model.

CHAPTER 8
Optimizing Model Presentation

A picture is art
A blueprint is practical
Can it be art, too?

We've just spent several chapters discussing the various technical components that go into building a data model, and learned a bit about the relational theory that helps make a data model structurally sound. Although these components are critical to the design of a data model, unless you present the model effectively to your audience, you may not get the buy-in and success you are looking for. Like many things in life, it's the presentation that matters, and the look and layout of your model can be critical in enhancing your audience's understanding of the underlying concepts which, ultimately, drives their acceptance of the model, and your project in general. This chapter covers Subject Areas, Diagrams, Formatting Themes, and Drawing Objects in CA ERwin Data Modeler, and how you can use these features to enhance the organization and presentation of your models.

Subject Areas

We discussed Subject Areas in Chapter 3 as a means of providing scope to your data modeling effort. In this section, we'll go into more detail regarding how to build and leverage Subject Areas in your data model.

Let's go back to the eMovies example that we've used in previous chapters, and that comes with each CA ERwin Data Modeler installation. By default, the model opens to a diagram showing the main **<model>**, which contains all objects in the model. Even with this relatively small model, you'll see that the amount of information can begin to become overwhelming, as shown in Figure 8.1.

Figure 8.1 <model> Diagram of eMovies Data Model

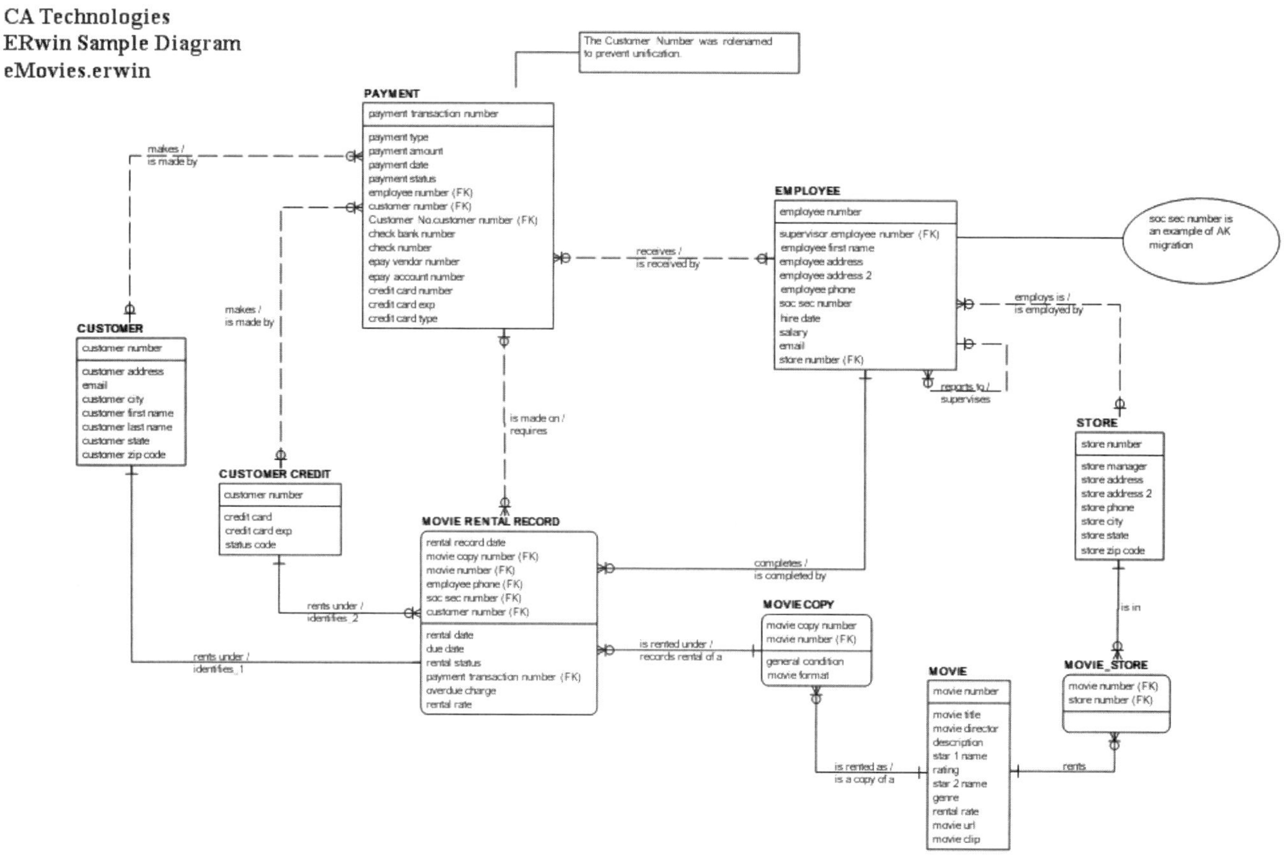

CA Technologies
ERwin Sample Diagram
eMovies.erwin

The Customer Number was rolenamed to prevent unification.

PAYMENT
payment transaction number
payment type
payment amount
payment date
payment status
employee number (FK)
customer number (FK)
Customer No.customer number (FK)
check bank number
check number
epay vendor number
epay account number
credit card number
credit card exp
credit card type

EMPLOYEE
employee number
supervisor employee number (FK)
employee first name
employee address
employee address 2
employee phone
soc sec number
hire date
salary
email
store number (FK)

soc sec number is an example of AK migration

CUSTOMER
customer number
customer address
email
customer city
customer first name
customer last name
customer state
customer zip code

CUSTOMER CREDIT
customer number
credit card
credit card exp
status code

MOVIE RENTAL RECORD
rental record date
movie copy number (FK)
movie number (FK)
employee phone (FK)
soc sec number (FK)
customer number (FK)
rental date
due date
rental status
payment transaction number (FK)
overdue charge
rental rate

STORE
store number
store manager
store address
store address 2
store phone
store city
store state
store zip code

MOVIE COPY
movie copy number
movie number (FK)
general condition
movie format

MOVIE
movie number
movie title
movie director
description
star 1 name
rating
star 2 name
genre
rental rate
movie url
movie clip

MOVIE_STORE
movie number (FK)
store number (FK)

makes / is made by
makes / is made by
receives / is received by
employs is / is employed by
reports to / supervises
is made on / requires
completes / is completed by
rents under / identifies_2
rents under / identifies_1
is rented under / records rental of a
is rented as / is a copy of a
rents
is in

To make the volume of information more manageable, and to 'zoom in' on particular areas of the business, several Subject Areas were defined, as are listed in the Model Explorer in Figure 8.2.

Figure 8.2 Viewing Subject Areas in Model Explorer

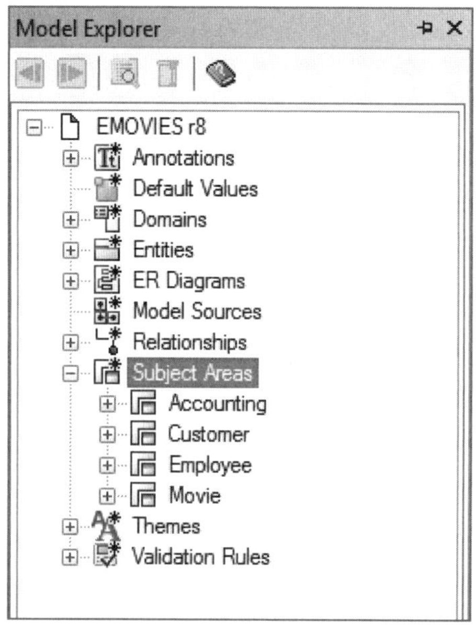

If we'd like to switch to one of these Subject Areas, there are several ways of doing this. One option is to select the Subject Area from the Model Explorer, right-click to invoke the context menu, and then choose **Switch to**, as shown in Figure 8.3.

Figure 8.3 Switching Subject Areas from the Model Tab in Model Explorer

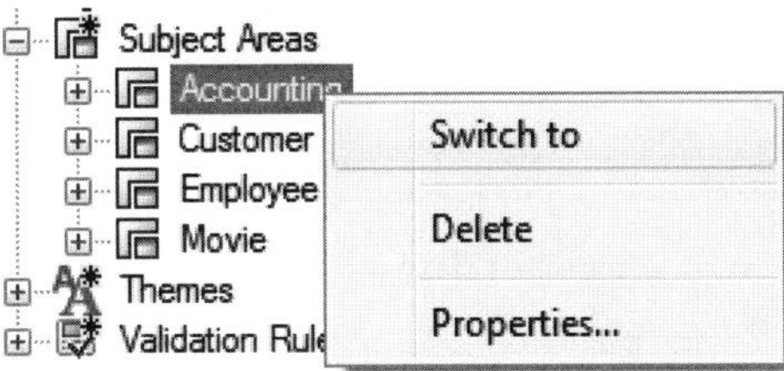

Another option is to move to the **Subject Area** tab, and use the drop-down menu to select the Subject Area you'd like to open, as shown in Figure 8.4.

Figure 8.4 Switching Subject Areas from the Subject Area Tab in Model Explorer

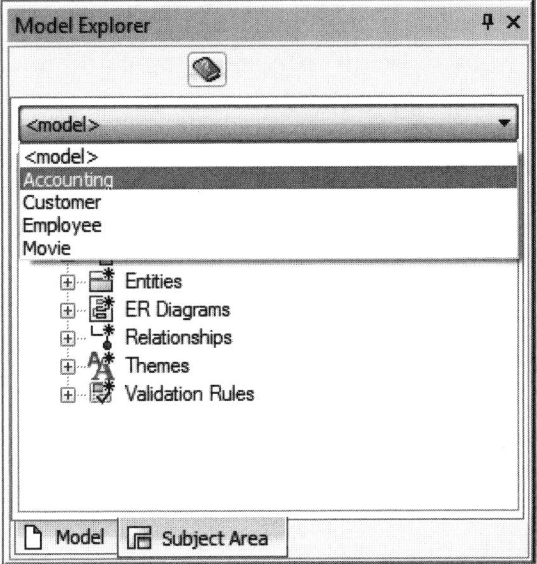

A third method for switching Subject Areas is to use the Subject Area Selection Tool, indicated by a downward-pointing arrow on the Display Toolbar, as shown in Figure 8.5.

Figure 8.5 Subject Area Selection Tool on the Display Toolbar

Once you invoke the selection tool, a drop-down menu appears, as shown in Figure 8.6, where you can choose a Subject Area to display. A checkmark indicates the current

Subject Area, and the highlighted area is the one selected. Once you select a Subject Area and release your mouse button, the current Subject Area is changed.

Figure 8.6 Switching Subject Areas Using the Display Toolbar

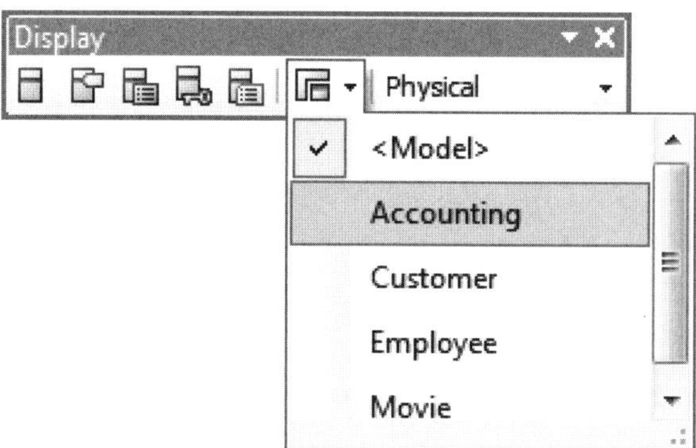

Any of these methods will change the selected Subject Area to **Accounting**, as shown in Figure 8.7. This Subject Area contains only the objects that relate to the Accounting business unit, which allows us to 'zoom in' on this topic and make the information more understandable and relevant to our audience.

Figure 8.7 Accounting Subject Area in eMovies

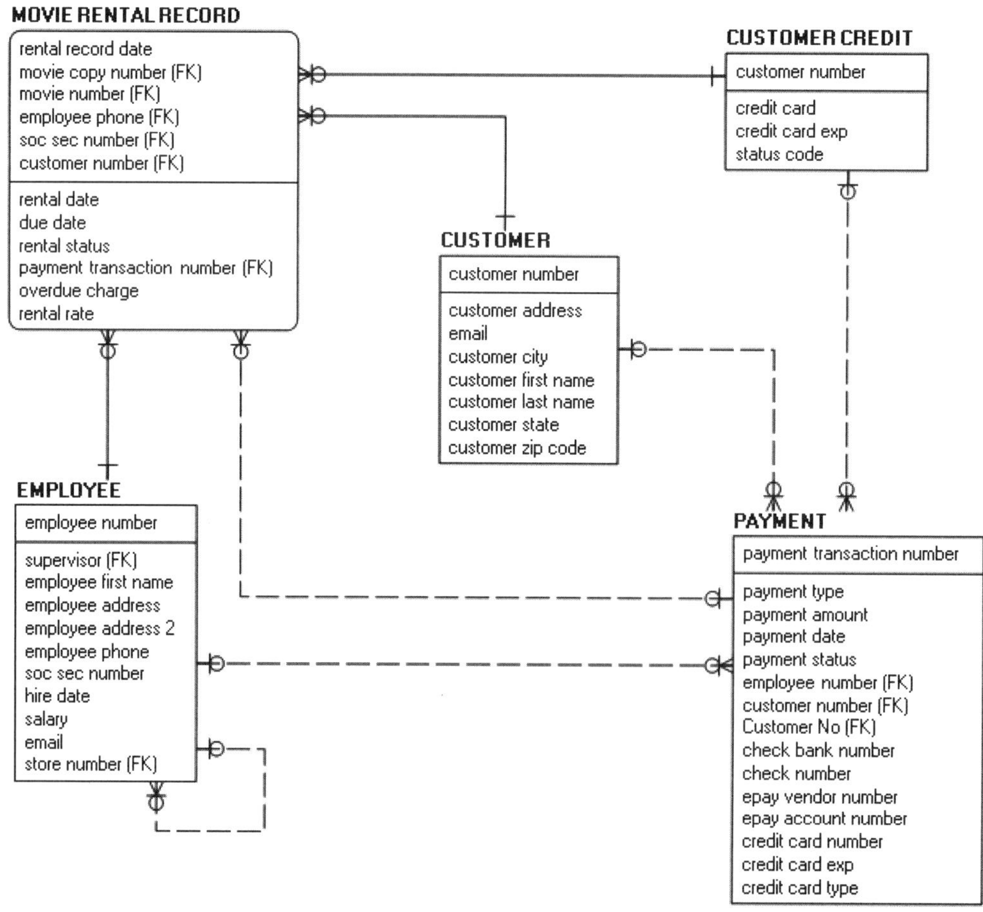

Now let's create a new Subject Area of our own. First, save the **eMovies.erwin** model as a new file, so that we can keep the default sample model intact. Go to **File|Save As** and save the model under the new name of **eMovies_practice.erwin**, as shown in Figure 8.8.

Figure 8.8 Saving a Backup Copy of eMovies

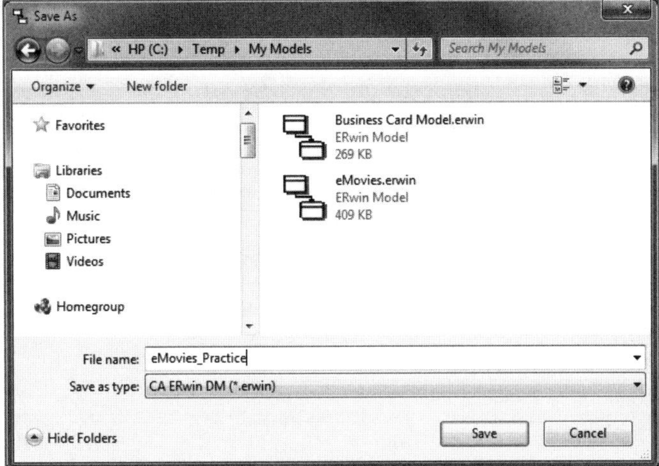

Now that we have a safe model to practice with, let's start building a new Subject Area. As a sample scenario, we've been asked by the business sponsor to look into the payments process and make sure that the existing application is working properly for an upcoming audit. For this review, we'll want to create a new Subject Area for the Payment business area. Select **Model|Subject Areas** from the **Main Menu** to invoke the Subject Area Editor, shown in Figure 8.9.

Figure 8.9 Subject Area Editor

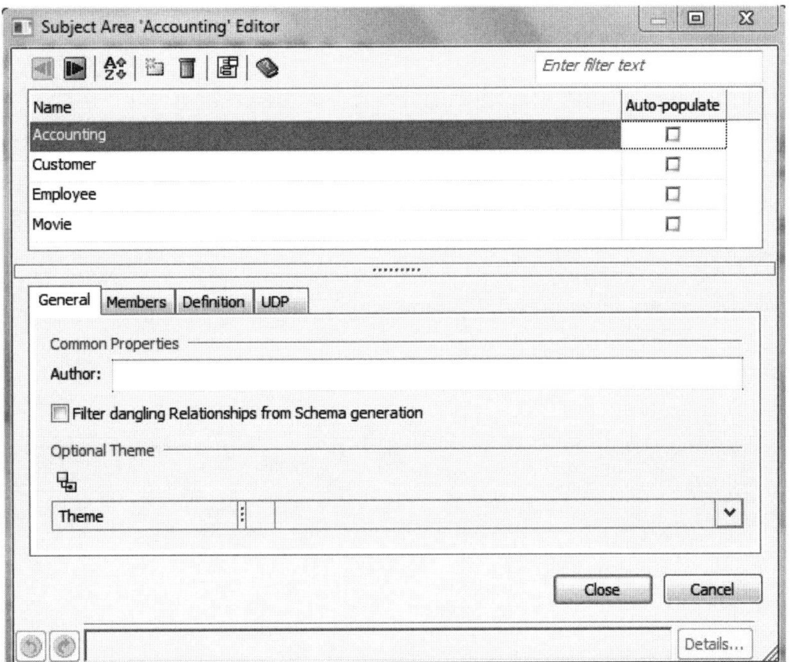

Select the **New** button on the toolbar to create a new entry, and type the name 'Payment' in the **Name** field, as shown in Figure 8.10.

Figure 8.10 Creating a New Subject Area for Payment

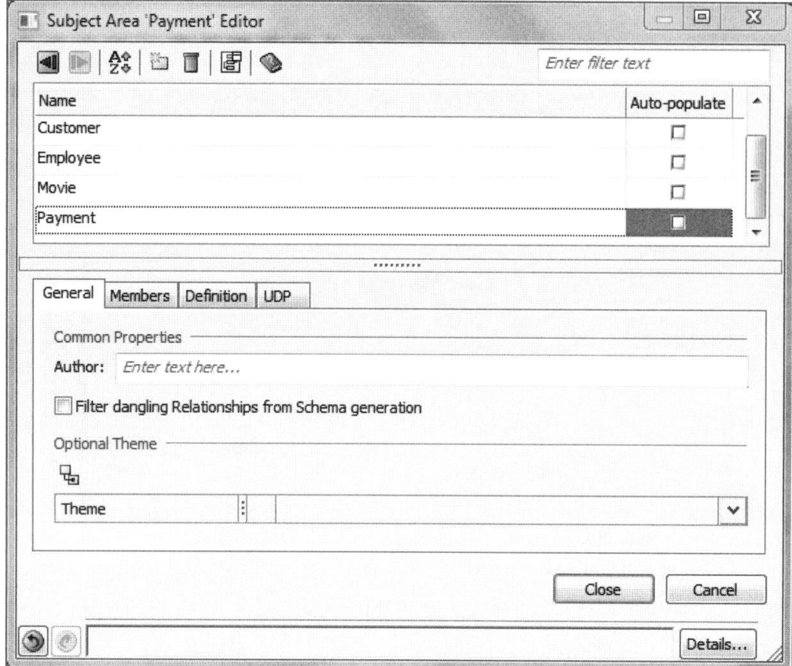

Now that we've created our subject area, we need to identify the relevant objects that relate to the payments process, which will be identified as members of the **Payment** subject area we just created. To define the members of the **Payment** Subject Area, move to the **Members** tab of the Subject Area Editor, as shown in Figure 8.11.

Notice that the left pane, **Available Objects**, lists all of the available objects in the model from which we can select to create our Subject Area. The right pane, **Included Objects**, shows the objects that are members of our subject area. In this case, the list is empty since we haven't yet defined any members. To define objects included in our Subject Area, we'll use the Available Objects Toolbar, shown in Figure 8.12.

Figure 8.11 Members Tab of the Subject Area Editor

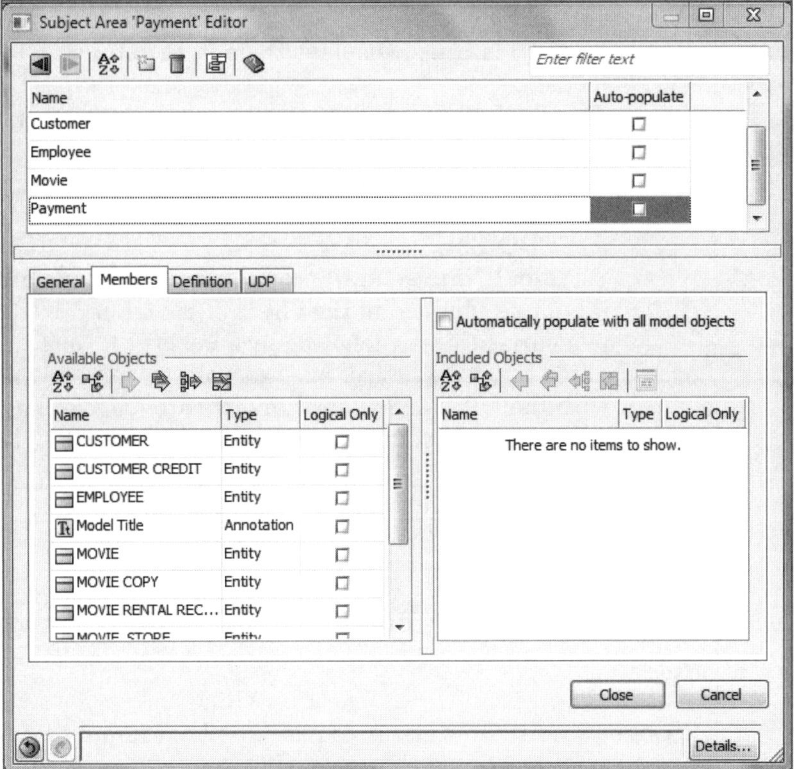

Figure 8.12 Available Objects Toolbar in Subject Area Editor

Table 8.1 defines the functionality and use of the buttons in the Available Objects Toolbar. We won't use all of these functions in our example, but this table may be handy to you for future reference.

Table 8.1 Available Object Toolbar in the Subject Area Editor

Icon	Option	Description
A↕Z	Sort Items	Sorts the available objects with the following options: • **Alphabetic:** Sorts in alphabetic order of the name of the object, i.e. 'A to Z' • **Reverse Alphabetic:** Sorts in reverse alphabetic order of the name of the object, i.e. 'Z to A' • **Alphabetic by Owner, Name:** Sorts in the alphabetic order of the owner of the object, and then the name of the object. Note: this applies only to physical objects, as logical objects do not have a (database) owner. For logical objects, only the name is used. • **Reverse Alphabetic by Owner, Name:** Sorts in the reverse alphabetic order of the owner of the object, and then the name of the object. Note: this applies only to physical objects, as logical objects do not have a (database) owner. For logical objects, only the name is used.

<table>
<tr><th>Icon</th><th>Option</th><th>Description</th></tr>
<tr><td></td><td>Choose Name display format</td><td>Defines the way object names are displayed in the editor. Options include:
<ul>
<li>Logical Names: Displays the names defined in the logical data model</li>
<li>Physical Names: Displays the names defined in the physical data model</li>
<li>Physical Names, show owner: Displays the names defined in the physical model, prefixed by the owner name, followed by a period (.), e.g. DBO.EMP</li>
<li>Physical Names, show owner for Non Current User: Displays the names defined in the physical model, prefixed by the names of non current users, followed by a period (.). Note that the current user name is not displayed. For example, if we have the following tables with the following owners, and we are logged in as DBO, the following information would be shown: CUST, DLB.EMP, SLH.PROD.
<table>
<tr><td>Table Name</td><td>Owner Name</td></tr>
<tr><td>CUST</td><td>DBO</td></tr>
<tr><td>EMP</td><td>DLB</td></tr>
<tr><td>PROD</td><td>SLH</td></tr>
</table></li>
</ul>
Notes:

1. Logical Only Models: If you are in a Logical-only model, the Choose Name display format button is grayed-out and inactive. In this case, all names will be displayed as logical names.

2. Physical-Only Models: If you are in a Physical-only model, the Choose Name display format button is active, but the Logical Names option is not displayed.</td></tr>
<tr><td></td><td>Move selected objects to Included Objects</td><td>Moves all objects that have been highlighted in the Available Objects section to the Included Objects section to be included in the Subject Area.</td></tr>
<tr><td></td><td>Move all objects to Included Objects</td><td>Moves all objects in the Available Objects section to the Included Objects section to be included in the Subject Area.</td></tr>
<tr><td></td><td>Move selected objects and neighboring objects to Included Objects</td><td>This button invokes the Spanning Neighborhood Editor (see Figure 8.14 and related discussion in the following paragraphs), which allows you to include the Ancestors and Descendants of the objects to be moved into the Subject Area.</td></tr>
</table>

Icon	Option	Description
	Include all objects contained in another Subject Area	Allows you to select another Subject Area, and include all of the objects from that Subject Area into the current Subject Area. Note: The objects are not removed from the selected Subject area, but will be included in both. When this button is selected, the **Subject Area Editor** is invoked, with a drop down menu allowing you to choose the Subject Area from which you'd like to include objects, as shown below. 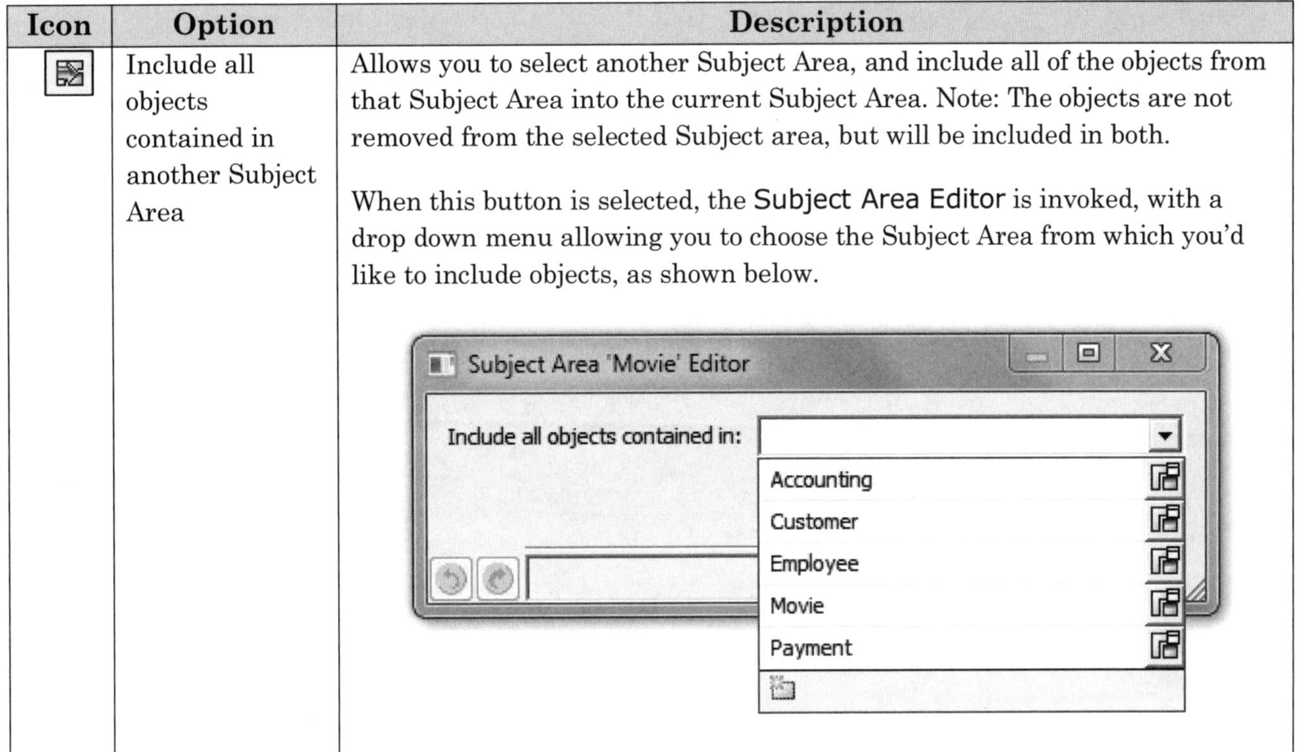

For our example, we want to select the subset of objects that relate to payments in our organization. Let's start by selecting the **Payment** entity, as shown in Figure 8.13. If you select the **Logical Only** option, only logical objects will be included in the subject area. In our example, we want to include both logical and physical model objects, so we'll leave it unchecked.

Figure 8.13 Selecting an Object to Include in a Subject Area

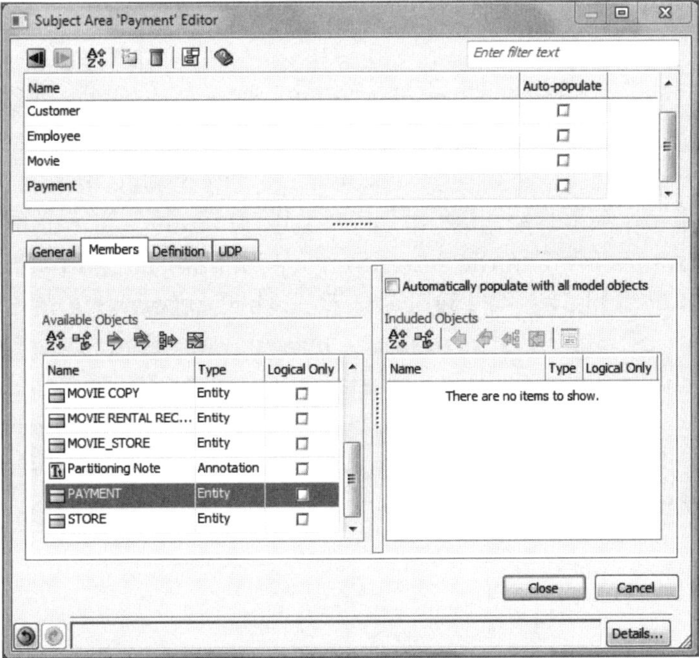

Now that we've selected the entity that's core to the payments process in our organization, **Payment**, CA ERwin Data Modeler can help us infer which other objects should be part of this Subject Area.

Select the **Move selected objects and neighboring objects to Included** button, and the Spanning Neighborhood Editor appears, as shown in Figure 8.14.

Figure 8.14 Spanning Neighborhood Editor

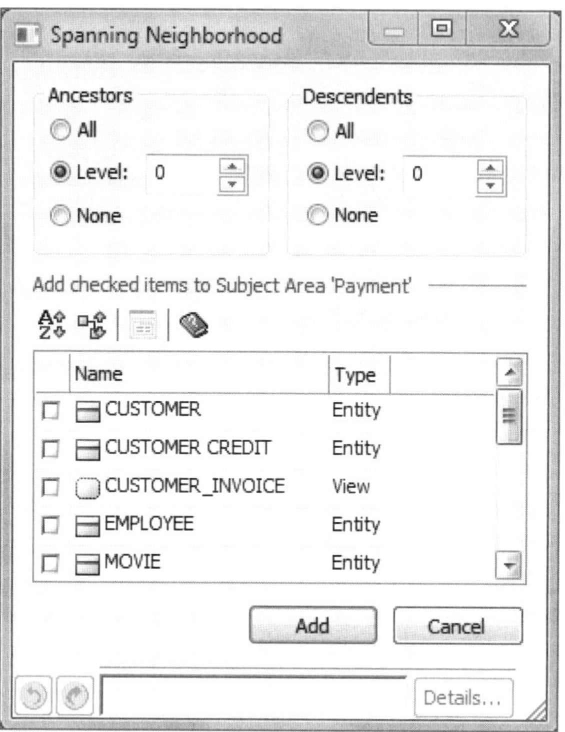

The Spanning Neighborhood Editor allows you include the entities and relationships that are related to the **Payment** entity. This is a very helpful feature, especially if you are working in a large complex data model. It allows you to isolate your model into one or more entities and everything that relates to them, which is useful for explaining the model to someone who just needs to see a subset of the model, or for performing impact analysis. Selecting an **Ancestor Level** of **1** will include all relationships of which **Payment** is the child, as well as the parent entity for that relationship. For example, in the portion of the model shown in Figure 8.15, both **Customer** and **Customer Credit** are parents, or Ancestors, of **Payment**. Choosing an **Ancestor Level** of **1** would automatically include **Customer**, **Customer Credit**, **Payment**, and the **Relationships** between these entities into the Subject Area. Selecting an **Ancestor Level** of **2** would include the parents of **Payment**, as well as the parents of **Customer Credit** and **Customer.**

Figure 8.15 Including Parent Entities in Subject Area

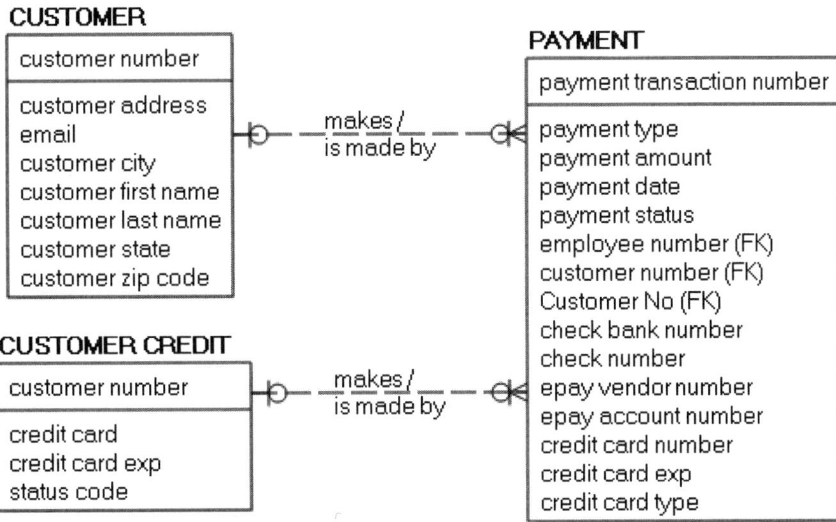

Levels for Descendants work in a similar way, but traverse to the children of the entity. In the subset of the model shown in Figure 8.16, both **Payment** and **Movie Rental Record** would be including using a **Descendant Level** of **1**, since **Movie Rental Record** is the child of **Payment**.

Figure 8.16 Including Child Entities in Subject Area

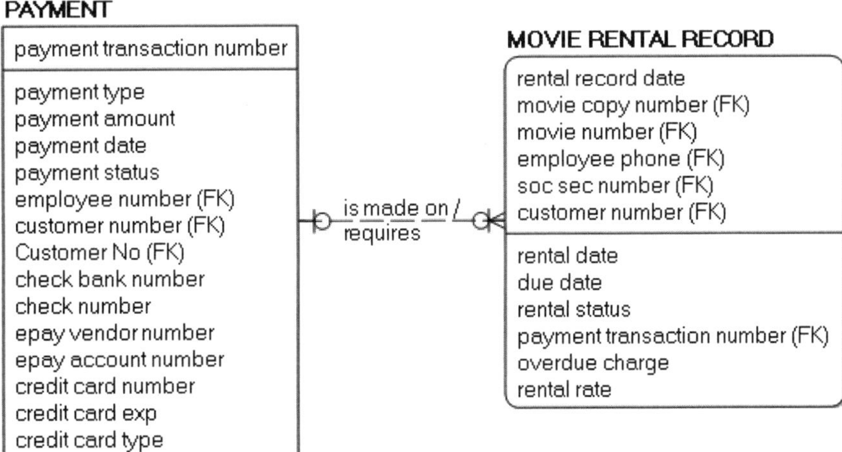

For our example, select both an **Ancestor Level** and **Descendant Level** of **1**, and you will see that both parents and children of **Payment** are included in the Subject Area, as well as the selected object itself, as shown in Figure 8.17.

Figure 8.17 Including Parents and Children in Subject Area

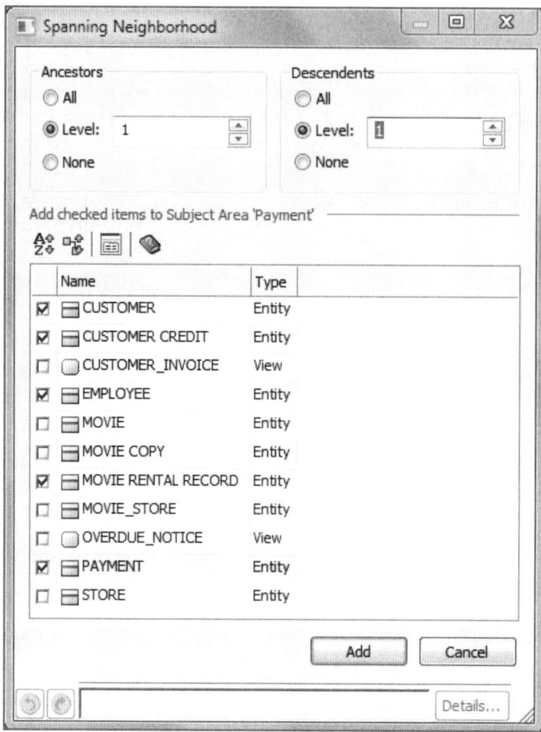

Click **Add**, and you'll be returned to the Subject Area Editor to see these new objects listed in the **Included Objects** section, as shown in Figure 8.18.

Figure 8.18 Included Objects for Payment Subject Area

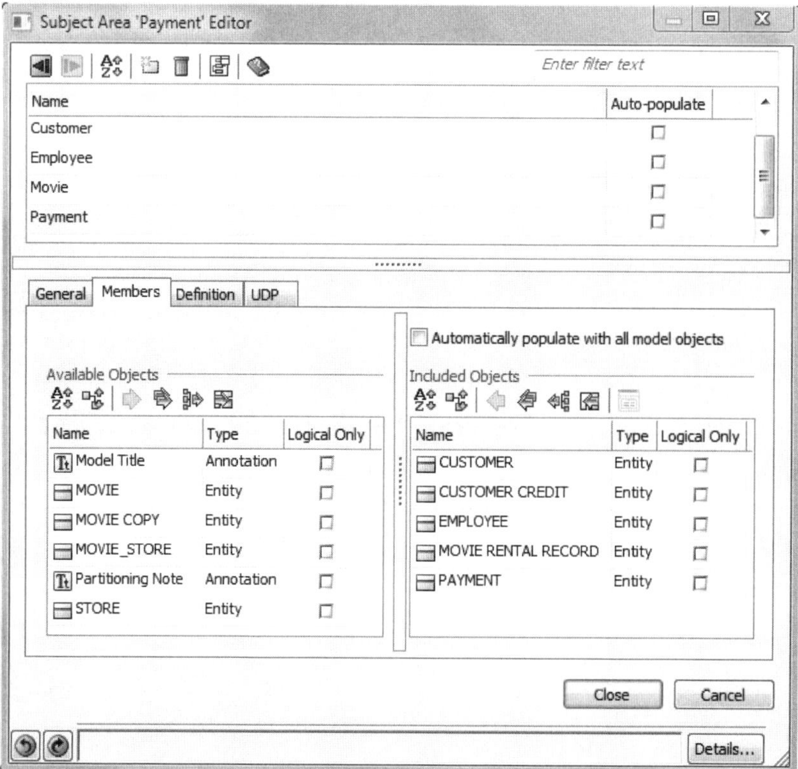

Select **Close** and you'll be returned to the model diagram, as shown in Figure 8.19. Notice that the objects in this Subject Area are now listed in the **Model Explorer**, but the Diagram window is empty.

Figure 8.19 Subject Area Objects in Model Explorer Only

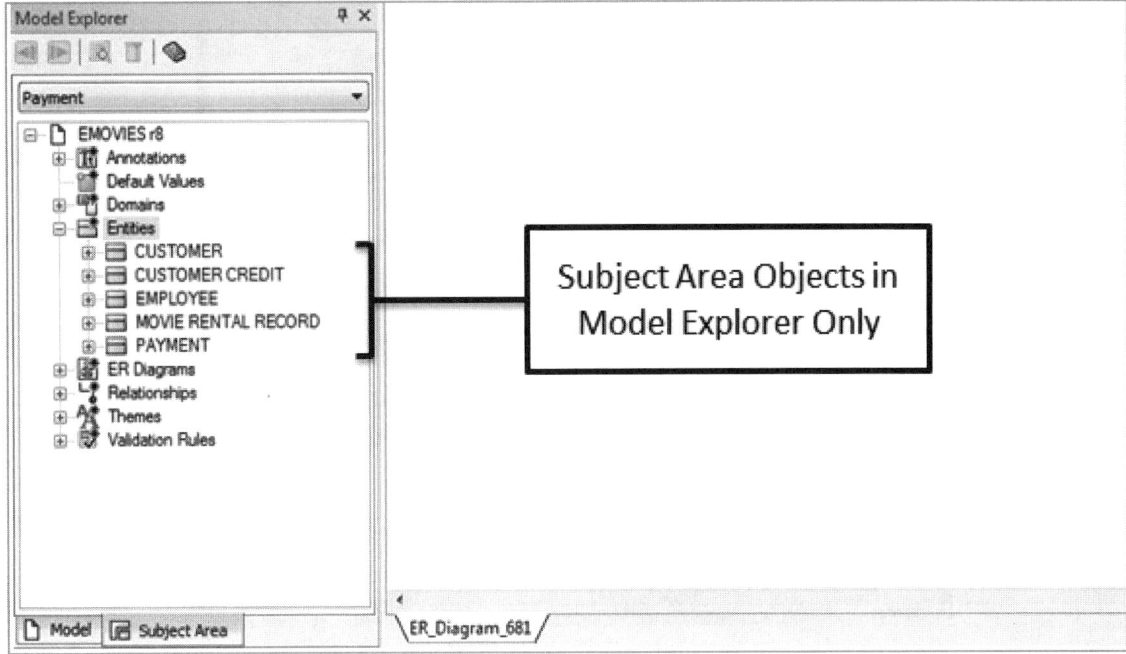

In CA ERwin Data Modeler r8, objects are not included by default on the diagram, as there is a clear separation between metadata information and display information. This leads us into the topic of our next section - Diagrams.

Diagrams

Diagrams are an ideal way to create customized views of your model for various audiences[8]. A business user might want to see entities and their definitions, for example, and a database administrator may want to see tables and their column details, such as data type, domain, null option, etc. Diagrams allow you to create custom views to suit each of these audiences.

[8] In previous versions of CA ERwin (r7.3 and earlier), Stored Displays were used as a concept similar to diagrams. In r8, Diagrams have a more clear separation between presentation (i.e. a diagram) and metadata (i.e. the model), which we'll explain further in this chapter.

It is important to understand the distinction between Diagram and Models in CA ERwin Data Modeler. The easiest way to think of this is that the Diagram is a 'picture', or visual representation, of a certain group of model objects, while a model contains the full set of model objects and the metadata defined for those objects. The model diagram in Figure 8.20 shows the relationship between Models, Subject Areas, and Diagrams in CA ERwin Data Modeler.

Figure 8.20 Relationship Between Model, Subject Area, and Diagram in CA ERwin Data Modeler

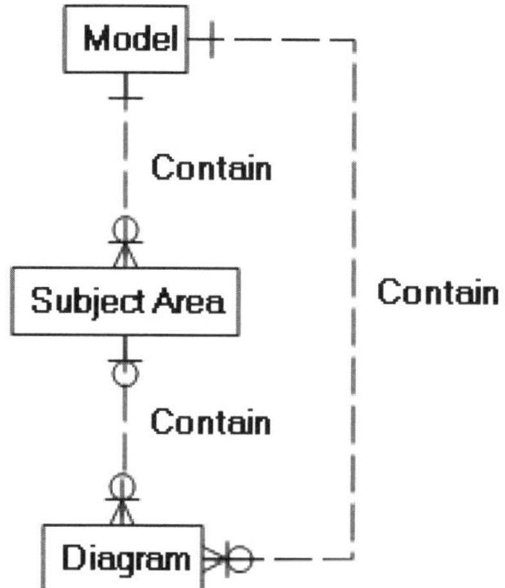

Since we've learned how to 'read' a data model from previous chapters (refer to Chapter 6 if you need a refresher), let's outline some of the business rules that this model defines:

- Each **Model** may contain one or many **Subject Area**s
- Each **Subject Area** may contain one or many **Diagram**s
- Each **Model** may contain one or many **Diagram**s

In summary, you can use Subject Areas to subset and organize your model objects by a particular topic, and Diagrams to visually organize your model objects with particular formatting and layout for different audiences. Neither Subject areas nor Diagrams are required, however. You can have a model that is simply a 'container' for all of the data objects and metadata about your organization, without having a 'picture' or diagram at all.

Let's walk through an example using the **eMovies_practice** model we created for our Subject Area discussion in the previous section. This model is also available for download at www.erwin.com/datamodelingmadesimple. If you recall in the previous chapter, Figure 8.19 shows that a default Diagram named **ER_Diagram_681**[9] was created with the new **Payment** Subject Area, but no objects were shown on that diagram. Let's add objects to the diagram now. Right-click on the diagram window and select **Properties** from the context menu, or simply double-click on the diagram 'white space'. When the Diagram Editor appears, move to the **Members** tab, as shown in Figure 8.21.

You'll see that there are a large number of tabs and options in the Diagram Editor but, for now, let's simply add our model objects for display on this diagram. You can selectively add objects using the **Available Objects** section but, in this case, we want to include all objects (for more information on how to use the **Available Options** toolbar, refer to the previous section).

[9] Note that diagrams are given a unique number upon creation, based on an internal algorithm. Your diagram number may be different from the one shown in this example, based on past model and diagram creation activities you may have performed.

Figure 8.21 Diagram Editor

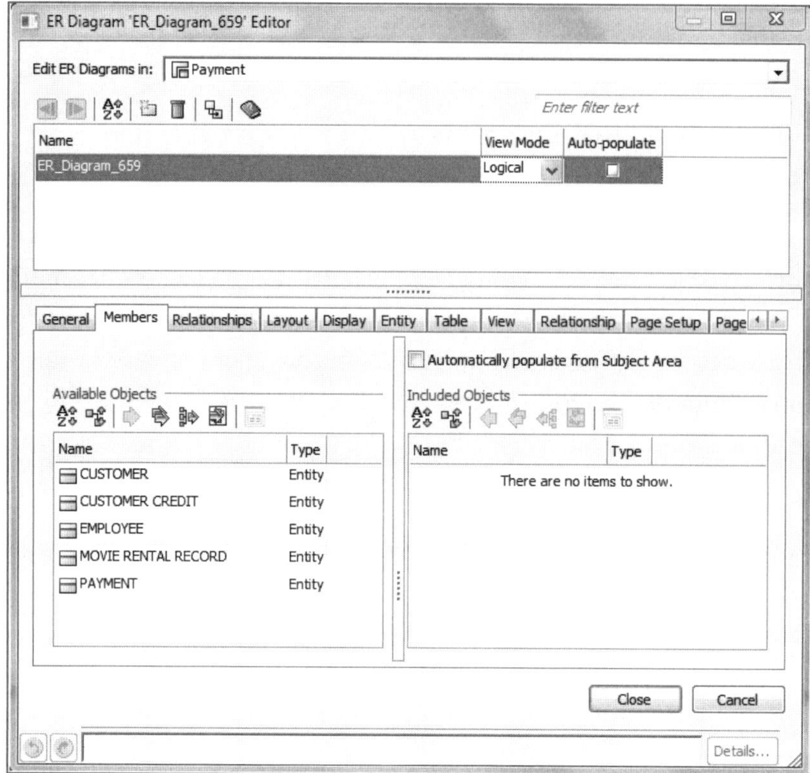

There are several easy ways to add all model objects to the diagram, as shown in Figure 8.22 by:

- Selecting the **Auto-populate** field next to the Diagram name. This field is useful when you wish to automatically populate multiple diagrams at the same time (Note that only a single diagram is listed in our example).
- Selecting the **Automatically populate from Subject Area** field (Note: This changes to **Automatically populate from Model** if the model is selected).
- Using the **Move all objects to Included Objects** on the **Available Objects** toolbar.

Figure 8.22 Easy Ways to Add All Objects to Diagram

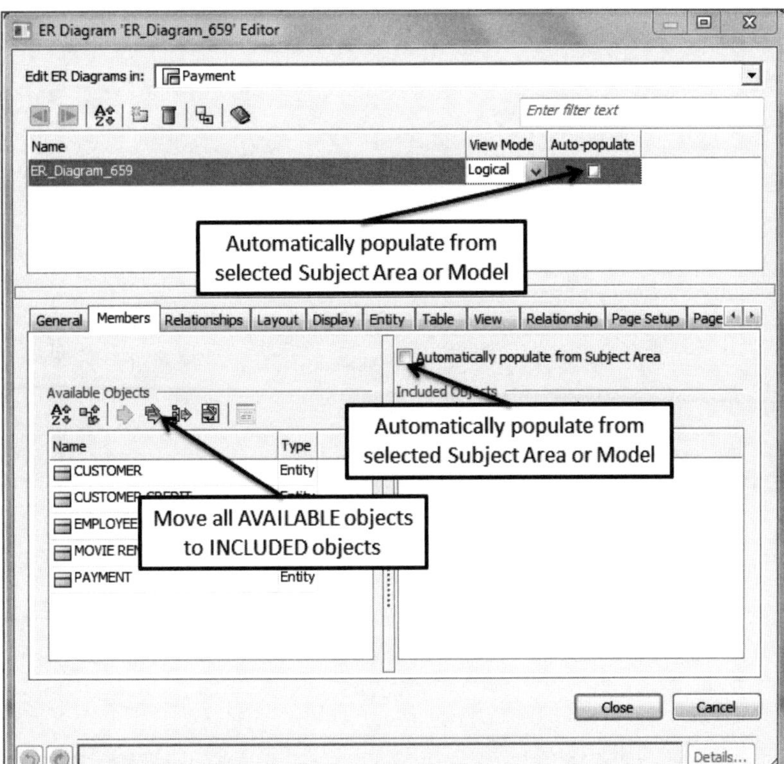

In this example, select the **Automatically Populate from Subject Area** check box. You'll then see all of the objects listed in the **Included Objects** section, as shown in Figure 8.23. Notice that the **Auto-Populate** checkbox is also automatically selected. Note that adding all objects to diagram is not recommended for large models, for both readability and performance reasons. One of the main purposes of a Diagram is to create an easily-readable presentation. With too many objects on a diagram, it easily becomes difficult to read and manage. The other aspect that contributes to readability is formatting and layout.

Figure 8.23 Adding Objects to a Diagram in the Diagram Editor

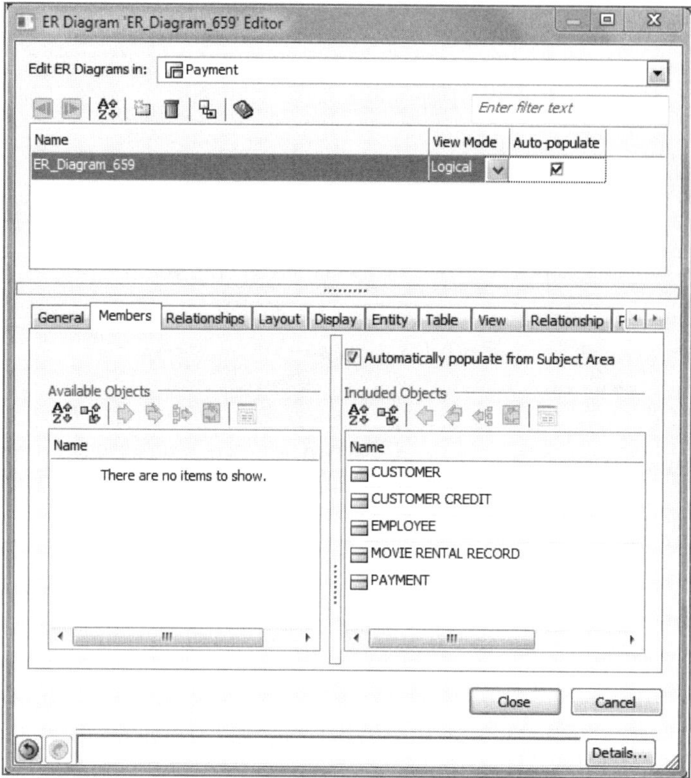

Select **Close** to return to the Diagram window, as shown in 8.24.

Figure 8.24 Default Layout for Model Objects Shown on a Diagram

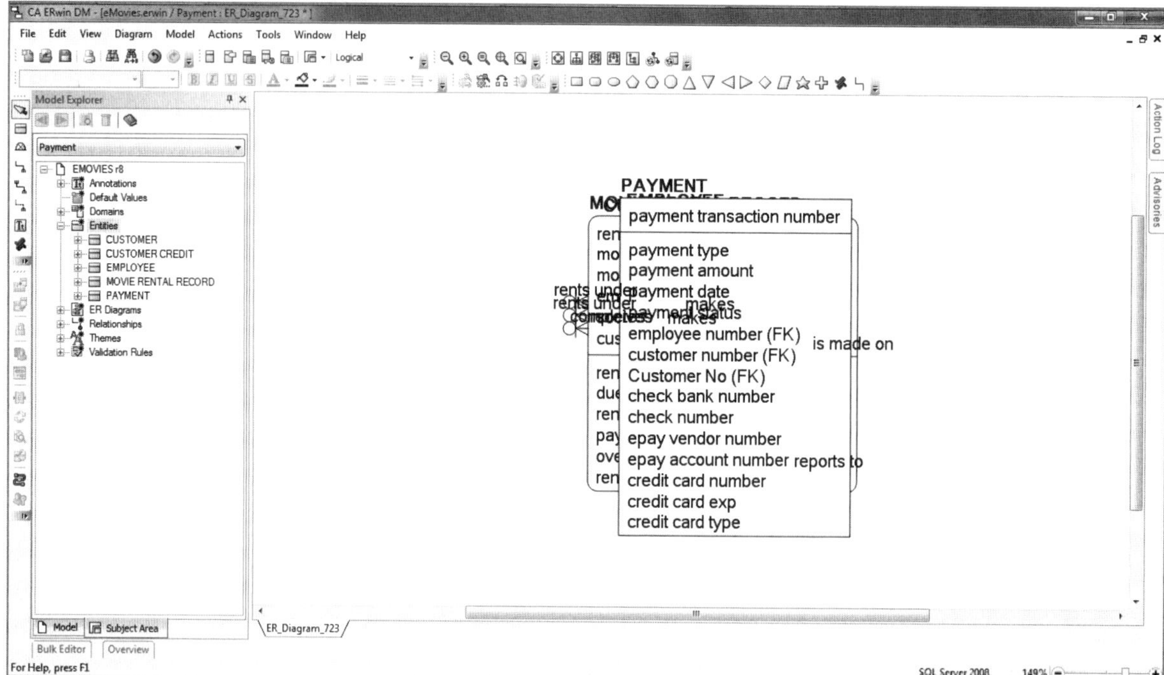

We now have our model objects listed on the diagram, but they are 'smooshed' together in an overlapping fashion. We'll want to layout our diagram in a more intuitive way. A simply way to lay out your model is using the auto-layout options found on the `Layout Toolbar`, shown in Figure 8.25.

Figure 8.25 Layout Toolbar

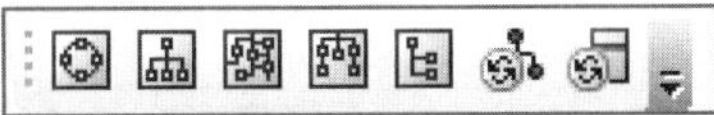

The button options in the `Layout Toolbar` are shown in Table 8.2, and are also referenced in Appendix A.

Table 8.2 Layout Toolbar Options

Icon	Option	Description
	Circular Layout	A circular layout displays objects in a ring-like, or circular pattern, as shown below.
	Hierarchical Layout	A hierarchical layout displays model objects in a top-down, org chart-style manner, as shown below.

Icon	Option	Description
	Orthogonal Layout	Orthogonal lines use right angles and perpendicular lines, and are traditionally used in data models. An orthogonal layout maximizes the use of right angles, as shown below. 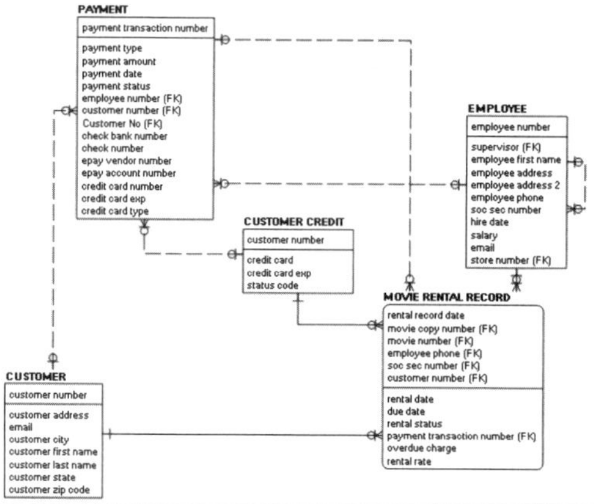
	Symmetric Layout	A Symmetric layout computes a layout with an even distribution of objects within the drawing area as shown below. 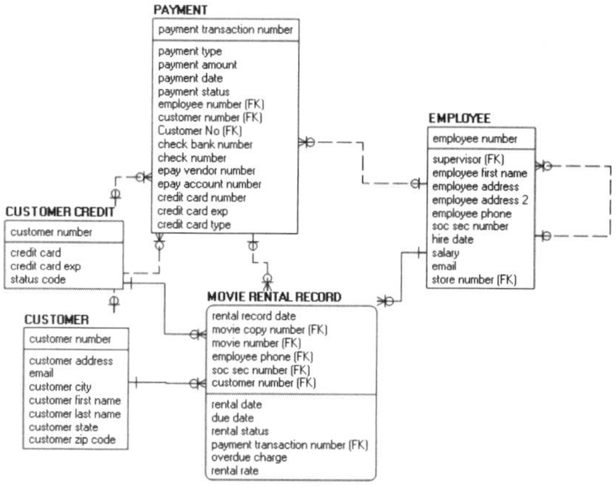
	Tree Layout	A Tree layout distributes the objects in using a branch-style paradigm, as shown below. 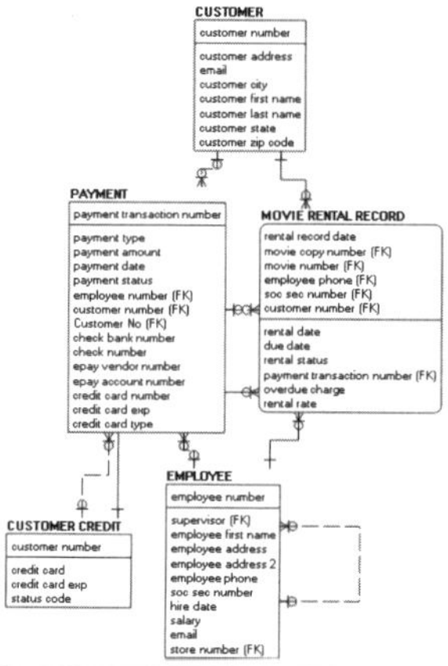

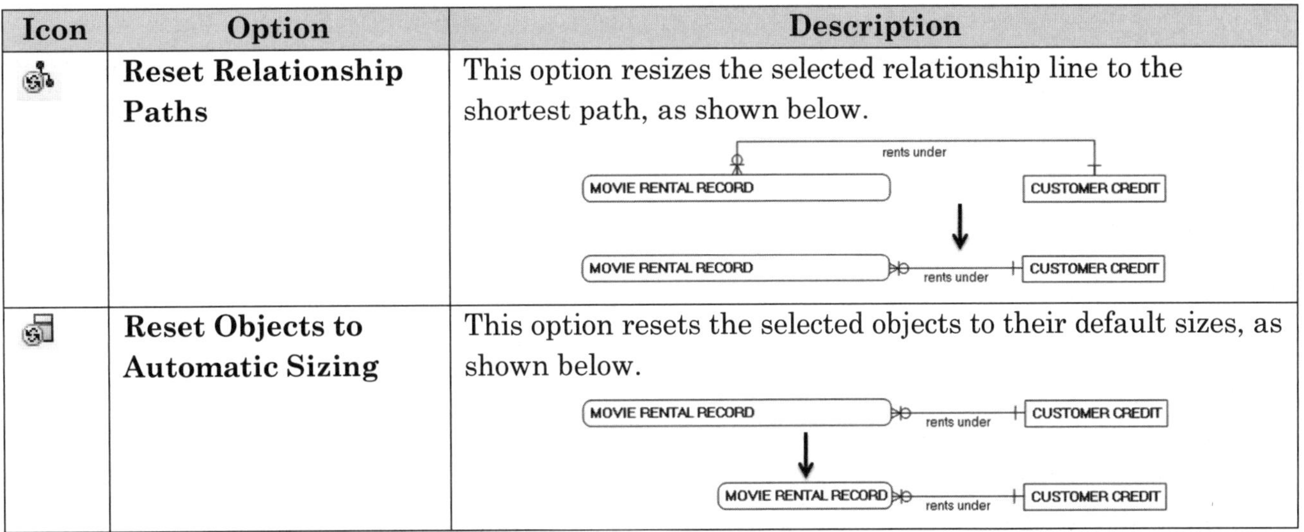

Icon	Option	Description
	Reset Relationship Paths	This option resizes the selected relationship line to the shortest path, as shown below.
	Reset Objects to Automatic Sizing	This option resets the selected objects to their default sizes, as shown below.

For our example, select **Hierarchical Layout** from the Layout Toolbar and the diagram will look similar to Figure 8.26.

Figure 8.26 Diagram Using Hierarchical Layout

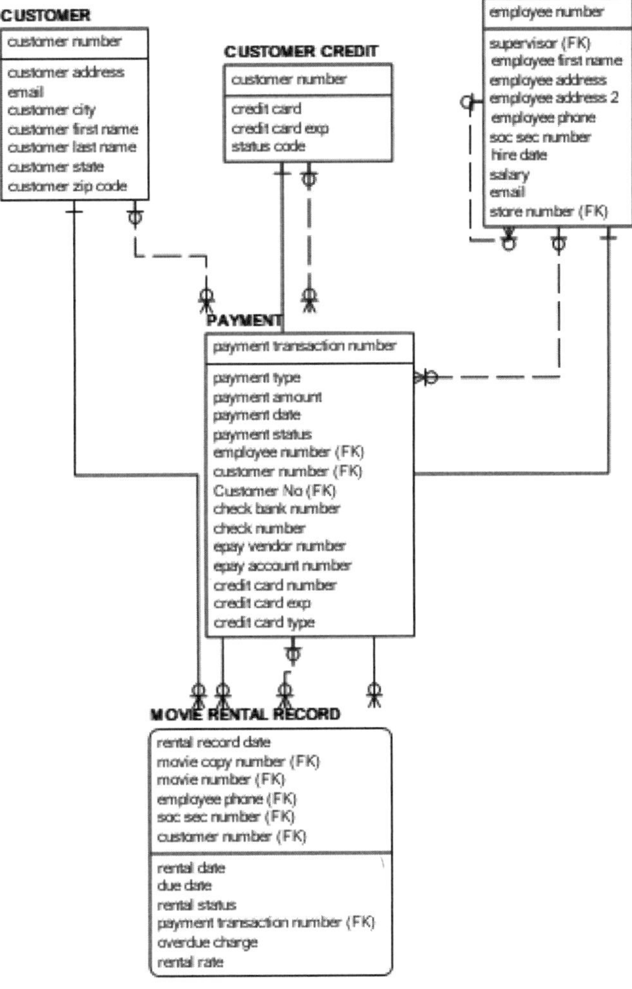

You may need to zoom out to see the full diagram, as shown in Figure 8.26. There are a number of diagram zoom options that you can use to increase or decrease the viewing focus. We'll cover these options in more detail later in this section. For now, simply use the Zoom Bar, shown in Figure 8.27, which is located in the lower right portion of the Workspace. Using an intuitive slider bar, you can increase or decrease the magnification percentage, which is shown on the left side of the Zoom Bar.

Figure 8.27 Zoom Bar

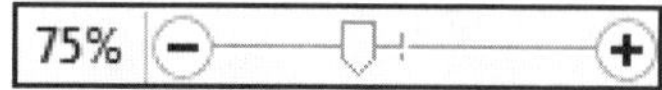

This diagram we created would work well to show to our data architecture team, but it's a bit complicated to show to our business sponsors. We'll want to create a separate display for them. Let's create a new diagram that will show just the entities and their definitions to our business sponsor. We could select **Diagram|New Diagram** from the **Main Menu**, which will create a new, blank diagram, but let's go directly into the Diagram Editor, since we'll immediately be making some changes to this diagram. Select **Diagram|Diagrams** from the **Main Menu**. The Diagram Editor will open, and you'll want to select the diagrams for the **Payment** Subject Area, as shown in Figure 8.28. Remember that Diagrams are associated with a particular Subject Area.

Figure 8.28 Selecting a Subject Area in the Diagram Editor

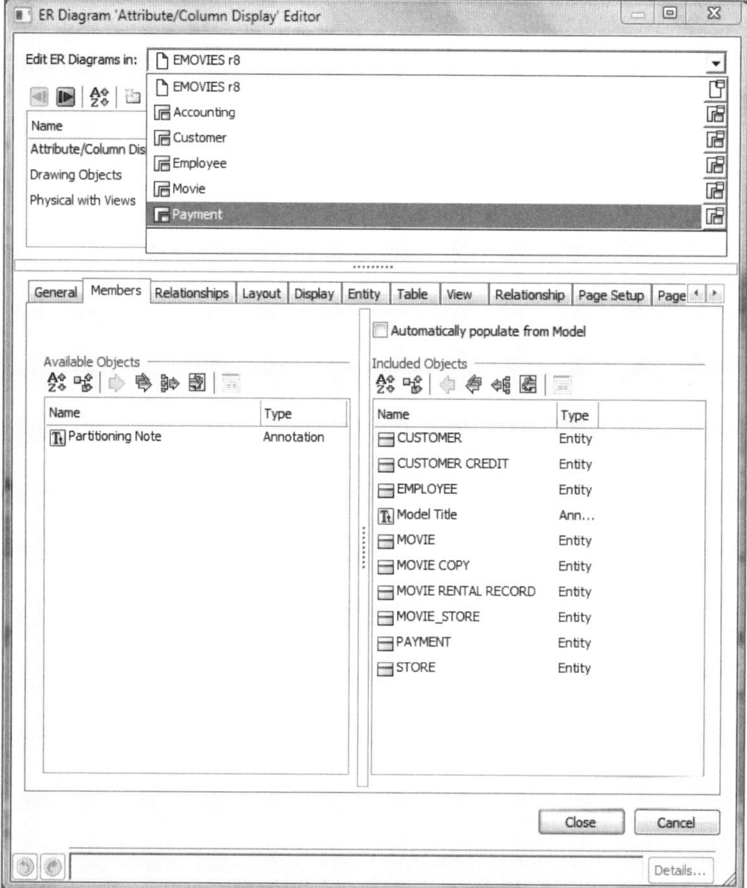

Once we've selected the **Payment** Subject Area, the diagrams for that Subject Area are listed. To add a new Diagram to this Subject Area, select the **New** toolbar button, as shown in Figure 8.29.

Figure 8.29 Creating a New Diagram within a Subject Area

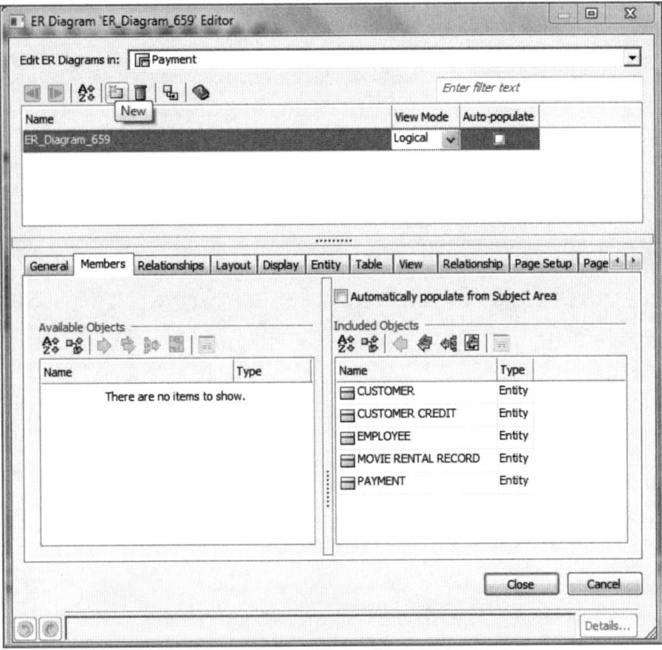

A new row will be created, where you can type the name of the new Diagram. Let's call this Diagram '**Business View**', and auto-populate the diagram with all objects from the **Payment** Subject Area using the **Auto-populate** check box, as shown in Figure 8.30.

Figure 8.30 Naming and Populating a New Diagram

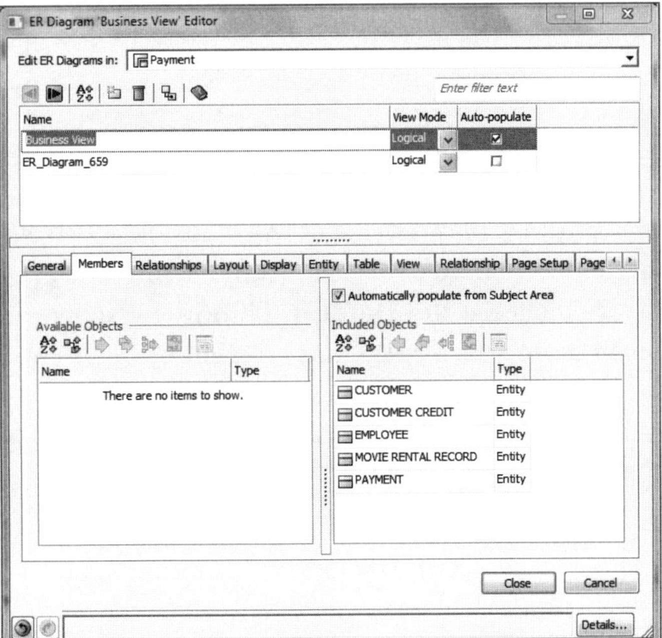

Since the audience for this Diagram is business users, we'll also want to define that the default view is the logical model diagram, not the physical model diagram, using the **View Mode** drop-down shown in Figure 8.31.

Figure 8.31 Specifying Logical vs. Physical View Mode for a Diagram

Now that we've created, named, and populated our diagram, we'll want to define the layout and formatting rules for this diagram. Let's start with the **General** tab, as shown in Figure 8.32.

Figure 8.32 General Tab of the Diagram Editor

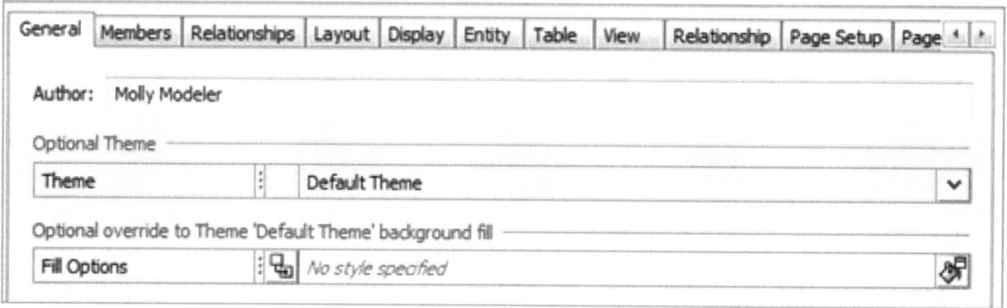

First, we'll need to outline the **Author** of this Diagram. Enter '**Molly Modeler**' in the **Author** field, as shown in Figure 8.33.

Figure 8.33 Defining Diagram Author

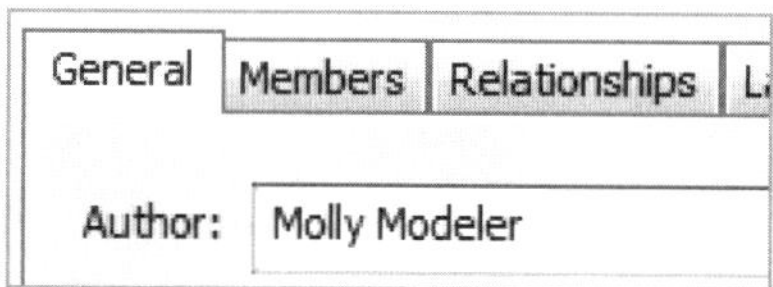

Next we'll choose the overall Display Theme of the diagram. We'll cover Display Themes in more detail in the next section but, for now, think of them as pre-defined settings for font, color, and style. We'll choose the **Default Theme**, as shown in Figure 8.34. We'll cover Display Themes in more detail in the next section.

Figure 8.34 Choosing a Diagram Display Theme

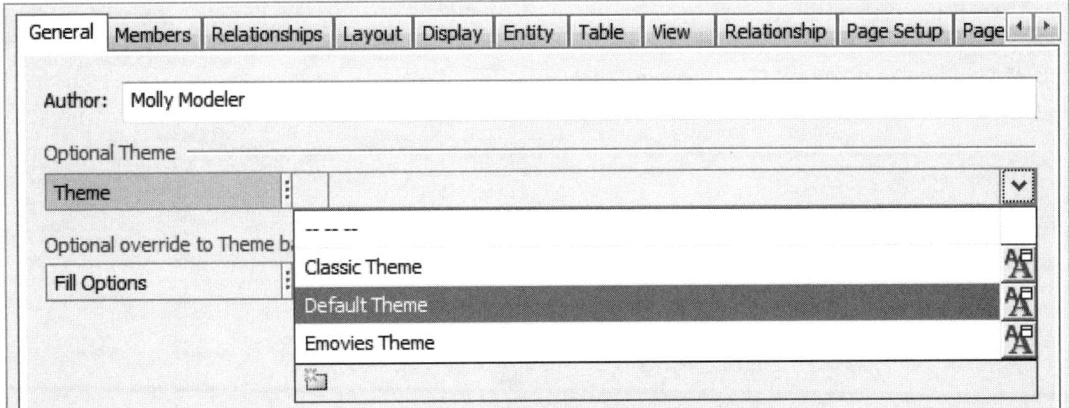

Notice that as you change the Display Theme in the **Diagram Editor**, the diagram which is open behind the editor changes to display this new theme. The **Default Theme** has a light blue patterned background, and entities with a shaded blue fill. We'd like more contrast between the entities and the background, so let's change the diagram fill to plain white. To make this change, we will override the default fill options with our own using the **Fill Options** field shown in Figure 8.35.

Figure 8.35 Overriding Fill Options for Diagram Background

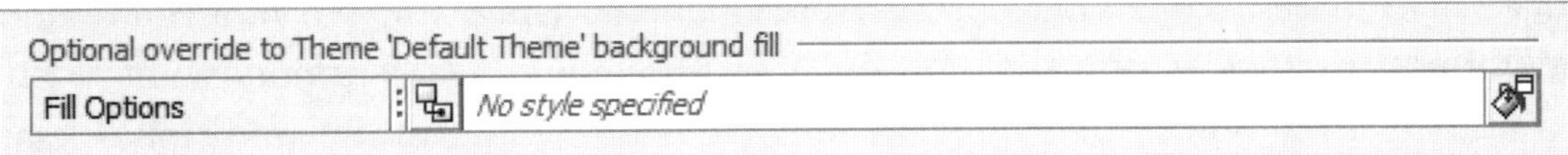

Click the fill icon to the right of the dialog and the Diagram Fill Editor appears, as shown in Figure 8.36.

Figure 8.36 Diagram Fill Editor

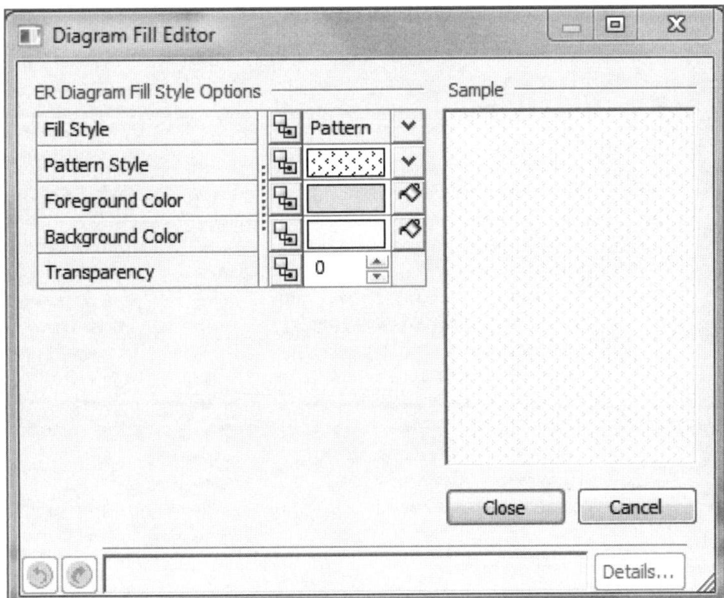

Select a **Fill Style** of Solid and a **Fill Color** of white, as shown in Figure 8.37, and then choose **Close** to exit this editor.

Figure 8.37 Defining Background Fill Style and Color

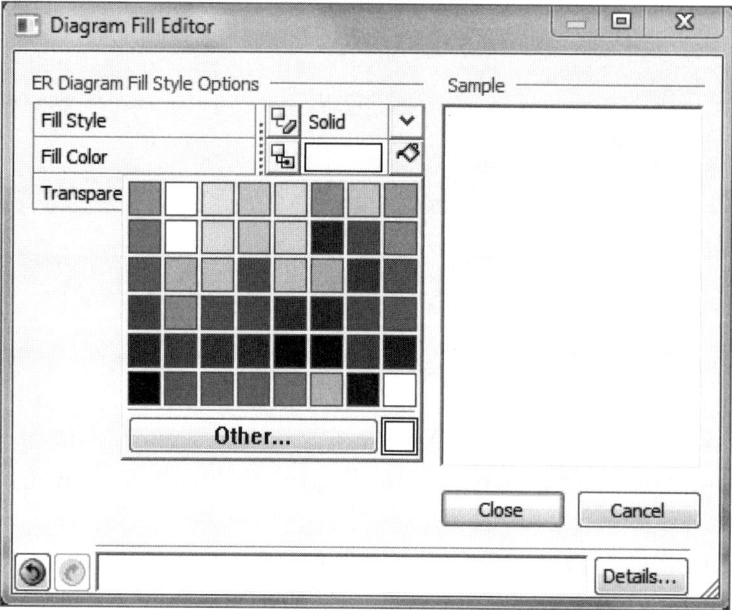

Next, we'll want to define what objects appear on the Diagram. We've already defined the **Members**, so we can skip that tab for now. In some cases, you may want to subset which entities in a subject area appear on a particular diagram for additional focus or discussion, but in this case we'll include all entities in this Subject Area.

But let's consider which relationships should appear on the diagram. Move to the **Relationships** tab, as shown in Figure 8.38.

Figure 8.38 Relationships Tab of the Diagram Editor

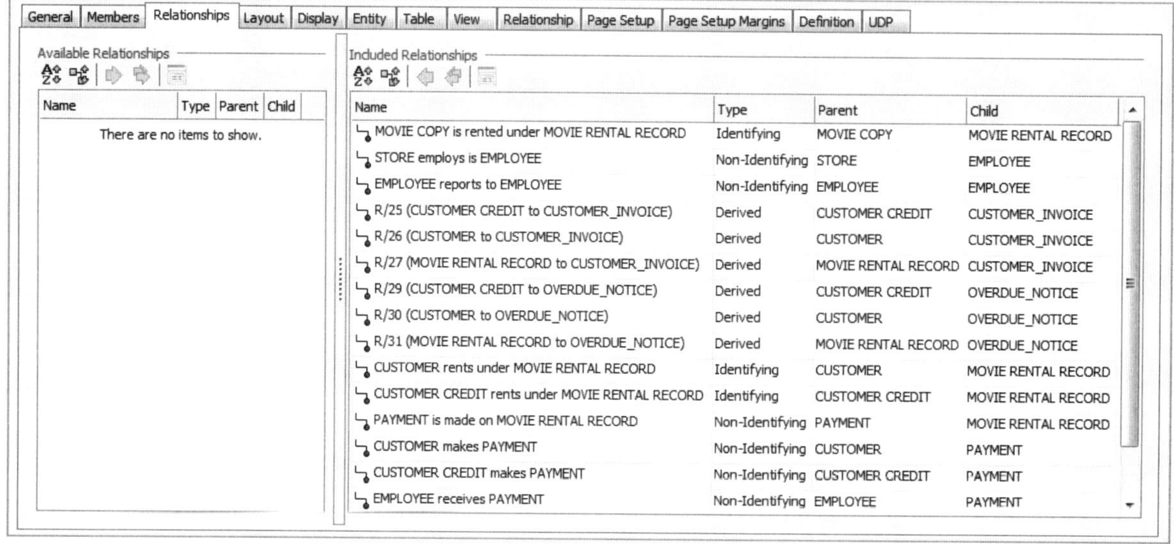

We'd like to use our **Business View** Diagram to help explain the Payments process in the organization to our business sponsor. Since we chose to seed our Diagram with all entities of the subject area, there may be some relationships to/from these entities that are not relevant to our particular discussion. One such relationship is the **EMPLOYEE reports_to EMPLOYEE** relationship, as shown in Figure 8.39. While this is a valid relationship, it's not relevant to our discussion around the Payments process, and will distract the reader of the diagram from the discussion at hand.

Figure 8.39 Employee reports to Employee Relationship

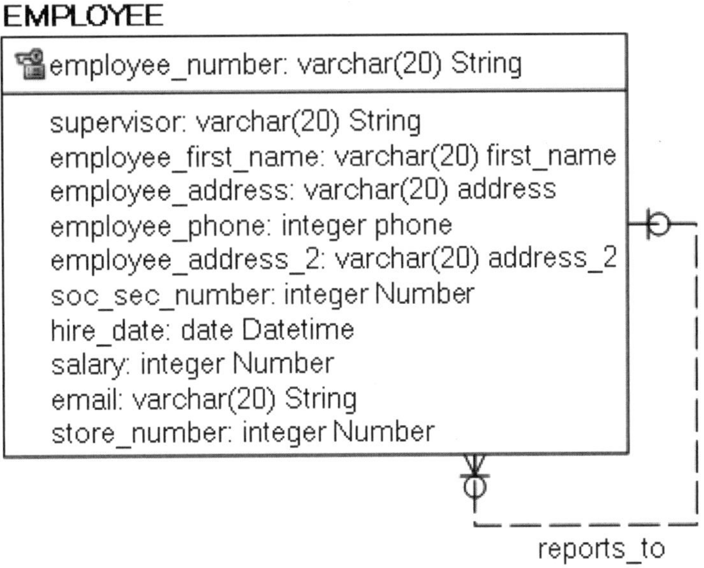

In this case, we'll hide this relationship from the diagram. Remember, the relationships will still exist in the model—we're just not going to show them on this particular diagram. By default, all relationships are shown, since we chose the **Auto-populate** option with this diagram. To change this, we'll have to first de-select the **Auto-populate** option, as shown in Figure 8.40.

Figure 8.40 De-selecting the Auto-populate option in order to Hide Relationships

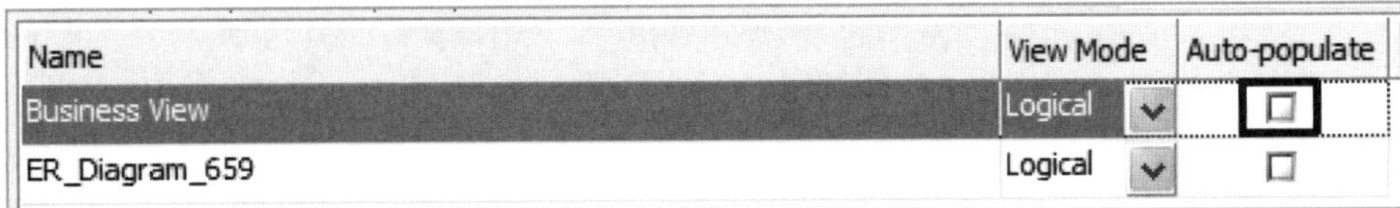

To hide this relationship from this diagram, first select the **EMPLOYEE reports to EMPLOYEE** relationship, then click the **Move selected objects to Available Objects** button, as shown in Figure 8.41.

Figure 8.41 Hiding Relationships using the Move selected objects to Available Objects Button

General | Members | Relationships | Layout | Display | Entity | Table | View | Relationship | Page Setup | Page Setup Margins | Definition | UDP

Available Relationships

Name	Type	Parent	Child
There are no items to show.			

Included Relationships

Move selected objects to Available Objects

Name	Type	Parent	Child
STORE employs is EMPLOYEE	Non-Identifying	STORE	EMPLOYEE
EMPLOYEE reports to EMPLOYEE	Non-Identifying	EMPLOYEE	EMPLOYEE
R/25 (CUSTOMER CREDIT to CUSTOMER_INVOICE)	Derived	CUSTOMER CREDIT	CUSTOMER_INVOICE
R/26 (CUSTOMER to CUSTOMER_INVOICE)	Derived	CUSTOMER	CUSTOMER_INVOICE
R/27 (MOVIE RENTAL RECORD to CUSTOMER_INVOICE)	Derived	MOVIE RENTAL RECORD	CUSTOMER_INVOICE
R/29 (CUSTOMER CREDIT to OVERDUE_NOTICE)	Derived	CUSTOMER CREDIT	OVERDUE_NOTICE
R/30 (CUSTOMER to OVERDUE_NOTICE)	Derived	CUSTOMER	OVERDUE_NOTICE
R/31 (MOVIE RENTAL RECORD to OVERDUE_NOTICE)	Derived	MOVIE RENTAL RECORD	OVERDUE_NOTICE
CUSTOMER rents under MOVIE RENTAL RECORD	Identifying	CUSTOMER	MOVIE RENTAL RECORD
CUSTOMER CREDIT rents under MOVIE RENTAL RECORD	Identifying	CUSTOMER CREDIT	MOVIE RENTAL RECORD
PAYMENT is made on MOVIE RENTAL RECORD	Non-Identifying	PAYMENT	MOVIE RENTAL RECORD
CUSTOMER makes PAYMENT	Non-Identifying	CUSTOMER	PAYMENT
CUSTOMER CREDIT makes PAYMENT	Non-Identifying	CUSTOMER CREDIT	PAYMENT
EMPLOYEE receives PAYMENT	Non-Identifying	EMPLOYEE	PAYMENT
EMPLOYEE completes MOVIE RENTAL RECORD	Identifying	EMPLOYEE	MOVIE RENTAL RECORD

You'll then see this relationships listed in the **Available Relationships** section, as shown in Figure 8.42. Note that if our intention is to hide *all* relationships on the diagram, another way to accomplish this is via the **Display Relationships** option on the **Relationship** tab, which we'll cover later on in this chapter.

Figure 8.42 Relationships Removed from Diagram via the Diagram Editor

General | Members | Relationships | Layout | Display | Entity | Table | View | Relationship | Page Setup | Page Setup Margins | Definition | UDP

Available Relationships

Name
EMPLOYEE reports to EMPLOYEE

Included Relationships

Name	Type	Parent	Child
MOVIE COPY is rented under MOVIE RENTAL RECORD	Identifying	MOVIE COPY	MOVIE RENTAL RECORD
STORE employs is EMPLOYEE	Non-Identifying	STORE	EMPLOYEE
R/25 (CUSTOMER CREDIT to CUSTOMER_INVOICE)	Derived	CUSTOMER CREDIT	CUSTOMER_INVOICE
R/26 (CUSTOMER to CUSTOMER_INVOICE)	Derived	CUSTOMER	CUSTOMER_INVOICE
R/27 (MOVIE RENTAL RECORD to CUSTOMER_INVOICE)	Derived	MOVIE RENTAL RECORD	CUSTOMER_INVOICE
R/29 (CUSTOMER CREDIT to OVERDUE_NOTICE)	Derived	CUSTOMER CREDIT	OVERDUE_NOTICE
R/30 (CUSTOMER to OVERDUE_NOTICE)	Derived	CUSTOMER	OVERDUE_NOTICE
R/31 (MOVIE RENTAL RECORD to OVERDUE_NOTICE)	Derived	MOVIE RENTAL RECORD	OVERDUE_NOTICE
CUSTOMER rents under MOVIE RENTAL RECORD	Identifying	CUSTOMER	MOVIE RENTAL RECORD
CUSTOMER CREDIT rents under MOVIE RENTAL RECORD	Identifying	CUSTOMER CREDIT	MOVIE RENTAL RECORD
PAYMENT is made on MOVIE RENTAL RECORD	Non-Identifying	PAYMENT	MOVIE RENTAL RECORD
CUSTOMER makes PAYMENT	Non-Identifying	CUSTOMER	PAYMENT
CUSTOMER CREDIT makes PAYMENT	Non-Identifying	CUSTOMER CREDIT	PAYMENT
EMPLOYEE receives PAYMENT	Non-Identifying	EMPLOYEE	PAYMENT
EMPLOYEE completes MOVIE RENTAL RECORD	Identifying	EMPLOYEE	MOVIE RENTAL RECORD

If you return to your diagram, you'll see that only the relevant relationships are shown, as displayed in Figure 8.43. (Note: Use the **Orthogonal Layout** option from the Layout Toolbar to organize the objects as shown below.)

Figure 8.43 Business View Diagram with Select Relationships Shown

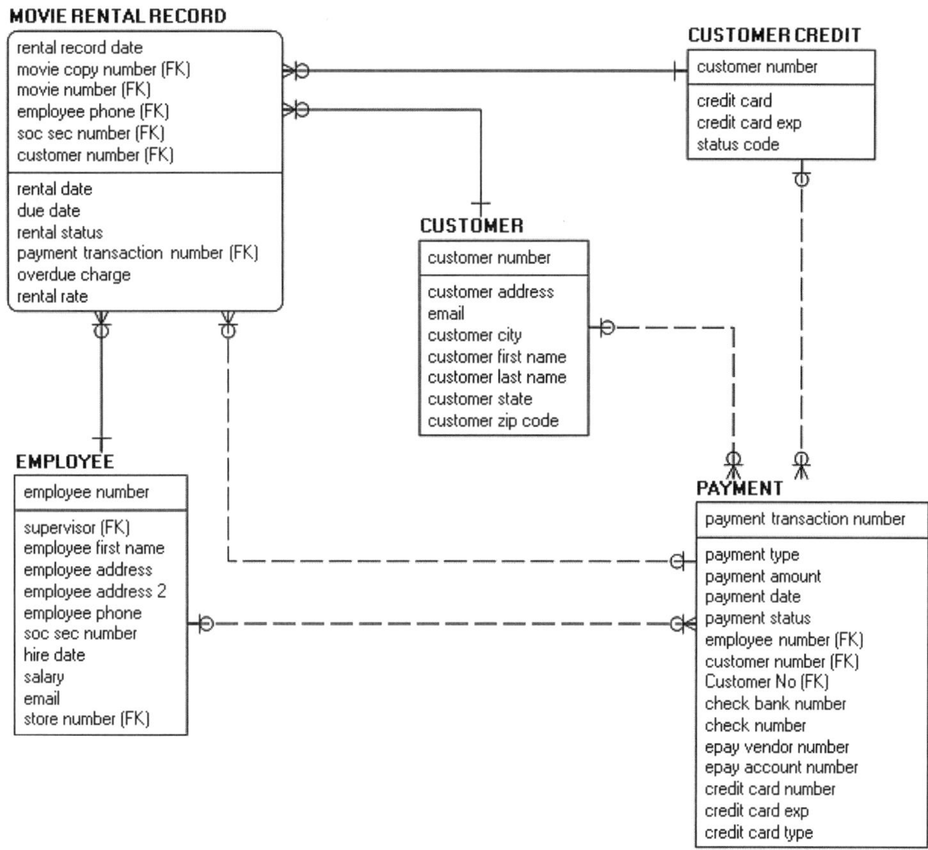

Reopen the Diagram Properties Editor and move to the **Layout** tab, as shown in Figure 8.44.

Figure 8.44 Layout Tab of the Diagram Editor

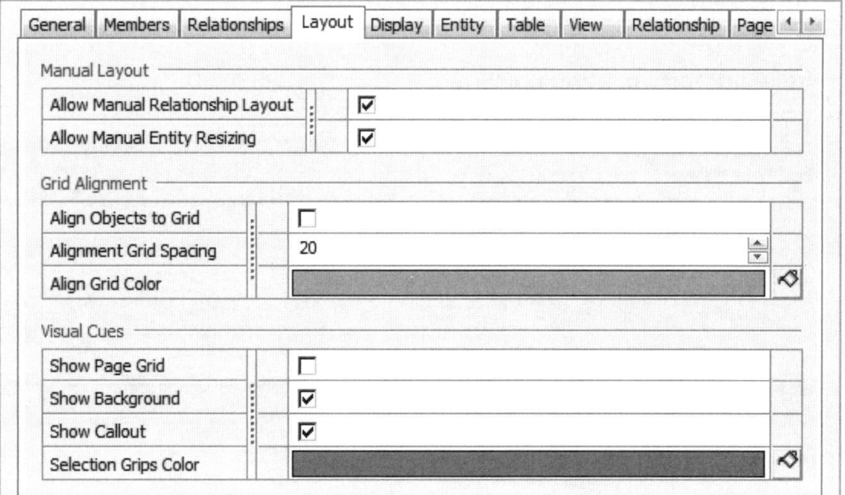

For the purposes of this **Business View** diagram, we won't need to change any of the settings, but you can refer to Table 8.3 for an overview of the options provided in the **Layout** tab.

Table 8.3 Options for Layout Tab of Diagram Editor

Option	Description
Allow Manual Relationship Layout	Allows you to manually layout relationship lines, rather than having the software determine placement for you.
Allow Manual Entity/Table Resizing	Allows you to manually resize the box surrounding entities, tables, or views. This is helpful, for example to allow the entire description to be viewed within an entity.
Align Objects to Grid	When this option is selected, an alignment grid appears behind the diagrams, as shown below. 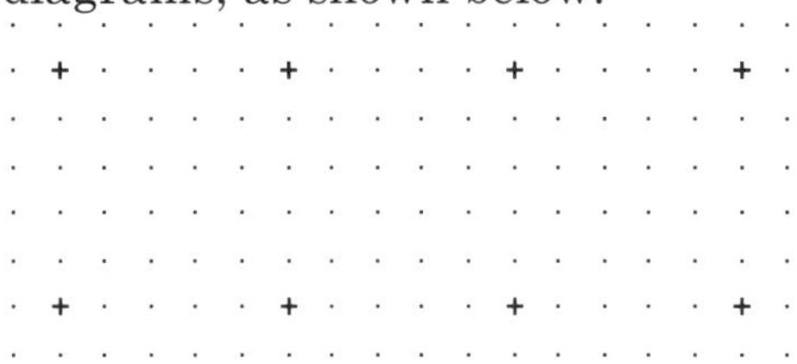 This grid aligns entities, tables, or views to the nearest vertical and horizontal gridlines. New objects 'snap' to the grid automatically. Existing objects are not automatically aligned with the grid unless they are copied, pasted, or moved. Note that this grid will not appear when printing—it only appears on the diagram.
Alignment Grid Spacing	Defines the distance in pixels between gridlines.
Align Grid Color	Defines the color of the diagram grid. To change the default color, click the color pick icon ( ) and pick a color.
Show Page Grid	Shows horizontal and vertical lines indicating where the page breaks exist for printing, as shown below. 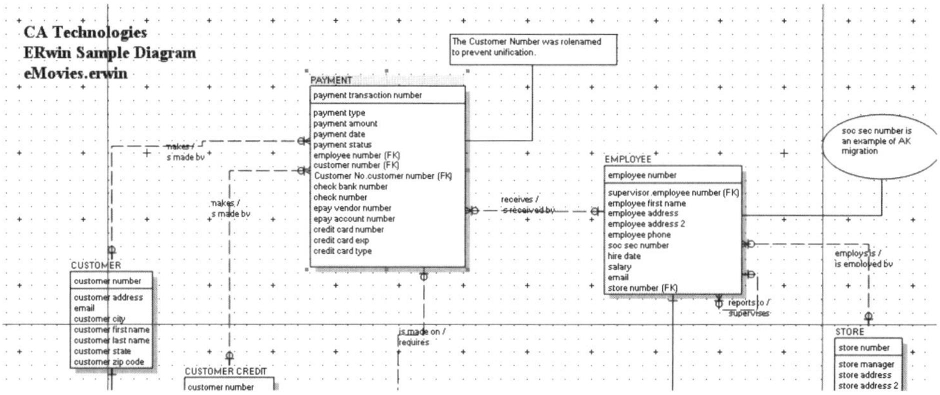 You can change the placement of these lines by selecting and dragging them, to change how diagram printing is determined.

Option	Description
Show Background	Indicates whether to show the background on the diagram, as defined by the diagram's Theme. For example, the diagram theme might have a dark blue background for display purposes on the monitor, but you may wish to disable this for printing purposes. Selecting this option does not change the background settings for the Theme itself—it simply 'turns off' the background on-demand.
Show Callout	Determines whether to display an identifying line drawn between a relationship verb phrase and the relationship it is associated with, shown below. This makes it easy to identify which verb phrase goes with a particular relationship, which is particularly useful on large or densely-populated diagrams. 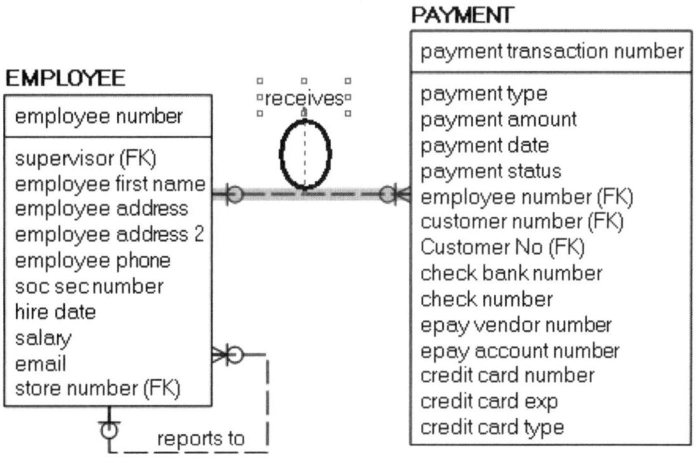
Selection Grips Color	Selection grips are the boxes that appear around an object when you select them with your cursor, indicating that they are enabled for edit or movement, as shown below. 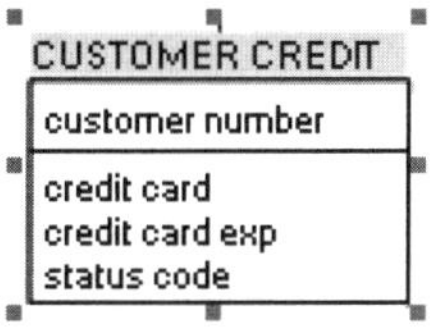 This option defines the color of the selection grips that surrounds an object. To change the default color, click the color pick () icon and select a color.

Next, move to the **Display** tab, as shown in Figure 8.45. This tab defines overall formatting and layout preferences for your diagram. In our case, since we'll be printing our diagram, we'll want to remove the shadows behind the entity boxes, since printing looks 'cleaner' without them. Un-checking the **Display Shadows** check box will remove the shadows from the diagram. We'll leave the other fields as the defaults for now, and Table 8.4 provides a full description of the other options on this tab that you can use for future reference.

Figure 8.45 Display Tab of the Diagram Editor

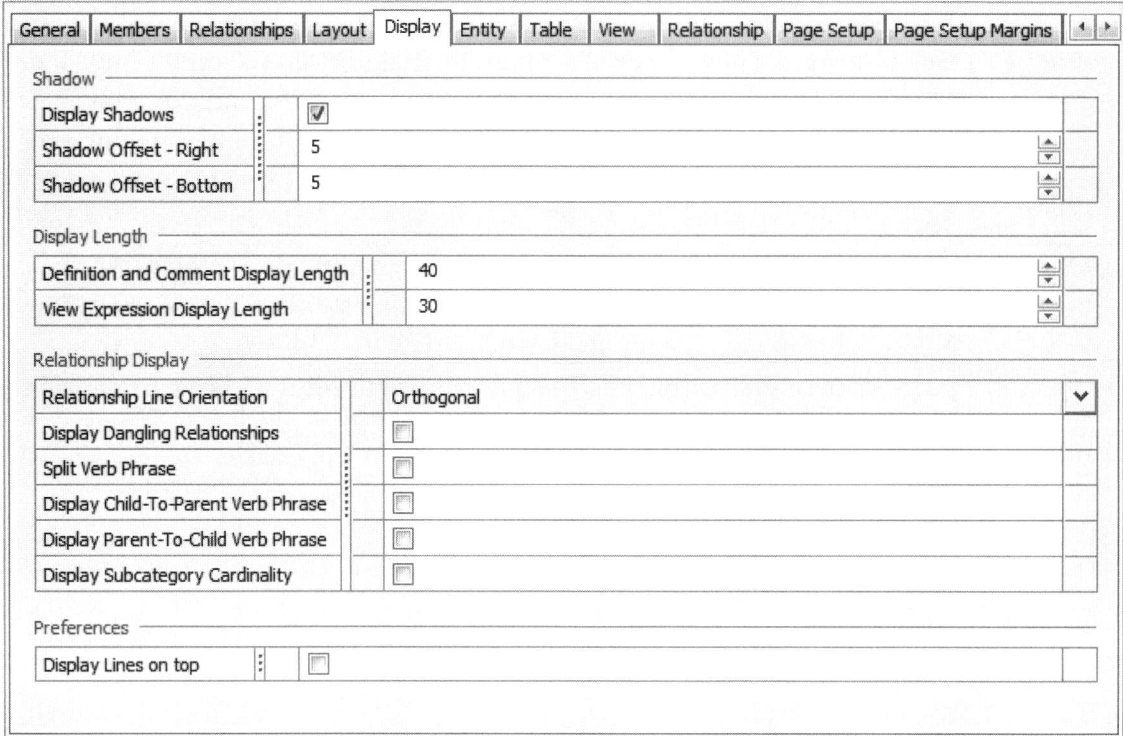

Table 8.4 Options for Display Tab of Diagram Editor

Option	Description
Display Shadows	Specifies whether or not to display shadows behind objects in the diagram. Applies to the following object types: entities, tables, and views.
Shadow Offset - Right	Specifies the number of pixels that the shadow box is shifted to the right. The default setting is 5, and you can increase or decrease this setting for a different look and feel. Note that this field is only relevant if the **Display Shadows** checkbox is selected.
Shadow Offset - Bottom	Specifies the number of pixels that the shadow box extends below the object. The default setting is 5, and you can increase or decrease this setting for a different look and feel. Note that this field is only relevant if the **Display Shadows** checkbox is selected.
Definition and Comment Display Length	Defines the ***number of characters displayed on a single line*** for the definition and comment fields. If the length of the definition or comment is longer than the number defined in this field, it will wrap to a second line, and you may have to resize the entity or table to see the entire text. Note also that entire words are kept intact. For example, if you define the length to be 40, and the 40th character is in the middle of a word, that word will be moved to the second line. The first line may be less than 40 characters as a result. Note that this does not restrict the length of the description itself, but rather the display of the definition on the diagram. If you are looking to restrict the length allowed for entry of this field (e.g. to meet a database platform limitation), use a domain to restrict the field length.

Option	Description
View Expression Display Length	Defines the ***number of characters displayed on a single line*** for the view expression.
Relationship Line Orientation	Determines the format in which lines are shown on the diagram. There are two options: • **Orthogonal:** Creates relationship lines at right angles. Orthogonal lines are traditionally used for relational models. • **Diagonal:** Creates diagonal relationship lines. Diagonal lines are traditionally used for dimensional models.
Display Dangling Relationships	Specifies whether or not to show dangling relationship on the diagram. Dangling relationships are relationships without a parent or a child. This can occur when an entity with a relationship to another entity is included in the diagram, but the related entity is not.
Split Verb Phrase	When this option is checked, the verb phrases are placed next to the respective parent or child object. When this option is not checked, verb phrases are shown together, separated by a slash. Note that this option is only relevant when the **Display Child to Parent Verb Phrase** and **Display Parent-to-Child Verb Phrase** are both checked (see below for more on these options). With this option selected, a relationship would be displayed like this: EMPLOYEE employee number supervisor (FK) employee first name employee address employee address 2 employee phone soc sec number hire date salary email store number (FK) completes is completed by MOVIE RENTAL RECORD rental record date movie copy number (FK) movie number (FK) employee phone (FK) soc sec number (FK) customer number (FK) rental date due date rental status payment transaction number (FK) overdue charge rental rate Without this option checked, the relationship would look like this: EMPLOYEE employee number supervisor (FK) employee first name employee address employee address 2 employee phone soc sec number hire date salary email store number (FK) completes / is completed by MOVIE RENTAL RECORD rental record date movie copy number (FK) movie number (FK) employee phone (FK) soc sec number (FK) customer number (FK) rental date due date rental status payment transaction number (FK) overdue charge rental rate

Option	Description
Display Child-to-Parent Verb Phrase	Defines whether the parent verb phrase for a relationship is shown on the diagram.
Display Parent-to-Child Verb Phrase	Defines whether the child verb phrase for a relationship is shown on the diagram.
Display Subcategory Cardinality	Displays the cardinality symbol for relationship lines in a supertype/subtype construct, as shown below. Note: For the **Display Subcategory Cardinality** option to work, you must select **Display Logical Relationship Name** on the **Relationship** tab. 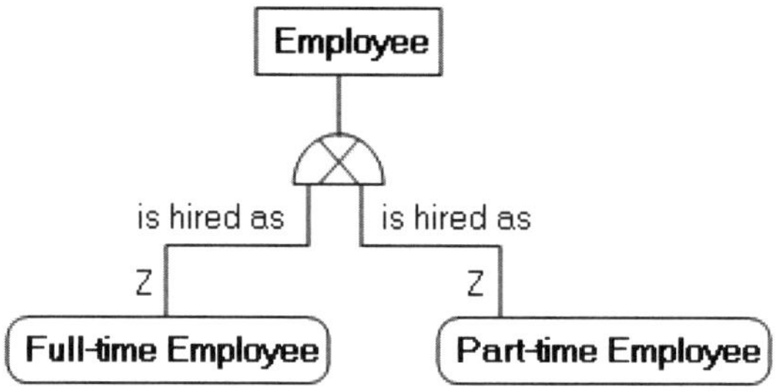
Display Lines on top	This option defines how lines are shown when a relationship line passes through an object. If this box is checked, the relationship line is shown on top of the object. If unchecked, it appears behind the object.

In addition to setting display options for the diagram overall, you can define display options specific to particular objects on the diagram, such as entities, tables, views, and relationships. Let's start by defining how entities are shown on this diagram, using the **Entity** tab, as shown in Figure 8.46.

Figure 8.46 Entity Tab of the Diagram Editor

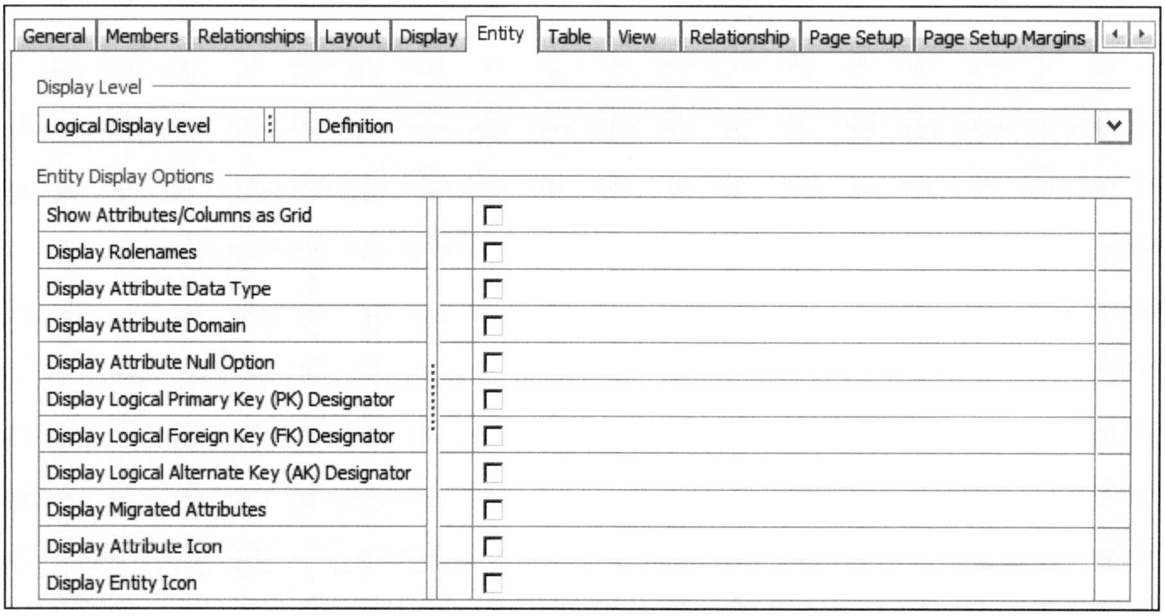

Since our audience for this particular diagram is business users, the key information we'll want to show them is the definitions of the logical entities. To change how entities are shown, select **Definition** from the **Logical Display Level** drop-down, as shown in Figure 8.47.

Figure 8.47 Showing Entity Definitions on a Diagram using the Entity Tab in the Diagram Editor

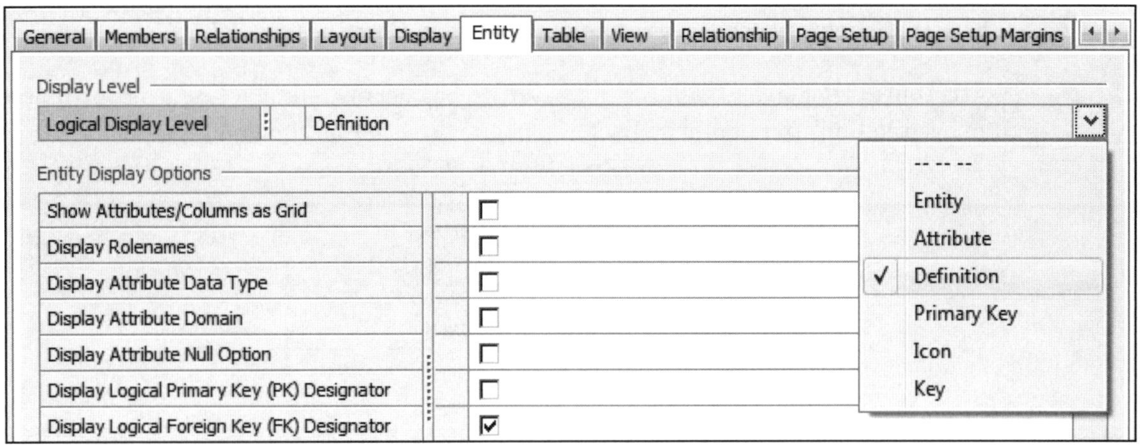

The entity display level is the only change we'll make for now, but there are a number of other helpful options on the **Entity** tab that you can use to customize your model display. Table 8.5 provides a full explanation of the properties on the **Entity** tab.

Table 8.5 Options for Entity Tab on the Diagram Editor

Option	Description
Logical Display Level	This option controls what information is displayed for an entity on the logical model diagram, allowing you to hide or show levels of detail, depending on the purpose of and audience for the model. Options include: **Entity:** Shows only the entity name, within the entity box:  MOVIE RENTAL RECORD **Attribute:** Displays attributes in the entity box separated by a line, with primary keys 'above the line' and non-primary keys 'below the line', as shown below. 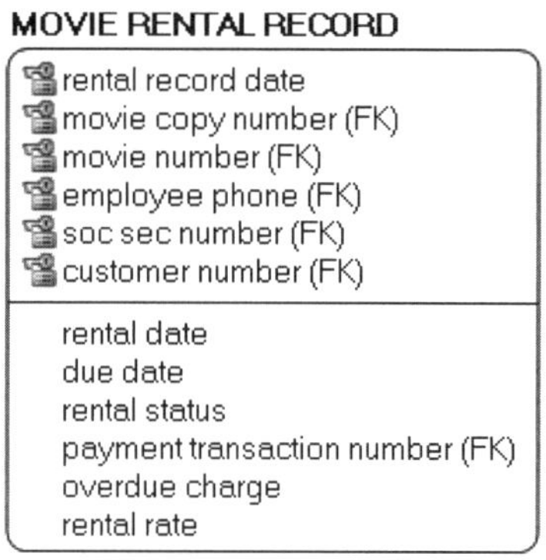 MOVIE RENTAL RECORD rental record date movie copy number (FK) movie number (FK) employee phone (FK) soc sec number (FK) customer number (FK) rental date due date rental status payment transaction number (FK) overdue charge rental rate **Definition:** Shows the definition of the entity within the box:  MOVIE RENTAL RECORD A MOVIE RENTAL RECORD is a record that is kept on every MOVIE in the STORE on who and when a MOVIE is rented **Primary Key:** Displays only the primary key within the entity, and no other attributes, as shown below. 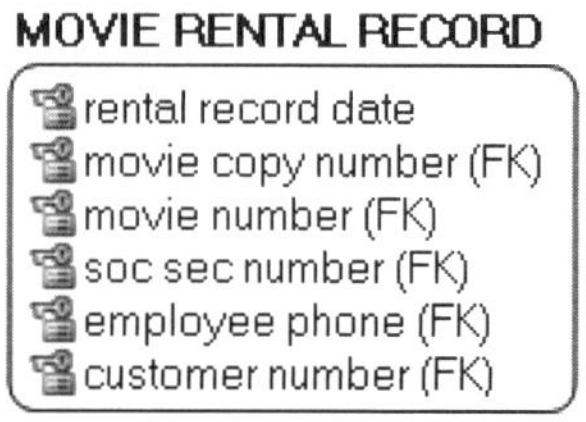 MOVIE RENTAL RECORD rental record date movie copy number (FK) movie number (FK) soc sec number (FK) employee phone (FK) customer number (FK) **Icon:** Displays the icon defined for the entity. By default, the entity icon is defined as a multi-colored box, as shown below, but you can change the icon that is displayed.  MOVIE RENTAL RECORD **Key:** Displays only the keys defined for the entity, as shown below. Note that this differs from the **Primary Key** option in that all keys are shown, including primary keys, foreign keys, and alternate keys. 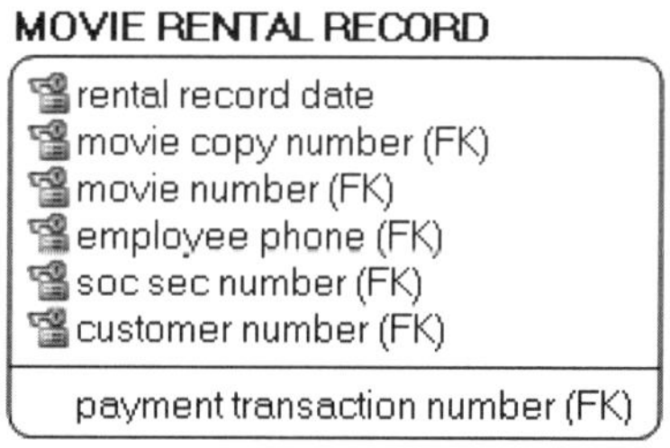 MOVIE RENTAL RECORD rental record date movie copy number (FK) movie number (FK) employee phone (FK) soc sec number (FK) customer number (FK) payment transaction number (FK)

Option	Description
Show Attributes/Columns as Grid	When this option is checked, all properties shown for a given attribute are aligned in an easily-readable grid, as shown below. MOVIE RENTAL RECORD rental record date DATE Datetime NOT NULL movie copy number INTEGER Number NOT NULL (FK) movie number INTEGER Number NOT NULL (FK) employee phone INTEGER phone NOT NULL (FK) soc sec number INTEGER Number NOT NULL (FK) customer number INTEGER Number NOT NULL (FK) rental date DATE Datetime NULL due date DATE Datetime NULL rental status VARCHAR(20) String NULL payment transaction number INTEGER Number NULL (FK) overdue charge INTEGER Number NULL rental rate INTEGER Number NULL Compare this with the same information displayed without this option checked: MOVIE RENTAL RECORD rental record date: DATE Datetime NOT NULL movie copy number: INTEGER Number NOT NULL (FK) movie number: INTEGER Number NOT NULL (FK) employee phone: INTEGER phone NOT NULL (FK) soc sec number: INTEGER Number NOT NULL (FK) customer number: INTEGER Number NOT NULL (FK) rental date: DATE Datetime NULL due date: DATE Datetime NULL rental status: VARCHAR(20) String NULL payment transaction number: INTEGER Number NULL (FK) overdue charge: INTEGER Number NULL rental rate: INTEGER Number NULL This option is only relevant when the display option shows attributes (e.g. **Attribute**, **Primary Key**, or **Key** display), and if more than one property is shown for attributes (e.g. **Name**, **Data Type**, **Null Option**). **Note:** This setting applies to all attributes and columns for entities, tables, and views on both the logical and physical models. I.e., you cannot show the logical model with the grid view and the physical model without—this setting applies globally to both.
Display Rolenames	When this option is selected, the role name for an attribute is shown, if it has been specified. A period is added after the role name, and then the base name is listed in the format: **`Rolename.basename`** Below is an example of an attribute with the role name shown. In this example, the role name is **supervisor** and the base name is **employee number**. EMPLOYEE employee number supervisor.employee number • • • Role names are discussed in more detail in Chapter 18.

Option	Description
Display Attribute Data Type	When this option is selected, the data type is listed after the attribute name, as shown below. **CUSTOMER** customer number INTEGER customer address VARCHAR(20) email VARCHAR(20) customer city VARCHAR(20) customer first name VARCHAR(20) customer last name VARCHAR(20) customer state VARCHAR(20) customer zip code Integer Note that this example is displayed in grid mode, using the **Show Attributes/Columns as Grid** option. Note also that when multiple attribute properties are shown, the default order is **Name**, **Data Type**, **Domain**, **Key indicator**.
Display Attribute Domain	When this option is selected, the attribute's domain is listed after the attribute name, as shown below. **CUSTOMER** customer number Number customer address address email String customer city city customer first name first name customer last name last name customer state state customer zip code zip code Note that this example is displayed in grid mode, using the **Show Attributes/Columns as Grid** option. Note also that when multiple attribute properties are shown, the default order is **Name**, **Data Type**, **Domain**, **Key indicator**.
Display Attribute Null Option	When this option is selected, null option for a given attribute is listed after the attribute name, as shown below. **CUSTOMER** customer number NOT NULL customer address NULL email NULL customer city NULL customer first name NULL customer last name NULL customer state NULL customer zip code NULL Note that this example is displayed in grid mode, using the **Show Attributes/Columns as Grid** option. Note also that when multiple attribute properties are shown, the default order is **Name**, **Data Type**, **Domain**, **Key indicator**.

Option	Description
Display Logical Primary Key (PK) Designator	Selecting this option causes an icon to be shown to the left of primary key attributes, as shown below. 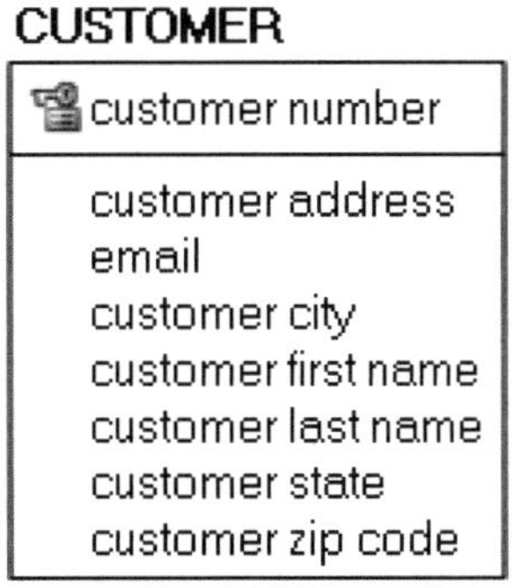 CUSTOMER customer number customer address email customer city customer first name customer last name customer state customer zip code
Display Logical Foreign Key (FK) Designator	When this option is selected, foreign key attributes are indicated by a **(FK)** indicator to the right of the attribute, as shown below. 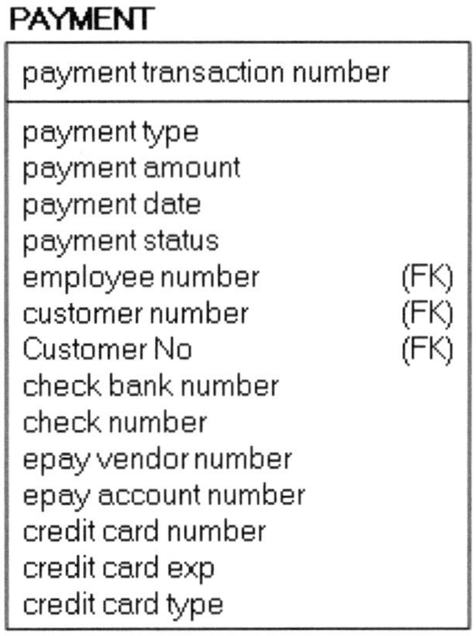 PAYMENT payment transaction number payment type payment amount payment date payment status employee number (FK) customer number (FK) Customer No (FK) check bank number check number epay vendor number epay account number credit card number credit card exp credit card type Note that when multiple attribute properties are shown, the default order is **Name**, **Data Type**, **Domain**, **Key indicator**.
Display Logical Alternate Key (AK) Designator	This option specifies that the alternate key and inversion entity indicators are shown on the diagram. When this option is selected, alternate key attributes are indicated by a **(AK)** indicator and inversion entity attributes as **(IE)**, as shown below. For more information on alternate keys, refer to Chapter 7. Note that when multiple attribute properties are shown, the default order is **Name**, **Data Type**, **Domain**, **Key indicator**. 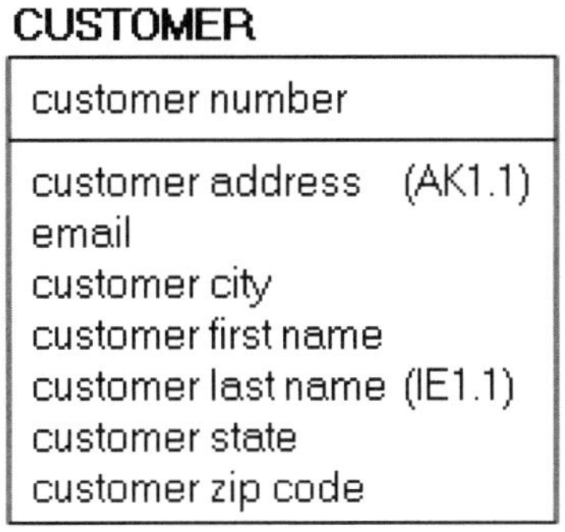 CUSTOMER customer number customer address (AK1.1) email customer city customer first name customer last name (IE1.1) customer state customer zip code

Option	Description
Display Migrated Attributes	Specifies whether to display migrated (foreign key) attributes in the diagram. If this option is left unchecked, no foreign keys are shown on the diagram, regardless of the setting for the **Display Logical Foreign Key (FK) Designator** option, which controls only how foreign keys are displayed, not whether they are shown or hidden.
Display Attribute Icon	When this option is selected, an attribute icon is shown to the left of each attribute name, as shown below. Note that attribute icons are inherited from the parent domain, so you may wish to customize this icon for various domain types. 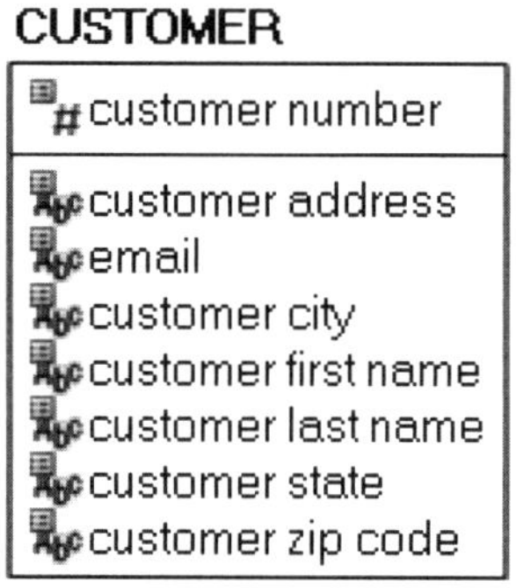 CUSTOMER customer number customer address email customer city customer first name customer last name customer state customer zip code
Display Entity Icon	When this option is selected, an attribute icon is shown to the left of the entity name, as shown below. Note that this is different from the Icon display level for an entity; in this case the entity is shown in full, but an icon is shown to the left of the entity name. 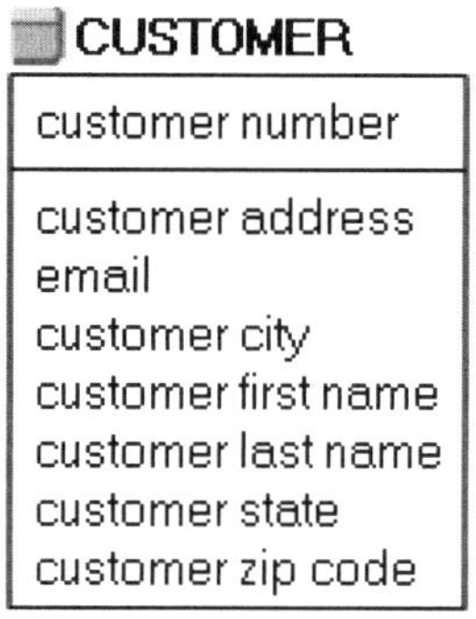 CUSTOMER customer number customer address email customer city customer first name customer last name customer state customer zip code

The changes we've just made in the **Entity** tab apply to the logical model. To modify the display for tables in the Physical model, we'll use the **Table** tab, as shown in Figure 8.48.

Figure 8.48 Table Tab of the Diagram Editor

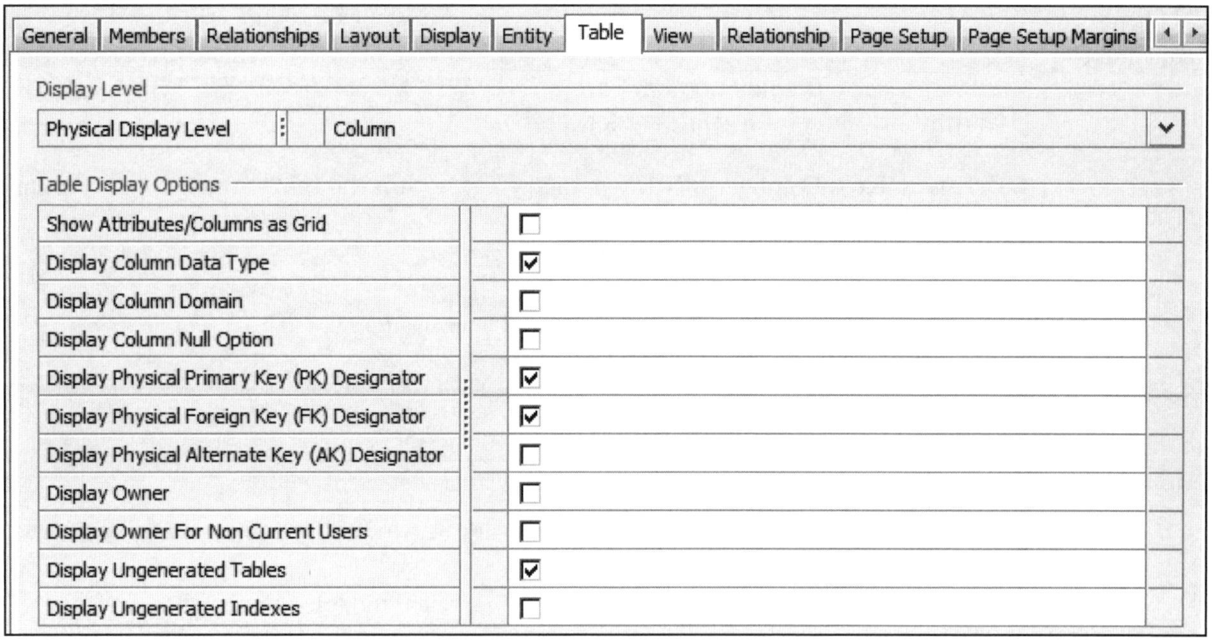

General | Members | Relationships | Layout | Display | Entity | Table | View | Relationship | Page Setup | Page Setup Margins

Display Level

Physical Display Level	Column

Table Display Options

Show Attributes/Columns as Grid	☐
Display Column Data Type	☑
Display Column Domain	☐
Display Column Null Option	☐
Display Physical Primary Key (PK) Designator	☑
Display Physical Foreign Key (FK) Designator	☑
Display Physical Alternate Key (AK) Designator	☐
Display Owner	☐
Display Owner For Non Current Users	☐
Display Ungenerated Tables	☑
Display Ungenerated Indexes	☐

Since this particular diagram is aimed at business users, we won't be focusing on physical objects such as tables, so we'll leave the default settings for now. Table 8.6 provides an overview and description of the options and settings on the **Table** tab.

Table 8.6 Options for Table Tab on the Diagram Editor

Option	Description
Physical Display Level	This option controls what information is displayed for a table on the physical model diagram, allowing you to hide or show levels of detail, depending on the purpose of and audience for the model. Options include: **Table:** Shows only the table name:  MOVIE_RENTAL_RECORD **Column:** Displays columns in the table box separated by a line, with primary keys 'above the line' and non-primary keys 'below the line', as shown below. Column order in the physical model is determined by the index order in the logical model. 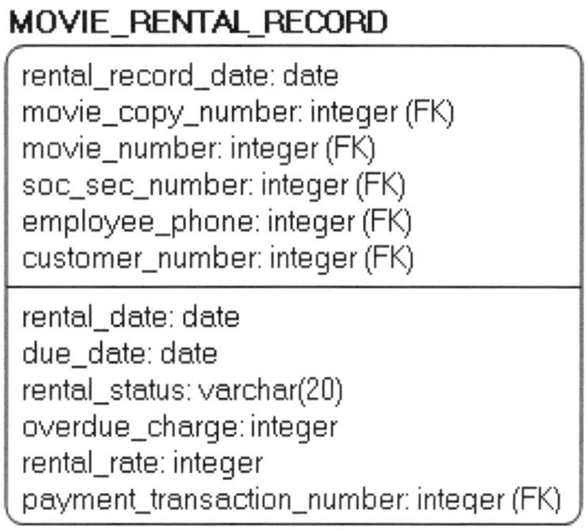 MOVIE_RENTAL_RECORD rental_record_date: date movie_copy_number: integer (FK) movie_number: integer (FK) soc_sec_number: integer (FK) employee_phone: integer (FK) customer_number: integer (FK) rental_date: date due_date: date rental_status: varchar(20) overdue_charge: integer rental_rate: integer payment_transaction_number: integer (FK)

Option	Description
Physical Display Level (continued)	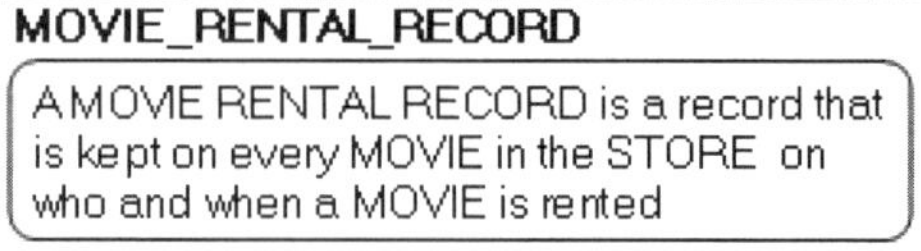 MOVIE_RENTAL_RECORD A MOVIE RENTAL RECORD is a record that is kept on every MOVIE in the STORE on who and when a MOVIE is rented **Comment:** Shows the comment for a table : **Primary Key:** Displays only the primary key within the table, and no other columns, as shown below. 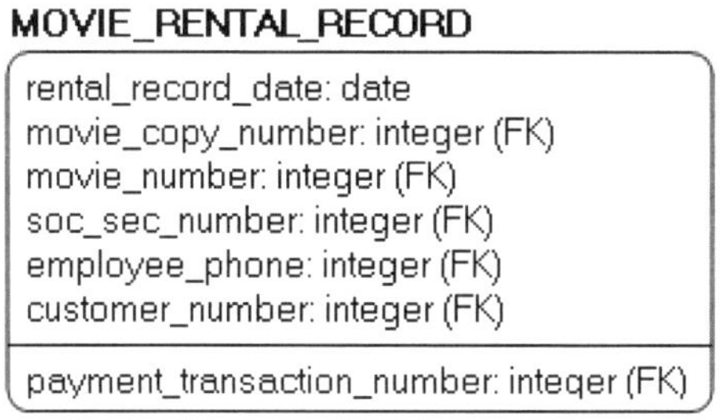 MOVIE_RENTAL_RECORD rental_record_date: date movie_copy_number: integer (FK) movie_number: integer (FK) soc_sec_number: integer (FK) employee_phone: integer (FK) customer_number: integer (FK) payment_transaction_number: integer (FK) **Physical Order:** Shows columns in the order in which they appear in the physical database, as shown below. **Note:** When forward engineering from the physical model, you can choose either physical order or column order for the generated schema. Column order is used to generate Primary Keys and **`ALTER`** statements. 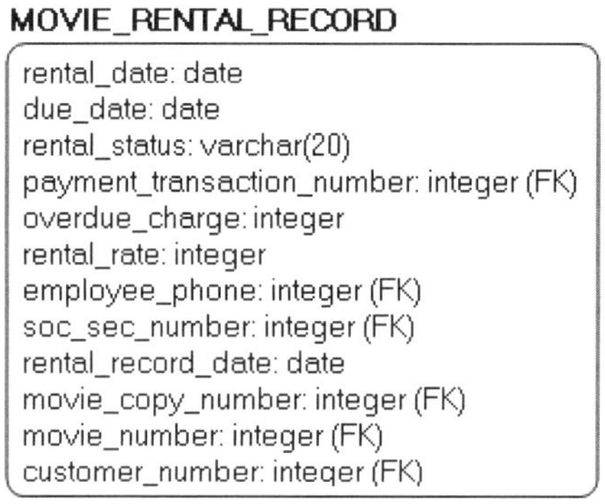 MOVIE_RENTAL_RECORD rental_date: date due_date: date rental_status: varchar(20) payment_transaction_number: integer (FK) overdue_charge: integer rental_rate: integer employee_phone: integer (FK) soc_sec_number: integer (FK) rental_record_date: date movie_copy_number: integer (FK) movie_number: integer (FK) customer_number: integer (FK) **Icon:** Displays the icon defined for the table. By default, the tables icon is defined as a multi-colored box, as shown below, but you can change the icon that is displayed.  MOVIE_RENTAL_RECORD **Key:** Displays only the keys defined for the table, as shown below. Not that this differs from the **Primary Key** option in that all keys are shown, including primary keys, foreign keys, and alternate keys. 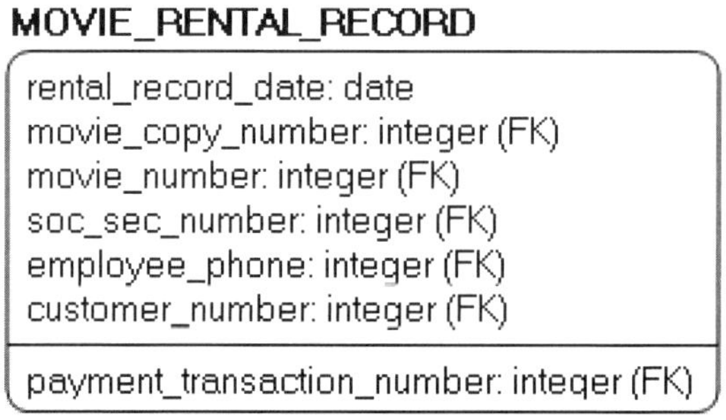 MOVIE_RENTAL_RECORD rental_record_date: date movie_copy_number: integer (FK) movie_number: integer (FK) soc_sec_number: integer (FK) employee_phone: integer (FK) customer_number: integer (FK) payment_transaction_number: integer (FK)

Option	Description
Show Attributes/Columns as Grid	When this option is checked, all properties shown for a given attribute are aligned in an easily-readable grid, as shown below. 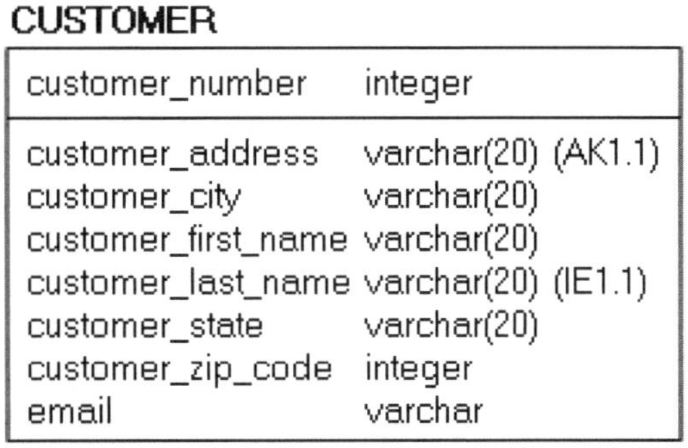 **CUSTOMER** customer_number integer customer_address varchar(20) (AK1.1) customer_city varchar(20) customer_first_name varchar(20) customer_last_name varchar(20) (IE1.1) customer_state varchar(20) customer_zip_code integer email varchar Compare this with the same information displayed without this option checked: 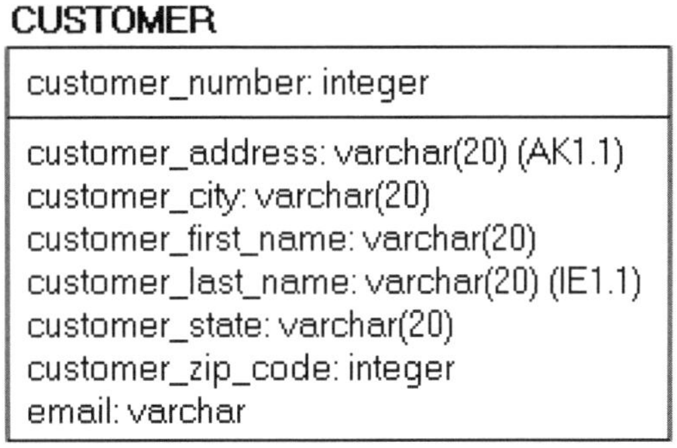 **CUSTOMER** customer_number: integer customer_address: varchar(20) (AK1.1) customer_city: varchar(20) customer_first_name: varchar(20) customer_last_name: varchar(20) (IE1.1) customer_state: varchar(20) customer_zip_code: integer email: varchar This option is only relevant when the display option shows columns (e.g. **Column**, **Primary Key**, **Physical Order** or **Key** display), and if more than one property is shown for attributes (e.g. **Name**, **Data Type**, **Key Indicators**). **Note:** This setting applies to all attributes and columns for entities, tables, and views on both the logical and physical models. I.e., you cannot show the logical model with the grid view and the physical model without—this setting applies globally to both.
Display Column Data Type	When this option is selected, the data type is listed after the column name, as shown below. 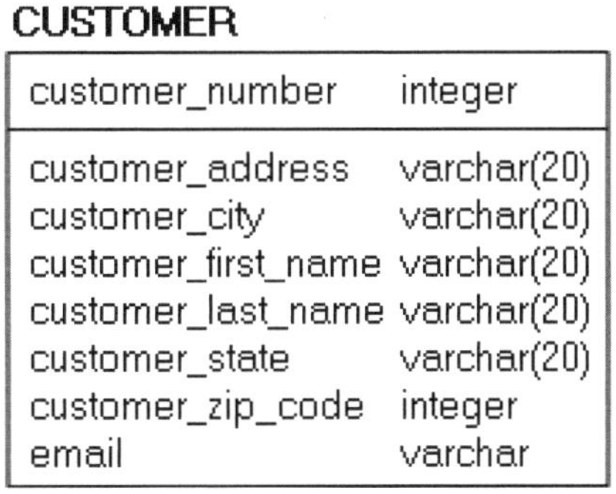 **CUSTOMER** customer_number integer customer_address varchar(20) customer_city varchar(20) customer_first_name varchar(20) customer_last_name varchar(20) customer_state varchar(20) customer_zip_code integer email varchar Note that this example is displayed in grid mode, using the **Show Attributes/Columns as Grid** option. Note also that when multiple attribute properties are shown, the default order is **Name**, **Data Type**, **Domain**, **Key indicator**.

Option	Description
Display Column Domain	When this option is selected, the column's domain is listed after the column name, as shown below. Note that this example is displayed in grid mode, using the **Show Attributes/Columns as Grid** option. Note also that when multiple attribute properties are shown, the default order is **Name**, **Data Type**, **Domain**, **Key indicator**. 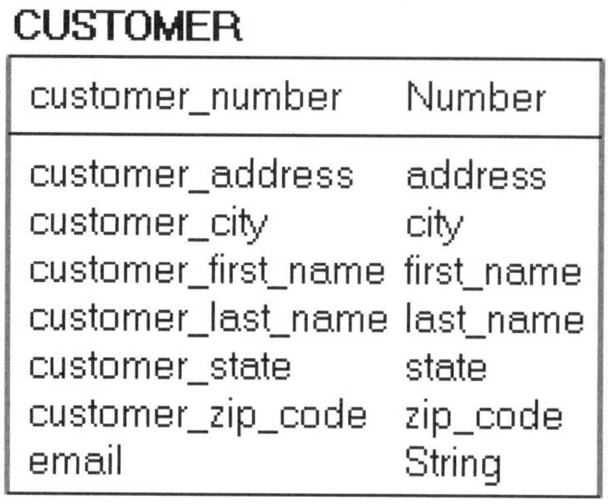 CUSTOMER customer_number Number customer_address address customer_city city customer_first_name first_name customer_last_name last_name customer_state state customer_zip_code zip_code email String
Display Column Null Option	When this option is selected, null option for a given column is listed after the column name, as shown below. Note that this example is displayed in grid mode, using the **Show Attributes/Columns as Grid** option. Note also that when multiple column properties are shown, the default order is **Name**, **Data Type**, **Domain**, **Key indicator**. 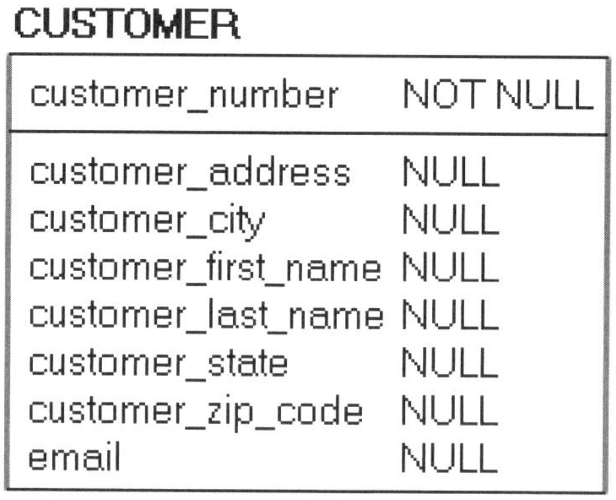 CUSTOMER customer_number NOT NULL customer_address NULL customer_city NULL customer_first_name NULL customer_last_name NULL customer_state NULL customer_zip_code NULL email NULL
Display Physical Primary Key (PK) Designator	Selecting this option causes an icon to be shown to the left of primary key column, as shown below. 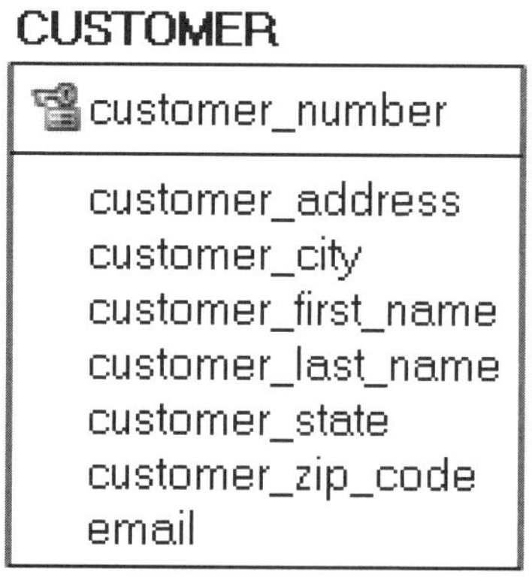 CUSTOMER customer_number customer_address customer_city customer_first_name customer_last_name customer_state customer_zip_code email

Option	Description
Display Physical Foreign Key (FK) Designator	When this option is selected, foreign key columns are indicated by a **(FK)** indicator to the right of the attribute, as shown below. Note that when multiple column properties are shown, the default order is **Name**, **Data Type**, **Domain**, **Key indicator**. PAYMENT payment_transaction_number payment_type customer_number (FK) customer_no (FK) payment_amount payment_date payment_status employee_number (FK) check_bank_number check_number epay_vendor_number epay_account_number credit_card_number credit_card_exp credit_card_type
Display Physical Alternate Key (AK) Designator	This option specifies that the alternate key and inversion entity indicators are shown on the diagram. When this option is selected, alternate key columns are indicated by a **(AK)** indicator and inversion entity columns as **(IE)**, as shown below. For more information on alternate keys, refer to Chapter 7. Note that when multiple column properties are shown, the default order is **Name**, **Data Type**, **Domain**, **Key indicator**. CUSTOMER customer_number customer_address (AK1.1) customer_city customer_first_name customer_last_name (IE1.1) customer_state customer_zip_code email
Display Migrated Attributes	Specifies whether to display migrated (foreign key) attributes in the diagram. If this option is left unchecked, no foreign keys are shown on the diagram, regardless of the setting for the **Display Logical Foreign Key (FK) Designator** option, which controls only how foreign keys are displayed, not whether they are shown or hidden.
Display Owner	Displays the table owner as a prefix to the table name, using the format **TABLEOWNER.TABLENAME**, for example **DBO.CUSTOMER**.
Display Owner for Non-Current Users	Displays the table owner information for tables owned by users other than the current user, using the format **TABLEOWNER.TABLENAME**, for example **DBO.CUSTOMER**. Note: The **Current User** can be defined using the **Actions|Database Connections** menu.
Display Ungenerated Tables	Displays tables that will not be generated when you forward engineer the schema. A table is generated only when you select the **Generate** check box in the Table Editor. See Chapter 19 for more information on forward engineering.
Display Ungenerated Indexes	Displays indexes that will not be generated when you forward engineer the schema. An index is generated only when you select the **Generate** check box in the Index Editor. See Chapter 19 for more information on indexes.

The next set of options we can define determines how Views are displayed on the diagram, using the **View** tab, shown in Figure 8.49. We'll discuss views in more detail in Chapter 19. You may wish to refer to this chapter, if you're not familiar with the concept of views, in order to better understand the options on this tab.

Figure 8.49 View Tab of the Diagram Editor

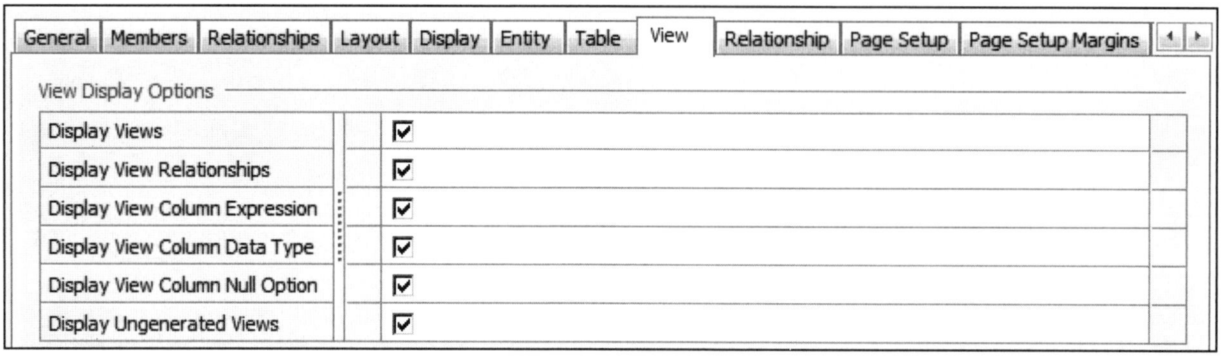

General | Members | Relationships | Layout | Display | Entity | Table | View | Relationship | Page Setup | Page Setup Margins

View Display Options

Display Views	☑
Display View Relationships	☑
Display View Column Expression	☑
Display View Column Data Type	☑
Display View Column Null Option	☑
Display Ungenerated Views	☑

Again, since this particular diagram is aimed at business users, we won't be changing any of the View display settings, but Table 8.7 describes the options in more detail for future reference.

Table 8.7 Options for Table Tab on the Diagram Editor

Option	Description
Display Views	Controls whether Views are shown on the diagram. If this option is selected, views will be shown. If unselected, views will not appear on the diagram.
Display View Relationships	Defines whether relationships to/from Views are shown on the diagram. **Note:** This option is only relevant if the **Display Views** option is checked.
Display View Column Expression	Displays the source table expression for view columns in the physical model, as defined in the **Expression** tab for the View Column. An example is shown below, where `<rental_rate * 1.5>` is the **View Column Expression**. 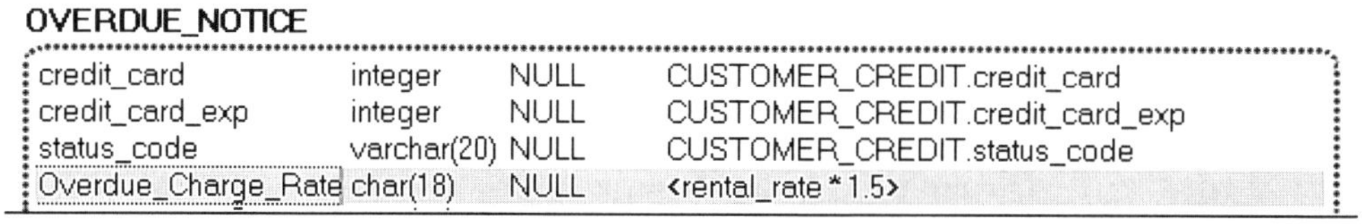 OVERDUE_NOTICE credit_card integer NULL CUSTOMER_CREDIT.credit_card credit_card_exp integer NULL CUSTOMER_CREDIT.credit_card_exp status_code varchar(20) NULL CUSTOMER_CREDIT.status_code Overdue_Charge_Rate char(18) NULL <rental_rate * 1.5> • • • **Note:** If you would like to see View column properties displayed in a grid view as shown above, use the **Show Attributes/Columns as Grid** option on the **Table** tab. This setting controls the display for attributes/columns on all views, tables, and entities.

Option	Description
Display View Column Data Type	When this option is selected, the data type is listed after the view column name, as shown below. OVERDUE_NOTICE credit_card integer credit_card_exp integer status_code varchar(20) • • • Note that this example is displayed in grid mode, using the **Show Attributes/Columns as Grid** option. Note also that when multiple attribute properties are shown, the default order is **Name**, **Data Type**, **Null Option, View Column Expression**.
Display View Column Null Option	When this option is selected, null option for a given view column is listed after the column name, as shown below. OVERDUE_NOTICE credit_card NULL credit_card_exp NULL status_code NULL • • • Note that this example is displayed in grid mode, using the **Show Attributes/Columns as Grid** option. Note also that when multiple column properties are shown, the default order is **Name**, **Data Type**, **Null Option,** and **View Column Expression**.
Display Ungenerated Views	Displays views that will not be generated when you forward engineer the schema. A view is generated only when you select the **Generate** check box in the View Editor. See Chapter 19 for more information on views.

The next tab in the Diagram Editor is the **Relationship** tab, shown in Figure 8.50.

Figure 8.50 Relationship Tab of the Diagram Editor

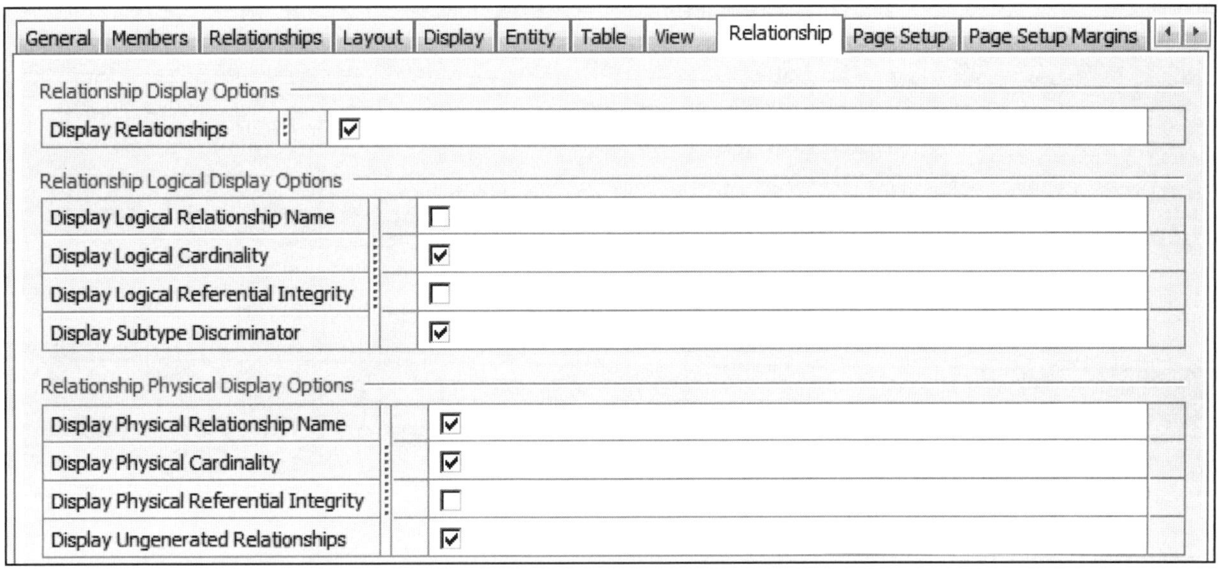

General | Members | Relationships | Layout | Display | Entity | Table | View | Relationship | Page Setup | Page Setup Margins

Relationship Display Options
- Display Relationships ☑

Relationship Logical Display Options
- Display Logical Relationship Name ☐
- Display Logical Cardinality ☑
- Display Logical Referential Integrity ☐
- Display Subtype Discriminator ☑

Relationship Physical Display Options
- Display Physical Relationship Name ☑
- Display Physical Cardinality ☑
- Display Physical Referential Integrity ☐
- Display Ungenerated Relationships ☑

Remember that we chose to hide a relationship using the **Relationships** tab earlier in this section. Note that if we want to show or hide *all* relationships on a diagram, the most direct method to do this is using the **Display Relationships** checkbox on the **Relationship** tab. There are many other options for controlling how relationships are shown, which are outlined in Table 8.8.

Table 8.8 Options for Relationship Tab on the Diagram Editor

Option	Description
Display Relationships	Indicates whether relationships are shown or hidden on the diagram. Unlike the **Relationships** tab, which allows you to specify selected objects for inclusion on the diagram, this is an 'all or nothing' flag, which does not affect inclusion within the Diagram, but display only.
Display Logical Relationship Name	Indicates whether to display the **Logical Relationship Name** on the diagram, as defined in the **Name** field of the Relationship Properties Editor on a logical model. **Note:** Don't confuse this with the **Display Child-To-Parent Verb Phrase** or **Display Parent -To-Child Phrase** display setting that are defined on the **Display** tab.
Display Logical Cardinality	Determines whether cardinality symbols are shown on the diagram, as defined by the **Cardinality** or **Cardinality Value** fields of the Relationship Properties Editor on a logical model. These symbols include: **P:** One or More (Cardinality)  CUSTOMER — P — MOVIE RENTAL RECORD **Z:** Zero or One (Cardinality)  CUSTOMER — Z — MOVIE RENTAL RECORD *n*: e.g. 3, 4, 5 (Cardinality Value)  CUSTOMER — 4 — MOVIE RENTAL RECORD
Display Logical Referential Integrity	Indicates whether to display referential integrity symbols (for example, U:R, I:R, D:C) for the relationships in the logical model, as defined on the **RI Actions** tab of the Relationship Properties Editor. Values in front of the colon include: • U: Update • I: Insert • D: Delete Letters after the colon include • R: Restrict • C: Cascade • SN: Set Null • SD: Set Default • NA: No Action **Note:** If you set the RI Action to '**None**', no symbols display. Below is an example of a relationship with Logical Referential Integrity shown: 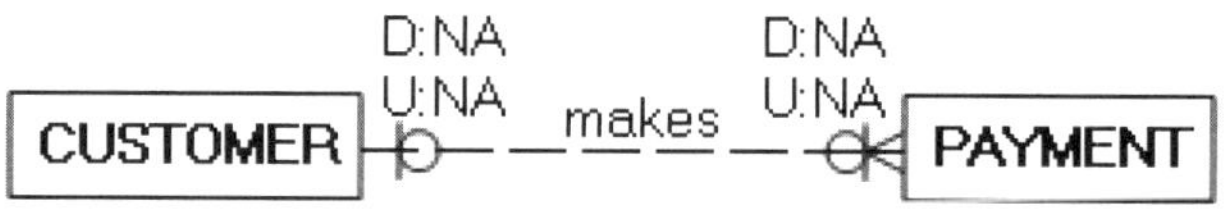 CUSTOMER D:NA U:NA — makes — D:NA U:NA PAYMENT

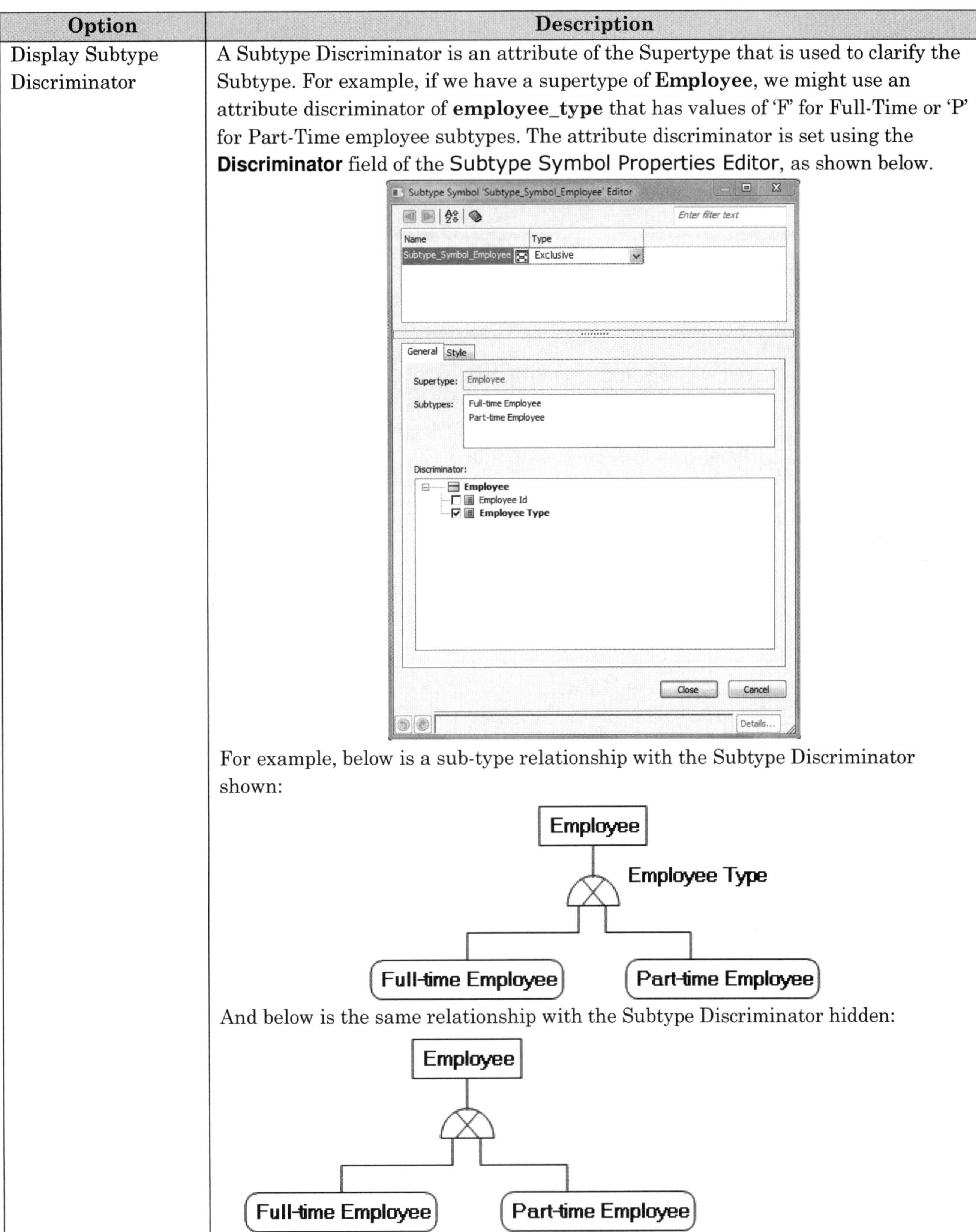

Option	Description
Display Subtype Discriminator	A Subtype Discriminator is an attribute of the Supertype that is used to clarify the Subtype. For example, if we have a supertype of **Employee**, we might use an attribute discriminator of **employee_type** that has values of 'F' for Full-Time or 'P' for Part-Time employee subtypes. The attribute discriminator is set using the **Discriminator** field of the Subtype Symbol Properties Editor, as shown below. For example, below is a sub-type relationship with the Subtype Discriminator shown: And below is the same relationship with the Subtype Discriminator hidden:

Option	Description
Display Physical Relationship Name	Indicates whether to display the Physical Relationship Name on the diagram, as defined in the **Foreign Key Constraint Name** field of the Relationship Properties Editor on a physical model.
Display Physical Cardinality	Determines whether cardinality symbols are shown on the diagram, as defined by the **Cardinality** or **Cardinality Value** fields of the Relationship Properties Editor on a physical model. These symbols include: **P:** One or More (Cardinality)  — CUSTOMER P MOVIE_RENTAL_RECORD **Z:** Zero or One (Cardinality) 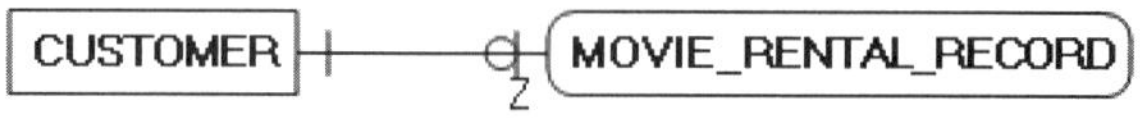 — CUSTOMER Z MOVIE_RENTAL_RECORD *n*: e.g. 3, 4, 5 (Cardinality Value)  — CUSTOMER 4 MOVIE_RENTAL_RECORD
Display Physical Referential Integrity	Indicates whether display referential integrity symbols (for example, U:R, I:R, D:C) for the relationships in the physical model, as defined on the **RI Actions** tab of the Relationship Properties Editor. Values in front of the colon include: • U: Update • I: Insert • D: Delete Letters after the colon include • R: Restrict • C: Cascade • SN: Set Null • SD: Set Default • NA: No Action **Note:** If you set the RI Action to 'None', no symbols display. Below is an example of a relationship with Physical Referential Integrity shown: 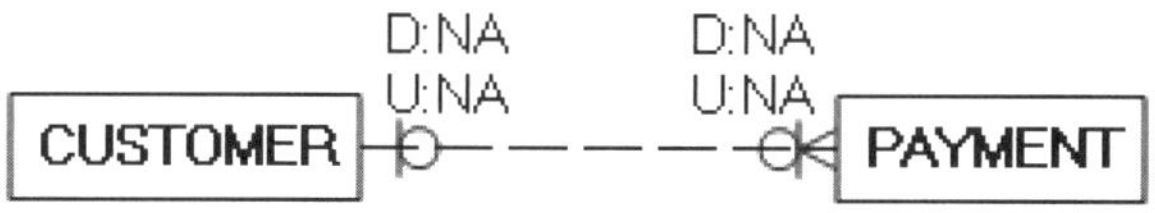 CUSTOMER D:NA U:NA — D:NA U:NA PAYMENT
Display Ungenerated Relationships	Indicates whether to display relationships that will not be generated when you generate the schema. A relationship is generated only when you select the **Generate** check box in the Relationship Properties Editor. See Chapter 6 for more information on relationships.

Now that we've finalized our diagram to address our business sponsors, we'll want to print our diagram. Let's move to the **Page Setup** tab, as shown in Figure 8.51, to define our printer settings.

Figure 8.51 Page Setup Tab of the Diagram Editor

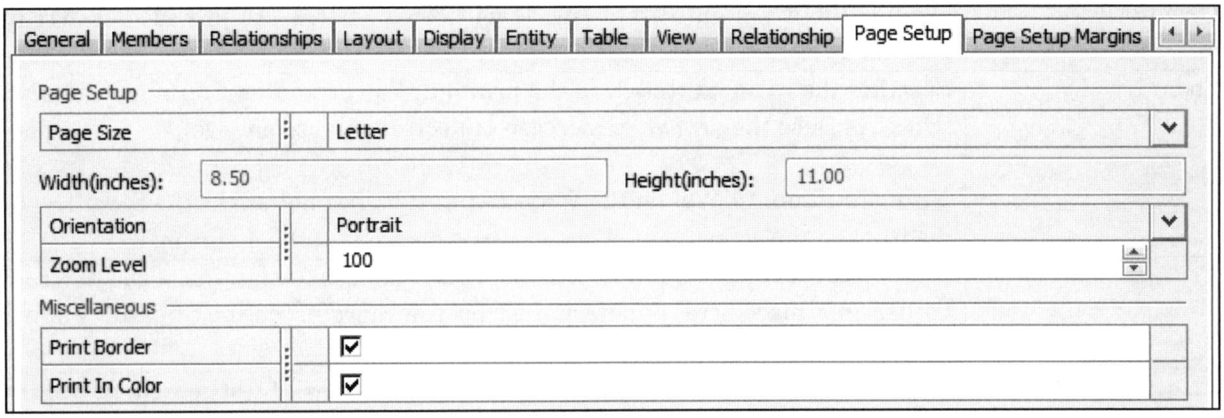

For our printout, we'll be using letter-sized paper, so we'll choose **Letter** from the **Page Size** drop-down menu, as shown in Figure 8.52.

Figure 8.52 Changing the Page Size for Diagram Printing

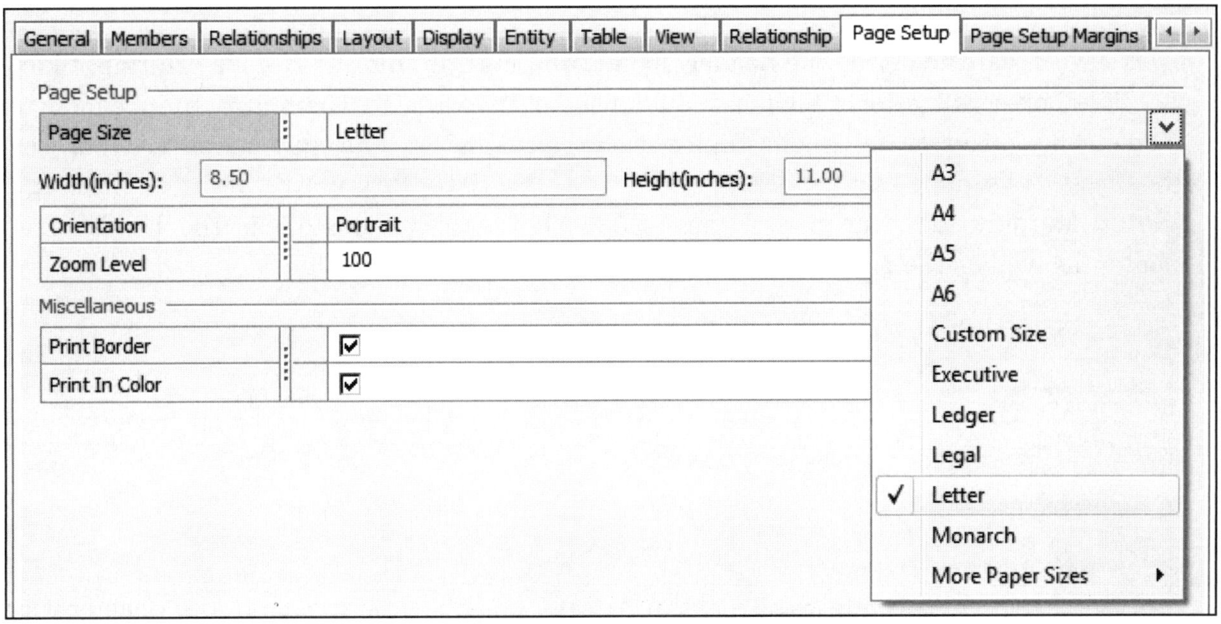

Table 8.9 provides an overview of the options on the **Page Setup** tab.

Table 8.9 Options for Page Setup Tab on the Diagram Editor

Option	Description
Page Size	Allows you to define specific page sizes for the paper in your printer. A drop-down list is provided where you can select a variety of formats, such as **Letter**, **Legal**, and even **Envelope**! (You know we are proponents of keeping a high-level data model to a single page—how about the 'back of an envelope'?) Note that you can also select a **Custom** size. If this option is selected, the **Width (inches)** and **Height (inches)** fields are enabled, where you can specify the exact size of the page.

Option	Description
Orientation	Defines the direction of the page layout. Two choices are provided: **Portrait** and **Landscape**.
Zoom Level	Specifies the zoom level used in the printout. You can enter a number directly in the text box or use the arrows to increase or decrease the zoom level. **Note:** The **Zoom Level** on the **Page Setup** tab does not affect the zoom level of the diagram on the screen, but of the physical printout of the diagram.
Print Border	If this box is checked, a border line is printed along the margins of the diagram. The border line placement is determined by the margins defined on the **Page Setup Margins** tab, which is explained later in this section.
Print In Color	If this box is checked, the diagram will print in color. If unchecked, it will print in black and white. **Note:** The **Print In Color** setting is independent of the colors of the diagram, i.e. the diagram may be in color on the screen, but if this box is unchecked, the printout will be in black and white.

Next, we'll want to define the header, footer, and margin information for printing. Since we'll be presenting to a business audience, we'll want to customize the header to something intuitive for them. Since we're focusing on the Payments area of the business, let's have our header read '**Data related to Payment**'. Move to the **Page Setup Margins** tab, shown in Figure 8.53, where we can customize the header and footer, as well as the page margins.

Figure 8.53 Page Setup Margins Tab of the Diagram Editor

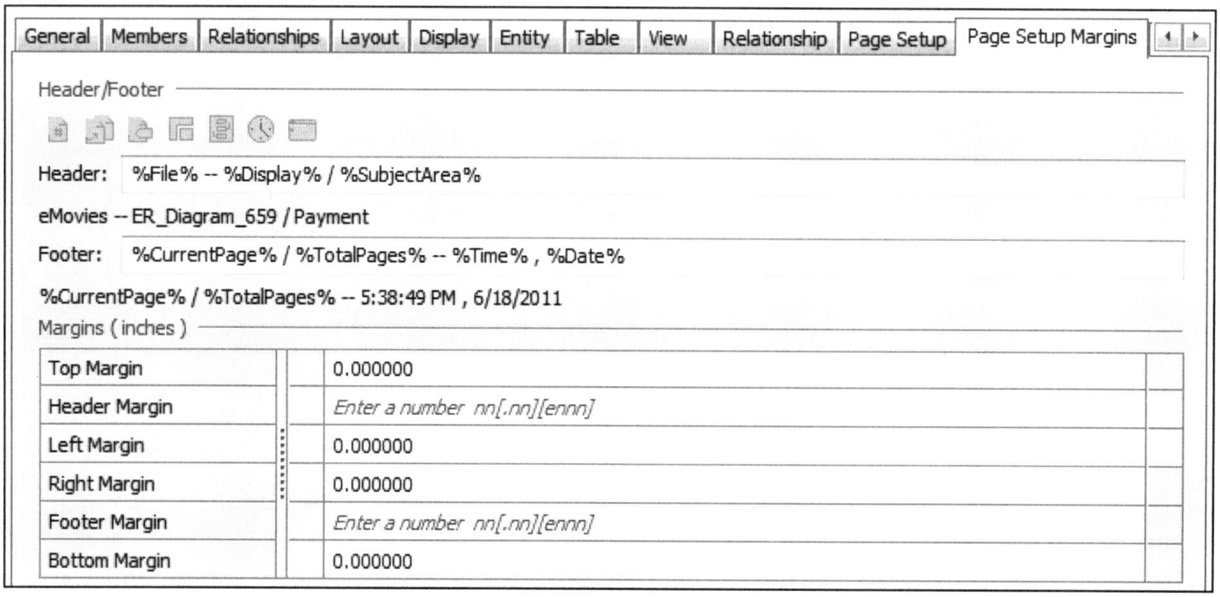

Place your cursor in the **Header** text box, and you'll see the Header/Footer Toolbar become active, as shown in Figure 8.54.

Figure 8.54 Header/Footer Toolbar

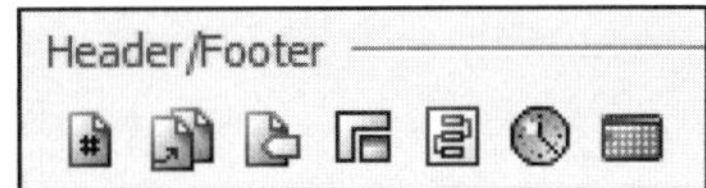

This menu provides shortcuts to a number of handy macro functions that insert commonly-used items into the header and footer, such as date/time, diagram name, etc. Table 8.10 provides a list of the macro options provided in the Header/Footer Toolbar.

Table 8.10 Header/Footer Toolbar

Toolbar Icon	Name	Description
	Current Page	Lists the current page (i.e. the '1' in '1 of 4'). Associated with the macro **%CurrentPage%**
	Page Count	Lists the total number of pages (i.e. the '4' in '1 of 4'). Associated with the macro **%TotalPages%**
	File Name	Prints the file name of the model, e.g. **eMovies_practice** Associated with the macro **%File%**
	Subject Area Name	Prints the name of the current Subject Area, e.g. **Payments** Associated with the macro **%SubjectArea%**
	Diagram Name	Prints the name of the current Diagram, e.g. **Business View** Associated with the macro **%Display%**
	Time	Shows the current time in HH:MM:SS AM/PM format, e.g. 2:19:51 PM Associated with the macro **%Time%**
	Date	Shows the current date, for example, MM/DD/YY representing. 3/31/11, or March 31, 2011. Note that the date format is picked up from the system preferences. Associated with the macro **%Date%**

Using these macros, we can customize our header. In addition to macros, plain text can be used. We'd like our header to read '**Data related to Payment**'. One way to generate this header is to simply type the text directly into the **Header** field, as shown in Figure 8.55.

Figure 8.55 Including Literal Text in a Diagram Header

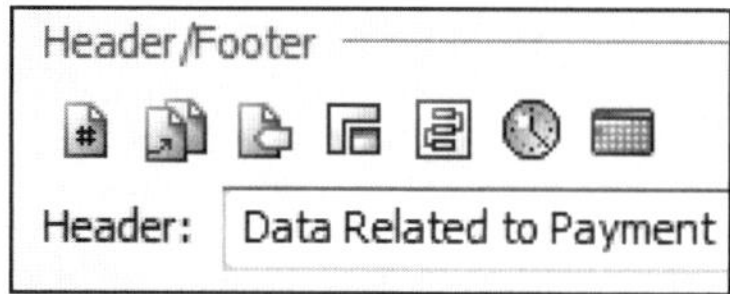

Since **Payment** is the name of our Subject Area, however, we can use a macro to translate this name for us. This is a flexible way to include Diagram names and other information that might change, so that the header is always up-to-date. To replace the hard-coded term with a more flexible macro, highlight the word **Payment**, and then click on the **Subject Area Name** button in the Header/Footer Toolbar, as shown in Figure 8.56.

Figure 8.56 Using Macros to Generate a Customized Header

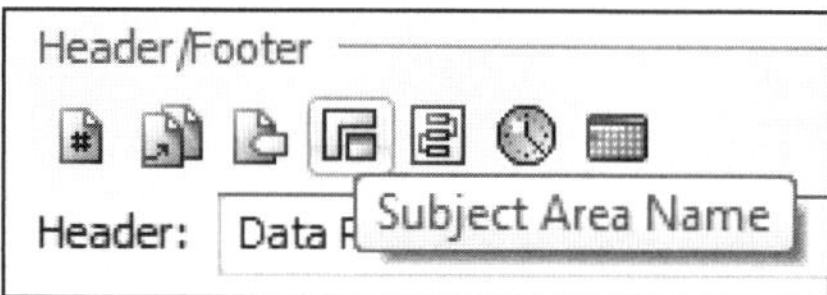

This will include the name of the Subject Area in place of the macro when the header is generated, as shown in Figure 8.57. Note that the full header text is shown below the **Header** field, so that you can preview the header text before you print, saving time and paper. Notice that in Figure 8.57, the header preview reads **Data related to Payment**, which is our desired result.

Figure 8.57 Using the %SubjectArea% Macro in a Diagram Header

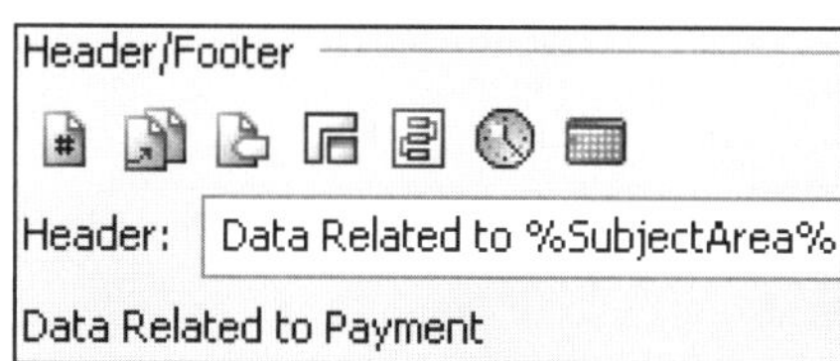

Table 8.11 lists the options for the **Page Setup Margins** tab.

Table 8.11 Options for Page Setup Margins Tab on the Diagram Editor

Option	Description
Header	Allows you to customize the header that appears at the top of the diagram, using a combination of plain text and macros. The Header/Footer Toolbar provides a quick way to enter commonly-used macros. The actual header text is previewed below the **Header** field.
Footer	Allows you to customize the footer that appears at the bottom of the diagram, using a combination of plain text and macros. The Header/Footer Toolbar provides a quick way to enter commonly-used macros.
Top Margin	Defines the size, in inches, of the margin at the top of the diagram.

Option	Description
Header Margin	Defines the size, in inches, of the header margin, which is the margin that appears *below* the header.
Left Margin	Defines the size, in inches, of the margin to the left of the diagram.
Right Margin	Defines the size, in inches, of the margin to the right of the diagram.
Footer Margin	Defines the size, in inches, of the footer margin, which is the margin that appears *above* the footer.
Bottom Margin	Defines the size, in inches, of the margin at the bottom of the diagram.

We've now set up our diagram in an intuitive way to display to our business users. Before we leave our Diagram Editor, we'll want to create a definition defining the purpose of this diagram. As each diagram is customized for a particular audience or purpose, a description is important. If another modeler views the diagram later and wonders why no data types are shown, they'll understand when they read the description of the audience and diagram purpose. Move to the **Definition** tab of the Diagram Editor, and type the following description, as shown in Figure 8.58.

Diagram Description	The audience for this diagram is the business sponsor, and the purpose is to explain the key business concepts and data-related rules around the Payment process in the organization.

Figure 8.58 Creating a Definition for a Diagram

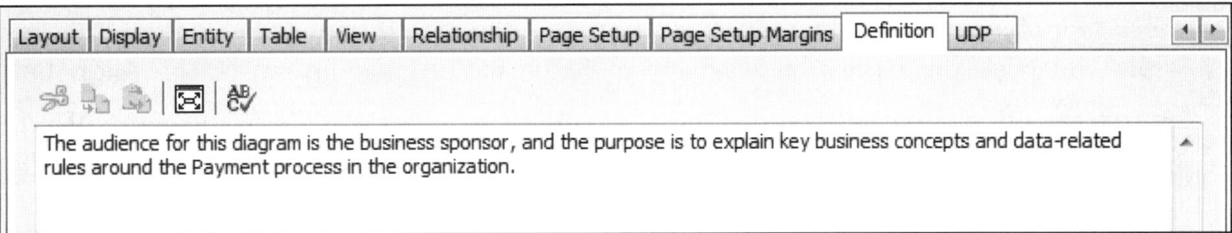

The next tab is the **UDP** tab, which can be used to attach custom metadata, or even documents containing additional information about the diagram; in this case, perhaps a document describing the payments process. We'll cover UDPs further in Chapter 14, so don't worry about this tab, for now.

Let's see how our diagram turned out. Select **Close** to return to the diagram, which should look similar to Figure 8.59. Use the **Hierarchical** layout option from the Layout Toolbar to re-organize your diagram objects. Since we are now showing descriptions, relative sizes of the entities have changed from our previous diagram layout in Figure 8.43, so we'll need to re-layout.

Figure 8.59 Business View Diagram

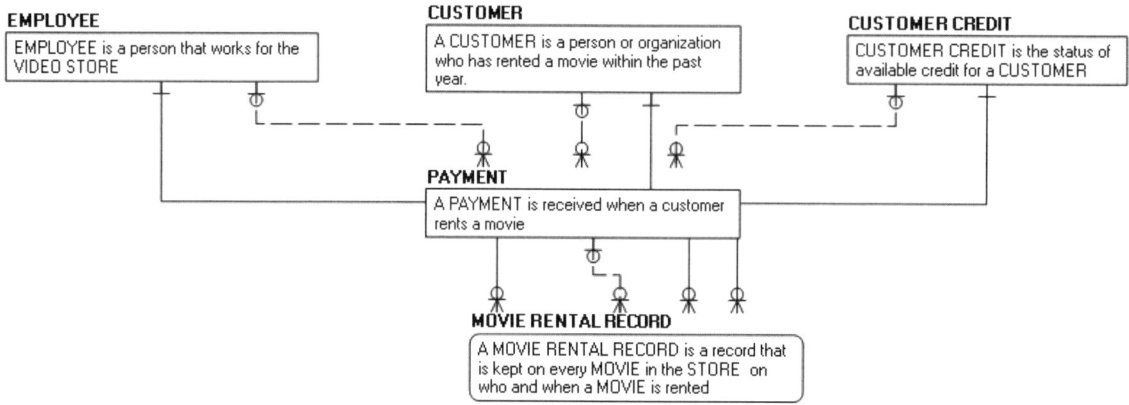

This is a nice presentation to display to your business users to discuss the data involved in the Payment process with them. Note that entity definitions are shown on the diagram, but no further detail such as attributes, data types, etc. This is a helpful view for creating conceptual or logical models to help define core business concepts and their definitions.

In looking at the model again, though, we realize that we're sticklers for perfection. Although the hierarchical auto-layout option did a fairly good job of presenting the objects on the diagram, it's really bothering us that the **Payment** and **Movie Rental Record** entities aren't left-justified. Luckily, we can make these fine-tuning adjustments with the help of the alignment buttons on the Alignment Toolbar. To align these two objects, highlight both objects on the diagram (holding down the CTRL key while you click the mouse on each object helps with this) and select the **Align Left** button on the Alignment Toolbar, as shown in Figure 8.60. We'll want **Movie Rental Record** to align with **Payment**, so click the **Payment** entity first when you're making your selection. The first object select is the one that stays in place—the second aligns to that selection. If the Alignment Toolbar isn't displayed on your screen, from the **Main Menu**, select **View|Toolbars** and then select **Alignment**.

Figure 8.60 Selecting the Align Left Option from the Alignment Toolbar

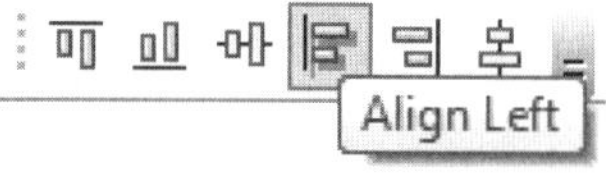

Your diagram will now look like Figure 8.61, with **Movie Rental Record** left-justified with **Payment**.

Figure 8.61 Using the Alignment Buttons to Fine-Tune Your Diagram Object Placement

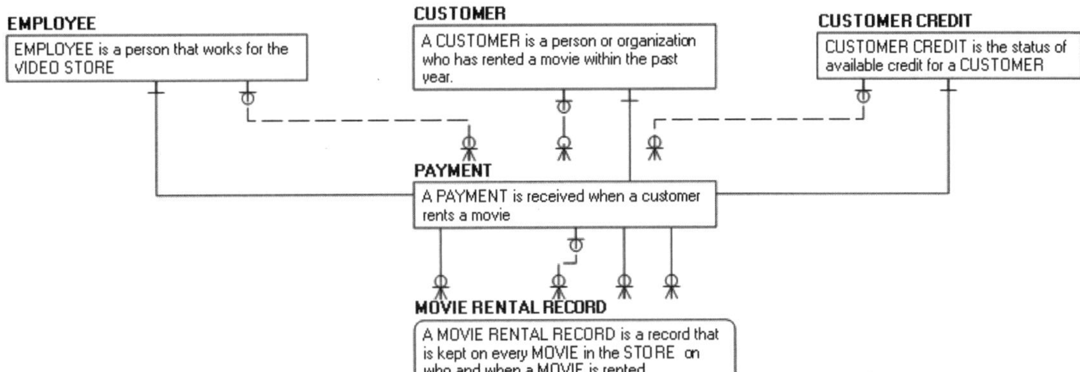

Now that we've aligned these two entities, we'll want to group them together so that they stay aligned if we move one of the objects. The **Group** option helps with this. Highlight the **Payment** and **Movie Rental Record** entities on the diagram, and then select **Diagram|Group** from the **Main Menu**. Once you've made this selection, you'll see that these two entities are bounded by a dashed box on the diagram, as shown in Figure 8.62. Click on another area of the diagram, and this box will disappear, but a (dotted) box will reappear if you select these objects again, indicating that they are grouped together. Move one of the objects and you will see that they both move together, which is a handy way of 'locking' design layouts in place once you've found an arrangement you like. If you need to change the layout down the road, you can simply highlight the objects and select **Diagram|Ungroup** to remove this behavior.

Figure 8.62 Objects Grouped on a Diagram

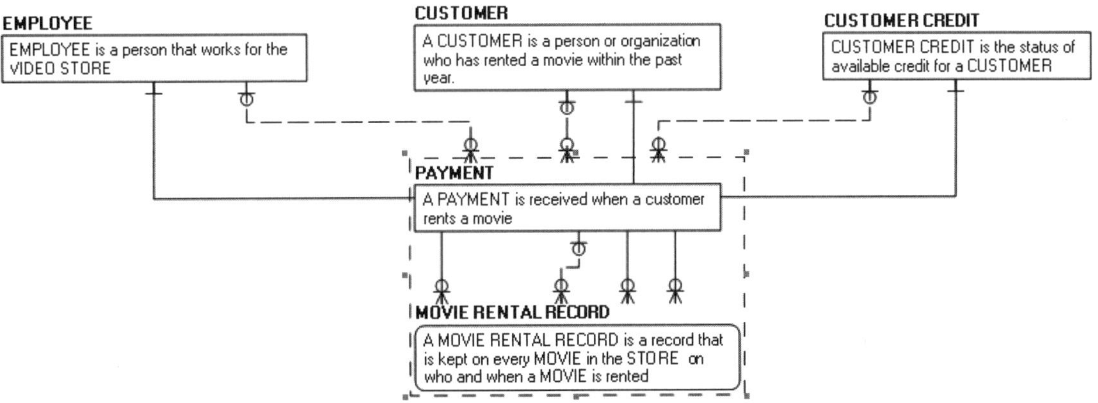

In this section, we've seen how diagrams can be used to create unique displays for various audiences in your organization. If you'd like an example of the finished model from this example, you can download the model `eMovies_practice_businessview.erwin` from the www.erwin.com/datamodelingmadesimple web site. The next section on formatting Themes will go further into ways to use color and other design aspects to add 'pizzazz' to your diagrams.

Formatting Themes

Themes provide a way to create custom formatting settings for specific audiences or use cases. For example, you may want to show your business-level model using colors, shading, italics, etc, while the physical model might be shown in simple black and white. Themes allow you to create these custom display settings that can be reused across other models and diagrams.

It is important to understand the concept of theme inheritance before we go into an example. Once you create a Theme, these properties are inherited by lower-level objects unless they are specifically overridden. For example, if you create a model with blue objects and a white background, all subject areas created within this model will have blue objects and a white background, as will all diagrams created within these subject areas. If, however, you override the model's theme for a particular subject area, with green objects on a blue background, for example, all diagrams within that subject area will inherit the theme of using green objects on a blue background. Within this diagram, you can select certain objects, and change them to a different color. Figure 8.63 provides an overview of the inheritance hierarchy for Themes.

Figure 8.63 Inheritance Hierarchy for Themes

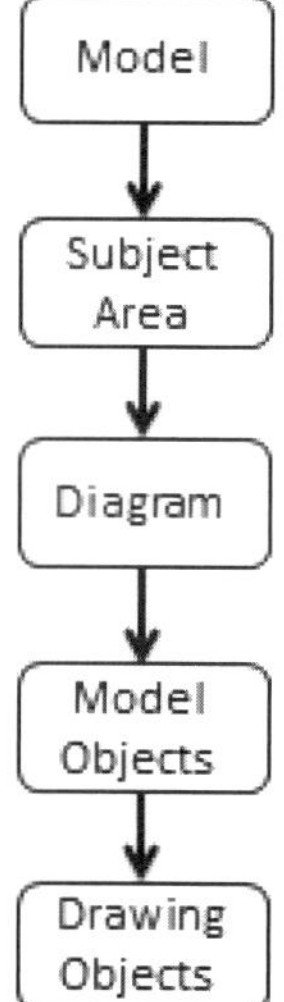

Let's walk through an example to better understand how Themes function within CA ERwin Data Modeler. Start by creating a new logical/physical model (for help on how to create a model, refer to Chapter 3). By default, a blank diagram is created using the **Default** Theme, which has a light-blue patterned background, as shown in Figure 8.64.

Figure 8.64 Diagram Using Default Theme

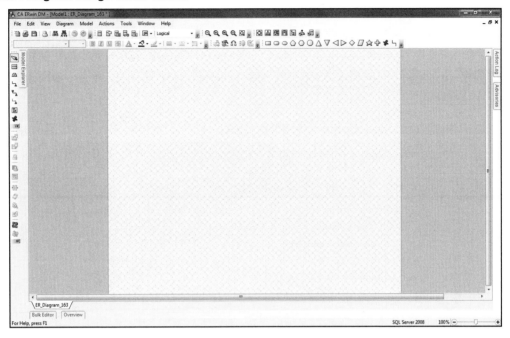

We'd like to change this to a more traditional black-and-white theme. We'll make this change at the Model level, so that all new and existing diagrams will inherit this theme. Select **Model|Model Properties** from the **Main Menu**, and move to the **Defaults** tab, as shown in Figure 8.65.

Figure 8.65 Default Tab of the Model Properties Editor

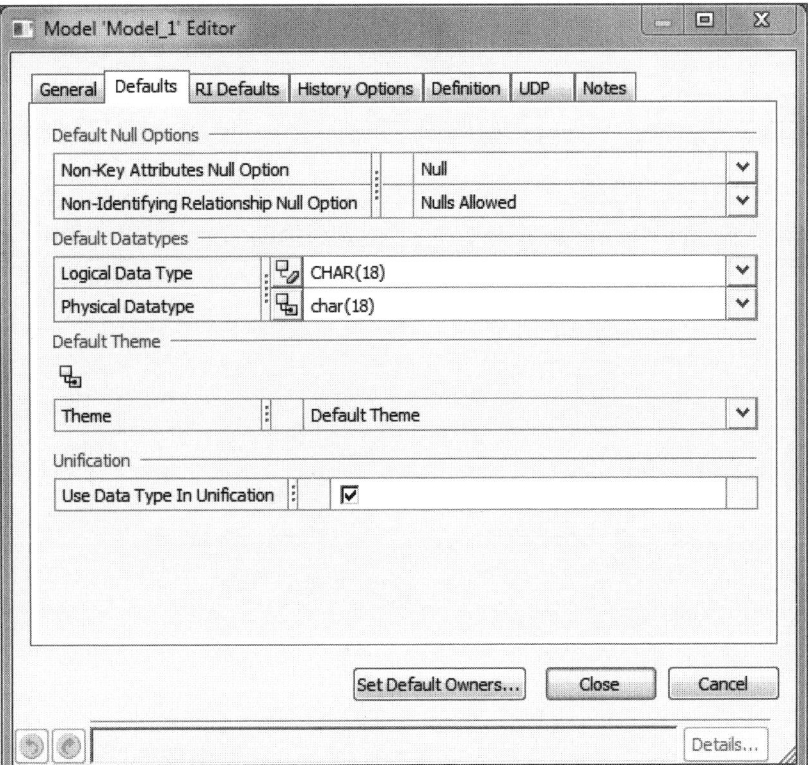

Notice that the **Theme** field is defined as **Default Theme**, which is the blue patterned background. We'll want to change this to the **Classic** theme, which has a more traditional black-and-white formatting. By using the drop-down menu, as shown in Figure 8.66, we can switch between the two themes provided with CA ERwin Data Modeler: **Default** and **Classic**. You can also create your own themes, which we'll do later in this section.

Figure 8.66 Changing to the Classic Theme at the Model Level

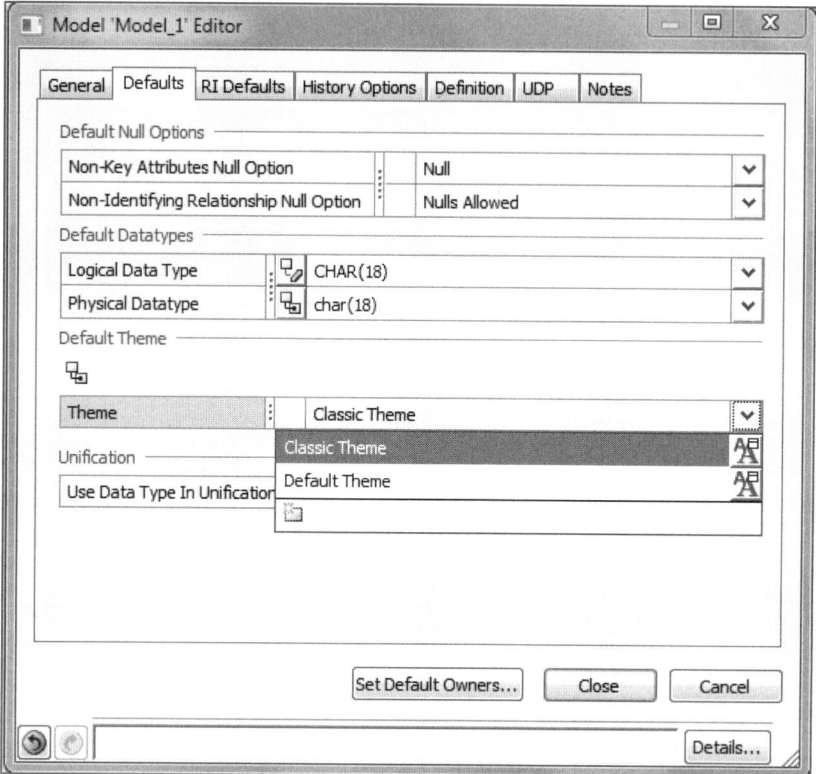

Once you've selected the **Classic** theme, you will see the open diagram change to a white background. Select **Close** to exit from the Model Properties Editor, and you'll see that the open diagram has a white background for a more classic look, as shown in Figure 8.67.

Figure 8.67 Diagram Using Classic Theme

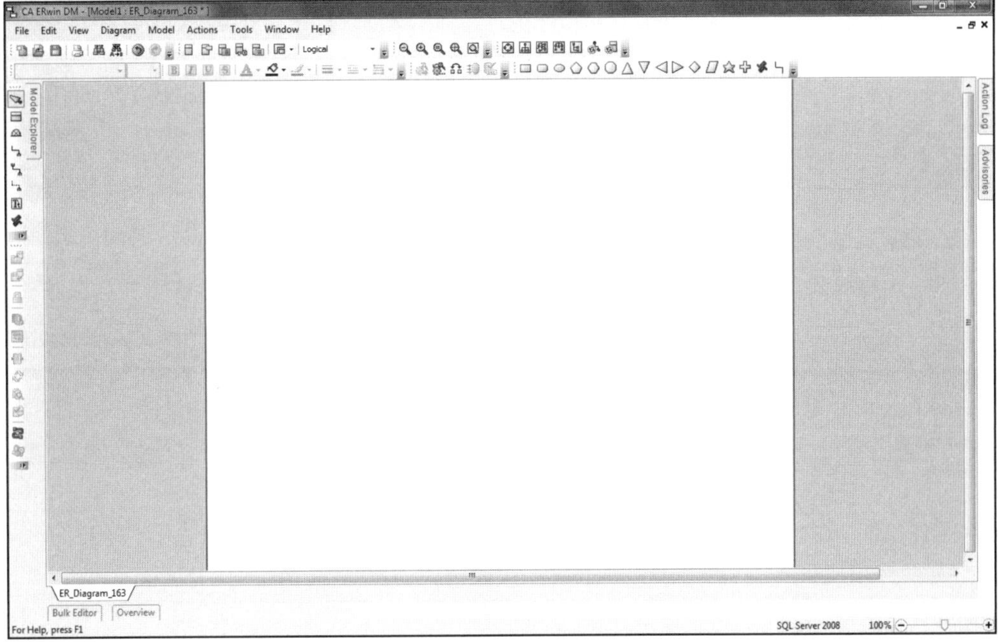

Although we'll want to use the classic look for the majority of our logical and physical model diagrams, for this particular diagram, we'd like to use some special fonts and shading to appeal to our business sponsor, who will be the audience for this diagram. In this case, we'll override the Model Theme and create our own special Theme for this Diagram. To do this, open the **Diagram Properties Editor** (invoke by double-clicking on the 'white space' of your diagram) and move to the **General** tab (for more information on the Diagram Properties Editor, refer to the section on Diagrams earlier in this section). Select the drop-down menu in the **Theme** field, and select the **New** option, as shown in Figure 8.68.

Figure 8.68 Creating a New Theme from within the Diagram Properties Editor

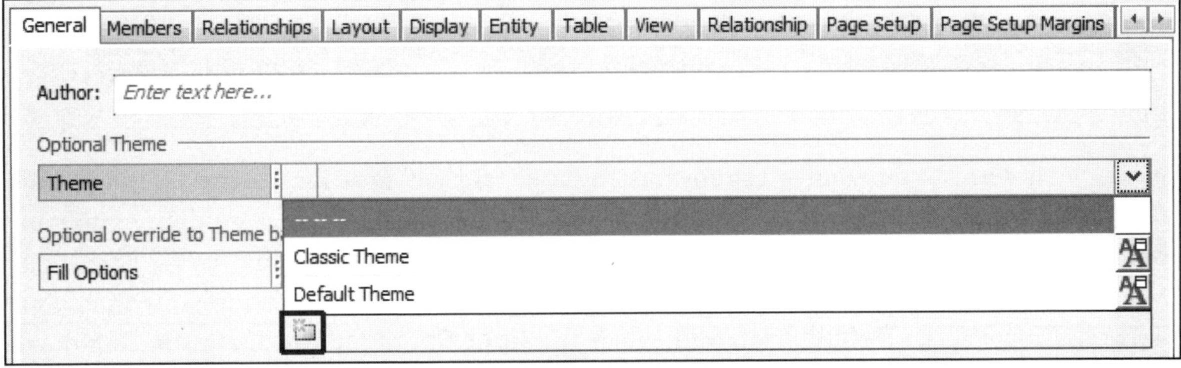

The Theme Editor appears, as shown in Figure 8.69, with a new Theme created using an automated numbering scheme. Notice that there are tabs to change the formatting for a number of objects such as **Entity**, **Attribute**, **Key**, etc. Some of the commonly-used settings such as **Diagram Fill**, **Entity Fill**, etc. are replicated along the top for ease-of-use.

Figure 8.69 Theme Editor

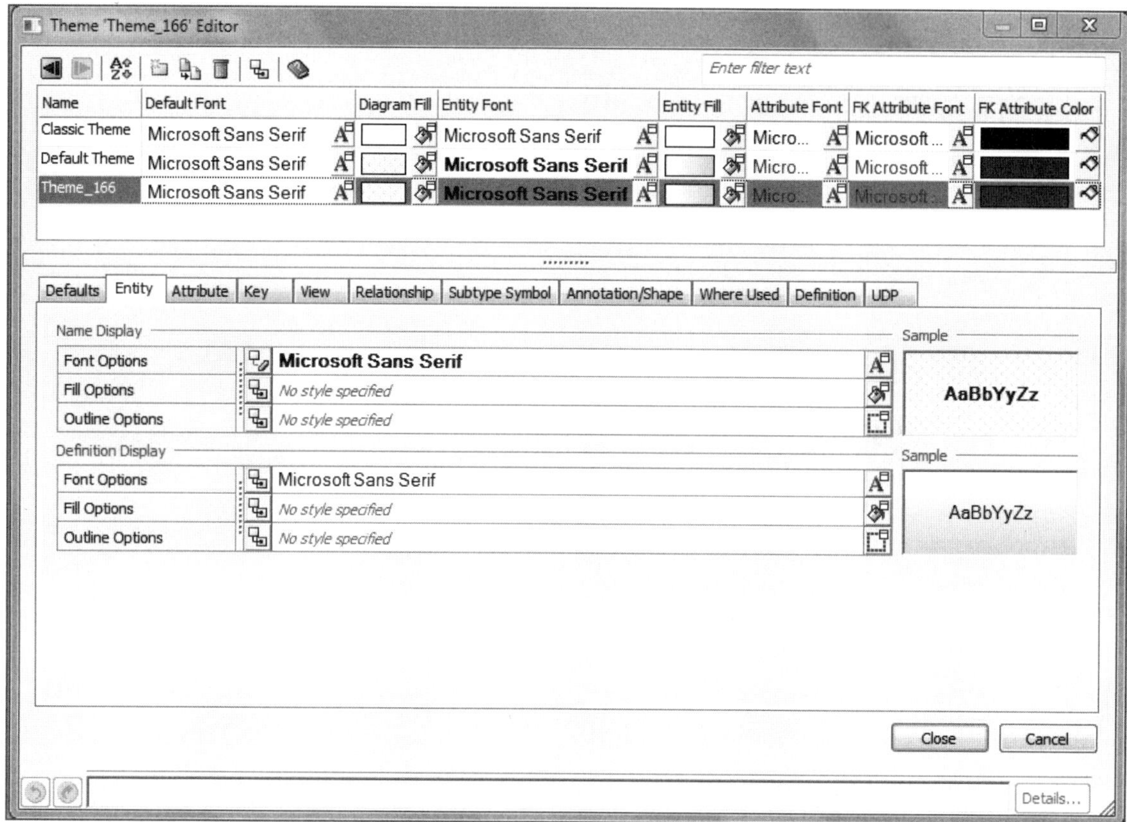

We'll want to change this automated name to something more intuitive. Enter the name **Business Theme** for the **Name** field, as shown in Figure 8.70.

Figure 8.70 Changing the Default Name for a New Theme

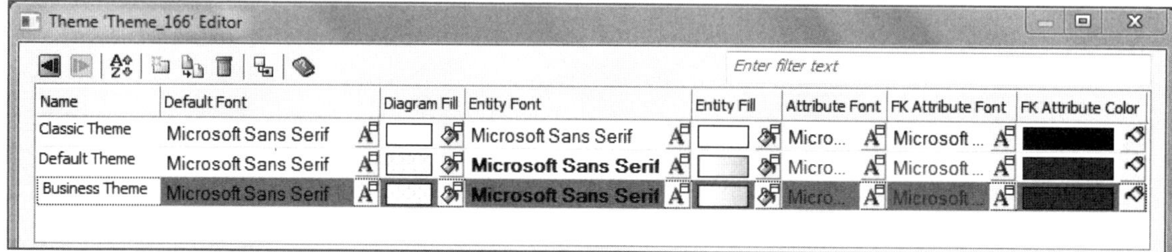

Next, we'll want to customize the formatting and font settings for our new Theme. The first change we'll make is to customize the font type. The branding guidelines for our business dictate that all marketing documents use the Arial font style. Since our business sponsors are accustomed to that style, we'll choose this font for our diagrams as well. Move to the **Defaults** tab and select the **Font Settings|Font Options** drop-down menu. In the General Font Editor that appears, select the **Arial** font, as shown in Figure 8.71.

Figure 8.71 Changing the Default Font for a Custom Theme

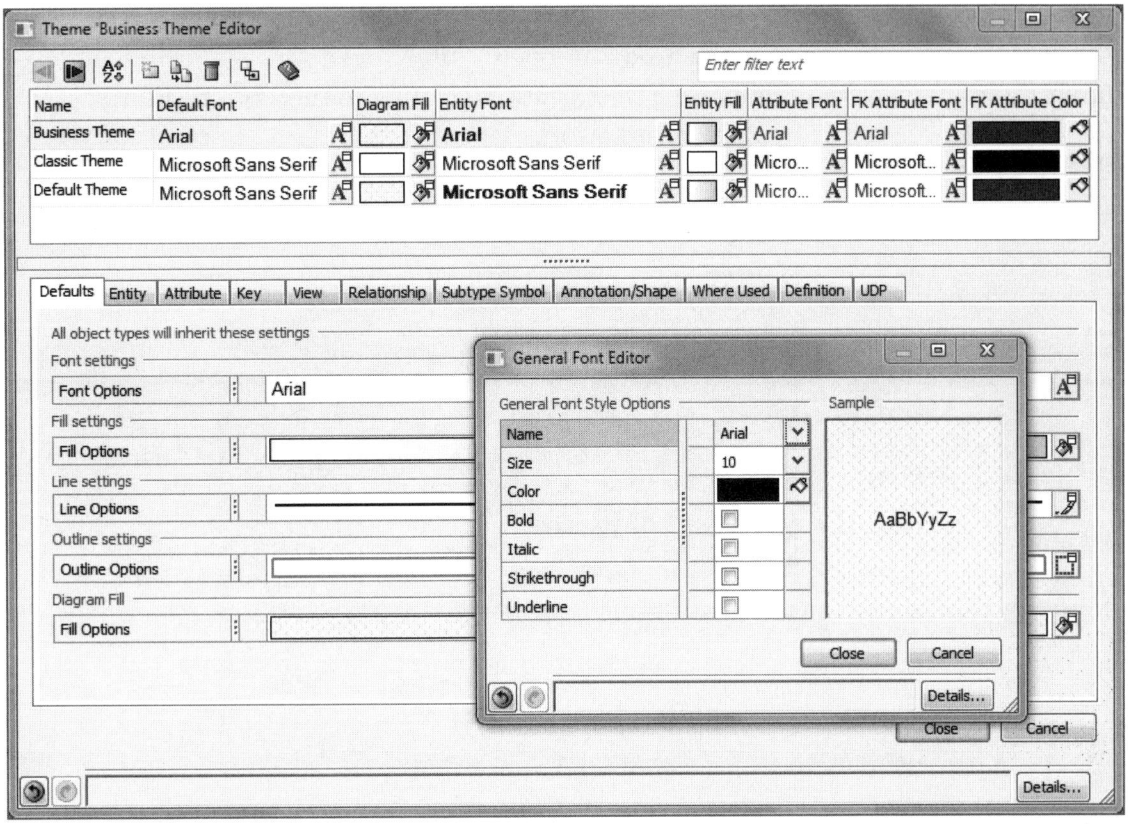

Close the **General Font Editor** and next we'll change the background color of the diagram, using the drop-down menu for the **Diagram Fill|Fill Options** field, as shown in Figure 8.72.

Figure 8.72 Diagram Fill Editor

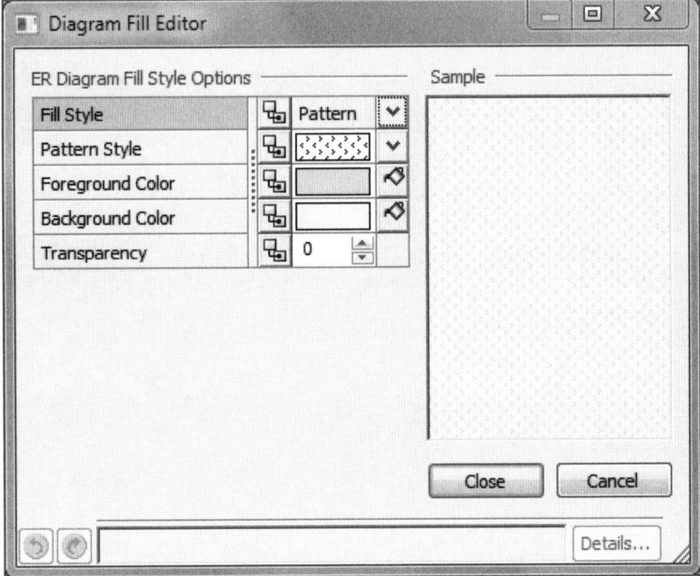

The default setting is a light-blue pattern. We'll change this to a solid, light gray by selecting a **Fill Style** of **Solid**, and a **Fill Color** of gray, as shown in Figure 8.73. Notice that the diagram color changes behind the open editor, even before closing. This is a handy way to preview your changes. Select **Close** to return to the Theme Editor.

Figure 8.73 Changing the Diagram Fill Style for a Custom Theme

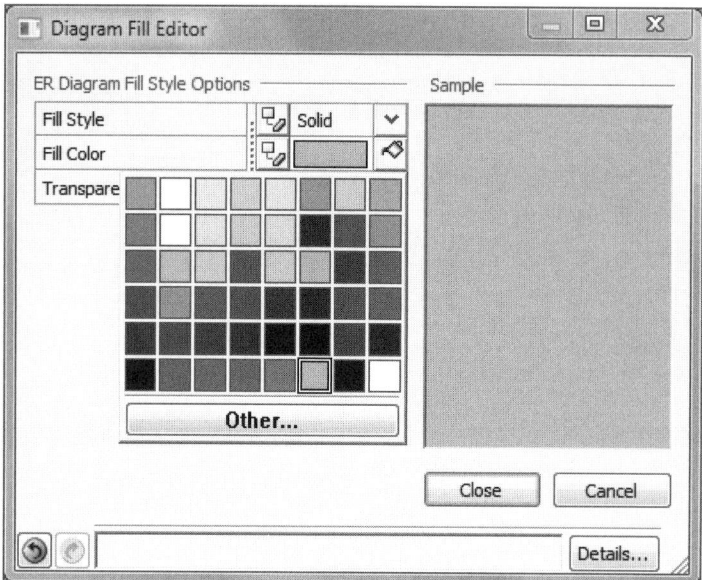

To contrast with the gray background, we'll make the background fill for our model objects such as entities, tables, and view a solid white. Use the drop-down menu for the **Fill setting|Fill Options** field, and the General Fill Editor appears, as shown in Figure 8.74.

Figure 8.74 General Fill Editor

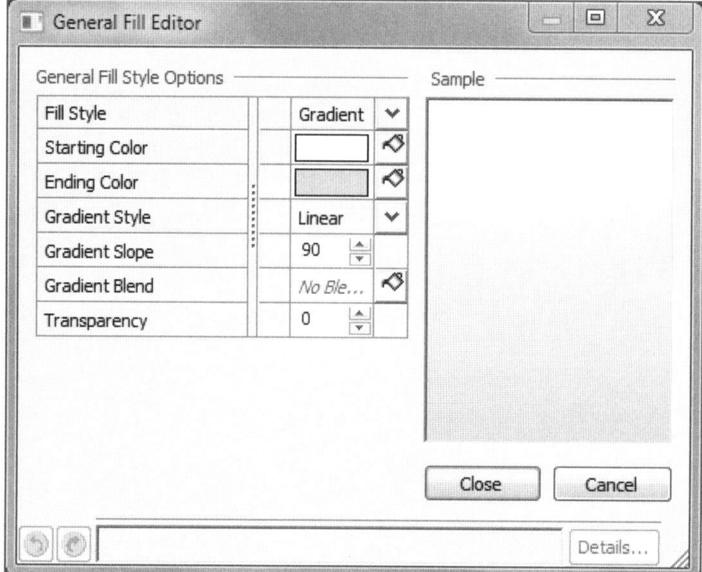

In the General Fill Editor, change the **Fill Style** to **Solid** and the **Fill Color** to white, as shown in Figure 8.75.

Figure 8.75 Changing the General Fill Style for a Custom Theme

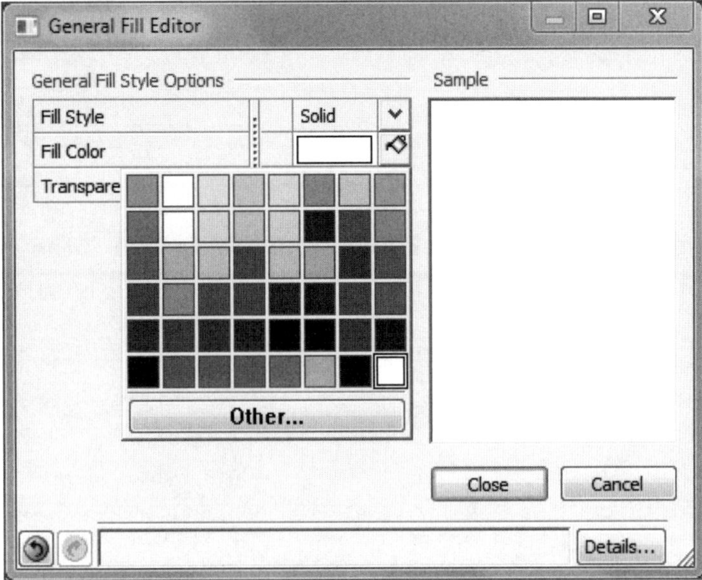

Select **Close** to return to the Theme Editor. You'll now see the settings we've changed, so that we have a font type of **Arial** on a gray diagram with white model objects, as shown in Figure 8.76.

Figure 8.76 Modified Theme Settings on the General Tab

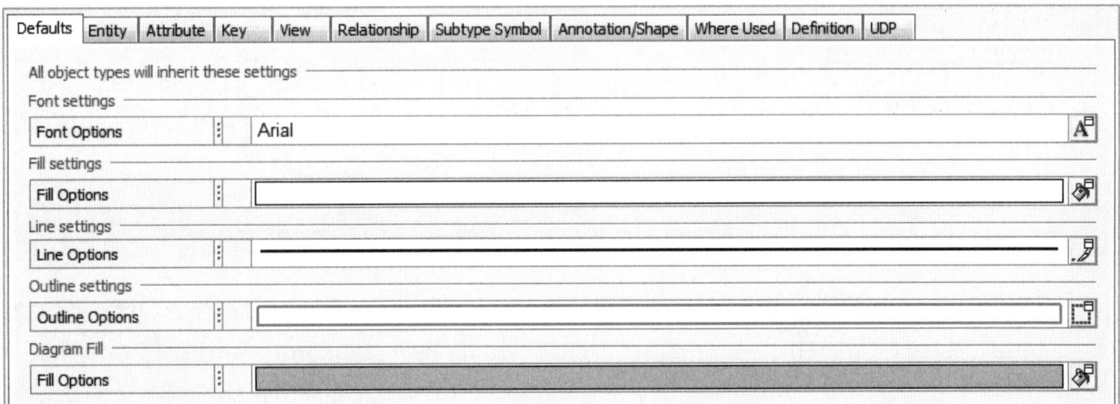

Remember the concept of theme inheritance. Since we've applied these themes to the entire diagram using the **Defaults** tab, these changes will cascade to the model objects themselves, such as Entities, Attributes, etc. To confirm this, move to the **Entity** tab, shown in Figure 8.77. You'll see that the **Font Options** have automatically been changed to **Arial**.

Figure 8.77 Model Object Inheritance of Diagram Theme Settings

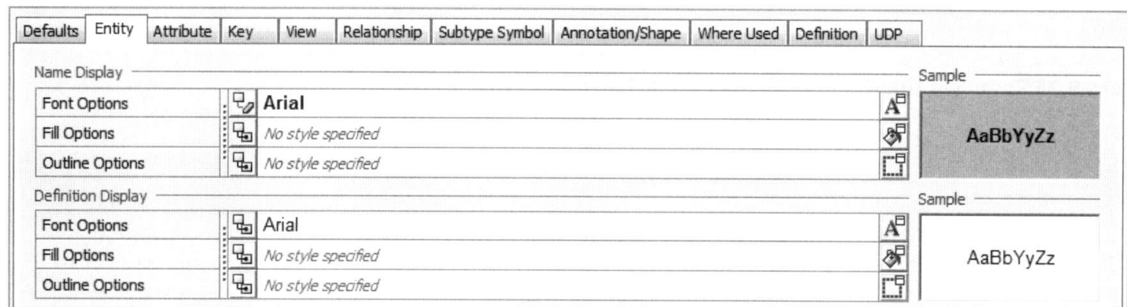

Selecting the drop-down menu for the **Fill Options** field verifies that the **Entity** object has inherited the fill option of solid white as well, as shown in Figure 8.78.

Figure 8.78 Model Object Inheritance of Fill Style Options

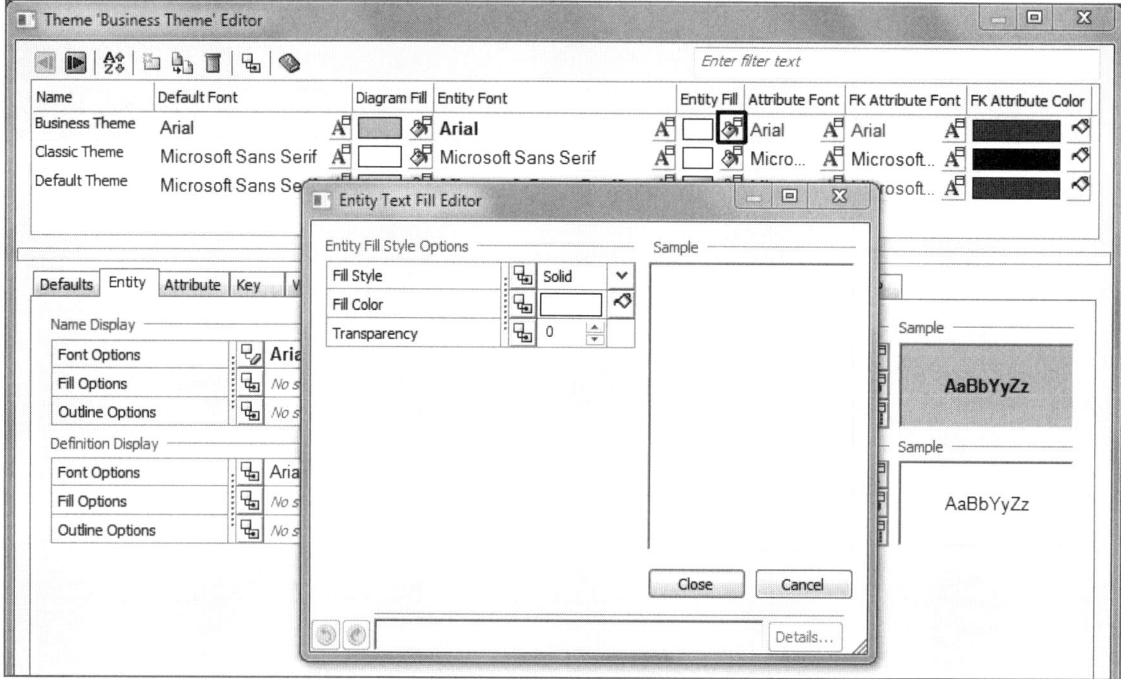

Select **Close** to exit the Entity Text Fill Editor and then **Close** to exist the Theme Editor and return to the diagram. Next, we'll create some sample entities to demonstrate how the new font and fill settings are display. Create five new entities on the diagram, named **Product**, **Order**, **Shipment**, **Payment**, and **Invoice** as shown in Figure 8.79. (For more information on how to create entities, refer to Chapter 4). You'll see that this creates a diagram with white objects on a gray background (not the prettiest combination, we know, but this book is in black and white, so we had to be creative!).

Figure 8.79 Diagram Using Newly-Created Business Theme

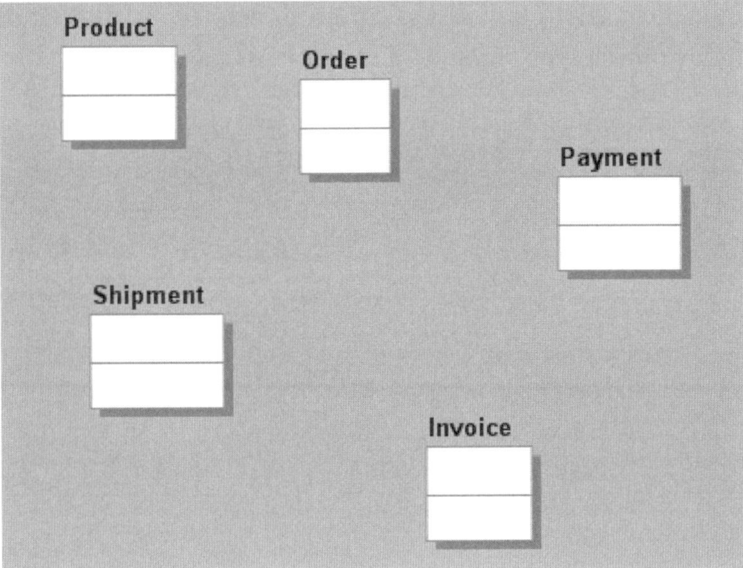

Just as we've overwritten the model Theme to create a specific diagram theme, we can also change the Theme for particular objects on the diagram. Say, for example, that we'd like to review **Product**, **Order**, and **Shipment** with our business sponsors for a design review meeting. We can highlight these entities using a particular color or formatting so that they stand apart from the others. To change the formatting for these three entities, multi-select the objects by holding down the CTRL key, and then placing the mouse on each of the entities. Once all three entities have been selected, right-click on one of the entities to invoke the context menu, and select **Override Fonts and Colors**, as shown in Figure 8.80.

Figure 8.80 Overriding Fonts and Colors for Specific Objects on a Diagram

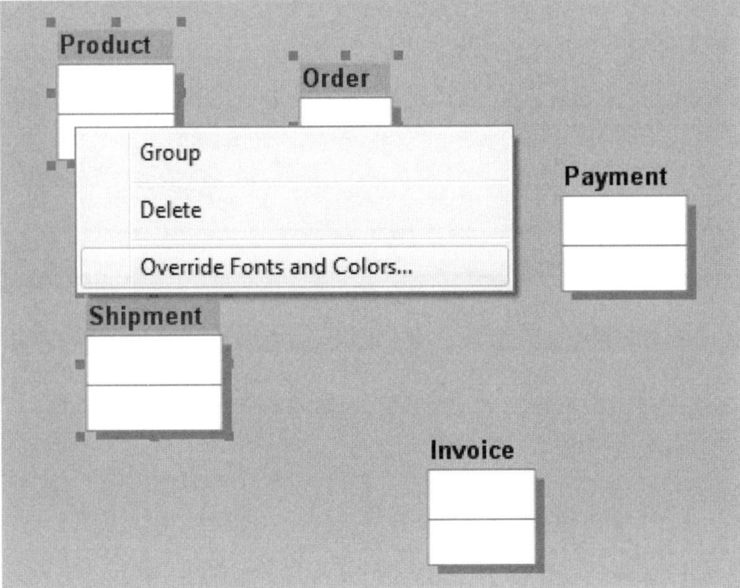

The Multiple Shape Object Editor appears, as shown in Figure 8.81. In this editor, you can specify common formatting for all selected objects using the **Style** tab, or define specific formatting by object type, such as Entity or Attribute.

Figure 8.81 Multiple Shape Object Editor

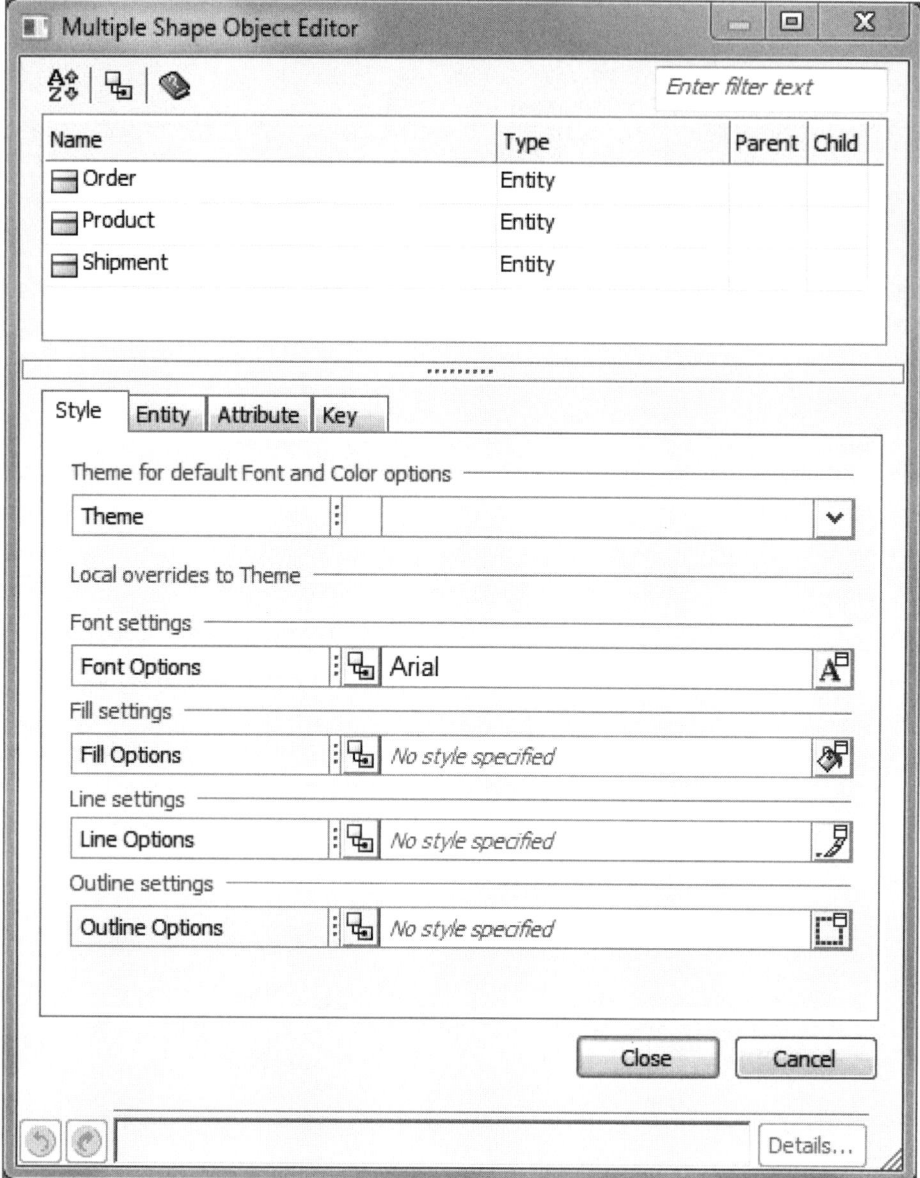

In this case, we'll use the **Style** tab to define a unique fill style for these objects, shown in Figure 8.82.

Figure 8.82 Style Tab in the Multiple Shape Object Editor

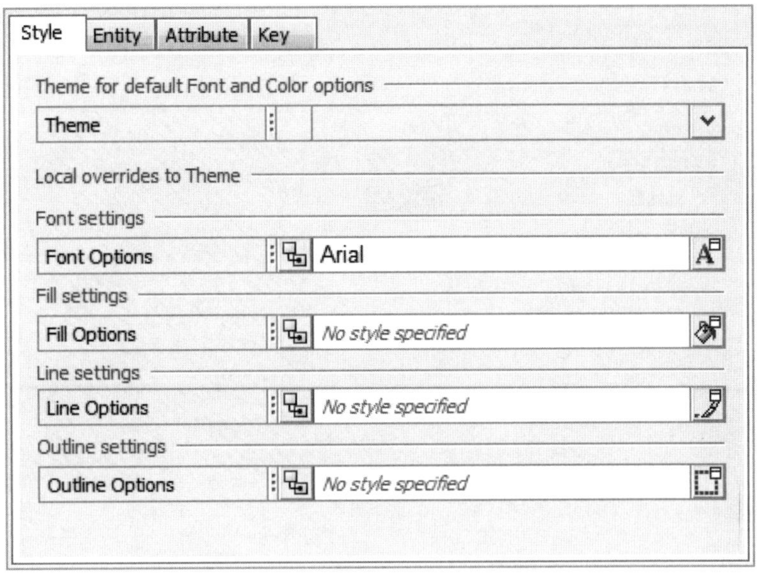

Select the drop-down menu for the **Fill Options** field, and the General Fill Editor appears, as shown in Figure 8.83.

Figure 8.83 General Fill Editor

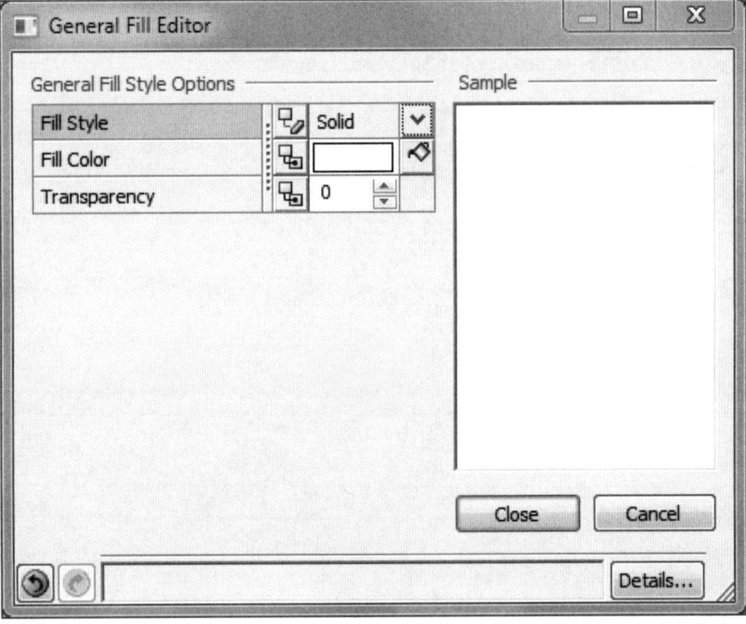

We'll use diagonal lines to highlight these objects, so select a **Fill Style** of **Pattern,** a **Pattern Style** of diagonal lines, and a **Foreground Color** of black, a shown in Figure 8.84.

Figure 8.84 Customizing the Fill Style for Selected Objects

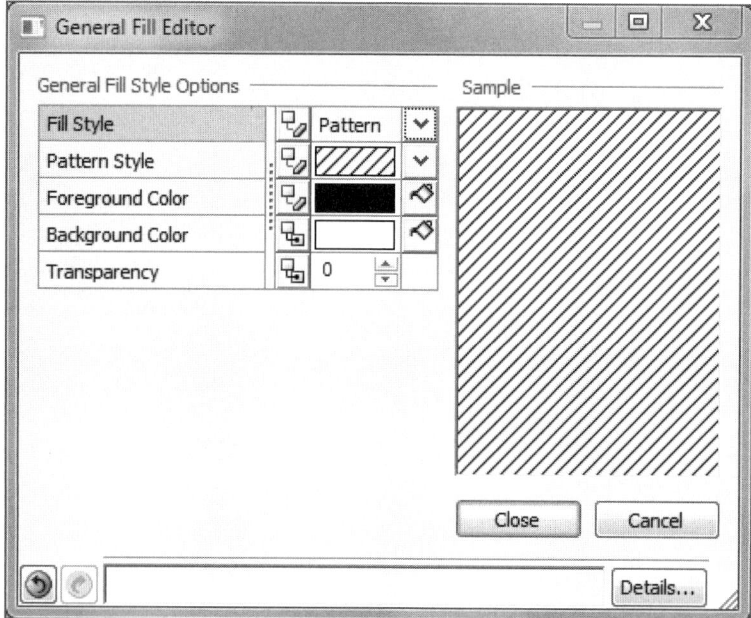

Select **Close** to return to the Multiple Shape Object Editor and **Close** again to return to the diagram, which should now look like Figure 8.85. With these entities highlighted using a separate color pattern, they can be easily identified during our review session.

Figure 8.85 Diagram with Custom Formatting for Selected Objects

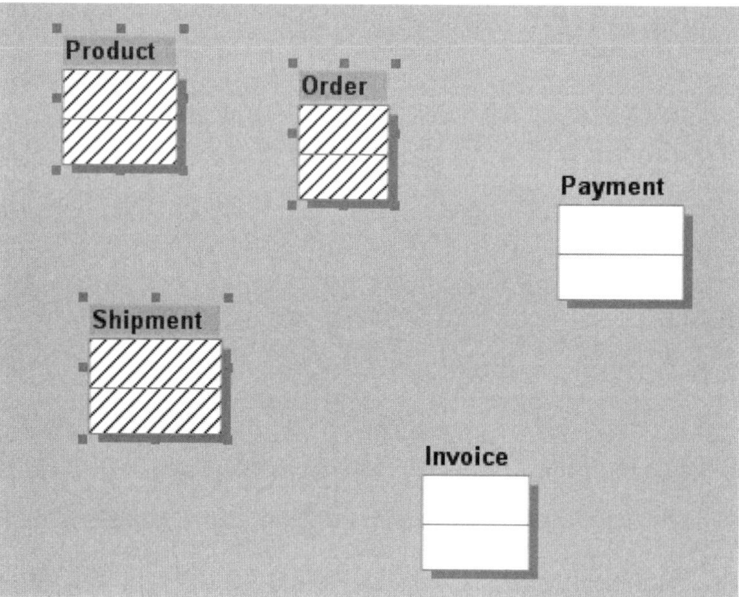

Before we leave the topic of Themes, let's create one more diagram, to reinforce the concept of Theme inheritance. Create a new diagram, using the **Diagram|New Diagram** menu. Notice that this new diagram, shown in Figure 8.86, uses the **Classic** theme that we defined for the model, not the Business Theme we created from the diagram. Since diagrams inherit their properties from the Model, it is the model's Theme that is used when a new diagram is created.

Figure 8.86 Diagrams Inherit Themes from the Model's Properties

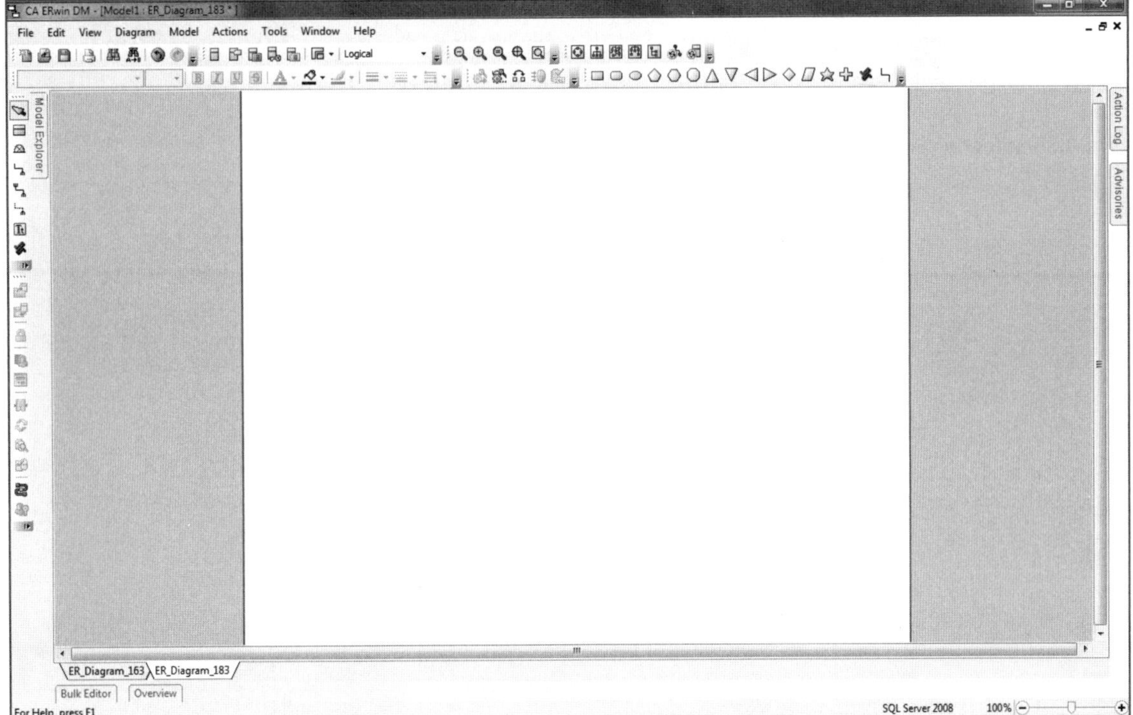

You should now have a good understanding of formatting Themes, and how inheritance can be used to cascade formatting selections throughout models, diagrams, and model objects. If you'd like an example of the finished model from this example, you can download the model **`Themes Example.erwin`** from the www.erwin.com/datamodelingmadesimple web site. In the next section, we'll discuss drawing objects, which can be used to add graphical elements to your model diagram.

Drawing Objects

Drawing objects can used to create visual elements in your diagram that not only make it easier to read, but can add meaningful contextual information as well. For example, in our previous scenario, we changed the shading of the three entities that are part of our scheduled design review. Another way to highlight these even more is to use a drawing shape. For example, we can draw a circle around the objects we'd like to review with our business sponsors. Using the model we created in our previous section (if you don't have this handy, you can download **`Themes Example.erwin`** from the www.erwin.com/datamodelingmadesimple web site), select the **Rounded Rectangle** object from the Drawing Toolbar, as shown in Figure 8.87.

Figure 8.87 Selecting a Rounded Rectangle from the Drawing Toolbar

Using this drawing shape, click on the diagram and drag the cursor so that you are 'lassoing' the three boxes you wish to highlight, as shown in Figure 8.88.

Figure 8.88 Selecting Area for Drawing Shape Placement

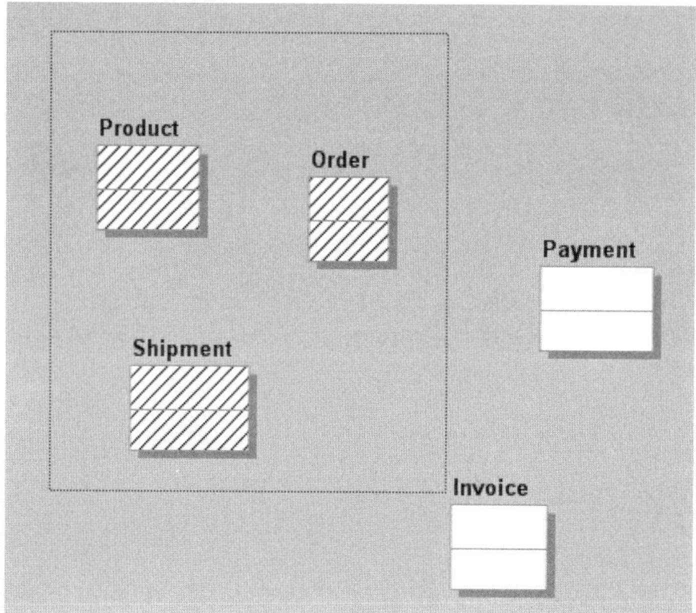

Release the cursor, and the rounded rectangle will be created on the diagram, as shown in Figure 8.89.

Figure 8.89 Using a Drawing Shape to Highlight Selected Objects

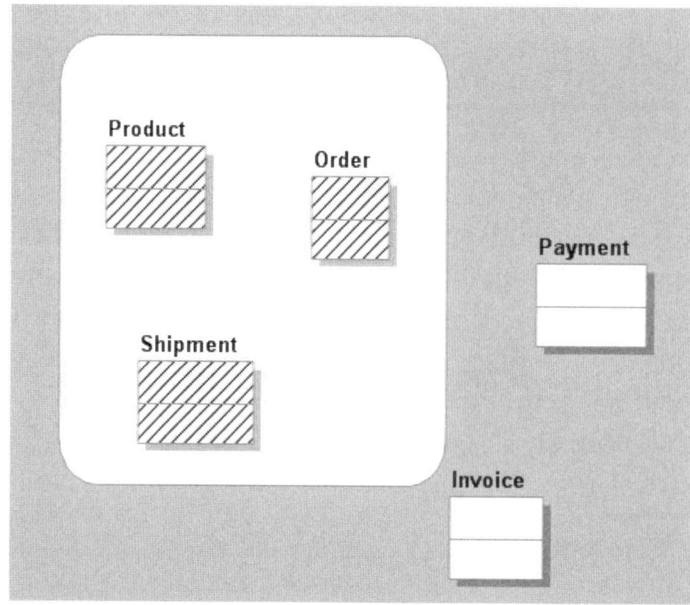

A nice feature of drawing shapes is that you can add additional text and metadata to the objects to add clarification and meaning. Let's add some additional information by double-clicking on the shape to invoke the ER Diagram Shape Properties Editor, as shown in Figure 8.90.

Figure 8.90 ER Diagram Shape Properties Editor

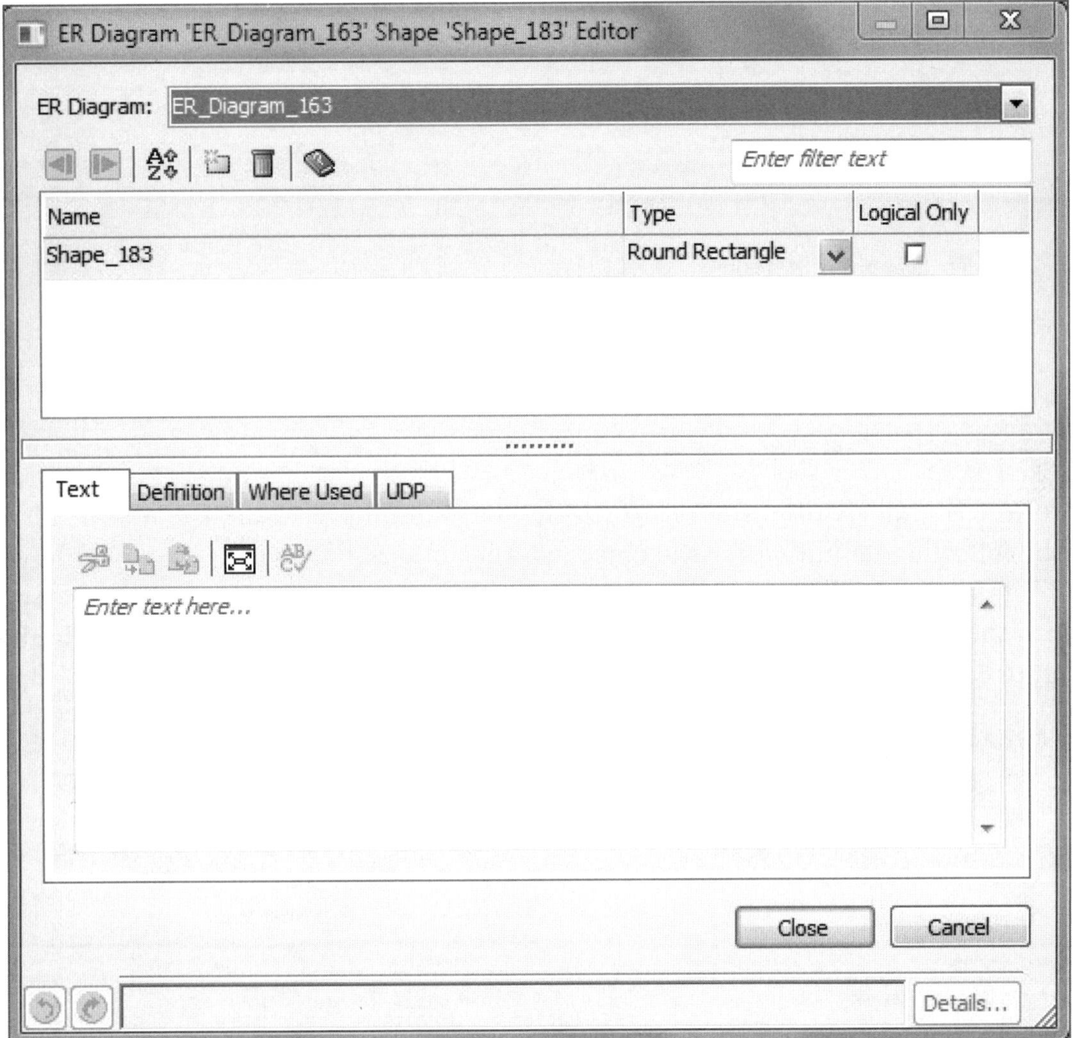

We'll use the fields in this editor to add context regarding the purpose of the shape. First, change the Name of the object to **Items for Review**. Next, add the text 'For Review; in the **Text** field box. This text will appear on the diagram. Lastly, check the **Logical Only** box, since we're only doing a design review on the logical model with the business sponsors. We'll review the physical model with the DBAs at a later date. These changes are shown in Figure 8.91.

Figure 8.91 Adding Context via Shape Properties

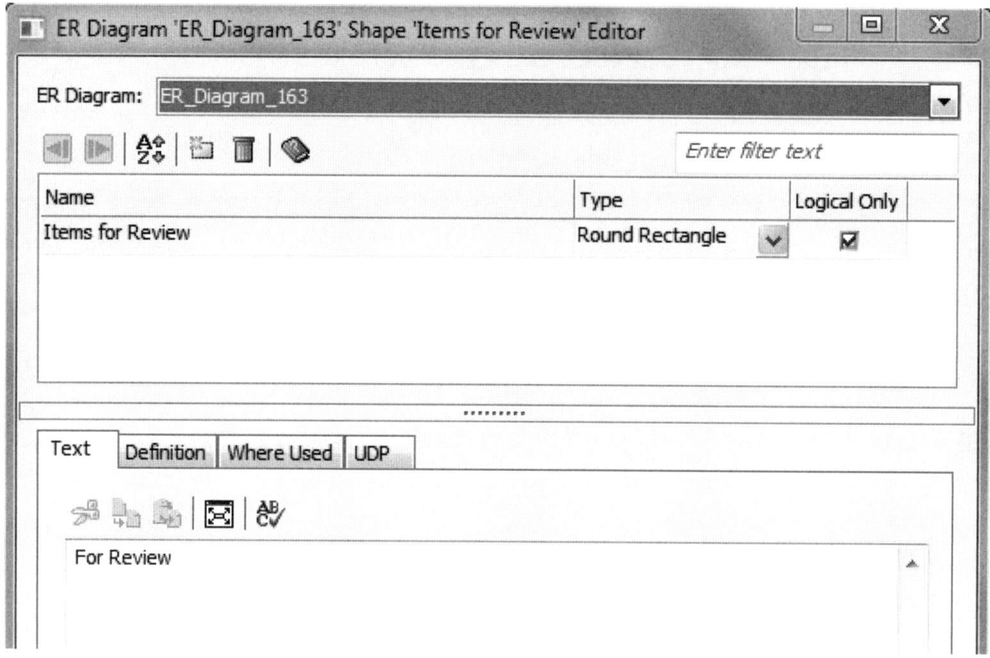

Before we close this editor and return to the diagram, move to the **Definition** tab, and add the following definition for the object, so that others reviewing this model have an idea of its purpose: "These objects are slated for the design review meeting on August 2nd with the Sales Accounting business sponsors". The completed **Definition** tab is shown in Figure 8.92.

Figure 8.92 Adding a Shape Definition

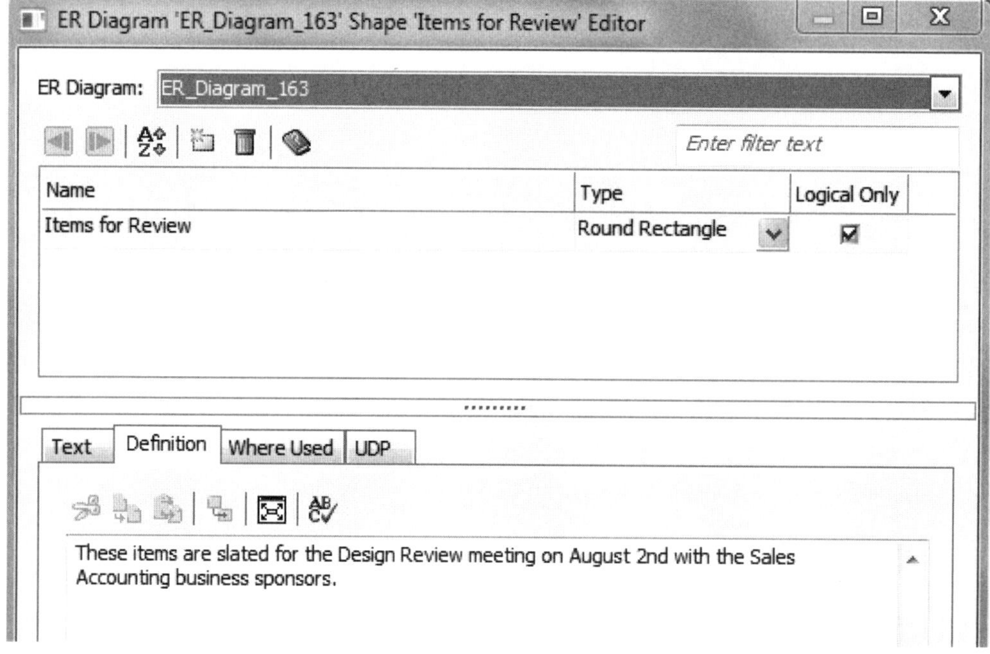

Select **Close** and you'll be returned to the diagram, as shown in Figure 8.93.

Figure 8.93 Drawing Shape with Textual Context Added

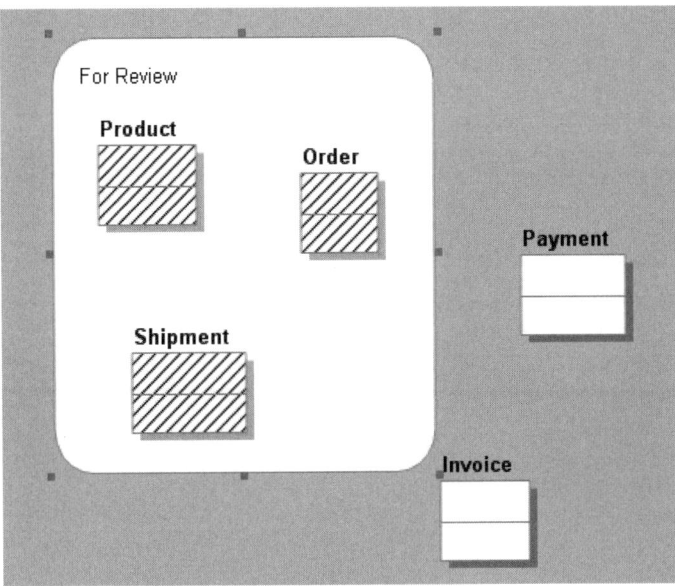

Another shape worth noting is the Annotation, which can act as a 'callout box' on your diagram to include notes and text fields that can easily attach to model objects. Let's add an Annotation to our diagram to see how this works. First, select the **Annotation** object from the Toolbox Toolbar, as shown in Figure 8.94.

Figure 8.94 Selecting the Annotation Object from the Toolbox Toolbar

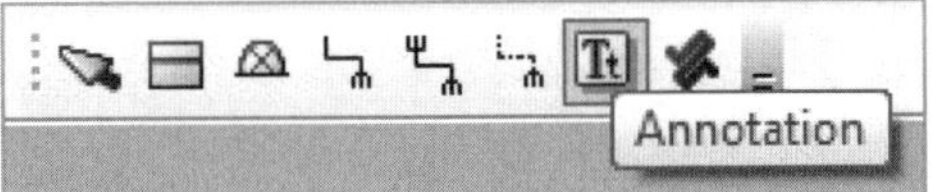

Click on the diagram to place the Annotation, as shown in Figure 8.95.

Figure 8.95 Placing an Annotation on the Diagram

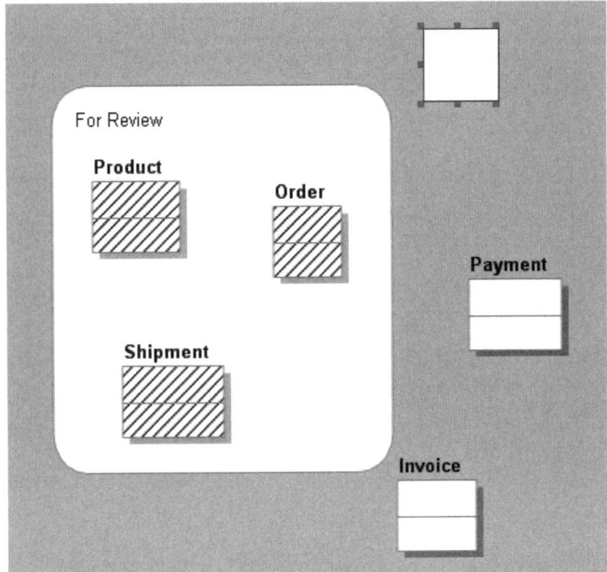

To add text to the Annotation, simply start typing, as it is dropped in auto-edit mode. Note that you may need to resize the object to show the entire text. In our example, we wanted to remember to ask Bob a question in this meeting--use the text in Figure 8.96.

Figure 8.96 Entering Text into an Annotation

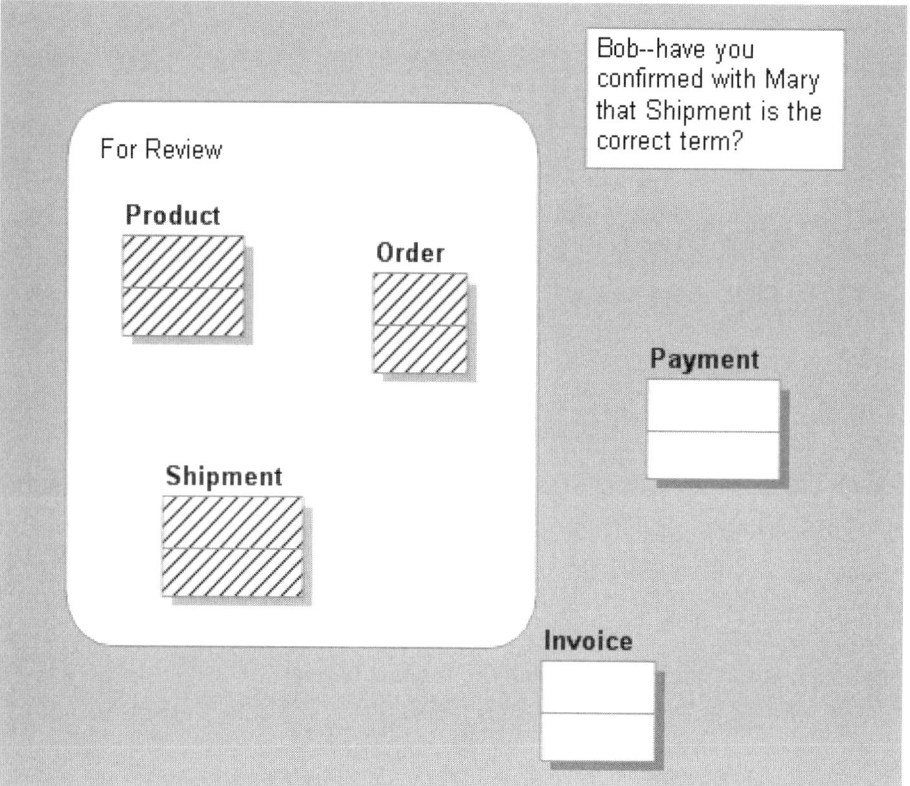

Another note about Annotations is that unlike drawing objects (which also can contain text) annotations are persisted across the model, not just the diagram, and therefore can be included as members in multiple diagrams or subject areas. The downside to this reusability is that annotations require more memory than drawing objects.

To associate this **Annotation** with the rectangle we created, use the **Connector** object to draw a line between the two objects, as shown in Figure 8.97. Using a **Connector** object is a better choice than a simple **Line** object, because a **Connector** acts similar to a relationship line in that it links a 'source' and 'target' object and moves automatically when you move the connected objects—you don't need to redraw the line every time the object is moved.

Figure 8.97 Selecting the Connector Object from the Drawing Toolbar

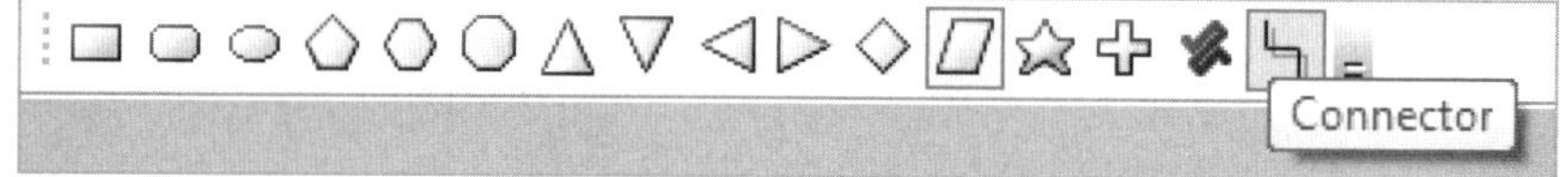

With the **Connector** button selected, click on the **Annotation** as the 'source' and the **Rounded Rectangle** as the 'target', which will create the linkage shown in Figure 8.98.

Figure 8.98 Linking Model Objects Using a Connector

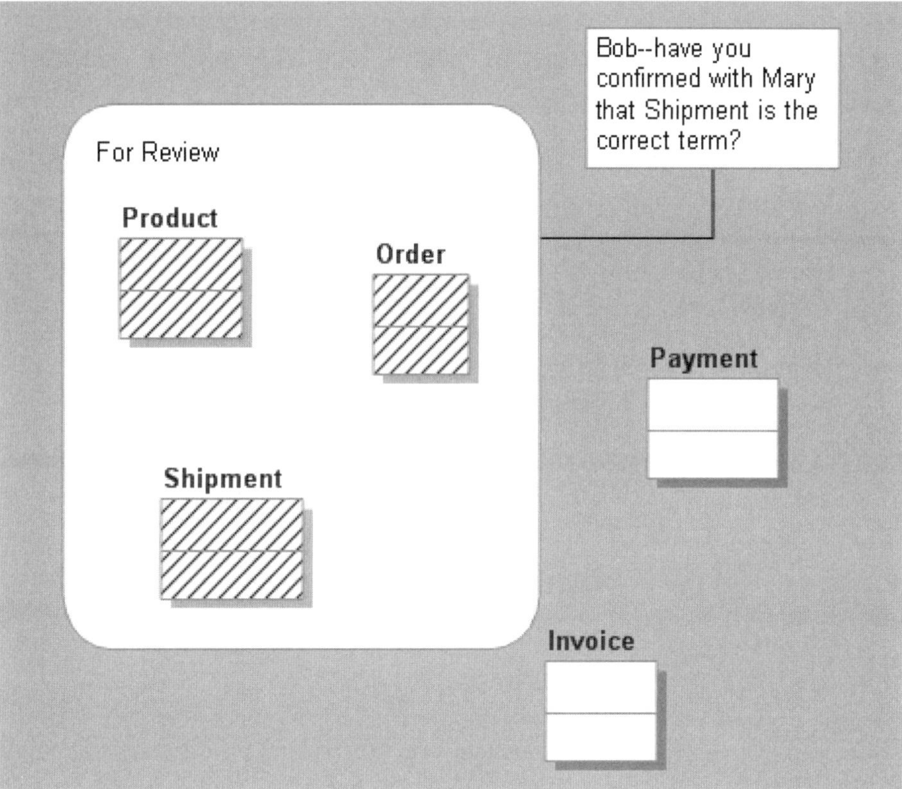

If you'd like an example of the finished model from this example, you can download the model **`Drawing Example.erwin`** from the www.erwin.com/datamodelingmadesimple web site.

There are a myriad of ways to use drawing objects in CA ERwin Data Modeler to enhance your model diagrams, limited only by your creativity. We've given you a taste of some options here. Go ahead and try a few scenarios on your own to get a feel for the possibilities.

Key Points

- Subject Areas allow you to define model scope and limit the model to certain business or functional areas.
- Diagrams allow you to define unique display options for various audiences.
- Model layout is important to the readability, and ultimate buy-in, of your model.
- Use colors and fonts to improve the readability of your diagram.
- Drawing objects can enhance your diagram by creating visual cues to highlight important areas.

CHAPTER 9
Personalizing Your Workspace

Working with data
Can be a complex process
My ERwin, my way!

In the last chapter, we discussed how to customize the organization and layout of your models for presenting to the various audiences in your organization. Equally important, however, is the environment that you see and use in your daily workflow of building and maintaining models. CA ERwin Data Modeler has a number of ways to personalize the workspace, toolbar, and workflow options to fit your needs. We'll cover a number of them in this section.

Personalizing the Workspace

The default CA ERwin Data Modeler workspace is shown in Figure 9.1, showing several of the main features of the CA ERwin Data Modeler Workspace highlighted with circled letters, 'A'-'I'. Chapter 3 provides a more detailed overview of the workspace—we include the workspace overview here as a reference, and starting point for our customization.

To view this default workspace, open the eMovies model, which is shown in Figure 9.1 (refer to Chapter 3 if you're not familiar with eMovies). While you'll see that there are a lot of helpful features and options, the workspace quickly becomes cluttered, leaving less room for the model diagram itself—where you'll likely spend the majority of your modeling efforts. You don't necessarily want to close the windows altogether, because you will use them from time-to-time, but you'd like to be able to visualize the entire diagram on the screen. One feature that helps with this challenge are on-demand user interface (UI) components, which can 'fly-in' on demand when needed, but otherwise remain minimized to avoid screen clutter.

Figure 9.1 Default CA ERwin Data Modeler Workspace

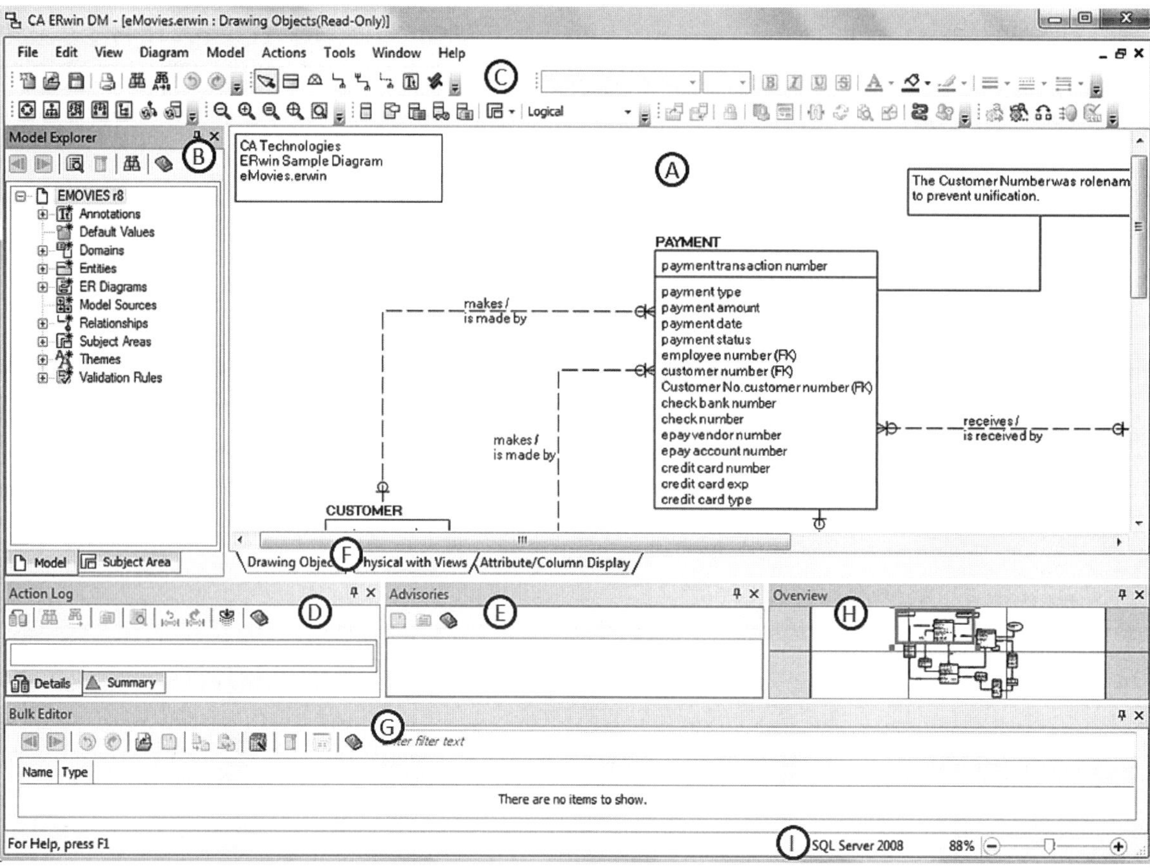

Key: A- Diagram Window, B- Model Explorer, C- Toolbars, D- Action Log Pane, E- Advisories Pane, F- Diagram Tabs, G- Bulk Editor Pane, H- Overview Pane, I- Status Bar

Let's change a pane to an on-demand UI component to show how this functionality works. One pane that is a good candidate for on-demand functionality is the Advisories Pane—most likely you won't need to view an advisory unless there is an issue, so you don't need this window displayed all of the time. To convert this pane to an on-demand UI component, click on the pushpin icon in the upper-right corner of the menu bar, as shown in Figure 9.2.

Figure 9.2 Using the Pushpin Icon to Create an On-Demand UI Component

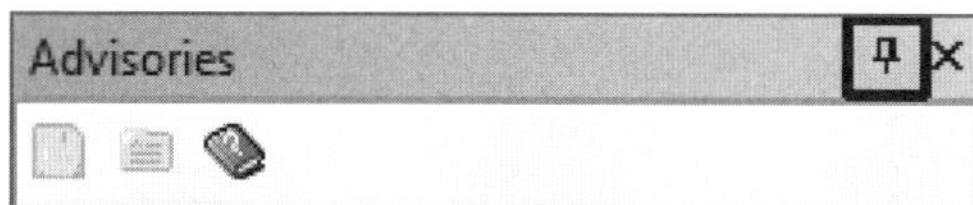

After clicking the pushpin, you will see that the Advisories Pane converts to an on-demand component resembling a folder tab, as shown in Figure 9.3. Note that your location might be slightly different, for example, below the action log, depending on the original placement of the pane.

Figure 9.3 Advisories Pane as an On-Demand UI Component

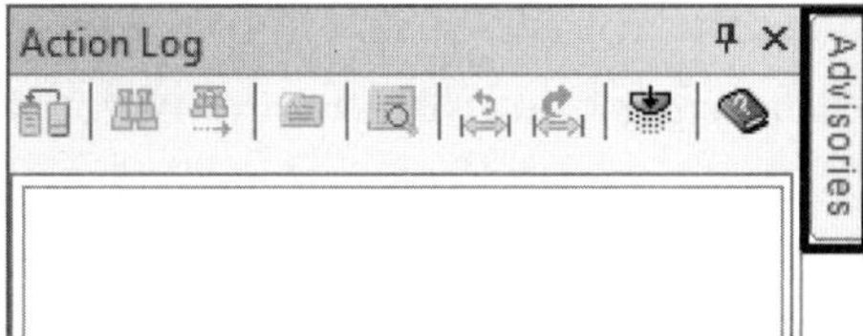

To invoke the on-demand functionality and see the contents of the pane, hover the cursor over or click the tab, and it activates the pane in a 'fly-out' manner, as shown in Figure 9.4. Notice that the pushpin icon is now lying on its side, indicating that the window is 'unpinned'.

Figure 9.4 Invoking the Advisories Pane On-Demand

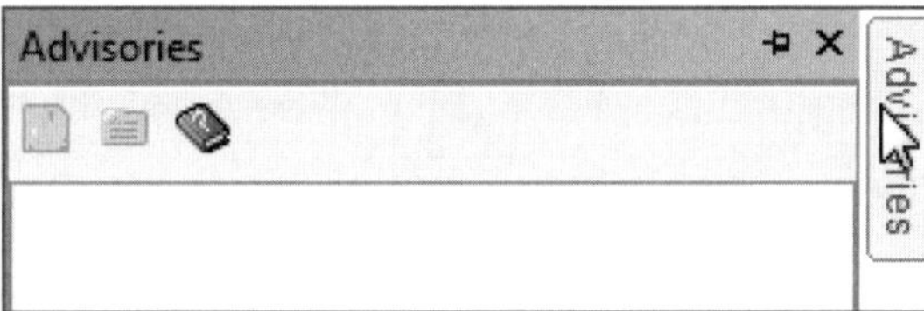

To hide this pane again, move your cursor away or click on another area of the workspace, and it auto-hides, reverting to the minimized view shown previously in Figure 9.3.

As you can see, this is a handy feature to maximize the diagram drawing area, without losing functionality. Give this a try yourself. Convert *all* of the workspace panes to on-demand components. Notice how this gives you a full-screen to work with for your diagram, as shown in Figure 9.5.

Figure 9.5 Maximized Diagram Drawing Area with All Workspace Panes On-Demand

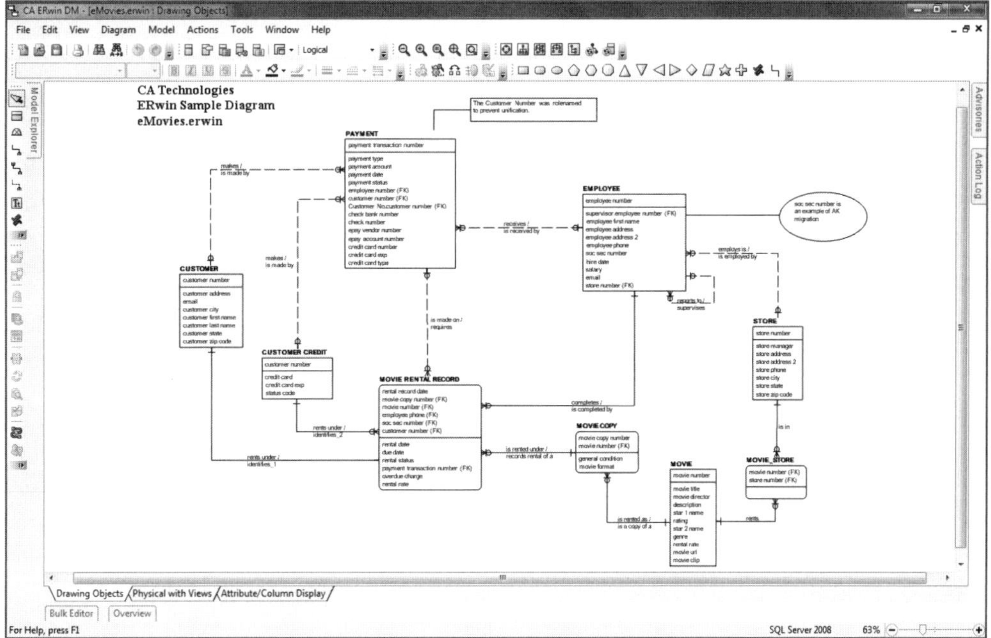

Another convenient option is to use a floating pane so that the window 'floats' above the diagram. This feature is especially helpful if you have more than one monitor. You can, for example, have your full diagram open on one monitor, with your Model Explorer, Bulk Editor, etc. open and active on a secondary monitor. A pane that is commonly converted to floating is the Bulk Editor, so let's use that for our example.

To convert a pane to floating from on-demand, the pane must first be docked or 'pinned' (i.e. not in on-demand mode). To pin a window so that it remains persistently open in the workspace, first click on the on-demand tab invoke the window pane. In our example, click on the Bulk Editor tab to invoke the Bulk Editor, as shown in Figure 9.6.

Figure 9.6 Invoking the Bulk Editor as an On-Demand UI Component

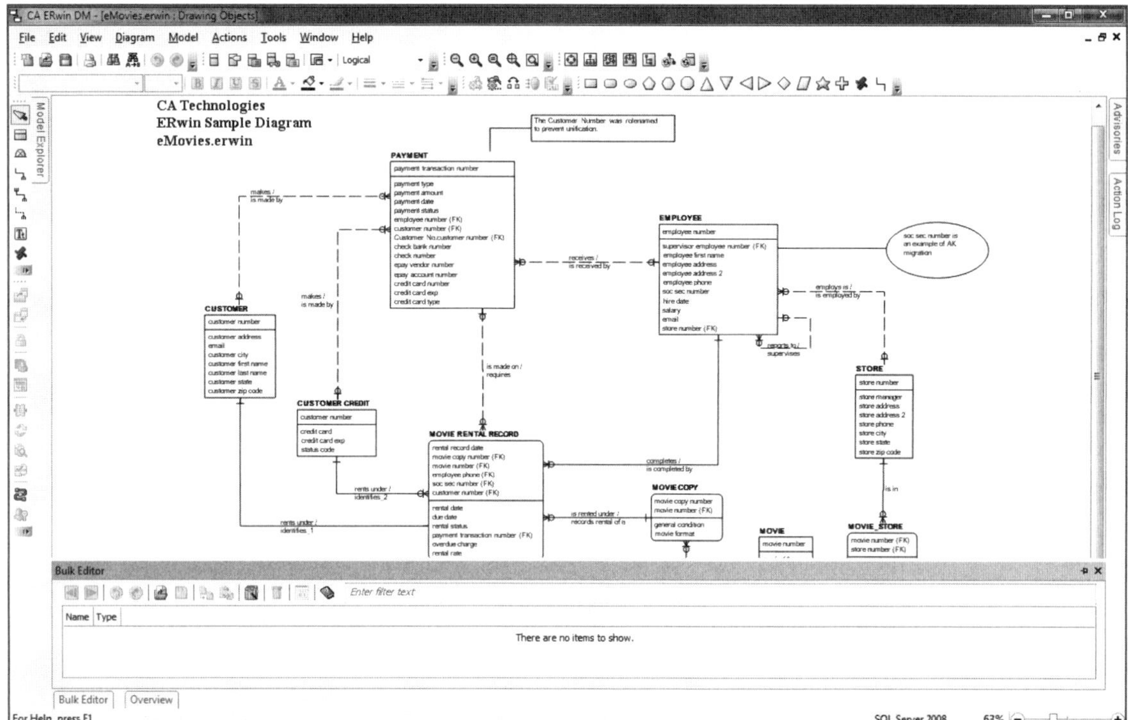

Notice that the pushpin icon is on its side, indicating that the window is 'unpinned'. Click on the pushpin icon to pin the window, and you will notice that the pushpin icon changes to vertical , and that the on-demand UI tab no longer appears, as shown in Figure 9.7.

Figure 9.7 Bulk Editor as 'Pinned' / Docked Window Pane

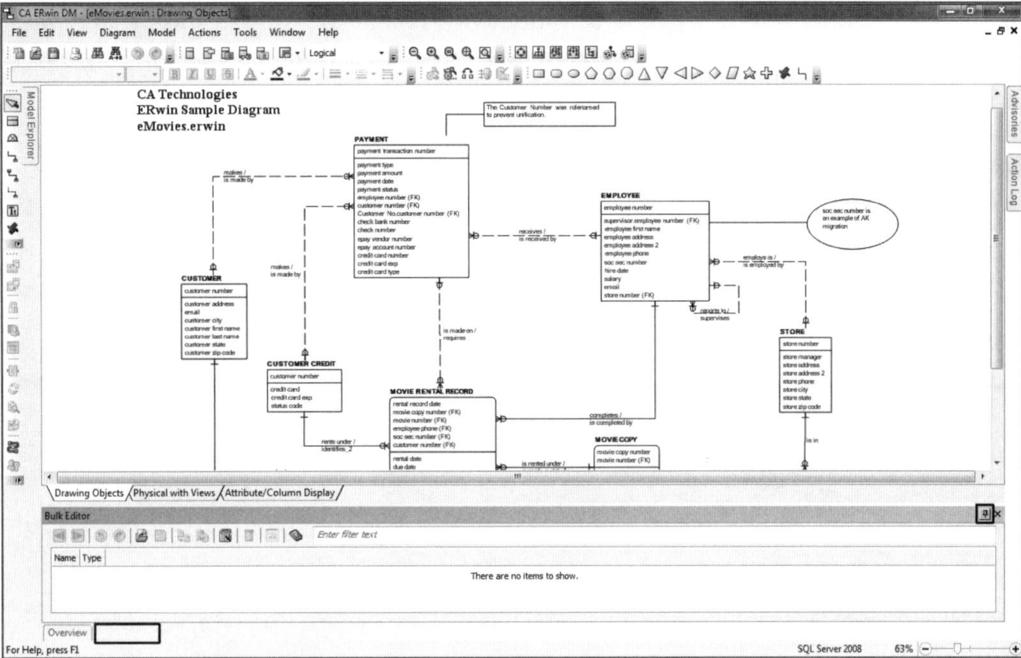

To cause the Bulk Editor pane to float above the diagram, and 'un-dock' from its current position, simply click on the menu bar, and drag the pane to the diagram area, as shown in Figure 9.8. You will see boxes with arrow indicators within them appear on the diagram, which are diagram hotspots for docking windows. Since we'd like the pane to float above the diagram, and not be docked to a particular position, we can ignore them for now. We'll cover these hotspots later in this section.

Figure 9.8 Converting Bulk Editor to a Floating Window

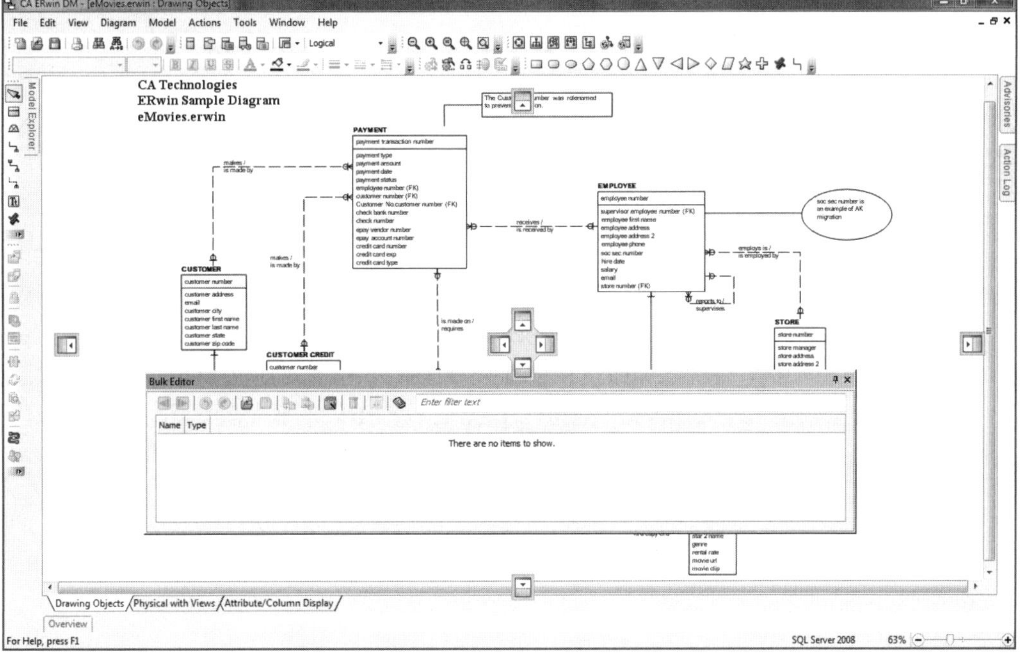

Release the mouse, and the Bulk Editor pane will appear as a floating window above the diagram, as shown in Figure 9.9. You can resize the pane, move the pane to a different position on the diagram, or even onto a second screen if you have dual monitors.

Figure 9.9 Bulk Editor as a Floating Window

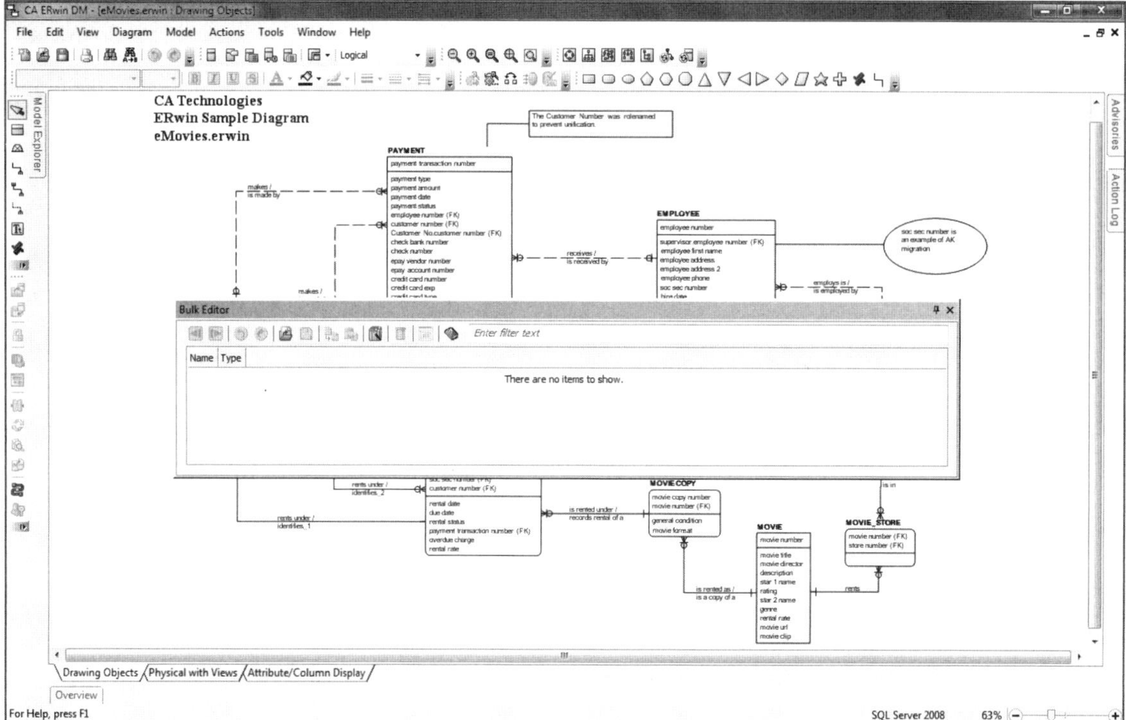

To return the Bulk Editor to its previous docked position, click on menu bar and begin to move window by dragging the cursor. Once you start moving the window, docking hotspots will appear on the diagram. Move the pane to the appropriate hot spot, and you will see a shadow appear, indicating where the window will be docked, as shown in Figure 9.10.

Release the mouse button, and the window becomes a docked window, as shown previously in Figure 9.7.

We've now covered three ways to manage the placement and functionality of window panes and CA ERwin Data Modeler: docked, which is a more traditional way of displaying panes, floating, which allows you to show panes above the diagram or even on another monitor, and on-demand, where panes fly-out as needed, leaving you with a maximized workspace to view and edit the diagram.

Figure 9.10 Shadow and Hot Spots Indicating Docking Position

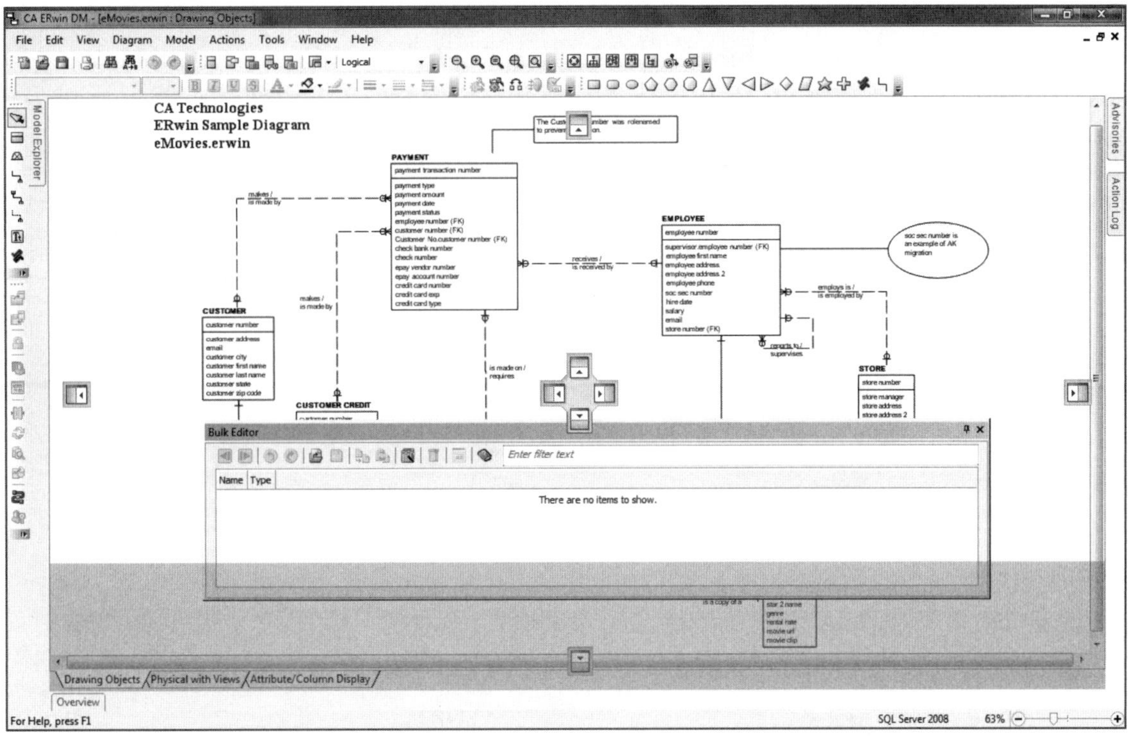

Customizing Toolbars

When you open the default workspace in CA ERwin Data Modeler, you'll see that there are a number of toolbars that help you quickly perform frequent tasks, as shown in Figure 9.11.

Figure 9.11 Default Toolbar Configuration in CA ERwin Data Modeler

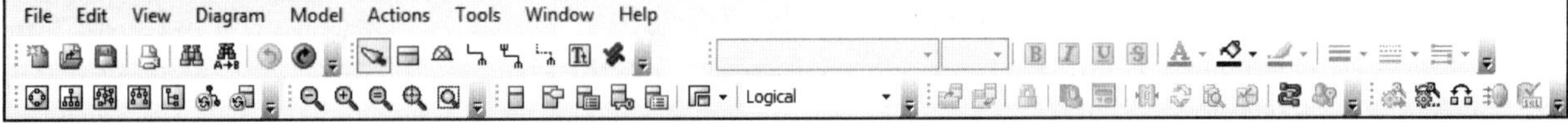

While some users find this default list of toolbars helpful, others feel that they clutter the workspace. Still others would like to see even more toolbars so that common tasks are shown. Luckily, the toolbars in CA ERwin Data Modeler can be completely customized to suit these difference preferences. For example, you can:

- Show or hide toolbars within the workspace
- Change the placement (docking position) of the toolbars within the workspace
- Show or hide individual buttons on the toolbars
- Add and customize new buttons on the toolbars

We'll cover all of these tasks in this section.

One of the most common tasks is to customize which toolbars you'd like to appear in your workspace. You may wish to hide particular toolbars that aren't commonly used, for example, to save space within the workspace. To show or hide a given toolbar, select **View|Toolbars** from the **Main Menu**, as shown in Figure 9.12. Select (check) a toolbar to make it visible in the workplace and clear (uncheck) to hide it.

Figure 9.12 Showing or Hiding Toolbars

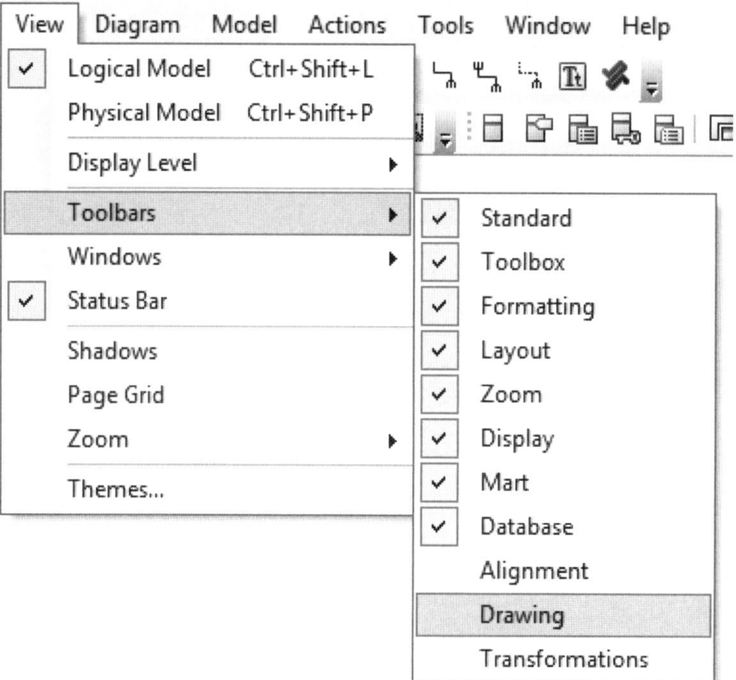

All of the toolbars are dockable and floatable so that you can drag them to dock along the edge of the workspace or let them float freely in the window if you prefer. For example, you may wish to have the Standard Toolbar appear along the left side of the workspace, instead of along the top. To move a toolbar from its default location, first select the toolbar handle at the left side of the toolbar, as shown in Figure 9.13.

Figure 9.13 Selecting the Toolbar Handle to Change Toolbar Location

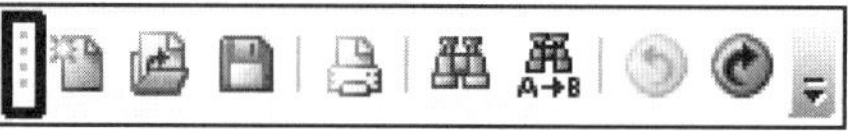

Next, drag the toolbar to the desired location and release the mouse. You can have the toolbar either float on the diagram, as shown in Figure 9.14.

Figure 9.14 Standard Toolbar as a Floating Toolbar

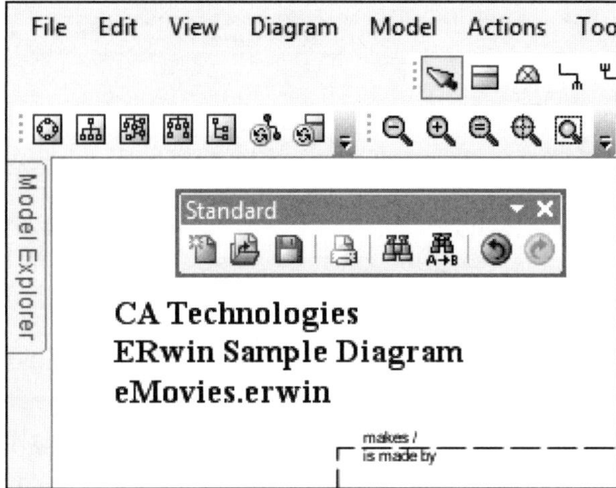

or docked along the left-hand side, as shown in Figure 9.15, which was our preference for this example.

Figure 9.15 Standard Toolbar Docked to the Left of the Workspace

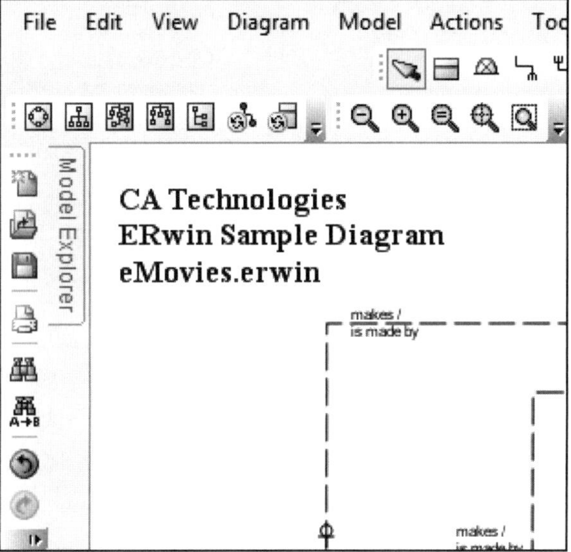

You can also customize which buttons are displayed on each toolbar. For example, you may wish to remove buttons that you do not use frequently to unclutter your workspace. For example, we may wish to hide some of the toolbar buttons on the Formatting Toolbar, which has quite a few default options. In our case, we'd like to remove the **Line pattern** and **Line ends** buttons. Since the patterns and endpoints of relationship lines have semantic meaning, we'd prefer to have the relationship semantics define the line formats (e.g. dashed line for a non-identifying relationship), and not have them overwritten by the modeler. To customize the toolbar buttons, first select the **Toolbar Options** menu, as indicated by a downward-pointing arrow at the rightmost side of the toolbar, shown in Figure 9.16.

Figure 9.16 Invoking the Toolbar Options Menu to Show/Hide Toolbar Buttons

The **Add or Remove Buttons** menu appears as shown in Figure 9.17.

Figure 9.17 Add or Remove Buttons Menu

Add or Remove Buttons

Select this menu, and a submenu appears showing a list of all toolbars that appear within the same docking position, as shown in Figure 9.18. For example, our first line of toolbars contains the `Toolbox Toolbar` and `Formatting Toolbar`, so these are the items that appear in the list.

Figure 9.18 Selecting a Toolbar for Customization

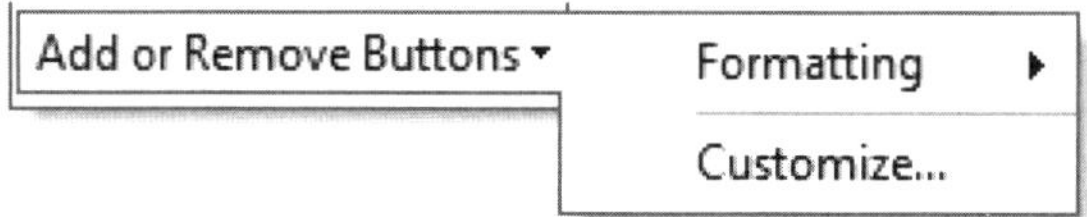

Select the **Formatting** menu item, and a list of toolbar buttons appears, as shown in Figure 9.19. A checkbox ✓ next to the button item indicates that the button is shown on the toolbar.

Figure 9.19 Customizing Buttons on the Formatting Toolbar

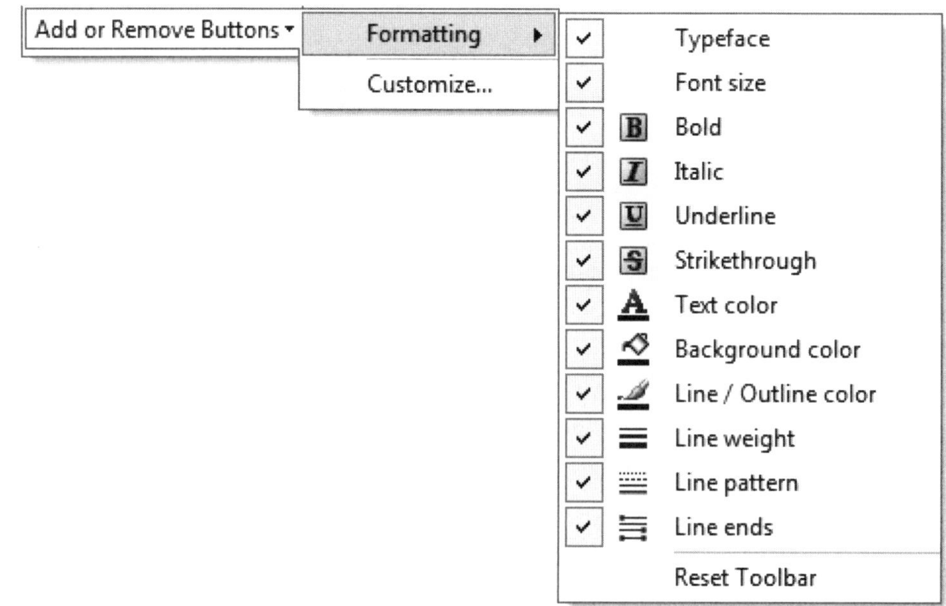

To hide the **Line pattern** and **Line ends** buttons, simply click on those menu options and the check box will be removed, as shown in Figure 9.20. Note also the **Reset Toolbar** menu item. If you change your mind, and would like to return to the default toolbar configuration, select this menu item to restore the defaults.

Figure 9.20 Hiding Toolbar Buttons

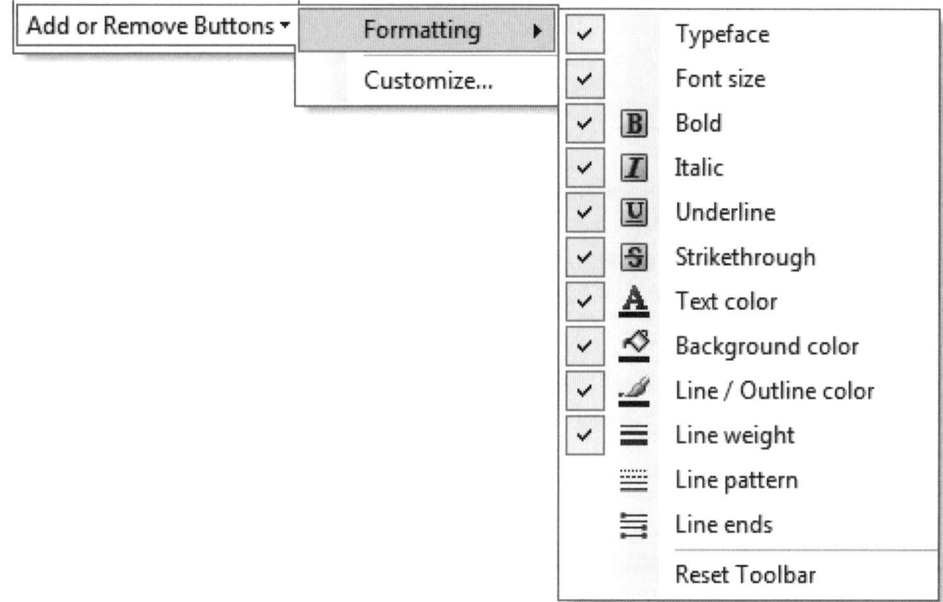

To exit this menu, simply click on another area of the workspace, and it will disappear. Once you've closed this menu, you'll see that the Formatting Toolbar appears with the **Line pattern** and **Line ends** buttons removed, as shown in Figure 9.21.

Figure 9.21 Customized Formatting Toolbar

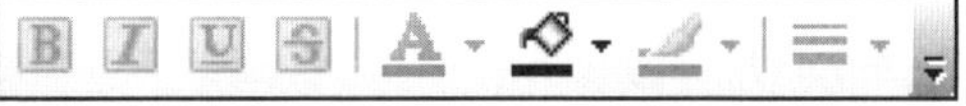

You can also create your own toolbars to house common functions that you would like quickly available. Say, for example, we'd like to have common diagram editing functions available on the toolbar. We can create a custom toolbar for these functions and add it to the workspace. To create a new toolbar, select **Tools|Customize** from the **Main Menu**, and the Customize Editor appears opened to the **Toolbars** tab, as shown in Figure 9.22. You can also invoke this menu from the toolbar menus, as shown in Figure 9.18.

Figure 9.22 Toolbars Tab of the Customize Editor

Within the Customize Editor, select the **New** button, and the New Toolbar Editor appears, as shown in Figure 9.23.

Figure 9.23 New Toolbar Editor

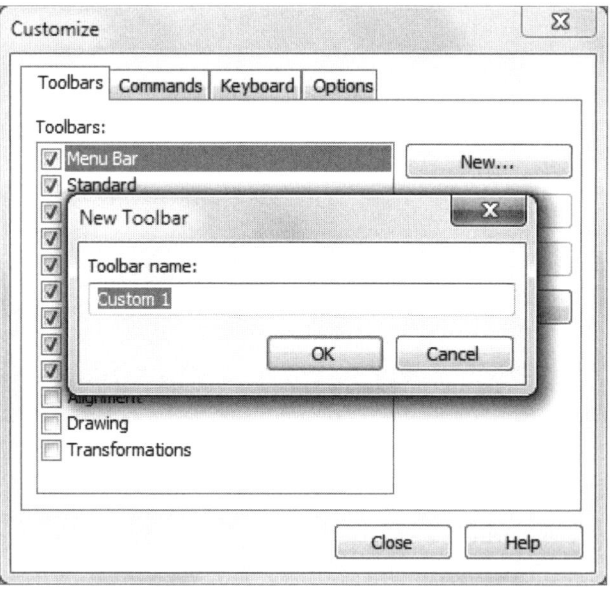

We'll call this toolbar the **Diagram Editing** toolbar, so type **Diagram Editing** in the **Toolbar name:** field and then press **OK**. The new **Diagram Editing Toolbar** now appears at the bottom of the **Toolbars** tab, as shown in Figure 9.24.

Figure 9.24 New Toolbar Shown in the Customize Editor

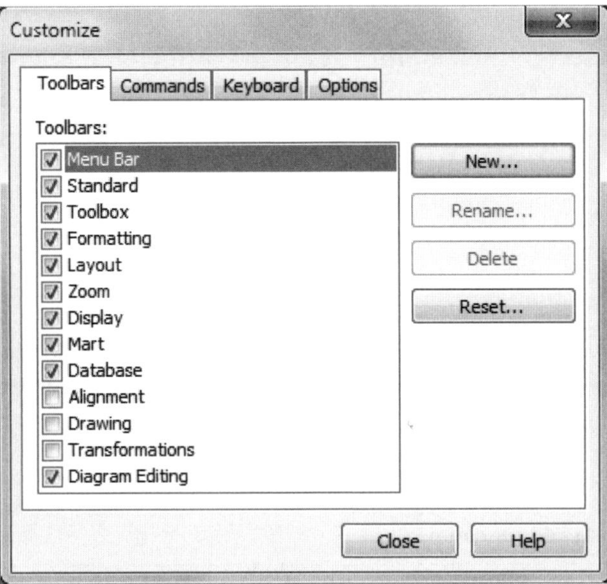

Notice that a blank toolbar is also created in the workspace, as shown in Figure 9.25.

Figure 9.25 Empty Toolbar Created in the Workspace

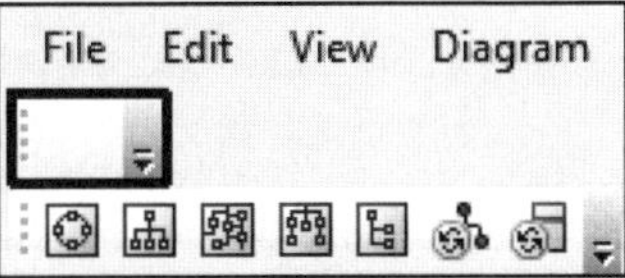

We'll want to add buttons to this empty toolbar. Move to the **Commands** tab of the Customize Editor and select **Diagram** from the **Categories** list box, as shown in Figure 9.26.

Figure 9.26 Commands tab of the Customize Editor

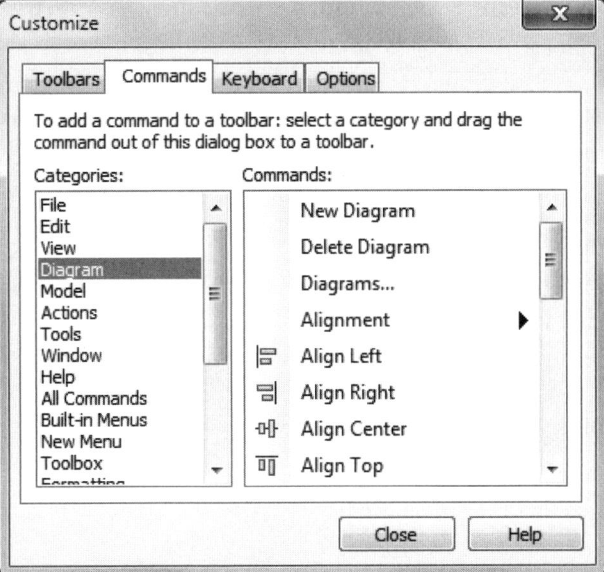

We'd like to be able to quickly add new diagrams to our model using this new toolbar, so select **New Diagram** from the **Commands** list box and drag it to the empty toolbar that we just created. Release the mouse and you'll see a button for **New Diagram** added to the toolbar, as shown in Figure 9.27. Note that there is no icon assigned for this particular action, so text is used.

Figure 9.27 Diagram Editing Toolbar with New Diagram Button Added

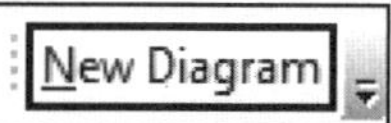

To flesh out this toolbar, add the **Delete Diagram** command from the **Diagram** category as well. Then, move to the **Edit** category and add the **Delete from Diagram**, **Undo**, and **Redo** commands to the toolbar. The finalized toolbar will look similar to Figure 9.28.

Figure 9.28 Finalized Diagram Editing Toolbar

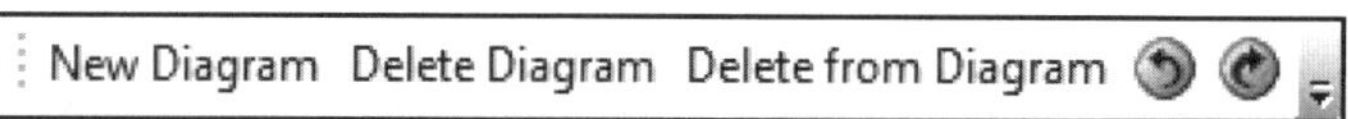

As you've seen, customizing and creating your own toolbars are an easy, flexible way to enhance your productivity by making common tasks available literally 'at the click of a button'.

Customizing Keyboard Shortcuts

Keyboard shortcuts are another way to make common functions readily available. There are a number of predefined keyboard shortcuts, and you can create your own as well. In this section, we'll discuss how to create your own customized keyboard shortcuts. To see a listing of existing shortcuts, and to create new shortcuts, select **Tools|Customize** from the **Main Menu**, and move to the **Keyboard** tab of the resulting Customize Editor, as shown in Figure 9.29. Appendix B provides a full listing of the predefined keyboard shortcuts for your reference.

The **Keyboard** tab lists available commands by category and displays their default key assignments. For example, Figure 9.29 shows that the **New** command in the **File** category can be invoked by pressing **`Ctrl+N`**. Let's create our own keyboard shortcut of **`Alt-Z`** for the **Save As** command, since we use that frequently. Select **Save As** from the **Commands** list box. Next, place your cursor in the **Press new shortcut key** field and hold down the **`Alt`** and **`Z`** keys simultaneously.

Figure 9.29 Keyboard Tab of the Customize Editor

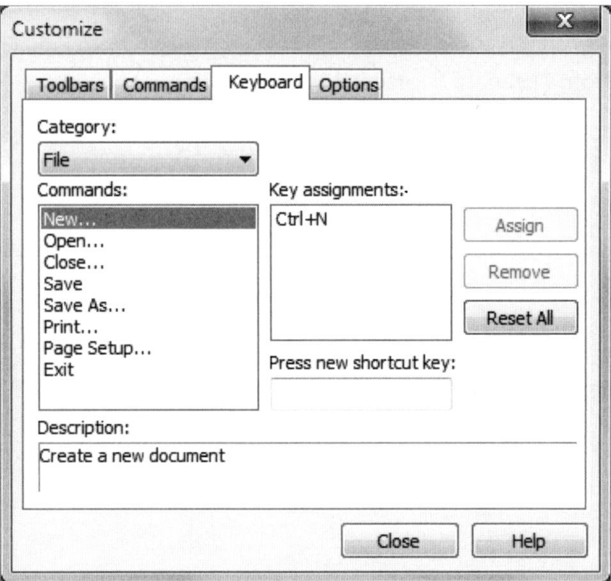

The text describing these shortcut keys will be automatically populated, as shown in Figure 9.30.

Figure 9.30 Defining a Custom Keyboard Shortcut

Next click the **Assign** button to associate this new shortcut key with the **Save As** command. Notice that the shortcut key description has now been moved to the **Key assignments** field, as shown in Figure 9.31. If this shortcut key had already been assigned to another command, you would have received an informational message indicating that the shortcut is already assigned, and giving you the option of overwriting the existing shortcut. In our case, however, no other commands were using the **`Alt+Z`** shortcut, so we did not have a conflict. You are also able to assign multiple key assignments for a given command, but in this case, we'll just use one key assignment to keep it simple.

Figure 9.31 Assigning a Custom Keyboard Shortcut

To test out our newly-created shortcut, select **Close** to return to the workspace window. Type **`Alt+Z`** and you'll see that the **Save As** menu is invoked. Nice work!

Using the Action Log and Undo/Redo

From time to time, we all make mistakes. Who has not been in the situation where you are working on a model or document and realize you need to undo an action or transaction you've just completed or, even worse, that you've completed 10 minutes ago—before you made several other changes that you'd like to keep. In CA ERwin Data Modeler, this is where the Action Log can help.

Most software products on the market today have an 'undo' feature, allowing you to reverse the last action you've performed, or even reverse the last *x* number of transactions in sequential order. CA ERwin Data Modeler goes a step beyond this traditional behavior and allows you to selectively choose which transactions you'd like to reverse.

The best way to demonstrate this behavior is through an example. First, create a blank logical model so that we can experiment without harming any existing models (refer to Chapter 3 if you need help with creating a model).

Once you've created this model, perform the following actions:

1. Create a new entity and name it **Customer**
2. Select the **Customer** entity on the diagram, then press the TAB key to move to the primary key area. Create a primary key attribute called **customer_id**.
3. Create a second entity called **Account**

Your model should look similar to Figure 9.32.

Figure 9.32 Sample Model to Test Action Log

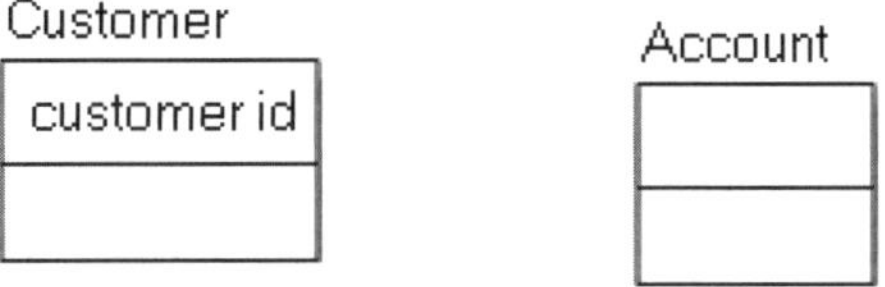

Let's take a look at the Action Log shown in Figure 9.33 to see how it has tracked these changes. Note that the first action, **Create Model**, is at the bottom, and the last action Set **Entity property Name**, is at the top. You can easily follow the sequence of your actions from creating the model, to creating and naming the entities and their attributes. Expanding the + sign next to each entry gives you more detail about each action, for example, what the name of the entity or attribute is that you defined.

Figure 9.33 Action Log

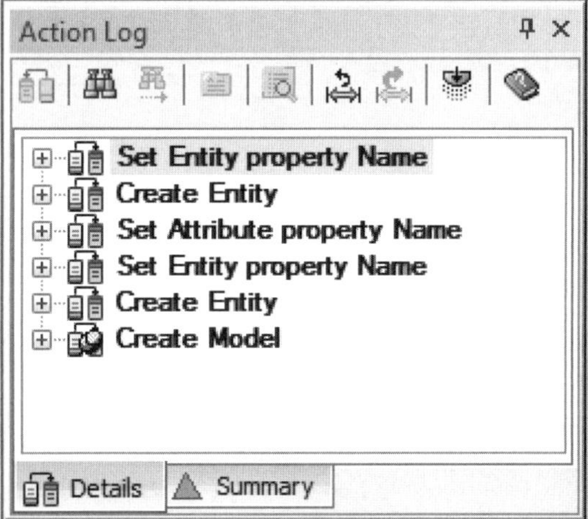

Say, for example, we've decided that we don't want the **customer_id** attribute in the model after all. To reverse only this change, while keeping the rest of the changes intact, select the **Set Attribute property Name** entry and expand the menu tree to show the **Created [Attribute] object: 'customer id'** action. Then, select the **Reverse** icon, as shown in Figure 9.34. Notice that there are several other steps that had occurred 'behind the scenes' in the action log after you had created the attribute-creating key groups, for example. This is part of the power of the Action Log-cleaning up all of the related actions and referential integrity rules that are needed as a result of a model change.

Figure 9.34 Reversing a Transaction Using the Action Log

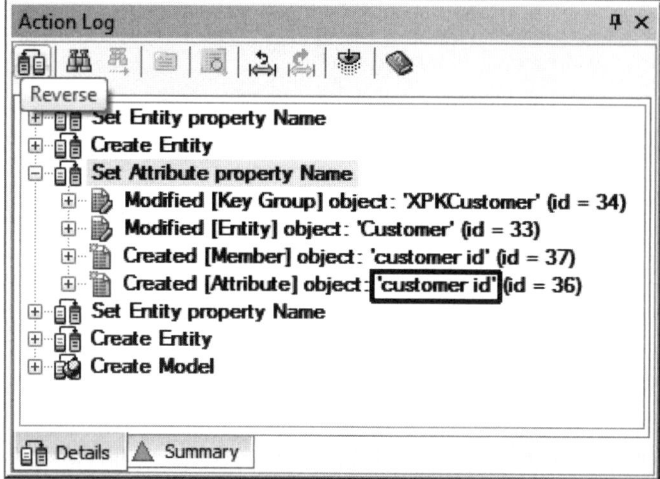

Your model will now have the **customer_id** attribute removed, but the other changes you made have remained intact, as shown in Figure 9.35.

Figure 9.35 Model After Reversing Attribute Creation

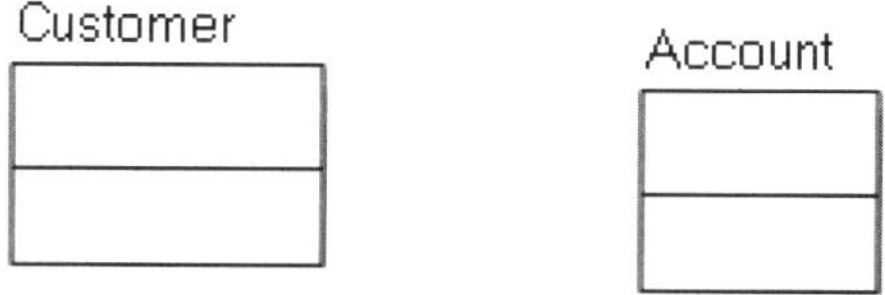

You'll also notice that the reversal is also tracked in the Action Log, as shown in Figure 9.36.

Figure 9.36 Tracking Reversals in the Action Log

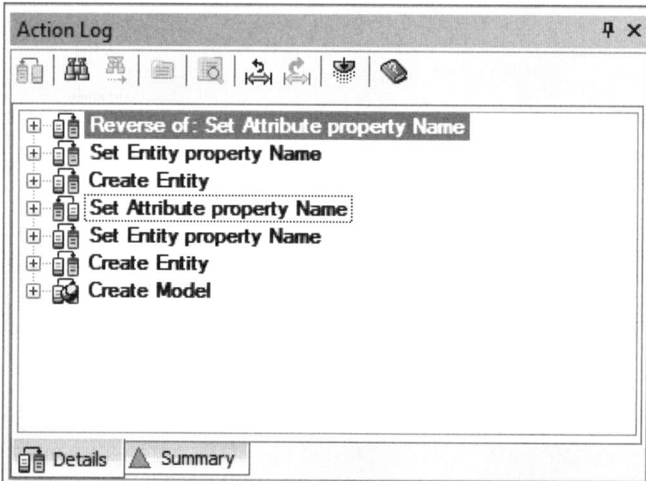

The traditional undo/redo found in other software products also exists in CA ERwin Data Modeler as well. **Undo** simply reverses the last item in the action log. For example, if you select **Edit|Undo** from the **Main Menu** (or use `Ctrl+Z`), you'll see that the Action Log shows the last item in normal (un-bolded) text and its corresponding icon uncolored, as shown in Figure 9.37.

Figure 9.37 Showing 'Undone' Actions

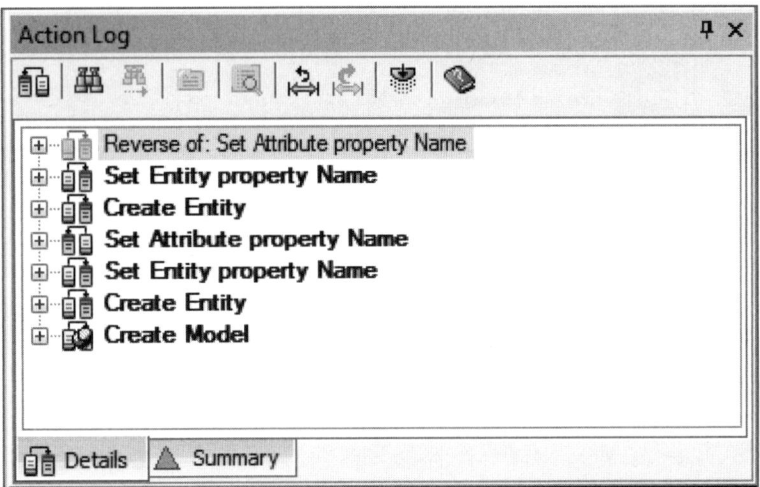

Since we've undone our last reversal, the **customer_id** entity will now re-appear in the model, as shown in Figure 9.38.

Figure 9.38 Re-creating an Attribute Using Undo

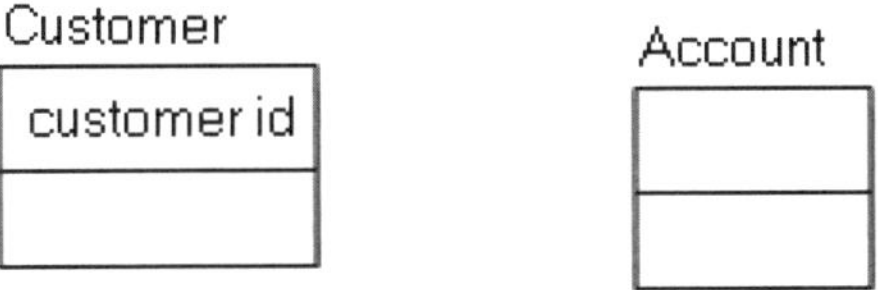

You can also reverse entire groups of changes—you don't need to select them one at a time. For example, perhaps we want to start completely from scratch and undo all of the changes we've made to the model so far. To do this, select the first action we performed, **Create Entity**, and then select the **Undo to Selected Transaction** icon, as shown in Figure 9.39.

Figure 9.39 Using the 'Undo to Selected Transaction' Feature

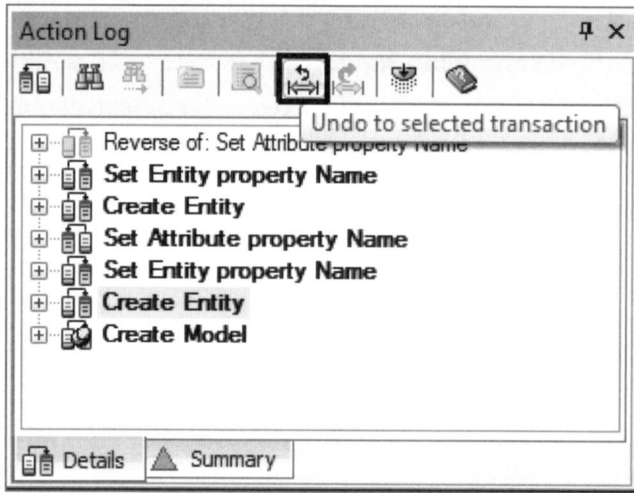

You'll now have a blank model, with all actions after **Create Model** grayed out in the Action Log, as shown in Figure 9.40.

Figure 9.40 Result of Undo to Selected Transaction Feature

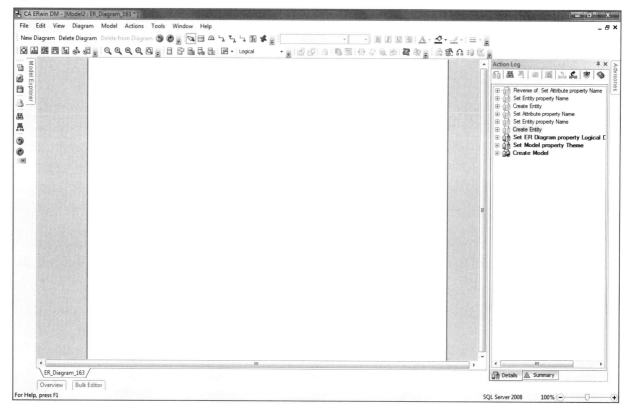

Note that the Action Log tracks all changes ***within a session***. A session persists as long as your model is open. A session doesn't correlate with a save, but with the open model. Once you close the model, the Action Log is cleared.

The Action Log is a very powerful feature that can help improve your productivity (and save your skin!) once you become familiar with it. So spend some time with sample models understanding how transaction reversals work.

Key Points

- The default workspace can be customizing by changing how windows are displayed and managed: docked, floating, on-demand, or hidden.
- Toolbars can be customized to hide/show toolbars, hide/show toolbar buttons, or create your own toolbar.
- Keyboard shortcuts can be customized to invoke common tasks with a keystroke pattern, e.g. Alt+Z.
- The Action Log is a powerful way to manage data model governance, with the ability to reverse transactions, even those transactions performed multiple steps earlier in your modeling session.
- Make use of the various customization options in CA ERwin Data Modeler to personalize the tool for your own unique workflow and usage.

One of the main benefits of data modeling is to create consistent, reusable design standards. Once we've created designs on both the business and technical level, we want to make sure that these designs are used across the organization in a consistent way. CA ERwin Data Modeler has a number of tools and techniques that support the reuse of your data model components.

Let's use an example to help explain how standards can assist with consistency and reuse. In our sample organization, we are integrating several customer databases and are struggling to create a consistent format for customer data. In looking at the various database systems that exist worldwide, here are just a few of the problems that we came up with:

- In the US, the standard length for the **last name** field is 20. In India, the standard length is 35, and names are truncated when entered into the US system.
- Several regions in Europe and Africa use the term **surname** instead of **last name** in their databases.

- In several Asian regions, the **last name** data element that is used in the US is considered the **first name**.
- Each region is using a different set of country codes.
- There are data quality issues in the **customer age** field. Some departments have been entering a value of '999' to indicate that the customer is deceased, which is not an approved entry, and is creating problems for reporting.
- And many, many more.

These issues are just a small subset of the typical data quality and standardization issues that arise.

This section will provide an overview of several of the main components of CA ERwin Data Modeler that help you create reusable standards to assist in solving these issues, including: Domains (Chapter 10), Validation Rules (Chapter 11), Naming Standards (Chapter 12), Data Type Standards (Chapter 13), User Defined Properties (Chapter 14), and Model Templates (Chapter 15). We'll also cover ways to share these standards across the organization through Reporting, Querying, and Editing (Chapter 16).

CHAPTER 10
Domains

Domains add focus
Prescribe values, length, and names
All elements one

Recall from Chapter 5 that a domain is a complete set of possible values that can be assigned to an element, and that domains can be used for validation criteria. Domains can be used to help create standardized data elements that have common formats, ranges, validation criteria, and even naming conventions.

For example, we may wish to create a reusable domain for the data element **first name**, shown in Figure 10.1. Once we've agreed on a common data type and length, we want to make sure that all attributes use the same criteria. We can also use domains to create naming conventions, and even standardized definitions. For example, you'll see that all attributes using this domain use the same convention of entity name + domain name: **customer first name**, **employee first name**, **vendor first name**. We can create these customized names and definitions with the help of CA ERwin Data Modeler's macro language.

Figure 10.1 Using Domains to Promote Consistency

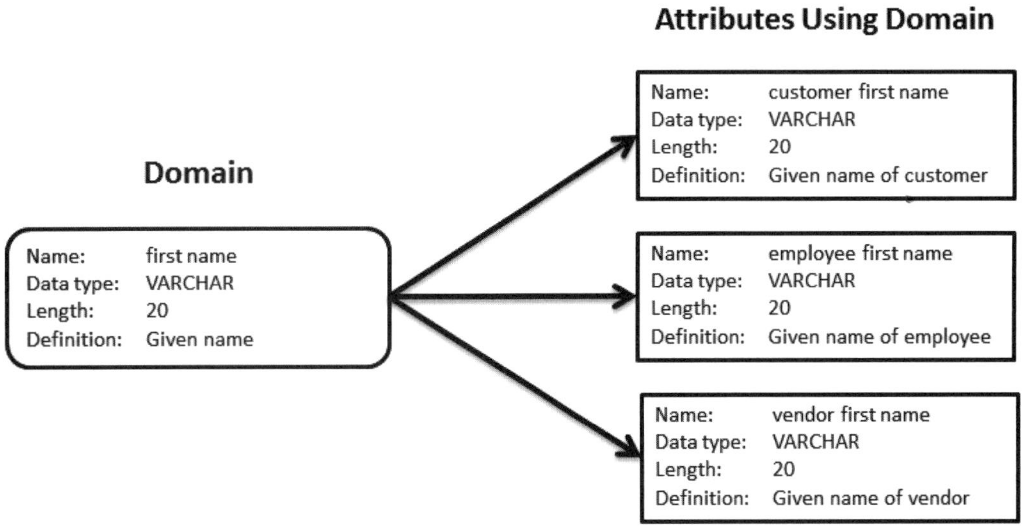

Creating Domains

CA ERwin Data Modeler's Domain Dictionary is a centralized storage point to create and maintain these reusable elements for use across the enterprise. To access the

Domain Dictionary, you'll need to have an open model. For this example, create a new logical/physical model with a target database of DB2 for LUW v9.7 and save it as **domain_example.erwin**. If you have difficulty with how to do this, refer to Chapter 3.

Select **Model|Domains** from the **Main Menu**. The Domain Dictionary appears as in Figure 10.2.

Figure 10.2 Domain Dictionary

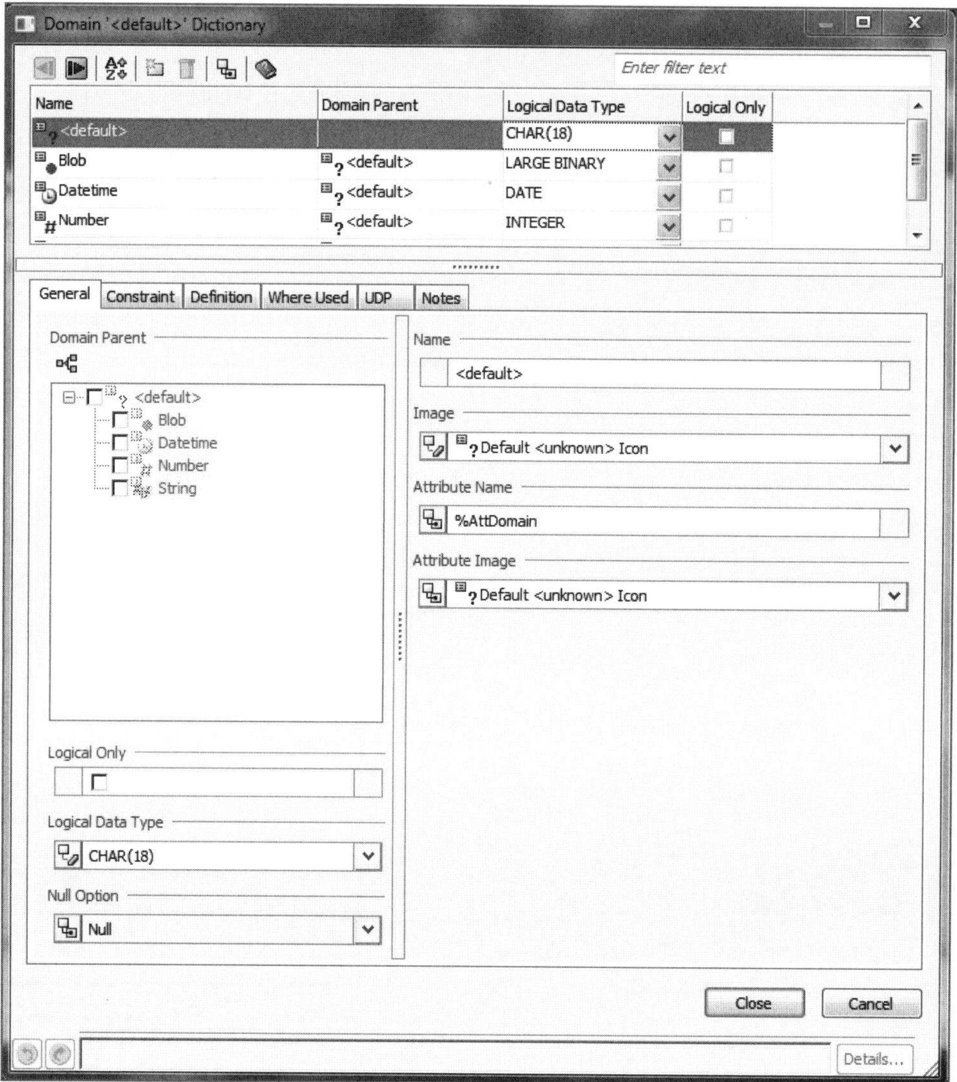

You'll see that the upper portion of the editor lists the **Name**, **Domain Parent**, and **Logical Data Type** for each domain. To explain the meaning of the **Parent** field, it's helpful to first discuss domain hierarchies and inheritance in CA ERwin Data Modeler. The concept of domain hierarchies is an important one for reuse, and it is worth going into more detail on this now, before we create our own domains.

Domain hierarchies allow you to reuse domain definitions through a process of inheritance. Child domains can inherit properties from their parent domain, as well as specify their own unique properties and/or override the properties of the parent. Changes made to a parent domain cascade to child domains for all inherited properties. If you choose to override certain properties in a child domain, these properties will not be affected by changes to the parent and will remain unique to the child domain.

For example, in Figure 10.3, we have inherited from the **String** domain that is part of the base installation of CA ERwin Data Modeler to create a **Region Code** domain. This domain defines region code as a two-character, uppercase entry. For example, **NY** and **US** would both be valid region codes. These two examples represent two different types of regions, however. **NY** represents the state of New York and **US** represents the country of the United States of America. We may want to inherit from the **Region Code** domain to further clarify the differences between a country code and a state code. For example, the **Country Code** domain has listed valid values from the ISO Country code list. It has also specified that a country code must be entered; blank entries are not allowed. For the **State** domain, we have included a different set of valid values that represents the fifty US states. Empty (null) values are allowed, since states are only applicable to the country value **US**. In fact, we might want to create a more generic domain here to represent not only US states, but regions within other countries as well.

Figure 10.3 Domain Inheritance

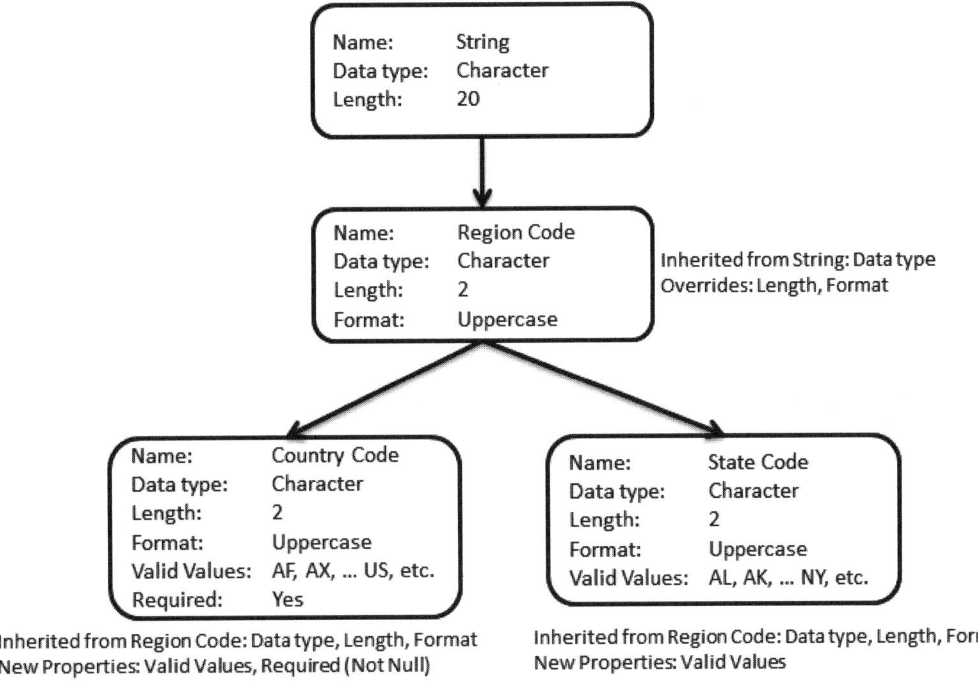

The concept of domains is so important in CA ERwin Data Modeler that every column or attribute is automatically attached to a domain upon creation. If you do not specify a domain, the **<default>** domain will be used. You can change this to a more customized domain at any time. Let's take a look at the **<default>** domain to get a better understanding of how domains are implemented and visualized in CA ERwin Data Modeler. One easy way to visualize the domain hierarchy is to sort the domains by their inheritance relationships to each other. The default sort order for domains is **Alphabetic**, but if you click on the **Sort Items** button, you can change the sort order, as shown in Figure 10.4.

Figure 10.4 Changing the Domain Sort Order

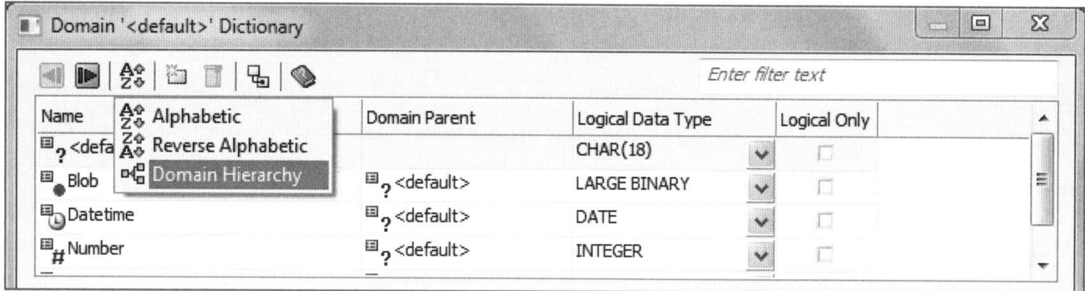

Changing the sort order to **Domain Hierarchy** results in the display shown in Figure 10.5. Notice that the domains **Blob**, **Datetime**, **Number**, and **String** are all inherited from the **<default>** domain. The **<default>** domain is assigned automatically to all attributes and columns that have not been assigned a domain by the designer. You'll notice that the **Logical Data Type** has been overridden for the **Blob**, **Datetime**, **Number**, and **String** domains. For example, the **Logical Data Type** for the **<default>** domain is **CHAR(18)**, while for the **Blob** domain it is **LARGE BINARY**. Note that in the physical model, these are automatically assigned based on the default data types set for the target server selected, so they may be different for each DBMS platform. When creating a new domain inherited from one of these pre-supplied domains, you can override the default data type and any of the other properties (except names and parent domains).

Figure 10.5 Sorting Domains Hierarchically

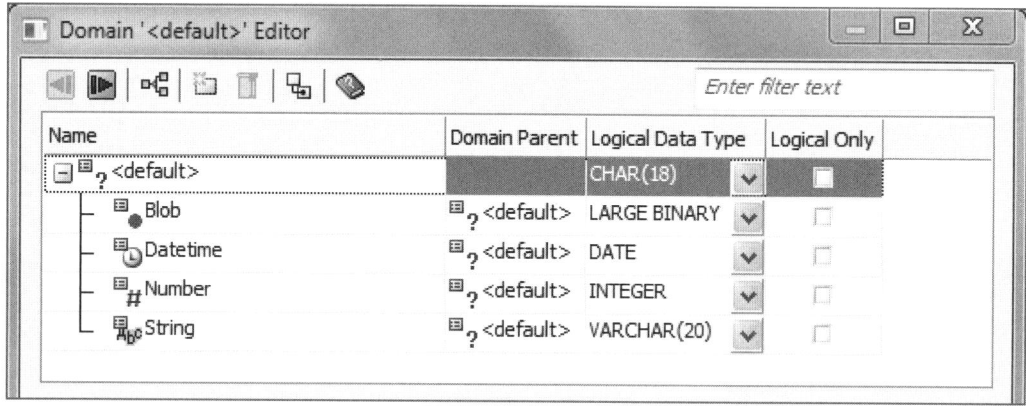

This hierarchy is also shown in the **General** tab, as shown in Figure 10.6.

Figure 10.6 Visualizing the Domain Hierarchy on the General Tab of the Domain Editor

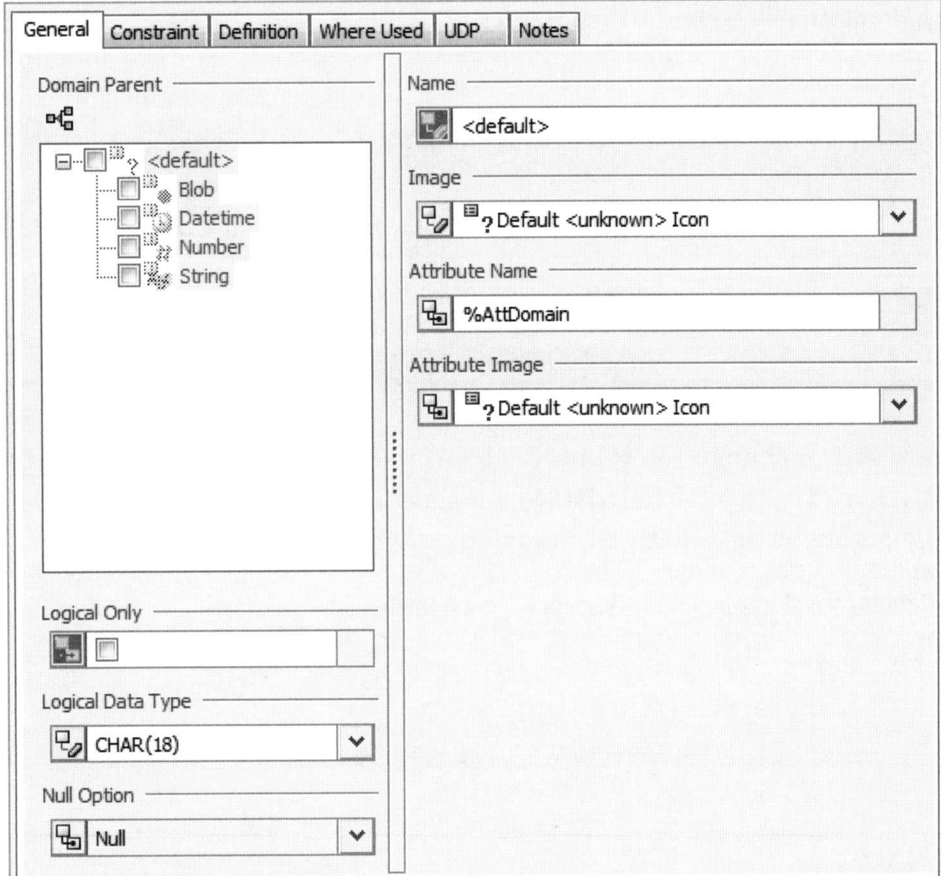

Now that we understand the general concept of domains, let's create a domain in CA ERwin Data Modeler. Recall from the introduction to this chapter that we discovered that the **last name** field in several of the databases was too short to accommodate the larger names in the India region. We want to create a standard to ensure that the default length for **last name** is long enough to hold all customer names in the system. From the Domain Editor shown in Figure 10.2, select the **String** domain from the domain hierarchy, as shown in Figure 10.7 (make sure that the sort order is set to **Domain Hierarchy**).

Figure 10.7 Inheriting from the String Domain

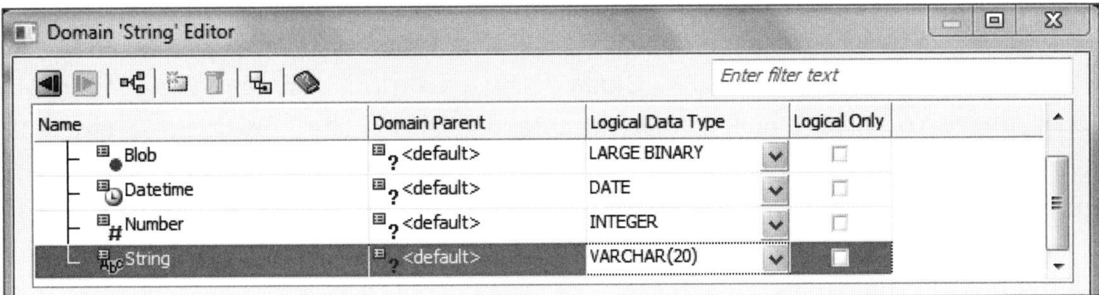

Next, select the **New** button . You'll see that a new domain is added as a child under the **String** domain, as shown in Figure 10.8.

Figure 10.8 New Domain Dialog

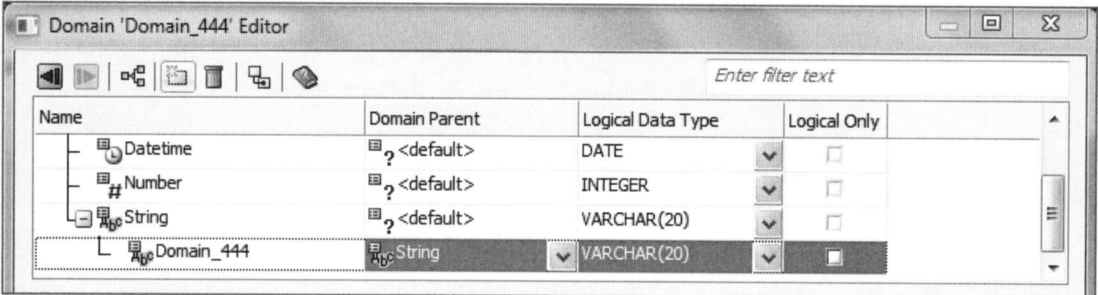

For this new entry, change the **Name** field to **Last Name** and the **Logical Data Type** from **VARCHAR(20)** to **VARCHAR(35)**, as shown in Figure 10.9. To change the data type, simply highlight the entry and change the number 20 to the number 35.

Figure 10.9 Defining the Name and Data Type for a New Domain

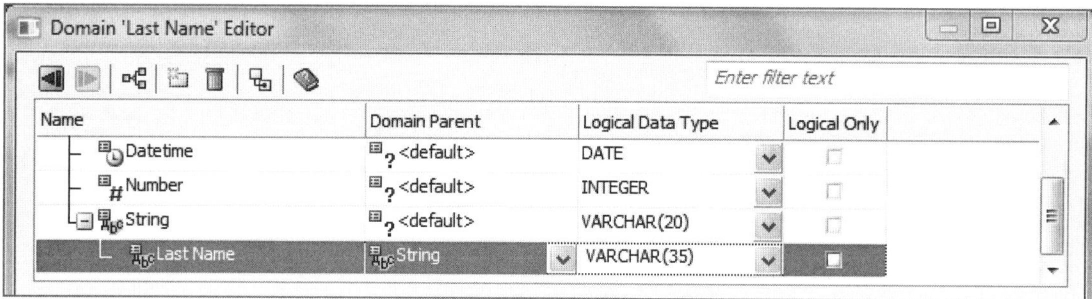

You've just created your first override by changing the data type of the child domain. To verify this, take a look at the **String** domain and see that the data type is still VARCHAR(20), while the data type of **Last Name** is VARCHAR(35).

We'll also want to change the **Null Option** for this domain. In the lower-left of the **General** tab, you'll see that the default **Null Option** is **Null**, which means that there can be empty values in this field. Since **Last Name** is a key piece of information in our database, we want to ensure that a value is entered every time, so we'll change this value to **Not Null**, using the drop-down menu, as shown in Figure 10.10.

Now that we've created a domain, let's use this domain to create a standardized attribute in a data model. **Close** the Domain Editor, and in the **domain_example.erwin** model we created earlier in this chapter, create a new entity called **Customer** on the diagram (for help regarding how to create an entity, refer to Chapter 4). Don't create any attributes for now—we'll do this using our new domain. But do make sure that your diagram display level is set to **Attribute Display Level** (see Chapter 4 for how to do this).

Figure 10.10 Changing the Null Option for a Domain

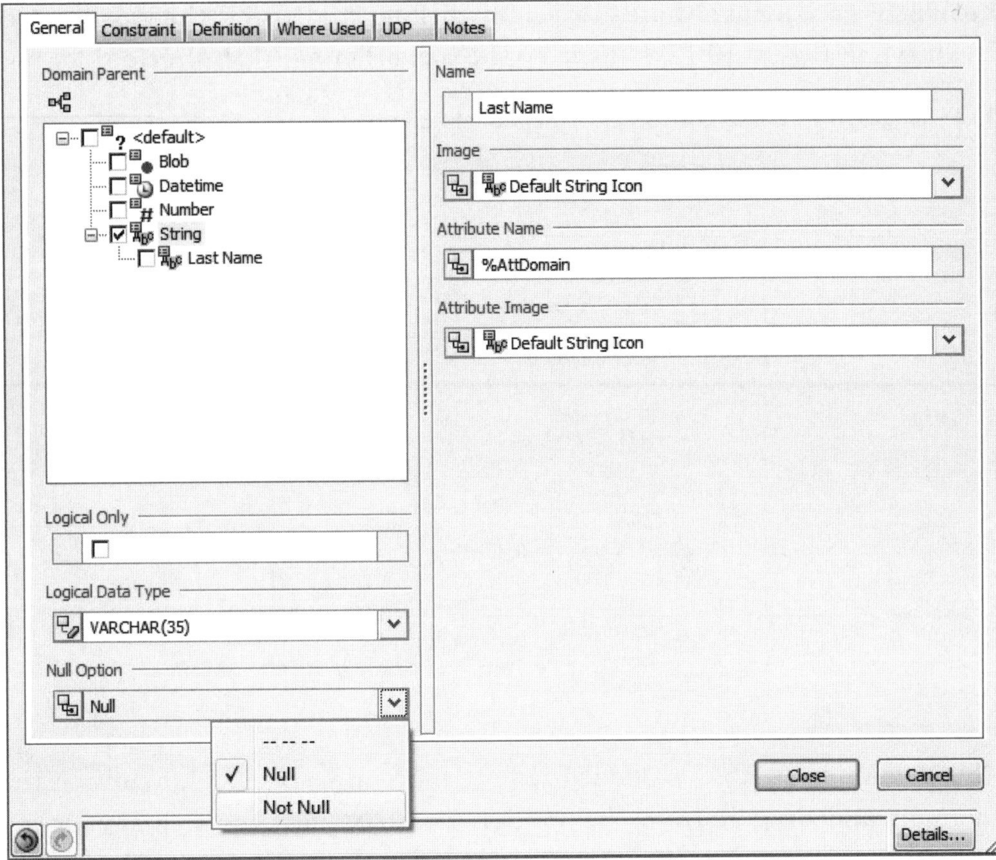

To find the domain we just created, expand the **Domains** node in the Model Explorer until you can see the **Last Name** domain, as shown in Figure 10.11.

Figure 10.11 Viewing Domains in the Model Explorer

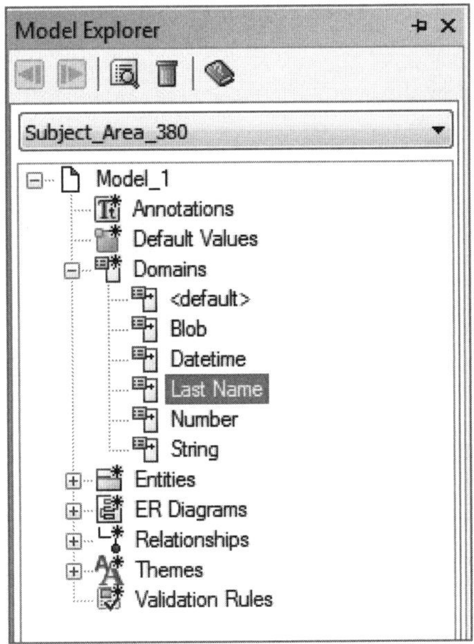

Note that as with the Domain Editor, you can choose to sort your domains **Alphabetically** or **Hierarchically** by right-clicking and using the resultant context menu, as shown in Figure 10.12. Let's keep the sort order as **Alphabetical** for now.

Figure 10.12 Changing the Domain Sort Order in the Model Explorer

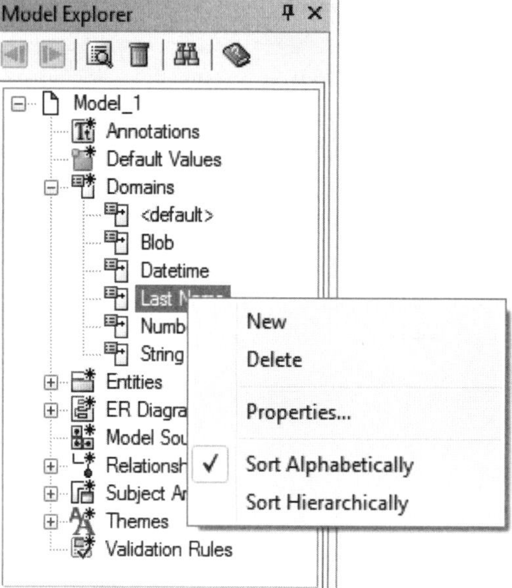

To use this domain to create a standardized attribute in your model, highlight the **Last Name** domain and drag it from the Model Explorer into the non-key area of the **Customer** entity. This will create an attribute called **Last Name**, as shown in Figure 10.13, which shows the domain being dragged, then dropped onto the entity.

Figure 10.13 Creating an Attribute Using a Domain

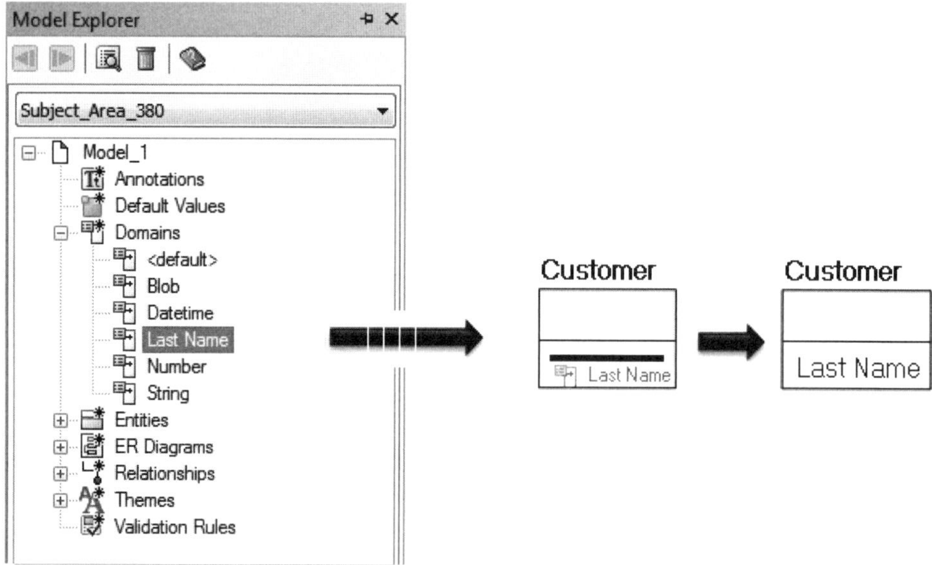

You can confirm that the correct domain was used and that the data type is correct using the Attribute Properties Editor (refer to Chapters 3 and 5 for more on the

Attribute Properties Editor), viewing the both the **Parent Domain** field and the **Domain** section of the **General** tab, shown in Figure 10.14. You'll also see that the data type, **VARCHAR(35)**, was correctly inherited from the **Last Name** domain. **Close** the Attribute Properties Editor for now.

Figure 10.14 Viewing the Domain Associated with an Attribute

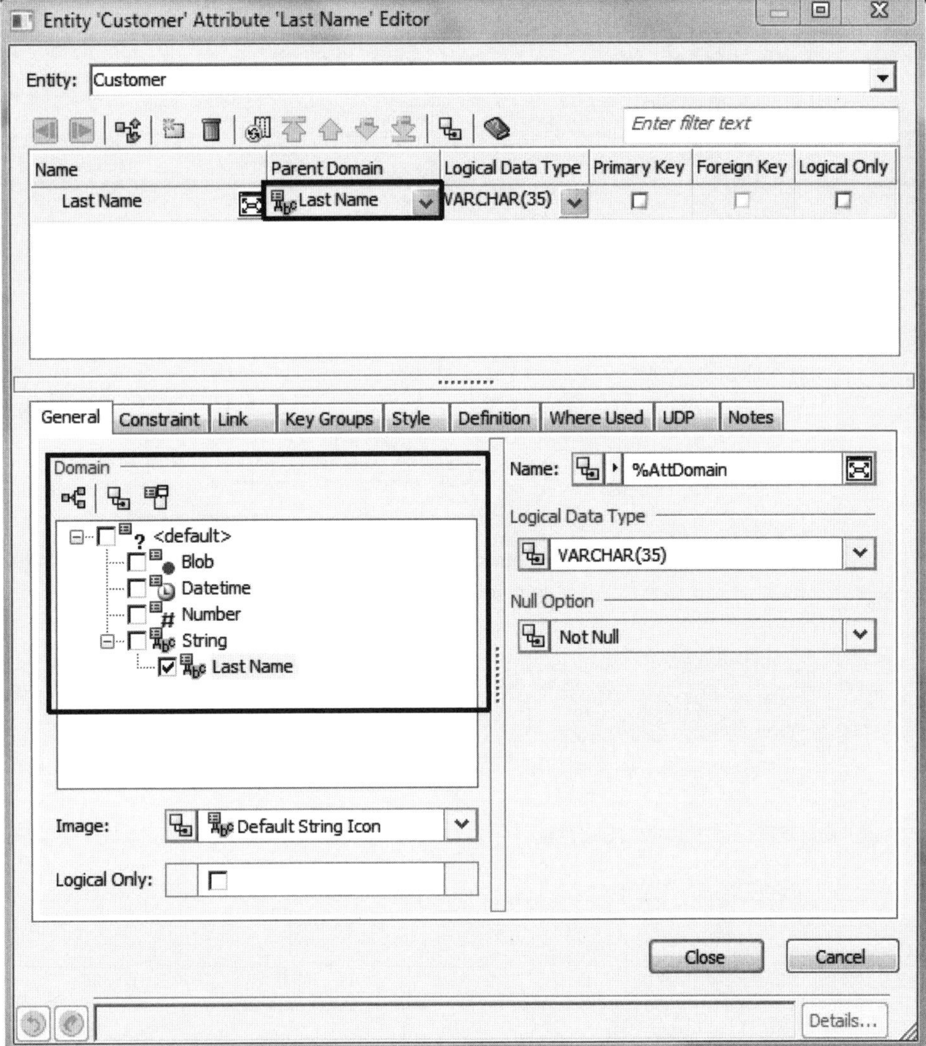

Using domains to seed attribute information is a helpful way to ensure consistency across the organization. However, for many organizations, using a generic name such as **Last Name** is seen as too vague. It is a common practice to add the entity name as a qualifier, such as **Customer Last Name**, to distinguish this attribute from, for example, **Employee Last Name**. CA ERwin Data Modeler's domain architecture is flexible enough to accommodate these customizations, using the CA ERwin Macro Language. Let's walk through an example of how macros can help define customized domain names.

Start by opening the Domain Editor and navigating to the **General** tab for the **Last Name** domain, as shown in Figure 10.15. Notice the field entitled **Attribute Name**. This field defines the name used for the attribute in the model when the domain is seeded into an entity. The default value in this case is `%AttDomain`.

Figure 10.15 Customizing the Default Attribute Name

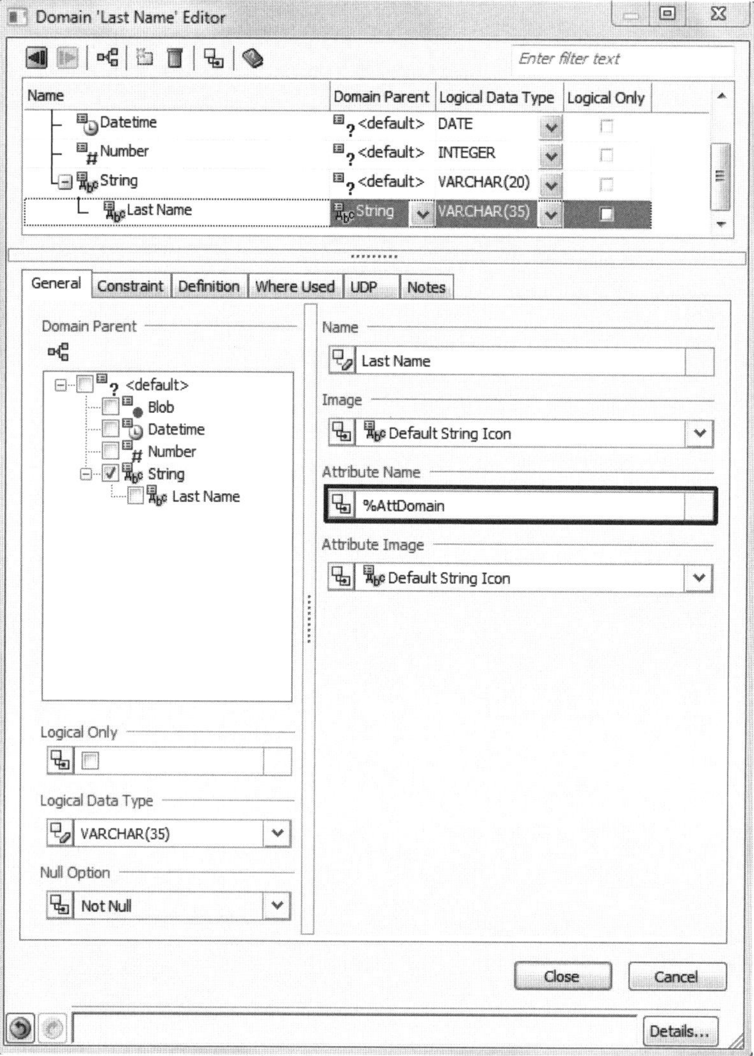

The `%AttDomain` macro returns the name of the domain attached to an attribute (e.g. **Last Name**). To append the name of the parent entity in front of the attribute name (e.g. **Customer Last Name**), we'll need to add the `%OwnerEntity` macro to this field. We'll also want to ensure that all attributes are lowercase, to adhere to the naming conventions of our organization. Edit the **Attribute Name** field so that it reads: `%Lower(%OwnerEntity %AttDomain)`, as shown in Figure 10.16.

Figure 10.16 Using Macros to Customize Domains

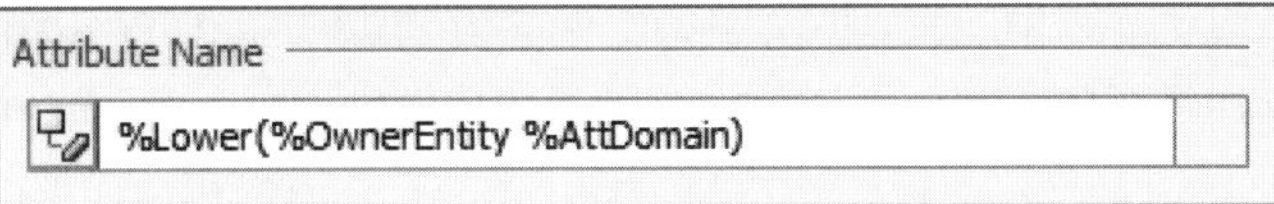

Figure 10.17 provides a schematic showing the function of each of the macros used for this domain.

Figure 10.17 Domain Macros Explained

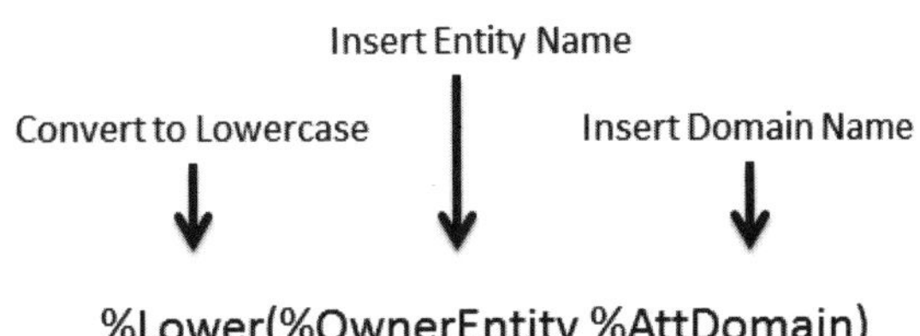

There are a wide range of Macros that can be used to customize CA ERwin Data Modeler. Table 10.1 shows a list of some macros that are commonly used in creating domains.

Table 10.1 Macros Commonly Used to Create Domains

Macro Name	Description
%OwnerEntity	Provides the name of the entity that owns the current attribute
%EntityName	Provides the entity name of the current entity
%AttName	Provides the attribute name
%AttDomain	Provides the logical domain name
%TableName	Provides the table name
%ColName	Provides the column name
%ColDomain	Provides the physical domain name
%EntityProp(UDP Name)	Provides the entity UDP value of the name specified
%TableProp(UDP Name)	Provides the table UDP value of the name specified
%Lower	Puts the object name in lower case
%Upper	Puts the object name in upper case

Now that we've inserted the macro definition to add the entity name to the beginning of the attribute name, click **Close** to return to the model diagram. You'll see that the **Last Name** attribute in the **Customer** entity has now been changed to **customer last name**, in lowercase letters, as shown in Figure 10.18.

Figure 10.18 Result of using Macros to Define Custom Domains

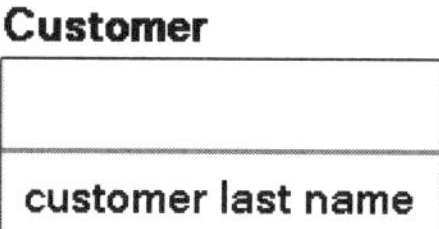

To show how the name will change based on the entity name, create a new entity called **Employee**, and drag and drop the **Last Name** domain onto the non-key area of this entity. You'll see that an entity named **employee last name** is created, as shown in Figure 10.19. You'll see that by using macros in your domains, you can create customized naming standards that are based on the entity name.

Figure 10.19 Two Attributes Using the Same Domain with Macro-based Naming

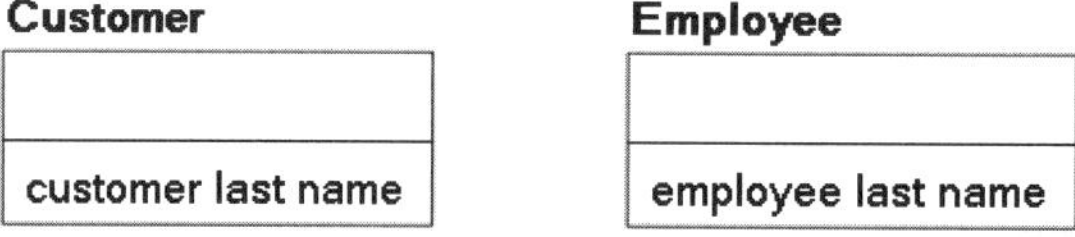

Once you start using domains in your model, it's helpful to see where a given domain has been used, particularly when assessing the impact that a change to this domain will make. To see where a particular domain has been implemented across your model, go to the Domain Editor, highlight the **Last Name** domain, and select the **Where Used** tab, as shown in Figure 10.20.

Figure 10.20 Showing Domain Usage via the Where Used Tab

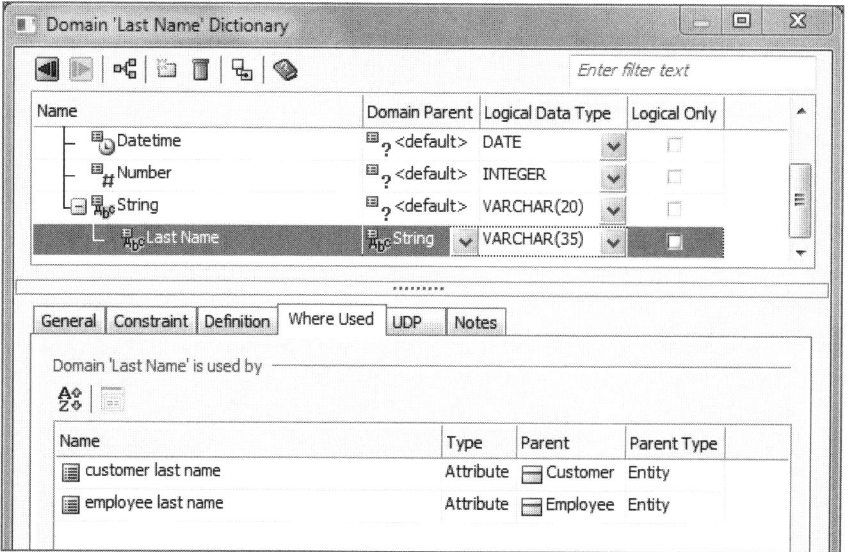

In this example, you'll see that the **Last Name** domain is used by the **customer last name** attribute in the **Customer** table, as well as the **employee last name** in the **Employee** table. This example is a simple one, but you can image how helpful this can be in a model where a particular domain is used by dozens of objects.

Another helpful way to show domain usage is to display the domain inheritance directly on the diagram itself. To do this, open the Diagram Editor for your diagram (see Chapter 8 for more on Diagrams), move to the **Entity** tab, and select the **Display Attribute Domain** option, as shown in Figure 10.21.

Figure 10.21 Showing Domains on a Diagram via the Diagram Editor

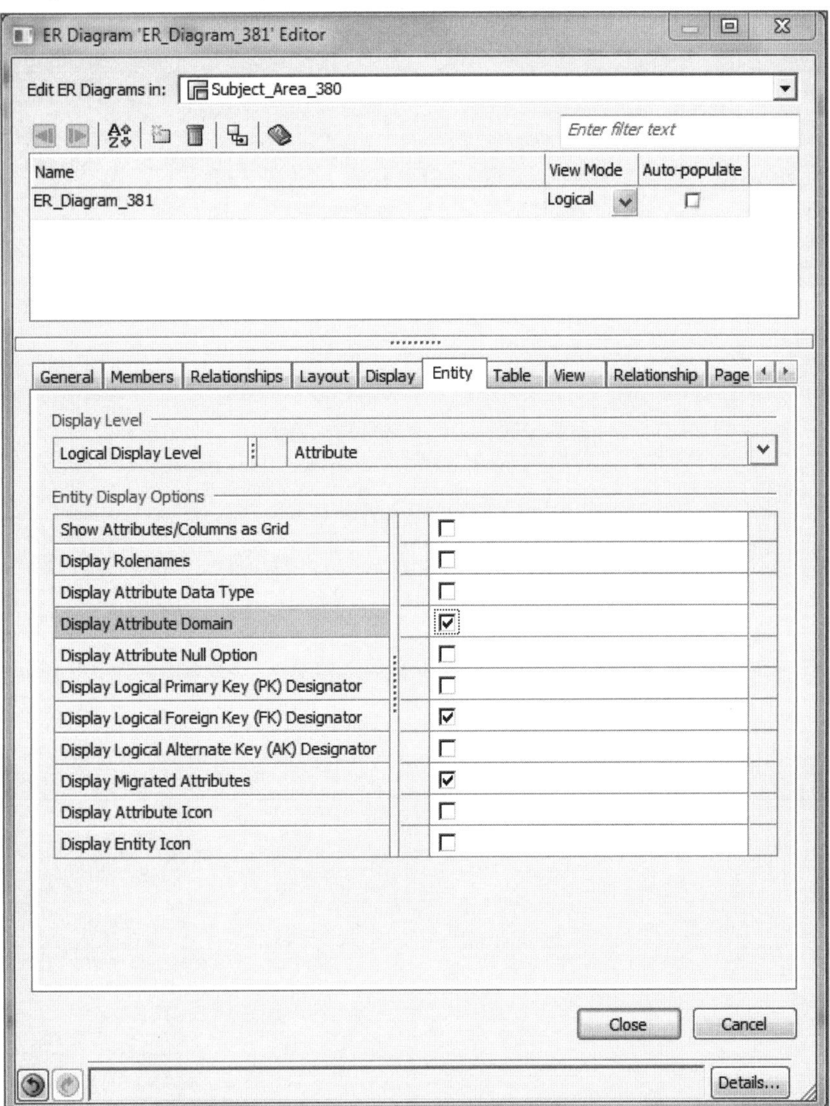

When you **Close** the Diagram Editor, your diagram should look similar to Figure 10.22, where you can see that both **customer last name** and **employee last name** both use the **Last Name** domain.

Figure 10.22 Showing Domains on a Diagram

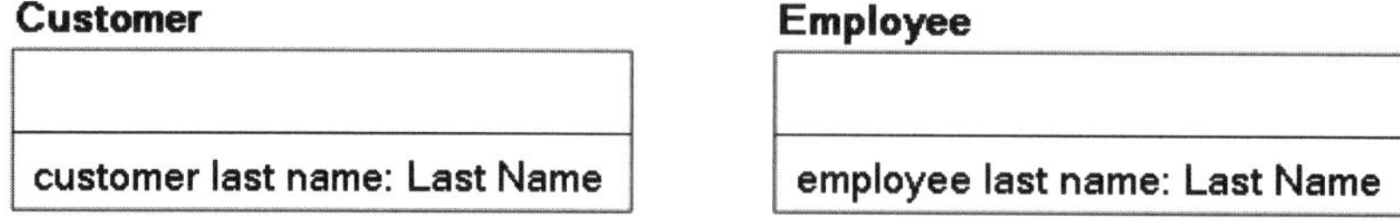

You aren't limited to standardizing just the name of attributes and columns using domains and the associated macros. You can also control attribute definitions, for example. To do this, open the Domain Editor, select the **Last Name** domain, and move to the **Definition** tab, as shown in Figure 10.23.

Figure 10.23 Standardizing Definitions using Domains

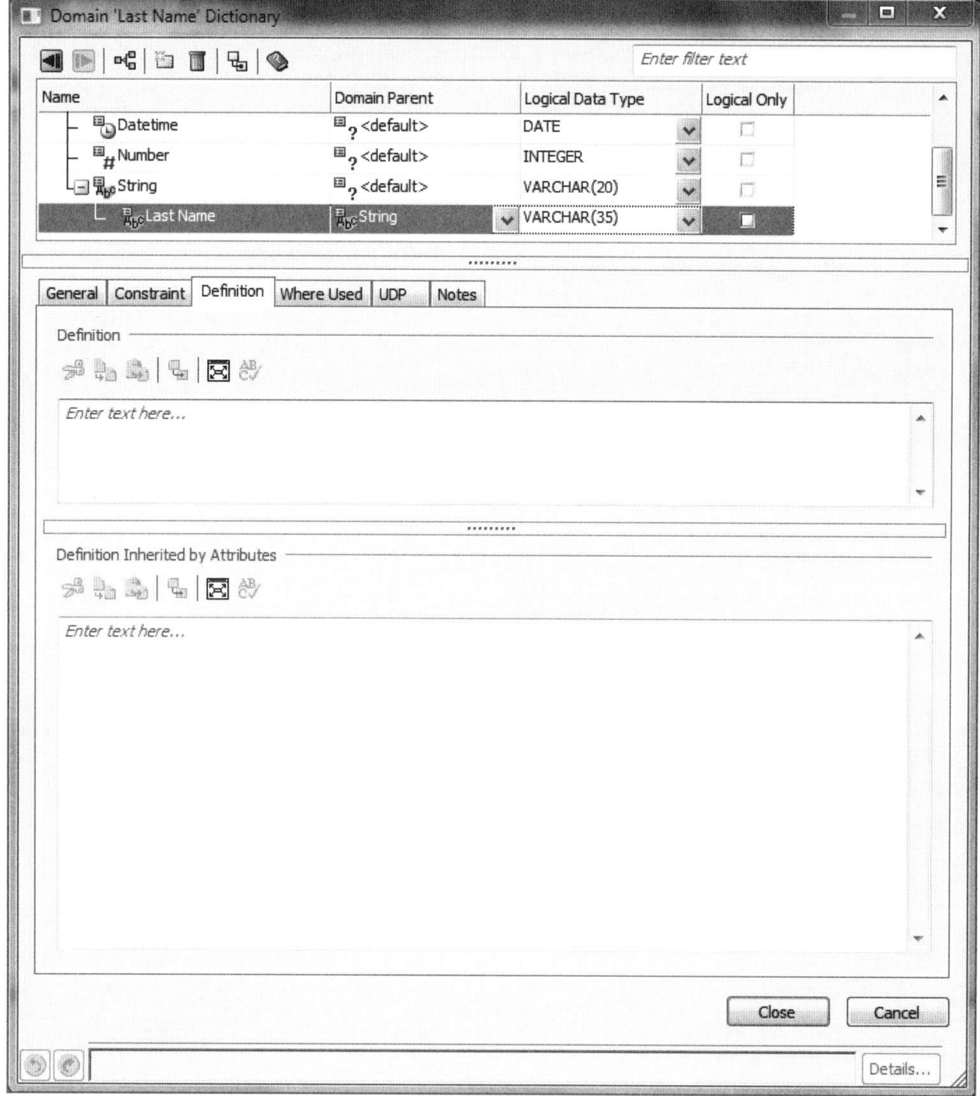

The **Definition** field contains the definition for the domain itself. It provides a general overview of the purpose and usage of the domain, as shown in Figure 10.24.

Figure 10.24 Creating a Domain Definition

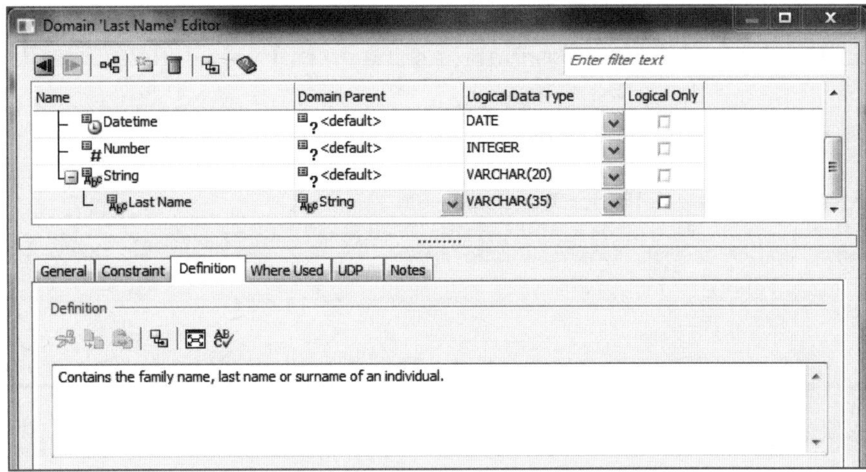

The **Definition Inherited by Attributes** field allows you to create a standardized definition that will be inherited by the attributes using this domain. This is another instance where macros come in handy. Say, for example, we wanted to clarify in the definition that the **last name** was the family name of the **Customer**, **Employee**, **Vendor**, or whatever entity type is using this domain. Rather than re-type a similar definition for each entity, which introduces the possibility of error or inconsistencies, we can create a standardized definition that can be customized for each entity via macros. For example, type the following text in the **Definition Inherited by Attributes** field: **`Family name of %OwnerEntity`**, as shown in Figure 10.25.

Figure 10.25 Using Domains and Macros to Standardize Definitions

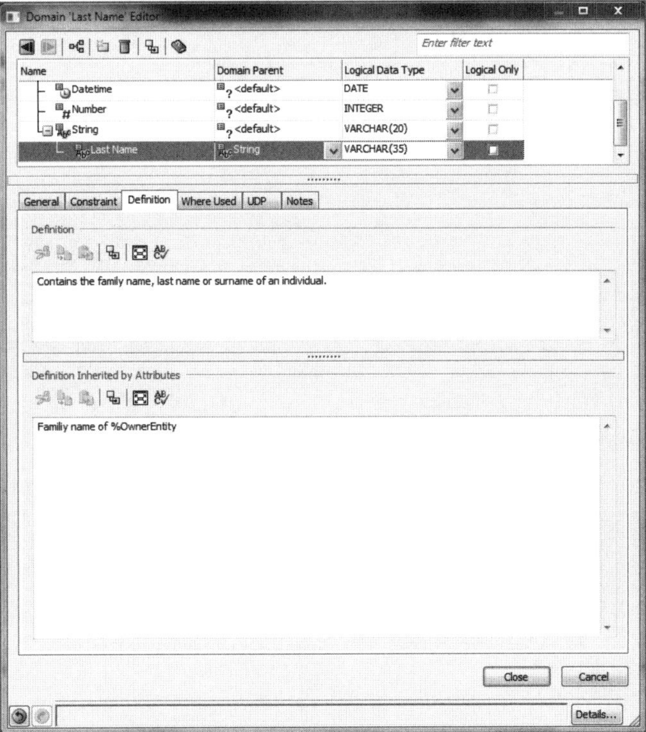

Click **Close** to return to the model diagram. To verify that this worked correctly, open the Attribute Properties Editor for the **Customer** entity and navigate to the **Definition** tab for the **customer last name** attribute, as shown in Figure 10.26. You'll see that the standard definition has been inherited from the attribute, and the name of the entity inserted where the macro was placed.

Figure 10.26 Inheriting Attribute Definition from a Domain

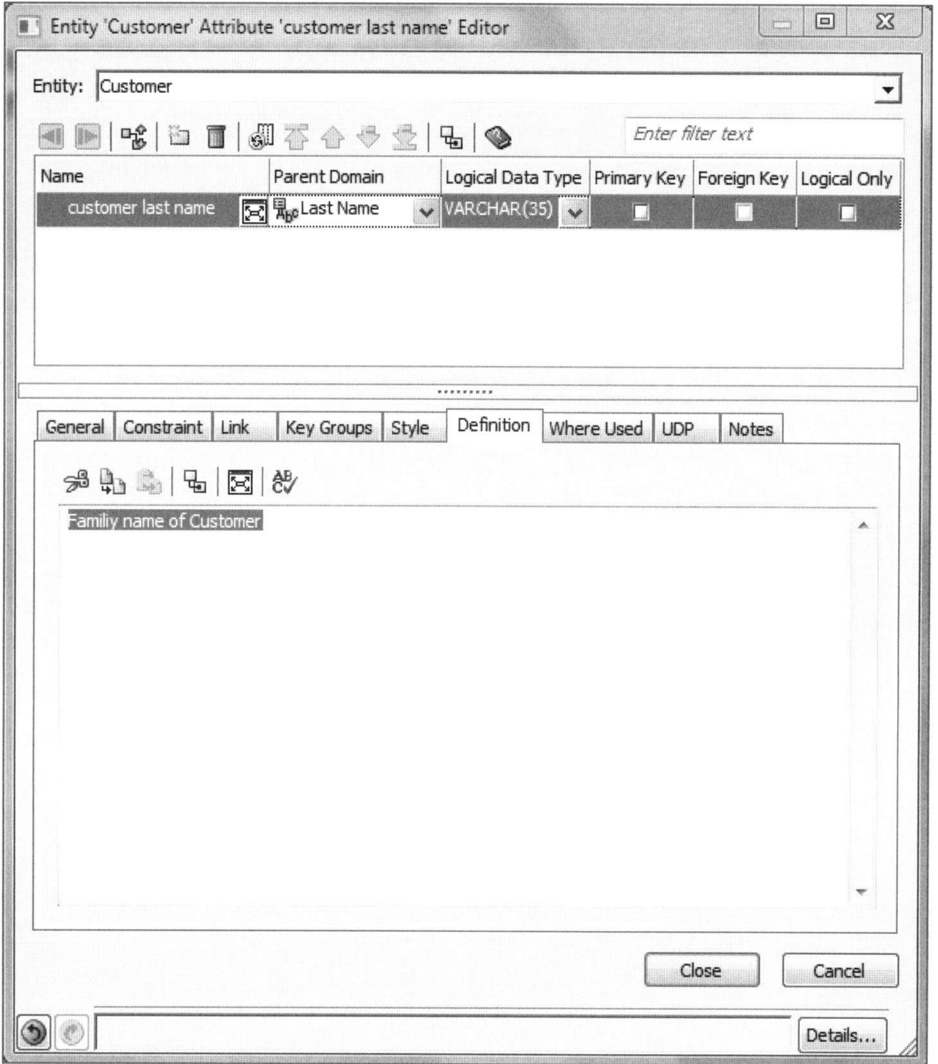

By now, you may be getting a better appreciation of the value of creating standards via domains. But at the same time, you may also feel a bit restricted by these controls. Are you locked in to these naming conventions once they've been created? Or can exceptions be made when there is a valid business reason? Fortunately, CA ERwin Data Modeler provides mechanisms which allow the user to override domain definitions, while at the same time maintaining a record of where domain definitions were changed. After all, once we've gone through the effort of creating these standards, we don't want them changed in a haphazard way.

As an example, let's change the name of the **customer last name** attribute that inherited its properties from the **Last Name** domain. Switch to the **General** tab in the Attribute Properties Editor, as shown in Figure 10.27.

Figure 10.27 Attribute Properties Editor

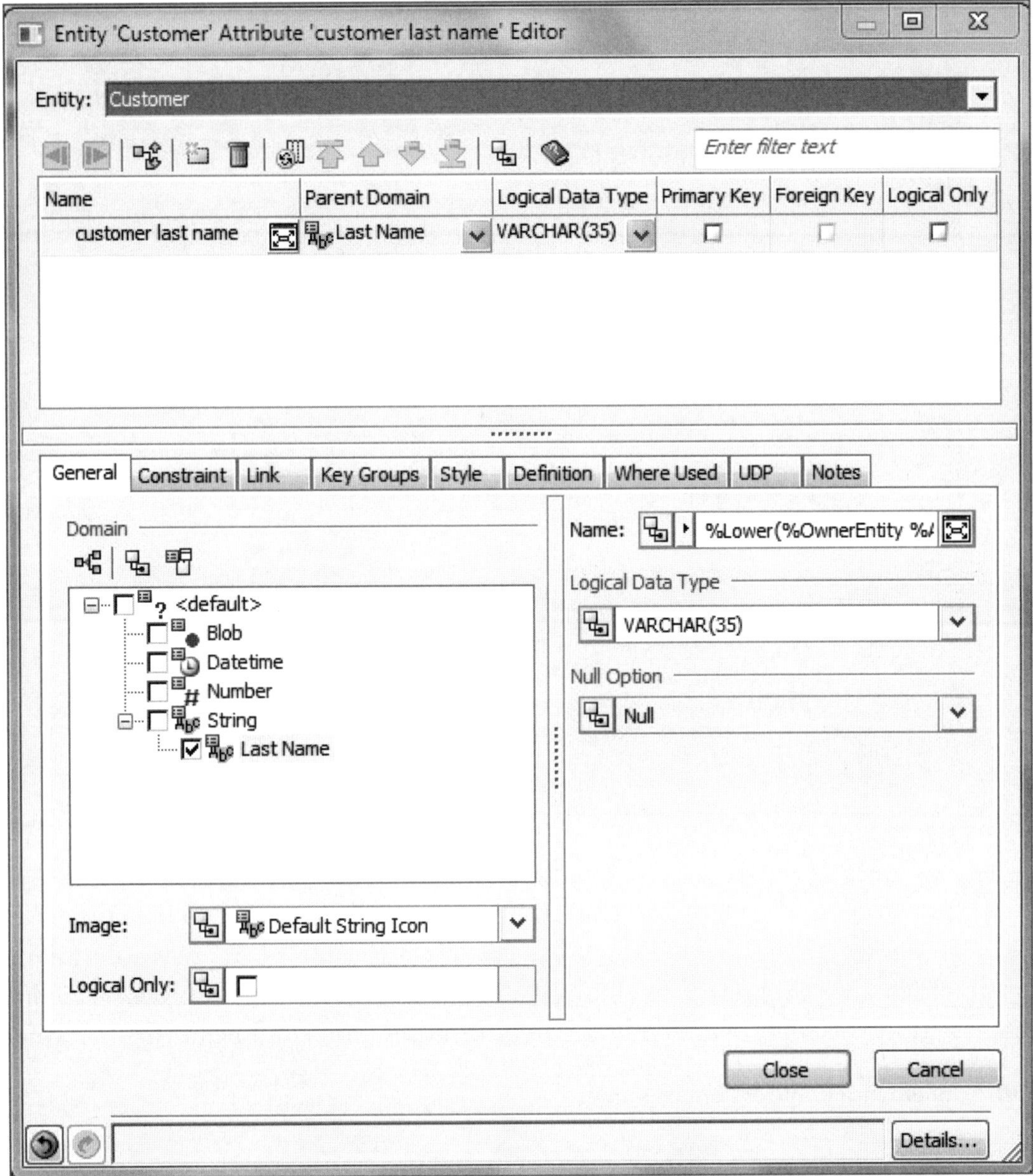

Change the value in the **Name** field to **cust last name**, as shown in Figure 10.28. Note that not only is the name itself changed, but the icon next to the field changes as well, to indicate that this value has been overridden .

Figure 10.28 Overriding a Domain's Naming Convention

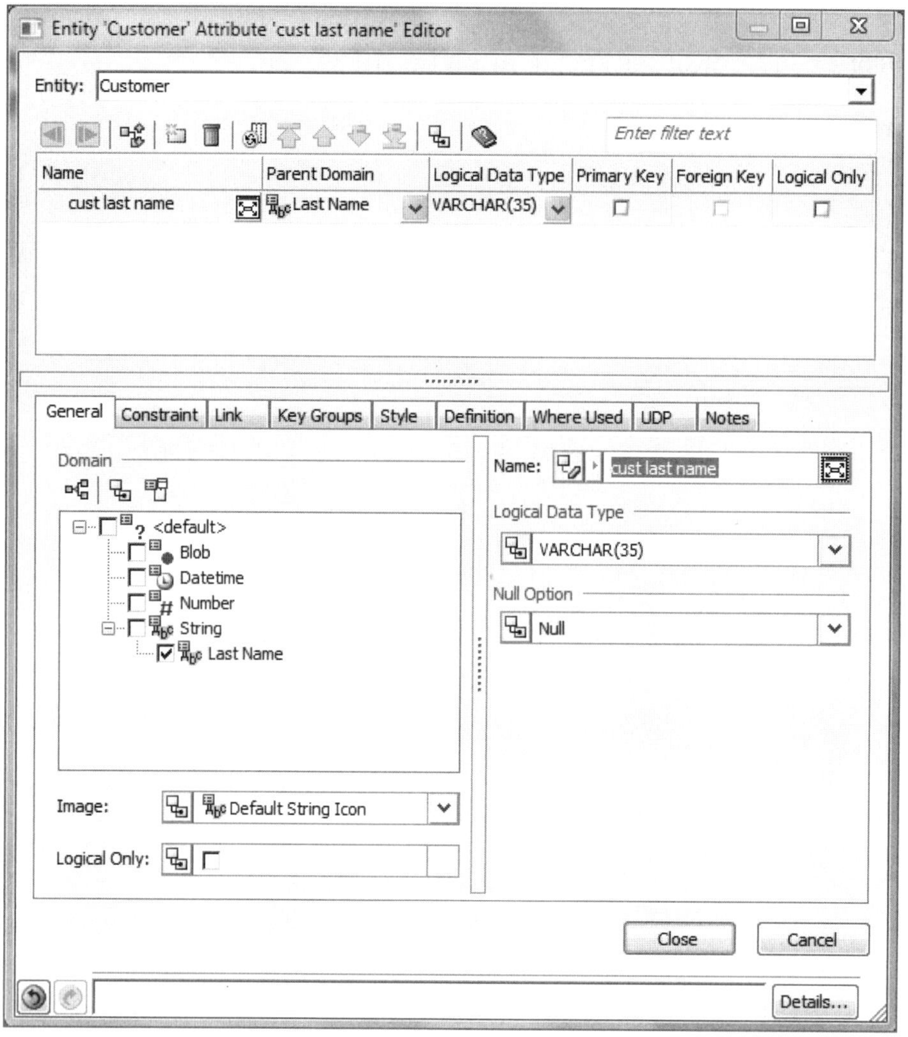

Click on this icon, and you'll see that there are options to **Inherit**, **Override**, or **Harden**, as shown in Figure 10.29. We'll cover these options in more detail in our discussion of Naming Standards in Chapter 12. For now, you can simply use this icon as an indicator that you have overridden the default name inherited from the domain.

Figure 10.29 Inheritance Icons for Domain Names

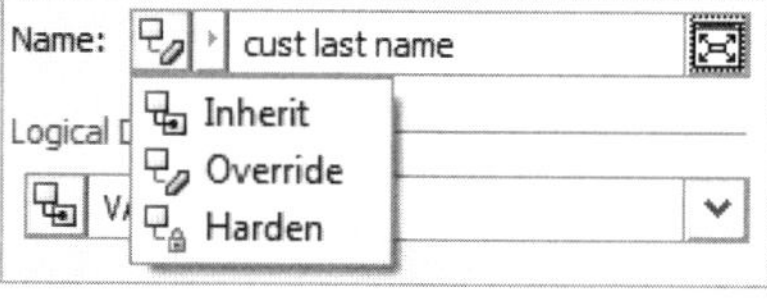

Now that you've exercised your power to override the name defined by the domain, you're starting to harbor some self-doubt. Although you enjoyed your taste of defying authority, you realize the error of your ways. Was this brief moment of power worth the risk to enterprise data standards? No, you say. You'd like to go back to the name defined by the domain. Never fear! CA ERwin Data Modeler has a mechanism to allow you to revert back to the domain standards using the **Reset Attribute Properties** feature. To invoke this, select the **Reset Property Inheritance** button from the toolbar, as shown in 10.30.

Figure 10.30 Reset Property Inheritance Toolbar Button

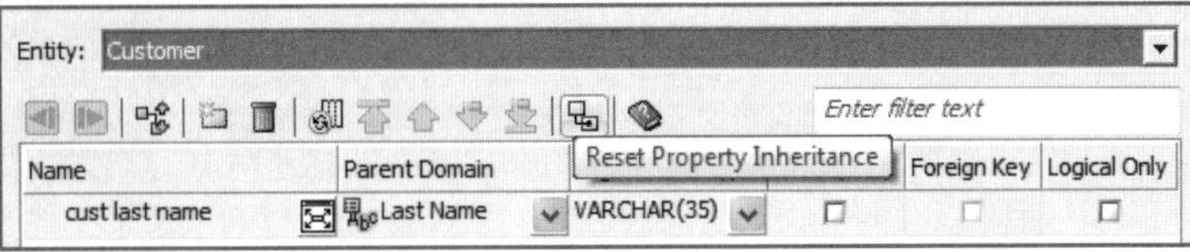

The Reset Attribute Properties Dialog appears, as shown in Figure 10.31. This dialog allows us to apply a domain retroactively to existing attributes. You'll see that there are many options to control whether we apply domain standards to all attributes or only selected ones, as well as controlling which properties to reset. For our example, choose to override properties for **Only Attribute 'cust last name'** and choose to reset only the **Name** property (deselect **Domain Parent**, or we'll override the changes we made to the parent domain, as well).

Figure 10.31 Reset Attribute Properties Dialog

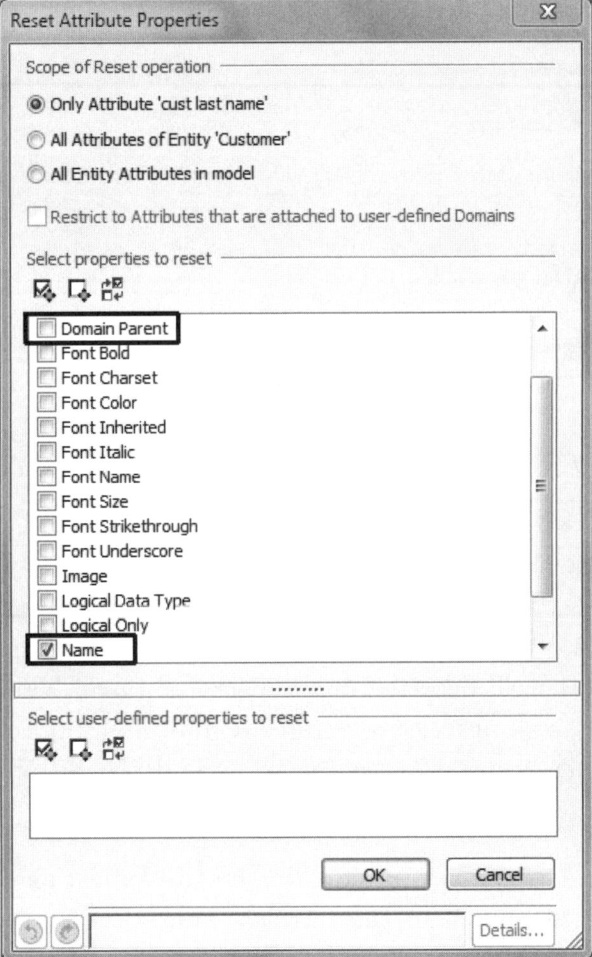

Click **OK** and you'll be returned to the Attribute Properties Editor, where you'll see that the attribute has been changed to **customer last name** to properly align with the domain definition, as shown in Figure 10.32.

Figure 10.32 Attribute Properties Editor Showing Reset Attribute Name

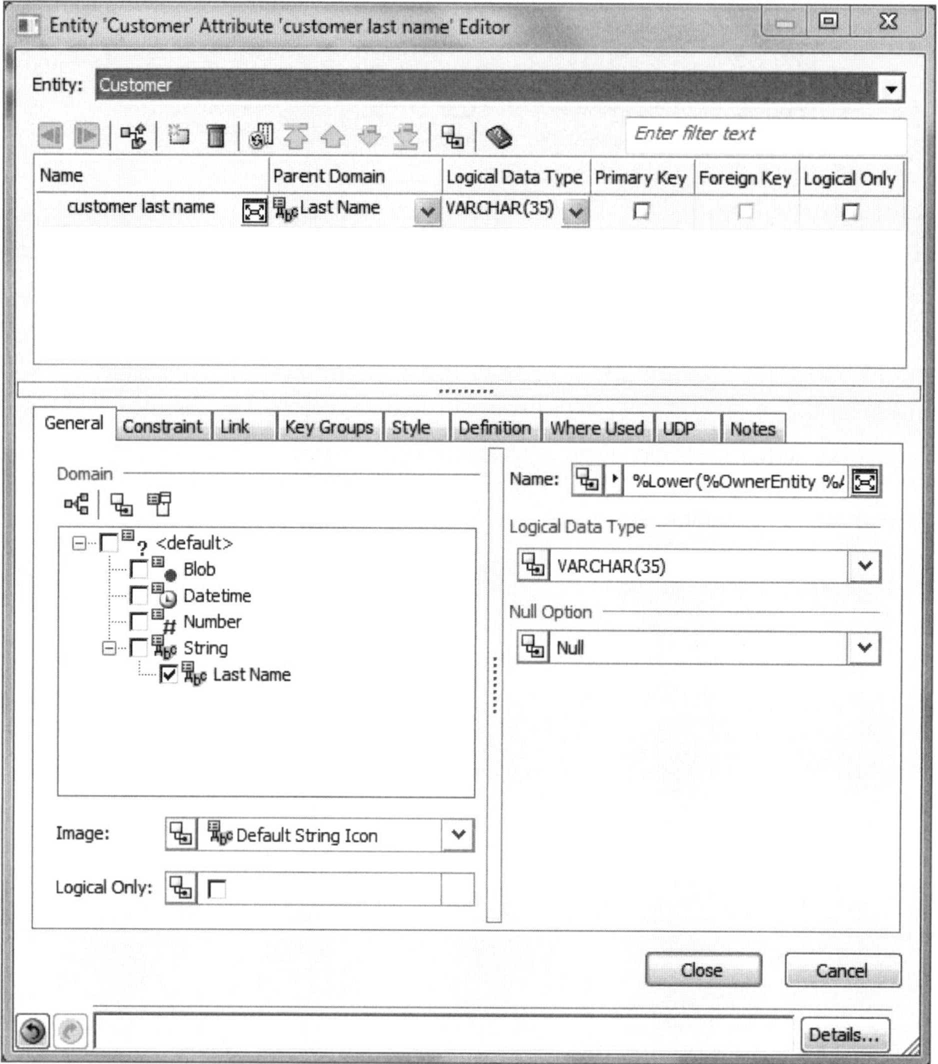

If the idea of allowing modelers to rename attributes that have been assigned to a domain makes you nervous, and you would like to disallow this behavior, you can 'harden' the attribute names so that they cannot be changed using the Name Hardening Wizard that we'll describe in the Chapter 12 on Naming Standards. Many organizations make it a best practice to enforce domain naming conventions without the ability to override. This decision is up to you, and is based on your individual best practices and business needs.

So far, we've described the creation of domains on the logical side of a data model. You can create and modify domains on the physical side as well. Note that the Domain

Editor is driven by the type of model you are currently editing. Switch to the physical model and open the Domain Editor, as shown in Figure 10.33.

Figure 10.33 Defining Domains for Physical Model Objects

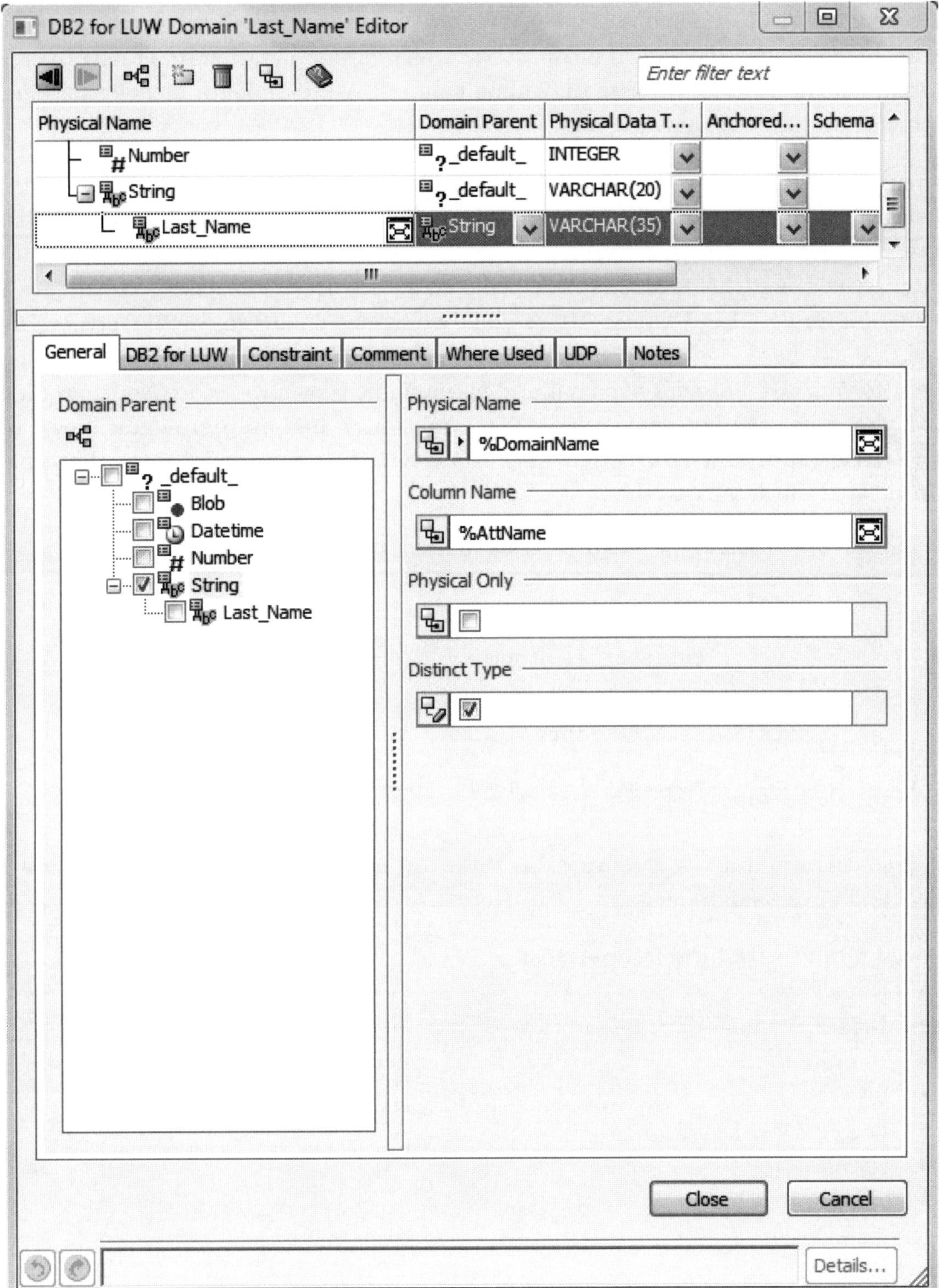

In the Physical mode, you'll notice that the tabs change slightly. For example, the **Description** tab is now the **Comment** tab, since physical databases use comments, not descriptions. Also, there will be a platform-specific tab that allows you to define formatting options that are specific to a given database platform which, in this example, is DB2 for LUW. The functionality of domains works in very much the same way for the physical mode as for the logical mode, so we won't go into detail here on how to create physical domain objects. Refer to the online help in CA ERwin Data Modeler for details on particular dialog options.

An important thing to remember for physical domains is that they will translate to physical data definitions, so the standards we've defined will cascade to our physical database implementations. For example, if we were to forward engineer the model we created, you'll see the following DDL, shown in Figure 10.34. We'll cover forward engineering in detail in Chapter 19, so don't worry about how to do this for now. Just know that the hard work you're doing in the logical and physical models now will have benefit to your database development and maintenance down the road. Notice in Figure 10.34 that the naming conventions (e.g. **customer_last_name**), data types (e.g. **VARCHAR2(35)**), and null option (e.g. **NOT NULL**) are translated to the column definitions in the database table.

Figure 10.34 Physical Domains Translate to Database Structural Definitions

```
CREATE TABLE Customer
(
        customer_last_name    VARCHAR(35) NOT NULL
);

CREATE TABLE Employee
(
        employee_last_name    VARCHAR(35) NOT NULL
);
```

The following are a list of the properties that can be standardized through macros for logical and physical data models.

Logical Model Attribute Properties:

- Data Type
- Default Value
- Definition
- Icon
- Logical Only Indicator
- Name
- Note
- Null Option
- UDPs
- Validation Rules

Physical Model Attribute Properties:

- All platform-specific properties including: display format, valid values, labels
- Average column width
- Comment
- Data Type
- Default Value
- Name
- Null Option
- Physical Only Indicator
- UDPs
- Validation Rules

So far, we've covered a great deal regarding the creation and usage of domains. We've mainly covered the usage of domains for formatting and naming, however. Recall from Chapter 6 that there are several types of domains including: Format, List, and Range. To cover the definition and usage of List and Range domains, we'll need to discuss Validation Rules, which is the topic of the next section.

Key Points

- The default workspace can be customized by changing how Domains can be used to help create standardized data elements that have common formats, ranges, validation criteria, and naming conventions.
- Domain hierarchies allow you to reuse domain definitions through a process of inheritance.
- Inherit, Override, and Harden options allow you to control how and whether domain values can be changed by the user.
- The **Where Used** tab helps in determining the impact of changing the properties of a given domain.
- Macros can be used to create domains -- for example, to append the name of the entity for a particular attribute.
- Domains in the physical model help ensure consistency in database development and maintenance.

CHAPTER 11
Validation Rules

Want consistency?
Enforce Validation Rules
Lists, values, and range

Validation rules help enforce the business rules of your organization by establishing a default value, list of values, or a range of acceptable values for an object. You can enforce validation rules through a domain, or assign them directly to a table, column, entity, or attribute. Defining validation rules as reusable components helps create consistency across the organization, as all groups are able to enforce the same business rules and valid value sets.

The following are some business rules that can be enforced through validation rules:

- A customer can order coffee in cup sizes of small, medium, or large
- The age of a contest participant must be between 18 and 65
- All customers in the loyalty program join at the Silver level before earning enough points to become Gold or Platinum
- The states in the New England region are: CT, NH, MA, ME, RI, VT.

Creating Validating Rules

Let's create a validation rule for the last business rule on the list: the states in the New England region. Note that you'll need to have a model open before this menu becomes active. For this example, we'll use **`domain_example.erwin`** model that we created in the last chapter. If you don't have this model available, you can download it at www.erwin.com/datamodelingmadesimple. Start by opening the Validation Rule Editor by selecting **Model|Validation Rules** from the **Main Menu**. The Validation Rule Editor is shown in Figure 11.1.

Figure 11.1 Validation Rule Editor for a Logical Model

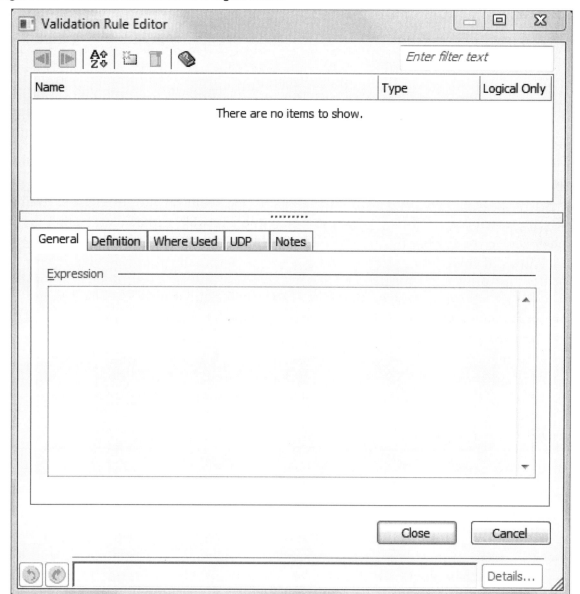

Validation rules can be created for both logical and physical data models. This example is based on a logical model. Validation rules that are created in the logical model are translated in the physical model to database constraints that enforce these rules. Since each database platform has unique syntax, it is helpful to create these rules at the logical level and allow CA ERwin Data Modeler to translate these rules into the correct syntax for your database platform(s).

Let's add our rule to define the valid states for the New England Region. Click the **New** button from the Validation Rule Editor and a new entry is added, as shown in Figure 11.2.

Figure 11.2 New Validation Rule Dialog

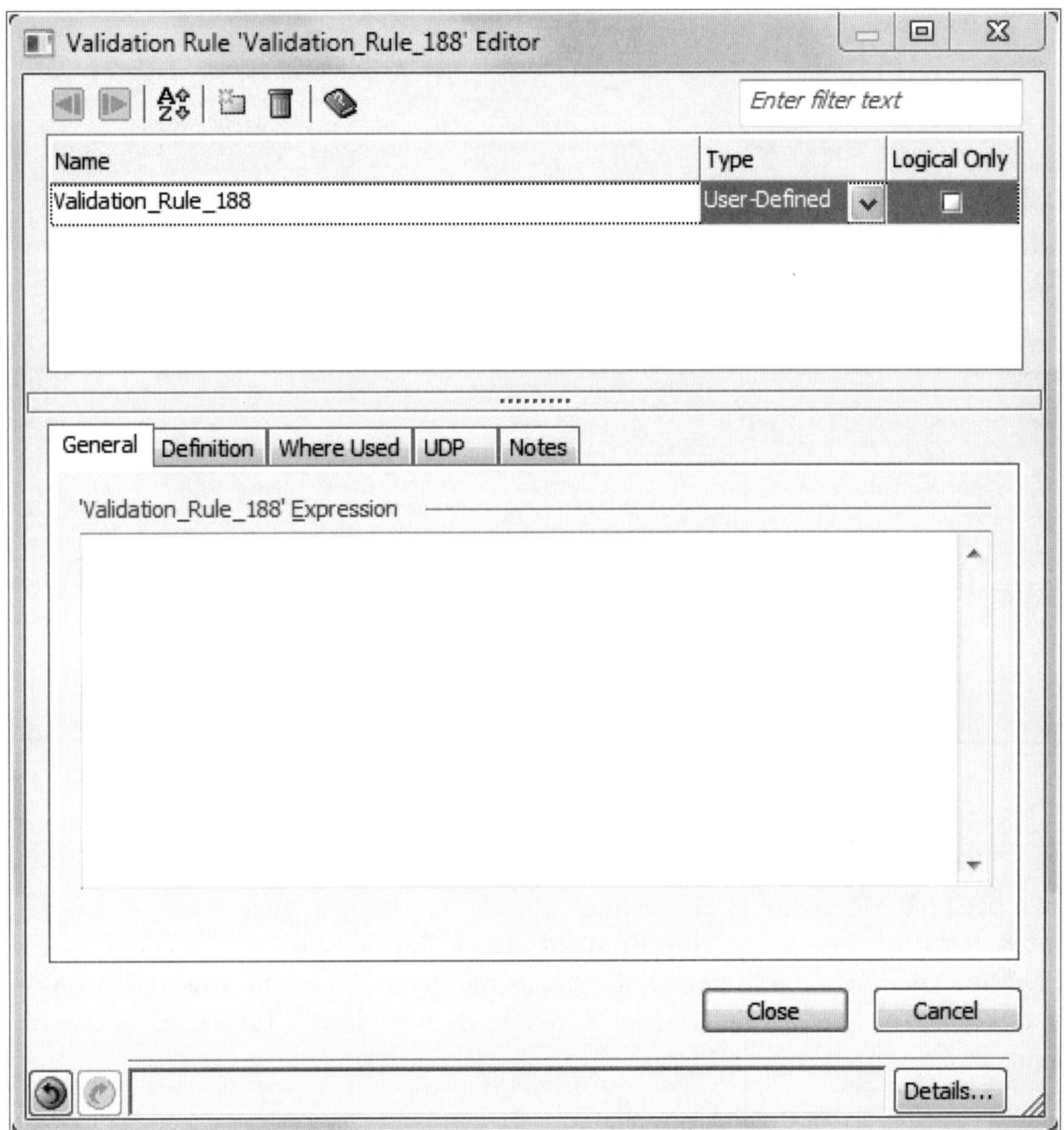

CA ERwin Data Modeler creates a default name for the validation rule, but we'll want to change this to a more user-friendly name. Type **New England States** into the **Name** field, as shown in Figure 11.3.

Figure 11.3 Naming a Validation Rule

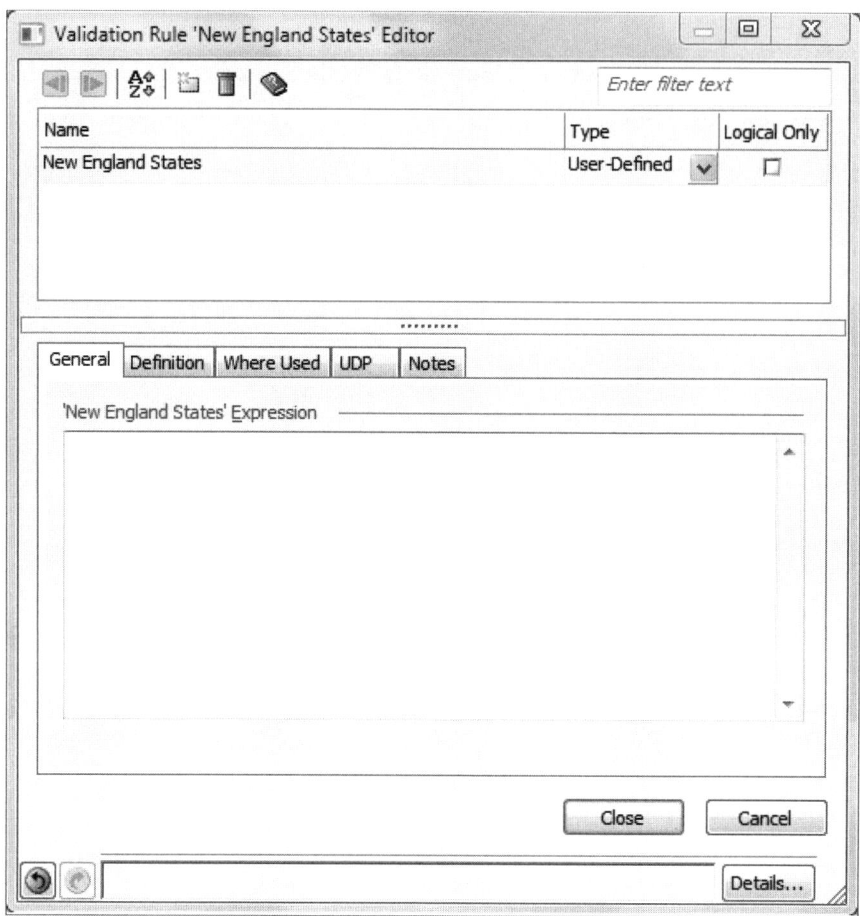

You'll see that the name of the validation rule has been defined as **New England States**, but if you look at the **'New England States' Expression** field, you'll see that the validation rule itself is still empty. To create the definition of the rule itself, we first need to choose the type of rule from the drop-down menu in the **Type** field, as shown in Figure 11.4.

Figure 11.4 Selecting the Validation Rule Type

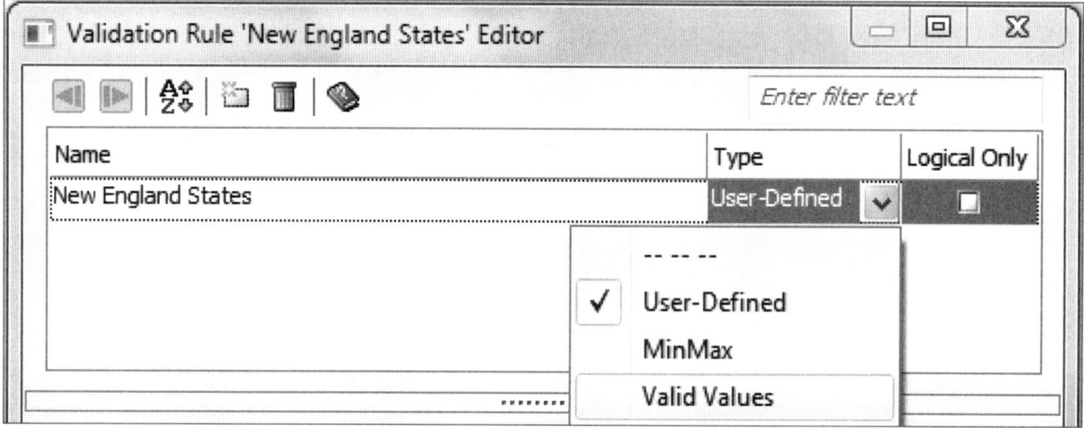

The valid options are:

- **User-Defined:** Allows custom code to be typed in by the user.
- **MinMax:** Allows the user to specify a minimum and/or maximum value to create a numeric test.
- **Valid Values:** Allows the user to specify a list of permitted values.

Since we're defining a list of valid states to be included in the region, select **Valid Values**, and the **General** tab will change to include the fields needed to define valid values, as shown in Figure 11.5.

Figure 11.5 General Tab for Valid Values Validation Rule

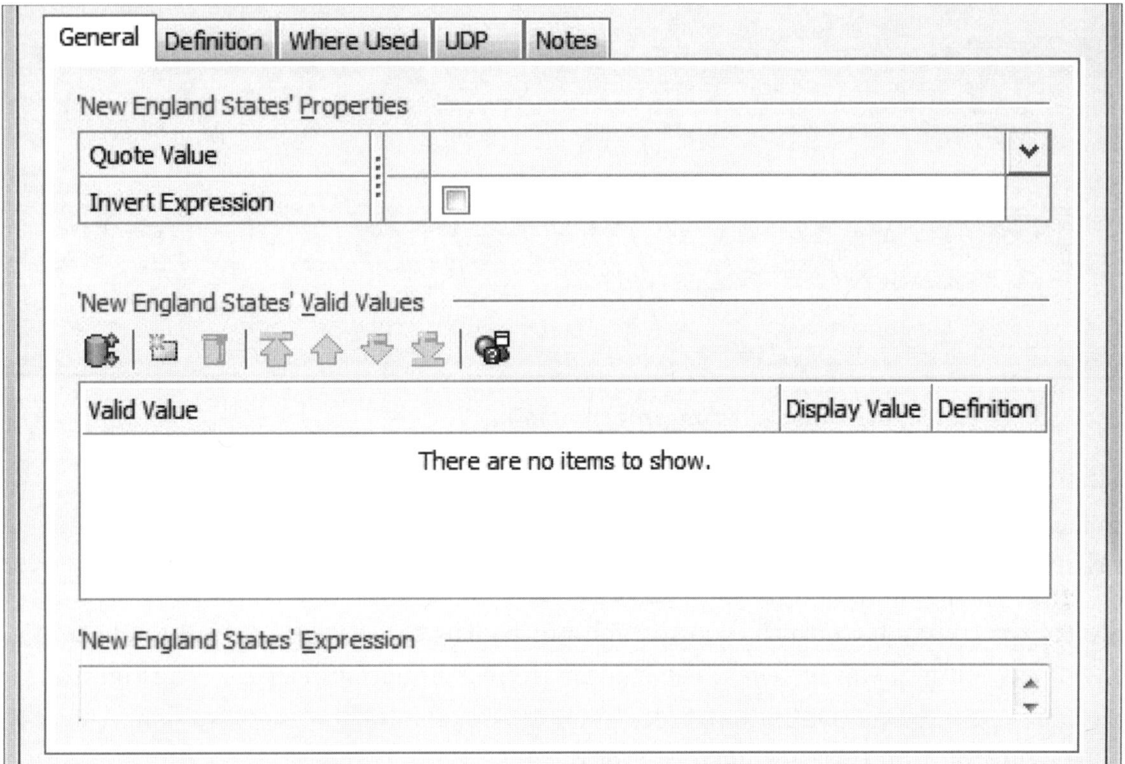

To add a valid value, select the **New** button from the Valid Values Toolbar, and a default entry is created, as shown in Figure 11.6.

Figure 11.6 Adding a New Valid Value

General | Definition | Where Used | UDP | Notes

'New England States' Properties

Quote Value

Invert Expression

'New England States' Valid Values

Valid Value	Display Value	Definition
Valid_Value_189		

'New England States' Expression

%AttFieldName IN ('Valid_Value_189')

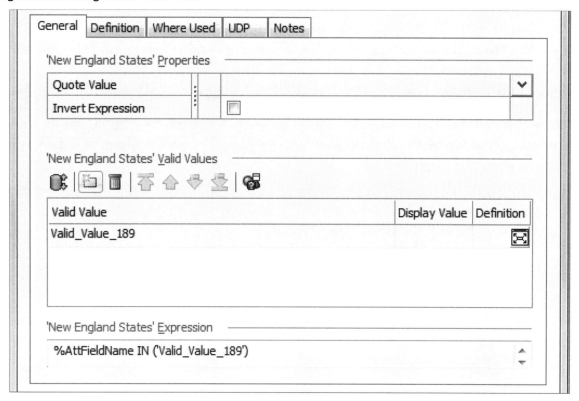

For our first entry, use the following information:

Valid Value: VT
Display Value: Vermont
Definition: The Green Mountain State

Note that you may have to change the column widths to accommodate the information. To widen a column, simply select the column divider line and drag it to the right or left. To enter text into the **Definition** field, click on the button, which opens the Valid Value Definition Editor, as shown in Figure 11.7.

Figure 11.7 Valid Value Definition Editor

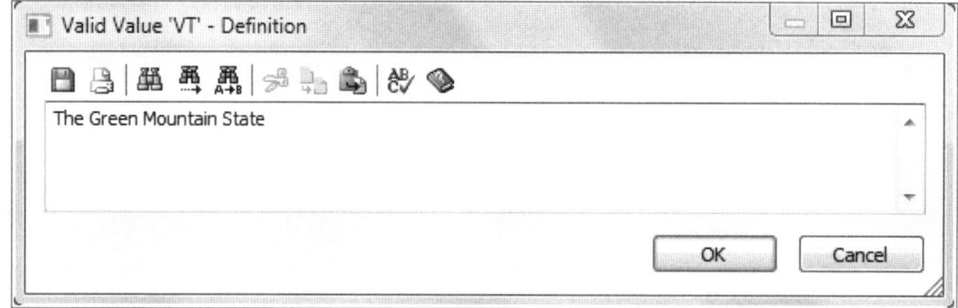

After you have entered this information, the **General** tab will look similar to Figure 11.8.

Figure 11.8 Modifying Valid Value Properties

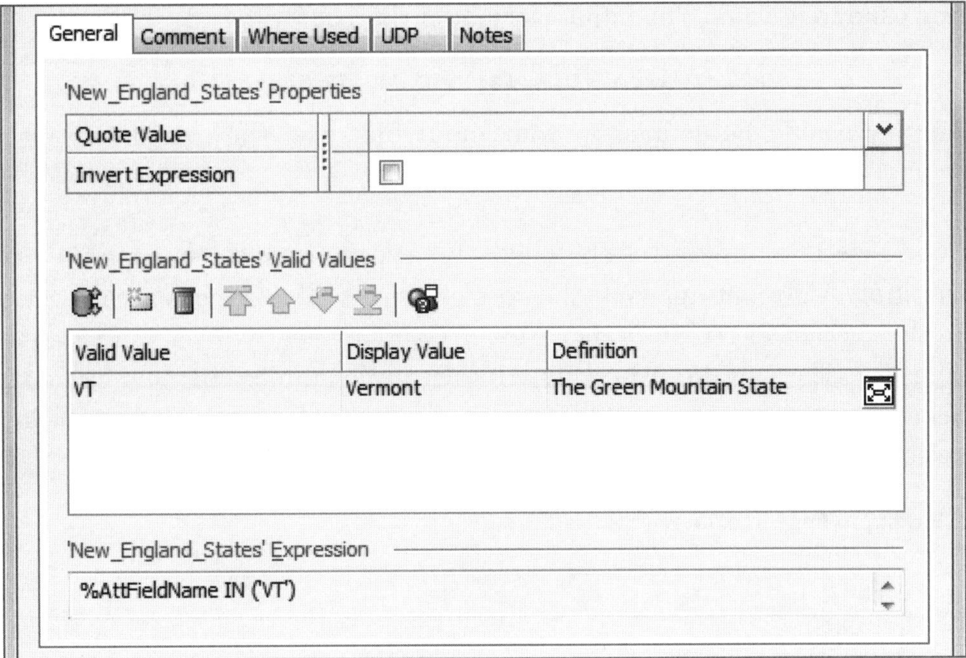

Next, we'll need to use the information listed in Table 11.1 to enter the remaining valid values.

Table 11.1 Valid Values for the New England States region

Valid Value	Display Value	Definition
VT	Vermont	The Green Mountain State
NH	New Hampshire	Live Free or Die
MA	Massachusetts	The Bay State
ME	Maine	Vacationland
CT	Connecticut	The Constitution State
RI	Rhode Island	The Ocean State

Rather than adding values one-by-one, a handy way to enter lists of information, is to import them directly from the source spreadsheet using a Comma Separated Value (CSV) format (Note: `.csv` is a format easily exported from Excel). We've saved the spreadsheet in Figure 11.1 in `.csv` format, and you can download it from www.erwin.com/datamodelingmadesimple. If you'd like to try this exercise on your own, download the **New England States.csv** file and save it to a directory named **My Documents\State Codes**. The import format of the **.CSV** file is defined as:

Valid value, Display value, Definition

No header row should be defined in your input file—just the raw data separated by commas.

To enter our New England States spreadsheet, click the **Import** button on the Valid Values Toolbar. A prompt appears, shown in Figure 11.9, asking whether you'd like to append to the current list. If you select **Yes**, the spreadsheet values will be appended to the existing list. Selecting **No** overwrites the list and includes the new values from the spreadsheet only. Since we've already entered one State Code, we don't want duplicates, so we'll select **No**, and will overwrite the existing list.

Figure 11.9 Prompt to Append or Overwrite Valid Values

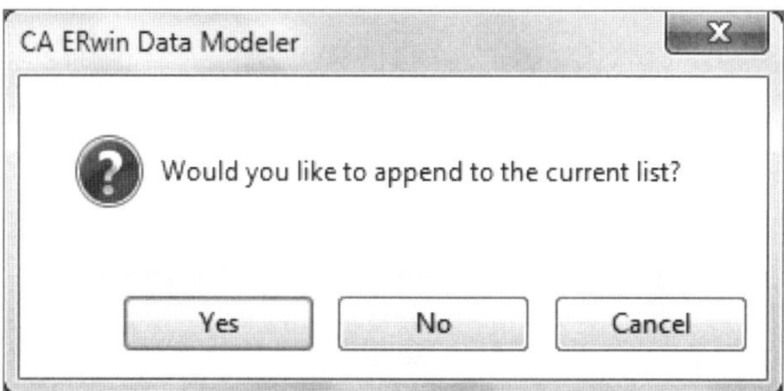

Next, you'll be prompted for the file to import. Select the **New England States.csv** from your **State Codes** directory, as shown in Figure 11.10.

Figure 11.10 Selecting a .CSV file to Import Valid Values

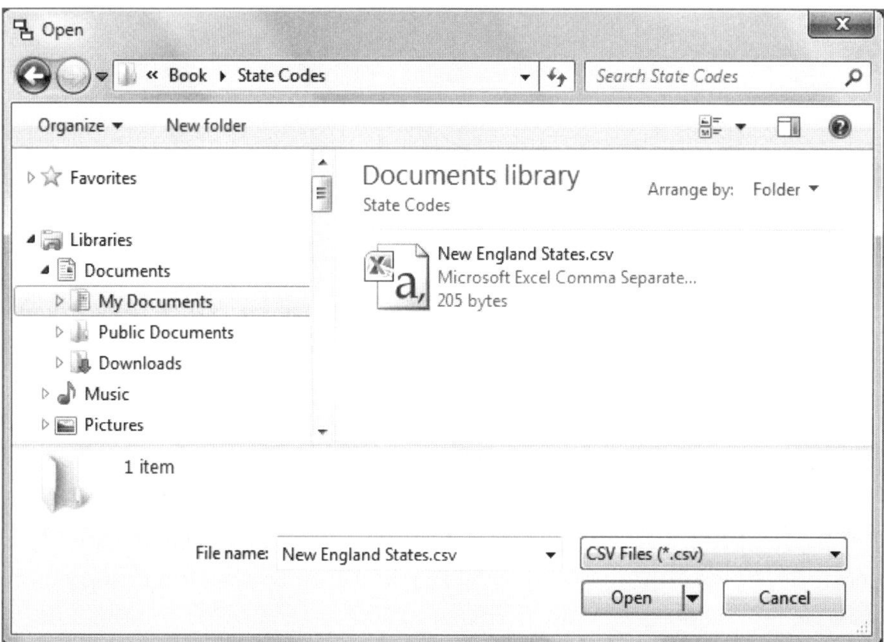

Select **Open** and the file will be imported. The new list will look similar to Figure 11.11.

Figure 11.11 List of Valid Values for New England States

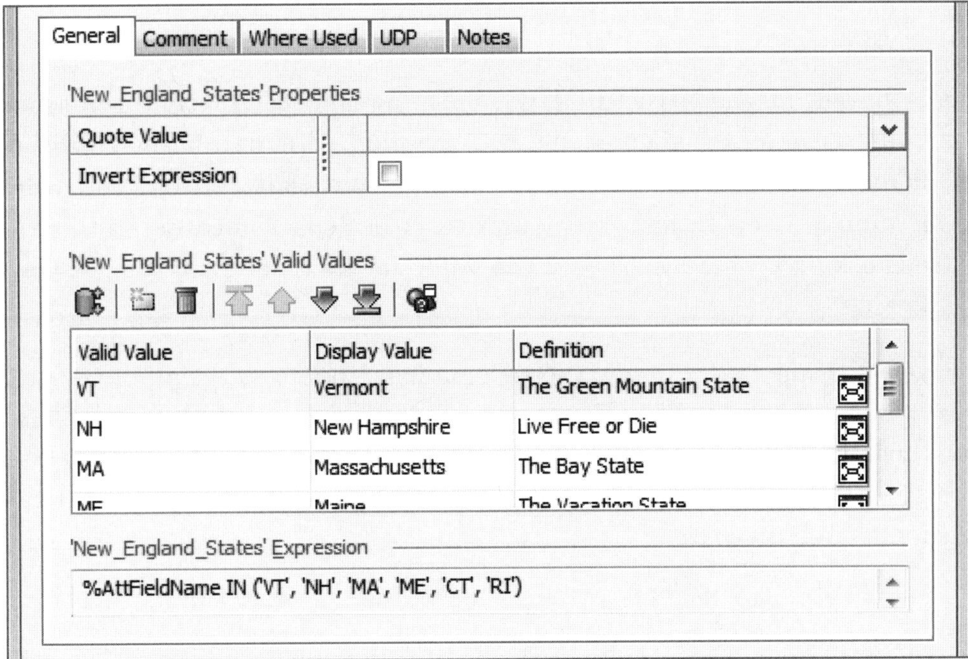

Note that by default, the entries are listed in the order that you entered them. To sort the values alphabetically, select the **Sort Items** icon from the Valid Values Toolbar. We'll choose to list the valid values in **Alphabetic** order, as shown in Figure 11.12. Note that this changes the display only, not the actual validation rule itself.

Figure 11.12 Sorting Valid Values Alphabetically

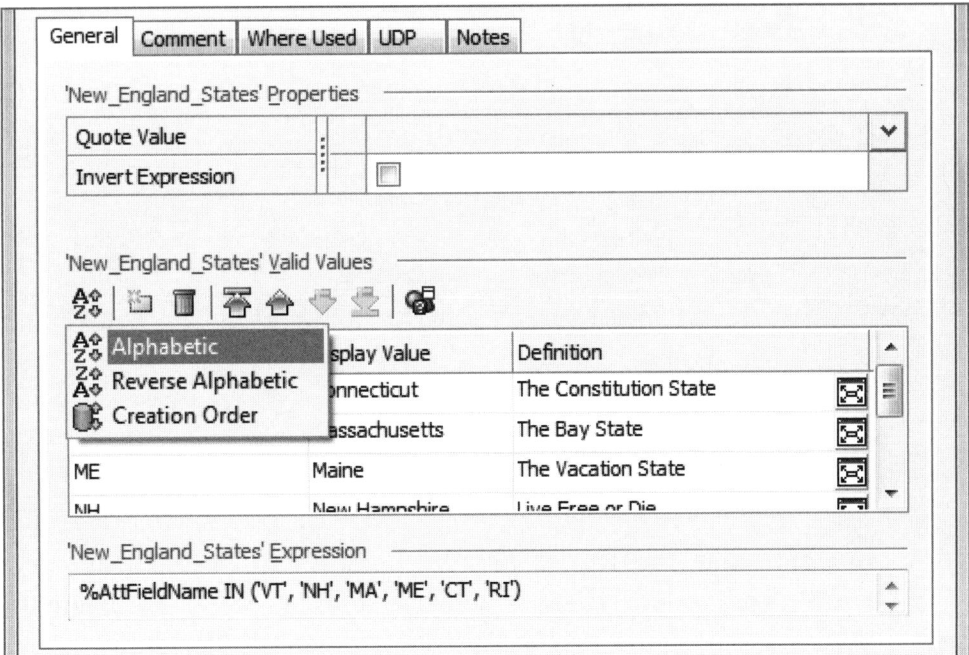

If you look in the **'New England States' Expression** field in Figure 11.2, you'll notice that a Validation Rule has been automatically created based upon the list you entered. In this case, the validation rule is

```
%AttFieldName IN ('VT', 'NH', 'MA', 'ME', 'CT', 'RI')
```

This rule is based on the Structured Query Language (SQL) that is used in most databases. This is a starting point for the creation of a database-specific script to enforce validation rules. **%AttFieldName** is a macro that returns the value of an attribute or column. Even without being an expert in SQL, you can read this rule fairly easily—it is checking to make sure that the value in the field is 'in' the list you defined in the valid value.

In some cases, you may want to use the reverse logic, i.e. to select all of the states that are 'not in' the list of valid values. For example, we might want to return all state codes except for those in New England. This is where the **Invert Expression** field comes into play. In Figure 11.13, you'll see that when we select the **Invert Expression** check box, the validation rule changes to:

```
%AttFieldName NOT IN ('VT', 'NH', 'MA', 'ME', 'CT', 'RI')
```

The **NOT** expression inverts the rule, or returns everything except what is shown in the list.

Figure 11.13 Using the Invert Expression Field

General | Comment | Where Used | UDP | Notes

'New_England_States' Properties

Quote Value	
Invert Expression	☑

'New_England_States' Valid Values

Valid Value	Display Value	Definition
CT	Connecticut	The Constitution State
MA	Massachusetts	The Bay State
ME	Maine	The Vacation State
NH	New Hampshire	Live Free or Die

'New_England_States' Expression

%AttFieldName NOT IN ('VT', 'NH', 'MA', 'ME', 'CT', 'RI')

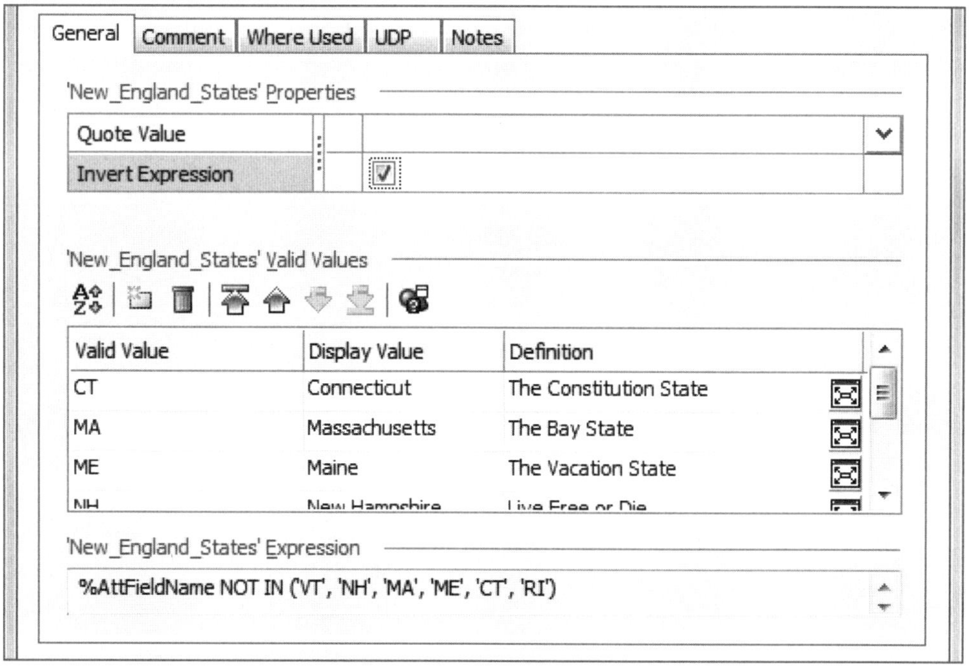

You might also notice that the values are, by default, enclosed within quotes, for example: 'VT', 'NH', and so on. Using quotation marks can be problematic when implementing SQL on your target database, so you may wish to remove them. To do

this, select **No** from the drop-down menu for the **Quote Value** field, as shown in Figure 11.14, and notice that the validation rule is written without quotes around the individual values:

```
%AttFieldName NOT IN (VT, NH, MA, ME, CT, RI)
```

Figure 11.14 Removing Quotes from Validation Rules

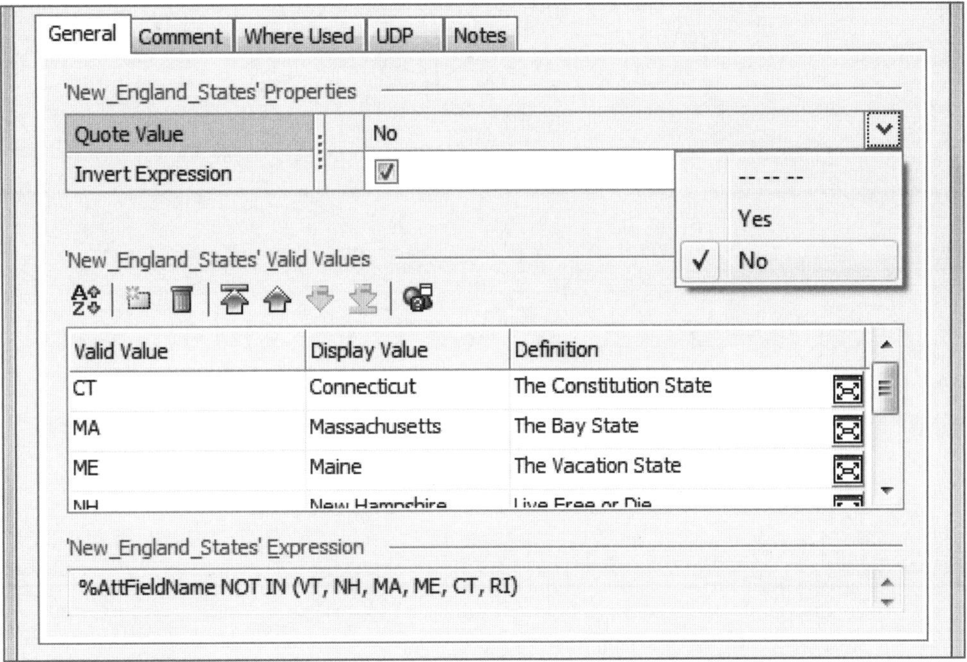

To implement Validation Rules, these rules can be associated with a domain or directly with an attribute or column. When implementing your physical database, these rules help with data quality, so that only valid values are entered. For example, our company may have a business rule that states that products cannot be shipped to customers in New England, since we don't have a commerce agreement in those states. **Close** the Validation Rule Editor, and in the logical model, add a **ship to state** attribute to the **Customer** entity, using a data type of **CHAR(2)** using the Attribute Properties Editor, as shown in Figure 11.15. (For more information on how to create attributes, refer to Chapter 5).

Figure 11.15 Adding ship to state Attribute

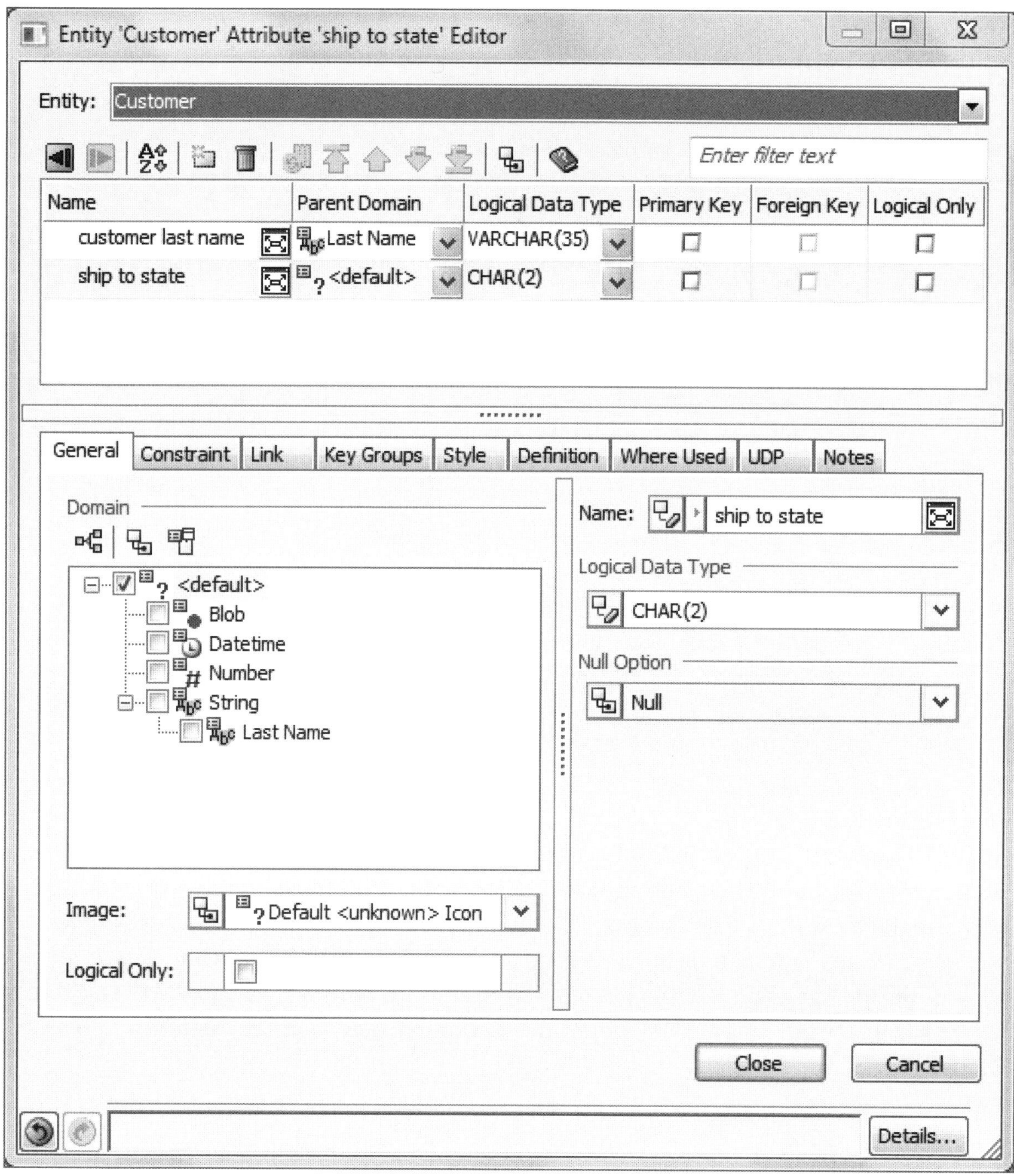

To add our Validation Rule, move to the **Constraint** tab, as shown in Figure 11.16.

Figure 11.16 Constraint Tab of the Attribute Properties Editor

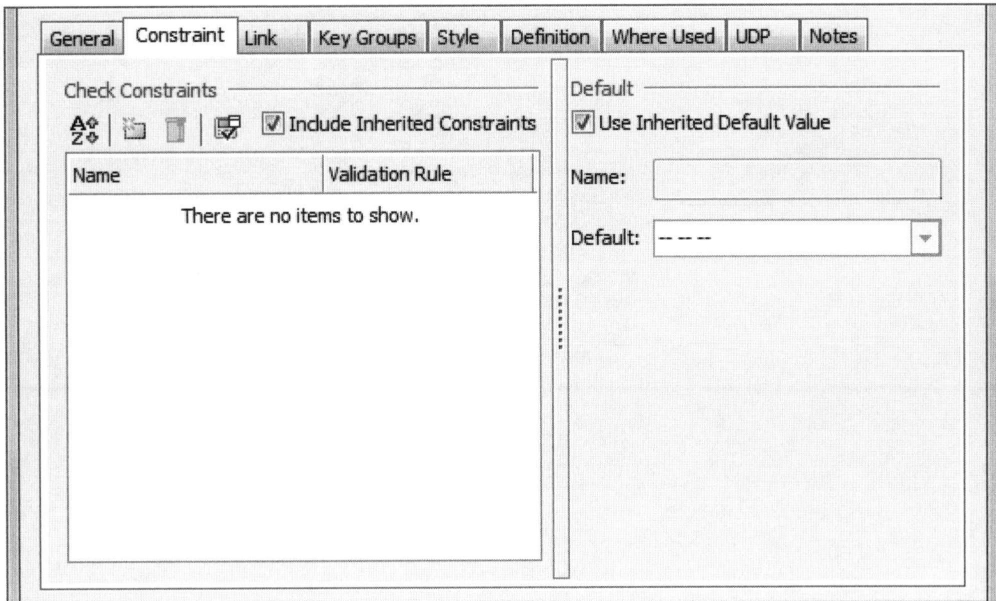

To add a Validation Rule, select the **New** button from the Check Constraints Toolbar, and a default value is created, as show in Figure 11.17.

Figure 11.17 Adding a New Validation Rule to an Attribute

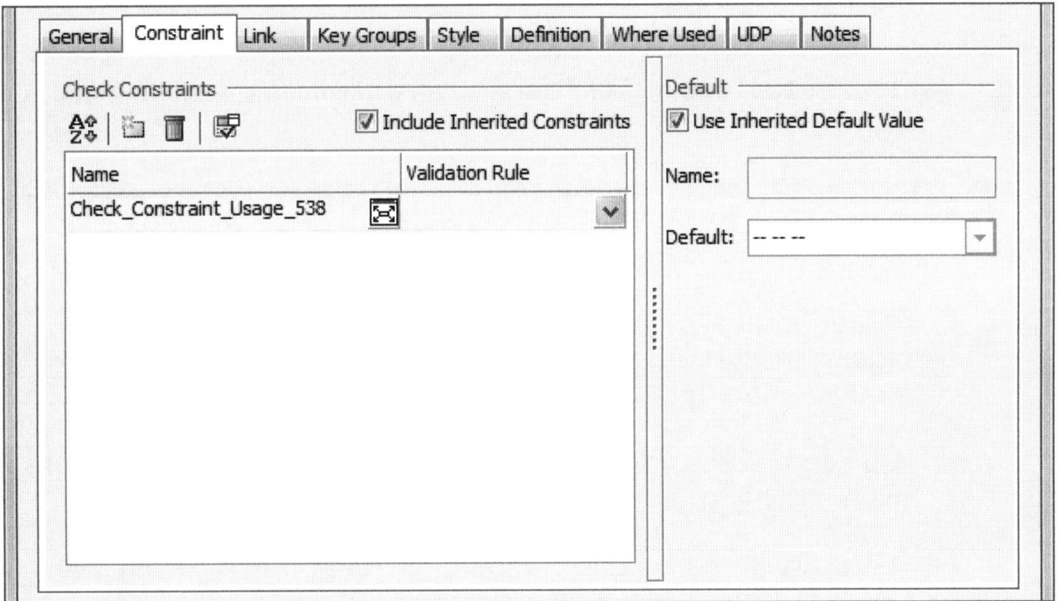

To change this default, use the **Validation Rule** drop-down menu, and select the **New England States** rule that we previously created, as shown in Figure 11.18. When the **Include Inherited Constraints** check box is selected, this property is inherited from the attribute's domain. Since we've selected a custom constraint in this case, and don't want to use any constraints that may have been defined in the parent domain, we'll want to uncheck that box.

Figure 11.18 Changing a Default Validation Rule

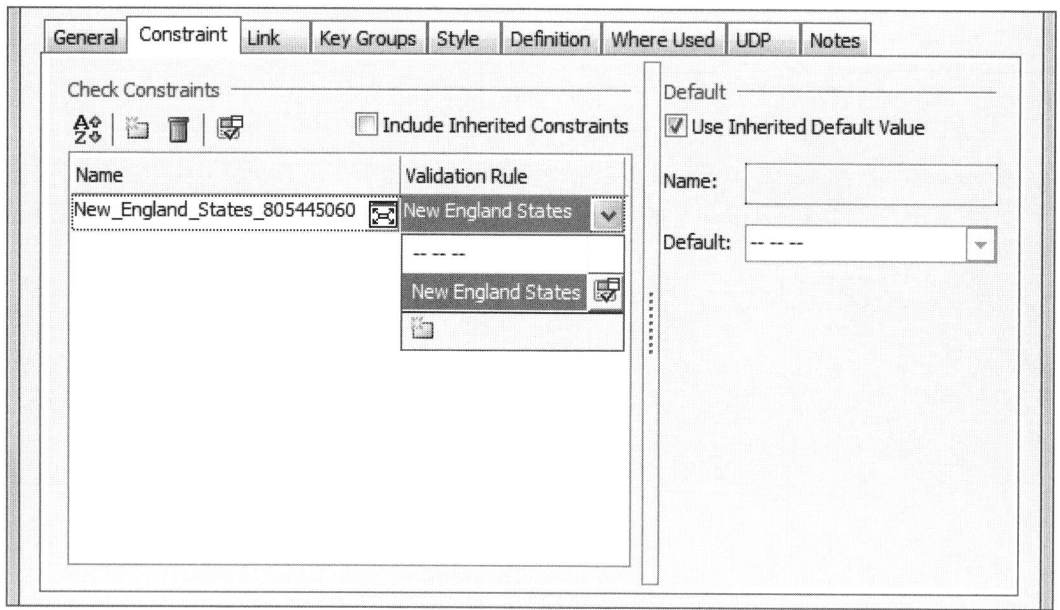

You've now successfully added a constraint to the **ship to state** attribute to enforce the rule that items cannot be shipped to states in the New England region. The validation rules we define in our model will be important when we implement the actual database, as it is these rules that help validate data as it is entered to control data quality.

If you'd like an example of the finished model from this example, you can download the model **`Validation Rules.erwin`** from the www.erwin.com/datamodelingmadesimple web site.

Key Points

- Validation Rules help enforce the business rules of your organization by establishing a default value, list of values, or a range of acceptable values for an object.
- You can enforce validation rules through a domain, or assign them directly to a table, column, entity, or attribute.
- There are three types of validation rules in CA ERwin Data Modeler: User-Defined, MinMax, and Valid Values.
- Valid values lists can be imported from an external format, such as a spreadsheet.

CHAPTER 12
Naming Standards

What is in a name?
Consistency and Reuse
Build understanding

Standardizing the way in which objects are named in your models is important to enforce consistency and reuse across the organization. It is hard enough to produce consistent definitions of core data assets such as **Customer**. This task becomes even more difficult when differing naming conventions hide the meaning of objects or make them difficult to locate. For example, there may be objects named **Cust**, **Customer**, **Cstmr**, **Client**, etc.—do these all have the same meaning, and is there data stored in these objects that should be consolidated?

Enforcing Naming Standards

Naming Standards can be enforced in CA ERwin Data Modeler to help ensure that modelers adhere to a consistent naming convention so that objects are named consistently, helping to promote reuse, increase data quality, and reduce overlap and data redundancy. Tools that assist in the creation of enterprise naming standards in CA ERwin Data Modeler are the Naming Standards Editor and Glossary. Through the Glossary, you can define a list of words and abbreviations that modelers can use to name entities, tables, attributes, columns, and domains. Naming Standards can be used in the following scenarios in CA ERwin Data Modeler:

- Deriving physical names from logical names in a logical /physical model
- Deriving a physical model from a logical model
- Deriving a logical model from a physical model
- Checking naming standard compliance in a logical or physical model

Naming Standards are developed outside of a given data model and are stored in a separate file with the extension **.nsm**. A naming standards (**.nsm**) file can then be attached to one or more data models or data model templates so that the standards can be enforced across models in the enterprise.

To define naming standards, you can invoke the Naming Standards Editor within CA ERwin Data Modeler by selecting **Tools|Standards|Naming Standards** from the **Main Menu** (note that a model must be open for this menu to be active). You can also invoke the Naming Standards Editor as a stand-alone application from the **CA ERwin Data Modeler** folder in the Windows **Start** menu. The Naming Standards Editor is shown in Figure 12.1.

Figure 12.1 Naming Standards Editor

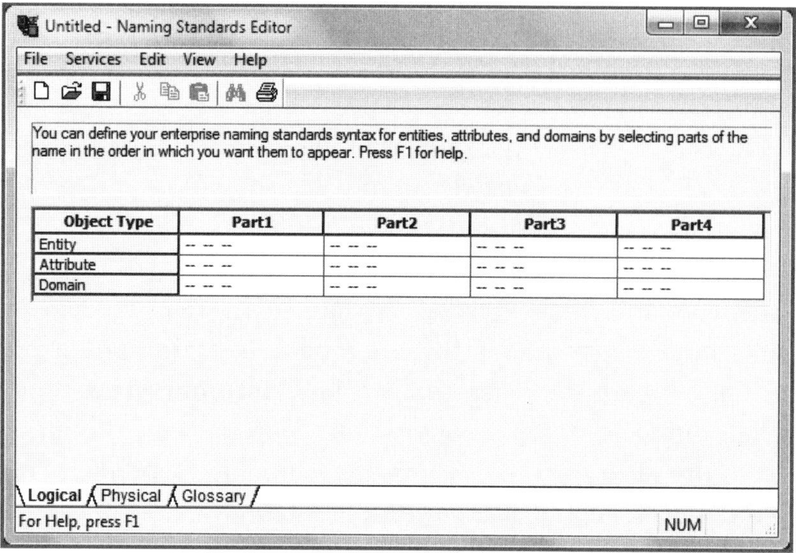

There are three tabs in the Naming Standards Editor:

- The **Logical** tab defines the naming standards syntax for entities, attributes, and domains.
- The **Physical** tab defines the naming standards syntax for tables, columns, and domains.
- The **Glossary** tab contains the words and abbreviations used to create standard object names across the enterprise.

Let's start by creating our core list of words and abbreviations by selecting the **Glossary** tab, shown in Figure 12.2.

Figure 12.2 Glossary Tab of the Naming Standard Editor

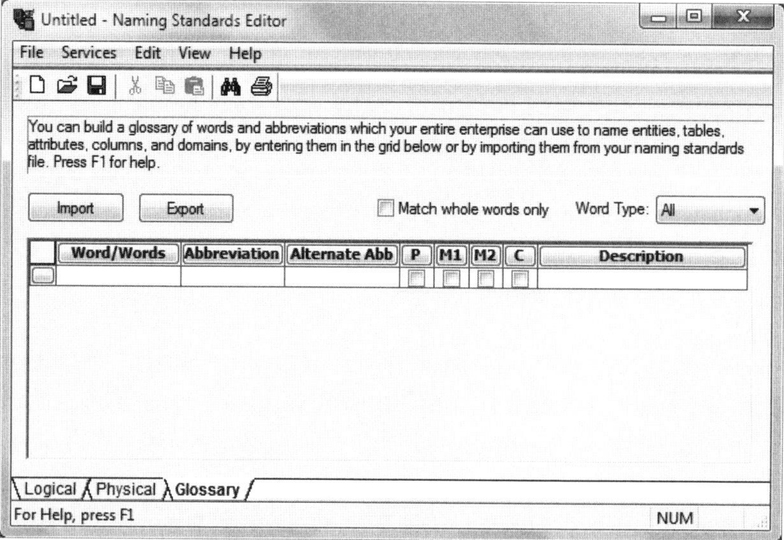

You can either create the Glossary manually, by entering words and abbreviations directly into the grid, or you can import the Glossary from an external file. For this example, we'll enter a few items manually to get a better understanding of each of the entries and what they mean. First, let's start with an overview of the Glossary properties and how they are used. Table 12.1 provides a list of the Glossary properties and what they mean.

Table 12.1 Glossary Properties and Their Definitions

Glossary Property	Definition
Word/Words	The business term or technical element that needs to be abbreviated, e.g. **customer**.
Abbreviation	The standard, approved abbreviation for the Word, e.g. **cust**.
Alternate Abbreviation	An alternate abbreviation that may be used by a particular region or application. This may be customized for a particular platform, or language/region. e.g. **cst**, **cliente**.
P (Prime)	A Prime Word typically describes the subject area of the data such as **Account**, **Employee**, or **Customer**.
M1 and M2 (Modifier 1 & 2)	A Modifier is a word that further defines or distinguishes the prime and class words. For example, you can use the modifier **Last** to further define the **Name** class word (e.g. **Last Name**). You can specify up to two modifiers.
C (Class Word)	A Class word designates the major classification of data that is associated with a model object such as **Date**, **Amount**, **Code**, or **Name**.

Let's use an example to explain this further. There are many different ways in which organizations implement data-naming conventions, and CA ERwin Data Modeler allows you to customize the way in which names are created based on your unique criteria. A popular naming convention in the industry is the 'modifier/prime word/modifier/class word' convention. We'll use this convention in our example. With this convention, every data element must have one prime word, one or more modifiers, and end in one class word (modifiers can apply to both prime and class words). Class words are standardized and documented (e.g. **date**, **amount**, **code**, etc.).

An example of a standardized business name for a data element is **full-time employee last name**. The main component (prime word) is **employee**, which is further qualified by the modifier **full-time** to distinguish this from a **part-time employee**. The class word indicating the type of data value contained in this data element is **name**, which is further qualified by a second modifier **last** to indicate the type of name (e.g. first, last, middle). Figure 12.3 explains this visually, labeling each portion of the business term with its corresponding Glossary property.

Figure 12.3 Example of Prime Word, Class Word, and Modifiers

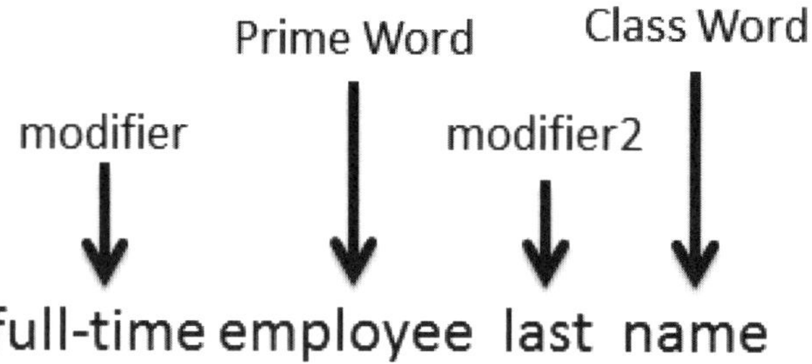

Let's enter the Glossary words that correspond to our example above. Referring to the example in Figure 12.3, we are able to determine the Glossary words and their types. In addition, we have created a set of standard abbreviations. In our example, we are working with two organizations that have merged, and we still have not integrated the two database environments. In the interim, we have two sets of standards: one from Company A, and one from Company B. Table 12.2 shows the list of words, as well as their corresponding type and abbreviation.

Table 12.2 Standards for Glossary

Word	Type	Abbreviation from Company A	Abbreviation from Company B (Alternate)
full-time	Modifier 1	ft	fte
employee	Prime	emp	empl
last	Modifier 2	lst	l
name	Class	nm	nme

Entering this information into the **Glossary** tab in the Naming Standards Editor will result in a list similar to Figure 12.4.

Figure 12.4 Populating the Naming Standards Editor

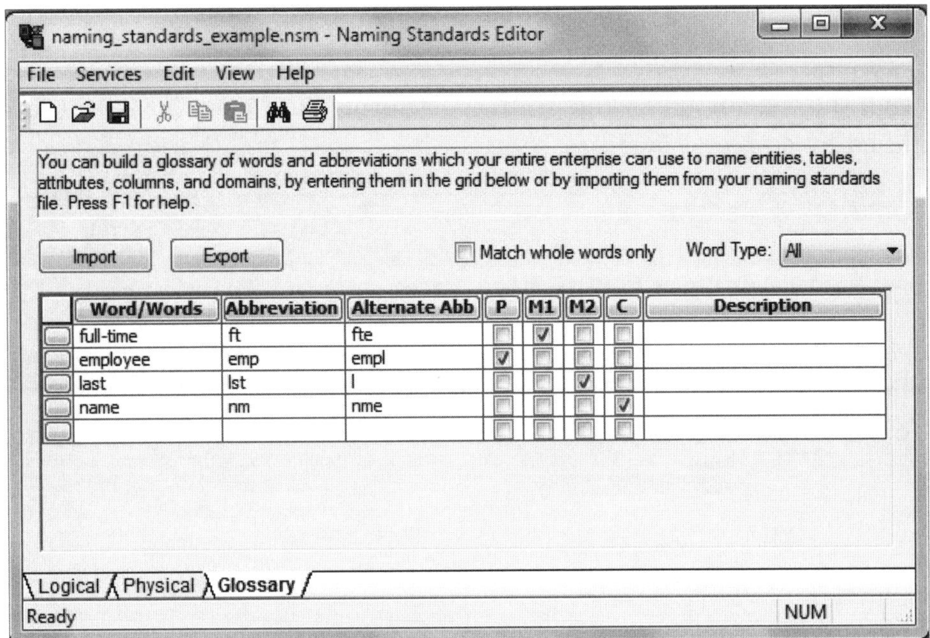

Rather than enter Glossary words manually, a helpful way to populate large numbers of glossary values is by importing from a spreadsheet using **.CSV** format using the **Import** button. The **.CSV** file for a Glossary word import must be in the format shown in Figure 12.5. The **Prime**, **Mod1**, **Mod2**, and **Class** indicators are entered as 'X'.

Figure 12.5 Format for Naming Standards .CSV File Import

```
Word, Abbreviation, Alt Abbreviation, Prime, Mod1, Mod2, Class, Description
```

For example, the **.CSV** version of the data we entered in Figure 12.4 is shown in Figure 12.6. A sample **glossary.csv** file can be found on www.erwin.com/datamodelingmadesimple if you'd like to give the **Import** option a try on your own.

Figure 12.6 CSV Version of Naming Standards Glossary

```
full-time,ft,fte,,X,,,
employee,emp,empl,X,,,,
last,lst,l,,,X,,
name,nm,nme,,,,X,
```

Now that we've entered our Glossary words, we want to enforce the word order syntax. In our case, we want to use the 'modifier/prime word/modifier/class word' convention for all attributes in our model. Figure 12.7 shows how the drop-down menus on the **Logical** tab can be used to define the word order for a given object type. In our example, we've defined that attributes use a **Modifier** for the first part, a **Prime** word as the second, a second **Modifier** for the third, and a **Class** word as the final portion.

Figure 12.7 Defining Word Order Syntax

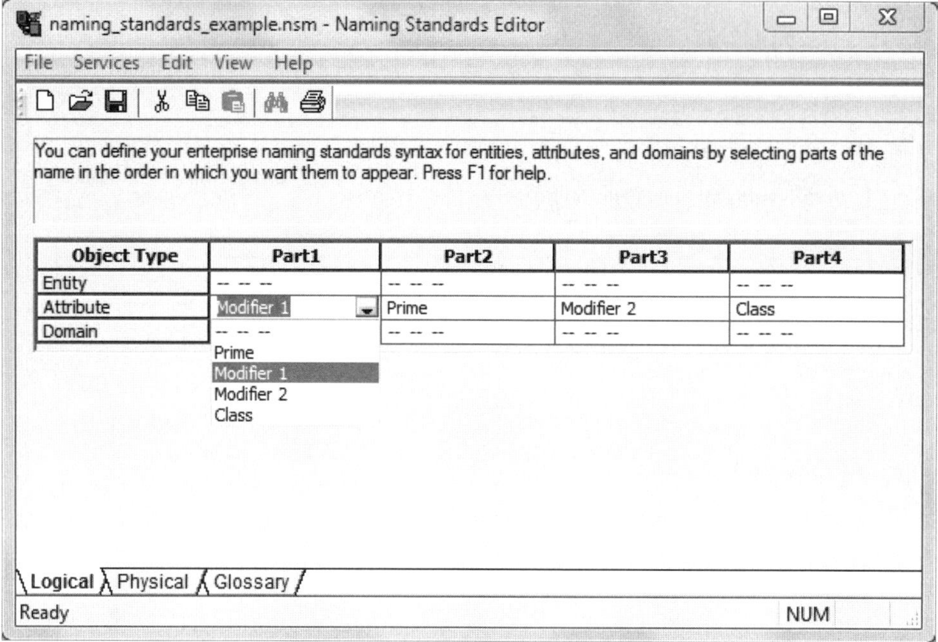

To save the Naming Standards file we just created, select **File|Save** or click on the **Save** button on the Naming Standards Toolbar. When prompted for a file name, use **`naming_standards_example.nsm`** for this example. A sample of this file can be found on www.erwin.com/datamodelingmadesimple.

Using Naming Standards in a Model

Now that we've created our Glossary, let's use this Glossary to enforce naming standards in our model. To ensure consistency in our organization, a key requirement we have is to use a standardized naming convention for logical and physical object names. As we discussed earlier, if objects are named differently across projects, it is difficult to get a consistent view of information.

First, create a Logical/Physical model with a target database of SQL Server 2008 (for help on how to create a model, refer to Chapter 3). Once your model is created, select **Actions|Model Naming Options** from the **Main Menu**. The Model Naming Options Editor appears, shown in Figure 12.8.

Figure 12.8 Model Naming Options Editor

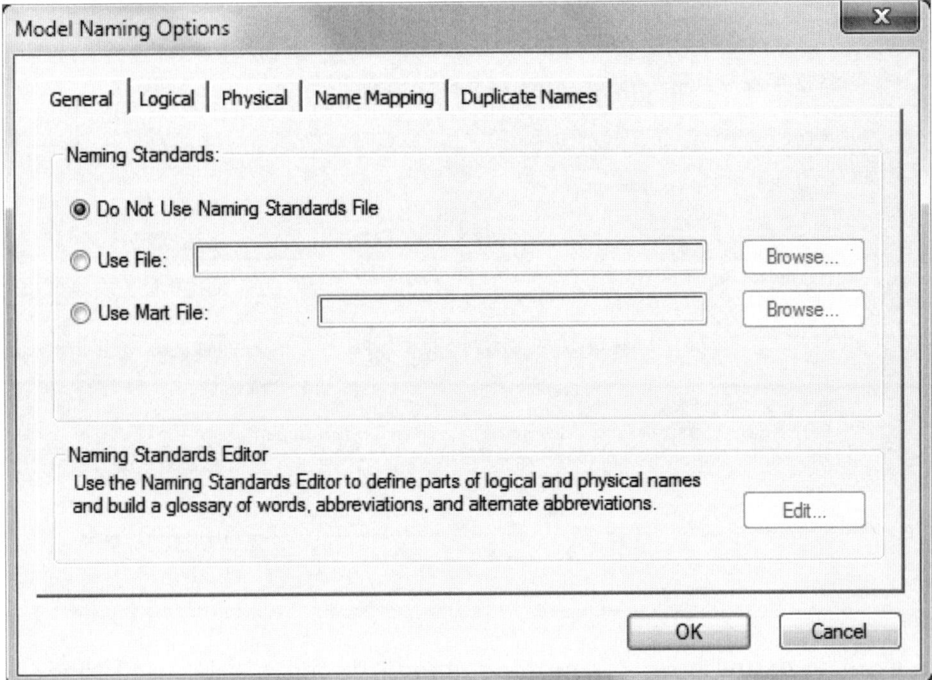

The Model Naming Options Editor contains the following tabs:

- The **General** tab contains the naming standard file that CA ERwin Data Modeler will use. By default, CA ERwin Data Modeler does not validate your object names or object naming conventions. To activate this validation, you'll need to create and specify a naming standards file.
- The **Logical** tab enables you to set the **Case** and **Maximum Length** for the listed object types for the Logical data model.
- The **Physical** tab enables you to set the **Case** and **Maximum Length** for the listed object types for the Physical data model.
- The **Name Mapping** tab can be used to set preferences for deriving a physical model object name from a logical model object name. Note that the naming preferences that you set for the physical model objects must conform to the naming rules of the target database.
- The **Duplicate Names** tab defined how duplicate names are handled in CA ERwin Data Modeler

First, we'll want to associate the naming standards file we just created to this new model. On the **General** tab, select the **Use File** radio button, and then the **Browse** button to locate the **`naming_standards_example.nsm`** file you created, as shown in Figure 12.9. A sample **`naming_standards_example.nsm`** file is also located at www.erwin.com/datamodelingmadsimple.

Figure 12.9 Associating a Naming Standards File with a Model

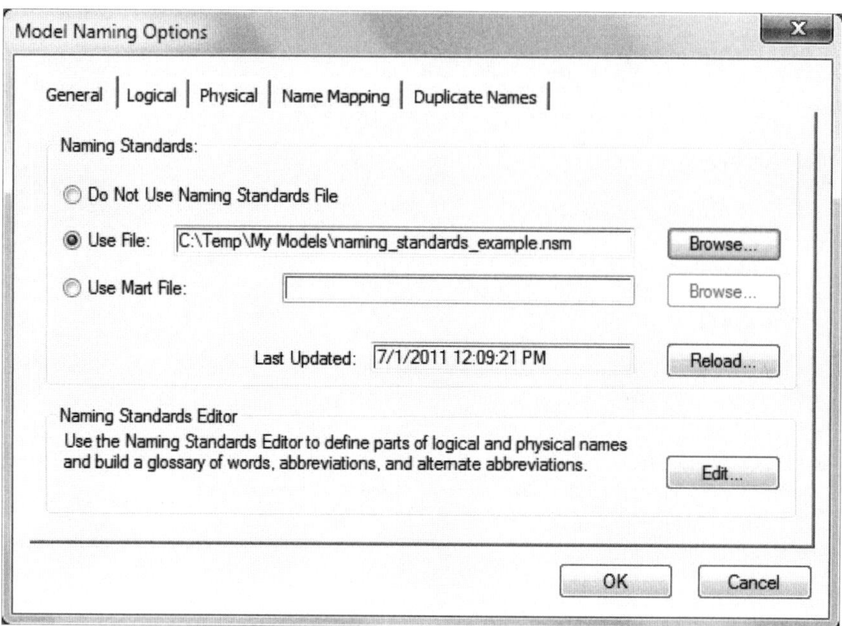

Next, we'll want to define how this naming standards file will be used to create names in our model. In our case, we want to use our Glossary to define a consistent naming convention for logical and physical objects. To implement this behavior, move to the **Name Mapping** tab, and select the **Use Glossary** column for the **Entity to Table** row in the **Object Type** column, as shown in Figure 12.10. This option will create logical and physical object names based on the Glossary, using the **Word** field from the Glossary for logical names and the **Abbreviation** field for the corresponding physical object names.

Figure 12.10 Creating an Entity to Table Name Mapping

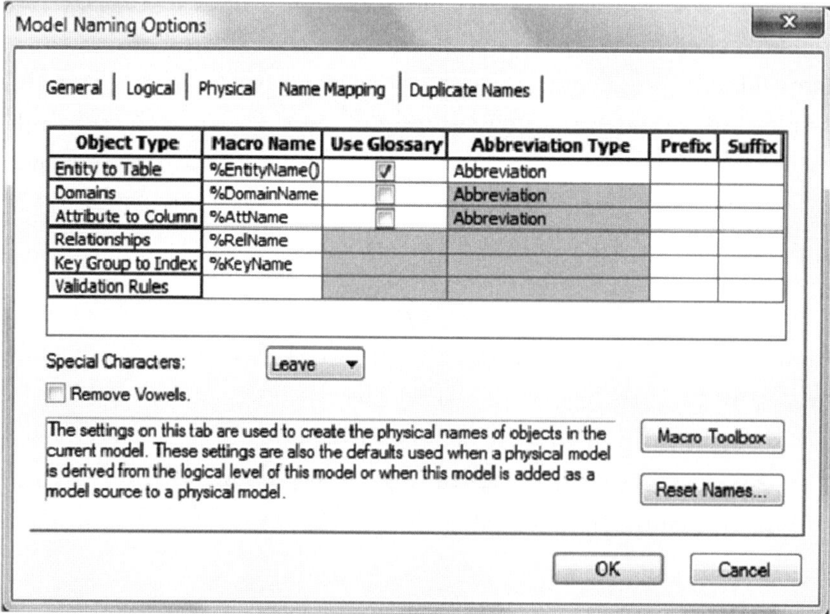

There are other tabs and options we can use to refine our naming standards implementation, but for now, let's stop here and click **OK** to return to your model to get a sense of how the naming standards work.

On your logical model diagram, create an entity named **Employee**, as shown in Figure 12.11. (In this example, we are using the **Entity Display Level**). For more information on how to create an entity and change entity display levels, refer to Chapter 4.

Figure 12.11 Employee Entity

Employee

Now switch to your physical model. You will see a table named **emp**, as shown in Figure 12.12.

Figure 12.12 emp Table

emp

In this example, the physical table name was automatically populated with the standard **Abbreviation** that was created in the Naming Standards file. Figure 12.13 shows a mapping between the terms in the Glossary we created, and the model objects on the diagram.

Figure 12.13 Mapping Glossary Terms with Model Objects

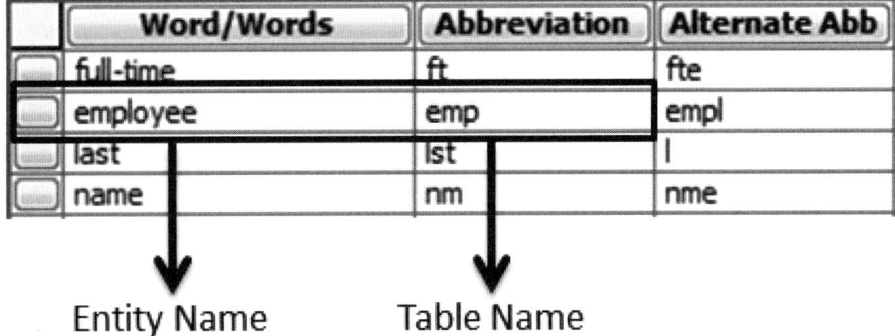

Word/Words	Abbreviation	Alternate Abb
full-time	ft	fte
employee	emp	empl
last	lst	l
name	nm	nme

Although the physical name was generated correctly, we notice a few things that aren't quite right. First, the table name looks strange in all lowercase. Our company standard is to have all table names in uppercase letters. To specify that particular model objects use uppercase versus lowercase text, use the **Case** field on the **Physical** tab of the Model Naming Options Dialog, as shown in Figure 12.14.

Figure 12.14 Specifying Uppercase Text for Model Objects

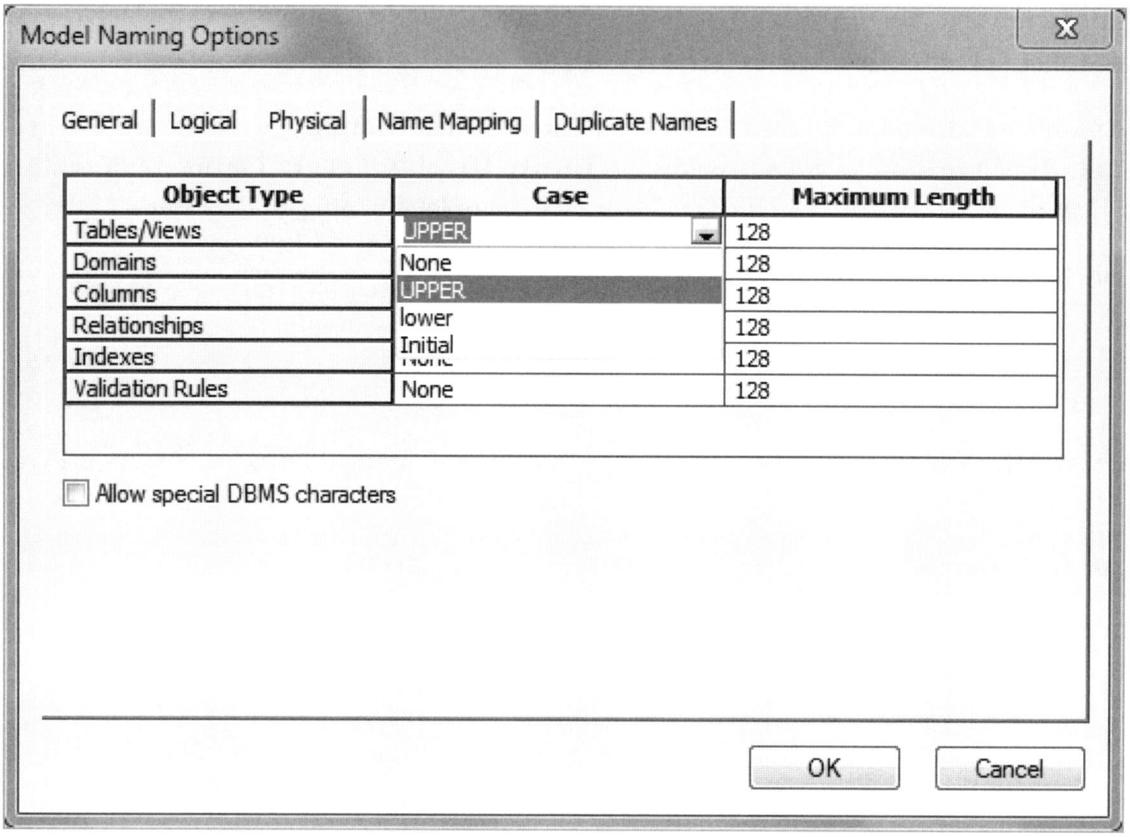

Object Type	Case	Maximum Length
Tables/Views	UPPER	128
Domains	None	128
Columns	UPPER	128
Relationships	lower	128
Indexes	Initial	128
Validation Rules	None	128

By changing the **Case** value to **UPPER** for **Tables/Views** and clicking **OK** to return to the model diagram, you'll see that the **EMP** table is now defined as uppercase, as shown in Figure 12.15. All future tables will also use uppercase text, whether they are defined in the Glossary or not. Try this for yourself by adding a few tables to your diagram—you'll see that they are all created with uppercase text.

Figure 12.15 EMP Table with Uppercase Letters Based on Model Naming Options

EMP

The database we're creating is a test system. Let's assume it's the preferred convention to add the prefix 'TST_' before all of the table names. We can also define prefixes and suffixes in the Model Naming Options dialog, as well. Open the Model Naming Options dialog again and type 'TST_' in the **Prefix** field for the **Entity to Table** object type on the **Name Mapping** tab, as shown in Figure 12.16. Note that while we're adding this prefix to just tables in our model, you can define both prefixes and suffixes for domains, columns, relationships, indexes, and validation rules as well.

Figure 12.16 Defining a Standard Prefix for Model Objects

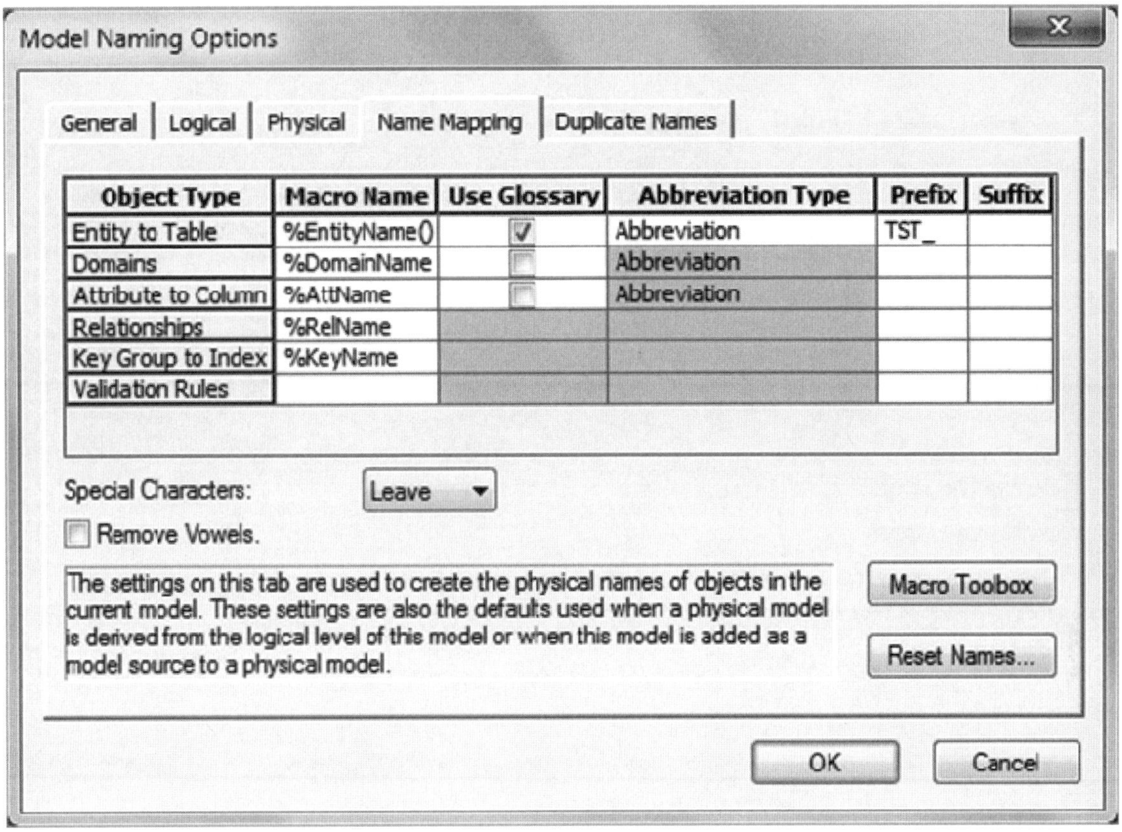

Model Naming Options

General | Logical | Physical | Name Mapping | Duplicate Names

Object Type	Macro Name	Use Glossary	Abbreviation Type	Prefix	Suffix
Entity to Table	%EntityName()	☑	Abbreviation	TST_	
Domains	%DomainName	☐	Abbreviation		
Attribute to Column	%AttName	☐	Abbreviation		
Relationships	%RelName				
Key Group to Index	%KeyName				
Validation Rules					

Special Characters: Leave

☐ Remove Vowels.

The settings on this tab are used to create the physical names of objects in the current model. These settings are also the defaults used when a physical model is derived from the logical level of this model or when this model is added as a model source to a physical model.

Macro Toolbox

Reset Names...

OK Cancel

Click **OK** to return to your model, and you'll notice that the prefix 'TST_' has been added to the **EMP** table, as well as any other tables you may have created in your model, as shown in Figure 12.17.

Figure 12.17 Adding a Prefix to the EMP Table Using Model Naming Options

Recall from our earlier discussion that we have two companies who are in the process of merging: Company A and Company B. While Company A uses the abbreviations we've defined in our example so far, Company B is still using their own abbreviations. We'll eventually want to move to a single naming convention across companies, but for now, we're maintaining two sets of abbreviations. Recall that we used the **Alternate Abbreviation** field to list Company B's abbreviation scheme (refer to Figure 12.4). To use these terms for our physical model, select **Alternate Abbreviation** as the **Abbreviation Type** on the **Name Mapping** tab of the Model Naming Options dialog, as shown in Figure 12.18.

Figure 12.18 Using Alternate Abbreviations for Model Naming Standards

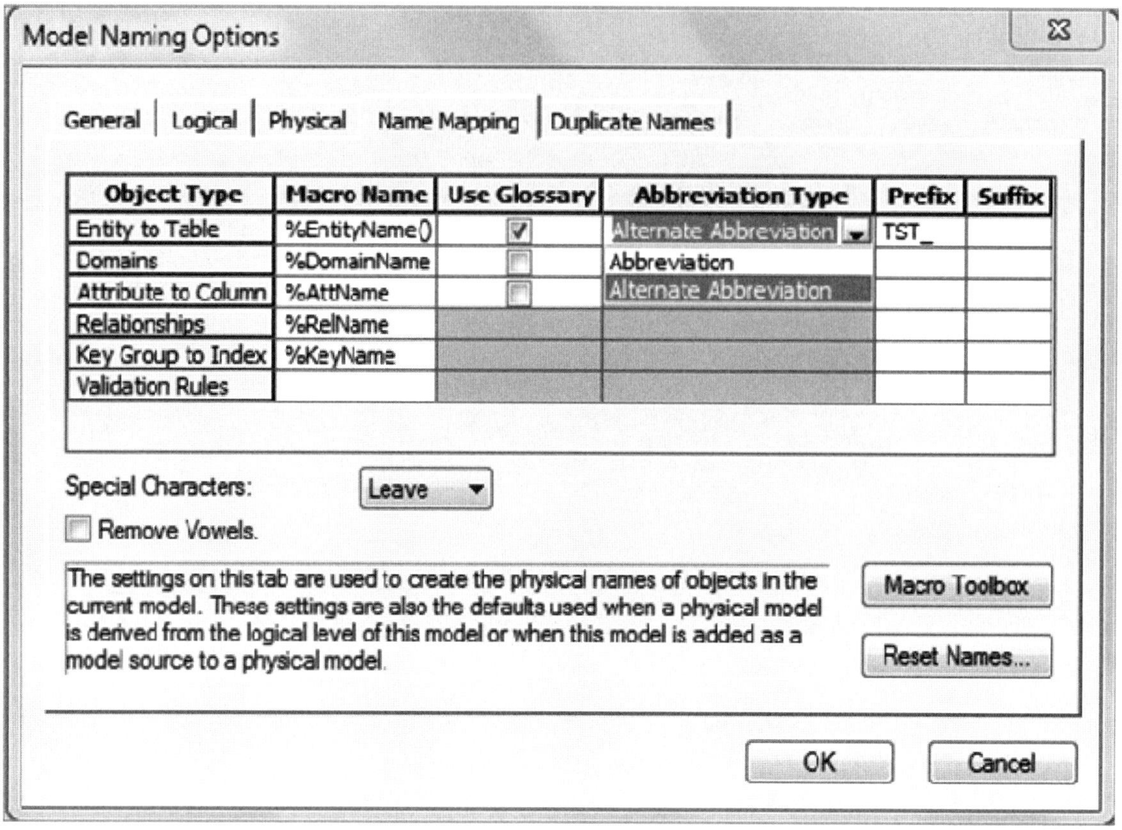

Model Naming Options

General | Logical | Physical | Name Mapping | Duplicate Names

Object Type	Macro Name	Use Glossary	Abbreviation Type	Prefix	Suffix
Entity to Table	%EntityName()	☑	Alternate Abbreviation	TST_	
Domains	%DomainName	☐	Abbreviation		
Attribute to Column	%AttName	☐	Alternate Abbreviation		
Relationships	%RelName				
Key Group to Index	%KeyName				
Validation Rules					

Special Characters: Leave

☐ Remove Vowels.

The settings on this tab are used to create the physical names of objects in the current model. These settings are also the defaults used when a physical model is derived from the logical level of this model or when this model is added as a model source to a physical model.

Macro Toolbox | Reset Names...

OK | Cancel

After making this change, click **OK** to return to the model diagram, and you will see that the **TST_EMP** table is now named **TST_EMPL**, according to the standards defined in our **Naming Standards** file, as shown in Figure 12.19. Save this model with a file name of `naming_standards_example.erwin`.

Figure 12.19 Using an Alternate Abbreviation for a Table Name

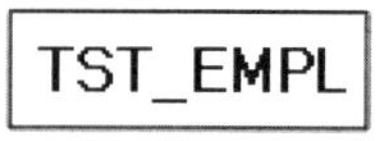

TST_EMPL

As you're beginning to see, there are numerous options you can choose to implement naming standards according to your organization's needs. Table 12.3 lists some common naming standards requirements and the menu options used to implement them in CA ERwin Data Modeler.

Table 12.3 Common Scenarios for Implementing Naming Standards

Scenario	How to Implement in CA ERwin Data Modeler
Disallow duplicate names in a model and force unique object names.	1. Select **Actions|Model Naming Options** from the **Main Menu** 2. Move to the **Duplicate Names** tab 3. Select the **Disallow Duplicate Names** radio button
Remove vowels from the names of physical model objects	1. Select **Actions|Model Naming Options** from the **Main Menu** 2. Move to the **Name Mapping** tab 3. Select the **Remove Vowels** check box
Limit the length of table names to 25 characters or fewer	1. Select **Actions|Model Naming Options** from the **Main Menu** 2. Move to the **Physical** tab 3. Define the **Maximum Length** field as 25 for the **Tables/Views Object Type** field. Names longer than 25 characters will be truncated
Enforce that all attribute names are in lower case	1. Select **Actions|Model Naming Options** from the **Main Menu** 2. Move to the **Logical** tab 3. Define the **Case** field as **Lower** using the drop-down menu for the **Attributes Object Type** field
Add a Suffix of '_TMP' to all column names.	1. Select **Actions|Model Naming Options** from the **Main Menu** 2. Move to the **Name Mapping** tab 3. Type **_TMP** in the **Suffix** field for the **Attribute to Column Object Type** field

Checking Naming Standards Compliance

In some cases, you may have inherited a model that did not use naming conventions during the initial creation phase. In this case, you might want to validate this model against an existing naming standards file, to see which object names are out of compliance. This is where the Check Naming Standards Compliance feature of CA ERwin Data Modeler comes in handy. Let's do a compliance check on the small model we just created.

While in the physical model, select **Tools|Standards|Check Naming Standards Compliance** from the **Main Menu.** The Check Name Standards Compliance Editor appears, as shown in Figure 12.20. Note that if we were in the logical model, the editor would show logical model objects such as entities, attributes, and domains.

Figure 12.20 Checking Naming Standards Compliance

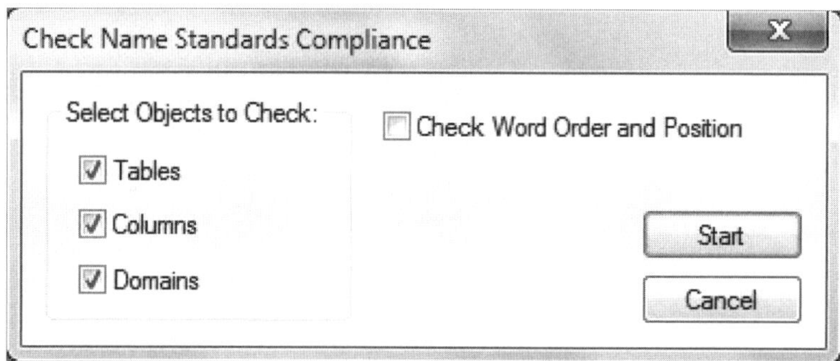

In this case, we'll just run a check on table names, so deselect the **Columns** and **Domains** options, as shown in Figure 12.21. We won't worry about the word order and position for now.

Figure 12.21 Including Only Tables in Naming Standards Compliance

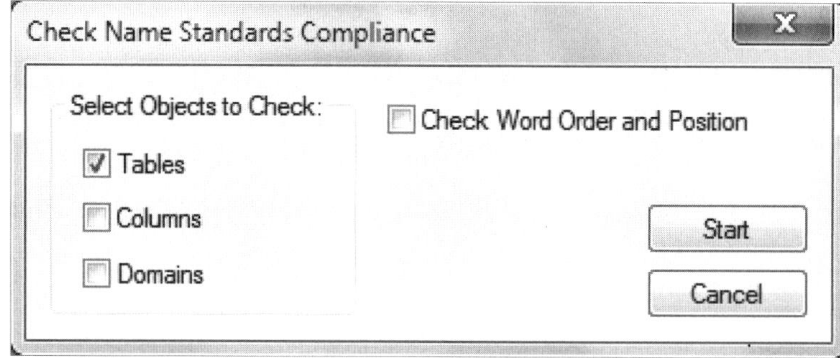

Select **Start** to run the compliance check. You'll see that an exception is found on the TST_EMPL table, as shown in Figure 12.22. Even though we've taken the table name from the Glossary, we neglected to add the **TST_** prefix to our Glossary. Select **Ignore** to move past this error for now, and make a note to return to the Glossary and add an entry for the **TST_** prefix.

Figure 12.22 Exception Report in Naming Standards Compliance Check

Check Name Standards Compliance

Table "TST_EMPL" has word(s) which are NOT defined in the Naming Standard File's glossary.

Non-conforming Name: TST_EMPL

Replace the Name With:

Ignore | Ignore All | Replace | Replace All | Cancel

This is the only exception found in the model and a message indicating that the name check is finished is displayed, as shown in Figure 12.23.

Figure 12.23 Name Check Completion Message

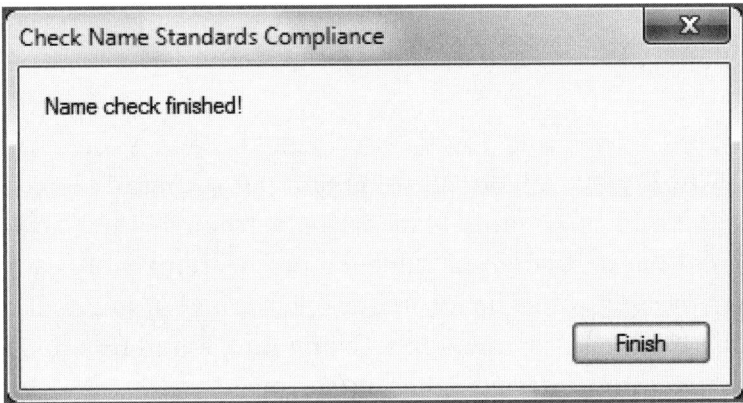

Select **Finish** to exit the Check Name Standards Compliance Editor and return to your model. You've now ensured that all object names comply with the naming standards in your organization.

Name Hardening Wizard

Although naming standards are beneficial to ensuring consistency and are a common best-practice in the industry, there are occasions where exceptions need to be made to the defined naming conventions. Particularly when legacy systems are inherited, it is not always practical to retroactively apply naming standards to an existing production system, for example. This is where Name Hardening comes into play within CA ERwin Data Modeler.

The Name Hardening Wizard provides a way to override inheritance of names and block name changes or resets within a model. Using the wizard, you can select the object types and object instances for which you need to set logical and physical names within the model instead of using the inherited name value. The wizard also includes the flexibility to specify whether to override name inheritance for all model objects, a subset of model objects, or a specific model object using the various pages of the wizard.

Let's use a simple example to get a feel for how the Name Hardening functionality works. Recall in our discussion of naming standards in the previous chapter, we used a naming standards file to define standard names for our logical and physical object names. This worked nicely in our 'top-down' design example, but let's consider the 'bottom-up' scenario where entity and table names were defined *before* we created our naming standards. Let's walk through that scenario. Create a logical/physical model and create a single entity called **Employee**, as shown in Figure 12.24. (In this example, we are using the **Entity Display Level**). For more information on how to create an entity and change entity display levels, refer to Chapter 4.

Figure 12.24 Employee Entity

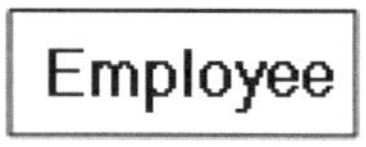

Employee

Switch to the physical model, and you will see that there is a corresponding table that has been named **Employee**, as well, since no naming standards have been applied, as shown in Figure 12.25. In this example, let's assume that this physical model describes an in-production database. Changing table names without first conferring with the DBAs and developers could cause havoc in our operational systems. Instead, we'll want to keep the existing table names, and apply the naming standards to any *new* tables we create. We'll re-address the existing table names on a case-by-case basis during team review meetings.

Figure 12.25 Employee Table

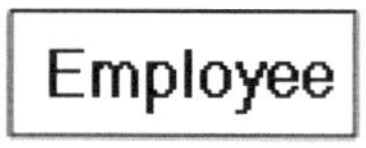

Employee

To make sure that the name of this table is not changed when we apply our naming standards file, we can use the Name Hardening. Select **Actions|Manage Name Hardening** from the **Main Menu** to invoke the Name Hardening Wizard, as shown in Figure 12.26.

Figure 12.26 Name Hardening Wizard

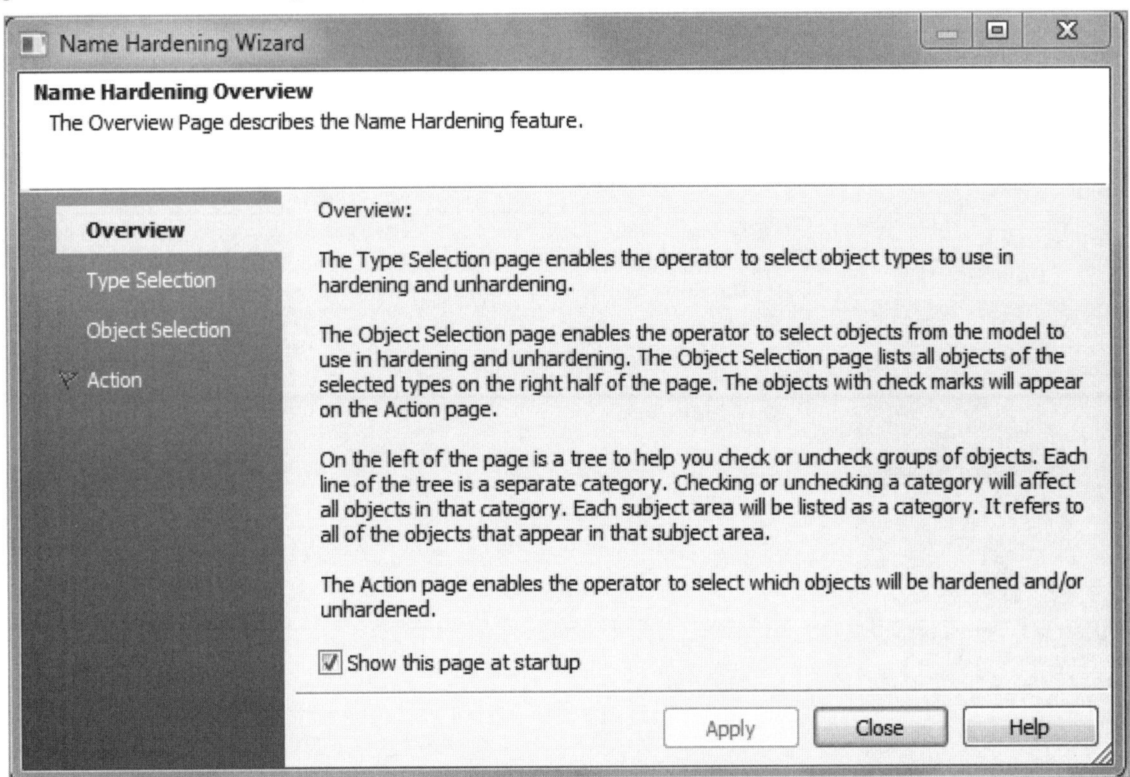

The first tab you will see is an **Overview** of the functionality of the wizard. If you don't wish to see this overview in the future, de-select the **Show this page at startup** check box.

To choose which object types to harden, move to the **Type Selection** tab, as shown in Figure 12.27. We've selected the **Table** object type in this example, since it is tables we're concerned about in our existing system. Note that since we invoked the Name Hardening Wizard from a physical model, only physical object types are listed. A list of which logical and physical model objects can be hardened are shown later in this chapter in Table 12.4.

Figure 12.27 Name Hardening Type Selection for a Physical Model

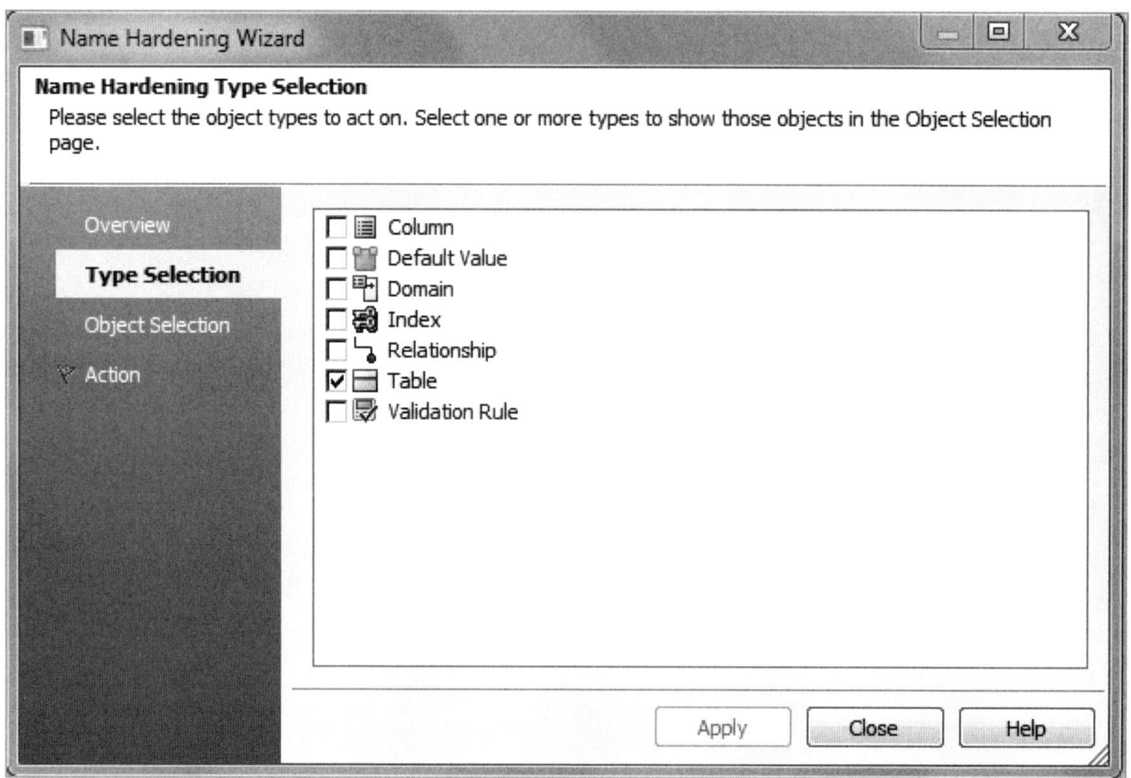

Once we've selected the type of objects to harden (tables, in our case), we can filter further to include specific model objects. Move to the **Object Selection** tab to see a list of tables in our model, as shown in Figure 12.28. All tables are selected by default, and in our case, we have only one table, so we don't need to make any changes. We'll keep the check box next to the **Employee** table, since we want to ensure that this table name is not changed.

Figure 12.28 Object Selection for a Physical Model

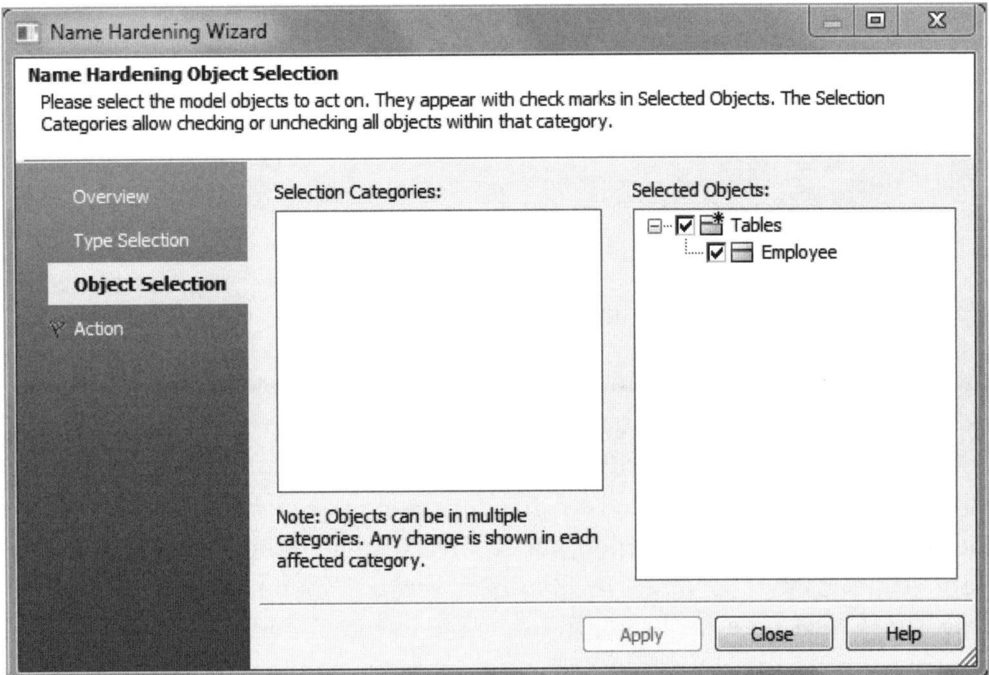

Next, move to the **Action** tab, and expand the **Entities** tree by clicking on the **+** as shown in Figure 12.29. Note that there is no check mark in the **Physical** column for the **Employee** table. This means that Name Hardening has not been enforced for this object.

Figure 12.29 Action Tab of Name Hardening Wizard

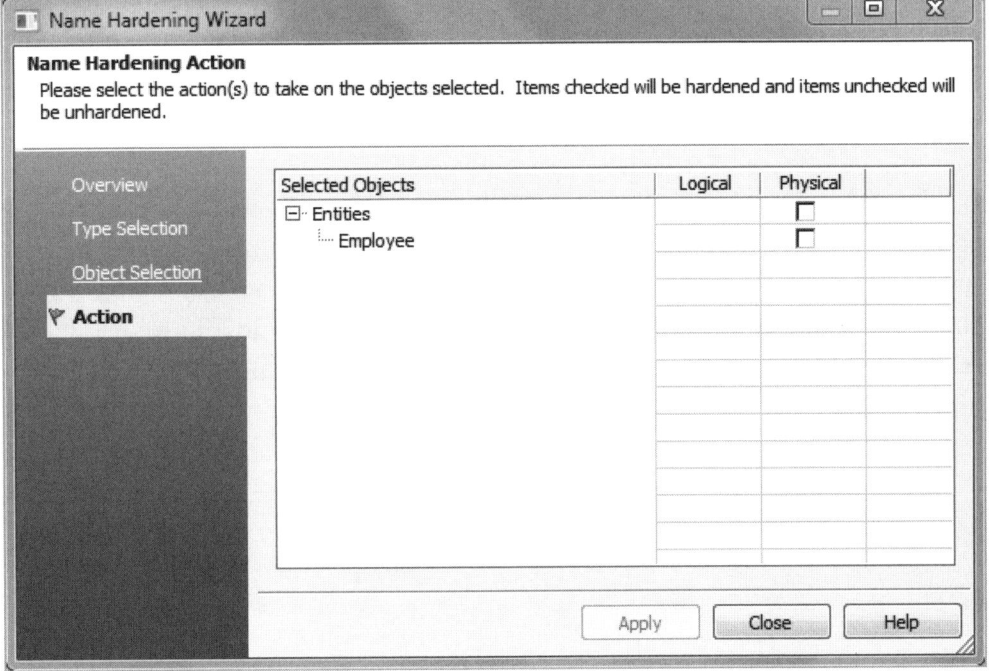

To harden the name of the **Employee** table, place a check mark in the **Physical** column, as shown in Figure 12.30.

Figure 12.30 Selecting Name Hardening for Model Objects

Selected Objects	Logical	Physical	
⊟ Entities		☑	
Employee		☑	

Select **Apply** to save your settings and then **Close** to return to your model diagram.

In this example, we used the Name Hardening Wizard to harden the name of this single table, to give you an overview of the functionality of the wizard for making bulk changes to a model. If we were truly hardening only a single table, we could make this change directly from the model diagram. To harden one or more objects from a diagram, select the object(s) you wish to harden, move your cursor to the diagram area (i.e. white space), and right-click to invoke the diagram context menu, shown in Figure 12.31. Hardening the **Employee** table in this fashion has the same result as the steps we outlined using the Name Hardening Wizard, and is a simpler workflow when working with a single object.

Figure 12.31 Hardening Object Names from a Diagram

Now that we've hardened the **Employee** table, let's apply some naming standards to this model, to see how the functionality differs from the example we used without name hardening in place. To keep it simple, let's simply apply a prefix of 'TMP_' to our table names, using the Model Naming Options Dialog as shown in Figure 12.32. For more information on how to use the Model Naming Options Dialog, refer to the previous section in this chapter.

Figure 12.32 Assigning a Table Prefix Naming Option

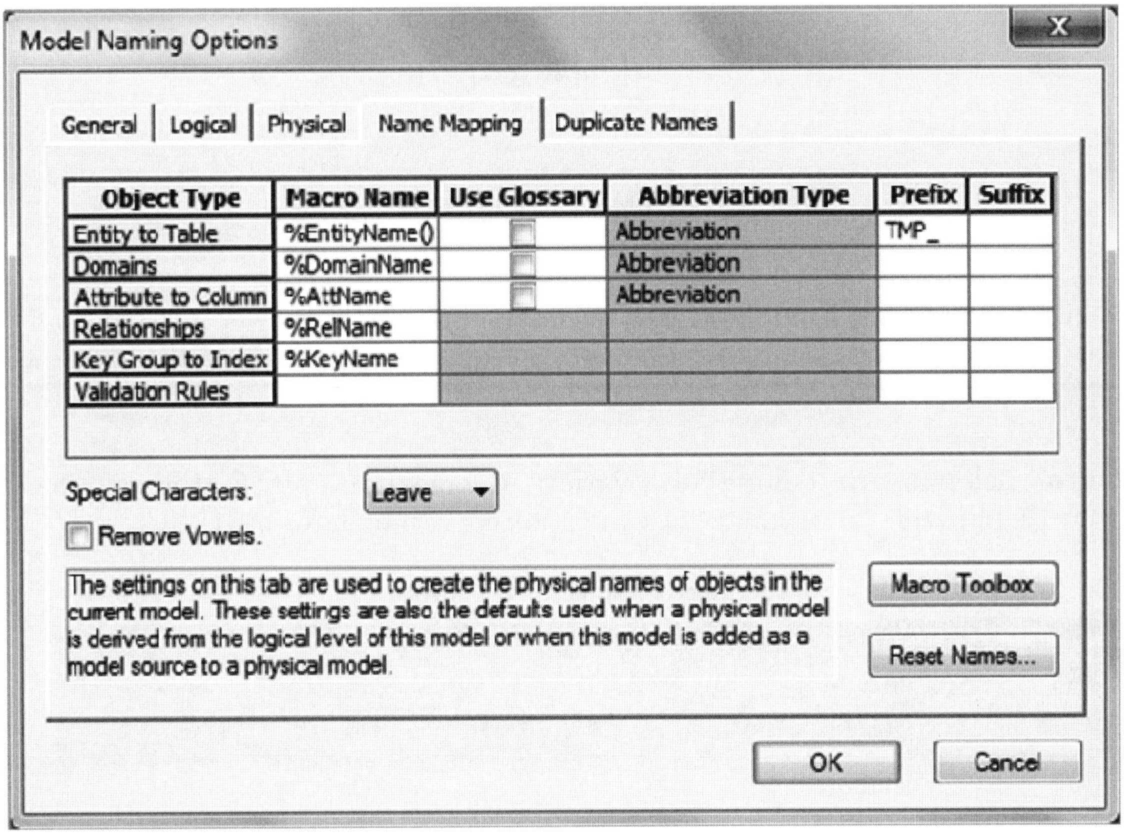

Model Naming Options

General | Logical | Physical | Name Mapping | Duplicate Names

Object Type	Macro Name	Use Glossary	Abbreviation Type	Prefix	Suffix
Entity to Table	%EntityName()	☐	Abbreviation	TMP_	
Domains	%DomainName	☐	Abbreviation		
Attribute to Column	%AttName	☐	Abbreviation		
Relationships	%RelName				
Key Group to Index	%KeyName				
Validation Rules					

Special Characters: Leave

☐ Remove Vowels.

The settings on this tab are used to create the physical names of objects in the current model. These settings are also the defaults used when a physical model is derived from the logical level of this model or when this model is added as a model source to a physical model.

Macro Toolbox

Reset Names...

OK Cancel

Click **OK** to return to your model and you'll see that the name of the **Employee** table has remained unchanged, as shown in Figure 12.33. Since we hardened the name of this table, no prefix was added.

Figure 12.33 Employee Table Name Unchanged Due to Name Hardening

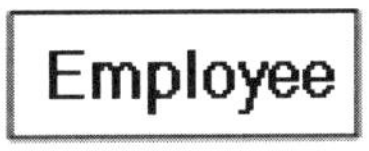

Employee

Let's add a new table, to show that the prefix will be successfully added for new tables moving forward which have not had their names hardened. Create a new table named **Product**. Notice that when you are finished naming the entity (for example, after pressing **`Enter,`** if naming directly on the diagram), the name is automatically changed to **TMP_Product**. Here you can see that unhardened objects are named according to the naming standards defined in the model, while hardened objects are not, as shown in Figure 12.34. This would be helpful, for example, if **Employee** were from a legacy application which could not be changed, and **Product** were part of a new development effort that needed to adhere to the common enterprise naming standards.

Figure 12.34 Hardened vs. Unhardened Objects Using Naming Standards

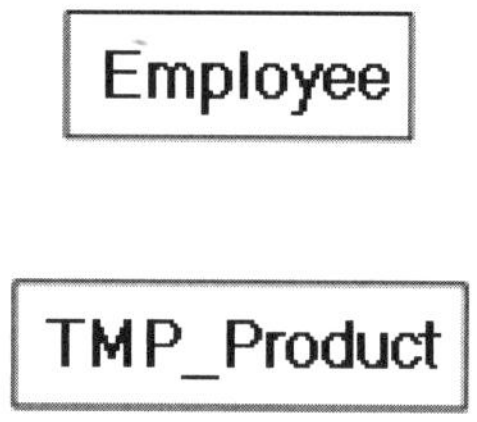

Employee

TMP_Product

If you'd like an example of the finished model from this exercise, you can download the model **`Name Hardening.erwin`** from the www.erwin.com/datamodelingmadesimple web site.

You can use name hardening for a variety of logical and physical model objects. Table 12.4 provides a summary of which objects can be hardened.

Table 12.4 Logical and Physical Model Objects Which Can Be Hardened

Logical Model Objects that can be Hardened	Physical Model Objects that can be Hardened
Attribute	Column
Default	Default Value
Domain	Domain
Entity	Table
Key Group	Index
Relationship	Relationship
Validation Rule	Validation Rule

Key Points

- Validation Rules help enforce the business rules of your organization by establishing a default value, list of values, or a range of acceptable values for an object.
- Naming Standards ensure that model objects adhere to a consistent naming convention.
- Naming Standards can be created outside of a data model and stored in a separate file with the extension .nsm, which can then be attached to one or more data models or data model templates.
- A Glossary can be created to define terms and their abbreviations, as well as their positions as Prime, Modifier, or Class Words.
- Name Hardening provides a way to leave certain objects unchanged when naming standards are applied, which is helpful when working with legacy systems.

CHAPTER 13
Datatype Standards

Storage of data
Is unique across platforms
Map to a standard

CA ERwin Data Modeler provides default logical-to-physical data type mappings for the major database platforms in the market. If your organization has its own data type mappings that differ from the defaults, you can change these mappings to suit your individual needs by creating a Datatype Standards file, which has the extension of **`.dsm`**.

There are two main use cases for creating mappings in a Datatype Standards file:

1. To create mappings between a logical model and one or more physical models

2. To create mappings between physical models, for example, if you are migrating from one database platform to another.

Creating Datatype Standards

Let's create a Data Type Standards file for the model we created in the previous chapter, **`naming_standards_example.erwin`**. This file is available for download on www.erwin.com/datamodelingmadesimple. Open this model and select **Tools|Standards|Datatype Standards** from the **Main Menu**. The Datatype Standards Editor appears, as shown in Figure 13.1. Note that data type standards functionality is not available in the Community Edition. You'll need to upgrade to the Standard or Workgroup Edition. There is a time-limited trial of the Standard Edition available on the erwin.com website if you'd like to try this feature.

By default, the **Logical Definitions** tab is shown. It lists the default data types that are included in each logical data model and which domain they are associated with. Fields highlighted in gray cannot be modified. For example, a **DATE** doesn't have a length associated with it, and the precision of types such as **BOOLEAN** and **BYTE** cannot be modified.

Figure 13.1 Datatype Standards Editor

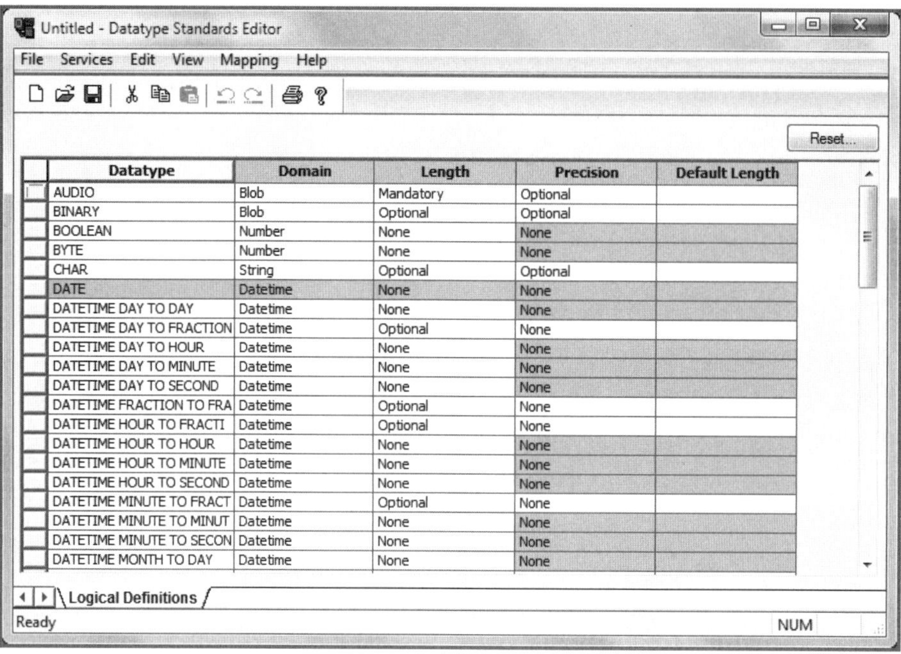

Datatype	Domain	Length	Precision	Default Length
AUDIO	Blob	Mandatory	Optional	
BINARY	Blob	Optional	Optional	
BOOLEAN	Number	None	None	
BYTE	Number	None	None	
CHAR	String	Optional	Optional	
DATE	Datetime	None	None	
DATETIME DAY TO DAY	Datetime	None	None	
DATETIME DAY TO FRACTION	Datetime	Optional	None	
DATETIME DAY TO HOUR	Datetime	None	None	
DATETIME DAY TO MINUTE	Datetime	None	None	
DATETIME DAY TO SECOND	Datetime	None	None	
DATETIME FRACTION TO FRA	Datetime	Optional	None	
DATETIME HOUR TO FRACTI	Datetime	Optional	None	
DATETIME HOUR TO HOUR	Datetime	None	None	
DATETIME HOUR TO MINUTE	Datetime	None	None	
DATETIME HOUR TO SECOND	Datetime	None	None	
DATETIME MINUTE TO FRACT	Datetime	Optional	None	
DATETIME MINUTE TO MINUT	Datetime	None	None	
DATETIME MINUTE TO SECON	Datetime	None	None	
DATETIME MONTH TO DAY	Datetime	None	None	

You can create new logical data types, if you wish to include additional options in your logical models. Let's add a data type to show how this works. Say, for example, we want to create a special type of String value. Let's add a new data type called **SPECIALSTRING** by entering this value in the empty row at the bottom of the list. We'll inherit from the **String** domain, and make **Length** and **Precision Optional**, as shown in Figure 13.2. For more information on domains and domain inheritance, refer to Chapter 10.

Figure 13.2 Creating a New Logical Datatype

Datatype	Domain	Length	Precision	Default Length
LONG	Number	None	None	
LONG FLOAT	Number	None	None	
LONG TEXT	String	Mandatory	Optional	
MONEY	Number	Optional	Optional	
NCHAR	String	Optional	Optional	
NUMBER	Number	Optional	Optional	
NUMERIC	Number	Optional	Optional	
NVARCHAR	String	Mandatory	Optional	
SECURITY_ID	Blob	None	None	
SHORT FLOAT	Number	None	None	
SMALLINT	Number	None	None	
SPATIAL	Unknown	None	None	
TEXT	String	Optional	Optional	
TIME	Datetime	None	None	
TIMESTAMP	Datetime	Optional	None	
UNIQUEID	Number	None	None	
VARCHAR	String	Mandatory	Optional	
VIDEO	Blob	None	None	
SPECIALSTRING	String	Optional	Optional	

Unknown
Blob
Datetime
Number
String

Let's save this Datatype Standards file, and associate it with our model, so we can see how our new datatype has been implemented. Select **File|Save** or click on the **Save** button 💾 on the **Datatype Standards Toolbar**. Name this file `datatype_standards_example.dsm`. Then select **File|Exit** to exit the editor.

To associate the Datatype Standards file with your model, select **Actions|Model Datatype Options** from the **Main Menu**. In the Model Datatype Options Dialog, select the **Use File** radio button, and then the **Browse** button to locate the `datatype_standards_example.dsm` file you created, as shown in Figure 13.3.

Figure 13.3 Associating a Datatype Standards File With a Model

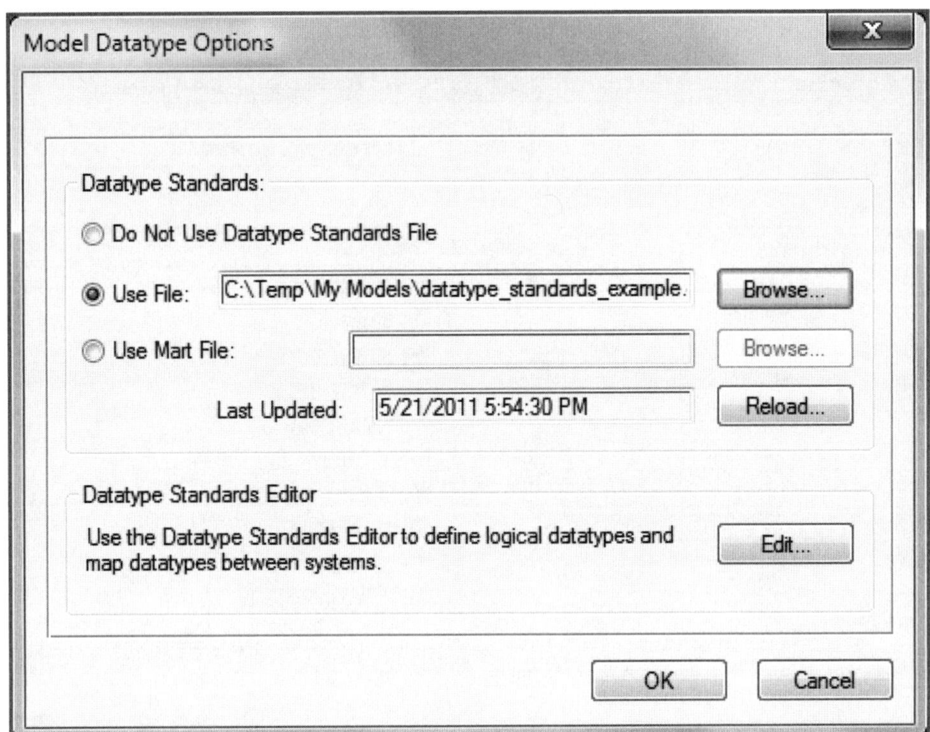

Click **OK** to exit this dialog. To see this new logical data type as part of your model, add a new primary key attribute to the **Employee** entity called **Employee Identifier** using the Attribute Properties Editor (for more information on how to create attributes, refer to Chapters 3 and 5.). When selecting the **Logical Data Type**, select your new data type **SPECIALSTRING** from the list, as shown in Figure 13.4. Then **Close** the editor to return to your model diagram.

Figure 13.4 Using a Custom Logical Data Type

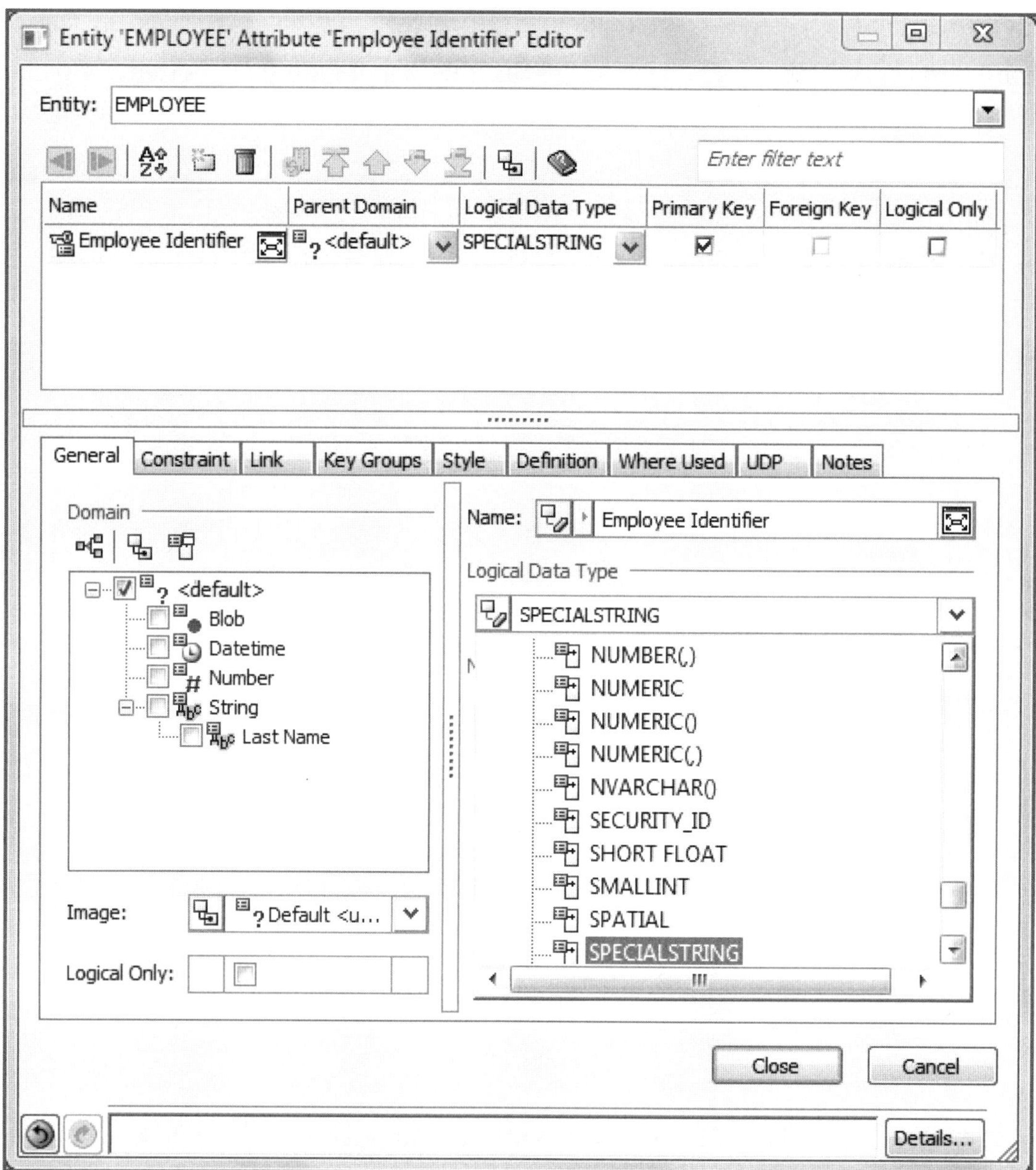

One reason to create a custom logical data type is to be able to specify a specific physical data type mapping. Let's go back to our datatype standards file and add physical data type mappings to it. Open the **Datatype Standards Editor** and select **Mapping|Insert New Mapping** from the menu, as shown in Figure 13.5.

Figure 13.5 Creating a New Datatype Mapping

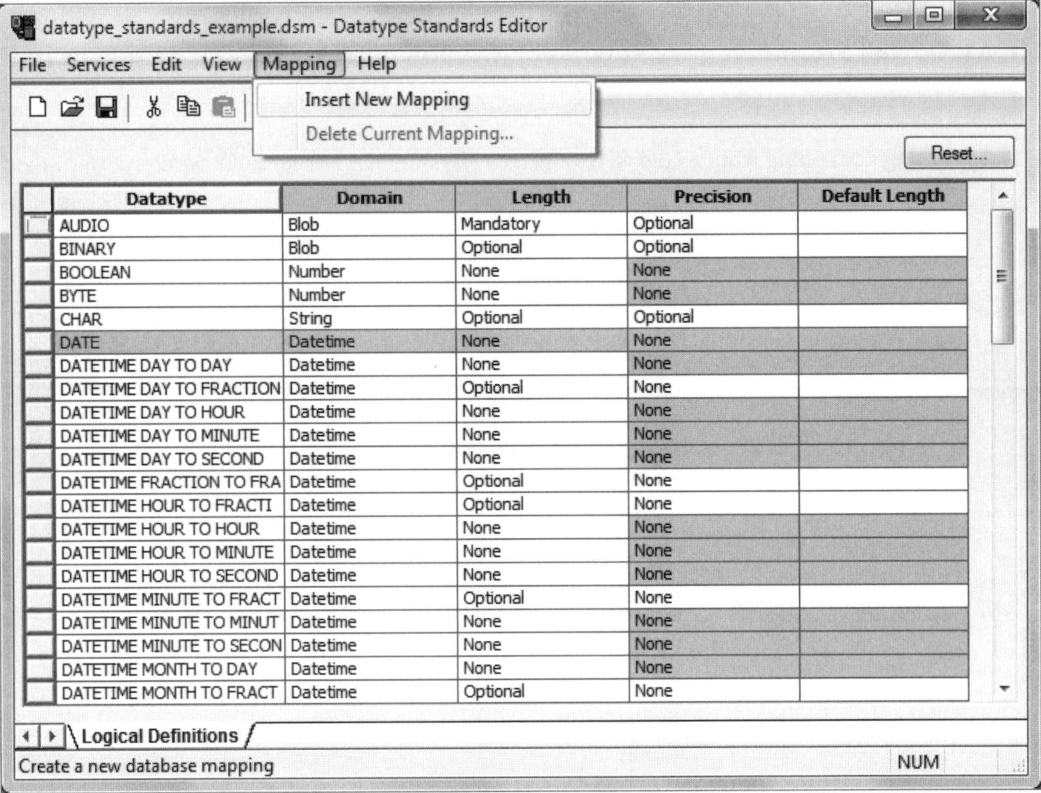

A **New Mapping** tab is created, as shown in Figure 13.6.

Figure 13.6 New Mapping Tab in the Datatype Standards Editor

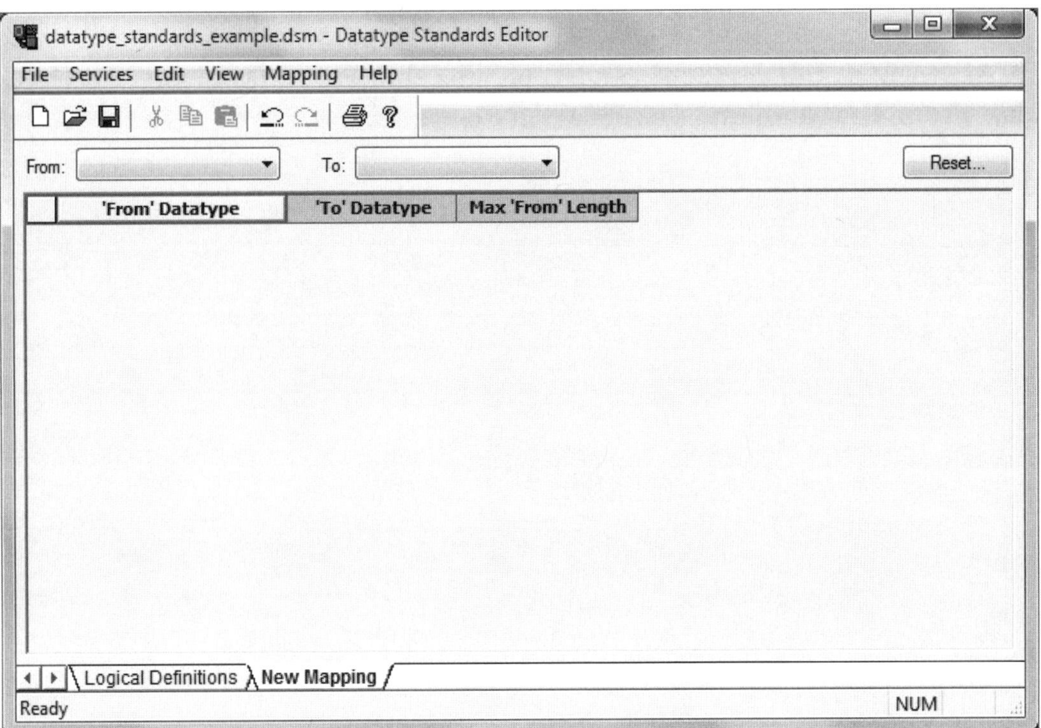

In this case, we want to define a custom mapping from a logical model to a physical model on the SQL Server 2008 platform. Using the drop-down menus provided, select **LOGICAL** for the **From** field and **SQL Server 2008** for the **To** field, as shown in Figure 13.7.

Figure 13.7 Creating a Mapping from a Logical Model to a Physical SQL Server 2008 Model

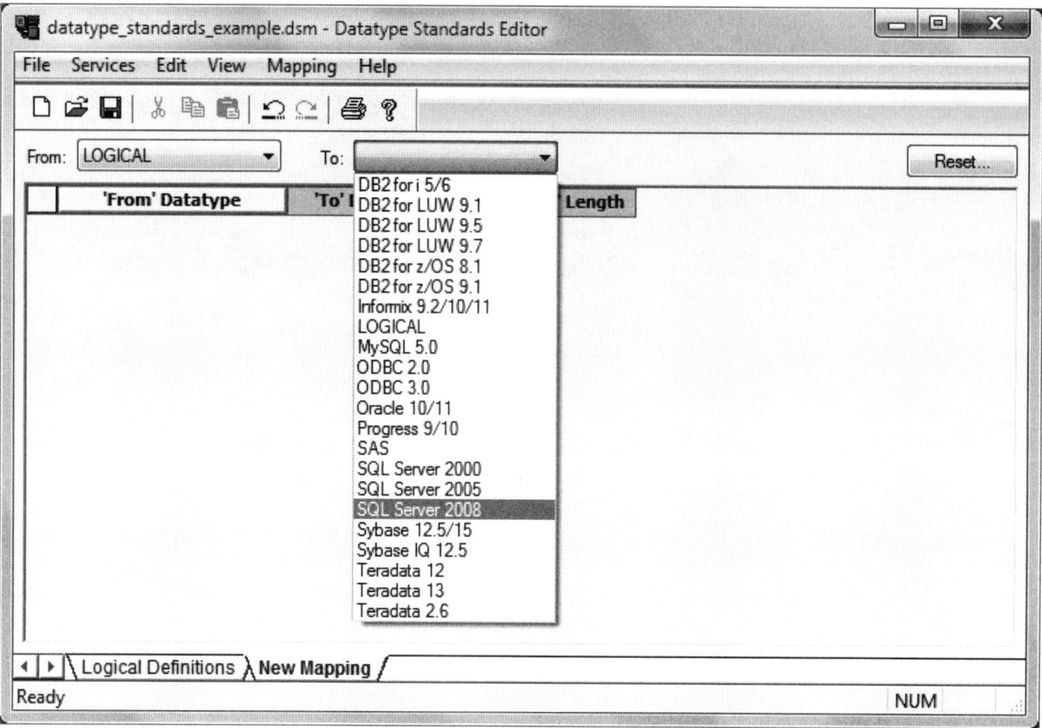

Once you've made these selections, the **New Mapping** tab changes its name to **LOGICAL to SQL Server 2008**, and populates the **'From' Datatype**, **'To Datatype'**, and **Max 'From' Length** columns as shown in Figure 13.8.

Figure 13.8 Mapping from a Logical Model to a Physical SQL Server 2008 Model

datatype_standards_example.dsm - Datatype Standards Editor

File Services Edit View Mapping Help

From: LOGICAL To: SQL Server 2008 Reset...

'From' Datatype	'To' Datatype	Max 'From' Length
AUDIO	varbinary	MAXIMUM
BINARY	binary	MAXIMUM
BOOLEAN	bit	
BYTE	tinyint	
CHAR	char	MAXIMUM
DATE	date	
DATETIME DAY TO DAY	datetime	
DATETIME DAY TO FRACTION	datetime	MAXIMUM
DATETIME DAY TO HOUR	datetime	
DATETIME DAY TO MINUTE	datetime	
DATETIME DAY TO SECOND	datetime	
DATETIME FRACTION TO FRACTION	datetime	MAXIMUM
DATETIME HOUR TO FRACTION	datetime	MAXIMUM
DATETIME HOUR TO HOUR	datetime	
DATETIME HOUR TO MINUTE	datetime	
DATETIME HOUR TO SECOND	datetime	
DATETIME MINUTE TO FRACTION	datetime	MAXIMUM
DATETIME MINUTE TO MINUTE	datetime	

Logical Definitions | LOGICAL to SQL Server 2008

Ready NUM

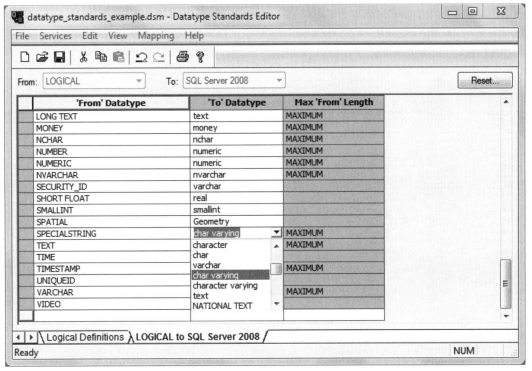

Let's create a physical SQL Server 2008 datatype for our **SPECIALSTRING** logical data type. Using the drop-down menu that shows a list of valid SQL Server 2008 datatypes, select **char varying** from the list, as shown in Figure 13.9.

Figure 13.9 Defining a Physical Datatype for a User-Defined Logical Datatype

datatype_standards_example.dsm - Datatype Standards Editor

File Services Edit View Mapping Help

From: LOGICAL To: SQL Server 2008 Reset...

'From' Datatype	'To' Datatype	Max 'From' Length
LONG TEXT	text	MAXIMUM
MONEY	money	MAXIMUM
NCHAR	nchar	MAXIMUM
NUMBER	numeric	MAXIMUM
NUMERIC	numeric	MAXIMUM
NVARCHAR	nvarchar	MAXIMUM
SECURITY_ID	varchar	
SHORT FLOAT	real	
SMALLINT	smallint	
SPATIAL	Geometry	
SPECIALSTRING	char varying	MAXIMUM
TEXT	character	MAXIMUM
TIME	char	
TIMESTAMP	varchar	MAXIMUM
UNIQUEID	char varying	
VARCHAR	character varying	MAXIMUM
VIDEO	text	
	NATIONAL TEXT	

Logical Definitions | LOGICAL to SQL Server 2008

Ready NUM

You can also change the mapping for existing data types. For example, perhaps we are starting a new international project and will need to store international character sets. We may wish to change the mapping for the **TEXT** logical data type to map to the physical data type **NATIONAL TEXT**, as shown in Figure 13.10.

Figure 13.10 Modifying an Existing Data Type Mapping

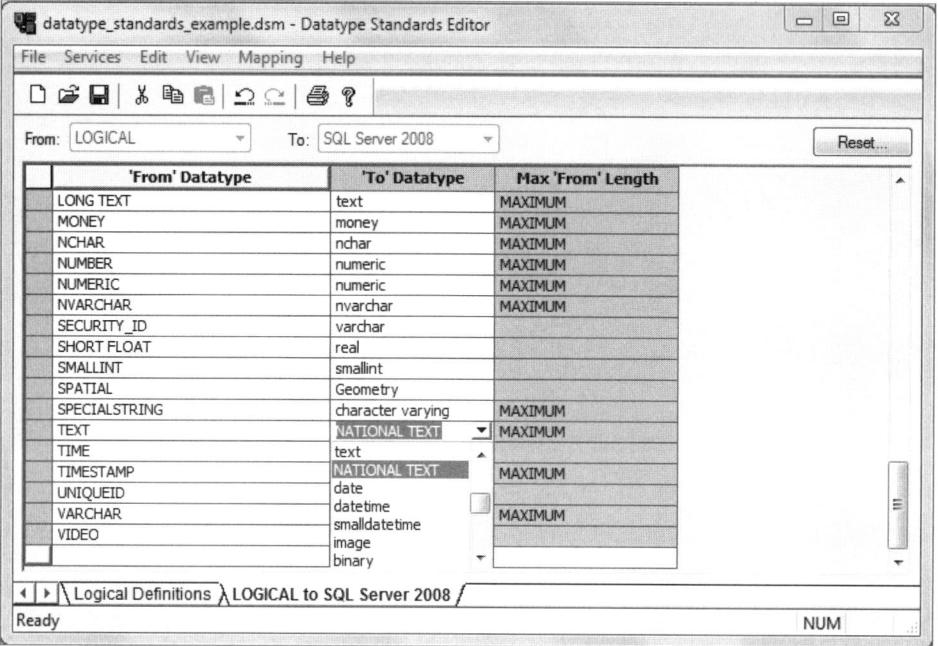

Now that we've made these changes, **Save** and exit from the Datatype Standards Editor. To apply these changes to our model, we'll need to 'reload' them into the open model. To reload the data type mappings, select **Actions|Model Datatype Options** from the **Main Menu** and click the **Reload** button from the resulting Model Datatype Options Dialog, as shown in Figure 13.11.

Figure 13.11 Reloading Datatype Mappings

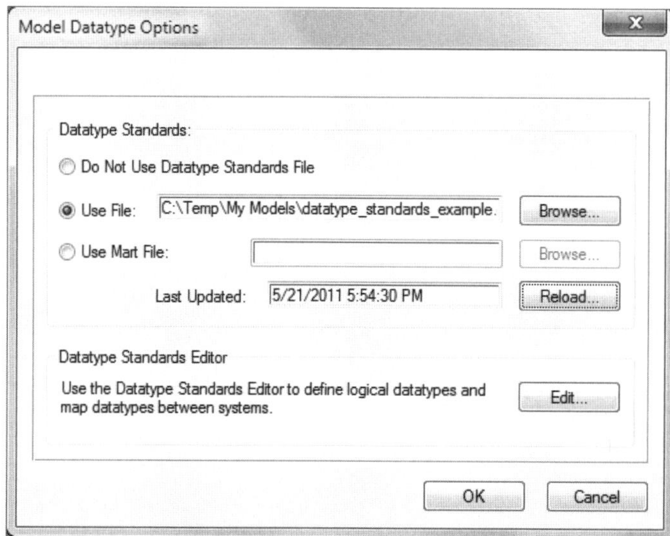

Now that we've applied the data type mappings, let's see how these changes are implemented in our model. Recall that we created a logical attribute called **Employee Identifier**, and gave it a data type of **SPECIALSTRING**. Go to the physical model and look at the corresponding column, named **Employee_Identifier**, and you'll see that the data type for this column is the same as that which we defined for the **SPECIALSTRING** data type: **char varying**, as shown in Figure 13.12.

Figure 13.12 Physical Datatype Mapping for a Customer Datatype

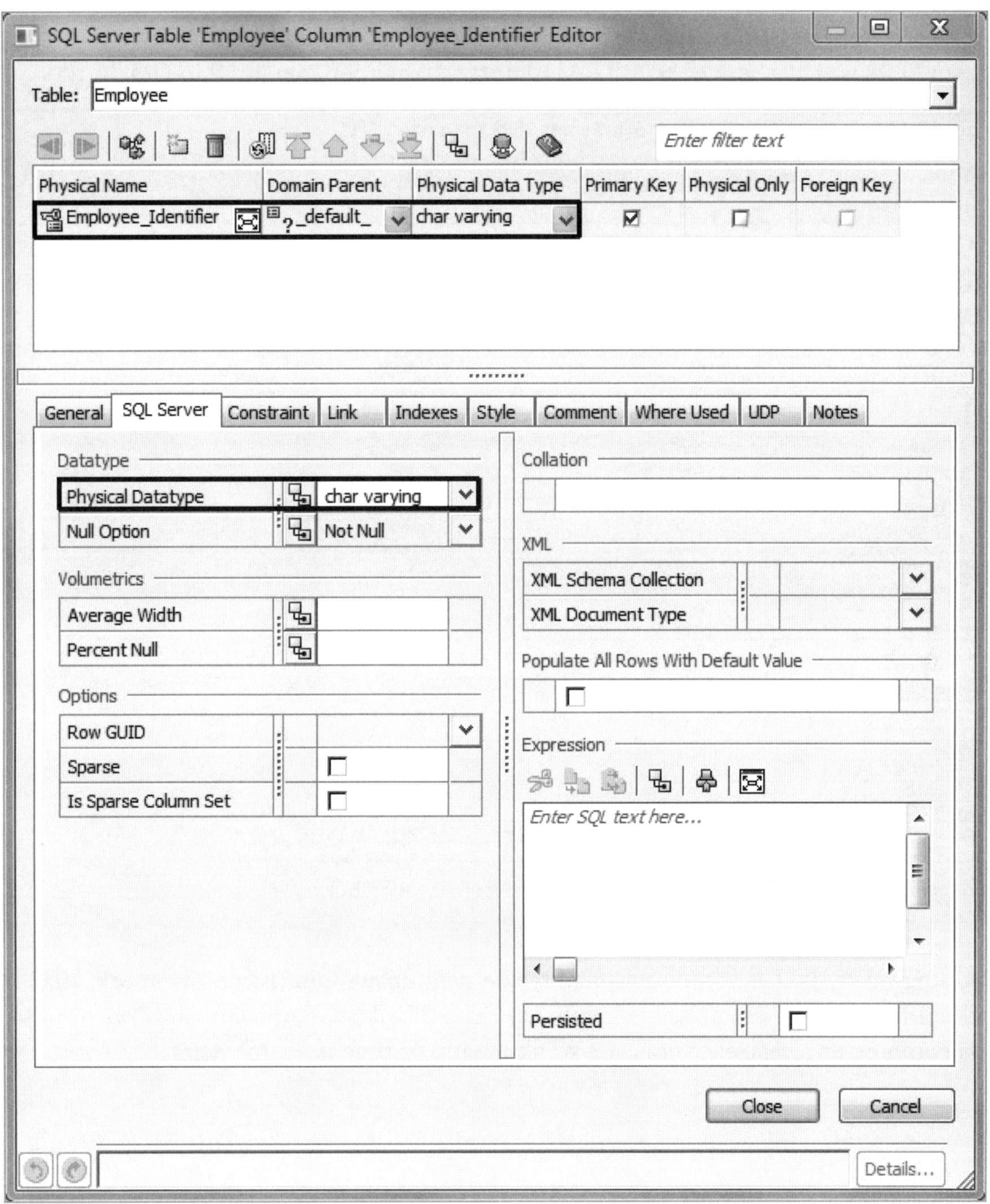

You can also create custom mappings from one database platform to another. Let's open our datatype standards file again and add a mapping from SQL Server 2008 to Oracle. Multiple mappings can be stored in the same file, so we can add this to our existing file. Select **Mapping|Insert New Mapping**, then select **SQL Server 2008** for the **From:** field, and **Oracle 10/11** for the **To:** field, as shown in Figure 13.13. Database-to-database mappings are helpful when migrating from one platform to another using models in the Design Layer Architecture. You can change the values to meet your unique needs, or simply use this mapping as a reference so that you will know how data types will be migrated. For example, as you can see in Figure 13.13, a **bigint** data type in SQL Server 2008 will be changed to a **REAL** datatype when implemented in Oracle 10g.

Figure 13.13 Datatype Mappings from SQL Server 2008 to Oracle 10/11

datatype_standards_example.dsm - Datatype Standards Editor

File Services Edit View Mapping Help

From: SQL Server 2008 To: Oracle 10/11 Reset...

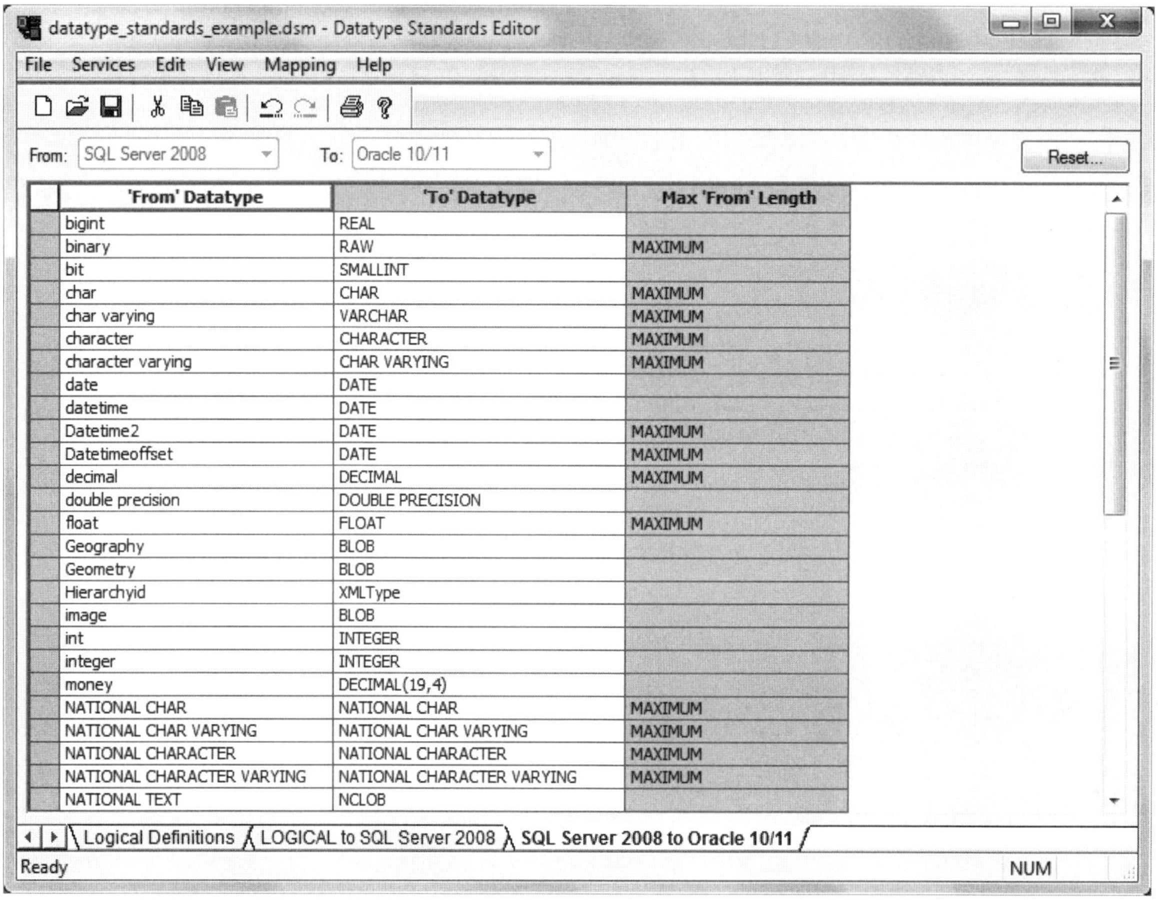

'From' Datatype	'To' Datatype	Max 'From' Length
bigint	REAL	
binary	RAW	MAXIMUM
bit	SMALLINT	
char	CHAR	MAXIMUM
char varying	VARCHAR	MAXIMUM
character	CHARACTER	MAXIMUM
character varying	CHAR VARYING	MAXIMUM
date	DATE	
datetime	DATE	
Datetime2	DATE	MAXIMUM
Datetimeoffset	DATE	MAXIMUM
decimal	DECIMAL	MAXIMUM
double precision	DOUBLE PRECISION	
float	FLOAT	MAXIMUM
Geography	BLOB	
Geometry	BLOB	
Hierarchyid	XMLType	
image	BLOB	
int	INTEGER	
integer	INTEGER	
money	DECIMAL(19,4)	
NATIONAL CHAR	NATIONAL CHAR	MAXIMUM
NATIONAL CHAR VARYING	NATIONAL CHAR VARYING	MAXIMUM
NATIONAL CHARACTER	NATIONAL CHARACTER	MAXIMUM
NATIONAL CHARACTER VARYING	NATIONAL CHARACTER VARYING	MAXIMUM
NATIONAL TEXT	NCLOB	

Logical Definitions / LOGICAL to SQL Server 2008 / SQL Server 2008 to Oracle 10/11

Ready NUM

Note, however, that if you do not modify the default mappings in a given tab, that tab will not be saved, and a message similar to Figure 13.14 will appear. Since we are using this mapping as a reference only, we won't modify or save it at this point.

Figure 13.14 Data Type Standards Save Error for Unchanged Information

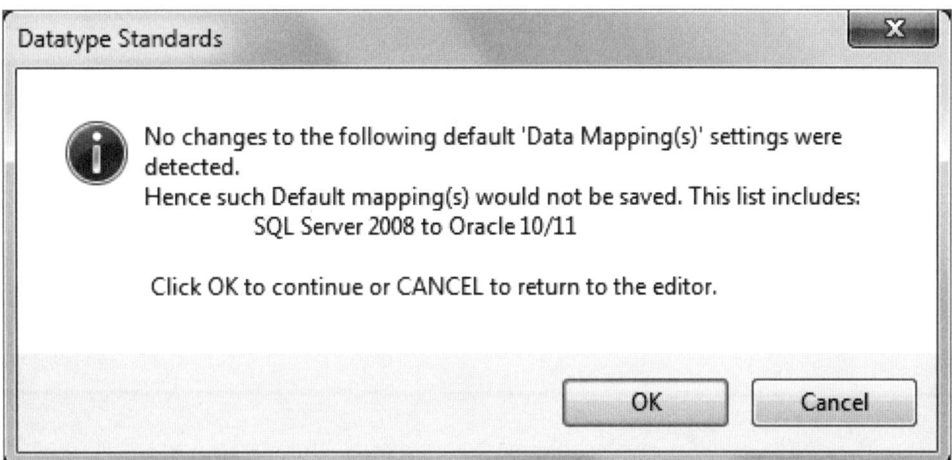

The main use of a datatype standards file is to create custom mappings for your organization, so only mappings that have modified data types are saved. In this case, we were able to use the data type standards as a reference for our database conversion as well.

We've saved this model as **`datatype_standards_example.erwin`**. If you'd like an example of the finished model from this exercise, as well as the `datatype_standards_example.dsm` we created in this chapter, you can download them from the www.erwin.com/datamodelingmadesimple web site.

Datatype mappings are a helpful way to either create custom mappings for logical-to-physical data model conversions, or for migrating from one data platform to another. They are also a handy reference for understanding what default mappings are used in data type conversion.

Key Points

- A Data Type Standards file can be used to create custom data type mappings from logical to physical models or from one physical platform to another.
- Data types are defined in an external Datatype Standards file, which has the extension of .dsm.
- Data type mapping can be used in translating from logical to physical models, or from one physical model to another.
- Custom logical data types can be created for mapping to physical data types.

CHAPTER 14
User-Defined Properties (UDPs)

Need a custom field?
Build a special UDP
Your model, your way

A data model contains a wealth of information about an organization's data, and CA ERwin Data Modeler has a wide range of properties and object types used to describe the details of this data. Since every organization's needs are unique, however, you may wish to add your own custom properties of the objects in your model. For example, you may wish to track the data steward for a particular entity, the security level of a given table, or attach a specifications document to a model. User-Defined Properties, or UDPs, allow you to create your own properties to add customized metadata documentation to your model.

Creating UDPs

Let's create some UDPs to get a better understanding of how and why they are used. Say, for example, that we are working on a data governance project in our organization. As part of this project, all entities must be assigned a steward, and all tables must be listed with a security classification. Since stewardship and security classifications are not listed as properties in CA ERwin Data Modeler by default, we'll need to create our own UDPs for these properties.

First, create a sample logical/physical model using SQL Server 2008 as a target DBMS platform (for more information on how to create a model, refer to Chapter 3). We'll start within the logical model to create a UDP for stewardship for the entities in our model. To enter the UDP library, select **Model|User Defined Properties** from the **Main Menu**, and the User Defined Properties Editor appears, as shown in Figure 14.1.

Figure 14.1 User Defined Properties Editor for Logical Objects

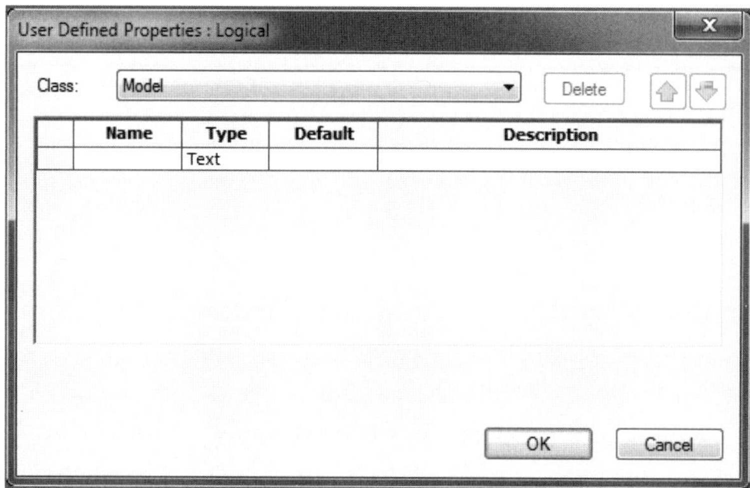

Next, we'll need to choose the class, or type of object, to which we'll assign a UDP. In this case, we're starting with entities. Select **Entity** from the **Class** drop-down menu, as shown in Figure 14.2.

Figure 14.2 Selecting an Object Class to Assign a UDP

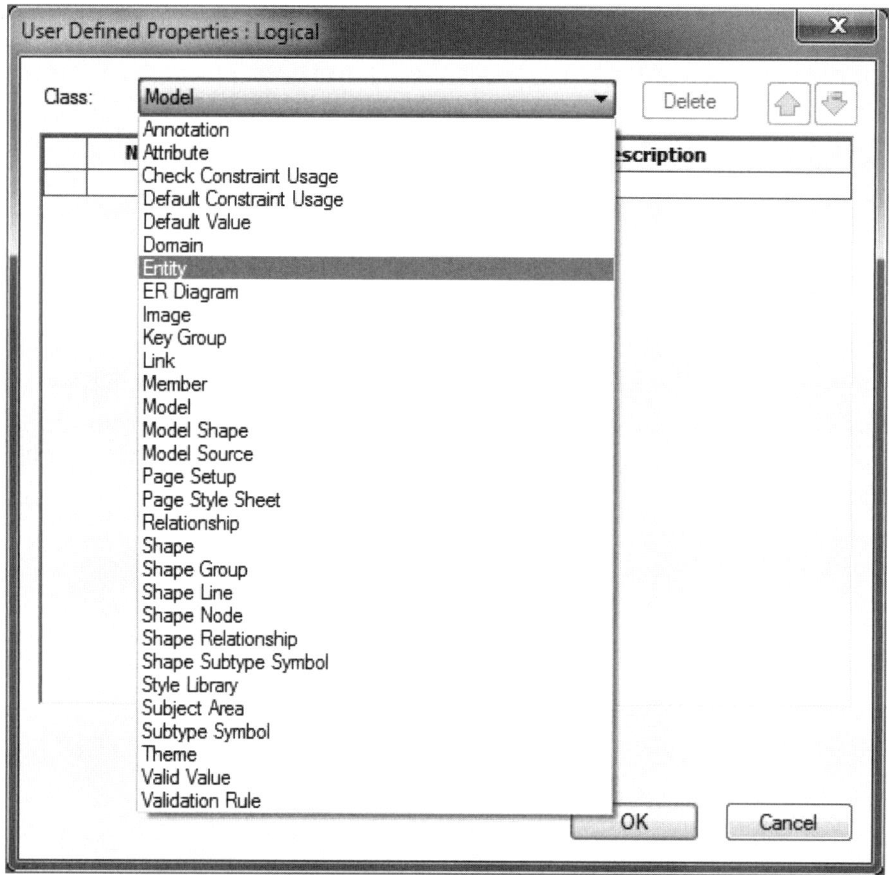

We'll need to define a name, type, default value, and description for our UDP. Enter the following information, as shown in Figure 14.3.

Name: Steward

Type: Text

Default Value: [none]

Definition: Person responsible for the definition of an entity

Figure 14.3 Creating a UDP for Stewardship Information

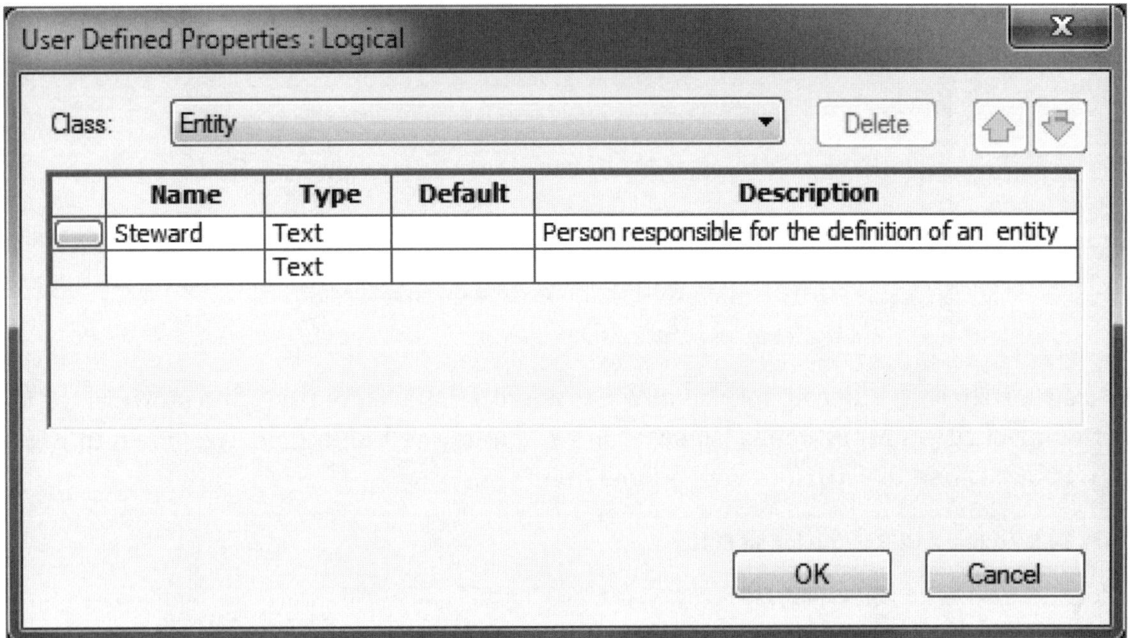

Now that we've created our **Steward** UDP, click **OK** to return to your model diagram. Create a sample entity called **Customer**, open the property editor for that entity, and move to the **UDP** tab, as shown in Figure 14.4. (For more information on creating and editing entities, refer to Chapter 4).

Figure 14.4 Viewing a UDP for an Entity

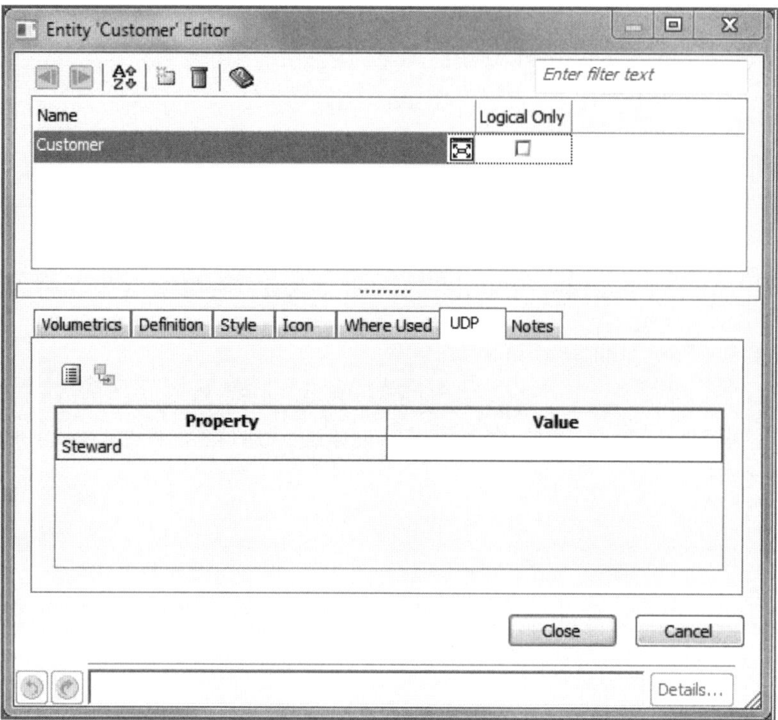

Notice that there is a listing for the new **Steward** UDP we created. The steward for this particular entity is Mary Jones, so enter her name in the **Value** field, as shown in Figure 14.5. Select **Close** to return to your model diagram.

Figure 14.5 Adding a UDP Value for an Entity

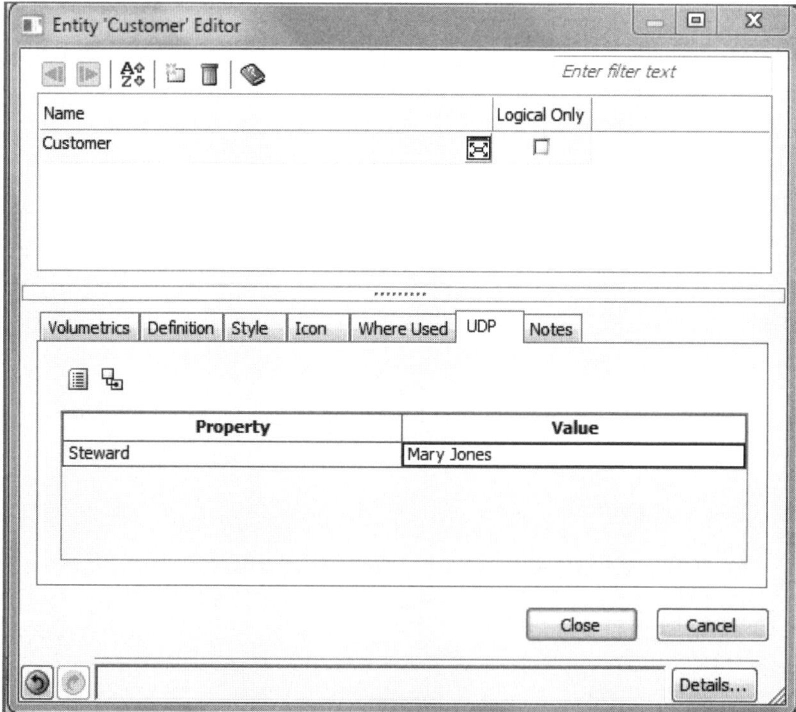

Next we'll need to create the security classification UDP for the tables in our model. To do this, switch to the physical model (for more information on switching between logical and physical models, refer to Chapter 3). You should see a table named **Customer**, which corresponds to the logical entity we created. Open the property editor for this table, and move to the **UDP** tab, as shown in Figure 14.6.

Figure 14.6 Viewing a UDP for a Table

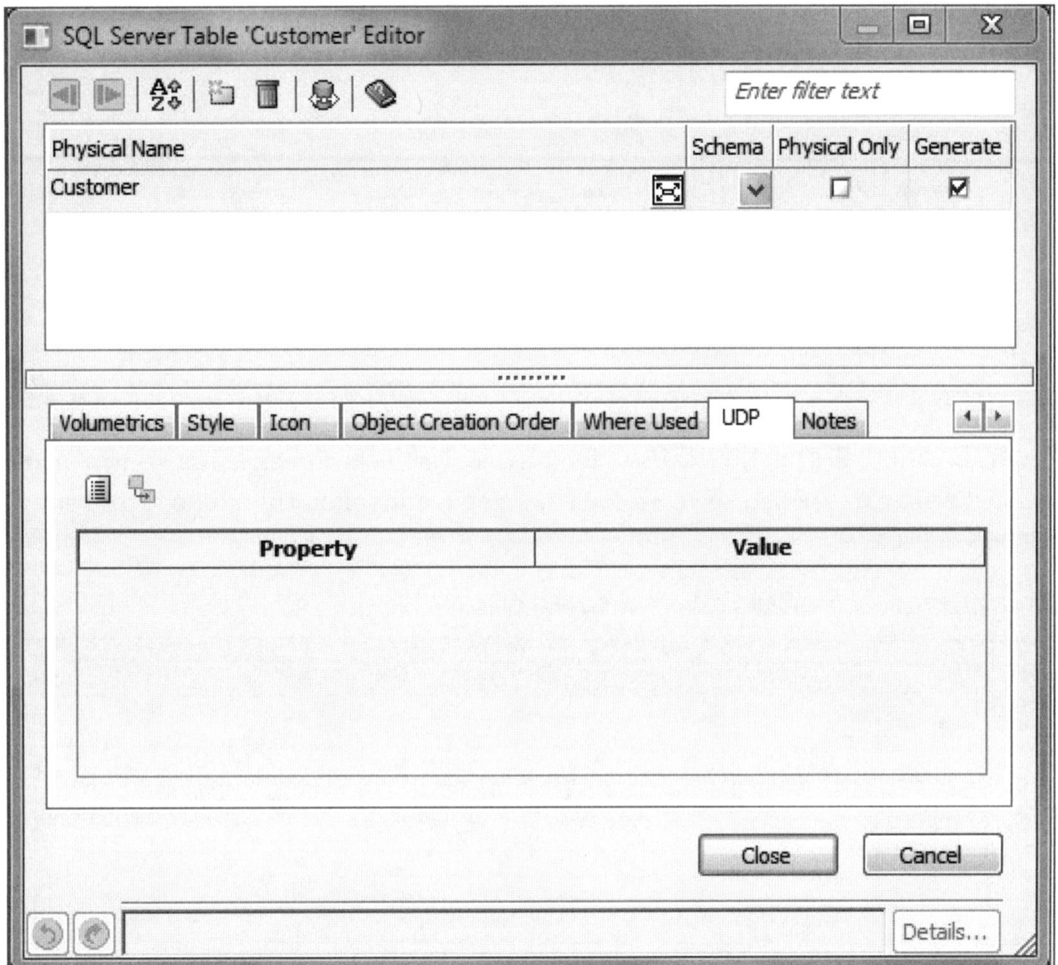

Notice that the **Steward** UDP we created for the logical entity is not displayed. UDPs are unique between logical and physical models so, since we created the **Steward** UDP for the logical entity, it will not be displayed for the physical table. This is fine, since we only need stewardship information for entities in our organization. We will need to create a security classification UDP for our tables in this model, however. We can invoke the User Defined Properties Editor directly from the Table Properties Editor by using the **User Defined Properties Editor** toolbar button, as shown in Figure 14.7.

Figure 14.7 Invoking the User Defined Properties Editor from the Table Properties Editor

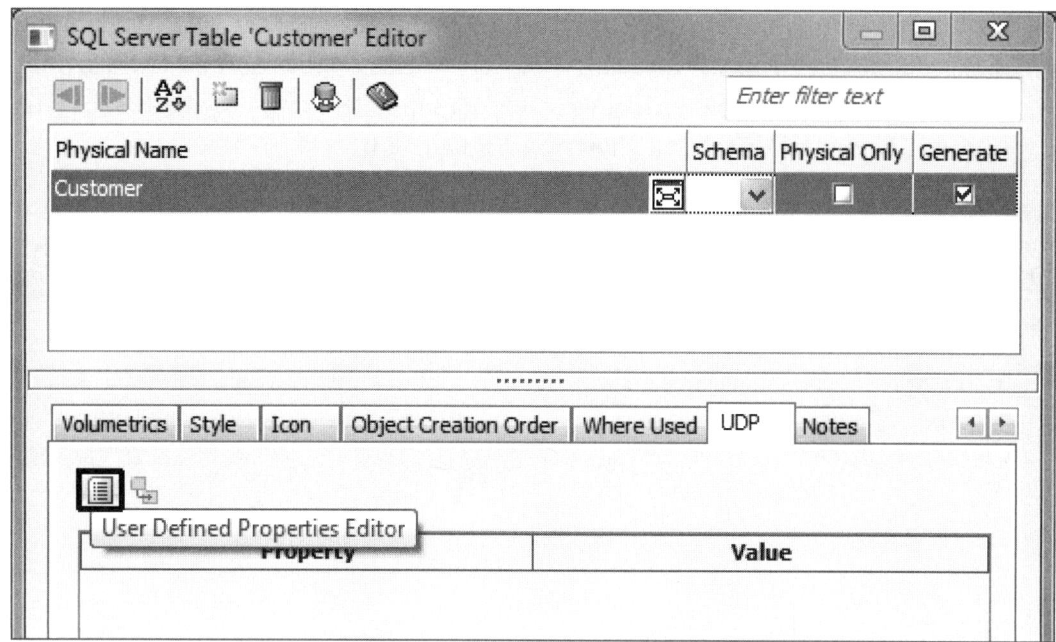

The User Defined Properties Editor for physical objects appears, as shown in Figure 14.8. The **Table** class is pre-selected for us, since we invoked this dialog from the Table Properties Editor.

Figure 14.8 User Defined Properties Editor for Physical Objects

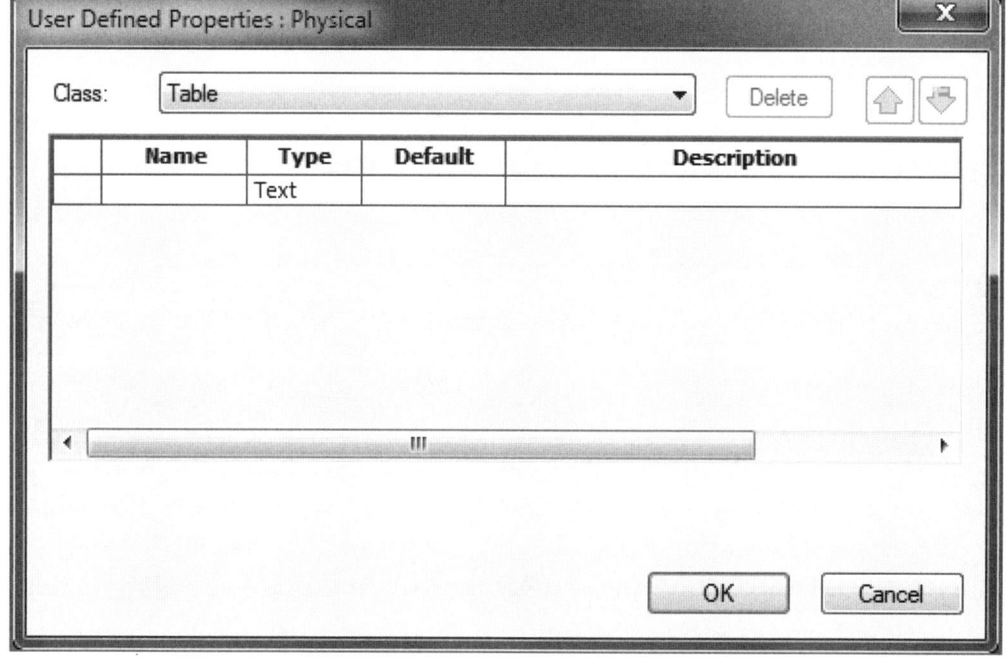

Next, we'll want to create a new UDP for table objects for our security classifications. In our organization, there are three levels of security classification: classified, secret, and top secret. We'll want to create a drop-down list with these values, so the data modeler

entering these values has an easy, error-free list to choose from. We'll create a list UDP, and use a comma-separated list for our entries. Enter the following information for this UDP, as shown in Figure 14.9.

Name: Security

Type: List

Default Value: Classified, Secret, Top Secret

Description: Security Classification

Figure 14.9 Creating a List Value UDP for a Table

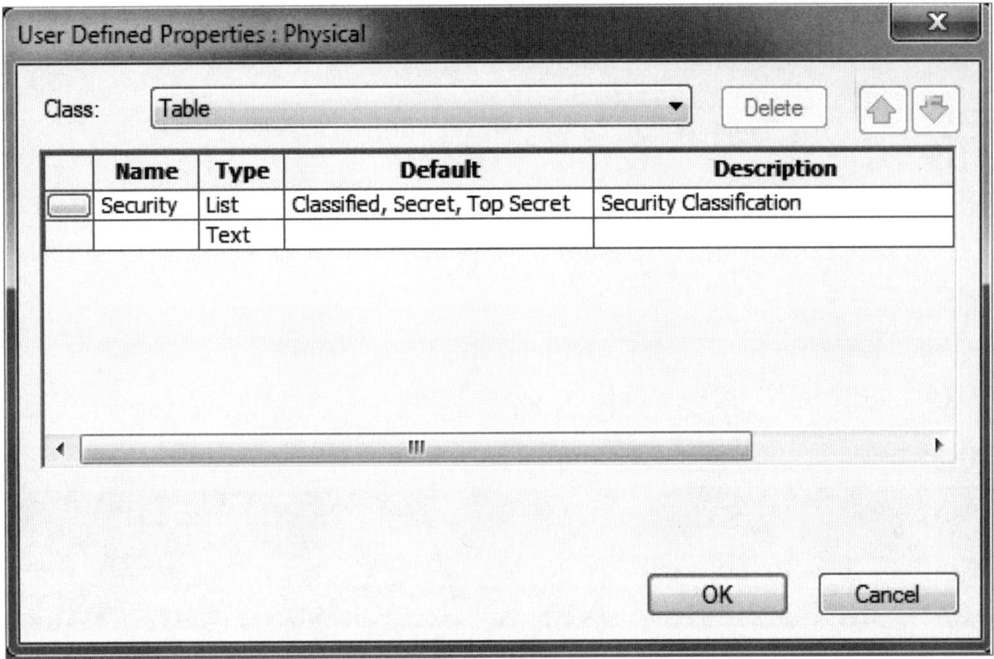

Click **OK** to return to the Table Properties Editor, where you'll now see a UDP called **Security** with a drop down list of values showing **Classified**, **Secret**, and **Top Secret**, as shown in Figure 14.10. By default, the field is populated with the first item on the list (in this case, Classified). To specify a value other than the first as the default, place a tilde (~) in front of the object that you'd like to appear as the default when creating the UDP value list.

Figure 14.10 Using a List UDP

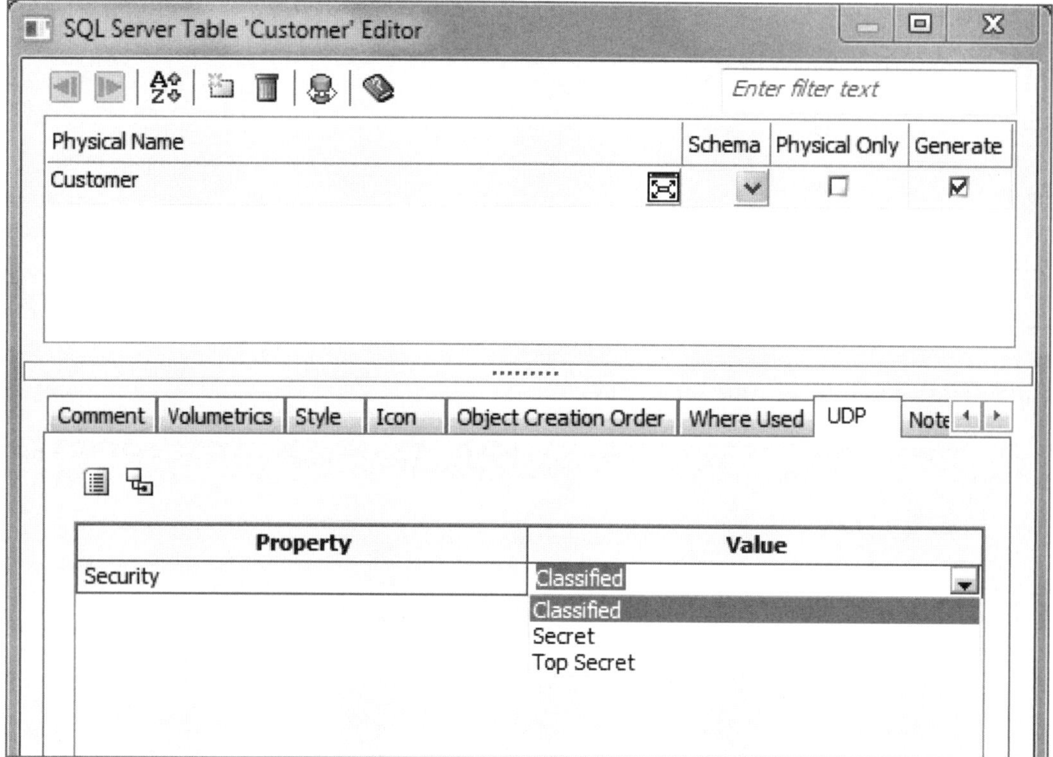

Table 14.1 lists the UDP types and their descriptions.

Table 14.1 UDP Types

UDP Type	Description
Command	A link to execute another application. This value provides a path to launch a document or another application from within this UDP value. This can be used, for example, to attach documents such as specification documents, to model objects.
Date	A calendar date in MM/DD/YY format.
Int	An integer number (e.g. 1, 2, 3…)
Real	A real number, with a decimal (e.g. 12.5, 18.72, 82.7 …)
Text	An ASCII text field
List	A list of values. When entering list values, entries are separated by a comma. The first item on the list is populated as the default value. To specify a value other than the first as the default, place a tilde (~) in front of the object that you'd like to appear as the default.

If you'd like an example the model we created in this chapter, the **udp_example.erwin** file is located on www.erwin.com/datamodelingmadesimple.

By now, you should have a general sense of what UDPs are and how they are implemented. Take the time to practice using them on your own, as they are a commonly-used feature in CA ERwin Data Modeler to add flexibility and customization to your models.

Key Points

- User-Defined Properties, or UDPs, allow you to create custom properties to add customized metadata documentation to your model.
- UDPs can be assigned to the majority of model objects including entities, tables, drawing shapes, diagrams, and even the model itself.
- There are several types of UDPs including Command, Date, Int, Real, Text, and List.
- Valid values can be defined for UDPs to assist with data entry and data quality.

CHAPTER 15
Model Templates

It's been done before
Don't frustrate with rebuilding
Use a template file

Once you've created a set of reusable standards in CA ERwin Data Modeler, you'll want to share them with others across the organization. Model templates are a great way to do this. You can save any model as a template to save its settings and contents for quick reuse. In this way, templates provide the ideal way of maintaining a consistent look and feel across different models, as well as standards for naming, domains, data types, etc. After you save a template, you can use it as the basis for creating new models.

In the past several chapters, we've created a number of organizational standards. We'd like a way to promote the usage of these standards that ensures consistency, but also make it easy for the team to implement. Templates are an ideal way to do this.

Creating Templates

Let's create a template to house the following model settings and standards:

- The standard database server for the organization is SQL Server 2008
- The corporate standard data modeling notation is Information Engineering (IE)
- All model diagrams should be developed in black and white to facilitate printing
- All entities, attributes, tables, columns, and domains should follow the corporate naming standards policy
- All logical entities are assigned an Information Steward.

There are a number of other settings you can store in a CA ERwin model template, but we'll limit our example to these for now. In fact, you can store any model setting or object using a model template. You can even store common entities and their definitions if you'd like these entities to be a standard across all models. Basically, a model template, saved using the file extension **`.erwin_tmpl,`** is the same as a CA ERwin model file **`(.erwin`**), with the added benefit of showing up in the template list when you create a model. Using an explicit template also makes a clear distinction between a template to be used as a 'seed' model, and a for-production model used for development or analysis.

Let's start the creation of our template by creating a new logical/physical model, as shown in Figure 15.1. (For help on creating a new model, refer to Chapter 3.) Since the corporate standard database is SQL Server 2008, we'll select that as our target database.

Figure 15.1 Using a Logical/Physical Model as the Starting Point for a Template

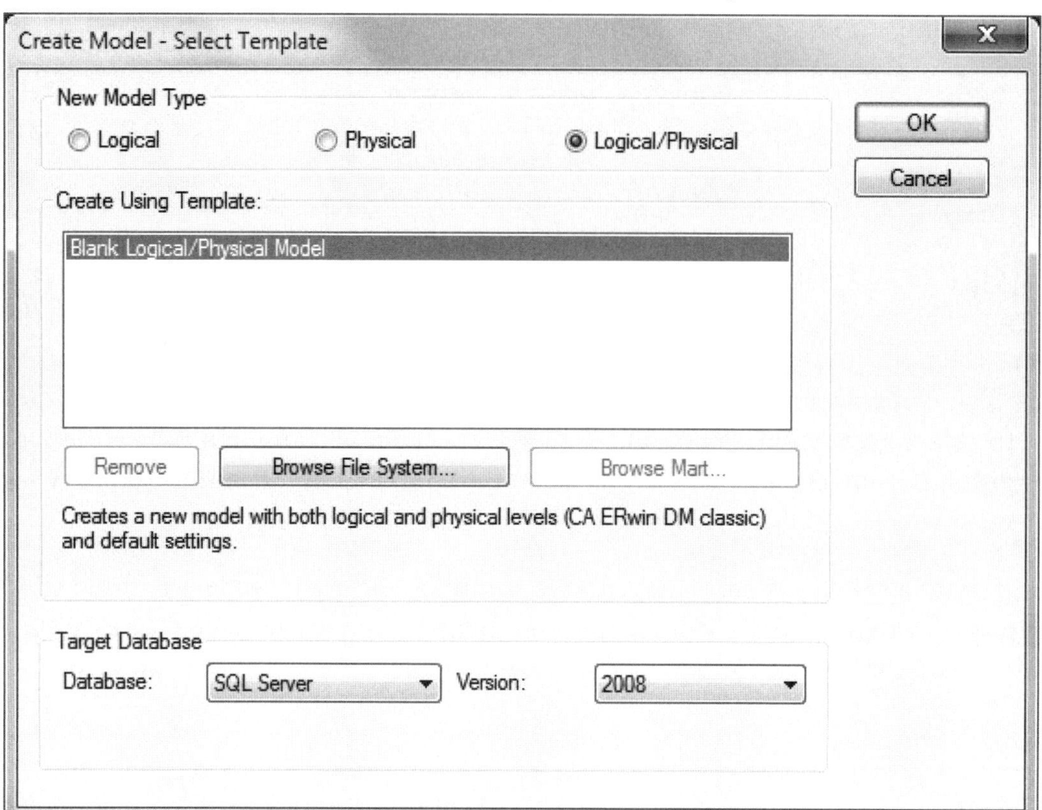

Notice that we'll need to select a template, which in this case is the default **Blank Logical/Physical Model** template. This might be slightly confusing, since we're in the process of creating a template, but think of this as inheriting from this template for basic property settings. Once we create a template, we can use this template as the starting point for other templates. For example, if we need a template for DB2 database, we can simply open the template we're creating for SQL Server and change the target database to DB2.

Select **OK** and you'll see the logical/physical model open to a default diagram. The first setting we'll want to change for this template is the modeling notation. We'll want to change the default to Information Engineering (IE), so that all models in the organization use the same notation style. Select **Model|Model Properties** and on the **General** tab, change the **Logical Notation** and **Physical Notation** fields to Information Engineering (IE), as shown in Figure 15.2.

Figure 15.2 Setting Model Template Notation to Information Engineering

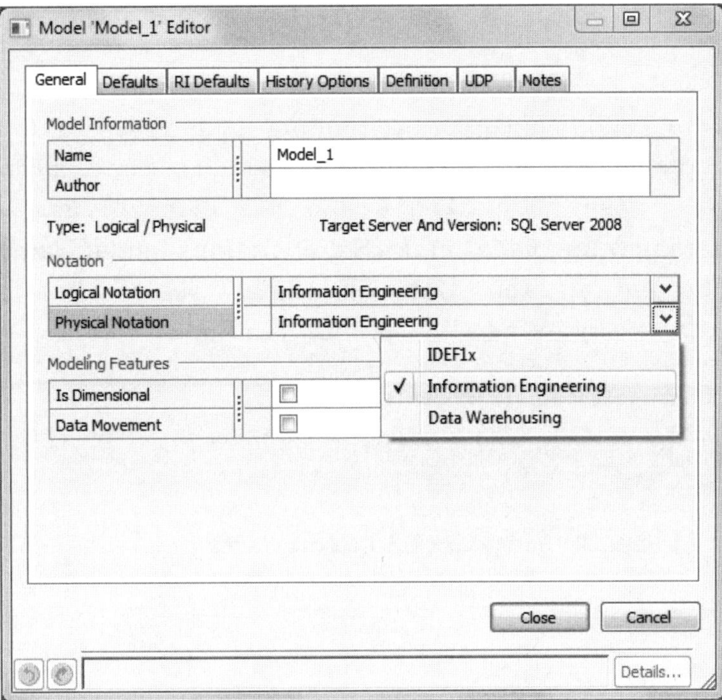

We also have a requirement that all model diagrams be displayed in black and white, to facilitate printing. As we learned in Chapter 8, we can use display Themes for this. Move to the **Defaults** tab, as shown in Figure 15.3, and select the **Classic** theme, which displays model diagrams in black and white.

Figure 15.3 Setting a Default Display Theme using a Template

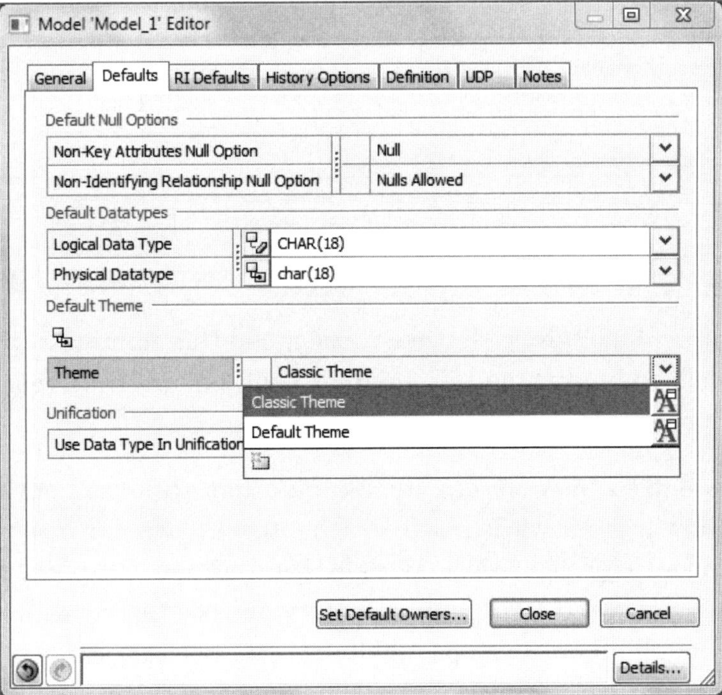

Now that we've changed the model notation and the default Theme, select **Close** to exit the Model Properties Editor. Notice that the open diagram now has a white background.

Next, we'll need to establish corporate naming standards. Let's use the naming standards file we created in Chapter 12 for this. If you don't have a copy of this file, you can download the **naming_standards_example.nsm** file from www.erwin.com/datamodelingmadesimple. Select **Actions|Model Naming Options** from the **Main Menu**, and in the **Use File** field, select the location for the **naming_standards_example.nsm** file, as shown in Figure 15.4.

Figure 15.4 Assigning Naming Standards to Model Template

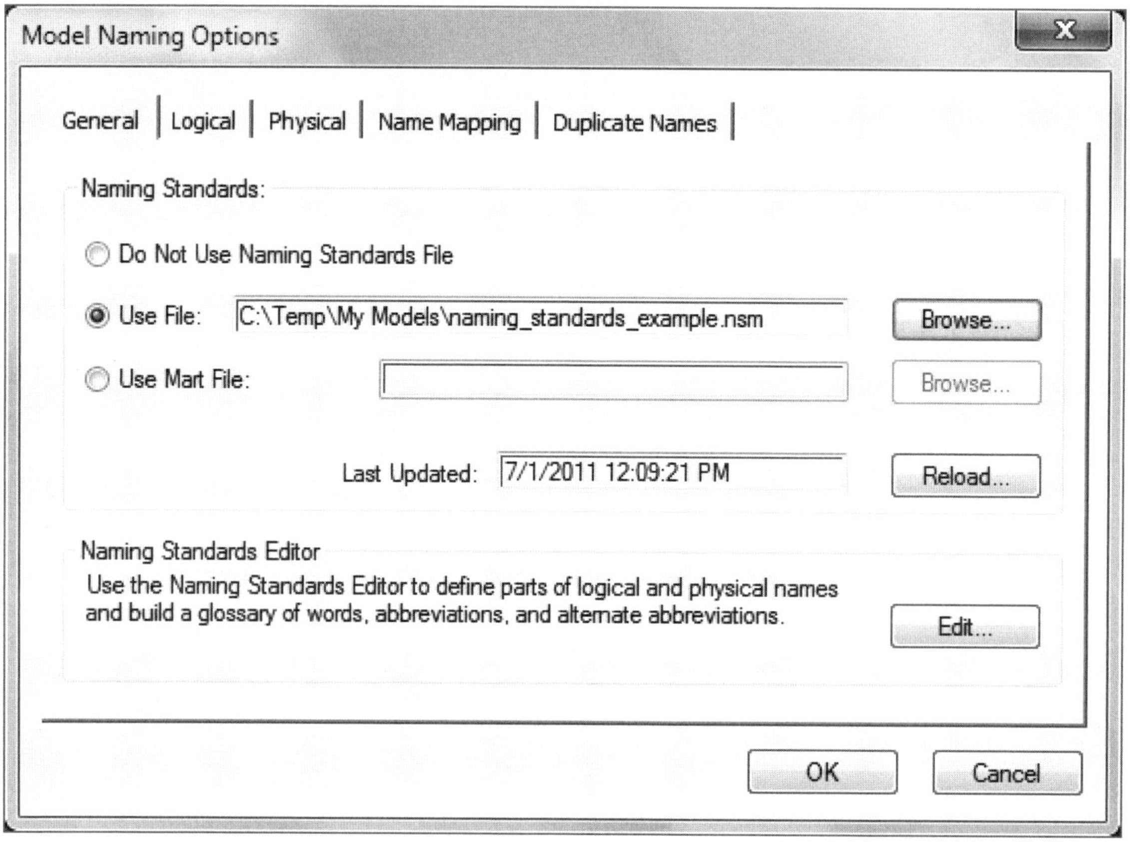

Select **OK** to exit this dialog. Now that we've assigned this naming standards file to our template, all models created using this template will ensure that objects adhere to the defined naming conventions for the organization.

The next requirement we have for our template is that all logical entities are assigned an Information Steward. As we learned in Chapter 14, we can use a UDP to assign stewardship to model objects. Select **Model|User Defined Properties** from the **Main Menu**, and create a **Steward** UDP for the **Entity** object type, as shown in Figure 15.5. We won't walk through all of the steps for this. If you need assistance, refer to Chapter 14 for more information.

Figure 15.5 Assigning a UDP for Entities using a Template

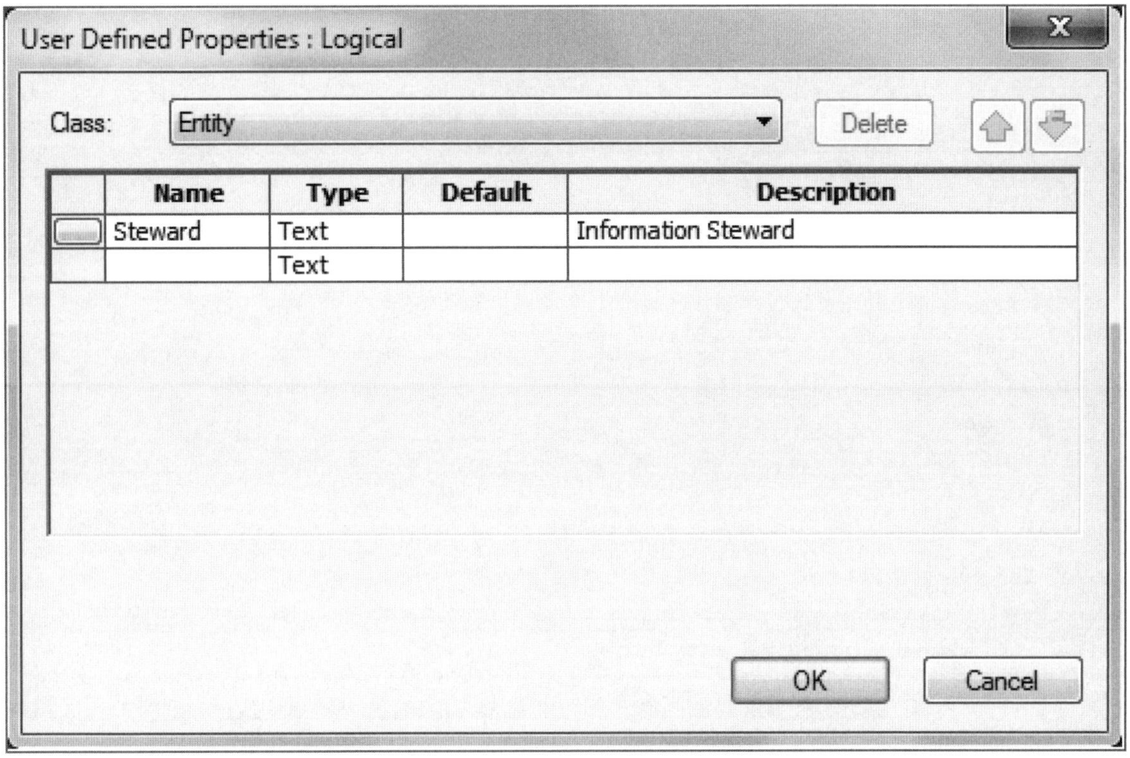

We've now created all of our model defaults for our template, from modeling notation, to look-and-feel, to naming standards. The next step is to save these defaults as a template, so that they can be easily reused. To do this, simply select **File|Save As**, and use a file type of **`.erwin_tmpl`**, as shown in Figure 15.6, using a file name of **`Corporate_SQLServer_Template.erwin_tmpl`**.

Figure 15.6 Saving a Model as a Template

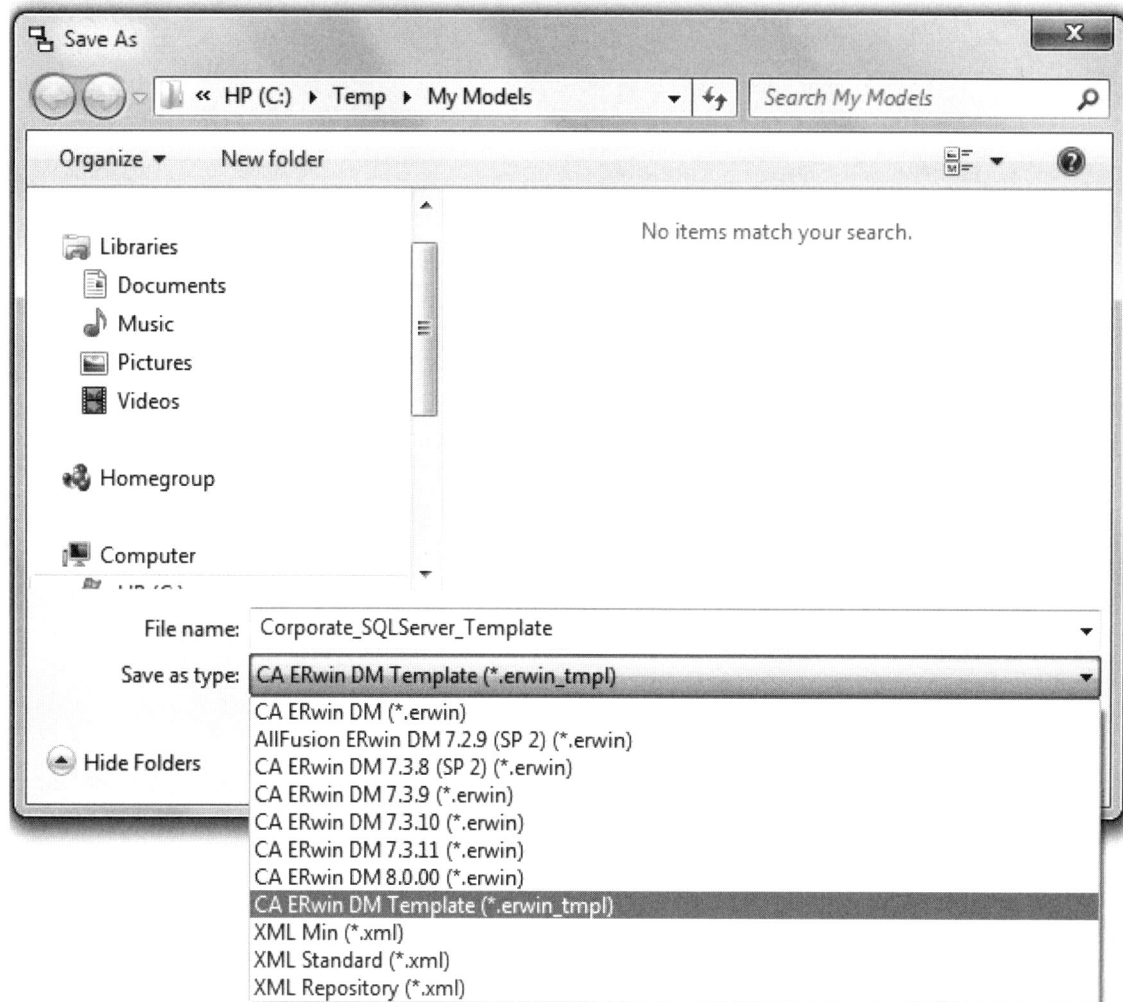

Let's see how we can use this template when we create a new model. Create a new Logical/Physical data model, and in the Create Model Dialog, use the **Browse File System** button to locate your **`Corporate_SQLServer_Template.erwin_tmpl`** file. One you've selected this file, you'll see that it appears in the list of available templates, as shown in Figure 15.7. Note that templates are specific to a particular model type. For example, since we created this template for a logical/physical model, we cannot use it for a logical only model.

Figure 15.7 Using a Template for New Model Creation

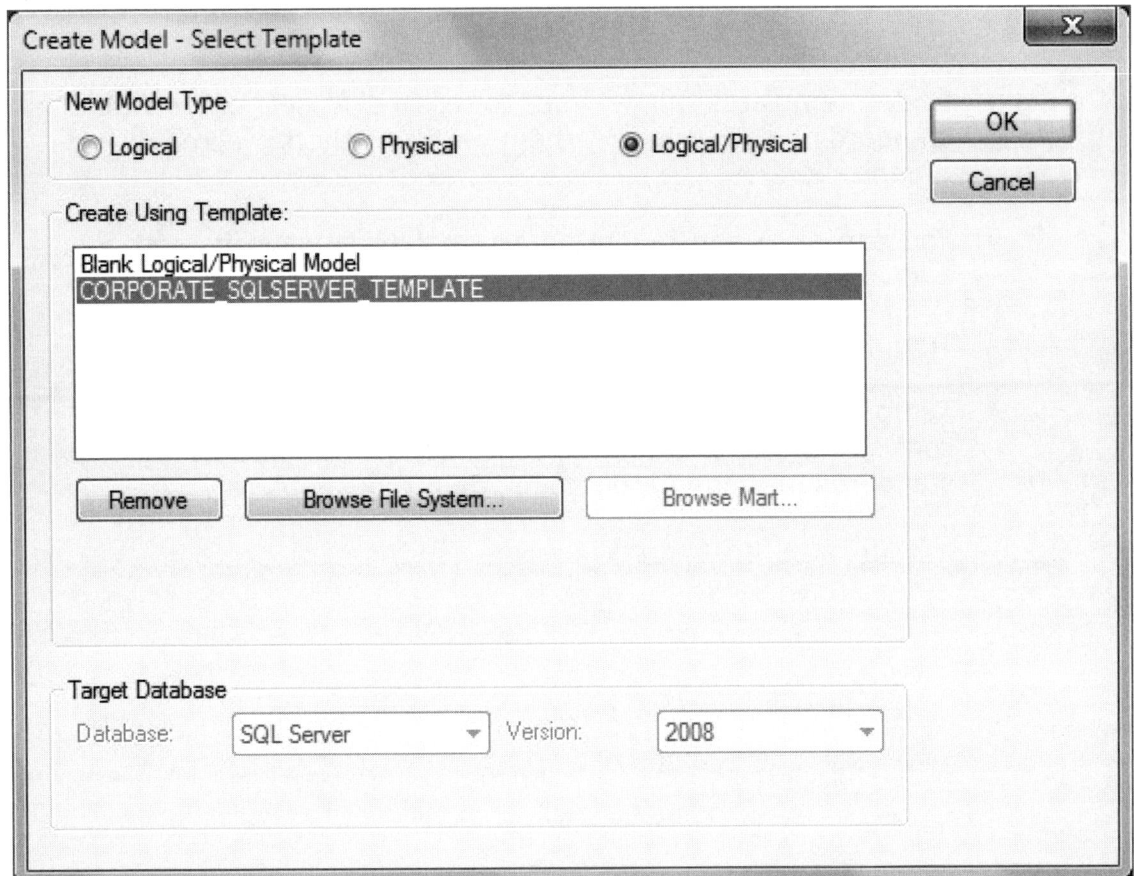

Highlight the **CORPORATE_SQLSERVER_TEMPLATE** template option, and select **OK** to open your new model. Browse around this model, and you'll see that our template settings are all in place. The model diagram appears in black and white, the model notation is Information Engineering, etc. Try creating a new entity and you'll see that the **Steward** UDP appears, as well.

If you'd like an example of the template we created in this chapter, you can download the **`Corporate_SQLServer_Template.erwin_tmpl`** file from www.erwin.com/datamodelingmadesimple.

Now that you have a basic understanding of templates and their usage, use them as both a time-saving and quality-enhancing tool in your daily tasks. If there is a common setting you find yourself re-defining with each model, create a template. If there is a diagram theme you prefer to use, create a template. If there are common UDPs that should be used by all models, you get the picture—create a template. Once you get used to this handy feature, you'll find yourself using templates on a regular basis to make your job easier.

Key Points

- Model templates allow you to create a set of reusable standards and share them with others across the organization.
- You can save any model as a template to save its settings and contents for quick reuse.
- Templates are saved with the file extension *.erwin_tmpl.
- Templates provide a simple method of maintaining a consistent look and feel across different models, as well as standards for naming, domains, data types, etc.

CHAPTER 16
Reporting, Querying, and Editing

Information shared
Promotes knowledge and reuse
Hidden, is failure

Communicating with the various stakeholders across the organization is a key part of achieving success and buy-in for your data modeling projects. After spending time and effort creating the business rules and data structure definitions in CA ERwin Data Modeler, it's important that this information be shared, in order to achieve the true benefits of reuse and standards. And not everyone needs or wants to read a data model (as surprising as that may be to us!). There are a number of ways to share information using CA ERwin Data Modeler: generating reports from SAP Business Objects Crystal Reports, creating queries into other reporting tools using the ODBC interface, using spreadsheet-style editing with the Bulk Editor, or even exporting metadata directly into other tools using the metadata bridges.

Reporting using SAP Business Objects Crystal Reports

Every commercial copy of CA ERwin Data Modeler is bundled with a developers' copy of SAP Business Objects Crystal Reports for advanced reporting capabilities. There are a number of out of the box-reports that you can leverage, which is the simplest way to get started.

Start by opening the eMovies model, which we'll use for our example (refer to Chapter 3, if you're not familiar with this). In our example, we'd like to share the logical attribute definitions with the business analyst team to verify that we're on the right track. In this case, we can use the predefined reports in CA ERwin Data Modeler to generate a report to show them, since many of the analysts are not familiar with data models, although they are familiar with the business rules and definitions of the organization. Select **Tools|Pinned Reports** from the **Main Menu**, and you'll see a list of the pre-defined reports that are included with CA ERwin Data Modeler, as shown in Figure 16.1.

Figure 16.1 Predefined Reports in CA ERwin Data Modeler

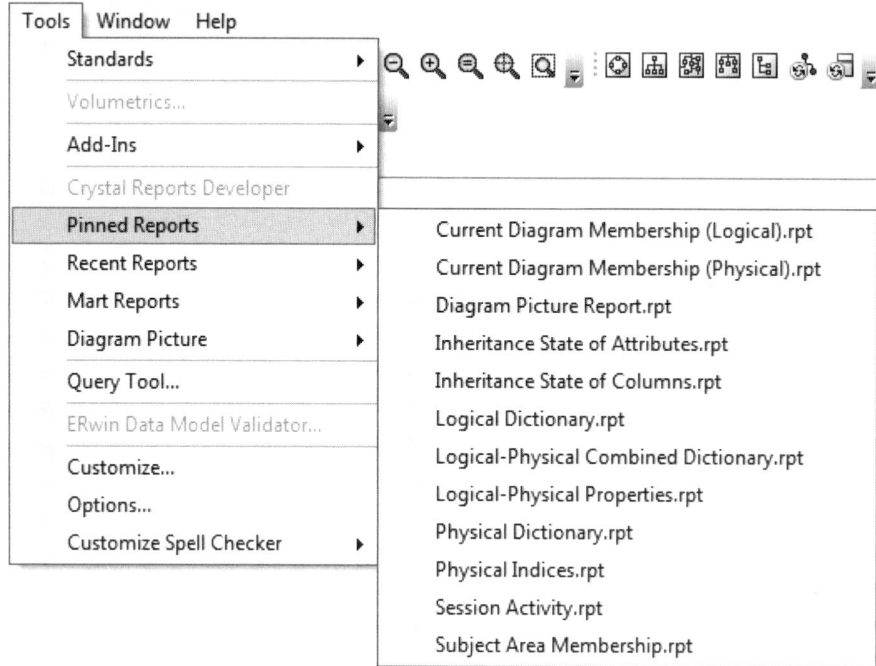

The **Logical Dictionary** report will suit our needs, so select that from the menu list. The CA ERwin Report Viewer appears, as shown in Figure 16.2, with a dialog asking for parameter values for the report.

Figure 16.2 CA ERwin Report Viewer - Enter Parameter Values Dialog

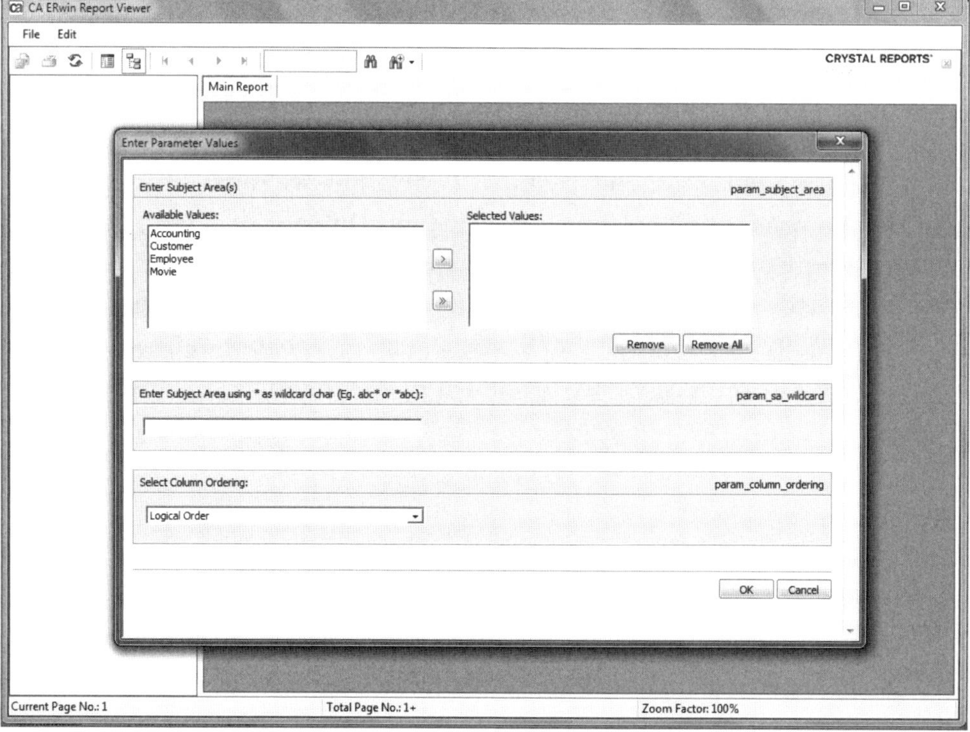

The first parameter requested is which Subject Area(s) you'd like to report on. In this case, we'd like to review the Accounting business area with the business analysts, so we'll select **Accounting** from the **Available Values** list box, as shown in Figure 16.3.

Figure 16.3 Selecting a Subject Area for a Pre-Defined Report

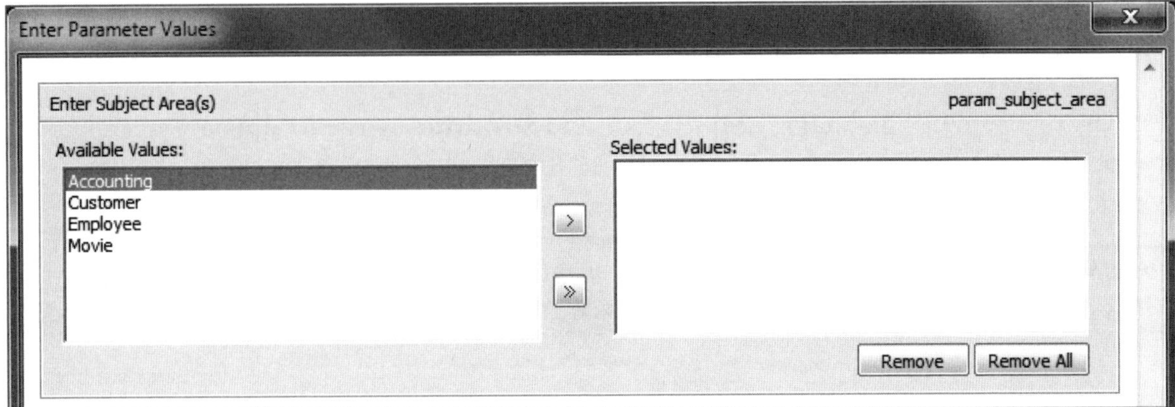

Use the arrow button [>] to move the **Accounting** Subject Area into the **Selected Values** list box, as shown in Figure 16.4.

Figure 16.4 Selecting the Accounting Subject Area

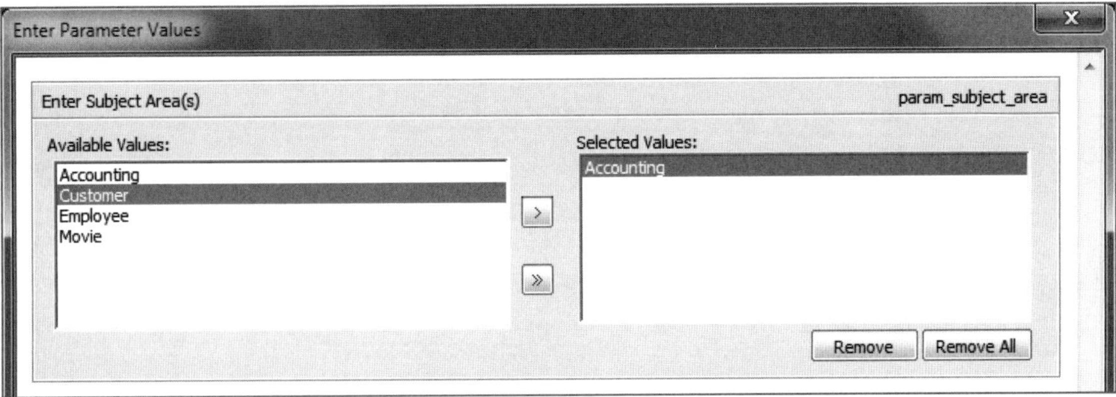

Next, we'll want to customize the order in which the attributes appear on the report. Since we're showing this report to business analysts, the most intuitive ordering would be alphabetical. If we were showing this same report to a DBA, for example, we might want to use the physical order. Select **Alpha Order** from the **Select Column Ordering** drop-down field, as shown in Figure 16.5.

Figure 16.5 Selecting Column Ordering for a Predefined Report

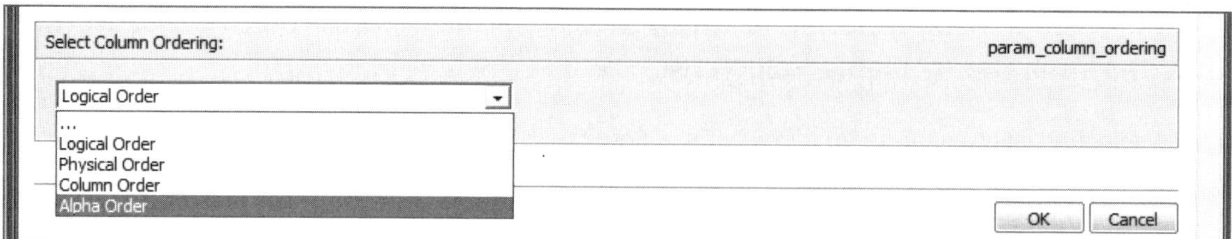

Select **OK** to complete this dialog and the **Logical Dictionary** report appears in the **CA ERwin Report Viewer**, as shown in Figure 16.6. This is a clearly formatted report that will be easily understandable to our business audience.

Figure 16.6 Logical Dictionary Report in the CA ERwin Report Viewer

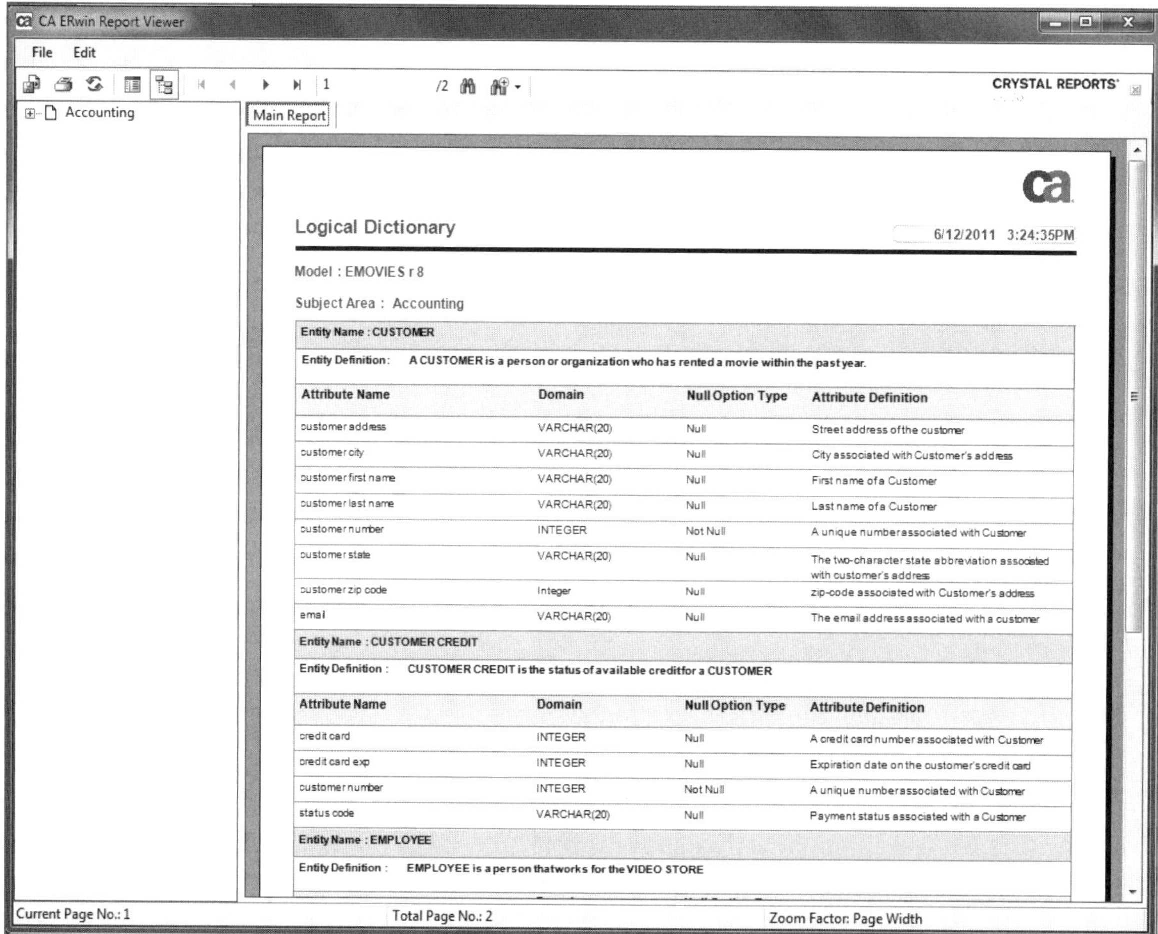

Logical Dictionary 6/12/2011 3:24:35PM

Model : EMOVIES r8

Subject Area : Accounting

Entity Name : CUSTOMER

Entity Definition: A CUSTOMER is a person or organization who has rented a movie within the past year.

Attribute Name	Domain	Null Option Type	Attribute Definition
customer address	VARCHAR(20)	Null	Street address of the customer
customer city	VARCHAR(20)	Null	City associated with Customer's address
customer first name	VARCHAR(20)	Null	First name of a Customer
customer last name	VARCHAR(20)	Null	Last name of a Customer
customer number	INTEGER	Not Null	A unique number associated with Customer
customer state	VARCHAR(20)	Null	The two-character state abbreviation associated with customer's address
customer zip code	Integer	Null	zip-code associated with Customer's address
email	VARCHAR(20)	Null	The email address associated with a customer

Entity Name : CUSTOMER CREDIT

Entity Definition : CUSTOMER CREDIT is the status of available credit for a CUSTOMER

Attribute Name	Domain	Null Option Type	Attribute Definition
credit card	INTEGER	Null	A credit card number associated with Customer
credit card exp	INTEGER	Null	Expiration date on the customer's credit card
customer number	INTEGER	Not Null	A unique number associated with Customer
status code	VARCHAR(20)	Null	Payment status associated with a Customer

Entity Name : EMPLOYEE

Entity Definition : EMPLOYEE is a person that works for the VIDEO STORE

Notice that in the upper-left corner of the report viewer is a group tree with a node labeled **Accounting**, as shown in Figure 16.7. Also notice that the **Toggle Group Tree** toolbar button [button icon] is enabled, which determines whether this tree is shown or hidden (in this case shown).

Figure 16.7 Report Viewer Group Tree

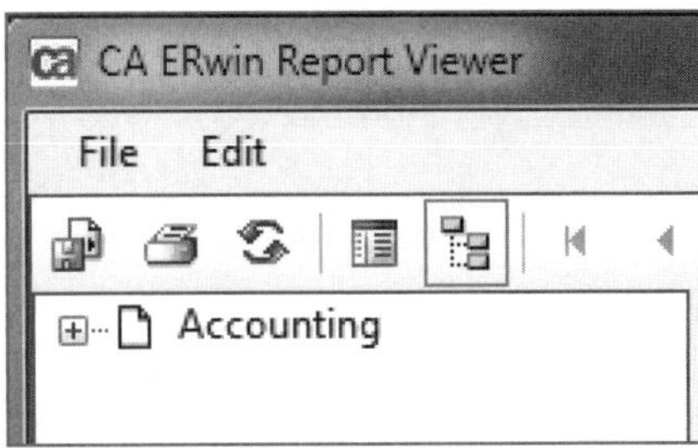

Expand the tree using the **+** sign, and you will see a list of the entities within the **Accounting** Subject Area, as shown in Figure 16.8.

Figure 16.8 Entity Listing in Group Tree of ERwin Report Viewer

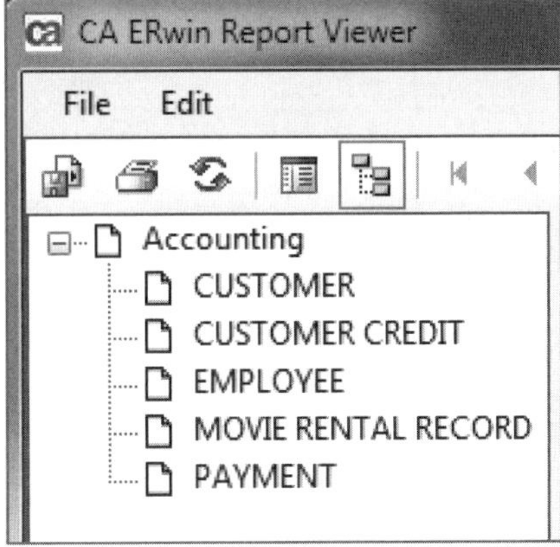

This listing is a helpful way to 'jump' to a given entity within the report. For example, select the **Payment** entity from the list and you will see that a red box appears around the **Payment** entity on the second page of the report, as shown in Figure 16.9.

Figure 16.9 Using the Group Tree to 'Jump' to a Selected Entity within a Report

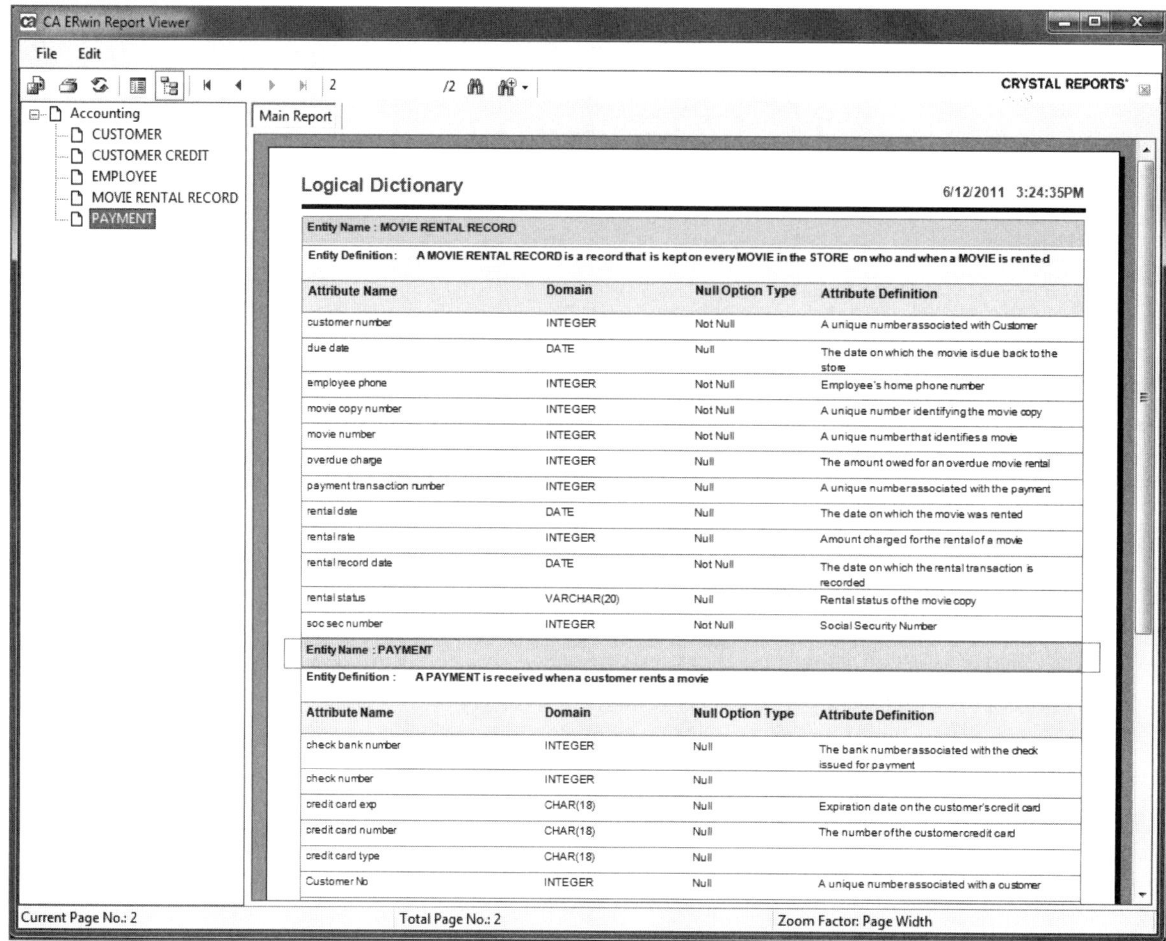

Logical Dictionary 6/12/2011 3:24:35PM

Entity Name : MOVIE RENTAL RECORD

Entity Definition: A MOVIE RENTAL RECORD is a record that is kept on every MOVIE in the STORE on who and when a MOVIE is rented

Attribute Name	Domain	Null Option Type	Attribute Definition
customer number	INTEGER	Not Null	A unique number associated with Customer
due date	DATE	Null	The date on which the movie is due back to the store
employee phone	INTEGER	Not Null	Employee's home phone number
movie copy number	INTEGER	Not Null	A unique number identifying the movie copy
movie number	INTEGER	Not Null	A unique number that identifies a movie
overdue charge	INTEGER	Null	The amount owed for an overdue movie rental
payment transaction number	INTEGER	Null	A unique number associated with the payment
rental date	DATE	Null	The date on which the movie was rented
rental rate	INTEGER	Null	Amount charged for the rental of a movie
rental record date	DATE	Not Null	The date on which the rental transaction is recorded
rental status	VARCHAR(20)	Null	Rental status of the movie copy
soc sec number	INTEGER	Not Null	Social Security Number

Entity Name : PAYMENT

Entity Definition : A PAYMENT is received when a customer rents a movie

Attribute Name	Domain	Null Option Type	Attribute Definition
check bank number	INTEGER	Null	The bank number associated with the check issued for payment
check number	INTEGER	Null	
credit card exp	CHAR(18)	Null	Expiration date on the customer's credit card
credit card number	CHAR(18)	Null	The number of the customer credit card
credit card type	CHAR(18)	Null	
Customer No	INTEGER	Null	A unique number associated with a customer

Another way to easily search for objects within the report is using the **Find Text** toolbar button, as shown in Figure 16.10. Typing the text 'Payment' in the text box will find all instances of that term that appear in the report, regardless of object type.

Figure 16.10 Searching for Text Strings using the Find Text Option in the CA ERwin Report Viewer

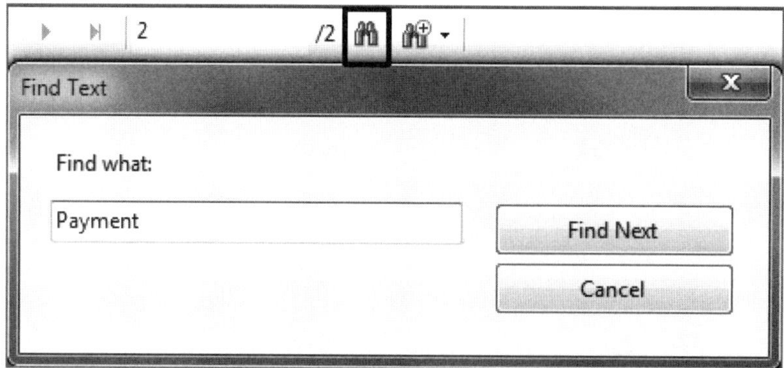

Next, we'll want to export our report into a format easily shared with the business analyst team, in this case **.PDF**. Select the **Export Report** toolbar button and the Export Report Dialog appears, as shown in Figure 16.11. In this dialog, you can name and save the report to a given location on your computer or network.

Figure 16.11 Saving a Report in .PDF format

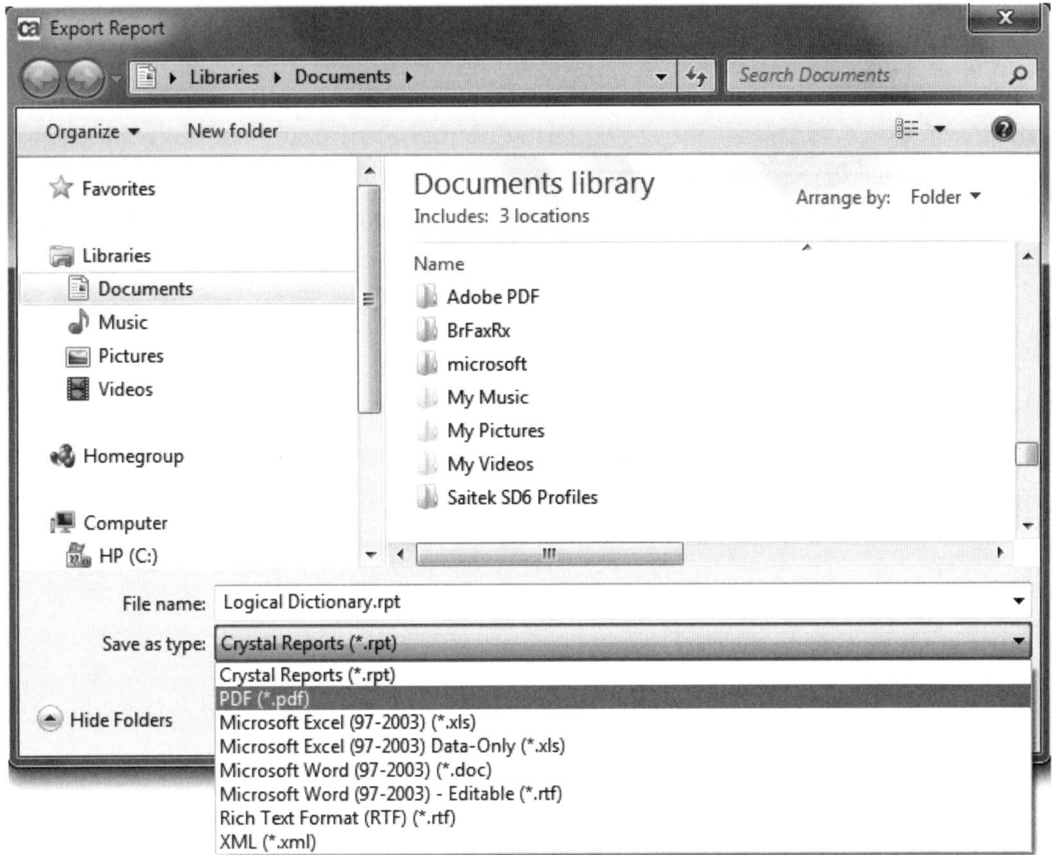

You can also create and customize your own reports using the full developer version of SAP Business Objects Crystal Reports included with CA ERwin Data Modeler (by selecting **Tools|Crystal Reports Developer** from the **Main Menu**). It's beyond the scope of this book to go into great detail on creating new reports with Crystal Reports, but an easy way to get started is to use the predefined reports as a guide, then add and remove fields from those reports. It's generally easier to start with a template as a guide than to create something new from scratch.

Reporting and Editing using the Bulk Editor

The Bulk Editor is a tool designed to edit large quantities of model metadata in a spreadsheet-style interface. Cross-object editing is also possible so that you can update multiple object types in a single interface. For example, tables, columns, annotations, and domains can all be edited in the same interface, without the need to switch to separate editors. As long as the objects have common properties (e.g. name, description), they can be edited together in 'bulk'.

Since metadata is often created and stored in spreadsheets across a typical organization, you can also easily import and export metadata from external sources through a `.csv` file import/export. This is a helpful way to gather and manage information from spreadsheets into the CA ERwin Data Modeler tool so that it can be integrated with a centralized source for enterprise models and metadata.

Let's walk through an example using the eMovies model (if you need help in locating and opening the eMovies file, refer to Chapter 3). In this example, we'd like update the data types for all attributes, columns, and domains in the model. Open the Bulk Editor, shown in Figure 16.12. (Note: If the Bulk Editor window is not active in your workspace, you may have to invoke it using the **View|Windows|Bulk Editor Pane** or using the `Ctrl+B` keystrokes).

Figure 16.12 Empty Bulk Editor Pane

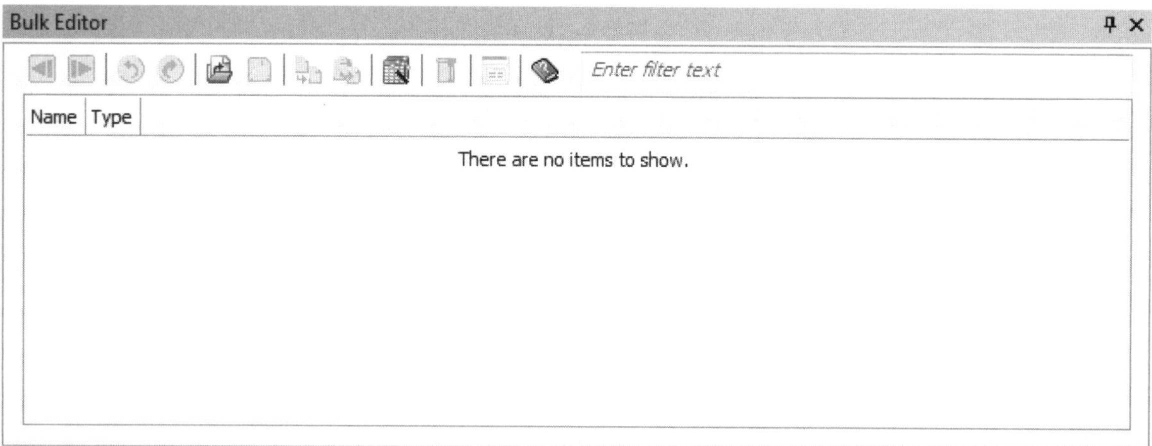

The Bulk Editor is empty by default, so we'll have to invoke the Bulk Editor Wizard to populate it with the values we're looking to edit. Select the **Bulk Editor Wizard** toolbar button, and the Bulk Editor Wizard will appear, as shown in Figure 16.13. The first page of the wizard provides a brief overview of the functionality of the Bulk Editor tool.

Figure 16.13 Invoking the Bulk Editor Wizard

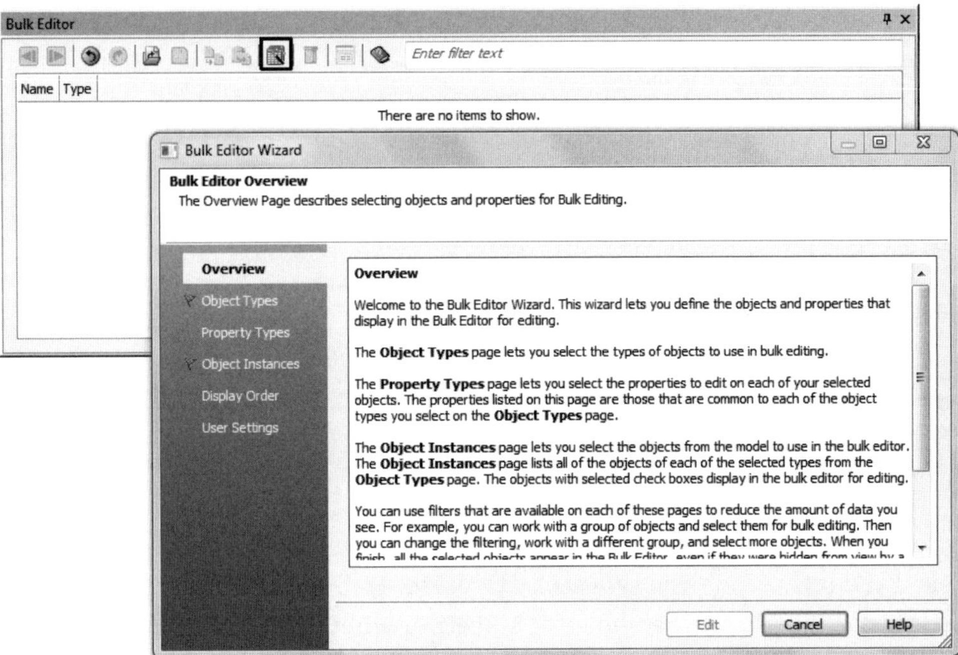

The first selection we'll need to make is what object types we'd like to view and edit. Select the **Object Types** menu item from the left-hand pane of the wizard, and a list of available object types appears, as shown in Figure 16.14.

Figure 16.14 Object Types Page of the Bulk Editor Wizard

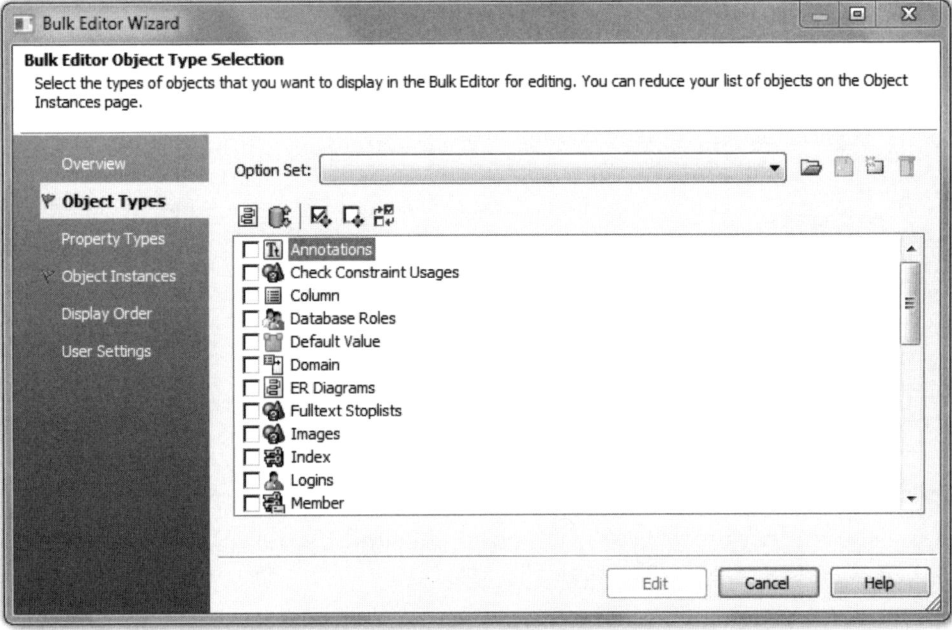

Since we'd like to edit the data types of attributes, columns, and domains in our example, we'll select **Column** and **Domain** from the list of objects, as shown in Figure 16.15.

Figure 16.15 Object Selection in the Bulk Editor Wizard

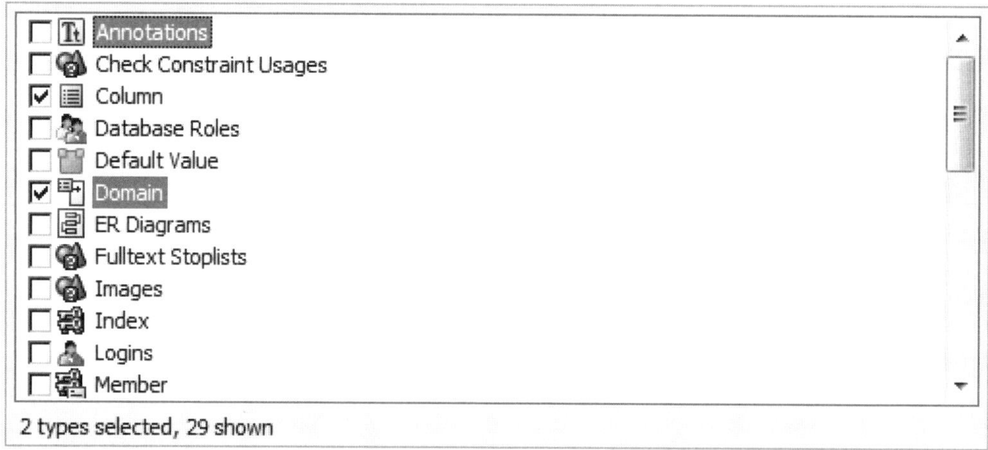

You may be wondering why there is no selection for **Attribute** in the list. This is where the display options fit in. Since the eMovies model we're using in our example is a logical/physical model, the object types of attribute and column are closely linked. In the Bulk Editor Wizard, you have the choice of selecting whether to view the logical or physical names. Select the **Display either Logical name or Physical names** button from the Bulk Editor Toolbar, and a drop-down menu will appear, as shown in Figure 16.16, which allows you to control how object names are viewed in the wizard.

Figure 16.16 Switching Logical/Physical Display in the Bulk Editor Wizard

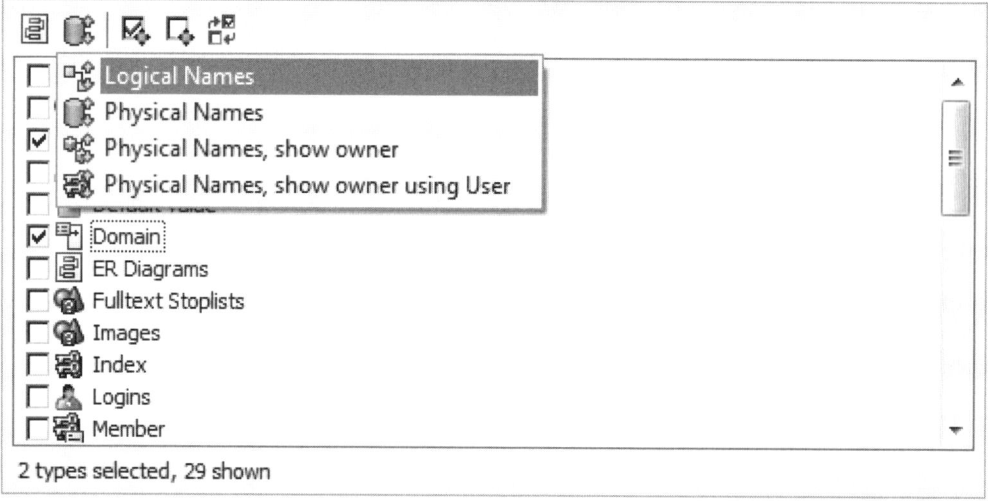

Choose **Logical Names** from the menu, and you'll see that the list changes to include **Attributes**, as shown in Figure 16.17, which is checked by default, since we have a closely linked logical/physical model in this case.

Figure 16.17 Showing Logical Display in the Bulk Editor Wizard

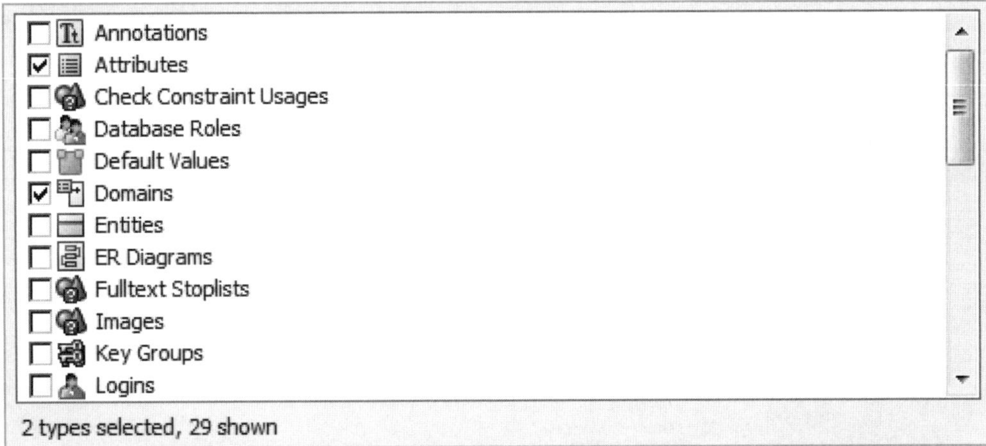

Now that we've chosen what object types to edit, we can select which properties to edit for these objects. Move to the **Property Types** menu item and the **Property Types** page appears, as shown in Figure 16.18. Note that the property types listed are only those that are ***common to all object types selected***. For example, had we chosen **Table** as an object type to include, the property type **Average Width** would not appear on the list, since that does not apply to tables.

Figure 16.18 Property Types Page of the Bulk Editor Wizard

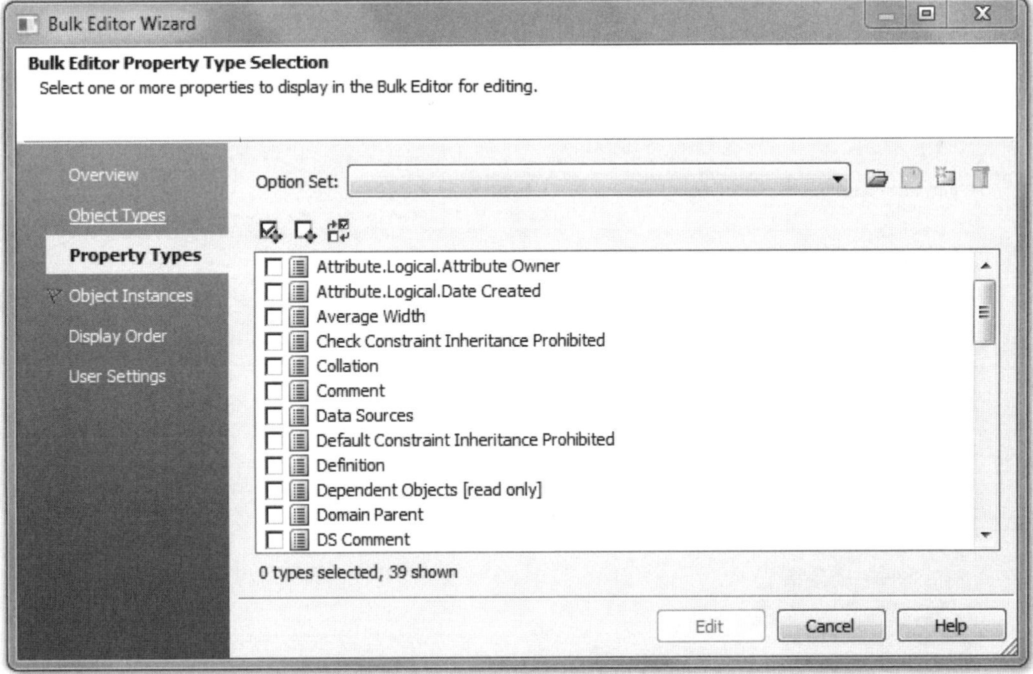

Select the property types **Domain Parent**, **Logical Data Type** and **Physical Data Type** from the list, as shown in Figure 16.19.

Figure 16.19 Selecting Property Types from the Bulk Editor Wizard

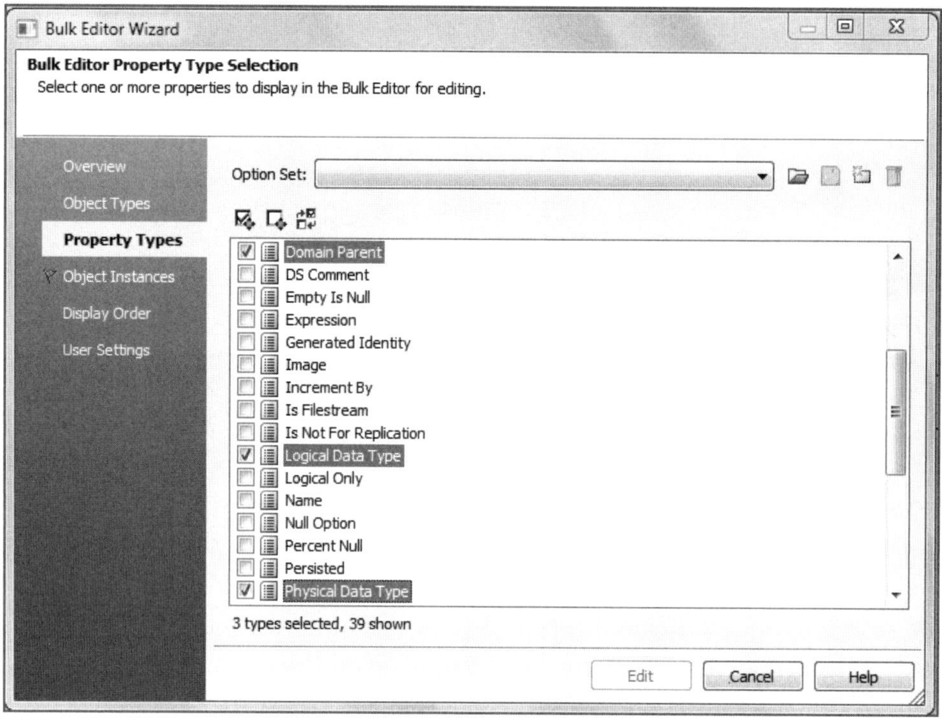

Now that we've defined the object types and their properties that we'd like to edit, we can further filter our criteria by selecting individual instances. Move to the **Object Instances** page, as shown in Figure 16.20.

Figure 16.20 Object Instances Page of the Bulk Editor Wizard

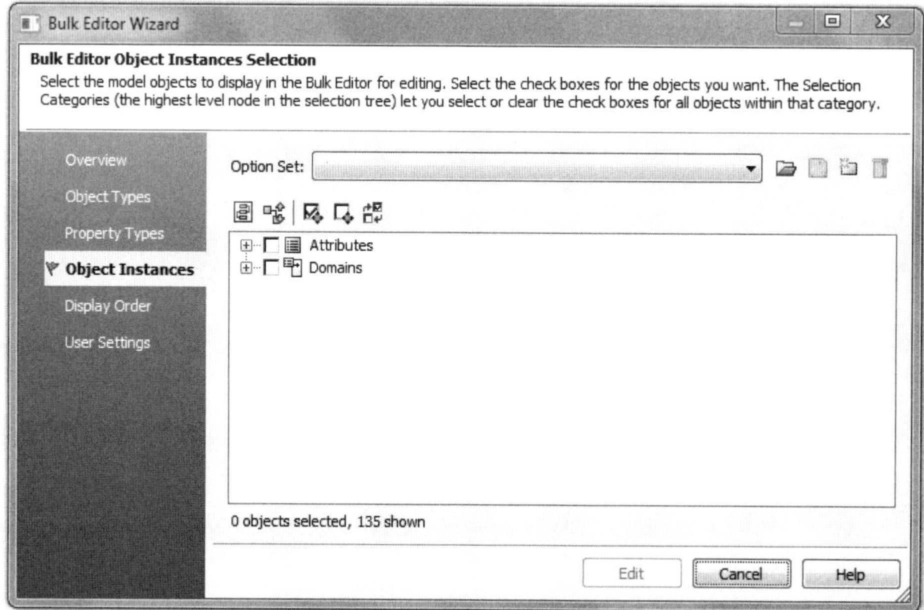

Expand the **Attributes** tree by clicking on the + sign, and you'll see a full list of the attribute instances that match our criteria in the model, as shown in Figure 16.21. You can use this select to filter your selection to certain instances you'd like to edit.

Figure 16.21 Displaying Individual Object Instances in the Bulk Editor Wizard

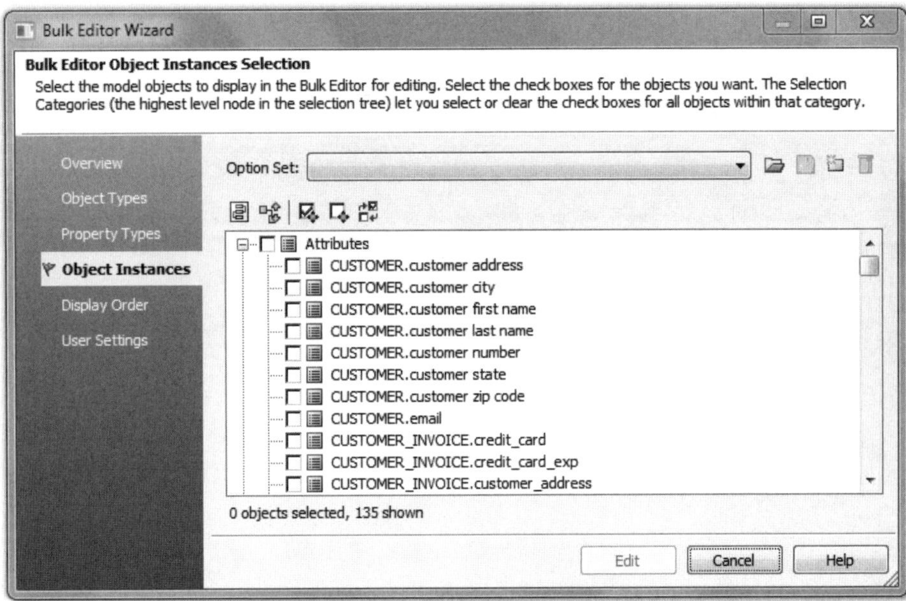

In our case, we'll want to have the ability to edit all instances (we can always filter them later in the Bulk Editor itself), so we'll use the checkbox next to the **Attributes** and **Domains** nodes to select all items within this node, as shown in Figure 16.22. Remember, although we're selecting **Attributes**, this will actually select both attributes and columns.

Figure 16.22 Selecting All Instances for Object Types in the Bulk Editor Wizard

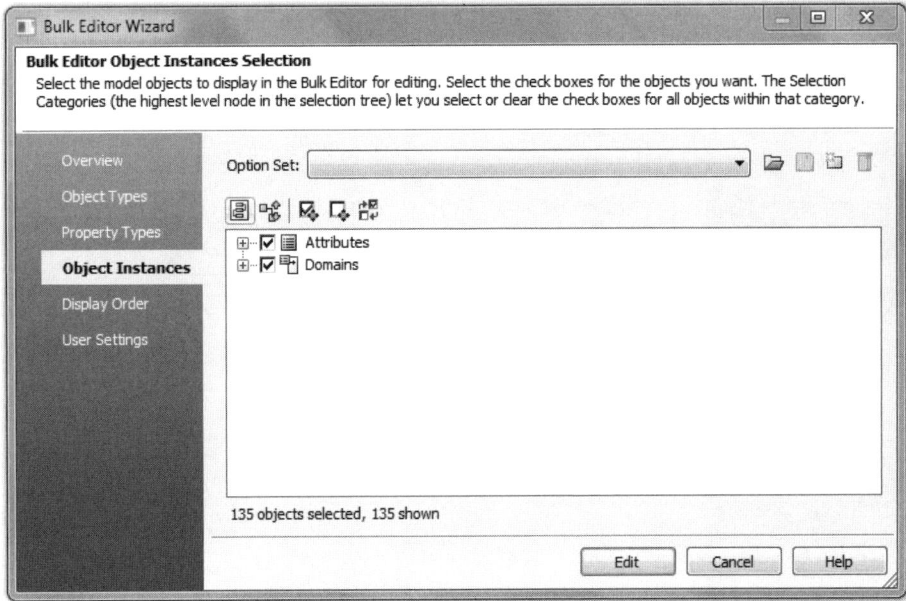

Next, we can customize the order in which objects are displayed by moving to the **Display Order** tab, as shown in Figure 16.23. The defaults indicate that **Attributes** will be listed before **Domains** for the row order (i.e. vertically), and that **Physical Data Type** will be listed before (i.e. to the left of) **Logical Data Type** for the column order. The default settings will work for us here, but we can easily change them by highlighting a selecting and moving the order using the arrow keys on the toolbar .

Figure 16.23 Display Order for Bulk Editor

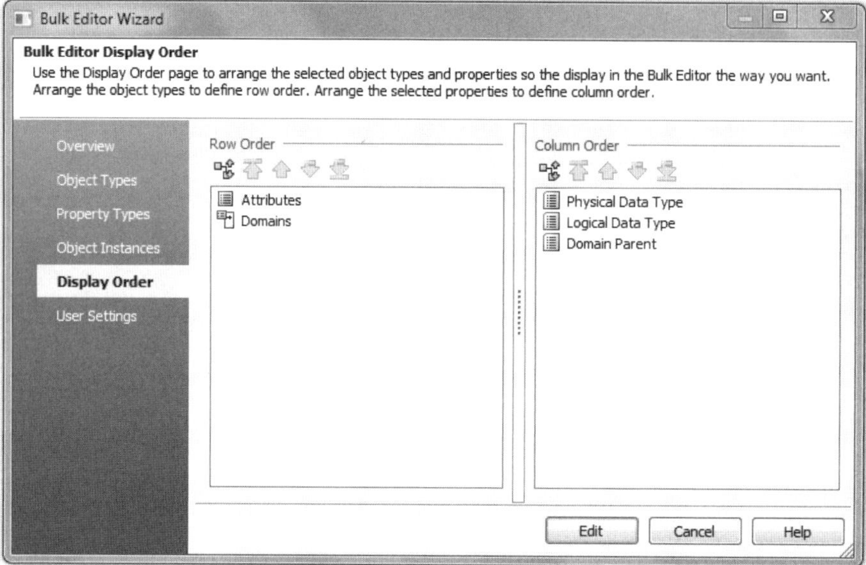

Lastly, we'll move to the **User Settings** tab to define common preferences, as shown in Figure 16.24.

Figure 16.24 User Settings in Bulk Editor Wizard

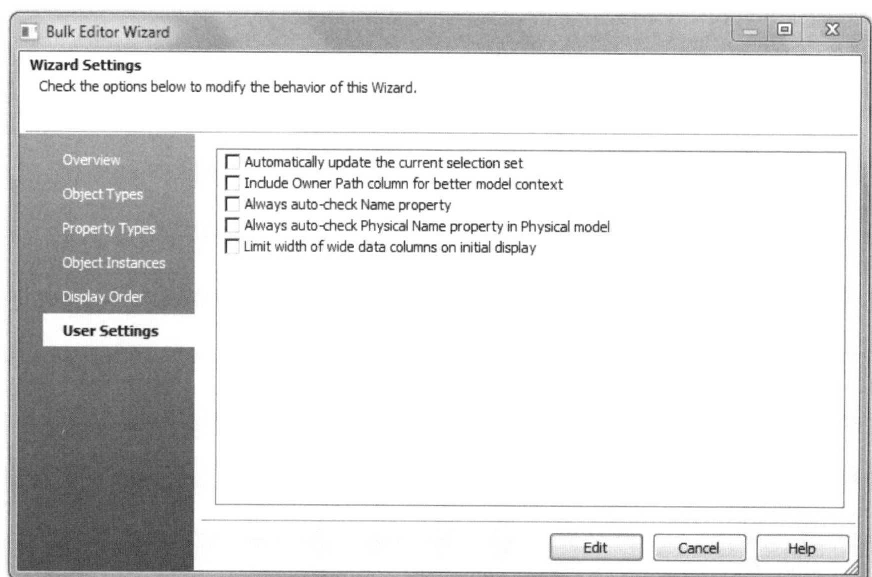

A brief explanation of these settings is as follows:

- **Automatically update the current selection set**: This option ensures that user settings reflect any changes previously made. If unchecked, user settings are based on default settings. (This only applies to subsequent invocations of the wizard.) Note: As of the 8.1 release, this option is not active.
- **Include Owner Path column for better model context**: In addition to the standard **Name** and **Type** columns, an **Owner Path** column will be added to the Bulk Editor to show the names of each object, in the hierarchy of objects, that owns the current object. For example, the table name for a given column.
- **Always auto-check Name property**: Specifies that the **Name** property is checked by default.
- **Always auto-check Physical Name property in the Physical model**: Specifies that the **Physical Name** property is checked by default, if you are working with a Physical or Logical/Physical model.
- **Limit width of wide data columns on initial display**: Restricts the width of columns that contain large amounts of text to 250 pixels upon the initial display in the Bulk Editor. All other columns are sized to match the best width so that a column's entire title and widest data value is displayed. Note: You can resize the columns once you're in the Bulk Editor to change these defaults.

We'll leave the default settings for our example.

Now that we've defined our settings and criteria, select **Edit** to invoke the Bulk Editor, as shown in Figure 16.25.

Figure 16.25 Bulk Editor Populated Metadata Based on Object and Instance Selections

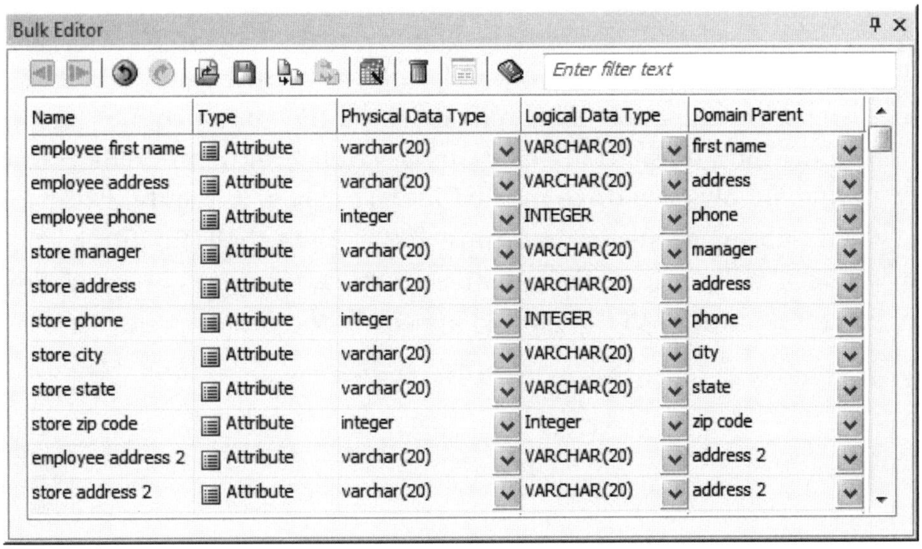

Bulk Editor

Enter filter text

Name	Type	Physical Data Type	Logical Data Type	Domain Parent
employee first name	Attribute	varchar(20)	VARCHAR(20)	first name
employee address	Attribute	varchar(20)	VARCHAR(20)	address
employee phone	Attribute	integer	INTEGER	phone
store manager	Attribute	varchar(20)	VARCHAR(20)	manager
store address	Attribute	varchar(20)	VARCHAR(20)	address
store phone	Attribute	integer	INTEGER	phone
store city	Attribute	varchar(20)	VARCHAR(20)	city
store state	Attribute	varchar(20)	VARCHAR(20)	state
store zip code	Attribute	integer	Integer	zip code
employee address 2	Attribute	varchar(20)	VARCHAR(20)	address 2
store address 2	Attribute	varchar(20)	VARCHAR(20)	address 2

With multiple object types, property types, and instances showing on the same screen, it's easy to view and edit the information that we're focused on in this example. For instance, a requirement from our sponsor is to be able to monitor movie rentals by time of day. The **DATE** data type for **rental date** isn't specific enough to track that. We'll want to change it to track both the date and hour. To make this change, simply move to the rental date field and use the drop-down field for the **Logical Data Type**, and select **DATETIME DAY TO HOUR**, as shown in Figure 16.26.

Figure 16.26 Changing a Physical Data Type Using the Bulk Editor

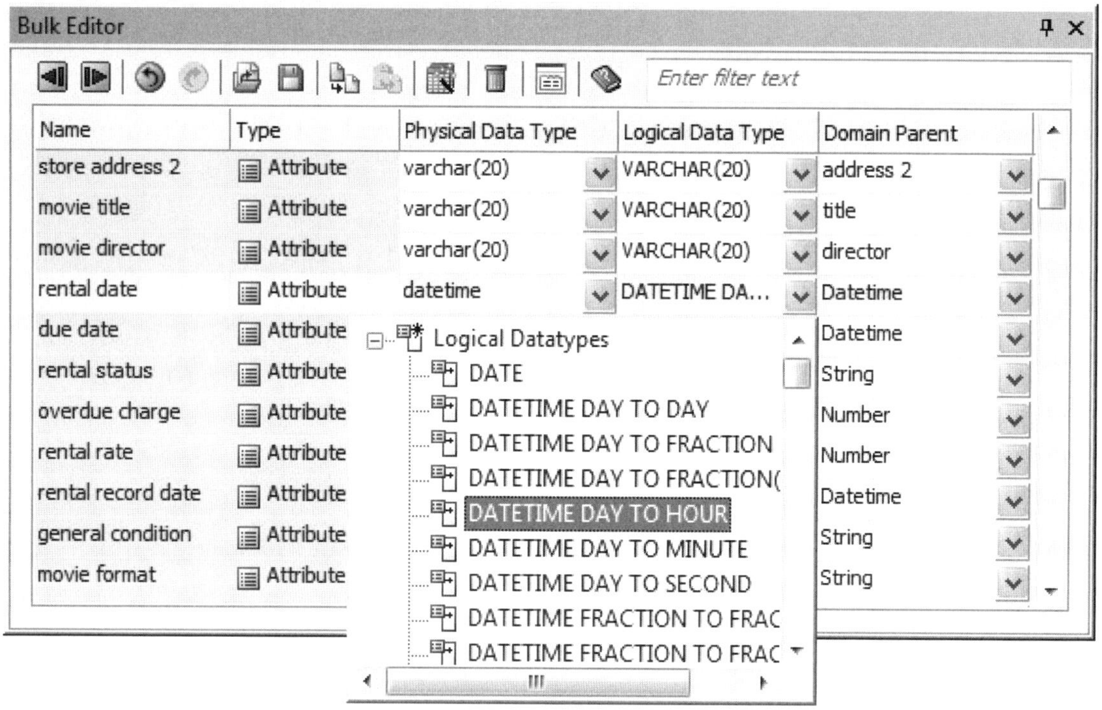

In this small data set, it was relatively easy to locate the **rental date** field. In a larger data set, it certainly would be more difficult, which is where the ability to filter comes in handy. If we wanted to filter the information shown in the Bulk Editor to fields that contain the word 'date', we could simply type **date** in the **Filter Text** box, and only instances that meet that criteria would appear, as shown in Figure 16.27. Note that this filter looks across all fields displayed in the Bulk Editor. For instance, if an attribute was named **Termination**, and the logical data type was **DATE**, it would appear in the filter results for 'date'.

Figure 16.27 Filtering Instances in the Bulk Editor

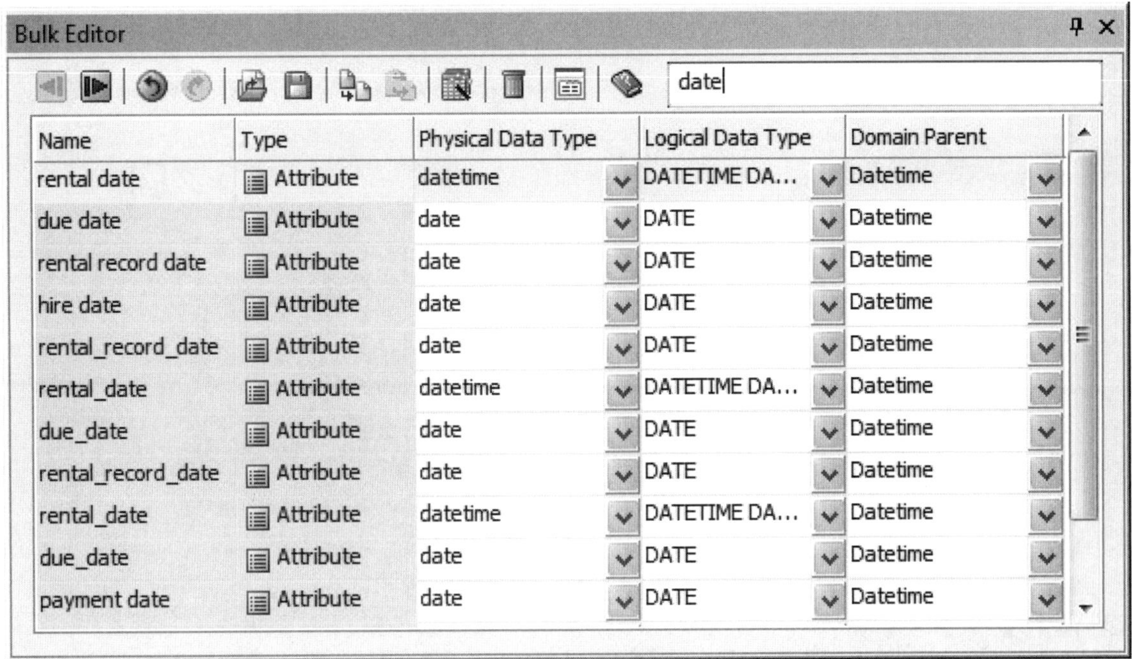

Name	Type	Physical Data Type	Logical Data Type	Domain Parent
rental date	Attribute	datetime	DATETIME DA...	Datetime
due date	Attribute	date	DATE	Datetime
rental record date	Attribute	date	DATE	Datetime
hire date	Attribute	date	DATE	Datetime
rental_record_date	Attribute	date	DATE	Datetime
rental_date	Attribute	datetime	DATETIME DA...	Datetime
due_date	Attribute	date	DATE	Datetime
rental_record_date	Attribute	date	DATE	Datetime
rental_date	Attribute	datetime	DATETIME DA...	Datetime
due_date	Attribute	date	DATE	Datetime
payment date	Attribute	date	DATE	Datetime

Now that we've made our edits, we'd like to export this information to a spreadsheet, to easily show to the developers in our next design meeting. Highlight all of the rows in the editor and select the **Save selected rows to CSV file** button from the toolbar menu. You will be prompted for a file location to save your file. Save this file as **`data_elements_emovies.csv`**, which can then be easily opened in your spreadsheet software. Note that CA ERwin Data Modeler also has the ability to import from a **`.csv`** file. If changes are made to this **`.csv`**, we're able to re-import the file and CA ERwin Data Modeler will reconcile the changes.

Since updating data types is something we do on a regular basis, we'd like to save these settings as an Option Set so that we can reuse them again. Return to the Bulk Editor Wizard by selecting the button from the toolbar, and move to the **Object Types** tab, which will look identical to Figure 16.14, since the editor saves our settings until we exit CA ERwin Data Modeler. Select the **Save current selections as new Options Set** button, and the Save Current Option Set Dialog appears, as shown in Figure 16.28, where you can save this option set as an external XML file, or within the model. If you save as XML, the option set can be used across multiple models, but only the **Object Types** and **Property Types** page selections are saved, not the **Object Selection** page selections, since those are specific to an individual model. We'll use an external XML file for our example.

Figure 16.28 Saving Bulk Editor Wizard Selections as an Option Set

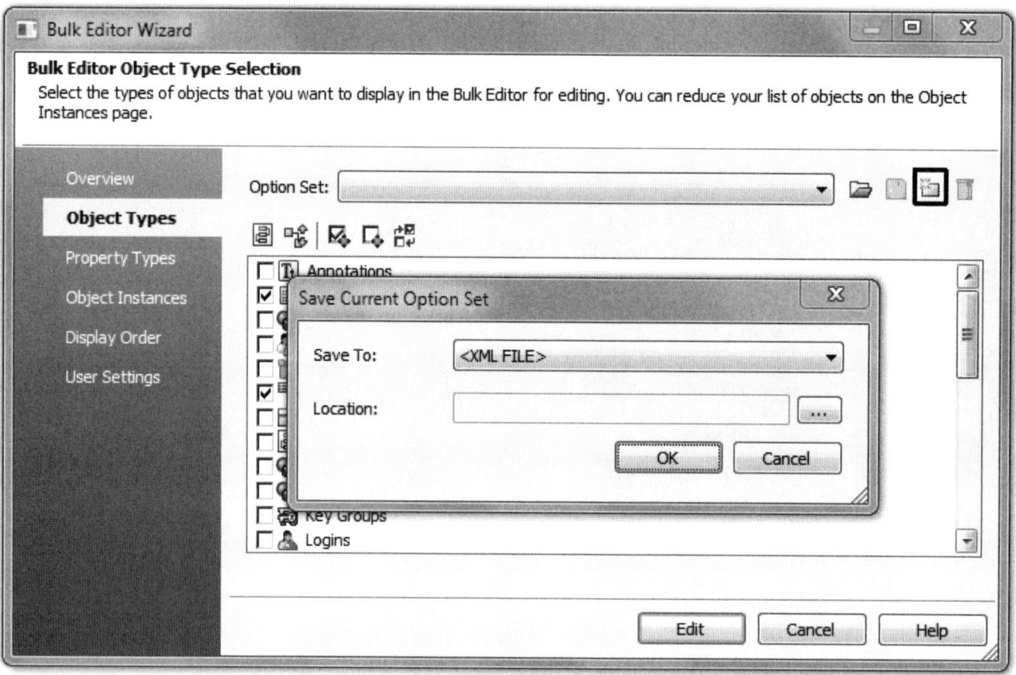

Select a location for your file using the **Location** field selector, and use a name of **`data type edit option set.xml`**, as shown in Figure 16.29.

Figure 16.29 Saving File Name and Location for a Bulk Editor Wizard Option Set

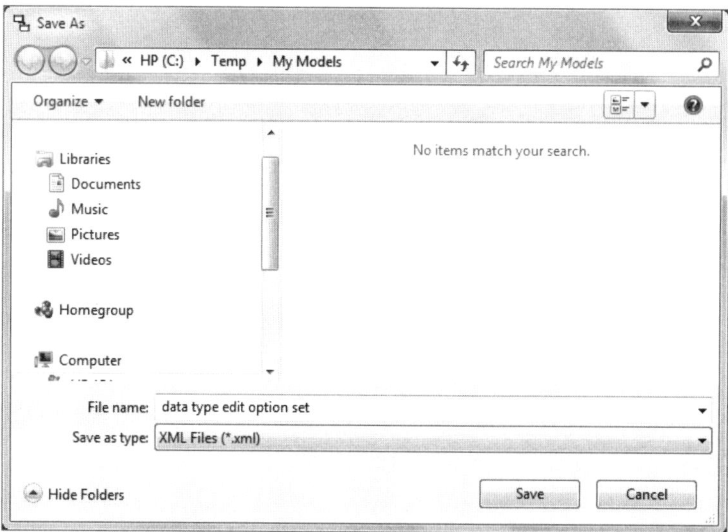

Once that you've saved these settings as an **Option Set**, you can easily reuse them for future editing sessions by opening the file using the **Open a stored Options Set** button next to the **Option Set** field. The option set we just created can be found on www.erwin.com/datmodelingmadesimple.

Now that you have a basic understanding of the Bulk Editor, try a few editing scenarios of your own, and you'll begin to see the power and ease-of-use of this interface.

Using the Query Tool

The Query Tool enables you to write SQL queries against an external database. This is particularly helpful to be able to compare your model design against 'real world' data values to validate against a sample data set. For example, in Figure 16.30, the physical data model design lists the **customer_number** column of the **CUSTOMER** table as an integer. Using the Query Tool to display the data values that exist in the actual database, we see that the **customer_number** field in the physical database contains alphanumeric values, indicating a mismatch between the model and the physical implementation. Note that there are other ways to do this type of comparison in CA ERwin Data Modeler, notably the Complete Compare feature, which would show the differences in the column data types. However, it is often helpful to see sample data as context. For example, in this case it looks like the customer number is using a code 'NC' or 'RC' at the end of the **customer_number**. Perhaps this means 'New Customer' and 'Renewing Customer'? We can't be sure from just the data, but it gives us more information as we begin our discussions with the database owners and our plans for resolving the differences.

Figure 16.30 Comparing Data Model with Physical Instance Data Using the Query Tool

Physical Data Model Design

CUSTOMER

customer_number	integer
customer_address	varchar(20)
customer_city	varchar(20)
customer_first_name	varchar(20)
customer_last_name	varchar(20)
customer_state	varchar(20)
customer_zip_code	integer
email	varchar

SQL Query

```
SELECT customer_number
FROM CUSTOMER
```

Physical Instance Data

129287123NC
293387432RC
989327483NC
923834923RC
889892838RC
....

In addition to querying external databases, you can also use the Query Tool to query the CA ERwin Data Model metadata, since metadata is exposed via an ODBC interface. In fact, it is this interface that allows the reporting to be done in Crystal Reports. It's beyond the scope of this book to go into too much detail on these queries, but let's use a simple query of the ERwin ODBC interface, since it's a common 'database' that we'll all have access to. In fact, no database is needed, as the ERwin application itself exposes its run-time metadata using ODBC—turning CA ERwin Data Modeler into a query-able database of sorts.

First, we'll need to activate the ODBC driver for our ERwin instance that's running. To do this, select **Tools|Options** from the **Main Menu**, and go to the **Integrations** tab, as shown in Figure 16.31. Click the **Start ODBC Driver for this instance** button (if it isn't already started), and the ODBC driver will be activated. Click **OK** to close this window, and the ODBC driver will continue running in the background.

Figure 16.31 Starting the ERwin ODBC Driver using the Tools|Options Menu

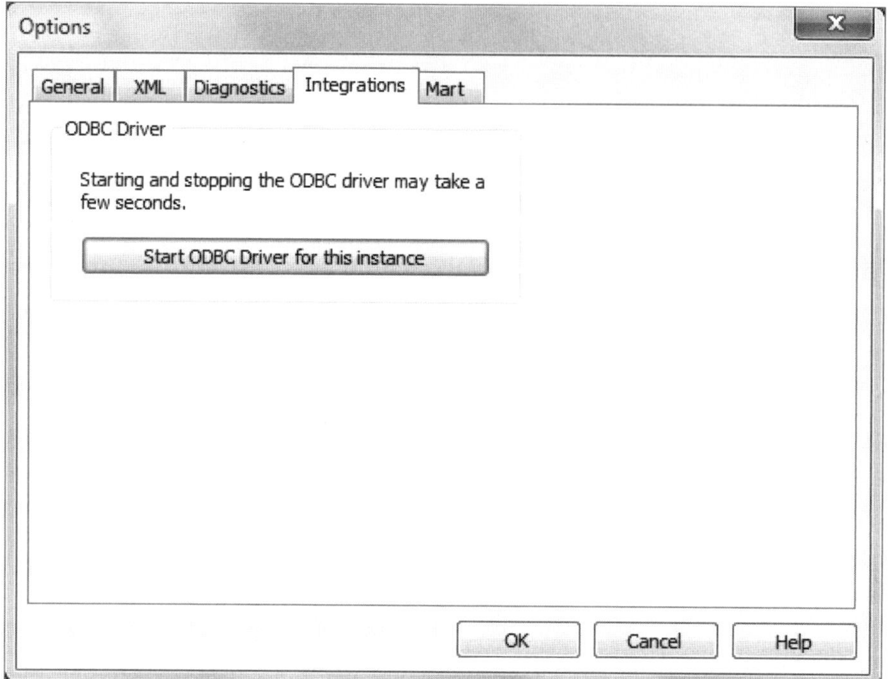

Next, using the eMovies model (refer to Chapter 3 if you need help with this), open the Query Tool by selecting **Tools|Query Tool** from the **Main Menu**. The Query Tool appears, as shown in Figure 16.32.

Figure 16.32 Query Tool

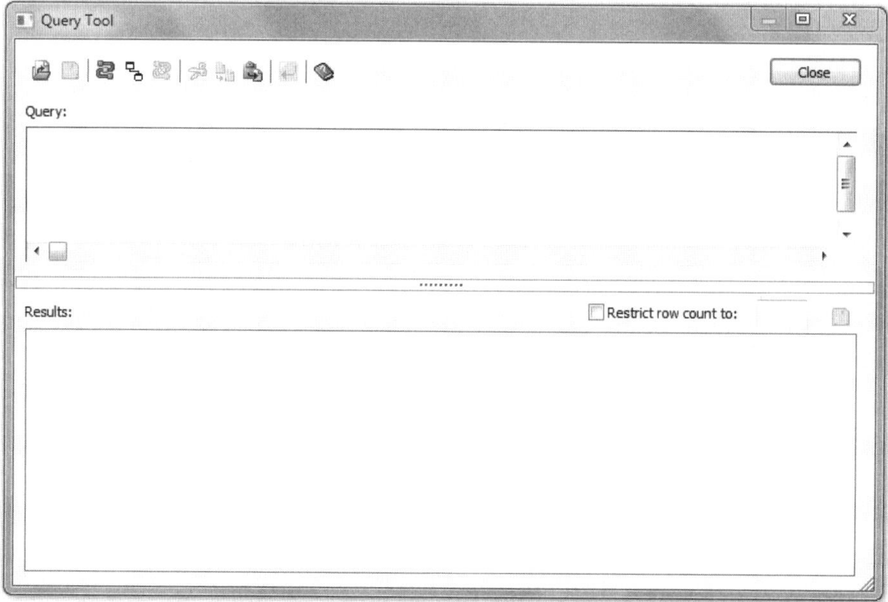

There are a number of documents available to help understand the ERwin metamodel. A good one to start with, for our purposes, is the **CA ERwin Data Modeler ODBC Reporting Guide.pdf** which is located in the **c:\Program Files\CA\CA ERwin Data Modeler r8\Doc** directory. In this file, you'll find a number of pre-written sample queries that you can use. We'll choose the query that lists the names of all logical entities, which is shown in Figure 16.33.

Figure 16.33 SQL Query against ERwin ODBC to Retrieve the Names of all Logical Entities

```
SELECT NAME
FROM em0.MV_LOGICAL_ENTITY@
ORDER BY 1
```

To execute this query in the Query Editor, first select the **Connect to ERwin ODBC** toolbar button. Next, type this query (or copy/paste from the Reporting Guide) into the **Query** text box and press the **Execute** button, as shown in Figure 16.34. In the **Results** text box, you'll see the query result set displayed; in this case, the names of all of the logical entities in the eMovies model.

Figure 16.34 Executing a SQL Query Using the Query Tool

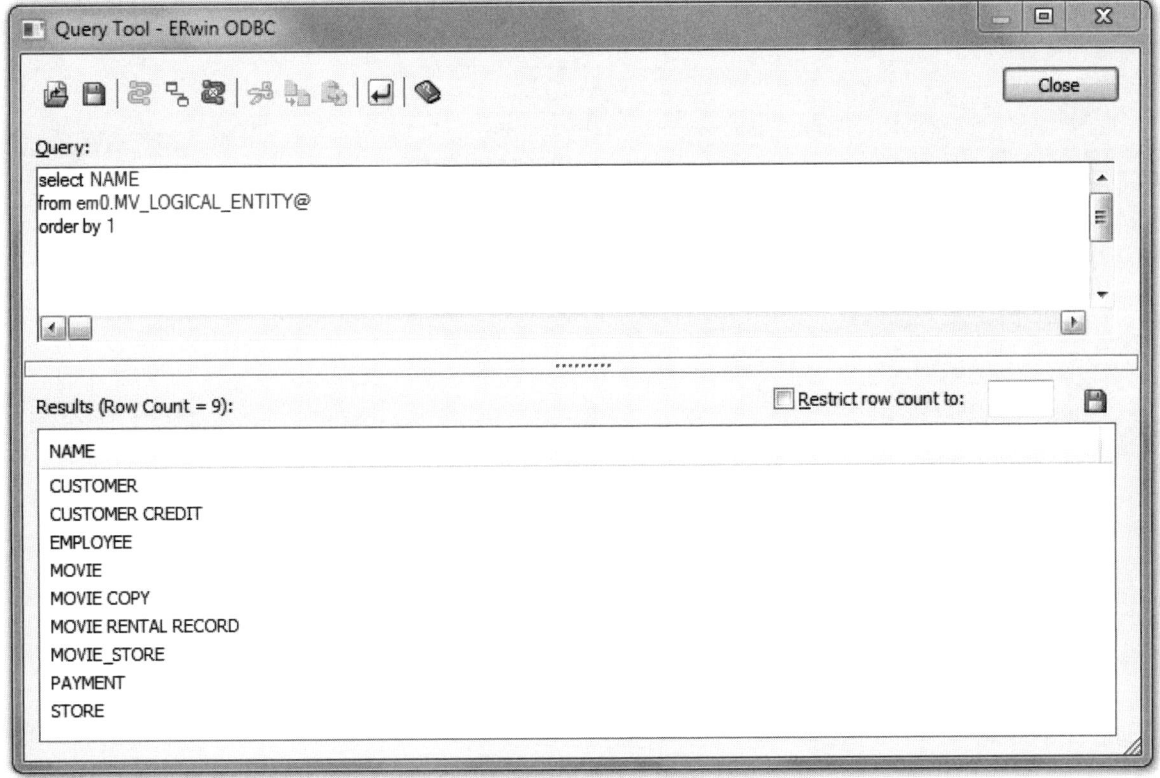

The Query Editor is an easy way to query external databases, or the ERwin metamodel itself, without having to leave CA ERwin Data Modeler and use a separate query tool.

Using Metadata Bridges

In addition to reporting and query features, CA ERwin Data Modeler has a powerful set of metadata bridges that allow you to import and export metadata directly into other tools. For example, the data structures and definitions you create can be shared with a Business Intelligence (BI) tool so that the BI team doesn't have to recreate them. This not only saves time, but ensures that common standards are being used across the organization. There are also bridges for MDM hubs, other data modeling tools, ETL tools, UML tools, XML design tools, and more—over 120 in all. It's beyond the scope of this book to go into detail on each of these, but we wanted to make you aware of them to have the ability to leverage ERwin metadata across the organization.

To access these metadata bridges, select **File|Import from External Format** or **File|Export to External Format**, according to your needs. Figure 16.35 shows an example of the **Destination** tab of the Export to External Format Wizard, which lists a subset of the tools supported.

Figure 16.35 Sample Destination Formats for Metadata Bridges

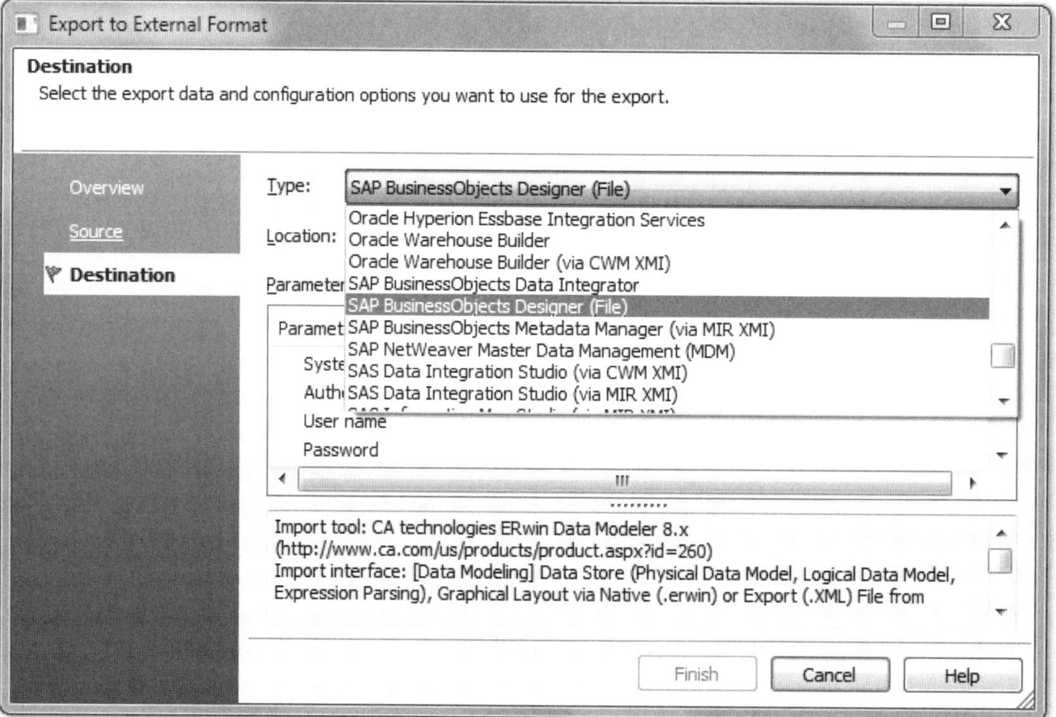

Give these metadata bridges a try in your organization. The documentation is fairly robust, so pay attention to the specific settings for the tool with which you're integrating.

Key Points

- CA ERwin Data Modeler is integrated with SAP Business Objects Crystal Reports, and contains a number of helpful out-of-the-box reports.
- The Bulk Editor is a tool designed to edit large quantities of model metadata with diverse object types in a spreadsheet-style interface.
- The Query Tool enables you to write SQL queries against an external database.
- CA ERwin Data Modeler has a powerful set of metadata bridges that allow you to import and export metadata directly into other tools.

SECTION IV
Conceptual, Logical, and Physical Data Models

Section IV explores the three different levels of models (conceptual, logical, and physical) and how to build them in CA ERwin Data Modeler. A conceptual data model (CDM) captures a very broad view, containing only the basic and critical concepts for a given scope, and representing a specific business need. The logical data model (LDM) represents a detailed business solution, capturing the business requirements without complicating the model with implementation concerns such as software and hardware. The physical data model (PDM) represents a detailed technical solution. It loses some of the exactness of the LDM, but this loss usually comes with gains in performance and usability within a given hardware and software set.

In addition to these three levels of detail, there are also two different modeling mindsets: relational and dimensional. Relational modeling captures how the business works, and captures business rules such as "A **Customer** must have at least one **Account**", or a "**Product** must have a **Product Short Name**." Dimensional modeling captures what the business uses to measure how it is doing. For example, examining sales at a day level and then, after getting the answer, looking at sales at a month or year level, or a product or brand level, or a city or country level. Dimensional modeling is all about playing with numbers by summarizing or aggregating data such as sales amount.

The table below summarizes these three model levels and two mindsets, leading to six different types of models.

Three Model Levels and Two Mindsets in Data Modeling

Types of models		Mindset: Relational	Mindset: Dimensional
	CDM	Key concepts and their business rules, such as a "**Customer** can place many **Orders**."	Key concepts focused around one or more measures, such as "I want to see **Gross Sales Amount** by **Customer**."
	LDM	All data elements required for a given application or business process, neatly organized into entities according to strict business rules and independent of technology, such as "Customer Number is guaranteed to bring back only one Customer Last Name."	All data elements required for a given reporting application, focused on measures and independent of technology, such as "I want to see **Gross Sales Amount** by **Customer** and view the Customer's first and last name."
	PDM	The LDM modified for a specific technology, such as database or access software. For example, "To improve retrieval speed, we need a non-unique index on Customer Last Name."	The LDM modified for a specific technology, such as database or access software. For example, "Because there is a need to view Gross Sales Amount at a **Day** level, and then by **Month** and **Year**, we should consider combining all calendar data elements into a single table."

Each of these six models will be explained in detail in this section, along with how to build them in CA ERwin Data Modeler using an example based on Baker Cakes, a small corporation whose focus is the sale and production of specialty decorated cakes. Chapter 17 focuses on conceptual data models, Chapter 18 on logical data models, and Chapter 19 on physical data models.

CHAPTER 17
Conceptual Data Models

Need a Consensus?
No common definitions?
All in the presentation

The highlighted row in Table17.1 shows the focus of this chapter - the conceptual data model (CDM).

Table 17.1 The CDM is the Focus of this Chapter

	Relational	Dimensional
CDM	**'One-pager' on how something works**	**'One-pager' on what is monitored**
LDM	Detailed business solution on how something works	Detailed business solution on what is monitored
PDM	Detailed technical solution on how something works	Detailed technical solution on what is monitored

A conceptual data model shows the key concepts in a particular area and how these concepts interact with each other.

Business Concept Explanation

A business concept is a key concept that is both *basic* and *critical* to your audience. 'Basic' means this term is probably mentioned many times a day in conversations with the people who represent the audience for the model. 'Critical' means the business would be very different or non-existent without this concept.

The majority of business concepts are easy to identify because they are common across industries, such as **Consumer**, **Customer**, **Employee**, and **Product**. An airline may call a **Customer** a **Passenger**, and a hospital may call a **Customer** a **Patient**, but they are still someone who purchases goods or services. Each concept will be shown in much more detail at the logical and physical phases of design. For example, the **Consumer** concept might encompass the logical entities **Consumer**, **Consumer Association**, **Consumer Demographics**, **Consumer Type**, and so on.

Many business concepts however, can be more challenging to identify, as they may be business concepts to your audience, but not to others in the same department, company, or industry. For example, a business concept named **Account** would most likely be a concept for a bank and for a manufacturing company. However, the audience for the bank conceptual data model might also require **Checking Account** and **Savings Account** to be on their model, whereas the audience for the manufacturing conceptual data model might, instead, require **General Ledger Account** and **Accounts Receivable Account** to be on the model.

In our example with the business card, a basic and critical concept can be **Address**, but **Mailing Address** can also be basic and critical. Should the conceptual data model for contact management contain **Mailing Address** as well? To answer this question, we need to know whether **Mailing Address** is basic and critical to your audience. The key point about conceptual data modeling is to model at a level where the audience for the model would agree that each concept is basic and critical.

Conceptual Data Model Explanation

Think of the conceptual data model as the roadmap for your organization's key information concepts. It is a set of symbols and text representing the key concepts and rules binding these key concepts for a specific business or application scope, for a particular audience, that fits neatly on one page[10]. Limiting the conceptual model to one page is important because it forces the modeler and participants to select only key concepts. On one page, for example, we can fit 10 or 20 or 50 concepts, but not 500. A good rule of thumb, therefore, is to ask yourself if the audience for this model would include this concept as one of the top 10 or 20 or 50 concepts in their business. This will rule out concepts that are at too low a level of detail. They will appear in the more detailed logical data model. If you're having trouble limiting the number of concepts, think about whether or not there are other concepts into which the ones you're discussing could be grouped. These higher concepts are the ones you should be including in the conceptual data model.

During the conceptual modeling phase, definitions of the concepts should be given a lot of attention. All too often, we wait until it is too late in the development process to get definitions. Waiting too long usually leads to not writing definitions altogether, or doing a rush job by writing quick definition phrases that have little or no usefulness. If the definitions behind the terms on a data model are nonexistent or poor, multiple interpretations of the business concept become a strong possibility. Imagine a business rule on our model that states that an employee must have at least one benefits package.

---

[10] Don't get tricky here. By 'one page', we mean 8 ½ x 11, 8 ½ x 14, or similar sized paper, but not a plotter-sized piece of paper!

If the definition of **Employee** is lacking, we may wonder, for example, whether this business rule includes job applicants, temporary help, and retired employees.

When the conceptual data model is complete (including concept definitions), it is a powerful tool that can provide a number of important business benefits:

- **Provides broad understanding**. We can capture extremely complex and encompassing business processes, application requirements, and even entire industries on a single piece of paper. This enables people with different backgrounds and roles to understand and communicate with each other on the same concepts, agreeing or debating on issues.
- **Defines scope and direction**. By visually showing concepts and their business rules, we can more easily identify a subset of the model to analyze. For example, we can model the entire logistics department, and then scope out of this a particular logistics application that we would like to build. The broad perspective of a conceptual data model can help us determine how planned and existing applications will coexist. It can provide direction and guidance on what new functionality the business will need next.
- **Offers proactive analysis**. By developing a high-level understanding of the application, there is a strong chance we will be able to identify important issues or concerns, saving substantial time and money later on. Examples include concept definition differences and different interpretations on project scope.
- **Builds rapport between IT and the business**. A majority of organizations have some level of internal communication issues between the business and IT departments. Building a conceptual data model together is a great way to remove or reduce these communication barriers. On one occasion, we sketched out a **Contact Data Mart** conceptual data model with a key business user, which built not just business understanding, but also a strong relationship with this user.

Before embarking on any large development effort, we first need to understand the business. For example, if an organization needs a new claims-processing system, it needs to have a common understanding of claims and related concepts. The conceptual model can be created simply to understand a business area, or as the beginning of a large development effort, such as introducing packaged software into your organization.

Types of Conceptual Data Models

As we've discussed in previous sections, there are two main types of conceptual data models: relational and dimensional. We'll walk through an example of each type of conceptual model in the following paragraphs.

RELATIONAL CONCEPTUAL MODEL

The relational conceptual model includes concepts, their definitions, and the relationships that show how these concepts interact with each other. Unlike the logical and physical data models, as we will see, conceptual models may contain many-to-many relationships. Let's go back to our business card example. A sample conceptual data model appears for this example in Figure 17.1.

Figure 17.1 Relational Conceptual Data Model for Business Card Contacts

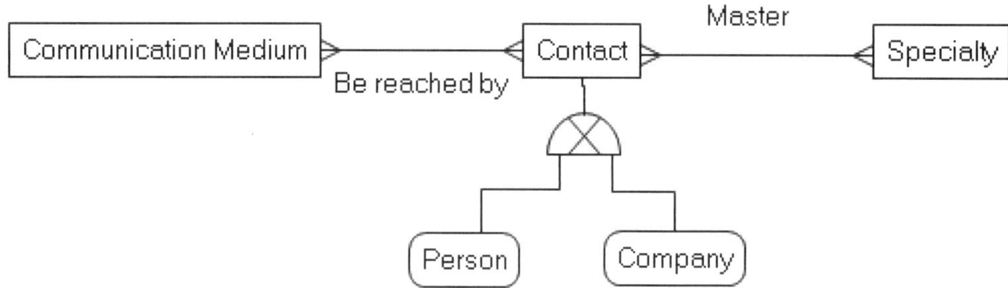

A large part of building a conceptual data model is arriving at definitions for key terms and concepts used by the business or organization. Although the meaning of these terms may seem simple and obvious at the outset, you'll soon find that there are important distinctions in the way the terms are used and defined by different areas of the organization. What is a **Contact**, for example? **Contact** can mean different things to different people or departments, much the same way as **Customer** can mean different things to different people or departments. Is a **Contact** the person in an organization whose phone number and email address we would like to capture? Is it the organization's phone number and email address itself? Or is the **Contact** the person's phone number or email address, and the person or organization becomes the **Contactee**? After hours of talking to people in different departments in the organization building this contact management application, we have come up with the following definition of **Contact**:

*A **Contact** is a person, a company, or a person at a company who our organization cares about knowing how to reach.*

Below is a full list of the concept definitions that we arrived at from our meetings with the project sponsor:

Communication Medium	A **Communication Medium** is a specific method of reaching a contact. It can be a specific phone number, email address, instant messaging user ID, etc.
Company	A **Company** is a distinct organization recognized by the government for tax reporting purposes.

Contact	A **Contact** is a person, a company, or a person at a company who our organization cares about knowing how to reach.
Person	A **Person** is a human being that could be living or deceased, fictional or real.
Specialty	A **Specialty** is an area of expertise that has recognition within a particular industry. Examples include: • Data modeling (within the Information Technology industry) • Juggling (within the Entertainment industry) • Singing (within the Musical industry)

Business Rules (listed in the order we would typically walk someone through the model):

- Each **Contact** must be reached by many **Communication Mediums**.
- Each **Communication Medium** must reach many **Contacts**.
- Each **Contact** must master many **Specialties**.
- Each **Specialty** most be mastered by many **Contacts**.
- Each **Contact** may be a **Person** or **Company**.
- Each **Person** is a **Contact**.
- Each **Company** is a **Contact**.

DIMENSIONAL CONCEPTUAL MODEL

To understand and document our reporting requirements, we can also build a dimensional conceptual model, such as the example in Figure 17.2. In this case, we'd like to build a report that shows us the number of people who have a particular specialty within a city and given quarter. For example, we might want to know the number of available data modelers in the New York City area in Q1, 2011.

Figure 17.2 Dimensional Conceptual Model for Business Card Contacts

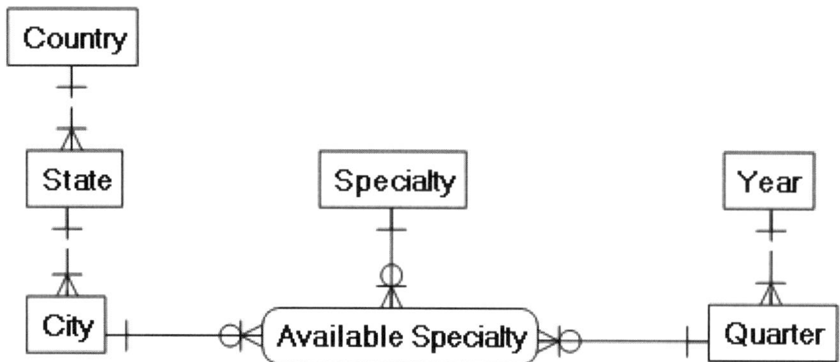

Concept definitions:

Available Specialty	**Available Specialty** is quantity of available resources within a given city and specified quarter that know a particular specialty. For example, there are 25 people in New York City in First Quarter 2011 who know data modeling.
City	A **City** is a parcel of land which is identified in terms of scope by a particular postal code.
Country	A **Country** is a recognized nation with its own government, occupying a particular territory, which is included in the ISO country code listing.
Quarter	A **Quarter** is any of the four financial accounting quarters within a fiscal year. Also referred to as Fiscal Quarter.
Specialty	A **Specialty** is an area of expertise that has recognition within a particular industry. Examples include: • Data modeling (within the Information Technology industry) • Juggling (within the Entertainment industry) • Singing (within the Musical industry)
State	In the United Sates, a **State** is one of the fifty states. Outside of the United states, this indicates a region or similar concept.
Year	A **Year** is a period of time containing 365 days, corresponding to a company's fiscal year. This may or may not coincide with the calendar year.

Navigation paths (listed in the order a user would typically navigate through the model):

- "I need to see the number of available specialists in a given city, in a particular quarter."

Notice that with a dimensional model, the focus is more on navigation than on business rules, as in a relational model.

How to Build a Conceptual Model

Following is a brief summary of the ten steps to complete a Conceptual Model (for more on this approach, please refer to *Data Modeling for the Business: A Handbook for Aligning the Business with IT using High-Level Data Models*, ISBN 9780977140077). We'll relate each of these ten steps to our fictional company, Baker Cakes, a small corporation whose focus is the sale and production of specialty decorated cakes, and show how a conceptual model helps them define their business requirements for a new application they're building.

1. **Identify model purpose.** Before starting any data modeling effort, first identify why the model needs to be built. The underlying reason for building a data model is communication. We build data models so we can ensure that we and others have a precise understanding of terminology and business rules. In this step, we identify our communication needs. What are we communicating? Who are we communicating it to? Always "begin with the end in mind", as Stephen Covey[11] would say. The most popular reason for building a conceptual model is to gain understanding of an existing area of the business. We can model a department such as Sales or Accounting, a line of business such as Home Mortgages, or even the entire organization. The Conceptual Data Model is also a very good place to start capturing the concepts and business rules for a new application. This way, terminology, rules, and definitions can be agreed upon prior to detailed project analysis.

   In our example, we're building a new application for Baker Cakes, who is looking to build a new application to manage their data. They currently have a small, home-grown application built in Microsoft Access, but it's not giving them the information they need. They'd like to start from scratch and build a new system. They would also like to improve their reporting—with the current system it's difficult for them to get basic sales revenue results.

[11] Steven Covey is the author of a popular self-help book entitled "7 Habits of Highly Effective People". Covey,S. 2004. *7 Habits of Highly Effective People*, New York, NY: Free Press.

2. **Identify model stakeholders.** Document the names and departments of those who will be involved in building the conceptual model, as well as those who will use it after its completion. Roles include architects, analysts, modelers, business users, and managers. Both business and IT roles are required for success. I remember one project I worked on where only IT people showed up to build the conceptual model. As enthusiastic as we all were to build the model and get support for the project, it was a losing effort because without the business, the model lost credibility and the project, therefore, lost financial support.

   Baker Cakes is a family-run business and our main stakeholder is Bob Baker, the owner/operator of Baker Cakes. Bob is in charge of making most decisions, from database design to icing color selection.

3. **Inventory available resources.** Leverage the results from Step 2, as well as identify any documentation that could provide useful content to the conceptual model. The two types of resources are people and documentation. People include both business and IT resources. Business people may be management and/or knowledge users. IT resources can span the entire IT spectrum, from analysts through developers, from program sponsors to team leads. From the people side, this step can be as simple as assigning actual people to the builder roles in Step 2. For example, if we are building a conceptual data model of the manufacturing section of our business, Bob, the business analyst who spent 20 years of his career working in the plant, would be an excellent resource to assign as a builder. Documentation includes systems documentation and requirements documents. Systems documentation can take the form of documentation for a packaged piece of software, or documentation written to support a legacy application. Requirements documents span business, functional, and technical requirements and can be an essential input to building the conceptual data model.

   Bob Baker is the main resource for defining the rules of the business. Having started this company from scratch, he knows everything there is to know about cakes and cake-making. Bob does not have a strong technical background, however. He recently hired an intern to build a database system for him in Microsoft Access, which did not work the way he wanted (which is why he's bringing us in now). That intern is long gone, and did not leave any system documentation. All we have is the physical database in Microsoft Access.

4. **Determine type of model.** Decide whether a relational or dimensional model would be most appropriate. Base your selection on the purpose of the model and the available resources.

To understand Mr. Baker's requirements so that we can get his application right this time, we will need to build a conceptual data model. Since the requirement is for an operational system, we'll need to create a relational conceptual model.

5. **Select approach**. There are three approaches for building a conceptual data model: top-down, bottom-up, and hybrid. Even though these approaches sound completely different from each other, they really have quite a lot in common. In fact, the major difference between the approaches lies in the initial information-gathering step. The top-down approach begins with a purely business needs perspective. We learn how the business works and what the business needs from the business people themselves, either through direct meetings with them, or indirectly, through requirements documents and reports. The business is allowed to dream - they should aim for the sky. All requirements are considered possible and doable.

   The bottom-up approach, on the other hand, temporarily ignores what the business needs and instead focuses on the existing systems environment. We build an initial conceptual data model by studying the systems that the business is using today. It may include operational systems that run the day-to-day business, or reporting systems that allow the business to view how well the organization is doing. Once the existing systems are understood at a high level, new concepts may be introduced or existing concepts modified to meet the business needs.

   The hybrid approach completes the initial information gathering step by usually starting with some top-down analysis and then some bottom-up analysis, and then some top-down analysis, etc., until the information gathering is complete. First, there is some initial top-down work to understand project scope and high level business needs. Then we work bottom-up to understand the existing systems. The whole process is a constant loop of reconciling what the business needs with what information is available.

   For Baker Cakes, we'll start with a top-down approach to 'start from scratch' and understand the business requirements. We don't want to ignore what was already created, though, so we'll at some point want to analyze the Microsoft Access application that was created. We'll end up using a hybrid approach, then, which is fairly common in the 'real world'.

6. **Complete audience-view model.** Produce a conceptual model using the terminology and rules that are clear to those who will be using the model. This is the first high-level model we build. Our purpose is to capture the viewpoint of the model's audience without complicating information capture by including how their perspective fits with other departments or with the organization as a whole. Our next step will reconcile the deliverable from this step with enterprise terminology.

Here our purpose is just to capture *their* view of the world. The initial model can be created by standing at a white board or flipchart with the users. Sometimes 30 minutes at a white board with a business user can reveal more about what they want than spending hours reading requirements documents.

We'll walk through creating the audience-view model for Baker Cakes in the next section on **Creating a Conceptual Model in CA ERwin Data Modeler**, as well as steps 7-10.

7. **Incorporate enterprise terminology.** Now that the model is well-understood by the audience, ensure the terminology and rules are consistent with the organization view. To build the enterprise perspective, modify the audience model to be consistent with enterprise terminology and rules. Ideally, this enterprise perspective is captured within an enterprise data model. You might have to schedule meetings between the people whose view is captured in the audience-specific model and those who share the enterprise perspective to resolve any terminology or definition issues.

8. **Signoff.** Obtain approval from the stakeholders that the model is correct and complete. After the initial information gathering, make sure the model is reviewed for data modeling best practices, as well as for meeting the requirements. The signoff process on a conceptual data model does not require the same formality as signoff on the physical design, but it should still be taken seriously. Usually, email verification that the model looks good will suffice[12]. In our example, Mr. Baker is our main stakeholder, and his approval is all that is needed.

9. **Market.** Similar to introducing a new product, advertise the data model so that all those who can benefit from it know about it. If the model has a relatively small scope, it is possible that the users who helped you build and validate the model are also the only ones who need to know about it, so marketing requires little effort. However, most conceptual data models span broad areas, so it is essential to let the appropriate business and IT resources know it is available to them. Techniques include 'Lunch-and-Learns', advertisements on corporate intranets, and presenting the model at periodic management meetings.

10. **Maintain.** Conceptual data models require little maintenance, but they are not maintenance-free. Make sure the model is kept up-to-date. The conceptual data model will not change often, but it will change, and we need to have formal processes for updating this model to keep it up to date. What works well is to have two additional steps in your software methodology: 1. Borrowing from a CDM, and 2.

[12] Validating whether the model has met data modeling best practices is often done by applying the Data Model Scorecard®, which is discussed in Data Modeling Made Simple.

Contributing back to the CDM. After the CDM is complete, and before starting a logical data model, for example, the CDM should be used as a starting point for further modeling. The second step in the methodology requires taking all of the learning from the project and making sure all new concepts are incorporated back into the CDM.

Creating a Conceptual Data Model

In following these ten steps to build a conceptual data model, you'll find that building the actual model in CA ERwin Data Model is comparatively simple. The biggest challenge, and biggest focus, for building the conceptual data model is to work with business stakeholders to get an understanding of the core data concepts, and make sure that they are defined and understood consistently across the organization. The conceptual data model is a vehicle for this communication process—it should be visually simple in order to communicate the core definitions and business rules to a non-technical audience.

To create a conceptual data model, CA ERwin Data Modeler uses a logical model as the starting point (refer to Chapter 3 for a discussion of the Design Layer Architecture). A common question is why CA ERwin Data Modeler uses the logical model to represent a conceptual data model, rather than having a specific model type for conceptual. A main driver for this is flexibility. Within the data modeling industry, there is no strong consensus when it comes to business-level data modeling; some organizations use four levels of data models, adding an even more abstract level above the conceptual for a thumbnail enterprise view; some organizations use different names for the conceptual data model, such as subject area model, business data model, or enterprise data model. In addition, there is a great deal of overlap in the notation between the conceptual and logical data model layers. In many ways, a conceptual data model can be seen as a logical model with less detail shown. Table 17.2 outlines some of the key differences between a conceptual data model and a logical data model.

Table 17.2 Comparing Conceptual and Logical Data Models

Conceptual Data Model	Logical Data Model
Defines key business concepts and their definitions	Represents the data needed, and the associated rules and data relationships at a detailed level
Main purpose is for communication and agreement on definitions and business logic	Provides enough detail for subsequent first cut physical design
Many-to-Many relationships OK	Many-to-Many relationships resolved
Attributes are optional. If shown, can be composite attributes to convey business meaning.	Attributes required. Primary and foreign keys defined.
Not normalized (Relational models)	Fully normalized (Relational models)
Concept names should use business terminology (e.g. Customer, Client)	Entity names may be more abstract (e.g. Party)
Many concepts are supertypes, although subtypes may be shown for clarity	Subtypes always shown (Relational models)
Should be a 'one pager'	May be larger than one page
Cross-functional & more senior people involved in conceptual data modeling process, with fewer IT folks	Multiple smaller groups of specialists and IT folks involved in logical data modeling process
'Looser' notation required – some formal construct needed, but ultimate goal is to be understood by a business user	Formal notation required

In CA ERwin Data Modeler, start by creating a blank logical-only model. (See Chapter 3 if you need help with how to create a logical model.) The first thing we'll want to do is to set some basic model properties, such as the name, notation type, etc. From the **Main Menu**, select **Model|Model Properties** to invoke the Model Properties Editor. On the **General** tab, we'll define the following information, as shown in Figure 17.3.

First we'll want to name the model, and make note of the authors (so they can hunt us down later!).

Name: Baker Cakes Conceptual Data Model

Author: Bob Baker, Donna Burbank, Steve Hoberman

Remember, the business owners should be key players in defining the conceptual data model—make sure to include them! Mr. Baker is as much a part of the team as the data architects.

Logical Notation: Information Engineering

Note: Information Engineering (IE) is the 'crow's foot' notation that is commonly used in a conceptual data model. From our experience, and after surveying other data architects and business analysts, we've found the IE notation to be the most intuitive to the non-technical audience.

Figure 17.3 Defining the Model Name, Authors, and Notation Style

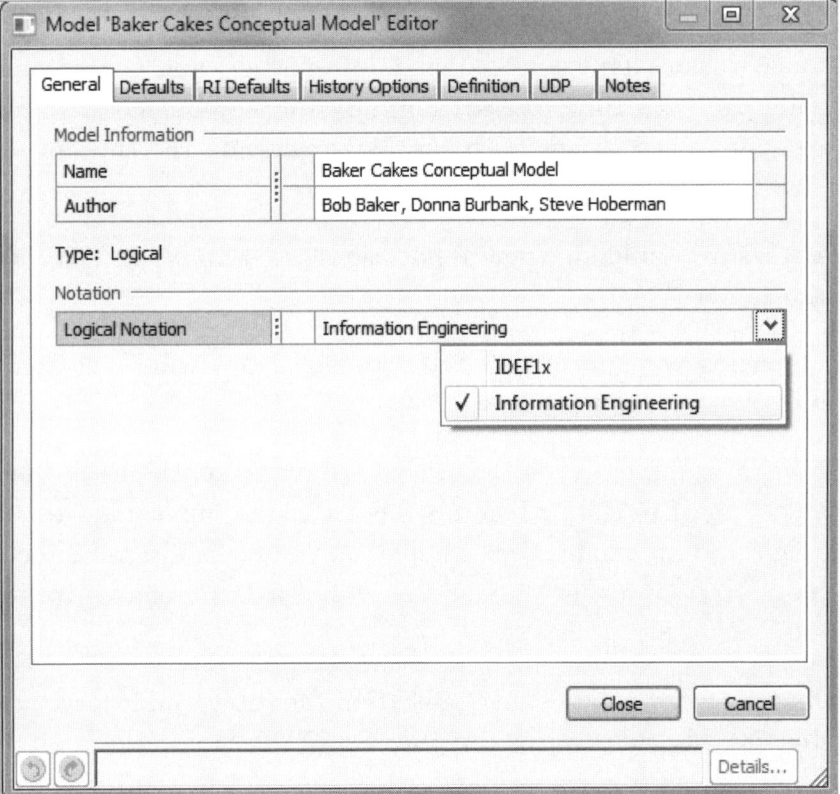

Next, we'll move to the **Definition** tab to create a clear and concise definition of the model, including the model purpose and scope, as shown in Figure 17.4. We don't need to walk you through this, but do remember to include the definition of the model. It is especially important to share the context with other members of the team. We don't want to be like that intern who left the application with no documentation!

Figure 17.4 Creating a Definition for the Conceptual Model

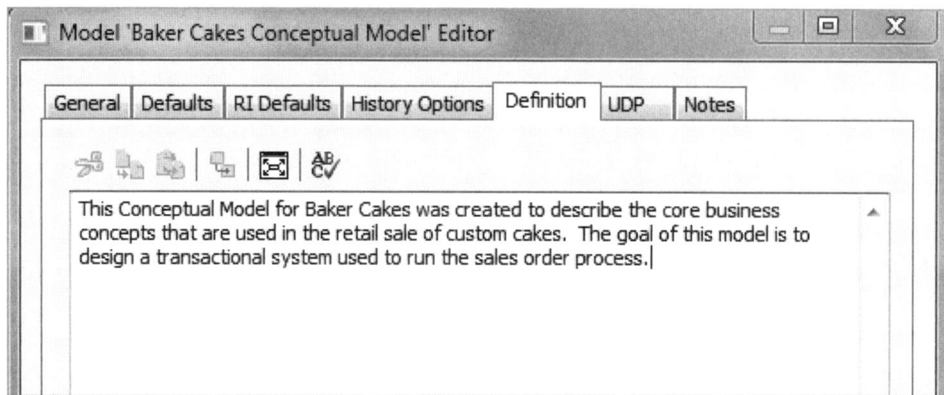

The remainder of the tabs can be left as-is for now—they will be more important as we delve into the logical and physical data models. Note that many of the settings and parameters we will be defining can be saved as a CA ERwin Model Template. We highly recommend creating a model template for the conceptual model type, and re-using this each time you build a conceptual data model. This will save you time, and help promote consistency. Model Templates are described in more detail in Chapter 15.

Select **Close** to save your changes to the model properties, and you will be returned to your blank model. Now it's time to start defining the key business concepts of Baker Cakes. We start our conversations with Mr. Baker around the concept of **Customer**. The following is a snippet of our discussion:

Steve: Before we start building your application, we wanted to ask you what your definition of a customer is.

Mr. Baker: I'm paying you how much? And you don't know what a customer is? I want my intern back.

Donna: What we're trying to say is that there are many subtleties in the definition of customer that we'll need to clarify before we start coding anything—to make sure we start with the right requirements. For example, do you normally sell directly to the end customer in your retail stores, or do you have wholesale purchases to distributors as well?

Mr. Baker: Oh, OK—good point. That application the intern built forgot to include our wholesale customers. My sales reports at the end of the month were all wrong. About 60% of our business comes from sales in our retail chains, but we also sell to distributors who sell to the grocery stores.

Steve: Great, that's an important distinction. We'd like to put together a high-level diagram outlining some of these concepts we just discussed, and run it by you quickly before we start building the application.

Mr. Baker: You mean one of those PowerPoint diagrams?

Steve: Well, sort of. The application we use is slightly different, but it will look similar to a PowerPoint diagram. The benefit of using this application is that we can generate our database code from it when we're done, so it will save us time and money in the long run.

Mr. Baker: Saving time and money is always a good thing. OK, I'm looking forward to seeing your diagram tomorrow. I have to run to a meeting now.

With this information from the business sponsor, we can now get started creating our conceptual data model. First we'll want to create the **Customer** concept. To create a business concept, use the **Entity** object from the Toolbox Toolbar, shown in Figure 17.5.

Figure 17.5 Using the Entity Object to Create a Business Concept

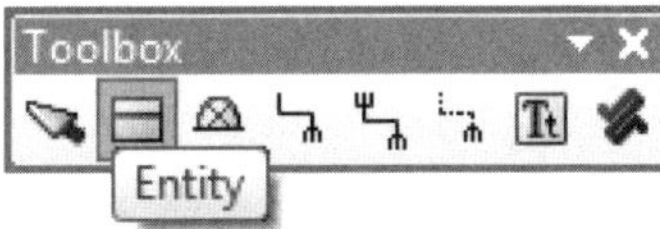

Create a concept called **Customer** on your diagram, as shown in Figure 17.6. Don't create any attributes for now—we'll do that in the logical data model.

Figure 17.6 Customer Concept

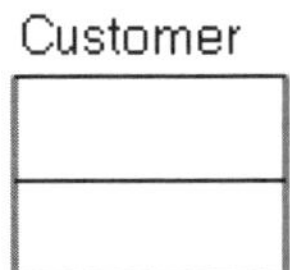

Since we're not defining attributes at this point, the line in the middle of the concept to denote the primary key looks a little strange. Let's change the display option to show just the entity (Refer to Chapter 4 for how to change entity display levels) and your model will look like Figure 17.7, which is similar to the 'PowerPoint look' that Mr. Baker is used to.

Figure 17.7 Using the Entity Display Level

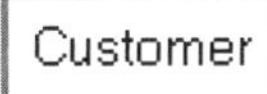

We learned from our business sponsor that a **Customer** can be either a **Retail Customer** or a **Wholesale Customer**. We can create a subtype relationship to show this, as shown in Figure 17.8. (Refer to Chapter 6 for more information on how to create subtypes.)

Figure 17.8 Conceptual Model Clarifying Customer using Subtypes

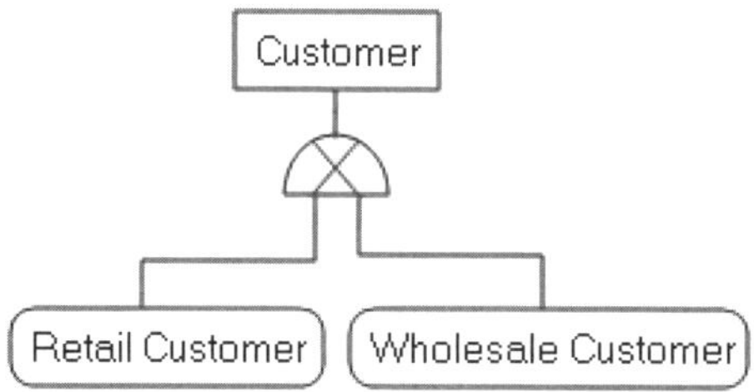

This model has a similar look to a PowerPoint diagram so that our business sponsor can easily understand it, but it also contains critical subtype information that will help us build our logical and physical models later on. In fact, let's name this Diagram as **PowerPoint View**, as shown in Figure 17.9. (For more information on Diagrams, refer to Chapter 8.)

Figure 17.9 Naming the High-Level View Diagram

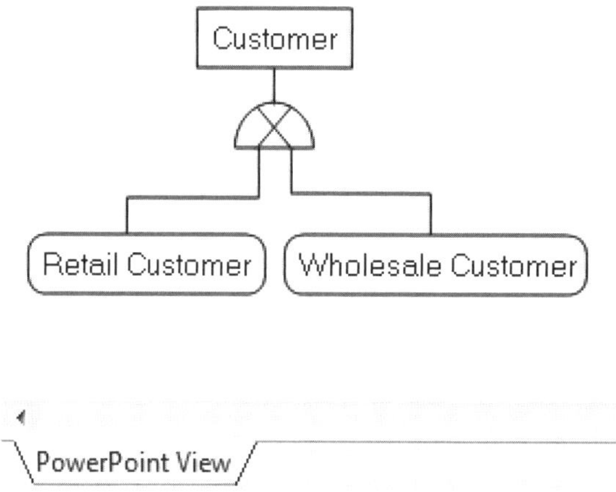

In addition to clarifying the differences between a customer as a **Retail Customer** or a **Wholesale Customer**, we want to create business definitions for these objects. Enter the following definitions for the concepts you've created (Refer to Chapter 4 for more information on adding entity definitions).

Concept definitions:

Customer	A **Customer** is a person who has obtained our product through purchase. Once a **Customer**, always a **Customer** so even **Customers** that have not obtained anything in 50 years are still considered **Customers**.
Retail Customer	A **Retail Customer** purchases goods or merchandise from a fixed location, such as a department store, boutique, or kiosk, or by mail, in small or individual lots for direct consumption by the purchaser.

Wholesale Customer	A **Wholesale Customer** is an industrial, commercial, institutional, or professional user who engages in the resale (sale without transformation) of new and used goods to retailers, or to other wholesale customers.

The **PowerPoint View** diagram we created earlier is a clear and helpful way to show the distinction of the various customer types, but we can't see the definitions, which are a critical part of the conceptual data model. Let's create a new Diagram called **Definition View**, and use the Definition display level this time option this time (refer to Chapter 4 if you need help with this). Your new Diagram should look similar to Figure 17.10.

Figure 17.10 Showing a Diagram using Definition View

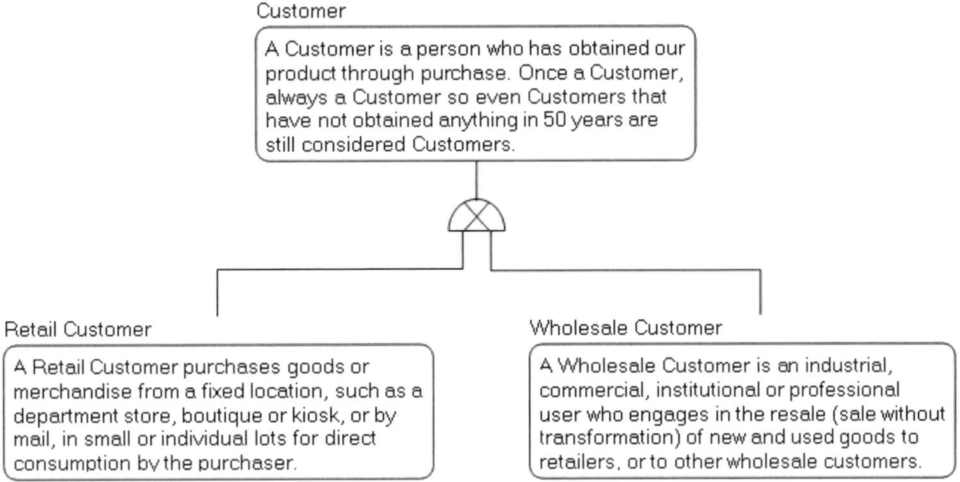

We were able to set up a quick, 15 minute meeting with Mr. Baker to verify that these definitions and our distinction between the various customer types were correct. Throughout the week, we were able to have several other brief meetings with Mr. Baker, and came up with the following concept definitions and business rules. Remember—a key part of working with your business sponsor is to fit into *their* schedule. Often, several brief meetings can accomplish more than a grueling day-long session in a conference room. It can often feel like a therapy session or an interview with all of the questions we need to ask about the business' data, so remember, keep it simple and keep it light. Don't burden the business user with too many questions at once.

Additional Concept definitions:

Sales Rep[13]
A **Sales Rep** is an individual currently working for the company who is responsible for taking an **Order** from a **Wholesale Customer**. All wholesale sales must be made through a **Sales Rep**.

Product
A **Product** is a completed cake offered for purchase. Partial products such as icing or ingredients are not offered for sale.

Style
The **Style** of cake is a distinctive design or flavor of one cake product over another. **Styles** are recognized and selected by **Customers**. Examples include Lemon Lovers and Chocoholics.

[13] Note that normally abbreviations are not recommended in a CDM, e.g. using "Representative" rather than "Rep". In this instance, however, the business users most commonly use the term "Sales Rep" in their daily language, so we chose to match the concept name to their typical usage.

Business Rules:

- Each **Customer** may be[14] either a **Retail Customer** or a **Wholesale Customer**.
- Each **Customer** must order many **Products.** (That will make our sales department happy! We'll clarify what this means further as we delve into the logical model.)
- Each **Product** must be ordered by many **Customers.**
- Each **Retail Customer** is a **Customer**
- Each **Wholesale Customer** is a **Customer**
- Each **Style** may group one or many **Products.**
- Each **Product** must be grouped by a **Style.**
- Each **Sales Rep** must call upon one or many **Wholesale Customers** (Only the big customers get real sales reps!).
- Each **Wholesale Customer** must be called upon by one **Sales Rep.**

Add these concepts and rules to the conceptual model you've created, using the **PowerPoint View** diagram. The result should look like Figure 17.11. Note that the **Sales Rep** to **Customer** relationship is a dashed line, indicating an independent relationship. The existence of a customer does not depend on the existence of a sales rep, and vice-versa.

Figure 17.11 Relational Conceptual Model for Baker Cakes

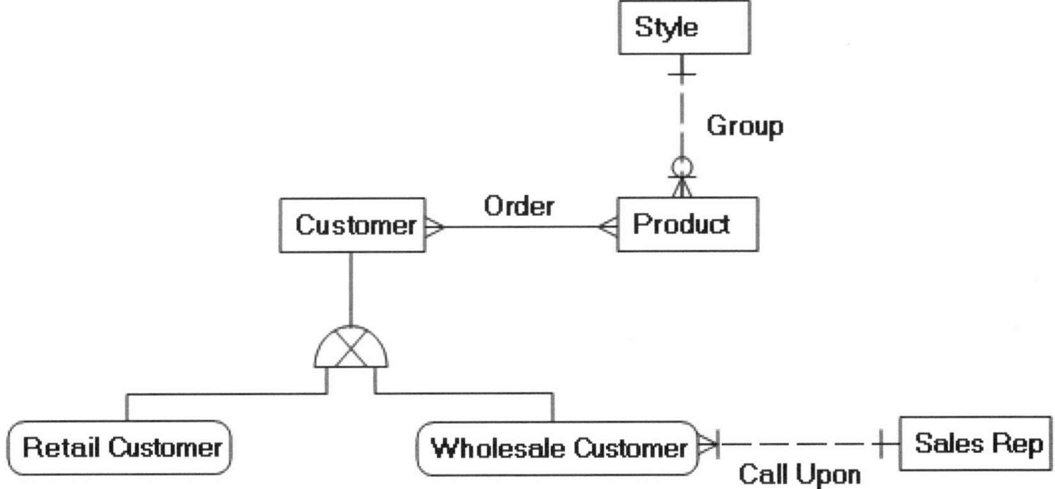

[14] The subtyping symbol in IE does not specify completeness, so there is a chance a supertype instance can exist without a subtype.

Save this model as **`Baker Cakes Conceptual.erwin`** . A fully-completed model with this name is also available on www.erwin.com/datamodelingmadesimple.

Now that we've created our conceptual model defining the business requirements, we can move on to the logical level to define more detailed business rules. We'll discuss logical models in the following chapter.

Key Points

- A concept is both basic and critical to your audience. Think of these as the key business terms your organization uses.
- A conceptual data model (CDM) is a set of symbols and text that represents key concepts and the rules binding these key concepts for a specific business or application scope and for a particular audience.
- The relational conceptual model documents the business rules and concept definitions around a defined portion of the organization.
- The dimensional conceptual model documents reporting requirements and navigation paths.
- Follow the ten-step approach to building a CDM.
- To build a conceptual data model in CA ERwin Data Modeler, use diagramming techniques in the logical model to keep the model simple, such as displaying by definition or by entity.
- Conceptual models can be created for both relational and dimensional models in CA ERwin Data Modeler.

CHAPTER 18
Logical Data Models

What does business need?
Forget the technology
Enter logical

The highlighted row in Table 18.1 shows the focus of this chapter, which is the logical data model.

Table 18.1 The LDM is the focus of this chapter

	Relational	Dimensional
CDM	'One-pager' on how something works	'One-pager' on what is monitored
LDM	**Detailed business solution on how something works**	**Detailed business solution on what is monitored**
PDM	Detailed technical solution on how something works	Detailed technical solution on what is monitored

A logical data model (LDM) takes the business need defined on a conceptual data model down to the next level of a business solution. That is, once you understand at a broad level the scope of an effort and what business people require to solve their problem, the next step is to come up with a solution for them in the form of an LDM.

Logical Data Model Explanation

A logical data model (LDM) is a business solution to a business problem. It is how the modeler captures the business requirements without complicating the model with implementation concerns such as software and hardware.

On the conceptual model, we might learn, for example, what the terms, business rules, and scope would be for a new order entry system. After understanding the requirements for the order entry system, we create a logical model containing all of the data elements and business rules needed to deliver the business solution system. For example, the conceptual model might show that a **Customer** places many **Orders**. The logical model would capture all of the details behind **Customer** and **Order**, such as the customer's name, their address, the order number, and what is being ordered.

While building the LDM, questions or issues may arise having to do with specific hardware or software such as:

- How can we retrieve this information in less than 5 seconds?
- How can we make this information secure?
- There is a lot of information here. What is the best way to manage storage space?

These questions focus on hardware and software. Although they need to be documented, they are not addressed until we are ready to start the physical data model. The reason these questions depend on technology is because if hardware and software were infinitely efficient and secure, these questions would never be raised.

Comparison of Relational with Dimensional Logical Models

There are both relational and dimensional logical data models. As we discussed in the last chapter, relational modeling is the process of capturing how the business works, while dimensional modeling is the process of capturing the information the business needs to monitor how well it is doing, typically for reporting.

Relational modeling contains business rules, such as "A **Customer** must have at least one **Account**", or a "**Product** must have a **Product Short Name**." A relational logical data model captures the business solution for how part of the business works. Figure 18.1 shows an example of the relational logical model for the business card model example we used in the previous chapter. We'll cover this model in more detail later in this chapter.

Figure 18.1 Sample Relational Logical Model for Business Card Contacts

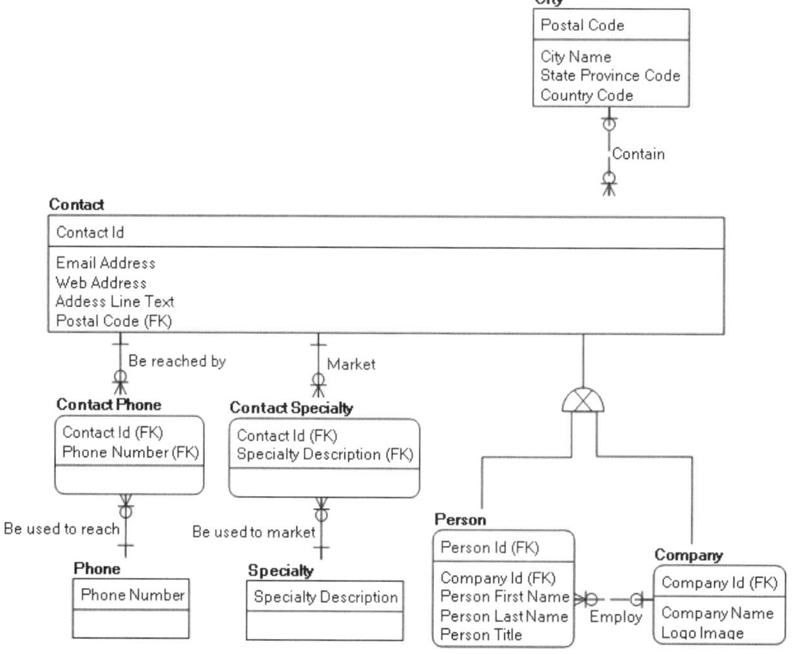

Dimensional modeling focuses on capturing and aggregating the metrics from daily operations that enable the business to evaluate how well it is doing by manipulating the numbers. For example, examining the measure **Gross Sales Amount** at a day level and then, after getting the answer, looking at **Gross Sales Amount** at a month or year level, or at a product or brand level, or a city or country level. The dimensional model is all about playing with numbers, typically for reporting. A sample logical dimensional model is shown in Figure 18.2.

Figure 18.2 Sample Dimensional Logical Model for Business Card Contacts

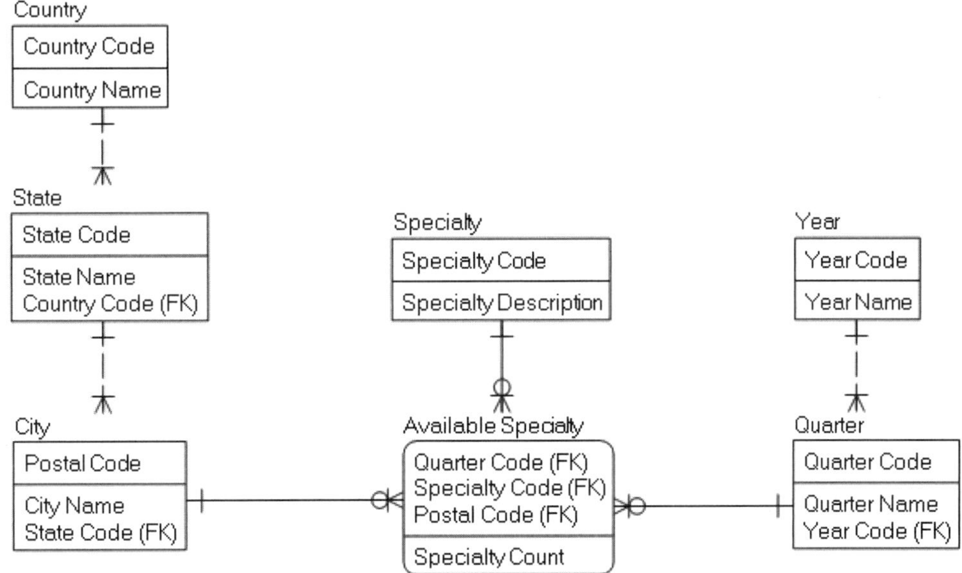

We'll explain both of these logical data model types in more detail in the rest of this chapter.

Normalization

Normalization is a key aspect of relational modeling, and an important one for you to get a grasp of before we go into the details of building a model. The simplest way to think of normalization is that normalization is the process of ***organizing data to reduce redundancy***. While normalization can become complex, the rules for normalizing data elements can be boiled down to a single sentence:

Make sure every data element is single-valued and provides a fact completely and only about its primary key.

The underlined terms require more of an explanation. 'Single-valued' means a data element must contain only one piece of information. If **Consumer Name** contains **Consumer First Name** and **Consumer Last Name,** for example, we must split

Consumer Name into two data elements: **Consumer First Name** and **Consumer Last Name**.

'Provides a fact' means that a given primary key value will always return no more than one of every data element that is identified by this key. If a **Customer Identifier** value of '123' for example, returns three customer last names ('Smith', 'Jones', and 'Roberts'), this violates this part of the normalization definition.

'Completely' means that the minimal set of data elements that uniquely identify an instance of the entity is present in the primary key. If, for example, there are two data elements in an entity's primary key, but only one is needed for uniqueness, the data element that is not needed for uniqueness should be removed from the primary key.

'Only' means that each data element must provide a fact about the primary key and nothing else. That is, there can be no hidden dependencies. For example, assume an **Order** is identified by an **Order Number**, as shown in Figure 18.3. The non-key attribute **Order On Time Indicator** contains value of either 'Yes' or 'No', providing a fact about whether the **Order Actual Delivery Date** is less than or equal to the **Order Scheduled Delivery Date**. **Order On Time Indicator,** therefore, provides a fact about **Order Actual Delivery Date** and **Order Scheduled Delivery Date**, not directly about **Order Number**, so it should be removed from the normalized model. **Order On Time Indicator** is an example of a derived data element, meaning it is calculated. Derived data elements are removed from a normalized model.

Figure 18.3 Order Entity with Hidden Dependencies within Attributes

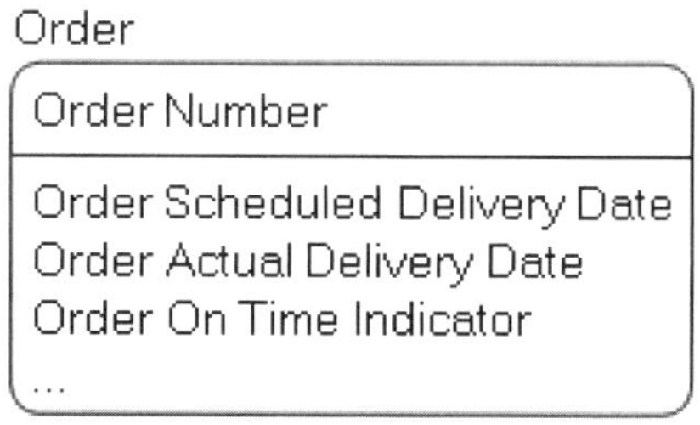

Order

Order Number

Order Scheduled Delivery Date
Order Actual Delivery Date
Order On Time Indicator
...

So, a general definition for normalization is that it is a series of rules for organizing something. The series of rules can be summarized as: *Every data element is single-valued and provides a fact completely and only about its primary key*. An informal definition we frequently use for normalizing is: *A formal process of asking business questions*. We cannot determine if every data element is single-valued and provides a fact completely and only about its primary key unless we understand the data. To understand the data we usually need to ask lots of questions. Even for an apparently simple data element such as **Phone Number,** for example, we can ask many questions:

- Whose phone number is this?
- Do you always have to have a phone number?

- Can you have more than one phone number?
- Do you ever recognize the area code as separate from the rest of the phone number?
- Do you ever need to see phone numbers outside a given country?
- What type of phone number is this? That is, is it a fax number, mobile number, etc.?

To ensure that every data element is single-valued and provides a fact completely and only about its primary key, we apply a series of rules or small steps, where each step (or level of normalization) checks something that moves us towards our goal. Most data professionals would agree that the most commonly used set of normalization levels is the following:

- first normal form (1NF)
- second normal form (2NF)
- third normal form (3NF)
- Boyce/Codd normal form (BCNF)[15]
- fourth normal form (4NF)
- fifth normal form (5NF)

Each level of normalization includes the lower levels of rules that precede it. If a model is in 5NF, it is also in 4NF, BCNF, and so on. Even though there are higher levels of normalization than 3NF, many interpret the term 'normalized' to mean 3NF. This is because the higher levels of normalization (that is, BCNF, 4NF, and 5NF) cover specific situations that occur much less frequently than the first three levels. Therefore, to keep things simple, this chapter focuses only on first through third normal forms.

Normalization provides a number of important benefits: (NOTE: In this section, the term data model may also represent the physical database that will be implemented from the data model)

- **Stronger understanding of the business**. The process of normalization ensures that we ask many questions about the data elements so that we know we are assigning them to entities correctly. The answers to our questions give us insight into how things work.
- **Greater application stability**. Normalization leads to a model that mimics the way in which the business works. As the business goes about its daily operations, the application receives data according to the rules that govern the business. The normalized model developed for the application leads to development of a database that has been structured to match these rules.

---

[15] BCNF was developed in 1974 by Raymond F. Boyce and Edgar F. Codd, two experts in the field of relational database theory.

- **Less data redundancy**. Each level of normalization removes a type of *data redundancy* from the model. Data redundancy occurs when the same information appears more than once in the same model. Removing redundancy helps ensure database stability, application reliability, and processing efficiency.
- **Better data quality**. By reducing redundancy and enforcing business rules through relationships, the data are less likely to get out of synch or violate these business rules. If an account must have at least one account owner, the data model can prevent accounts with invalid or missing account owners from occurring.
- **Faster development of new models**. A degree of common sense is applied to the place to which data elements are assigned during the normalization process. Therefore, it becomes easier to identify and reuse normalized structures in a new model. For example, all data elements that require **Account Identifier** for uniqueness appear in **Account**. The result is increased consistency across models and faster application development.

INITIAL CHAOS

We have all put together puzzles at one time or another. After you open the box and dump out the pieces, the sight can be overwhelming: hundreds, maybe thousands, of tiny pieces in a large pile. The pile is in a state of chaos. As we pick each piece up and examine it, we understand its properties in the form of its shape. We lack knowledge at this point about how these puzzle pieces connect with each other. We begin the process of fitting the pieces together and, after much effort, we complete our masterpiece. Each puzzle piece is in its proper place.

The term *chaos* can be applied to any unorganized pile, including data elements. We may have a strong understanding of each of the data elements, such as their name and definition, but we lack knowledge about how the data elements fit together. We understand each piece of the puzzle, but we do not yet understand the connections between the pieces. In our business card example, we do not know the relationship between **Mailing Address** and **Phone Number** before normalizing. Just as we need to determine the appropriate place for each piece within our puzzle, we need to determine the appropriate place for each data element within our model.

Recall our four business cards from Figure 1.2, repeated here as Figure 18.4.

Figure 18.4 Four Business Cards from Steve's Nightstand

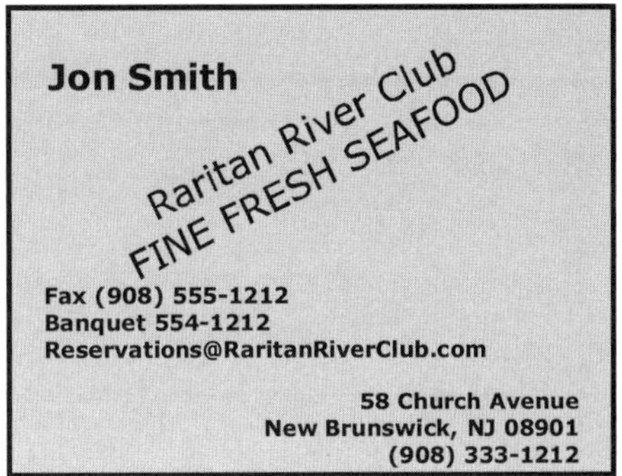

In this business card example, chaos starts off as one pile of data elements. In other words, all the data elements can be initially assigned to one entity, the business card itself. See Figure 18.5.

Figure 18.5 Initial Set of Data Elements in Chaotic State

Business Card

- Person Name
- Person Title
- Company Name
- Web Address
- Email Address
- Phone Number
- Logo Image
- Specialty Description

As was noted earlier, it is sometimes easier to think of an entity as a set of spreadsheet columns. Each data element in the entity is a separate column, and the rows in the spreadsheet represent the entity instances. Table 18.2 is a spreadsheet showing the data elements from Figure 18.5 as columns and the four business cards from Figure 18.4 as rows.

Table 18.2 Four Sample Business Cards in Spreadsheet Format

Card	Person Name	Person Title	Company Name	Web Address	Email Address	Mailing Address	Phone Number	Logo Image	Specialty Description
1	Steve Hoberman	Presi-dent	Steve Hoberman & Associates, LLC	www. stevehoberman.com	me@ stevehober-man.com	10 Main St New York, NY 10021	212-555-1212	Entity Model. jpg	
2	Steve Jenn		findsonline .com	findsonline.com	Steve@ findsonline.com Jenn@ findsonline.com		(973)555-1212		Internet auction experts
3	Bill Smith		The Amazing Rolando		BillSmith@TheAmazingRolando.com		732-555-1212		Magic for all occasions Walk around magic Children's parties
4	Jon Smith		Raritan River Club		Reservations @ RaritanRiver Club.com	58 Church Avenue New Bruns-wick, NJ 08901	(908)333-1212 (908)555-1212 554-1212		Fine fresh seafood

We hit a very interesting data modeling challenge in this step. It is a challenge that many of us face on the job when we first start a modeling project. The challenge is whether to model the medium or the content of the medium. In other words, do we model the form, report, or in this case the business card? Or do we model the contents of the form, report, or business card?

We need to ask a basic question to know whether we need to model the medium or the contents of the medium: *Why are we building this data model?* If we are building it for a business card company to automate the process of printing business cards, then the business card entity is appropriate. If we are building it for an organization or person to manage their contact information, then the business card is no longer the important concept. Rather, the contents of the business card are important and the business card serves as a grouping mechanism or source for our information.

To make the business card exercise even more fun, let's assume we are modeling this for a contact management organization, and the model you build will be the foundation for a new contact management application. In other words, we will model the content instead of the medium. Therefore, let's update the model as shown in Figure 18.6.

Figure 18.6 Contact Management Data Elements in Chaotic State

Contact

Person Name
Person Title
Company Name
Web Address
Email Address
Phone Number
Logo Image
Specialty Description

Normalizing is a process of asking questions. After asking the key question on model purpose, we now have another important question: What is a **Contact**? This is where we realize how important definitions are to the analysis and modeling process. In this case, we're able to leverage the definition we arrived at from building the conceptual data model in Chapter 17, which is:[16]

*A **Contact** is a person, a company, or a person at a company who our organization cares about knowing how to reach.*

Now that we know what a **Contact** is, how would a business person request a specific **Contact**? We need to ask how a **Contact** is identified. We need something that, at least initially, makes a contact unique. If we are replacing an existing contact management system, we can investigate what makes a contact unique in that system and use the same primary key here. If this is a new contact management system, we need to interview business people and consult requirements documents to determine what data element or data elements can uniquely identify a contact.

Let's assume that this is for a new system and the manager of the department building the system would like the system to create a new unique identifier for each contact. The manager would like this **Contact Id** combined with the contact's email address to guarantee uniqueness. See Figure 18.7 for the **Contact** model with this new primary key added.

[16] Note that the definition is not always necessarily the same for concepts and entities with the same name on the conceptual and logical models. An analysis needs to be done to ensure that the purpose, meaning, and usage are the same. For example, if we're building a logical model to match an application's terminology, the application's usage of **Contact** may be different from the organization's usage of **Contact**.

Figure 18.7 Contact Entity with Primary Key

Contact

Contact Id
Email Address

Person Name
Person Title
Company Name
Web Address
Phone Number
Logo Image
Specialty Description

In normalizing, you have to ask a business expert many questions or examine a lot of actual data to answer the questions themselves. Table 18.3 shows the same data from Table 18.2 with the rows divided to show the impact of defining a contact by **Contact Id** and **Email Address**. Note that a business card can have more than one contact. Note also that **Contact Id** is just a meaningless number, and therefore the values do not have to be a sequential counter.

Table 18.3 Four Sample Business Cards in Spreadsheet Format Segmented by Contact

Card	Contact Id	Email Address	Person Name	Person Title	Company Name	Web Address	Mailing Address	Phone Number	Logo Image	Specialty Description
1	123	me@stevehoberman.com	Steve Hober-man	Presi-dent	Steve Hoberman & Associates, LLC	www.steve hoberman. com	10 Main St New York, NY 10021	212-555-1212	Entity Model. jpg	
2	54	Steve@findsonline.com	Steve		findsonline.com	findsonline.com		(973)555-1212		Internet auction experts
	58	Jenn@findsonline.com	Jenn		findsonline.com	findsonline.com		(973)555-1212		Internet auction experts
3	42	BillSmith@TheAmazingRolando.com	Bill Smith		The Amazing Rolando			732-555-1212		Magic for all occasions Walk around magic Children's parties
4	14	Reservations@RaritanRiverClub.com	Jon Smith		Raritan River Club		58 Church Avenue New Brunswick, NJ 08901	(908)333-1212 (908)555-1212 554-1212		Fine fresh seafood

Now we are going to remove redundancies and assign each data element to its proper entity, following the first three levels of normalization. Recall our initial definition of normalization: *Every data element is single-valued and must provide a fact completely and only about its primary key.* To formalize this slightly, and to more accurately fit the description for the first three levels of normalization, we can rephrase this definition of normalization into: *Every data element must provide a fact about the key, the whole key, and nothing but the key.* First Normal Form (1NF) is the "Every data element must provide a fact about the key" part. Second Normal Form (2NF) is "the whole key" part, and Third Normal Form (3NF) is the "nothing but the key" part.

FIRST NORMAL FORM (1NF)

1NF ensures that "Every data element must provide a fact about the key". 'Key' refers to the primary key of the entity. 'Provide a fact about' is the key phrase, which we defined earlier and will elaborate on here. It means that for a given primary-key value, we can identify, at most, one of every data element that depends on that primary key. For example, assume **Department Number** is the primary key to the **Department** entity. Table 18.4 shows some sample values.

Table 18.4 Sample Values for Department

Department Number	Department Name
A	Accounting
A	Marketing
B	Information Technology
C	Manufacturing

In this example, **Department Number** A identifies two values for **Department Name**: Accounting and Marketing. Therefore, **Department Name** does not provide a fact about **Department Number**, and this example violates 1NF.

Ensuring each data element provides a fact about its primary key includes correcting the more blatant issue shown in Table 18.4, as well as addressing repeating groups and multi-valued data elements. Specifically, the modeler needs to:

- Move repeating data elements to a new entity
- Separate multi-valued data elements

Resolve Repeating Data Elements

When there are two or more of the same data element in the same entity, they are called repeating data elements. The reason repeating data elements violate 1NF is that for a given primary key value, we are getting more than one value back for the same data element. Repeating data elements often take a sequence number as part of their name.

In our contact example, by examining the sample data in Table 9.3 and asking lots of questions of business experts, we learn that a **Contact** can have more than one phone number and specialty description. We see that Jon Smith has three phone numbers: *(908)333-1212, (908)555-1212, 554-1212*. We see that The Amazing Rolando has three specialty descriptions: *Magic for all occasions*, *Walk around magic,* and *Children's parties*.

We can find ourselves asking many questions just to determine if there are any repeating data elements we need to address. We can have a question template, such as:

"Can a" <<insert entity name here>> "have more than one" <<insert data element name here>> "?" For example, "Can a **Contact** have more than one **Email Address**?" You'll need to ask a similar question for the following data elements as well: **Person**

Name, Person Title, Company Name, Web Address, Mailing Address, Phone Number, Logo Image, and **Specialty Description.**

Note that you might find yourself rephrasing some of these techie-sounding questions to make them more understandable to a business person. "Can a **Contact** have more than one **Email Address**?" might be better phrased as "Do you ever have the need to reach a **Contact** by more than one **Email Address**?"

Assuming that the four business cards we are examining contain a good representative set of data (and that's a big assumption), and that the businesspeople provide answers to our questions that are consistent with this data, a more accurate version of our **Contact** model would reflect that a contact can have, at most, three phone numbers and, at most, three specialties, as shown in Figure 18.8.

Figure 18.8 More Accurate View of Contact

Contact
Contact Id Email Address
Person Name Person Title Company Name Web Address Mailing Address Phone 1 Number Phone 2 Number Phone 3 Number Logo Image Specialty 1 Description Specialty 2 Description Specialty 3 Description

If a **Contact** can have three phone numbers, there is a good chance that one day there will be a **Contact** that has four phone numbers, or maybe ten. So in general terms, a **Contact** can have one or many phone numbers, and also one or many specialties. So we need to create separate entities for phone number and specialty, as shown in Figure 18.9.

Figure 18.9 Repeating Groups Moved to New Entities

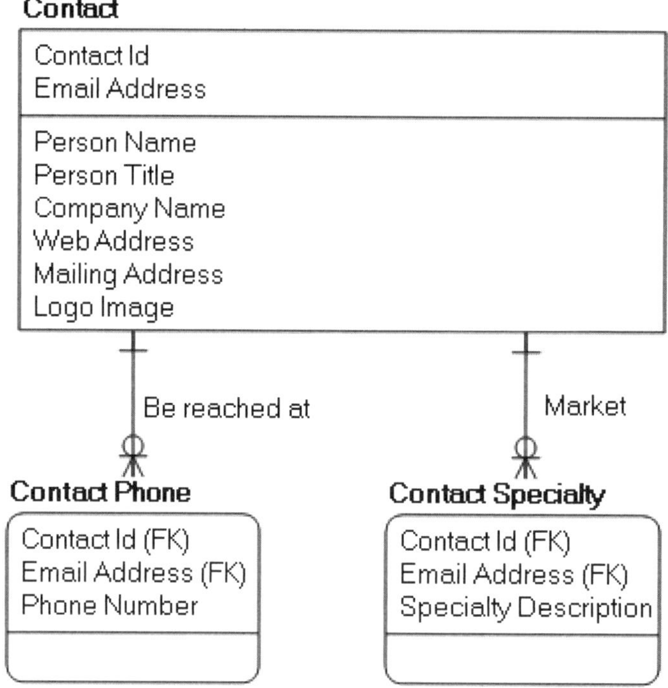

To resolve a repeating data element, you can see that we need to create a one-to-many relationship or a many-to-many relationship with a new entity that contains the repeating data element.

We are not yet done with completely resolving repeating groups, though. What other questions do we need to ask?

We already asked whether a contact can have more than one of each of its data elements. We also need to ask the other side of the equation, which is - can the values in these repeating data elements belong to more than one contact?

We need to make sure a one-to-many relationship from **Contact** to **Contact Phone**, and from **Contact** to **Contact Specialty** is correct, and that it is not a many-to-many relationship. So these two business questions need to be answered, as well:

- Can the same **Phone Number** belong to more than one **Contact**?
- Can the same **Specialty Description** belong to more than one **Contact**?

By looking at the sample data in Table 18.3 and confirming with businesspeople, we learn that the same phone number and specialty can belong to more than one contact, as Jenn and Steve from findsonline.com both share the phone number *(973)555-1212* and specialty *Internet Auction Experts*. Therefore, a more accurate model with repeating groups resolved is shown in Figure 18.10.

Figure 18.10 Repeating Groups Resolved

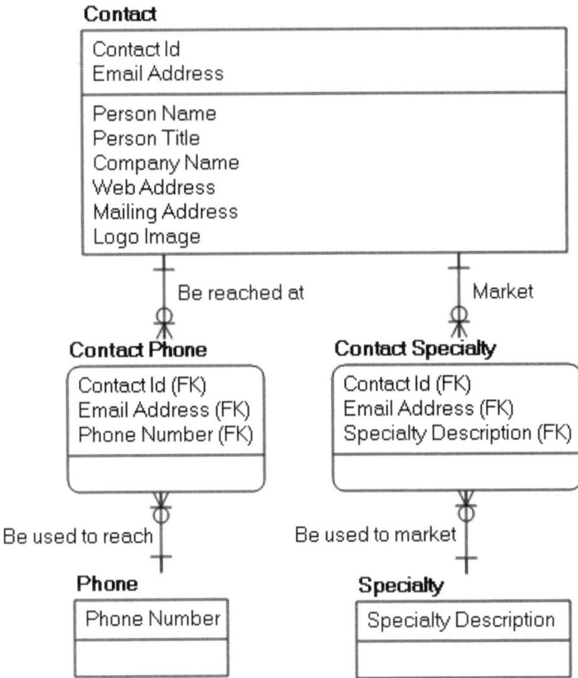

Note that what currently makes the phone number and specialty description unique at this point, is the **Phone Number** and **Specialty Description** themselves, respectively. These are not ideal primary keys, but they serve to illustrate normalization in this example.

Resolve Multi-valued Data Elements

Multi-valued means that within the same data element, we are storing at least two distinct values. There are at least two different business concepts hiding in one data element. For example, **Name** may contain both a first name and last name. **First Name** and **Last Name** can be considered distinct data elements, and therefore, "John Smith" stored in **Name**, is multi-valued, because it contains both "John" and "Smith."

By examining the data in Table 18.3 and the data model in Figure 8.10, and by asking even more questions, we can identify those data elements that need to be broken up into more refined data elements.

We may find ourselves asking many questions just to determine if there are any multi-valued data elements we need to identify. We can have another question template, such as:

"Does a" <<insert data element name here>> "contain more than one piece of business information?" For example, "Does a **Contact Id** contain more than one piece of business information?" You'll need to ask a similar question for the following business elements as well: **Contact Id**, **Email Address, Person Name, Person Title, Company Name,**

Mailing Address, Logo Image, Web Address, **Phone Number**, and **Specialty Description**.

Often a modeler will encounter multi-valued data elements that do not need to be separated into distinct data elements. This is common when the distinct data element parts are not of interest to the business or industry and the data element is considered to be in its atomic form, even though it contains more than one piece of information. For example, **Phone Number** contains an area code and may contain a country code. We might, therefore, decide to show country code and area code as separate data elements on the model. However, do your business people ever need to see the area code or do they view phone number as the most granular form? The answer to this question determines whether the modeler breaks apart the **Phone Number** data element.

Assume that in our contact example, **Person Name** and **Mailing Address** are the only two data elements that require being shown in a more granular form. The model in Figure 18.11 resolves these two multi-valued data elements and is therefore in 1NF.

Figure 18.11 Contact Data Model with Multi-Valued Data Elements Resolved, and therefore in 1NF

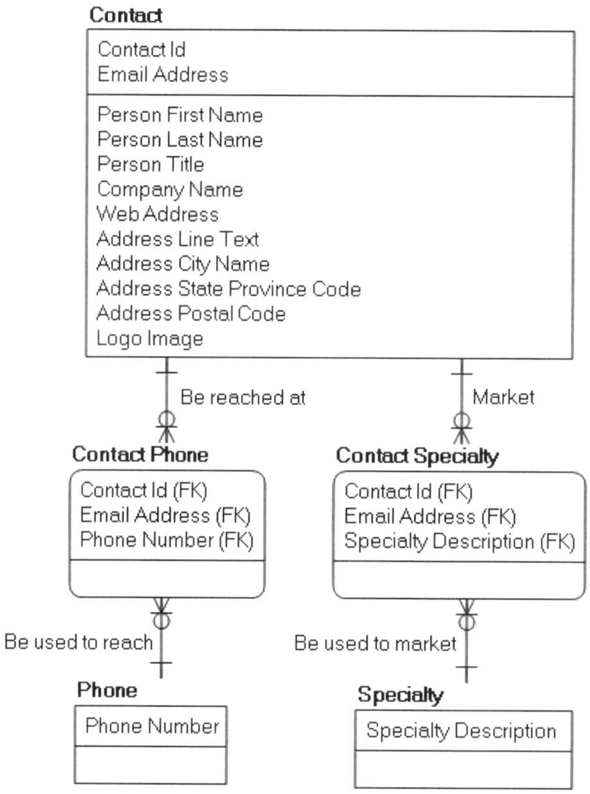

Contact
Contact Id
Email Address
Person First Name
Person Last Name
Person Title
Company Name
Web Address
Address Line Text
Address City Name
Address State Province Code
Address Postal Code
Logo Image

Be reached at

Market

Contact Phone
Contact Id (FK)
Email Address (FK)
Phone Number (FK)

Contact Specialty
Contact Id (FK)
Email Address (FK)
Specialty Description (FK)

Be used to reach

Be used to market

Phone
Phone Number

Specialty
Specialty Description

SECOND NORMAL FORM (2NF)

Recall the summary of all three normalization levels: *Every data element must provide a fact about the key, the whole key, and nothing but the key.* First Normal Form (1NF) is the "Every data element must provide a fact about the key" part. Second Normal Form

(2NF) is "the whole key" part. This means each entity must have the minimal set of data elements that uniquely identifies each entity instance.

For example, in Figure 18.12, we have **Employee Assignment**.

Figure 18.12 Example of Model not in 2NF

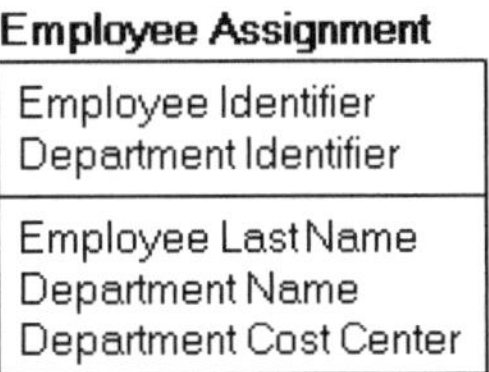

The primary key of **Employee Assignment** is **Employee Identifier** and **Department Identifier**. Do we have the minimal primary key for each of the non-key data elements? We would need to confirm with business experts whether the **Employee Identifier** is unique within a department or unique across the whole company. Most likely it is unique across the whole company, so we therefore do not have the minimal primary key for each of the non-key data elements. **Employee Last Name** probably needs only **Employee Identifier** to retrieve one value. Similarly, both **Department Name** and **Department Cost Center** most likely need only **Department Identifier** to retrieve one of their values. Therefore, we need to modify this model to get it into 2NF, as shown in Figure 18.13.

Figure 18.13 One Option for Putting the Model in 2NF

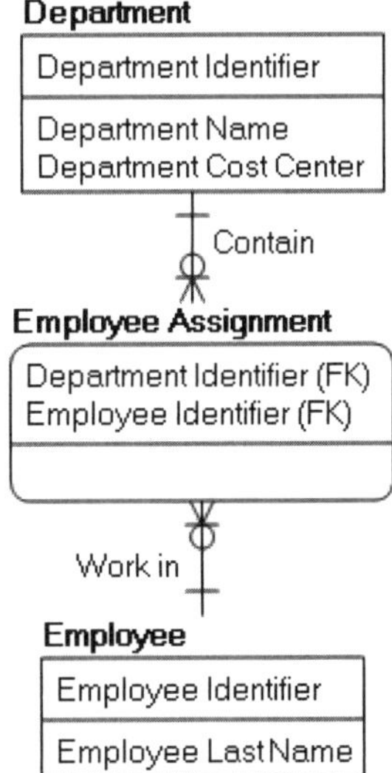

Now **Department Name** and **Department Cost Center** are facts about only **Department Identifier**, and **Employee Last Name** is a fact about only **Employee Identifier**. The entity **Employee Assignment** links employees with their departments. This is a 'special' entity that is called an associative (or sometimes an association) entity. An associative entity is an entity which resolves a many-to-many relationship. It is important to resolve a many-to-many relationship on the logical model because entities 'connect' to each other through foreign keys, and an associative entity provides the linking of foreign keys to travel from one side of the many-to-many relationship to the other side.

Normalization is a process of asking business questions. In this example, we could not complete 2NF without asking the business "Can an **Employee** work for more than one **Department**?" If the answer is "Yes" or "Sometimes", then the model in Figure 18.13 is accurate. If the answer is "No", then the model in Figure 18.14 prevails.

Figure 18.14 Another Option for Putting the Model in 2NF

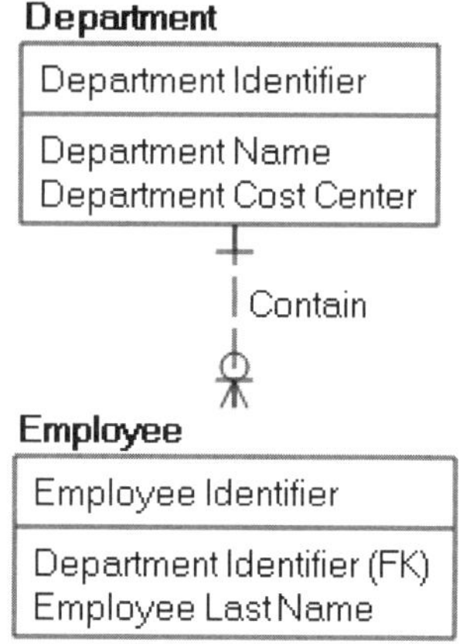

This model assumes answers to two other business questions:

- Can a **Department** exist without an **Employee**?
- Can an **Employee** exist without a **Department**?

The answers from the business would be "Yes, a **Department** can exist without an **Employee**" and "No, an **Employee** cannot exist without a **Department**".

As with 1NF, we will find ourselves asking many questions to determine if we have the minimal primary key. We can have another question template, such as:

"Are all of the data elements in the primary key needed to retrieve a single instance of" <<insert data element name here>>?" In our **Contact** example, the 'minimal set of primary key instances' are **Contact Id** and **Email Address.** So a valid question for our contact example would be: "Are both **Contact Id** and **Email Address** needed to retrieve a single instance of **Person First Name**?" You'll need to ask a similar question for the following data elements as well: **Person First Name, Person Last Name, Person Title, Company Name, Web Address, Address Line Text, Address City Name, Address State Province Code, Address Postal Code, Address Country Code,** and **Logo Image.**

We realize the answer to all of these questions is "No", we do not need both the **Contact Id** and **Email Address** in the primary key of **Contact**. Either one of these is enough to uniquely identify a contact and return a single instance of any of the data elements in **Contact**. Therefore, we only need one of these in the primary key. Let's use **Contact Id** as the primary key, and make **Email Address** an alternate key. The updated model is shown in Figure 18.15.

Figure 18.15 Contact Model in 2NF

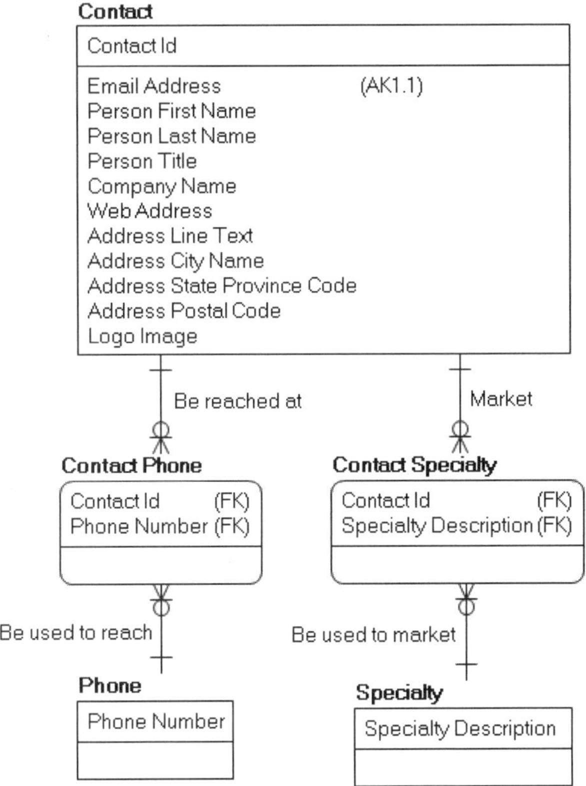

Asking the previous list of questions at this point might lead us to a more descriptive and refined model. For example, we realize there are people and company information in this entity. We can therefore make our model more descriptive and capture more business rules if we introduce subtyping into this structure.

Subtyping captures many more rules, but before we can show them, we need to confirm them with the business by asking more questions. For example, here are the questions we would need to ask to arrive at the model in Figure 18.16:

- Which data elements in **Contact** are shared by both a **Person** and **Company**?
- Which data elements are just for a **Person**?
- Which data elements are just for a **Company**?
- Which relationships to **Contact** are shared by both a **Person** and **Company**?

Note that we learn that the **Logo Image** is really just for a **Company** and not for a **Person**. In this case, then, we'll want to create a subtype relationship with **Contact** as the supertype with two subtypes: **Person** and **Company**, as shown in Figure 18.16. In a subtyping structure, the primary key from the supertype is also the primary key for each subtype. By default, the primary key for the subtype has the same name as the primary key for the supertype, so you'll see in Figure 18.16 that **Contact Id** is the primary key for **Contact**, as well as for the subtypes **Person** and **Company**. (For more information on subtypes, refer to Chapter 6).

Figure 18.16 Contact Model in 2NF Updated with Subtyping

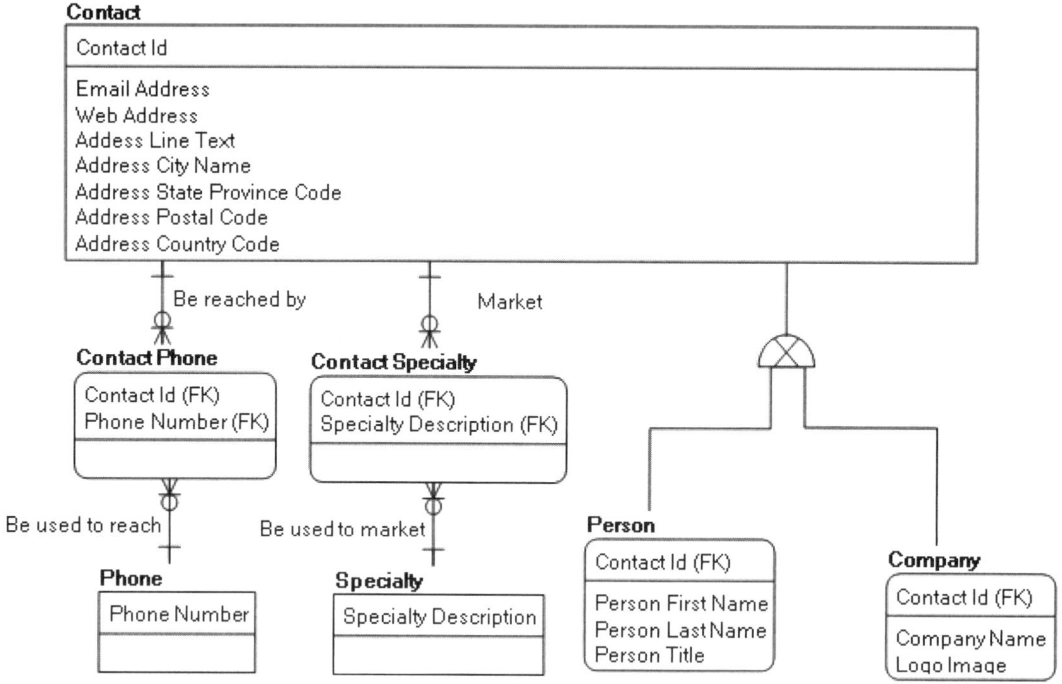

The modeler often renames the subtype primary keys to make them more meaningful. Renaming any foreign key, including a subtype's primary key, is called role naming. For example, we can role name **Contact Id** in **Person** to **Person Id** and **Contact Id** in **Company** to **Company Id**. **Person Id** and **Company Id** still contain the same value as **Contact Id**, but renaming the subtype's primary key facilitates better communication. Figure 18.17 contains the model with the new role names.

Figure 18.17 Contact Model in 2NF Updated with Role Names

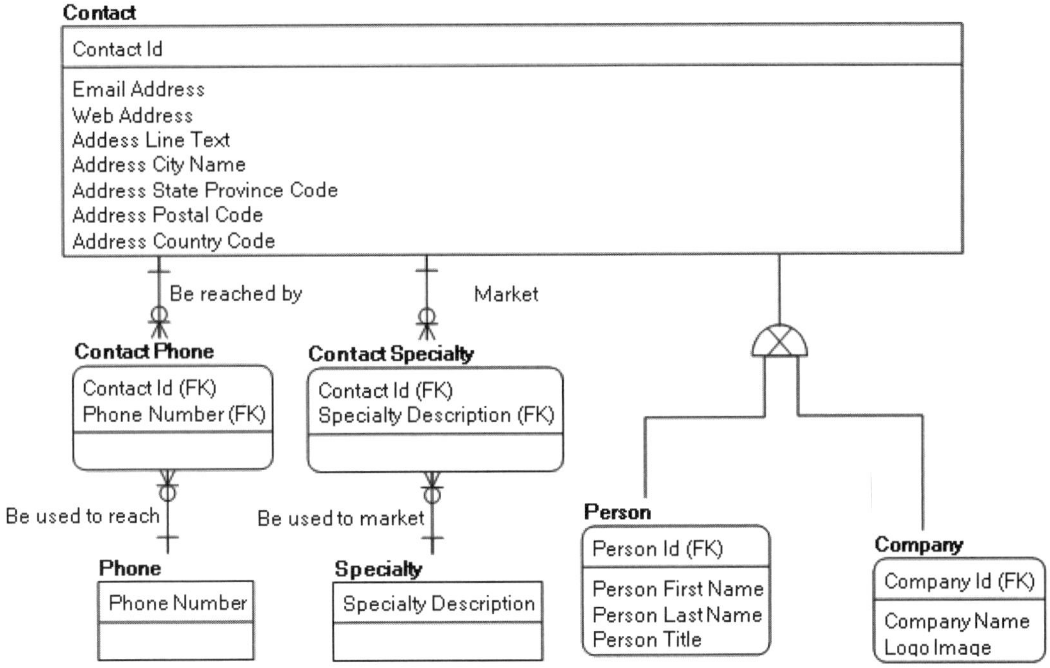

An important relationship that was assumed in Figure 18.15 is missing here. **People** work for **Companies**. By having the data elements together in the same entity in Figure 18.15, we assumed this was the case. Now, we have to show it explicitly in Figure 18.17. Can a **Person** work for more than one **Company**? Can a **Company** contain more than one **Person**? These questions need to be answered by the business.

Let's assume the answers to these questions are that a **Person** can only work for one **Company**, but doesn't have to work for a **Company** at all, and that a **Company** can employ many **People**, but doesn't have to employ any **People**. The updated model is shown in Figure 18.18, where a new relationship has been added between **Company** and **Person**.

Figure 18.18 Contact Model in 2NF Updated with Person Company Relationship

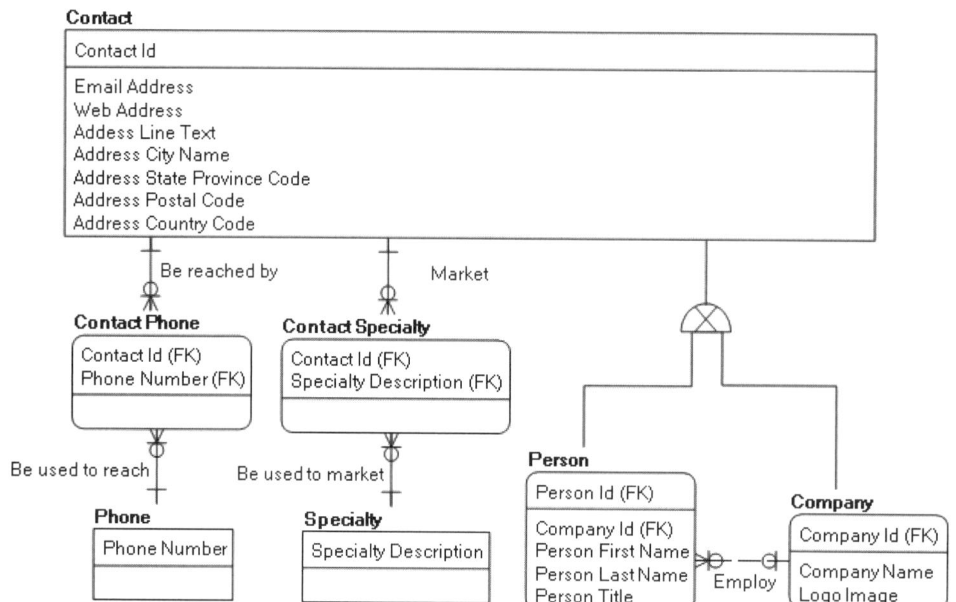

THIRD NORMAL FORM (3NF)

Again, recall our summary of all three normalization levels: *Every data element must provide a fact about the key, the whole key, and nothing but the key.* First Normal Form (1NF) is the "Every data element must provide a fact about the key" part. Second Normal Form (2NF) is "the whole key" part, and Third Normal Form (3NF) is the "nothing but the key" part.

3NF requires the removal of hidden dependencies. Each data element must be directly dependent on the primary key, and not directly dependent on any other data elements within the same entity. Alternate and foreign keys are excluded from this test.

The relational logical data model communicates which data elements are facts about the primary key and only the primary key. Hidden dependencies complicate the model and make it difficult to determine how to retrieve values for each data element. To resolve a hidden dependency, you will either need to remove the data element that is a fact about non-primary key data element(s) from the model, or you will need to create a new entity with a different primary key for the data element that is dependent on the non-primary key data element(s).

As with 1NF and 2NF, we will find ourselves asking many questions to uncover hidden dependencies. We can have another question template, such as: "Is" <<insert data element name here>> "a fact about any other data element in this same entity?" For the **Contact** entity, you may ask: "Is **Web Address** a fact about any other data element within this same entity?" You'll need to ask a similar question for the following data elements as well: **Web Address**, **Address Line Text**, **Address City Name**, **Address State Province Code**, **Address Postal Code,** and **Address Country Code**.

We learn from asking these questions that there are some hidden dependencies within the address data elements. If we know the postal code, we can determine the city, state province, and country. Therefore, by moving city, state province, and country to a different entity named **City**, as shown in Figure 18.19, our model is now in 3NF.

Figure 18.19 Contact Model in 3NF

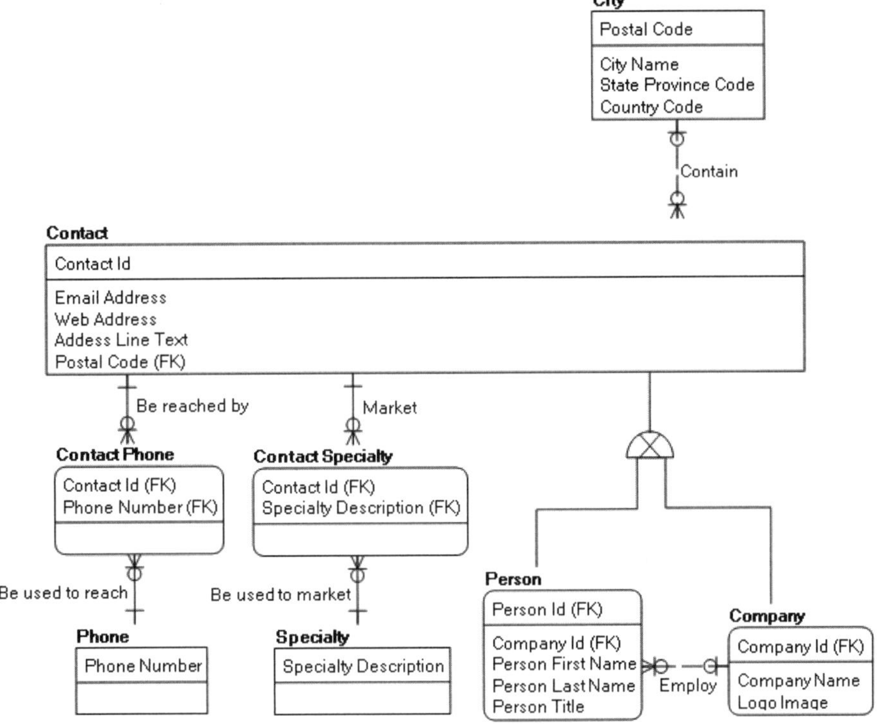

You may be wondering why we did not also move country and state province to their own entities. After all, if we know the city, we should know the state province, and if we know the state province, we should know the country. The reason we did not break these apart is because we do not have enough information to guarantee we can find the single country for a given state province or the state province for a given city. There is a Long Beach in New York State and a Long Beach in California, for example.

Note that we needed to ask even more questions to determine the right cardinality on the relationship line between **City** and **Contact**:

- Does a **Contact** have to have a **City**?
- Does a **City** have to contain at least one **Contact**?

We learned from the business that no, a contact does not have to have a city. We also learned that there could be cities in which no contacts reside. Therefore, the answer to the second question is "No".

You will find that the more you normalize, the more you go from applying rules sequentially to applying them in parallel. For example, instead of first applying 1NF to your model everywhere, and then when you are done applying 2NF, and so on, you will find yourself looking to apply all levels at once. This can be done by looking at each entity and making sure the primary key is correct and that it contains a minimal set of data elements, and that all data elements are facts about only the primary key.

Creating a Logical Data Model

Let's go back to our Baker Cakes example. In the last chapter, we created a Conceptual data model, shown again for reference in Figure 18.20, to define the core business concepts and relationships of the organization. We'll now want to refine the model, and add more detail.

Figure 18.20 Relational Conceptual Model for Baker Cakes

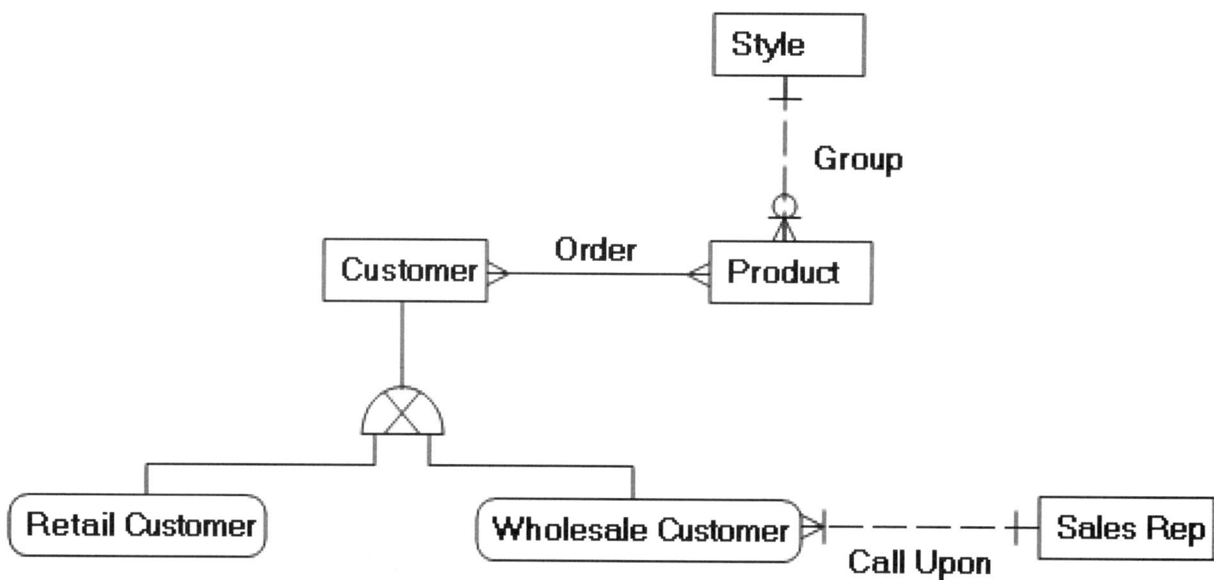

Let's use this Conceptual model as a starting point for our 'top-down' design. If you don't have it handy, you can download a sample `Baker Cakes Conceptual.erwin` model from www.erwin.com/datamodelingmadesimple.

To derive a logical model from the conceptual model we created, select **Actions|Design Layers|Derive New Model** from the **Main Menu**. (For more information on Design Layers, refer to Chapter 3.) The Derive Model Wizard appears, as shown in Figure 18.21.

Figure 18.21 Derive Model Dialog

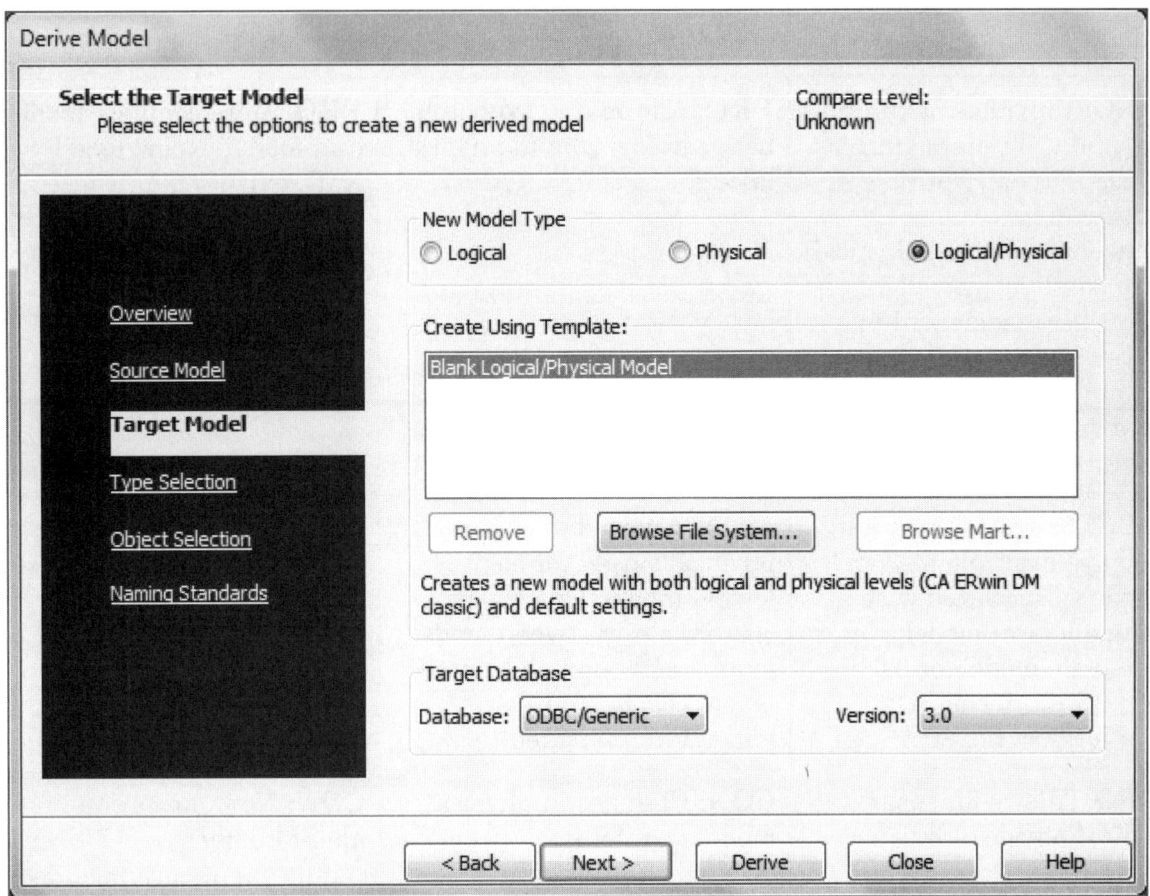

You'll see that there are three choices for the type of model: **Logical**, **Physical**, and **Logical/Physical**. In this case, we'll choose a **Logical/Physical** model. Table 18.5 summarizes some of the pros and cons of using the various model types: Logical only, Physical only, and Logical/Physical.

Table 18.5 Comparison of the Various Model Types in CA ERwin Data Modeler

Logical Only	Logical/Physical	Physical Only
PRO: Provides maximum flexibility in managing design layers. Multiple layers (e.g. conceptual/logical/physical) are possible, as well as multiple models within a layer (e.g. multiple logical or physical models relating to a single conceptual or logical).	**PRO:** Automated synching between logical and physical layers.	**PRO:** More compact model and model export (e.g. for XML export) if only a physical schema is needed.
PRO: Provides the ability to have multiple physical models associated with a single logical model (e.g. a separate model for each DBMS platform: SQL Server, Oracle, etc.)	**CON:** Limited to a single physical target for each logical model. One to one relationship between model layers (although additional layers can be manually added and managed).	**PRO:** Often faster and simpler to build by reverse engineering, if only physical model is needed.
PRO: Allows for separate logical/physical design constructs, for example rolling down a subtype relationship in the physical model, but keeping it intact in the logical.	**CON:** Changes in physical model (e.g. for denormalization) are automatically changed in the logical, and vice-versa. Although this can be a positive as well, it is a negative when you'd like to keep separate logical and physical designs.	**CON:** No information about business requirements are included if a logical model is not created (this is a very big CON!!).
CON: Requires synching with model source to align logical and physical models.		

Since we've selected to combine our logical model with our physical model, we're asked to choose our physical database platform. We're using Microsoft Access, so we'll choose the **ODBC/Generic** option using **Version 3.0**, which provides generic script for a variety of database platforms, including Microsoft Access. This will also allow us to easily change database platforms down the road if we want to change to a more scalable system.

Selecting **Next** will take us to the **Type Selection** tab, shown in Figure 18.22.

Figure 18.22 Object Type Selection in Derive Model Wizard

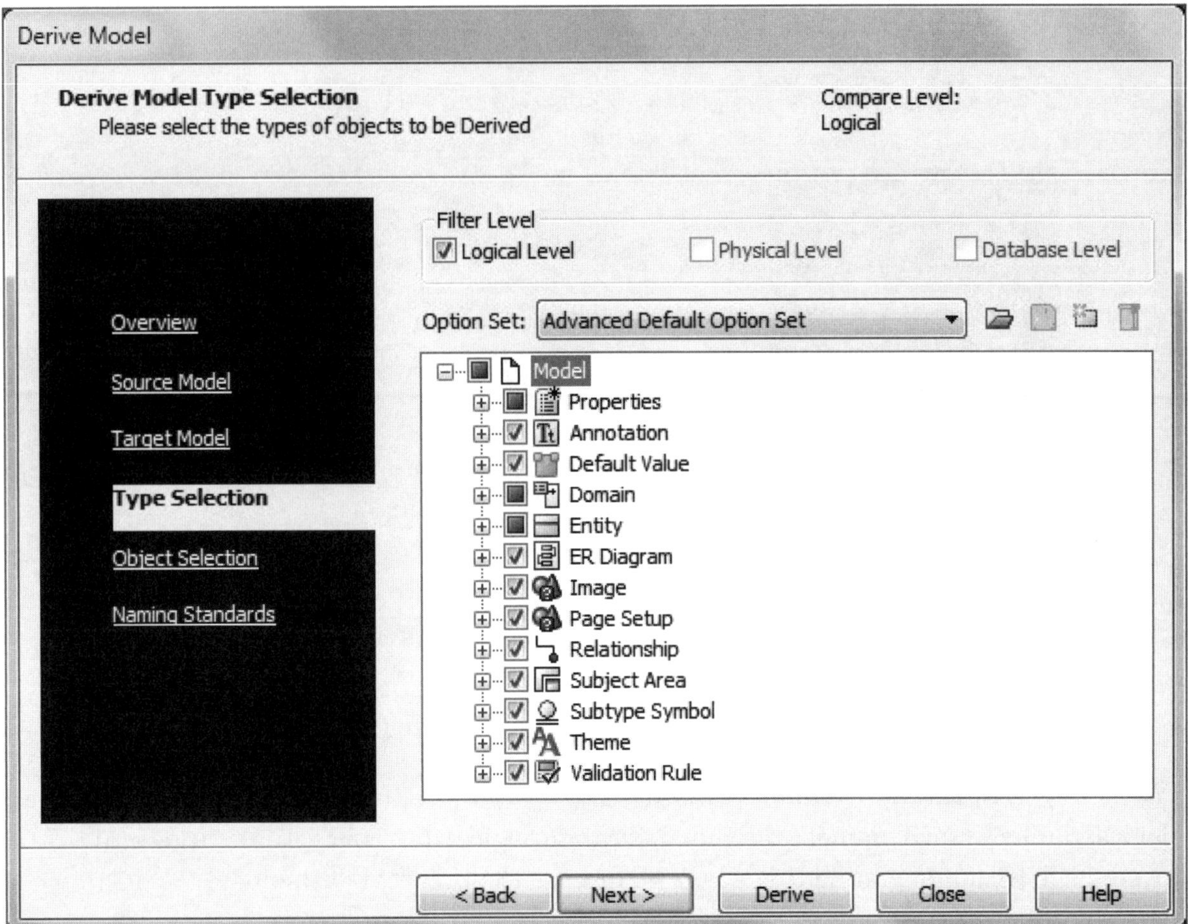

In the **Type Selection** tab, you're able to select which object types you'd like to include from the source model in the new model you're creating. For example, you might limit your derivation to only model objects, such as Entities and Relationships. Or you might want to include formatting information such as the display Themes or Page Setup options you've created. CA ERwin Data Modeler provides two option sets as defaults: the **Advanced Default Option Set**, which selects all objects and properties, and the **Standard Default Option** set, which selects only a subset of physical objects such as Entities and Relationships, but does not include Diagram options and layout Themes, for example. You can create your own custom option sets as well. This is a common best-practice for ensuring consistency across the organization, and to save you time the next time you create a model. For our example, though, we'll use the **Advanced Default Option Set**.

Next, move to the **Object Selection** tab, as shown in Figure 18.23. This tab allows you to select or filter specific object instances in the model derivation process. For example, you may want to exclude the **Sales Rep** entity from our logical model. For our purposes, though, we'll want to include all objects, so we'll leave this tab unchanged.

Figure 18.23 Object Selection in Derive Model Wizard

Derive Model

Source Model Object Selection
Please select the objects you want to linked to the derived model

Compare Level:
Logical

Overview
Source Model
Target Model
Type Selection
Object Selection
Naming Standards

Choose Objects Using Sets
Subject Areas
Key Groups

Selected Objects:
Baker Cakes Conceptual Model
Entities
Relationships
Subtype Symbols

Hide unselected objects

< Back | Next > | Derive | Close | Help

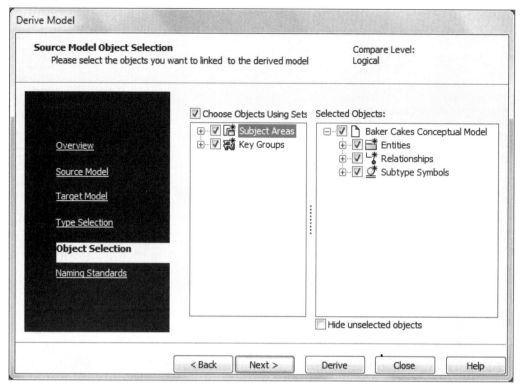

We'll skip the **Naming Standards** tab for now. Naming Standards are available to map logical and physical names, but not logical to logical (or conceptual to logical). We'll come back to naming standards when we discuss the physical data model.

Select the **Derive** button and the wizard will close to reveal your new default logical data model, shown in Figure 18.24. At this point, the logical model looks the same as the conceptual model. We'll need to modify and enhance this model using the skills we learned earlier in this chapter.

Figure 18.24 Logical Data Model Derived from Conceptual - Before Modifications

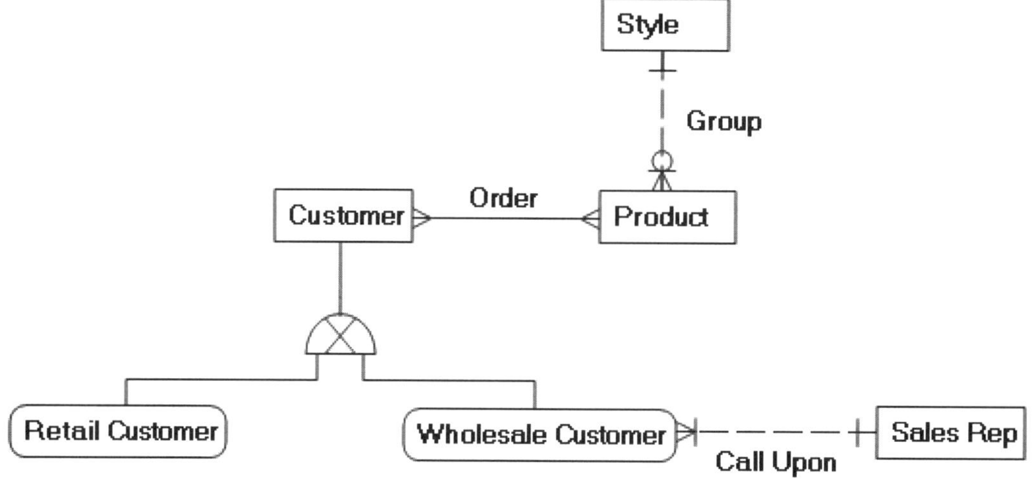

Before we go further, we'll want to change some key model properties and save the model with a new name. First, change the **Model Name** to **Baker Cakes Logical Physical Model** (see Chapter 3 or Chapter 17 if you need help with changing the model name). Next, change the name of the **PowerPoint View** diagram to **Logical Detail View** (see Chapter 8 if you need help with diagrams). Save the model as **`Baker Cakes Logical Physical.erwin`**.

Now it's time to add detail to our logical model. Recall that this additional detail on business rules and attributes is a distinguishing factor between the conceptual and logical model. Let's start by adding some attributes to our entities. We'll begin with the **Sales Rep** entity. In our conversations with Mr. Baker, we discovered that he had a spreadsheet he used to keep track of his sales staff. We decided to use this spreadsheet as a starting point for our model, as shown in Table 18.6.

Table 18.6 Spreadsheet with Sales Rep Information

Employee ID	Employee Name	Dept. Code	Dept. Name
1982746	Wanda Wang	IS	Inside Sales
9873631	Robert Bishop	OS	Outside Sales
8874251	Melissa Johannesen	IS	Inside Sales
Etc.			

The simplest way to start is simply add each column heading as an attribute in our **Sales Rep** entity. Enter the following attributes: **Employee ID**, **Employee Name**, **Department Code**, **Department Name**. Note that you'll want to change your diagram display level to **Attribute Display Level**. (For more information for changing the diagram display level, see Chapter 4. For more information on how to enter attributes, see Chapter 5.) Your entity should now look similar to Figure 18.25.

Figure 18.25 Adding Attributes to Sales Rep Entity

Our model has limited value if we simply mimic what was entered into a spreadsheet, however, without using any of the data modeling theory we've learned. Let's apply some of our new skills. First, let's define the unique identifier, or primary key. In this case, Baker Cakes uses a unique identifier for each employee. Since there are no duplicates, and the **Employee ID** uniquely identifies a given **Sales Rep**, we can use that as the primary key. Make this change, and your model should look similar to Figure 18.26. (For more information on how to define primary keys, see Chapter 7.)

Figure 18.26 Defining a Primary Key for the Sales Rep Entity

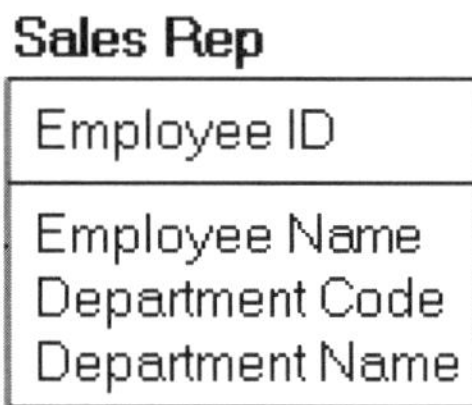

Next let's think about normalization. Does every data element provide a fact about the key, the whole key, and nothing but the key? **Department Code** and **Department Name** are attributes that jump out as not describing **Sales Rep**, which violates 1NF. The word 'Department' in front of them gives a clue that they describe another entity other than **Sales Rep**. Let's create a new entity called **Department** and move those attributes to that entity instead (for help on how to create an entity refer to Chapter 4). To move an attribute from one entity to another, select the 'source' entity and then hover over the attribute name on the diagram until the icon changes to a hand. Next, simply drag and drop the attribute in the desired location (indicated by a bold line) of the 'target' entity, as shown in Figure 18.27.

Figure 18.27 Moving an Attribute from One Entity to Another for Normalization

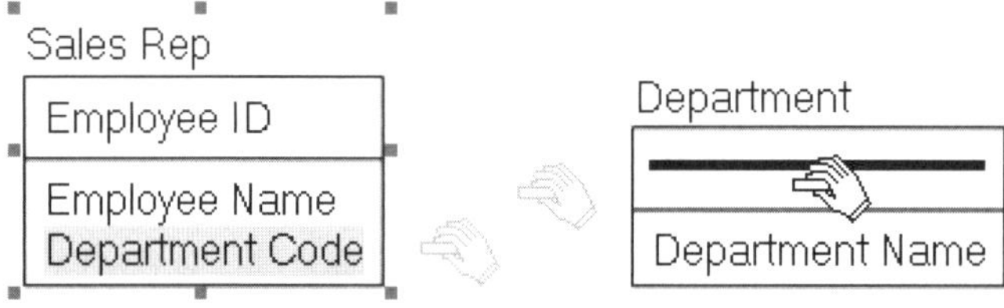

We've confirmed with Mr. Baker that the **Department Code** is a unique identifier for a given department, so we'll make that the primary key, as shown in Figure 18.28.

Figure 18.28 Assigning a Primary Key to the Department Entity

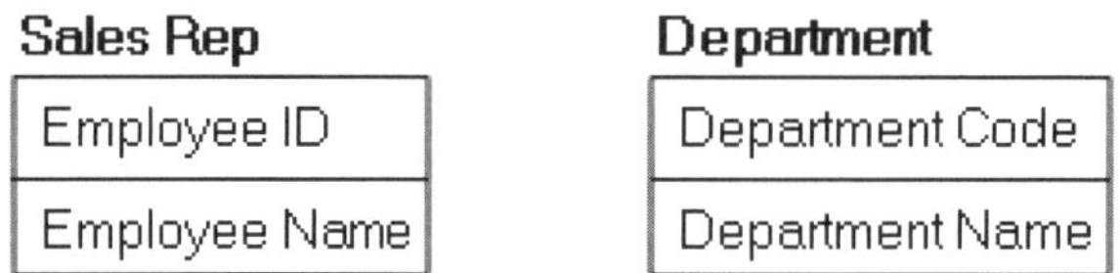

Next we'll need to add the relationship between **Department** and **Sales Rep**. We've confirmed the following business rules with our sponsor:

- A **Department** can exist without a **Sales Rep**
- A **Sales Rep** can exist without a **Department** assigned to them
- Each **Department** may contain one or more **Sales Rep**s
- Each **Sales Rep** can be assigned to only one **Department**

Based on this information, we'd select a one-to-many non-identifying relationship between **Department** and **Sales Rep**, as shown in Figure 18.29. Remember to add the verb phrases and show the parent verb phrases on the diagram (refer to Chapter 6 for more information on creating relationships). Also notice that **Department Code** is now automatically listed as a foreign key in the **Sales Rep** entity (refer to Chapter 7 for more on foreign keys).

Figure 18.29 Relationship between Department and Sales Rep

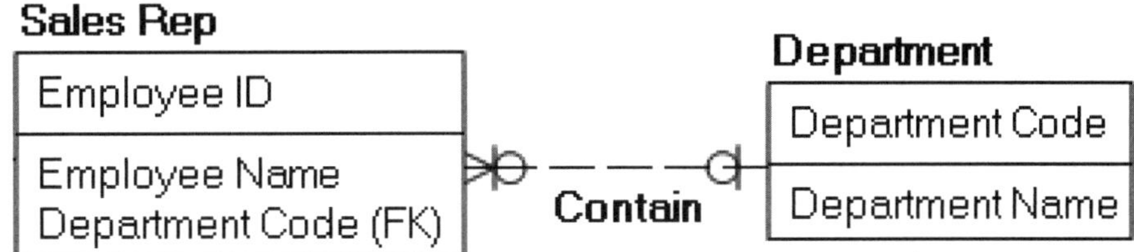

Continuing our normalization exercise, the other violation we see is in the **Employee Name** attribute. Since we see in the spreadsheet that the **Employee Name** field actually contains both a first name and last name (e.g. Wanda Wang), this would be considered a multivalued data element. We'll want to break this into two separate attributes: **Employee First Name** and **Employee Last Name**. In this case, rename the **Employee Name** attribute to **Employee First Name**, and add a new attribute called **Employee Last Name**, as shown in Figure 18.30.

Figure 18.30 Resolving Multivalued Elements in the Name Attribute

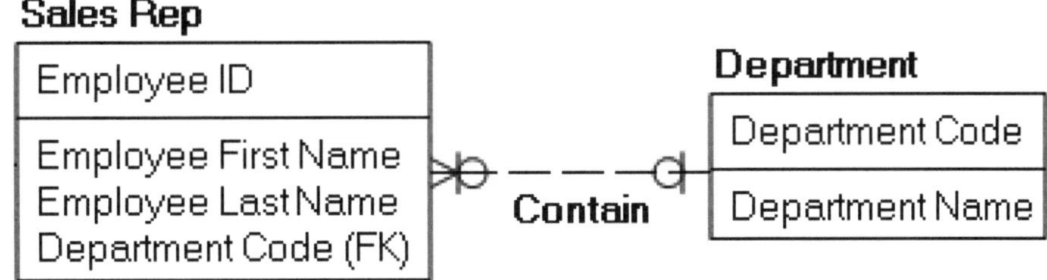

Congratulations! You've normalized your first data model.

Now that we have some attributes defined, we'll need to add more detail to these attributes, such as their length, nullability, etc. Let's start with the **Employee Last Name** attribute. First, we'll need to consider the length. What is the longest last name we would typically have for a **Sales Rep**? Before we bother our business sponsor with this question, let's look at some same data in the existing database. In looking at spreadsheet Mr. Baker provided us (refer to Table 18.6), we see that the longest last name is Johannesen, which is 10 characters long. Before we consider this the longest name, however, we decided to double-check with Mr. Baker.

Mr. Baker: Oh, I'm glad you asked that. We just hired a new rep from India, and Mr. Thiruvanamthapuram's name wouldn't fit into that Access database we had built. His name kept getting cut off to 'Thiruvanamthapu' on the commission reports, which didn't make him too happy. The consultant said that it was better to keep the names short to save space in the database, so I just added his full name to the 'Comments' field so we'd have it on file.

From Mr. Baker's comments, we discover a few things that went wrong with the original implementation. First, by basing the requirements on the physical implementation only, key business requirements were overlooked. It's not worth saving space by shortening the data type of an attribute if we lose key information that way. Starting with a logical model helps flesh out these requirements. As a result of poor design, business users often create their own work-arounds to get the information they need. In this case, Mr. Baker ended up placing long last names in the **Comments** field. Because this is not documented in the model, and is known only to Mr. Baker, it will cause problems down the road with data queries and updates, as well as migration to the new system.

For our **Employee Last Name** attribute, we decide to use a length of 40 characters to account for long names, as well as the potential for hyphenated or compound names. Before we simply assign a data type and length, however, let's think about reuse. Are there other areas in the model where a name might be used? Would a reusable domain be a good fit here? In looking at our model, we'll likely have names for our **Retail Customers**, so let's plan ahead and use a domain for this data element.

Domains were covered in detail in Chapter 10, so we won't go step-by-step here. Instead, we'll simply list the fields that need to be defined and show the results. Create a new domain with the following values:

Parent Domain type:	String
Name:	Last Name
Logical Data Type:	VARCHAR(40)
Null:	Not Null (i.e. a last name is required)
Attribute Name:	%OwnerEntity %AttDomain (e.g. Customer Last Name)
Definition:	The Last Name domain provides a consistent length of 40 characters and a naming standard of Entity Name + Domain Name.
Definition Inherited by Attributes:	The %OwnerEntity %AttDomain is the family name, or surname, of an individual.

The Domain Properties Editor for this new domain should look similar to Figure 18.31. **Close** this editor and return to the model diagram.

Figure 18.31 Creating a Last Name Domain

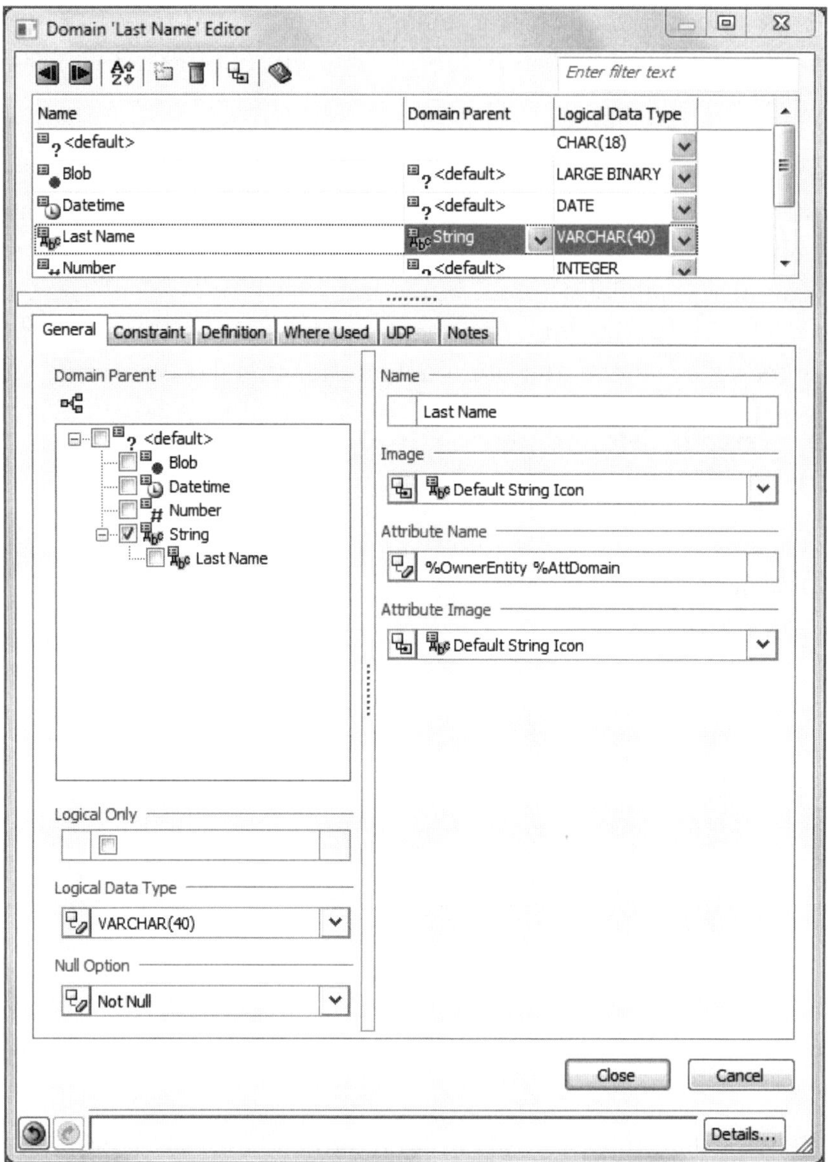

Now we'll want to use this domain for our **Employee Last Name** attribute, to ensure a consistent data type, null option, etc. In this case, however, we do not want the domain to define the attribute's naming convention. Recall that in the **Last Name** domain, we used the macro language to enforce a naming standard of **`%OwnerEntity %AttDomain`**, which would, in this case, be **Sales Rep Last Name**. Since we'd like to keep **Employee Last Name** in this case, we'll want to use Name Hardening before we apply the domain. (Name Hardening is covered in more detail in Chapter 12).

Open the Attribute Properties Editor for the **Employee Last Name** attribute, and use the drop-down menu to the right of the **Name** field to select the **Harden** option to enforce name hardening, as shown in Figure 18.32.

Figure 18.32 Using Name Hardening Before Applying a Domain

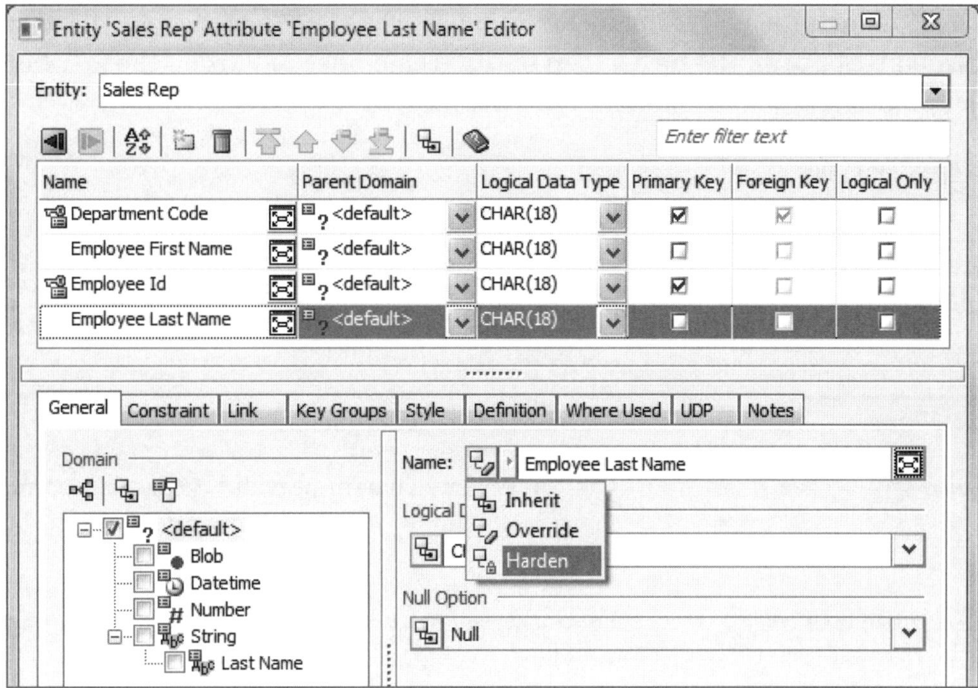

Now that we've ensured that the attribute name will not change, let's assign the **Last Name** domain to this attribute. To do this, simply check the box next to the **Last Name** domain in the **Domain** list box, and you'll see that the **Logical Data Type** changes to **CHAR(40)** and the **Null Option** changes to **Not Null**, as shown in Figure 18.33.

Figure 18.33 Using a Domain to Define the Logical Data Type and Null Option

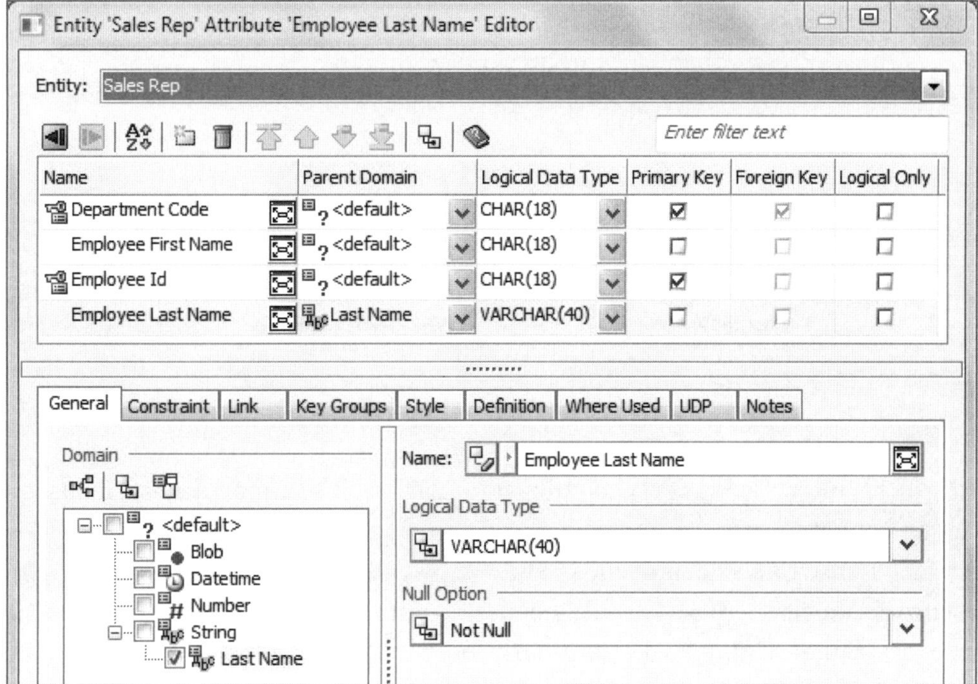

We'll want to follow similar standard for **Employee First Name**, so follow the same steps above to create a new domain for **First Name**, and assign it to the **Employee First Name** attribute on the **Sales Rep** entity (remember to harden the attribute name first). The properties for the domain are as follows:

Parent Domain type:	String
Name:	First Name
Logical Data Type:	VARCHAR(25)
Null:	Not Null
Attribute Name:	%OwnerEntity %AttDomain
Definition:	The First Name domain provides a consistent length of 25 characters and a naming standard of Entity Name + Domain Name.
Definition Inherited by Attributes:	The %OwnerEntity %AttDomain is the given name of an individual, e.g. Mary

Now that we've added some more detail around our **Sales Reps** at Baker Cakes, let's move to **Customer** information. Recall from our model that the **Customer** entity involves a supertype/subtype construct, as shown in Figure 18.34, which shows that a **Customer** can either be a **Retail Customer** or a **Wholesale Customer** (but not both).

Figure 18.34 Customers can be Retail Customers or Wholesale Customers

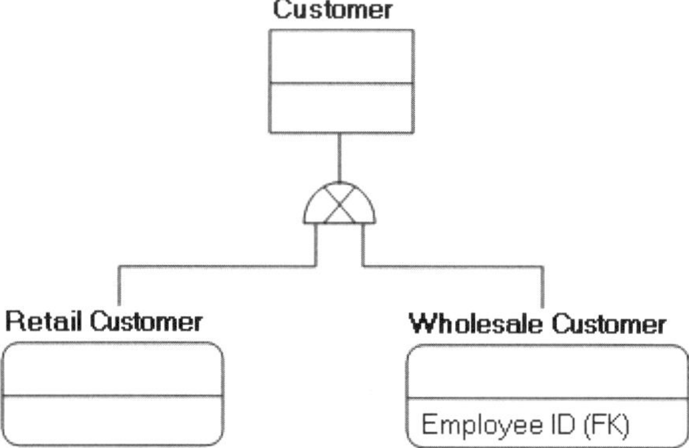

In defining attributes for supertype/subtype entities, it's important to focus on which attributes are shared across all entities, and which are unique to the subtype entities. Let's first focus on what information is shared by all entities, which will be included in the **Customer** entity. First, we'll need to determine the unique identifier for **Customer**. At Baker Cakes, all customers, both retail and wholesale, are assigned a unique customer id, so **Customer ID** is a logical candidate for our identifier, or primary key. Since this applies to all customers, place the primary key on the **Customer** entity, as shown in Figure 18.35. (For help in defining primary keys, refer to Chapter 7).

Figure 18.35 Defining a Unique Identifier for Customer Information

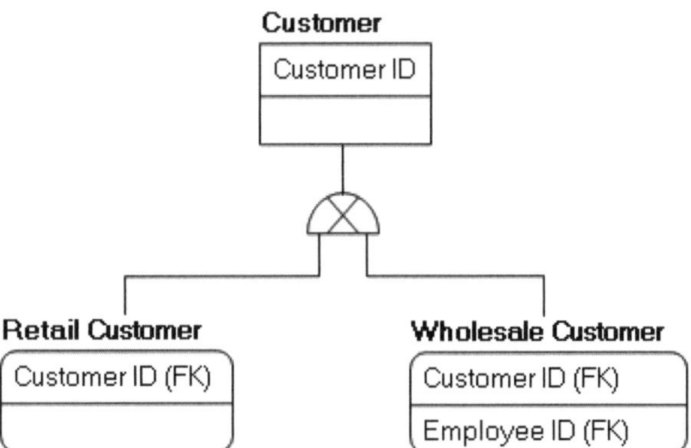

Note that **Customer ID** attribute cascades to the **Retail Customer** and **Wholesale Customer** entities as foreign keys. Recall our subtype discussion in Chapter 6, which explained that the subtyping relationship implies that all of the properties from the supertype are inherited by the subtype.

Next, let's focus on the attributes that are unique to retail and wholesale customers. One distinction is that retail customers are individuals, referred to by their first and last names, while wholesale customers use their company name. Let's start with the **Retail Customer** entity and add attributes for first and last name by using the domains we created earlier. An easy way to use a domain as a 'seed attribute' is to simply drag the domain from the Model Explorer. Drag both the **First Name** and **Last Name** domains to the **Retail Customer** entity, as shown in Figure 18.36. Note that the attribute name is automatically created as `%OwnerEntity %AttDomain`, as defined by the macro script we included in the domain definition.

Figure 18.36 Using Domains to Create Attributes

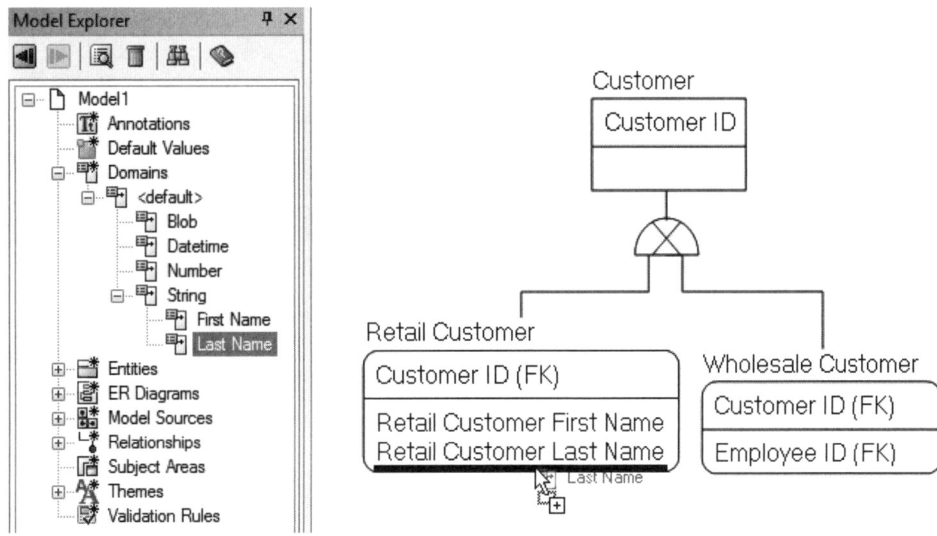

For the **Wholesale Customer** entity, we'll need to add an attribute to store company name information, but in this case we won't use a domain, since this is the only place where a company name will likely be used in our model. If this changes in the future, we can always add a domain later on. Create a non-key attribute for the **Wholesale Customer** entity using the following information:

Name: Company Name

Logical Data Type: CHAR(35)

Null Option: Not Null

Definition: The Company Name is the complete legal name of a firm-- the title by which a formally organized or incorporated firm is known as a legal entity.

The supertype/subtype relationship now appears as shown in Figure 18.37.

Figure 18.37 Customer Supertype/Subtype with Attribution

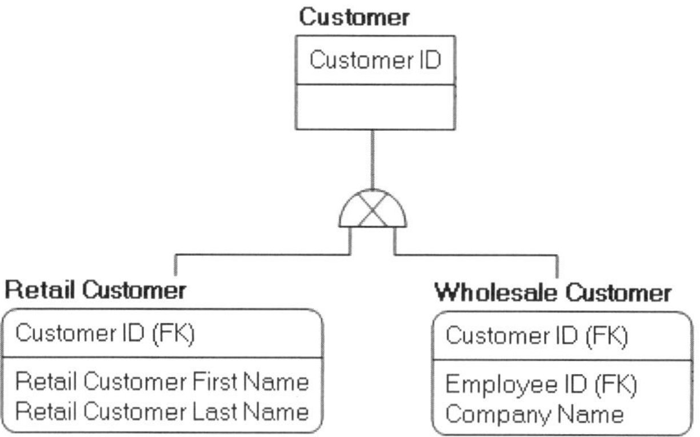

Let's add the necessary attributes to the rest of the entities in the model. You should have the hang of this by now, so we won't walk you through each step. On your own, add the following attributes to the model.

Product entity:

Attribute Name	Primary Key	Logical Data Type	Null Option	Description
Product ID	Yes	CHAR(18)	Not Null	The Product ID is a unique identifier for each product.
Product Name	No	CHAR(30)	Not Null	The Product Name is the customer-facing descriptor of the product, e.g. Layer Cake.

Style entity:

Attribute Name	Primary Key	Logical Data Type	Null Option	Description
Style ID	Yes	CHAR(18)	Not Null	The Style ID is a unique identifier for each style.
Style Name	No	CHAR(35)	Not Null	The Style Name is the customer-facing descriptor of the product style, e.g. Lemon Lovers.

After you've added these attributes, your model should look similar to Figure 18.38.

Figure 18.38 Relational Logical Model with Attributes for Baker Cakes

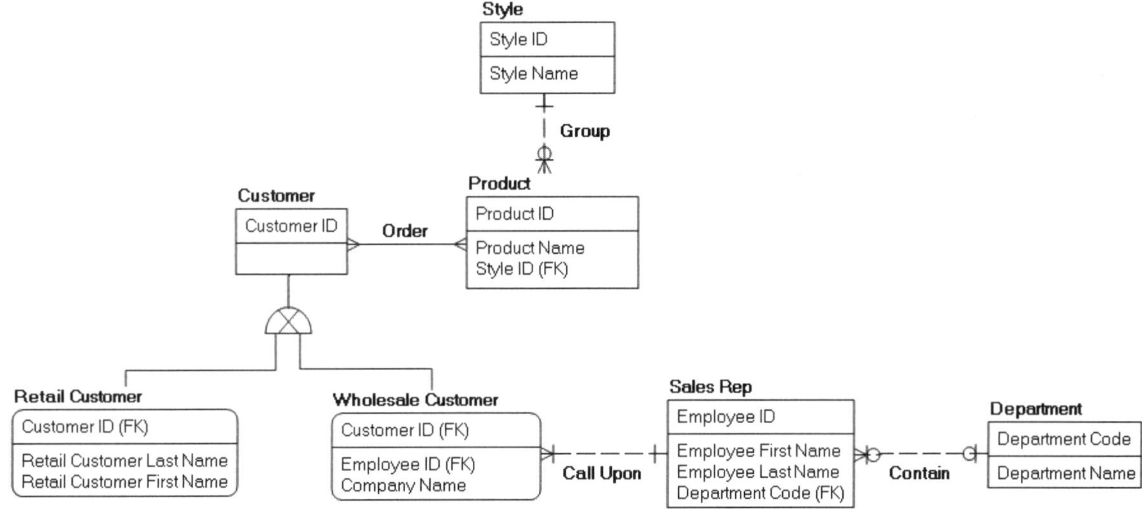

The model is starting to come together. We're getting close to having a comprehensive description of Baker Cake's data environment. But there is one thing that stands out as unresolved. Notice the many-to-many relationship between **Order** and **Product**. As we discussed earlier in this chapter, it's ideal to resolve all many-to-many relationships in the logical model before using it as a guide to create the physical model. Not only does it make our first cut at physical implementation easier, but in this case, there is a business reason behind resolving this, as well.

In our existing model, we're able to show that a particular **Customer** placed an **Order** for one or more **Products**, but we're not able to identify individual items within that order. For example, Mary Smith may have placed an order for a Lemon Lovers Layer Cake and a Chocoholics Sponge Cake. If Sponge Cakes are suddenly placed on backorder, we do not have a way to identify the particular line item on the order for this particular product. We'll resolve this issue by resolving the many-to-many relationship between **Customer** and **Product** with an associative entity.

In CA ERwin Data Modeler, we're able to resolve many-to-many relationships automatically with the help of Transforms. Simply highlight the many-to-many relationship and select **Actions|Transformations|Resolve Many to Many Relationship** from the **Main Menu**. Notice that the result of this action is the creation of a new associative entity named **Customer Product**, as shown in Figure 18.39. The default name is a concatenation of the source and target entity names.

Figure 18.39 Using Transforms to Resolve Many-to-Many Relationships

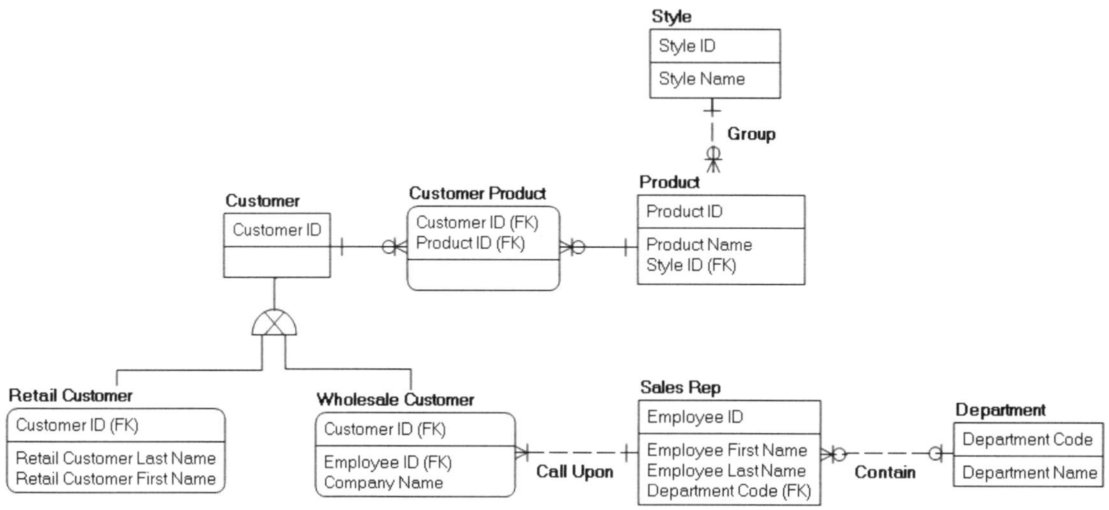

Notice also that the primary key for **Customer Product** is the superset of the primary keys of the source and target entities, **Customer** and **Product**. What this tells us is that the information that uniquely identifies a particular line item on an order is **Customer ID** and **Product ID**. So, with this information, we can now determine that our **Customer** (e.g. Mary Smith) has placed an order for a given **Product** (e.g. Layer Cake).

Happy with this solution, we showed our model to Mr. Baker to confirm that we had created this new entity correctly.

Mr. Baker: What's a 'Customer Product'?

Donna: That's a construct we've created to allow you to identify the items purchased by a given customer. For example, the fact that Mary Smith ordered a Lemon Lovers Layer Cake.

Mr. Baker: You mean an order? We track all of that by the order ID, and we'd know not only what she ordered, but how many, and on what date. I'm definitely starting to think I want my intern back.

OK, so we did a few things wrong this time. Not only were we using 'techie terms' that didn't resonate with the customer, but we hadn't fleshed out all of the business rules. And all that discovered from resolving a many-to-many relationship (and, of course talking with the business sponsor).

To resolve this, first we'll rename **Customer Product** to **Order**, to use a more business-friendly term. Also, since Mr. Baker indicated that he identifies an order by an order ID, we can change the relationship types between **Customer** and **Order** and **Product** and **Order** to non-identifying, i.e. we don't need a **customer ID** or **product ID** to retrieve an **Order**. We'll also add verb phrases as well. For example, a **Customer** 'places' an **Order** and a **Product** 'appears on' an **Order**.

In addition, we'll add the following attributes to the **Order** entity:

Attribute Name	Primary Key	Logical Data Type	Null Option	Description
Order ID	Yes	CHAR(18)	Not Null	The Order ID is a unique identifier for each Order.
Order Date	No	DATE	Not Null	The Order Date was the date on which the order was placed by the Customer.

The model should now look similar to Figure 18.40.

Figure 18.40 Defining the Order Entity

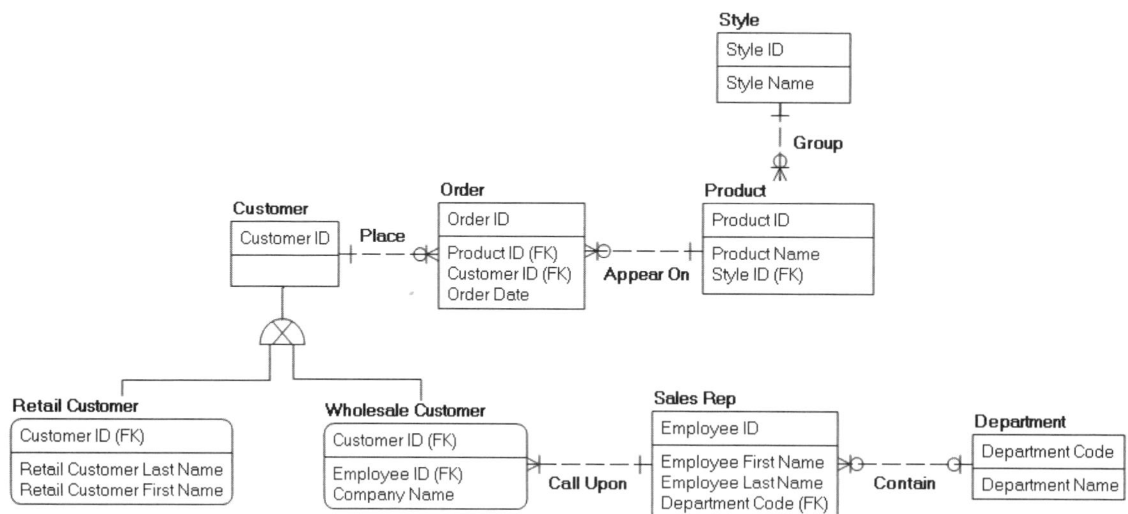

These modifications are closer to our solution, but we still aren't able to identify the number of items purchased. For example, did Mary Smith order five Lemon Lovers Layer Cakes or two? For this, we'll need to create another entity to track individual orders.

To keep track of individual items on an order, we'll add a new entity **Order Line**, between **Order** and **Product**. Delete the relationship between **Product** and **Order**, and add new relationships to/from **Order Line**. Since, in this case, we need a **Product ID** and an **Order ID** to identify and retrieve an **Order Line**, we'll use an identifying relationship for both of these new relationships. The business rules are as follows:

- Each **Order** must contain one or more **Order Lines**
- Each **Product** may appear on one or more **Order Lines**

Next, add two new attributes with the following properties for the **Order Line** entity:

Attribute Name	Primary Key	Logical Data Type	Null Option	Description
Order Line Quantity	No	Integer	Not Null	The Order Line Quantity is the countable number of products purchased by a customer, in whole numbers. Partial products cannot be ordered.
Unit Price Amount	No	Decimal (4,2)	Not Null	The Unit Price Amount is the predetermined price for a Customer of a single unit sold of a Product.

Your model should now look similar to Figure 18.41.

Figure 18.41 Adding the Order Line Entity

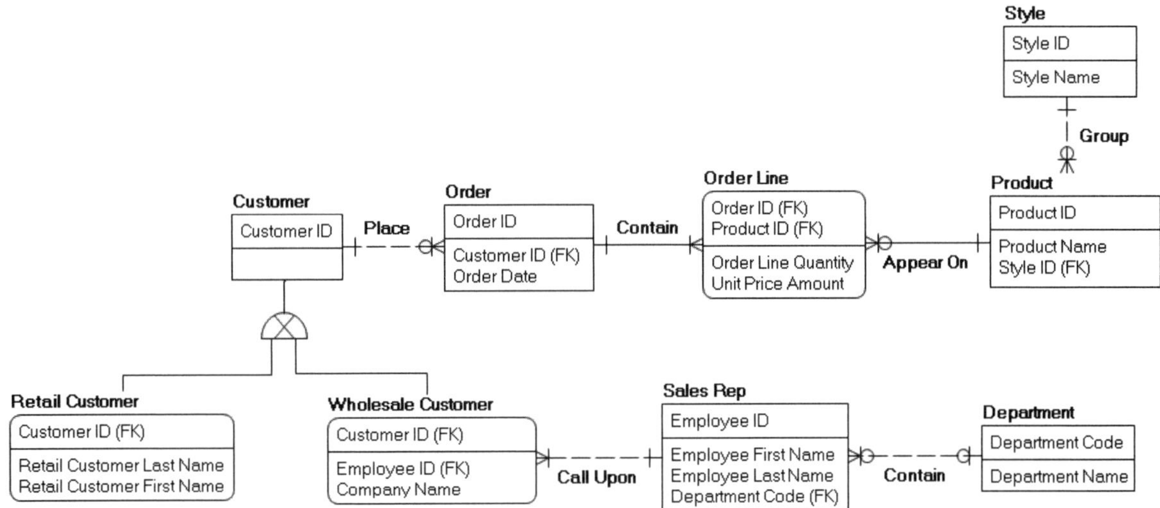

We now have a robust relational logical data model complete with attributes, domains, business rules, etc. The completed model is available for download at www.erwin.com/datamodelingmadesimple.

Key Points

- A logical data model (LDM) represents a detailed business solution.
- A relational logical model represents how the business works. A dimensional logical model represents what the business is monitoring.
- Normalizing is a formal process of asking business questions. Normalization ensures that every data element is a fact about the key (1NF), the whole key (2NF), and nothing but the key (3NF).
- CA ERwin Data Modeler's Design Layer Architecture gives you flexibility in how you create your logical data model, whether using a combined logical/physical model, or a single logical model with multiple physical models.
- CA ERwin Data Modeler's Transforms help you with common normalization tasks such as resolving many-to-many relationships.
- Domains can help you standardize attribute data types and naming conventions in CA ERwin Data Modeler.

CHAPTER 19
Physical Data Models

Let's get Physical
Consider environment
Time to make it real

The highlighted row in Table 19.1 shows the focus of this chapter, which is the physical data model.

Table 19.1 The PDM is the Focus of this Chapter

	Relational	Dimensional
CDM	'One-pager' on how something works	'One-pager' on what is monitored
LDM	Detailed business solution on how something works	Detailed business solution on what is monitored
PDM	**Detailed technical solution on how something works**	**Detailed technical solution on what is monitored**

A physical data model (PDM) takes the business solution defined on a logical data model to the next level of a technical solution. That is, once you solve the problem independent of software and hardware concerns, then you can make adjustments for software and hardware. This chapter will explain the most popular techniques used to make adjustments to a business solution to create an efficient technical solution. We will explain the PDM and then discuss the techniques of denormalization, views, indexing, and partitioning. Although these techniques apply to both relational and dimensional models, their names may differ depending on which type of model they are applied to. We will explain these terminology differences in this chapter, as well. We will conclude with a discussion on how to adjust your physical data model to accommodate data value changes, and introduce the concept of a slowly changing dimension.

Physical Data Model Explanation

The physical data model (PDM) is the logical data model modified for a specific set of software or hardware. On the CDM, we might learn, for example, what the terms, business rules, and scope would be for a new order entry system. After understanding the need for an order entry system, we create an LDM representing the business solution. It contains all of the entities, data elements, and relationships needed to deliver the system. For example, the conceptual model will show that a **Customer** places many **Orders**. The LDM will capture all of the details about the **Customer** and **Order**, such as the customer's name, their address, and the order number. After understanding the business solution, we move on to the technical solution and build the PDM.

While building the PDM, we address the issues that have to do with specific hardware or software such as:

- How can we retrieve this information in fewer than 5 seconds?
- How can we make this information secure?
- What is the best way to manage storage space?

Note that in the early days of data modeling, when storage space was expensive and computers were slow, there were major modifications made to the PDM to make it work. In some cases, the PDM looked like it was for an entirely different application than the LDM. As technology improved, the PDM started looking more like the LDM. We should continue to see this trend as better hardware and software lead to fewer compromises on the PDM, resulting in a PDM that looks more like its LDM.

Denormalization

Denormalization is the process of selectively violating normalization rules and reintroducing redundancy into the model (and therefore, the database). This extra redundancy can reduce data retrieval time, which is the primary reason for denormalizing. We can also denormalize to create a more user-friendly model. For example, we might decide to denormalize company information into an entity containing employee information, because usually when employee information is retrieved, company information is also retrieved.

The faster retrieval and user-friendliness, however, come with the price of extra redundancy on the model, which could, in turn:

- **Cause update, delete, and insert performance to suffer.** When we denormalize, we often repeat the value of one or more data elements, which minimizes table joins and improves retrieval time. However, if we must change the value that we are repeating, we must change it everywhere it occurs, which generally has a negative performance impact.
- **Introduce data quality problems.** By having the same value appear multiple times, we substantially increase opportunities for data quality issues when those values change. Denormalizing also reduces the number of relationships on the model, thereby reducing the number of business rules enforced on our model.

- **Take up more space.** In a table with a small number of records, the extra storage space incurred by denormalization is usually not substantial. However, in tables with millions of rows, every character could require megabytes of additional space. Although space is cheap, one must consider the impact of additional storage – especially in hosted (e.g., "cloud") database environments.
- **Stunt growth of the application.** When we denormalize, it becomes harder to enhance structures to meet new requirements. Before we add data elements or relationships, we need to understand all the rules that were explicitly shown through relationships on the logical data model and are now hidden on the physical data model.

There are five denormalization techniques:

- Standard
- FUBES
- Repeating groups
- Repeating data elements
- Summarization

We will apply each of these five techniques to the contact logical data model from the previous chapter, repeated here in Figure 19.1.

Figure 19.1 Contact Logical Data Model

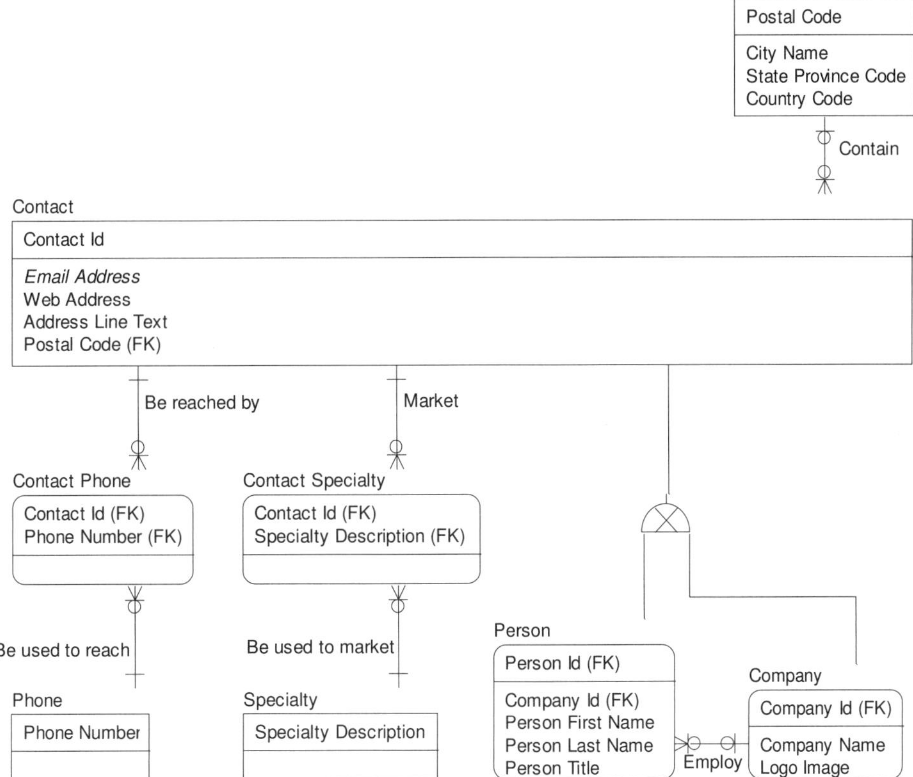

STANDARD

The standard method is the most common of the five denormalization techniques. The parent entity in the relationship disappears, and all the parent's data elements and relationships are moved down to the child entity. You'll recall that the child entity is on the many side of the relationship and contains a foreign key back to the parent entity, which appears on the one side of the relationship.

Although the standard technique is traditionally applied to a one-to-many relationship, we can illustrate the standard technique using the subtyping structure from Figure 19.1. The subtyping structure must be resolved on the physical data model, as there is no subtyping relationship defined in a relational database. There are three ways of resolving the subtyping symbol on the physical data model:

- Identity
- Rolling down
- Rolling up

Identity is the closest to subtyping, itself, because the subtyping symbol is replaced with a one-to-one relationship for each supertype/subtype combination. The main advantage of identity is that all of the business rules at the supertype level and at the subtype level remain as in the logical. That is, we can continue to enforce relationships at the supertype or subtype levels, as well as enforce that certain data elements be required at the supertype or subtype levels. The main disadvantage of identity is that it can take more time to retrieve data, as it requires navigating multiple tables to access both the supertype and subtype information. Identity is not a form of denormalization, but it is shown in Figure 19.2 for completeness.

Figure 19.2 Identity Method of Resolving Subtyping

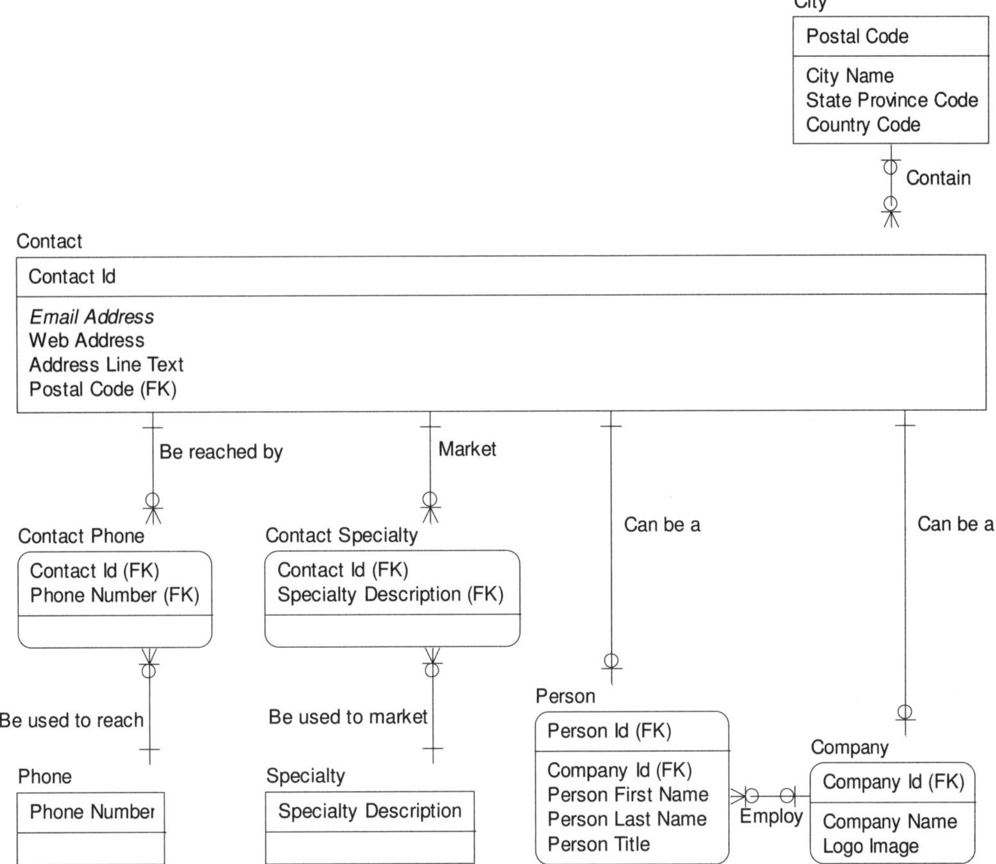

In this example, we can continue to enforce certain rules at the supertype level, such as a **Contact** can have only one **City** and must have one **Email Address**. We can also enforce rules at the subtype level, such as a **Person** can work for one **Company**, and **Person Last Name** is a required data element and must always contain a value.

Rolling down is when the supertype is 'rolled down' into each subtype, moving all of the data elements and relationships from the supertype into each subtype, then removing the supertype from the data model. Rolling down can produce a more user-friendly structure than identity or rolling up, because subtypes are often more concrete concepts than supertypes, making it easier for the users of the data model to relate to the subtypes. For example, users of our contact model would probably feel more comfortable with the concepts of **Person** and **Company**, rather than the concept of **Contact**. However, we are repeating relationships and data elements, which could reduce any user-friendliness gained from removing the supertype. In addition, the rolling down technique enforces only those rules present in the subtypes. This could lead to a less flexible data model, as we can no longer easily accommodate new subtypes without modifying the data model. See Figure 19.3 for what rolling down would look like in our Contact example.

Figure 19.3 Rolling Down Method of Resolving Subtyping

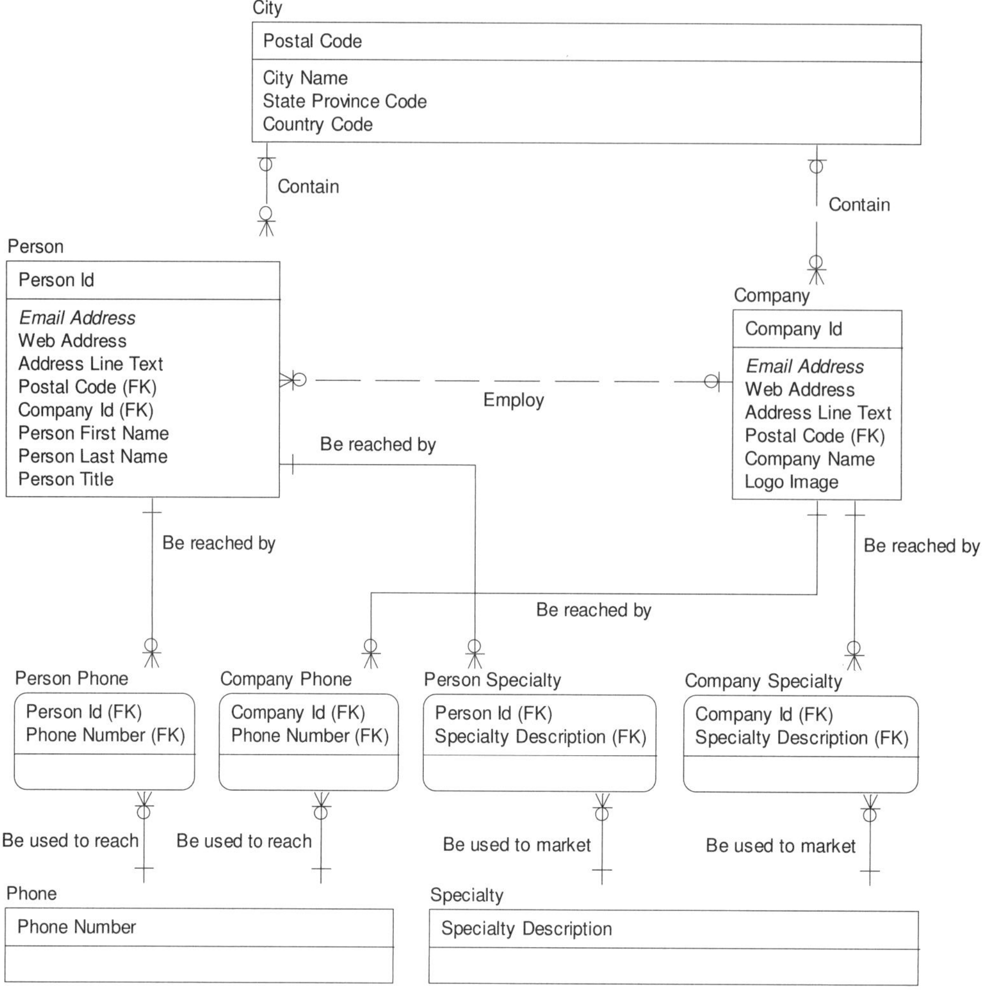

In the rolling down technique, we no longer have the **Contact** concept and everything at the supertype level was copied down into each subtype. Notice that although we have the user friendly concepts of **Person** and **Company**, we also have the redundancy of extra relationships to **Phone**, **Specialty**, and **City**, as well as repeating **Email Address**, **Web Address**, and address information for each subtype.

Rolling up is when each subtype is 'rolled up' into the supertype, moving the data elements and relationships from each subtype up into the supertype. The subtypes disappear and all data elements and relationships only exist at the supertype level. Rolling up adds flexibility to the data model because new types of the supertype can be added, often with no model changes. However, rolling up can also produce a more obscure model, as the audience for the model may not relate to the supertype as well as they would to the subtypes. In addition, we can only enforce business rules at the supertype level, not the subtype level. See Figure 19.4 for rolling up in our contact example.

Figure 19.4 Rolling Up Method of Resolving Subtyping

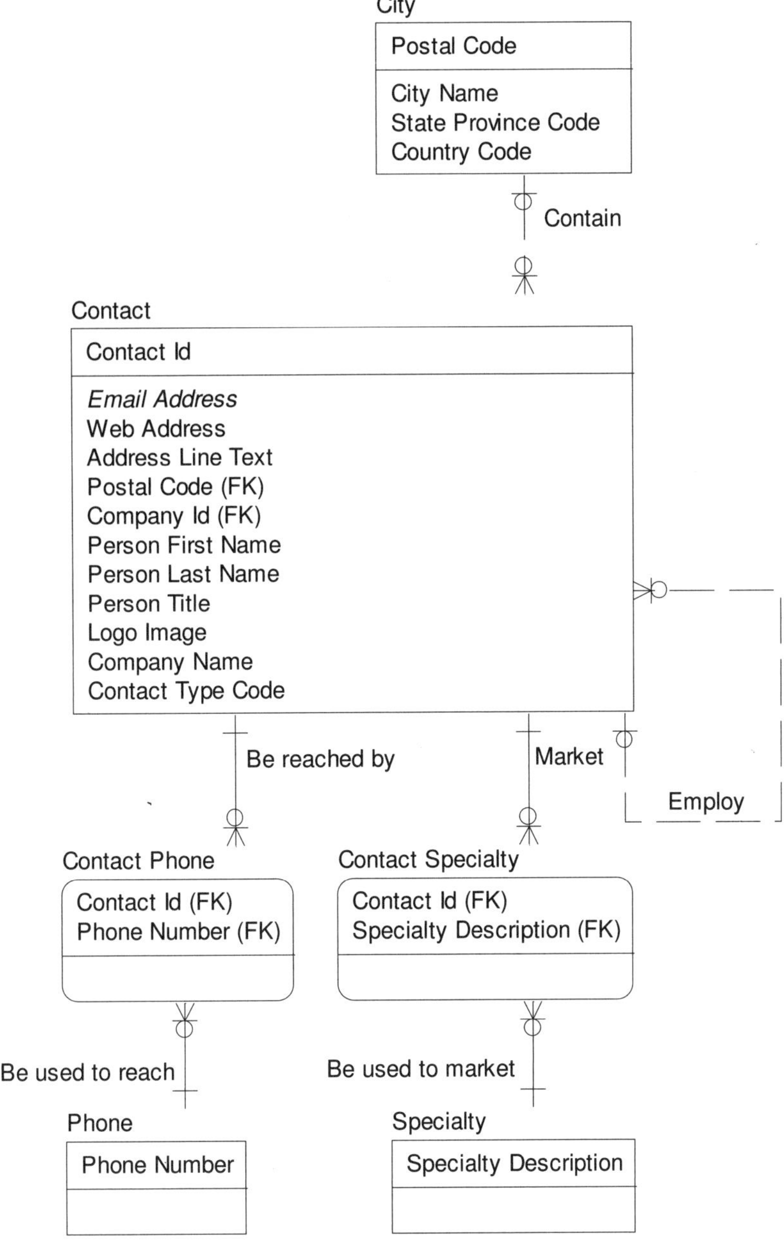

When we roll up, we need a way to distinguish the original subtypes from each other. Therefore, we add a data element that distinguishes people from companies, in this case **Contact Type Code**. Two of the values of **Contact Type Code** would represent **Person** and **Company**.

Using rolling up, we still retain the business rules for **Contact**, yet lose the rules that were only enforced for **Person** or **Company**. For example, we cannot make **Company Name** a mandatory data element in **Contact** because a **Person** does not have a **Company Name** and may not be assigned to a **Company**.

In addition to choosing denormalization because of the need for faster retrieval time or for more user friendly structures, the standard way of denormalizing can be chosen in the following situations:

- **When you need to maintain the flexibility of the normalized model.** Folding the data elements and relationships together using the standard approach still allows one-to-one and one-to-many relationships to exist. In Figure 19.4 for example, we did not lose the flexibility that a **Contact** can be a **Person** or Company (it is just harder to see and enforce).
- **When you want to reduce development time and complexity.** Often there is a direct relationship to the number of tables and relationships on a model, and the amount of effort to develop the application. A developer will need to write code that jumps from one table to another to collect certain data elements, and this can take time and add complexity. Denormalizing into fewer tables using the standard method means the data elements and relationships from different entities now exist in the same entity. In Figure 19.4 for example, if the developer needs to retrieve both the person and company name, they can easily do so from the same entity **Contact**.

FUBES

FUBES (fold up but easily separate) is an acronym I made up for a technique that uses the standard method of denormalizing while also allowing access to just the data elements from the parent side of a one-to-many relationship. There is an additional data element that contains a level code and additional instances for each of the parents. In Figure 19.5 for example, we have a subset of the logical data model for **Calendar**.

Figure 19.5 Subset of the Calendar Logical Data Model

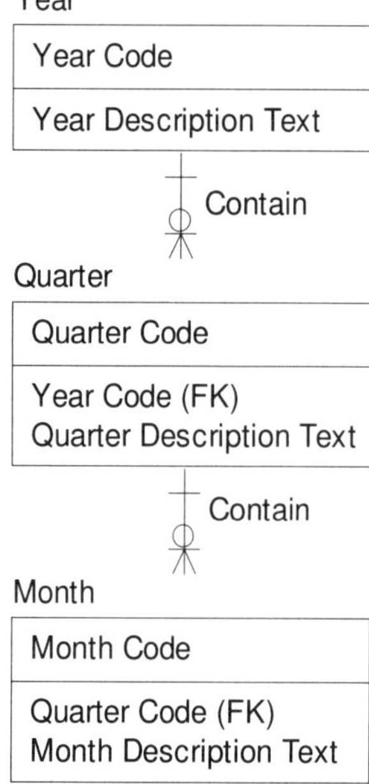

Table 19.2 contains sample values for each of these entities.

Table 19.2 Sample values for Figure 19.5

Year

Year Code	Year Description Text
2007	Two Thousand Seven
2008	Two Thousand Eight
2009	Two Thousand Nine

Quarter

Quarter Code	Year Code	Quarter Description Text
Q12009	2009	First Quarter Two Thousand Nine
Q22009	2009	Second Quarter Two Thousand Nine
Q32009	2009	Third Quarter Two Thousand Nine

Month

Month Code	Quarter Code	Month Description Text
Jan2009	Q12009	January Two Thousand Nine
Feb2009	Q12009	February Two Thousand Nine
Mar2009	Q12009	March Two Thousand Nine

If we decide to denormalize these three entities using the FUBES option, we would have the one entity in Figure 19.6.

Figure 19.6 FUBES being applied to Calendar

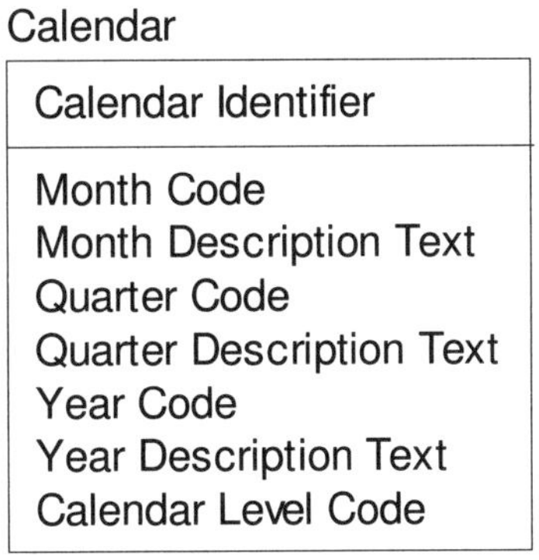

Table 19.3 contains sample values for this table.

Table 19.3 Sample values for Figure 10.6

Cal Id	Mo Code	Mo Desc	Qtr Code	Qtr Desc	Yr Cd	Yr Desc	Level Cd
1					2007	Two Thousand Seven	Year
2					2008	Two Thousand Eight	Year
3					2009	Two Thousand Nine	Year
4			Q12009	First Quarter Two Thousand Nine	2009	Two Thousand Nine	Quarter
5			Q22009	Second Quarter Two Thousand Nine	2009	Two Thousand Nine	Quarter
6			Q32009	Third Quarter Two Thousand Nine	2009	Two Thousand Nine	Quarter
7	Jan2009	January Two Thousand Nine	Q12009	First Quarter Two Thousand Nine	2009	Two Thousand Nine	Month
8	Feb2009	February Two Thousand Nine	Q12009	First Quarter Two Thousand Nine	2009	Two Thousand Nine	Month
9	Mar2009	March Two Thousand Nine	Q12009	First Quarter Two Thousand Nine	2009	Two Thousand Nine	Month

You may be wondering what value FUBES provides. After all, we are adding a substantial amount of redundancy when using FUBES, because we have all of the redundancy of the standard option plus we are repeating each parent for the child, and repeating all of the parents for that parent. That is, repeating each quarter in our example, plus repeating year for each quarter.

FUBES should be chosen when there is value in denormalizing, but there is a still a need to access parent instances. Having an instance for each parent allows us to achieve better report performance, as we can directly tie to parent levels without having to roll up from the child. We can store sales at a year level, for example, and save the time of summarizing monthly level sales up into a year level. The value is that results can be retrieved extremely fast if we are doing reporting at the parent levels, in this example at the quarter and year level. For example, see Figure 19.7.

Figure 19.7 Sales reporting with the Calendar FUBES structure

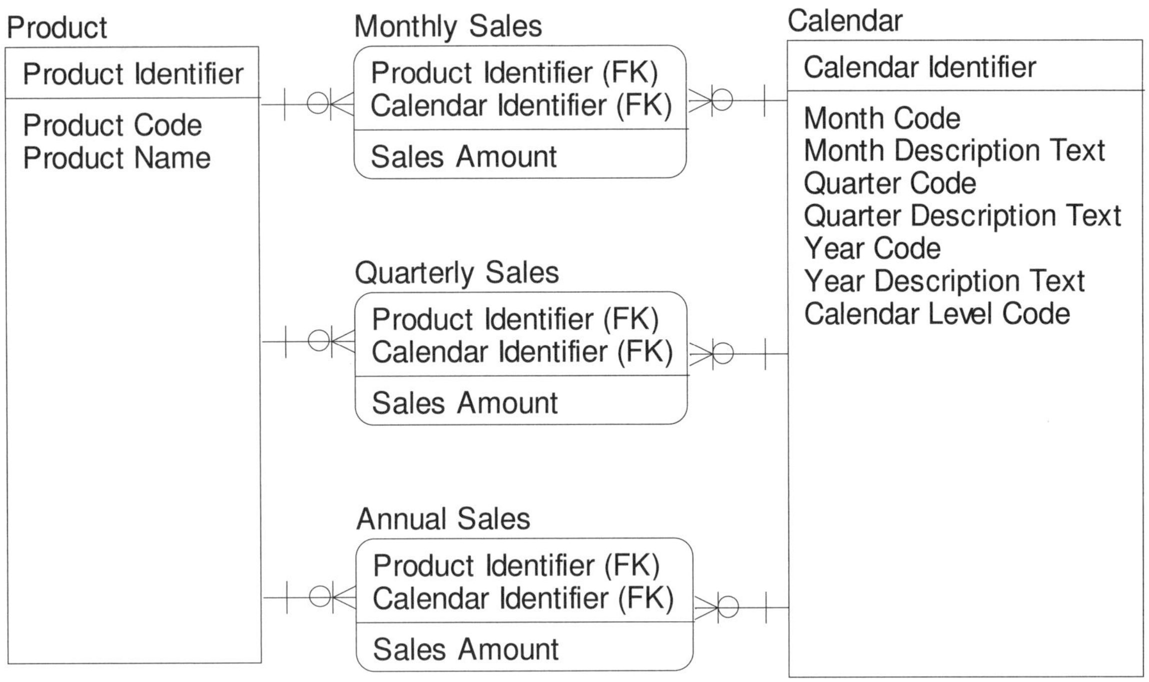

In Figure 19.7 we are summing and loading sales data at the month, quarter, and year levels. If there is a need to retrieve annual sales for 2008, we can quickly find this number because we are storing the **Sales Amount** for 2008 in **Annual Sales**, which references the **Calendar** instance where **Calendar Level Code** equals 'Year' and **Year Code** equals '2008'.

REPEATING GROUPS

In the repeating-groups technique, the same data element or group of data elements is repeated two or more times in the same entity. Also known as an *array*, a repeating group requires making the number of times something can occur static. Recall that in 1NF we removed repeating groups. Well, here it is, being reintroduced again. An example of a repeating group appears in Figure 19.8.

Figure 19.8 Repeating Groups in our Contact Example

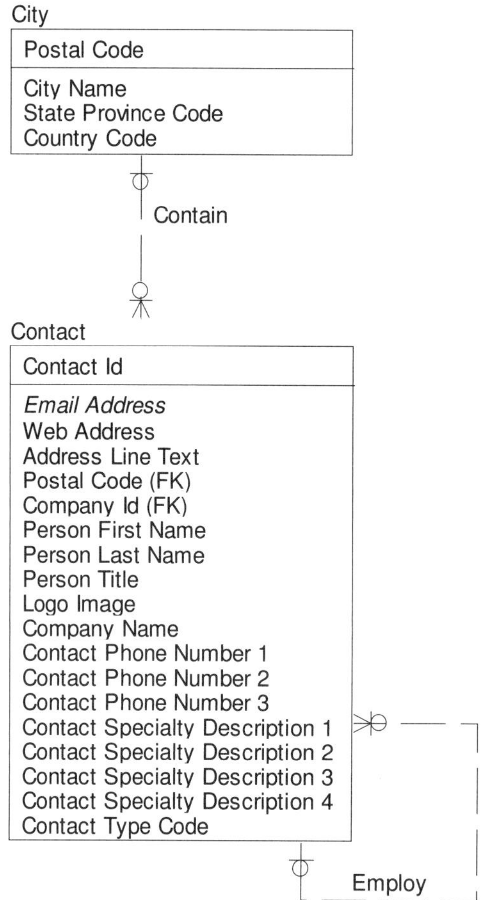

In this example, we can have up to three phone numbers for a **Contact** and up to four specialties. In addition to choosing denormalization because of the need for faster retrieval time or for more user friendly structures, repeating groups may be chosen in the following situations:

- **When it makes more sense to keep the parent entity instead of the child entity.** When the parent entity is going to be used more frequently than the child entity, or if there are rules and data elements to preserve in the parent entity format, it makes more sense to keep the parent entity. For example, in Figure 19.8, if **Contact** is going to be accessed frequently, and when **Contact** is accessed, **Phone Number** and **Specialty Description** are also occasionally accessed.
- **When an entity instance will never exceed the fixed number of data elements added.** In Figure 19.8, we are only allowing up to three phone numbers for a contact, for example. If we have four phone numbers for Bob the **Contact**, how would we handle this? Right now, we would have to pick which three of them to store.

- **When you need a spreadsheet.** A common use is to represent a report that needs to be displayed in a spreadsheet format. For example, if a user is expecting to see a sales report in which sales is reported by month for the last 12 months, an example of a repeating group containing this information is shown in Figure 19.9. At the end of a given month, the oldest value is removed and a new value is added. This is called a *rolling 12 months*. Faster performance and a more user-friendly structure lead us to add repeating groups and purposely violate 1NF, in this example.

Figure 19.9 Sales Summary Report Entity with Repeating Group

Sales Summary Report
Product Identifier Month Code Year Code
Current Month - 1 Total Sales Amount Current Month - 2 Total Sales Amount Current Month - 3 Total Sales Amount Current Month - 4 Total Sales Amount Current Month - 5 Total Sales Amount Current Month - 6 Total Sales Amount Current Month - 7 Total Sales Amount Current Month - 8 Total Sales Amount Current Month - 9 Total Sales Amount Current Month - 10 Total Sales Amount Current Month - 11 Total Sales Amount Current Month - 12 Total Sales Amount

REPEATING DATA ELEMENTS

Repeating data elements is a technique in which you copy one or more data elements from one entity into one or more other entities. It is done primarily for performance because by repeating data elements across entities, we can reduce the amount of time it takes to return results. If we copy **Customer Last Name** from the **Customer** entity to the **Order** entity, for example, we avoid navigating back to **Customer** whenever just **Customer Last Name** is needed for display with order information.

Repeating data elements differs from repeating groups because the repeating groups technique replaces one or more entities and relationships, while the repeating data elements technique retains the existing entities and relationships and just copies over the data elements that are needed. For example, to apply the repeating groups technique to **Customer** and **Order**, we'd need to determine the maximum number of orders a customer can place, then remove the **Order** entity and its relationship to **Customer** and repeat three or four or however many times all of the order data elements within **Customer**. The repeating data elements technique would just involve copying over the data elements we need and keeping everything else intact.

See Figure 19.10 for an example of this technique using our contact example. In this example, there was a need to view the country along with contact information. Therefore only the **Country Code** data element needed to be copied to **Contact** and the **City** entity and its relationship remains intact.

Figure 19.10 Repeating data Elements in our Contact Example

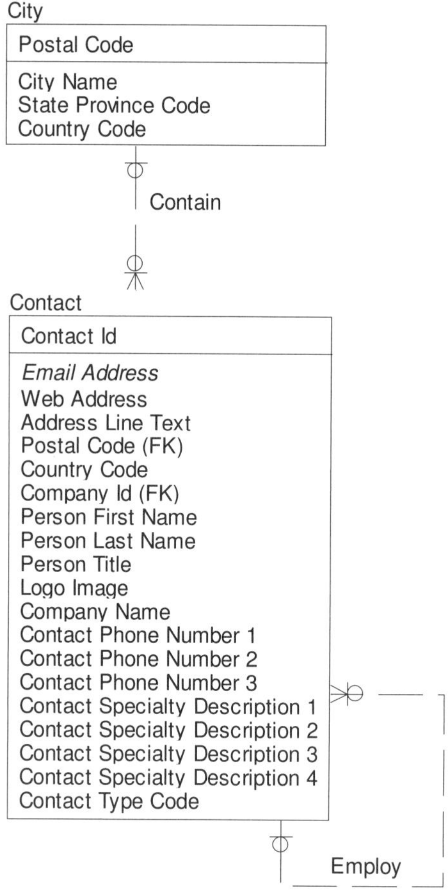

In addition to choosing denormalization because of the need for faster retrieval time or for more user friendly structures, repeating data elements can be chosen in the following situations:

- **When the repeated data element or elements are accessed often and experience little or no changes over time.** If, for example, **Country Code** changed frequently, we would be required to update this value on **City** and for each of the contacts related to **City**. This takes time to update and could introduce data quality issues if not all updates were performed correctly or completely.
- **When the standard denormalization option is preferred but space is an issue.** There might be too huge an impact on storage space if the entire parent entity was folded up into the child and repeated for each child value. Therefore,

only repeat those parent data elements that will be used frequently with the child.

- **When there is a need to enforce the business rules from the LDM.** With the repeating data elements technique, the relationships still remain intact. Therefore, the business rules from the logical data model can be enforced on the physical data model. In Figure 19.10 for example, we can still enforce that a **Contact** live in a valid **City**.

SUMMARIZATION

Summarization is when tables are created with less detail than what is available in the business. **Monthly Sales**, **Quarterly Sales**, and **Annual Sales** from Figure 19.7 are all summary tables derived from the actual order transactions.

In addition to choosing denormalization because of the need for faster retrieval time or for more user friendly structures, summarization can be chosen when there is a need to report on higher levels of granularity than what is captured on the logical data model. **Annual Sales** for example, provides high level summary data for the user, and therefore the user (or reporting tool) does not have to spend time figuring out how to produce annual sales from detailed tables. The response time is much quicker because time does not need to be spent summarizing data when it is requested by a user; it is already at the needed summarization level, ready to be queried.

Views

A view is a virtual table. It is a dynamic "view" or window into one or more tables (or other views) where the actual data is stored. A view is defined by a query that specifies how to collate data from its underlying tables to form an object that looks and acts like a table but doesn't physically contain data. A query is a request that a user (or reporting tool) makes of the database, such as "Bring me back all **Customer Ids** where the **Customer** is 90 days or more behind in their bill payments." The difference between a query and a view, however, is that the instructions in a view are already prepared for the user (or reporting tool) and stored in the database as the definition of the view, whereas a query is not stored in the database and may need to be written each time a question is asked.

Returning to our contact example, let's assume the users continuously ask the question "Who are the people that live in New Jersey?" We can answer this question in a view. Figure 19.11 contains the model from Figure 19.10 with the addition of a view to answer this question.

Figure 19.11 View Added to Answer Business Question

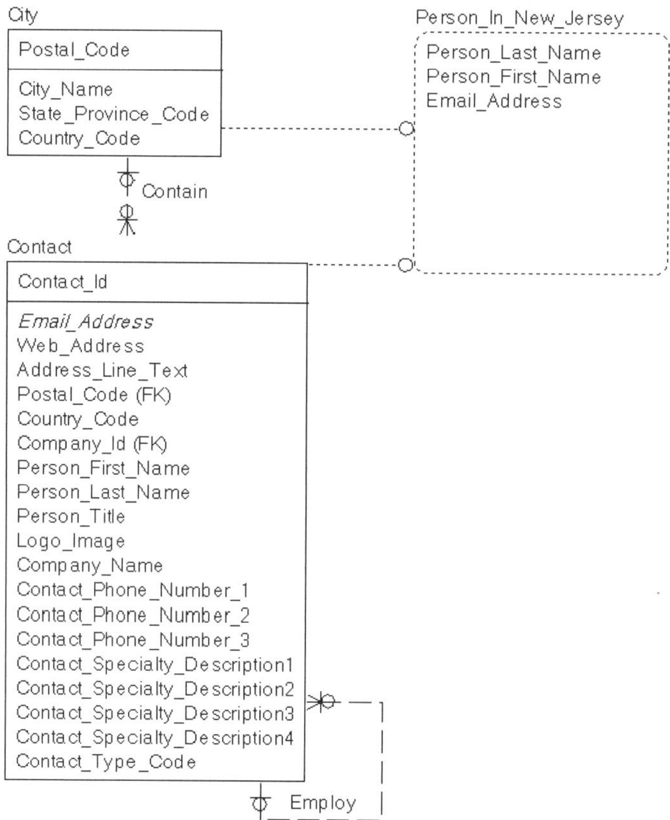

A view is shown as a rounded box with a dotted-line border. In this model, it is called **Person_In_New_Jersey**[17]. This view needs to bring together information from the entity **City** and from the entity **Contact** to answer the business question. The instructions to answer this business question are written in a query language a database can understand, usually in the language SQL (pronounced 'sequel'). Figure 19.12 contains the SQL language to answer this business question.

Figure 19.12 SQL language to answer question "Who are my Contacts that live in New Jersey?"

```
SELECT Contact.Person_Last_Name, Contact.Person_First_Name,
Contact.Email_Address

FROM City, Contact

WHERE (City.Postal_Code=Contact.Postal_Code)

AND (City.State_Province_Code='NJ')

AND (Contact.Contact_Type_Code = 'Prsn');
```

[17] Note: It is common to create a special naming convention to differentiate views from other objects, for example, appending a _VIEW suffix to the end of the name or adding a V_ prefix to the beginning of the name.

SQL is powerful for the same reason that data modeling is powerful: with a handful of symbols, one can communicate a lot. In English, this SQL statement is saying "Give me the last name, first name, and email address of the **Contact(s)** whose postal code matches a postal code in the **City** table that has a state code of 'NJ' and who is a person (and not a company)".

Views are a popular choice for assisting with security and user-friendliness. If there are sensitive data elements within a database table that only certain people in the company have access to, then views are a great way to hide these sensitive data elements from the common user. Views can also take some of the complexities out of joining tables for the user or reporting tool.

In fact, we can use views in almost all situations where we are using denormalization. At times, views can offer all of the benefits of denormalization *without the drawbacks associated with data redundancy and loss of referential integrity*. A view can provide user-friendly structures over a normalized structure, thereby preserving flexibility and referential integrity. A view will keep the underlying normalized model intact, and at the same time present a denormalized or flattened view of the world to the business.

Indexing

An index is a pointer to something that needs to be retrieved. An analogy often used is the card catalog, which in the library, points you to the book you need. The card catalog will point you to the place where the actual book is on the shelf, a process that is much quicker than looking through each book in the library until you find the one you need. Indexing works the same way with data. The index points directly to the place on the disk where the data is stored, thus reducing retrieval time. Indexes work best on data elements whose values are requested frequently but rarely updated.

Primary keys, foreign keys, and alternate keys are automatically indexed just because they are keys. A non-unique index, also known as a secondary key, is when an index based on one or more non-key data elements is added to improve retrieval performance. Where to add non-unique indexes depends on the types of queries being performed against the table.

For example, we may want to add indexes to the **Contact** table from Figure 19.11 to increase the retrieval performance of the **Person_In_New_Jersey** view query. In the model shown in Figure 19.13, you'll see we added several alternate keys. First, we added an alternate key (AK) on the **Email_Address** column. In addition, we created a non-unique index on **Person_Last_Name** (IE1.1) and **Person_First_Name** (IE.1.2), to assist with the retrieval performance of these instances. For more information on alternate keys, refer to Chapter 7.

Figure 19.13 Adding Indexes to Contact Table to Improve View Query Performance

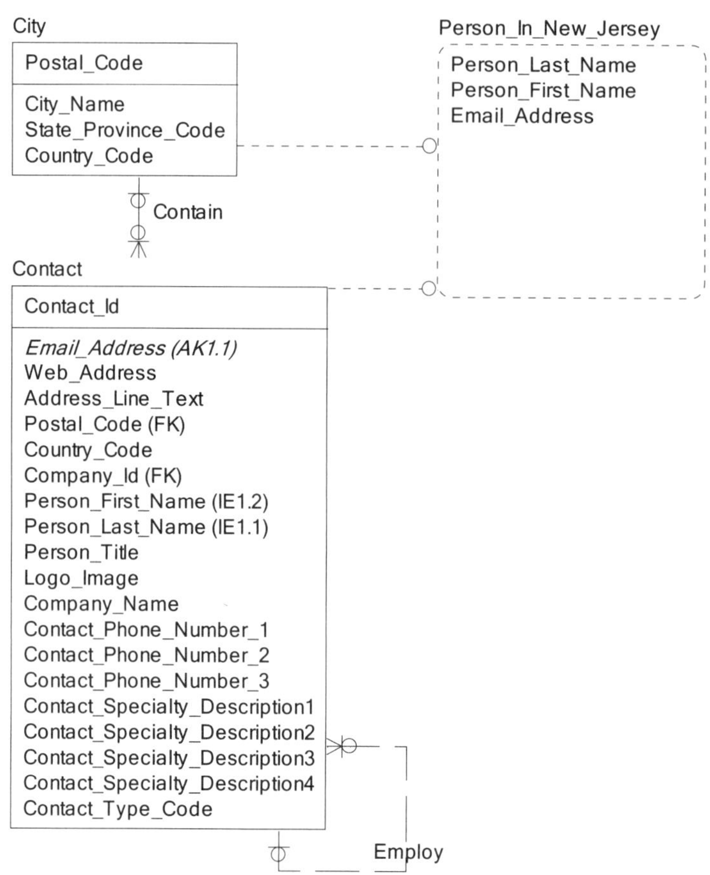

Partitioning

In general, a partition is a structure that divides or separates. Specific to the physical design, partitioning is used to break a table into rows, columns or both. An attribute or value of an attribute drives how the records in a table are divided among the partitions. There are two types of partitioning - vertical and horizontal. To understand the difference between these two types, visualize a physical entity in a spreadsheet format where the data elements are the columns in the spreadsheet and the entity instances are the rows. Vertical means up and down. So vertical partitioning means separating the columns (the data elements) into separate tables. Horizontal means side to side. So horizontal partitioning means separating rows (the entity instances) into separate tables.

An example of horizontal partitioning appears in Figure 19.14. This is our data model from Figure 19.10, modified for horizontal partitioning. In this example, we are horizontally partitioning by **Contact Last Name**. If a contact's last name starts with a letter from 'A' up to and including 'H', then the contact would appear as an instance of the entity **Contact A Through H**. If a contact's last name starts with a letter from 'I' up to and including 'Z', then the contact would appear as an instance of the entity **Contact I Through Z**.

Figure 19.14 Horizontal Partitioning in our Contact Example

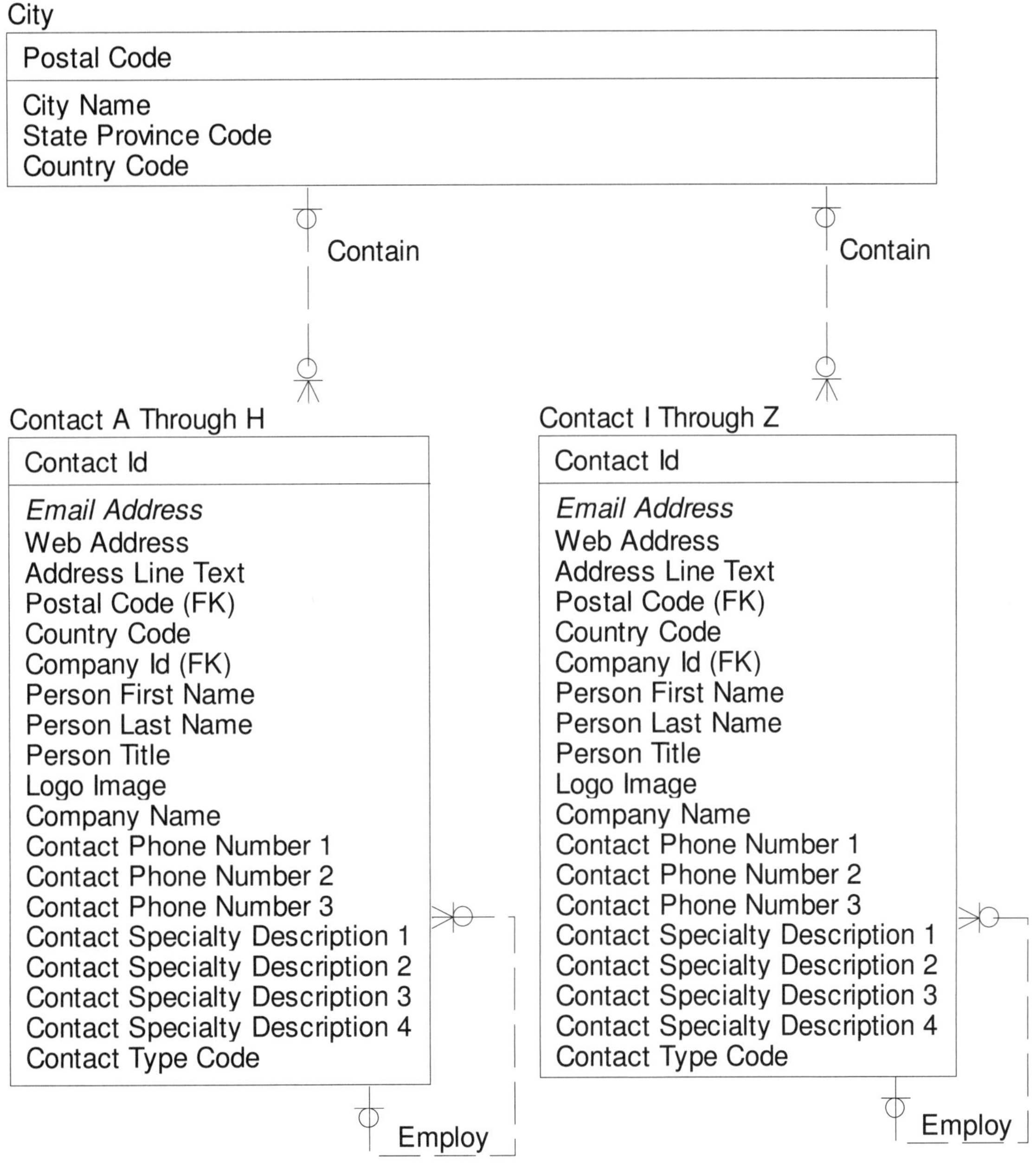

An example of vertical partitioning appears in Figure 19.15. Also, based on the example from Figure 19.10, we have vertically partitioned the phone numbers into a separate table and the specialties into a separate table. This might have been done for space or user access reasons.

Figure 19.15 Vertical Partitioning in our Contact Example

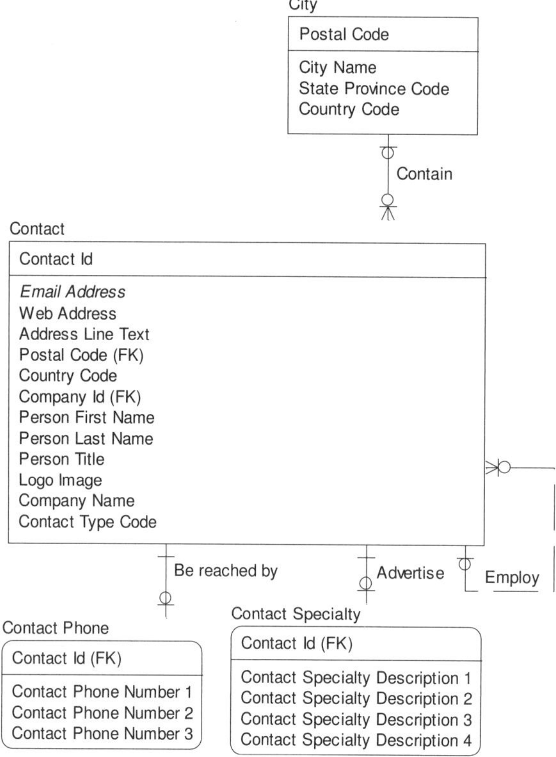

Creating a Physical Data Model

Let's apply what we've learned about physical data modeling to our Baker Cakes example. We now have a fairly good understanding of the business rules and requirements for the organization's data, and can begin to consider the physical design and implementation. Recall our logical data model for Baker Cakes that we created in Chapter 18, shown in Figure 19.16.

Figure 19.16 Relational Logical Data Model for Baker Cakes

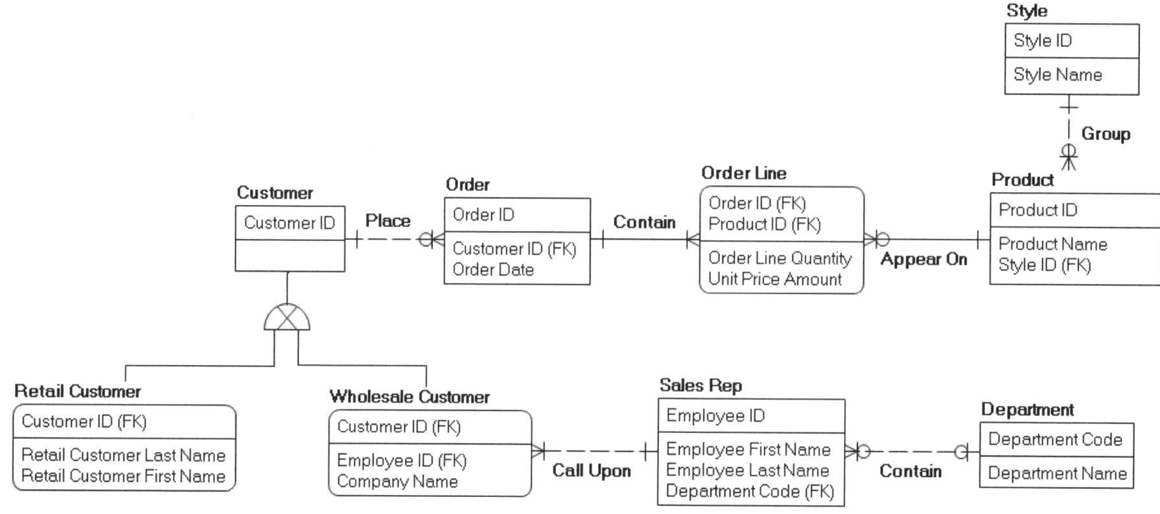

From this 'top down' conceptual and subsequent logical model design, we can create our first cut physical data model. Since we are using a combined logical/physical data model in our example, a physical data model was automatically created for us as we generated the logical model. Switch to the physical model, as shown in Figure 19.17. (If you need help with this, refer to Chapter 3). You'll notice that it looks very similar to our logical model, with the exception of the naming conventions, for example. As we discussed earlier, unless we modify the physical model for performance or query reasons, the physical model could remain normalized, similar to the logical model.

Figure 19.17 Relational Physical Data Model for Baker Cakes

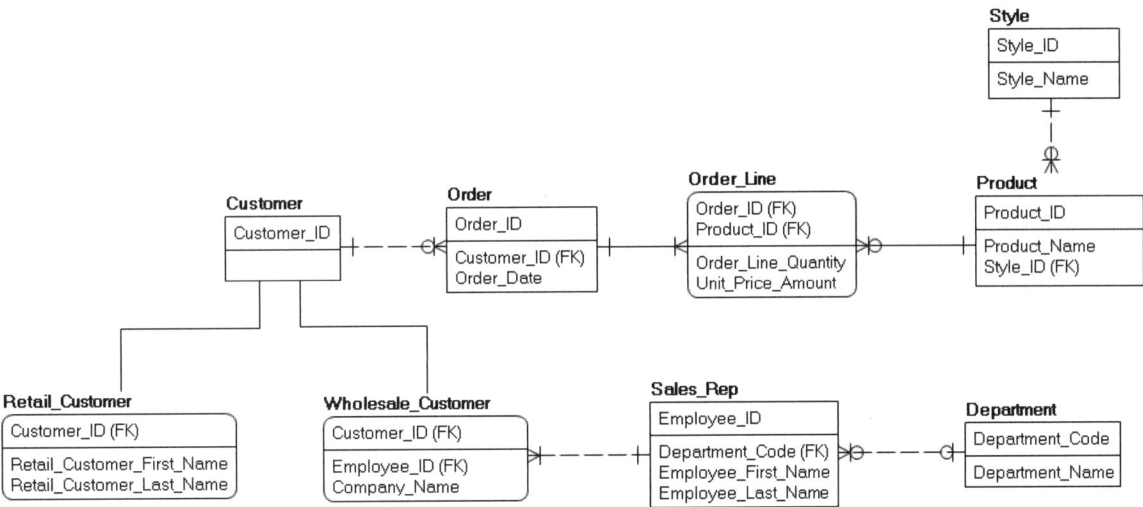

But before we move too far along with the 'top down' approach, we also need to consider the 'bottom up' approach-- that is, considering the physical database implementations that already exist. From existing implementations, we can get a sense of the technical requirements or modifications that were made for performance, queries, etc., and perhaps even discover some business requirements we may have missed.

As you recall, the intern who previously worked for Baker Cakes had created an Access database to store customer and order information. This database is a valuable source of information, and we'll want to review it as part of our analysis. The easiest way to generate a physical data model for this system is through a process called reverse engineering. Reverse engineering reviews the database structures and data dictionary information from source databases, and generates a physical data model from this information. Let's reverse engineer the Access database used by Baker Cakes.

REVERSE ENGINEER

To begin, select **Actions|Reverse Engineer** from the **Main Menu**. The **Reverse Engineer** wizard appears, as shown in Figure 19.18, with the **Select Template** panel shown, which allows you to indicate which model template you'd like to use, as well as the target database and type of model. We'll create a **Physical** only model with a target database of **ODBC/Generic 3.0**, and we'll use the default template.

Figure 19.18 Identifying Model Template Information in the Reverse Engineer Wizard

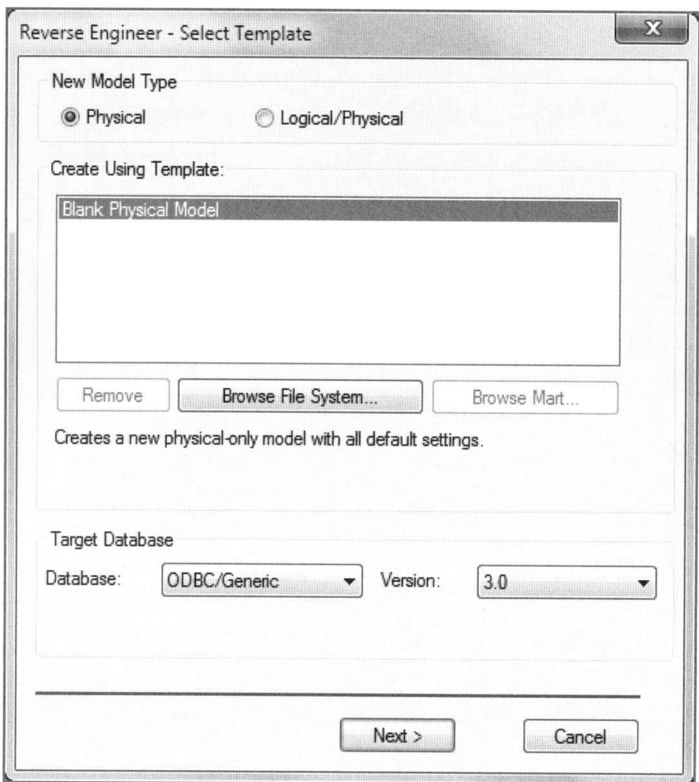

Select **Next** to move to the **Set Options** panel, as shown in Figure 19.19. This panel allows you to define your data source, and provide parameters for the reverse engineering process, such as which objects to include, how primary keys should be handled, and how and whether model object names should be manipulated.

Figure 19.19 Setting Options in the Reverse Engineer Wizard

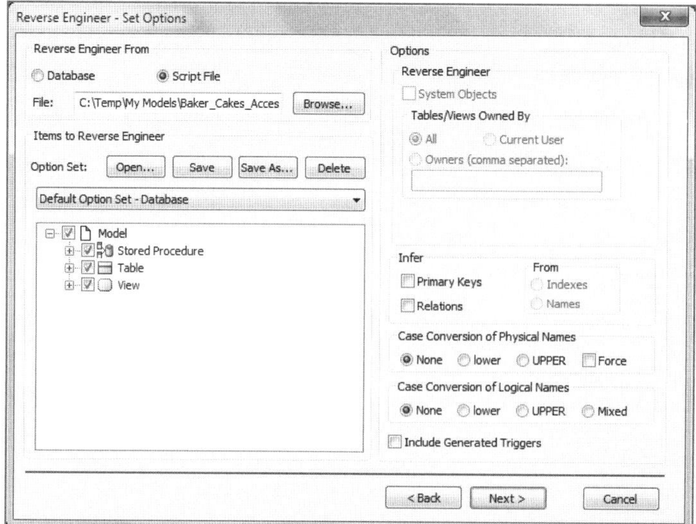

The **Reverse Engineer From** box allows you to select your source database, either by accessing the database directly, or by using a script file. In our case, we do not have access to the database itself, so we asked the database administrator to generate a DDL script for us to use. This script, named `Baker_Cakes_Access.ddl` can be downloaded from www.erwin.com/datamodelingmadesimple so that you can try this example on your own. In the **Reverse Engineer From** box, select the **Script File** radio button, and enter the location of the `Baker_Cakes_Access.ddl` file in the **File** text box, as shown above in Figure 19.19.

By expanding the object tree in the **Items to Reverse Engineer** box, shown in Figure 19.20, you can define which specific objects you'd like to include in your physical model. For example, we may only want to include tables and columns, but not stored procedures or views. Once you've defined a set of objects, you can save these settings as an Option Set, which can be reused for future reverse engineering procedures. For example, you could define one Option Set that includes only tables and columns, another that just includes views and stored procedures, and another that includes all objects in the database. In our example, we'll use the **Default Option Set**, which includes all objects.

Figure 19.20 Defining Items to Reverse Engineer

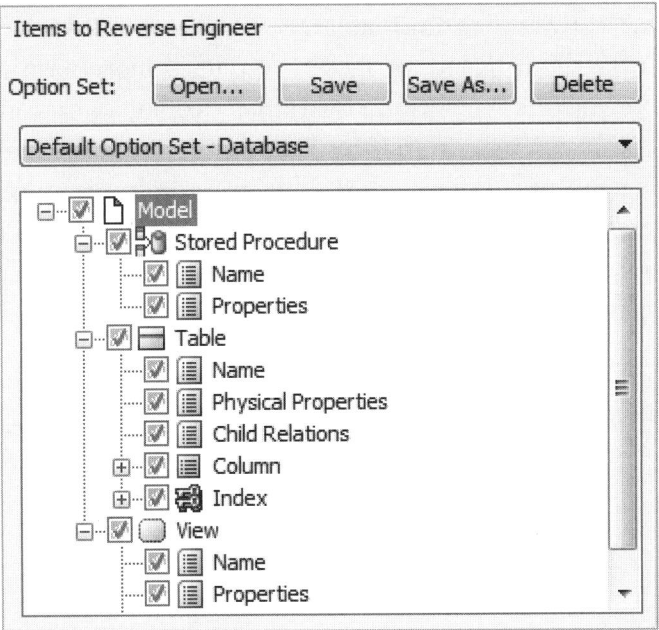

In the **Reverse Engineer** box, shown in Figure 19.21, you're able to further clarify which objects to include. These objects require a connection to the database to be accessed, so are grayed out in our example, since we're using a DDL script file. The **System Objects** checkbox specifies whether to include database system objects, which are tables created by the DBMS manufacturer for their own storage. In general, if you are focusing on user-created tables that include data related to the organization, you won't select this box. The **Tables/Views Owned By** box allows you to filter database objects by owner. Most DBMS systems have the concept of database object ownership as part of their security, and you can choose, for example, tables that are owned by a particular user in the organization. Again, since we are using a script file, and not accessing the database directly, this box is grayed-out in our example.

Figure 19.21 Choosing to Include System Objects, and Object by Owner/User

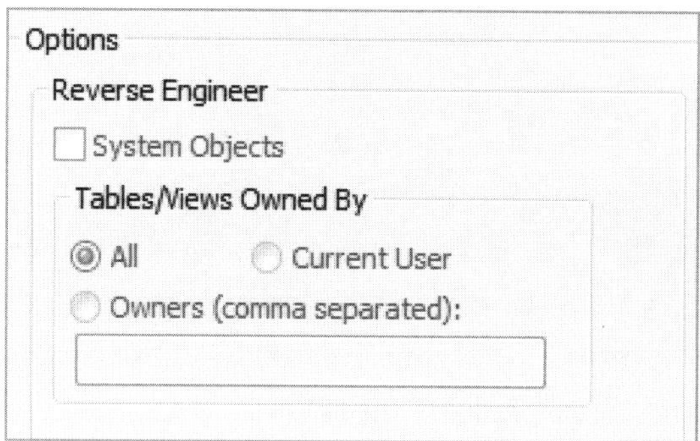

The next selection is whether to have CA ERwin Data Modeler infer relationships or primary keys, as shown in Figure 19.22. In general, if the target database or DDL script file supports primary key and foreign key declarations, you do not need to use this option. But, in some cases, either the DBMS does not support these options, or they were not implemented by the administrator who created the database. In these instances, you can infer them based on indexes and/or object naming. If you choose to **Infer Primary Keys**, primary key columns for tables are based on indexes defined in the database, if they exist. If you choose to **Infer Relations**, you have the option of inferring them from either the defined table indexes, or from column names. In this case, a relationship is inferred between two tables if all of the primary key columns of the parent are in the child table. In our example, we will not have CA ERwin Data Modeler infer primary keys or indexes, and will instead rely on the information as defined by the database creator.

Figure 19.22 Inferring Primary Keys and Relations in Reverse Engineering

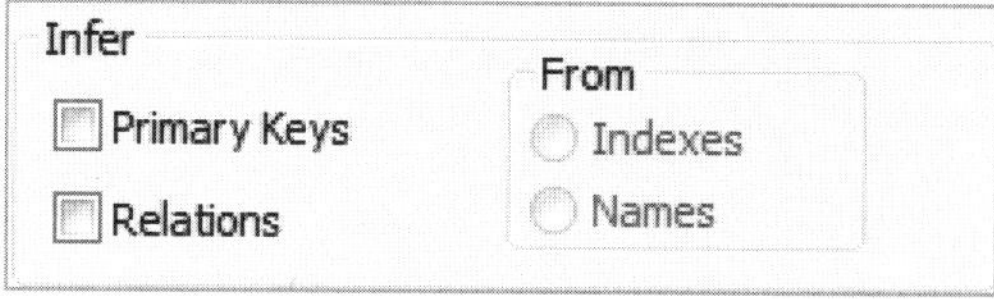

The next decision we'll need to make is how to handle case conversion for our object names, shown in Figure 19.23. For example, we can enforce that all objects are in lowercase or uppercase. If we are using a combined logical/physical model in our reverse engineer, we can also specify the default case handling for logical objects as well. If **Force** is selected, the physical names are treated as an override, so that they are not affected by subsequent name changes in the logical model. (This won't apply in our example, since we're using a logical only model.) We'd like to use the case convention defined by the database creator, so we'll select **None**.

Figure 19.23 Handling Case Conversion of Logical and Physical Names

Case Conversion of Physical Names

(◉) None ( ) lower ( ) UPPER [ ] Force

Case Conversion of Logical Names

(◉) None ( ) lower ( ) UPPER ( ) Mixed

The last option is the **Include Generated Triggers** checkbox. This option specifies whether or not CA ERwin Data Modeler-generated triggers are loaded during the reverse engineer process. CA ERwin Data Modeler allows you to implement referential integrity (RI) triggers that maintain the integrity between two related tables. For example, if a row in a parent table is inserted, updated, or deleted, an RI trigger defines how to handle rows in other tables that have a foreign key value that matches the primary key in the row being added, updated, or deleted. Since our database was not created by CA ERwin Data Modeler, we will not select this option.

Select the **Next** button, and you'll see the physical data model created by the reverse engineering process, as shown in Figure 19.24. Wow! You'll see that this is certainly a small model, with only a single table in it! In looking at the design, it appears as if the intern used the database much like a spreadsheet, basically creating a single table with attributes that represent the typical columns that would appear in a spreadsheet. From what we've learned about normalization in previous chapters, we know that this is not an ideal way to build a database.

Figure 19.24 Physical Model Reverse Engineered from Access Database

Customer
Name
Loyalty_Code Order_No Date Product Qty Unit_Price

In fact, when we ask the database administrator to run a query on this table to see some sample data, shown in Table 19.4, we see some potential redundancy and data quality errors right away. For example, are Mary Smith and M Smith the same customer?

Table 19.4 Sample Data from Customer Access Database

Name	Loyalty_Code	Order_No	Date	Product	Qty	Unit_Price
Mary Smith	BC857487	128	10/12/2011	Lemon Lovers Layer Cake	2	$19.95
M Smith		129	10/12/2011	Chocoholics Sponge Cake	1	$15.95
Joe McCabe	DB858635	130	10/12/2011	Strawberry Breeze Layer Cake	5	$19.95
Lisa Zhou	AB857416	131	10/15/2011	Rad Raspberry Pound Cake	1	$17.95

But let's not ignore this database entirely—there may be key information in it that we can learn from. Are there columns/attributes we've missed? Did the database creator build the database to match a particular query or report that is needed by the business?

One column that jumps out at us is the **Loyalty_Code** column, which we have not included in our original design. We check with Mr. Baker, and he tells us that all customers, both retail and wholesale, can have a customer loyalty number, which is an eight character alphanumeric code, if they choose to sign up for the loyalty program. We'll want to add this column to our physical model, and make sure a logical attribute exists for it as well. Before we go any further, save this model with a model name of **Physical Access Model** and a file name of **`Baker Cakes Physical Access.erwin`**, and close the file.

COMPLETE COMPARE

An easy way to merge information from one model to another is using the Complete Compare tool within CA ERwin Data Modeler. Complete Compare allows you to compare your data model with another data model, a DDL file, or a physical database. It discovers differences between the compared models, files, or databases, and allows you to selectively synchronize or merge objects between them. To invoke the Complete Compare tool, select **Actions|Complete Compare** from the **Main Menu**. The Complete Compare Wizard appears, with the **Left Model Selection** panel open, as shown in Figure 19.25.

Figure 19.25 Complete Compare Wizard - Left Model Selection

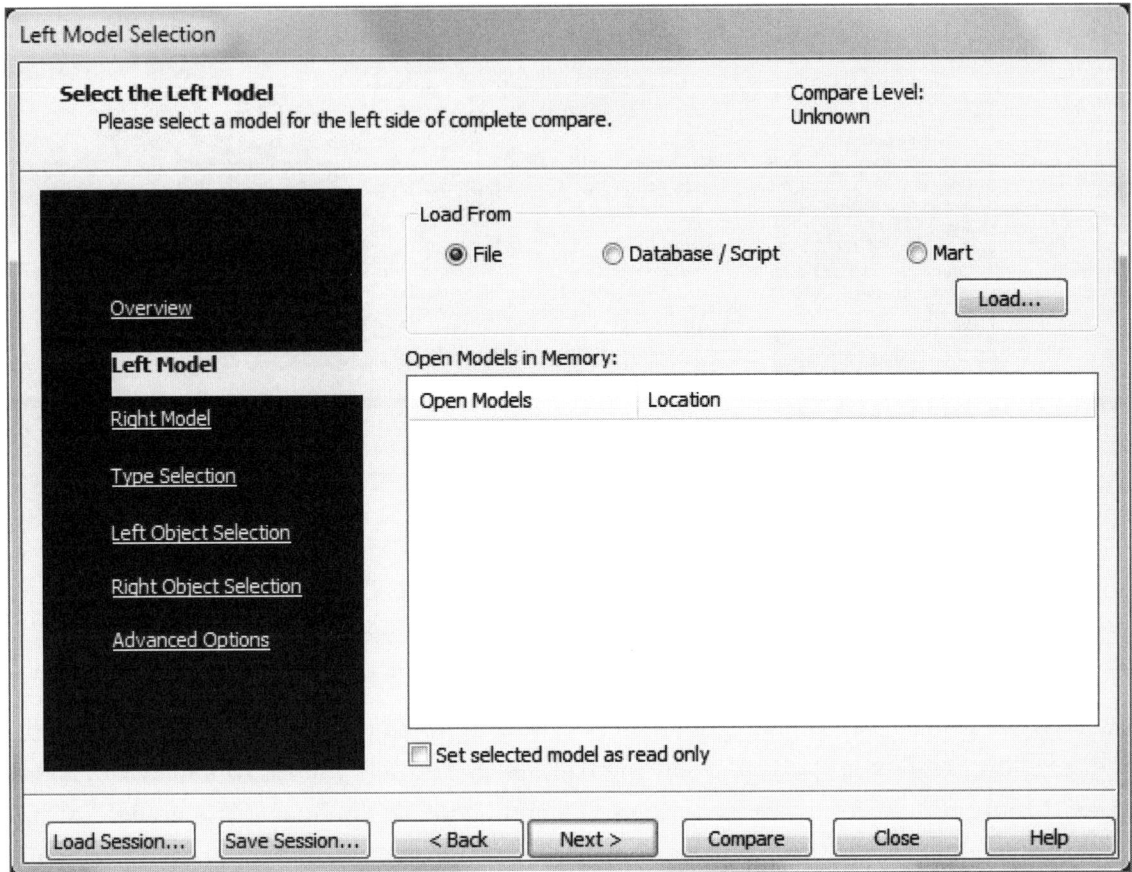

The terms 'Left Model' and 'Right Model' are arbitrary designations for the two models (or scripts or databases) that you'd like to compare. An easy way to think if this is to think about comparing two pieces of paper that have models written on them. To compare the two, you might hold one in your left hand and the other in the right, to evaluate them side-by-side. CA ERwin Data Modeler provides a similar view for you to compare your models—with one appearing on the left and the other on the right. It's up to you to choose which model you'd like to see on which side. In our example, we'll use the `Baker Cakes Logical Physical.erwin` file as the **Left Model**. With the **File** radio button selected, click on the **Load** button, and choose the location and file name for this model from your hard drive. Once you've selected the file, the file name will appear in the **Open Models in Memory** list box, and the model will be opened behind the wizard, as shown in Figure 19.26.

Figure 19.26 Selecting the Left Model in Complete Compare

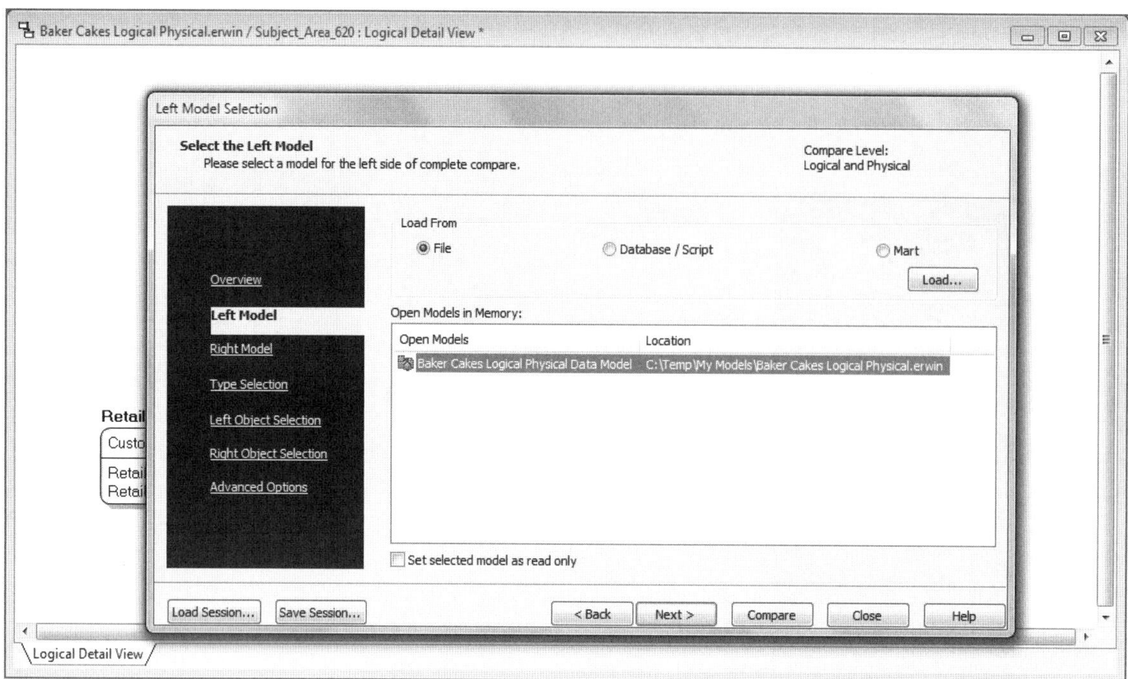

Now that we've chosen the left model, select **Next** to move to the **Right Model Selection** panel. Follow similar steps you performed to select the left model to select the `Baker Cakes Physical Access.erwin` file as the right model. You'll see this model listed in the **Open Models in Memory** box, and opened behind the wizard as well, as shown in Figure 19.27.

Figure 19.27 Selecting the Right Model in Complete Compare

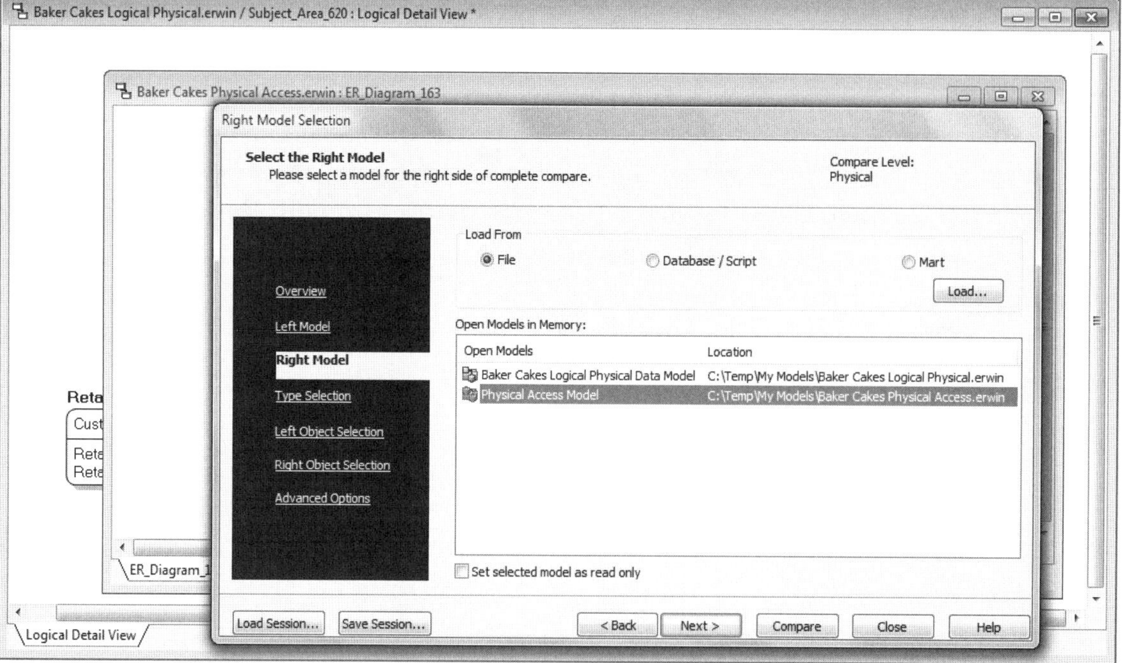

Notice that there is a **Set selected model as read-only** check box at the bottom of the wizard. This is a handy way to help ensure that you are only changing the model you've intended to. In our case, we'd like to modify the **Baker Cakes Relational Logical Physical model**, but leave the **Baker Cakes Physical Access** model intact. To ensure this, highlight the **Baker Cakes Physical Access** row, and check the **Set selected model** as read-only check box, as shown in Figure 19.28. You can never be too careful!

Figure 19.28 Setting a Model as Read Only in the Complete Compare Wizard

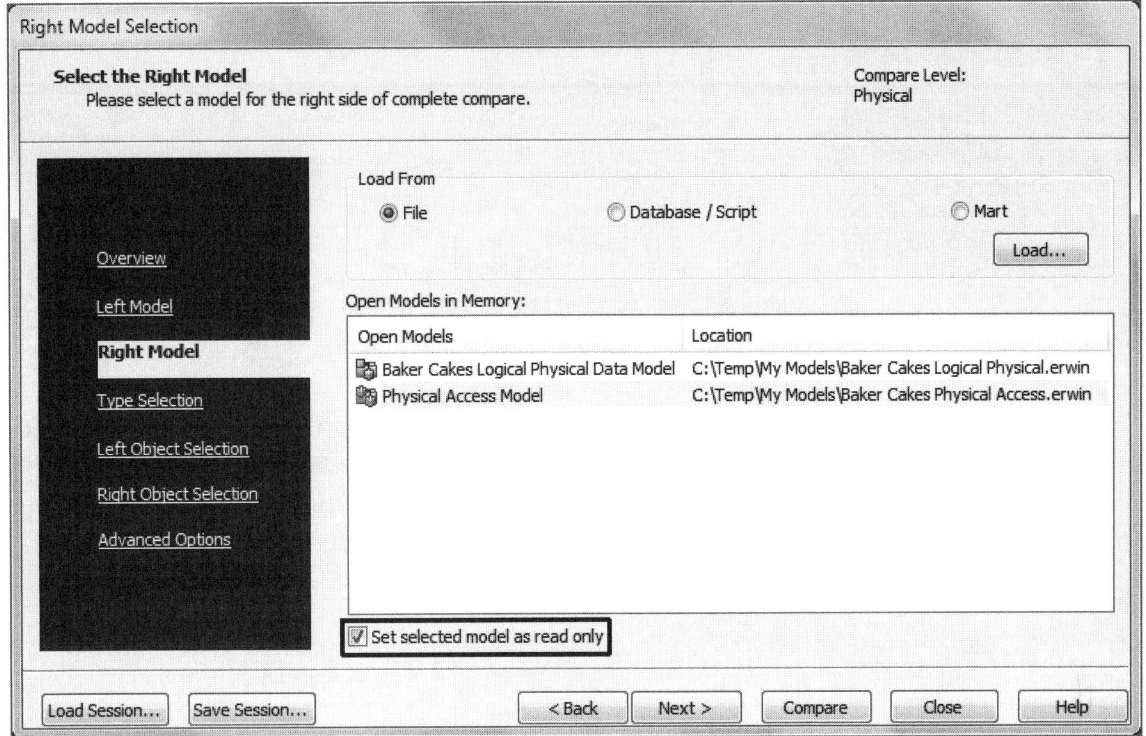

Select **Next** to move to the **Type Selection** panel, as shown in Figure 19.29. Here we can choose which object types to compare. For example, we can compare every object in the model, including colors and fonts, as well as physical metadata such as column length, domain definitions, etc. As you can imagine, comparing every model object can quickly become complex, so it's a good idea to create Option Sets to compare only the particular objects you're interested in. In our example, our main goal is to merge a column from one model to another, so we'll want to keep it simple, and limit our comparison to tables and columns only.

Figure 19.29 Object Type Selection in the Complete Compare Wizard

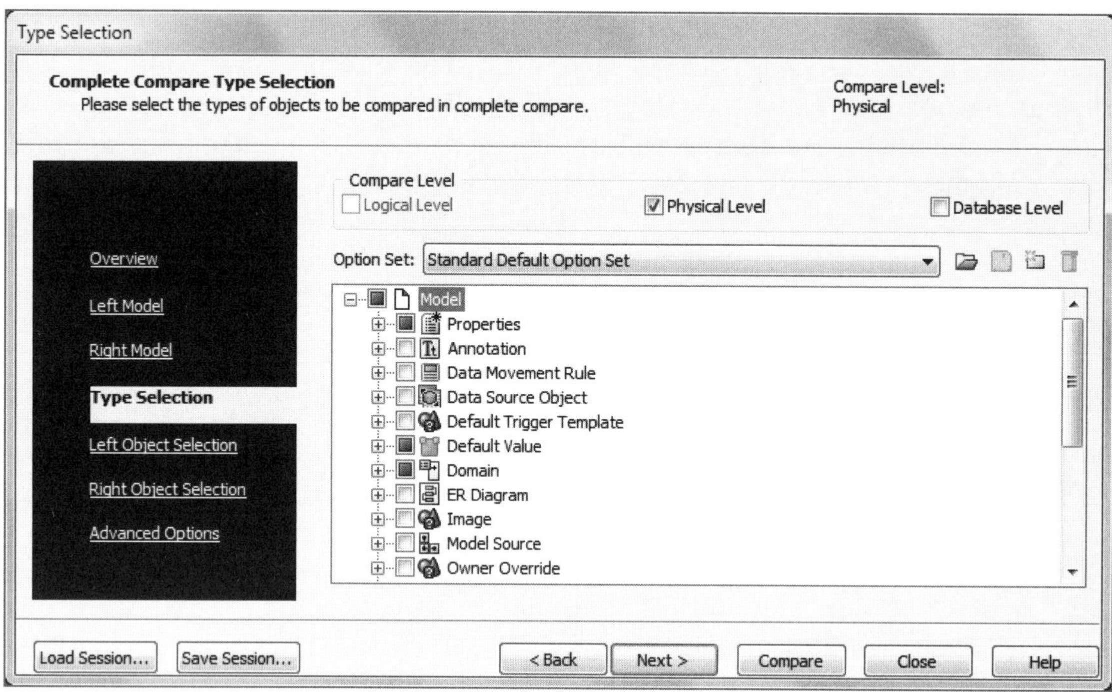

In the model menu tree, shown in Figure 19.30, clear all selections except for the **Table** and **Column** objects. Note: an easy way to select/clear all objects is by selecting/deselecting the topmost item on the tree. For example, toggling the topmost **Model** object will have a cascading effect on all objects below it.

Figure 19.30 Filtering Objects in the Type Selection Panel

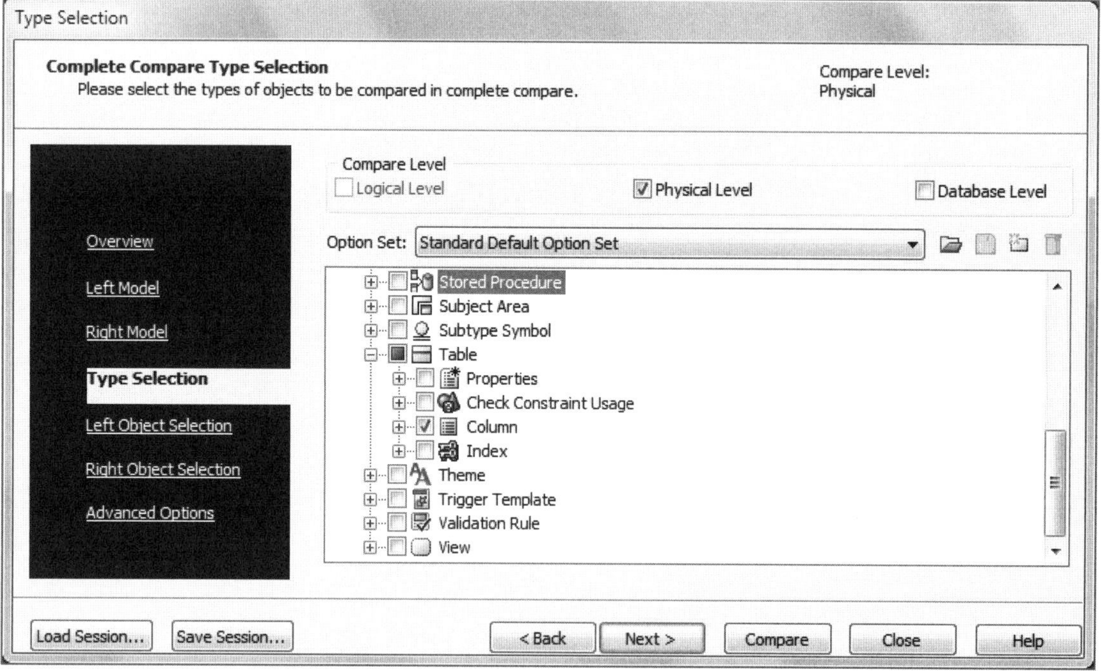

To save this Option Set so that we can reuse it for other Complete Compare operations, select the **Save current selections as a new Options Set** icon, and the **Save Current Option Set** dialog appears, as shown in Figure 19.31.

Figure 19.31 Saving an Option Set for Complete Compare

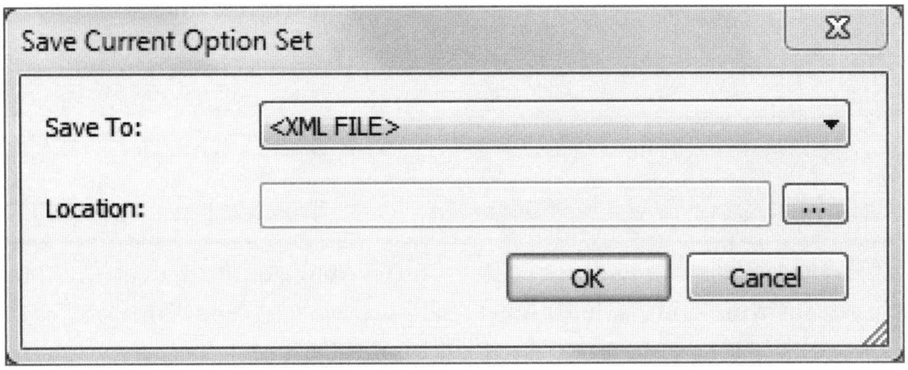

Save Current Option Set
Save To: <XML FILE>
Location:
OK Cancel

In the **Save To** drop-down editor, you have the option of saving an option set as an external XML file, or directly into a given model, as shown in Figure 19.32.

Figure 19.32 Saving an Option Set to an XML file or Model

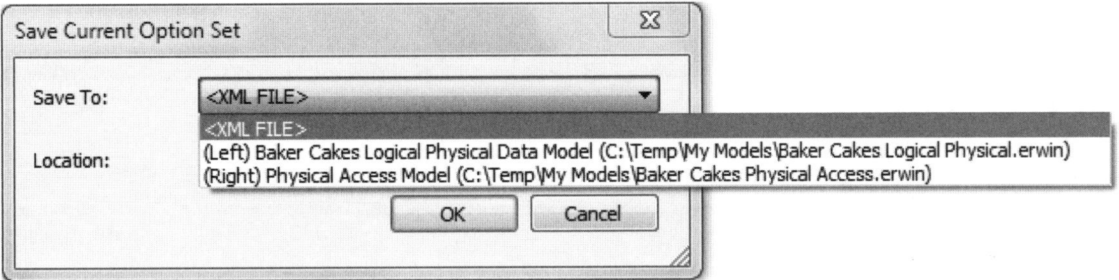

The benefit of saving to an XML file is that it can be easily shared across multiple models. The downside is that it is a separate file to have to maintain and manage. The benefit of saving the option set directly into a model is that all information is stored within a single file, making it easier to manage, but with the downside that it cannot be shared with other models. (But remember, you can always use Complete Compare to merge this option set into another model!)

In our example, we'll save this option set as an external XML file named **`Table_Column_CC.xml`**, as shown in Figure 19.33. This file is available on www.erwin.com/datamodelingmadesimple for your reference.

Figure 19.33 Saving an Option Set as an XML File

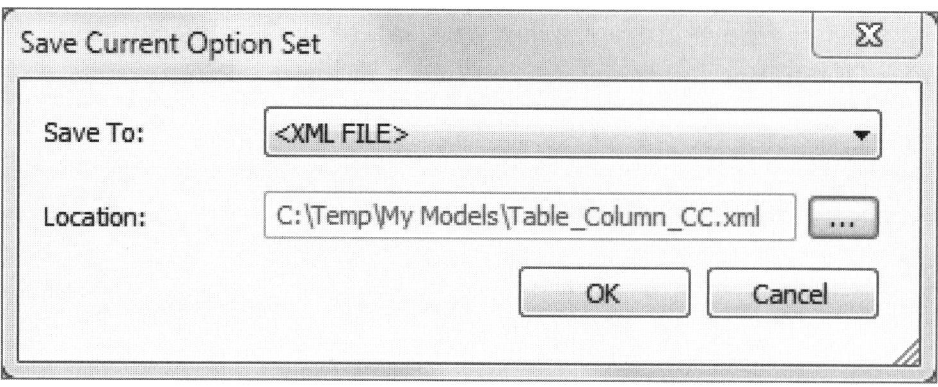

In addition to object *types*, we can also filter our comparison by object *instances* as well. For example, rather than compare all objects in a model, we can limit our comparison to specific tables. Select **Next** to move to the **Left Model Object** selection panel, as shown in Figure 19.34.

Figure 19.34 Left Object Selection in the Complete Compare Wizard

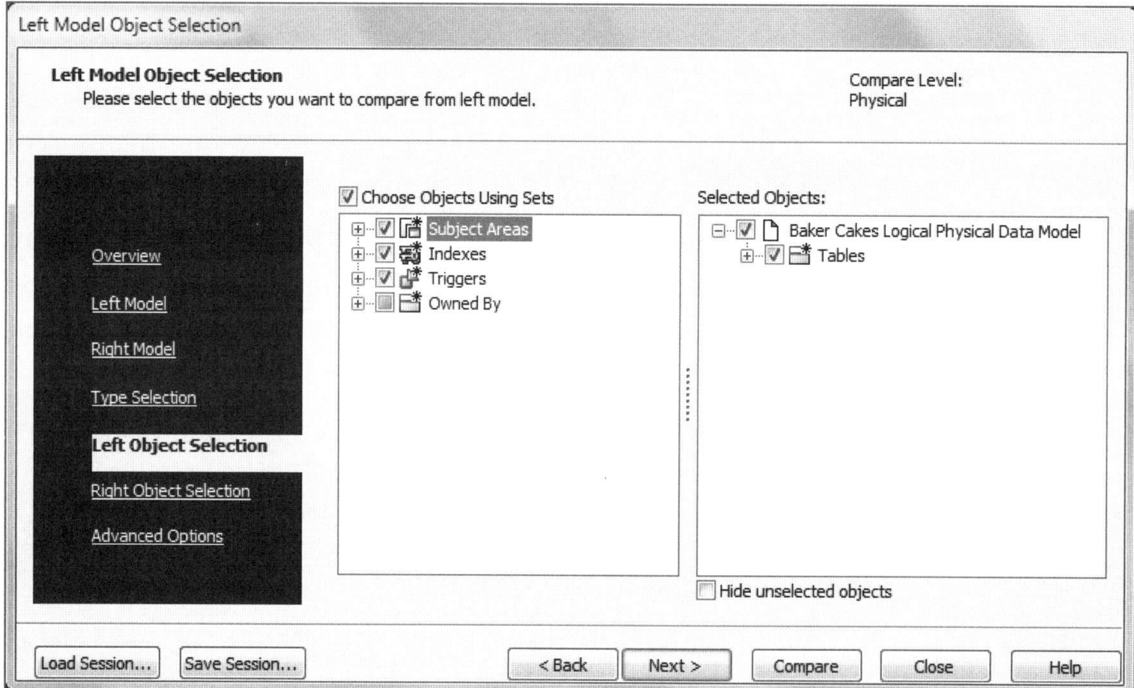

In our example, we know want to merge a column into the **Customer** table, so we can limit our comparison to just that table. In other cases, we might want to select all tables, so that we can see which tables might appear in one model, but not in the other, for example. In the **Selected Objects** box, clear all selections except for the **Customer** table, as shown in Figure 19.35.

Figure 19.35 Limiting Complete Compare to a Selected Table

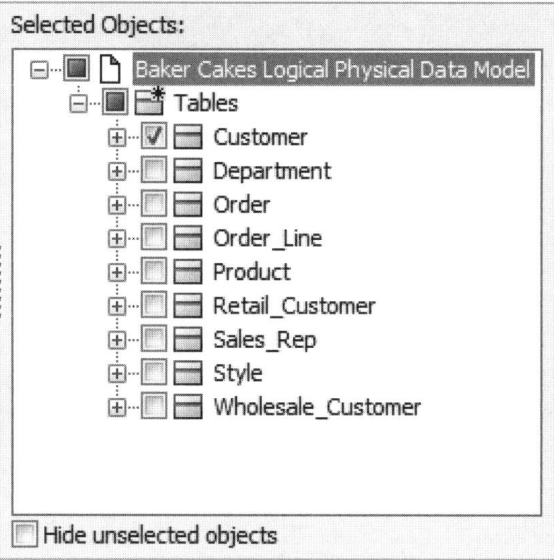

For our right model, there is only one table, so we won't need to do any filtering here. Select **Next** to move past the **Right Object Selection** panel, which is similar in functionality to the previous panel for the left model.

Select **Next** to move to the **Advanced Options** panel, shown in Figure 19.36. Table 19.5 lists a description for each of these objects. In our example, we'll deselect the **Prefix Owner**, since we're not using database owners in our model.

Figure 19.36 Advanced Options Panel for Complete Compare Wizard

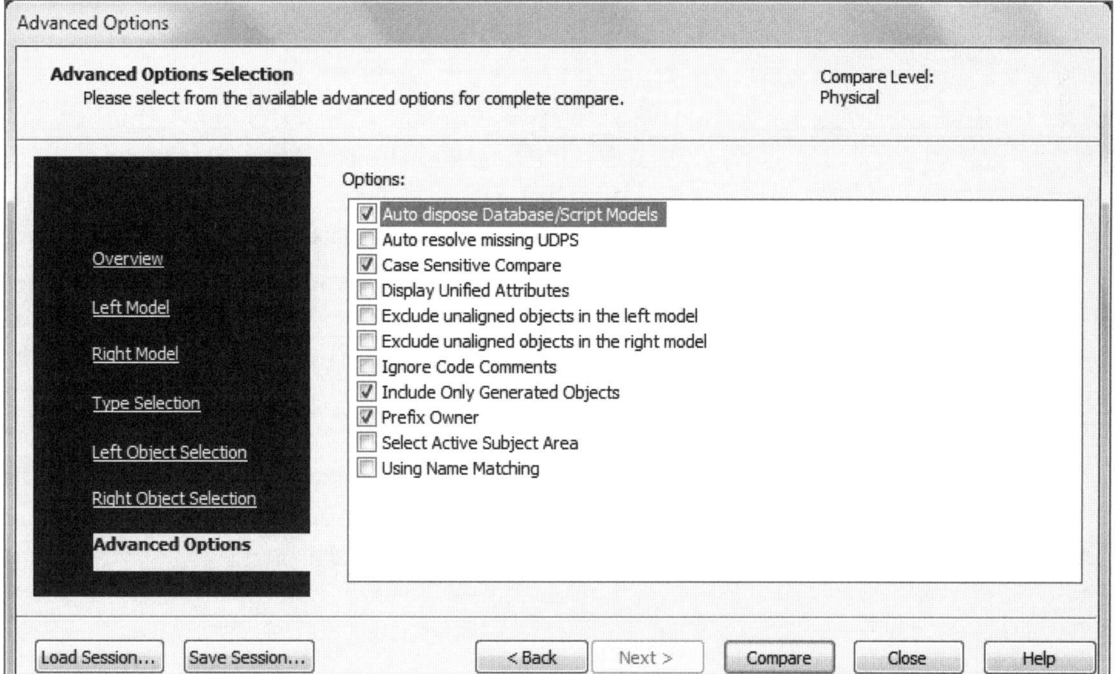

Table 19.5 Advanced Options Panel Properties for Complete Compare Wizard

Option	Definition
Auto dispose Database/Script Models	This option automatically closes the model when you complete the Complete Compare session. Note: The option to save the model is not displayed.
Auto resolve missing UDPs	When Complete Compare detects missing UDPs or property differences for common UDPs, a **Type Resolution** box appears allowing you to selectively choose how resolution is handled. If you select this option, all missing UDPs are automatically copied to the target model.
Case Sensitive Compare	With this option selected, Complete Compare uses case as a comparison criteria (e.g. uppercase vs. lowercase).
Using Database Id Matching (Informix, Sybase, and SQL Server only)	With this option selected, objects are aligned based on the DB ID property, if one is present.
Using Object Id Matching (DB2 z/OS only)	With this option selected, objects are aligned based on the Object ID property, if one is present on the object.
Display Unified Attributes	This option simplifies the display of foreign-key attributes in the **Resolve Differences** dialog. If selected, a Unified Attributes group object is used to display all unified attributes (role-named or not) of the same unified set of attributes.
Exclude unaligned objects in the left model	This option excludes unaligned objects from the ***left*** model in the **Resolve Differences** dialog, making it easier to distinguish between changes in a model subset you are working with (such as a subject area or submodel) and a larger model of which the subset is a part.

Option	Definition
Exclude unaligned objects in the right model	This option excludes unaligned objects from the ***right*** model in the **Resolve Differences** dialog, making it easier to distinguish between changes in a model subset you are working with (such as a subject area or submodel) and a larger model of which the subset is a part.
Ignore Code Comments	Ignoring Code Comments excludes comment blocks from the body of a trigger before including it in the compare process.
Prefix Owner	Matching by prefix table owner aligns objects based on both the name and owner name property.
Select Active Subject Area	This option automatically selects the active subject area you are working with for the Complete Compare process.
Using Name Matching	With this option, relationship, index, and index members are aligned based on name, in addition to the normal criteria used to align these objects.
Tablespace in Database (DB2 z/OS only)	When this option is set, objects are aligned based on both the IN_TABLESPACE and IN_DATABASE properties, if present on the object.
Include Only Generated Objects	This option only aligns on objects that will generate SQL during forward engineering. Each editor for a physical model object includes a **Generate** check box, which indicates that you want to generate SQL for this object during forward engineering. Note: When working with a database-level compare, the **Include Only Generated Objects** check box is selected by default.

Now that we've set up all of our comparison options, we're ready to run the Complete Compare process. Select the **Compare** button, to invoke the **Resolve Differences** dialog, shown in Figure 19.37.

Figure 19.37 Resolve Differences Dialog in Complete Compare

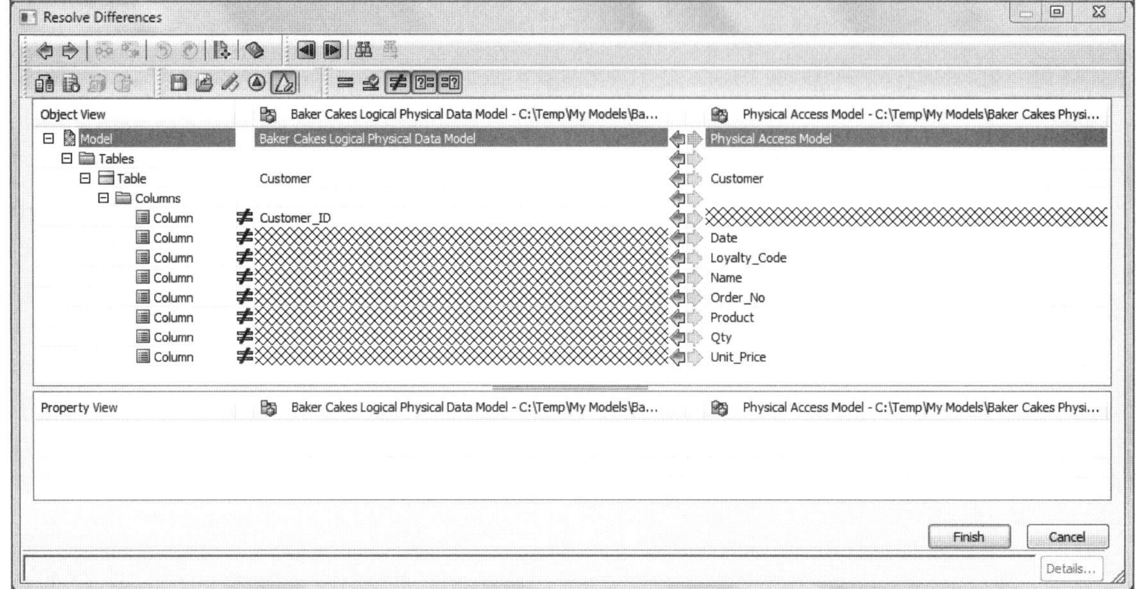

The **Resolve Differences** dialog shows a visual, side-by-side comparison of the **Customer** table from the physical model we created on the left and the **Customer** table that was reverse engineered from the Access database on the right. You can easily see that the Access **Customer** table on the right has many more columns than the one on the left. We don't want to include all of these columns, per our normalization discussion earlier, but we do want to include the **Loyalty_Code** column in our physical model. From this dialog, we can easily merge one or more columns from the right model into the left model.

To perform the merge, start by selecting the **Loyalty_Code** column from the right model, as shown in Figure 19.38. In the bottom panel, you'll see a listing of all of the properties of this column, such as the data type, null option, etc.

Figure 19.38 Selecting a Column to Merge in Complete Compare

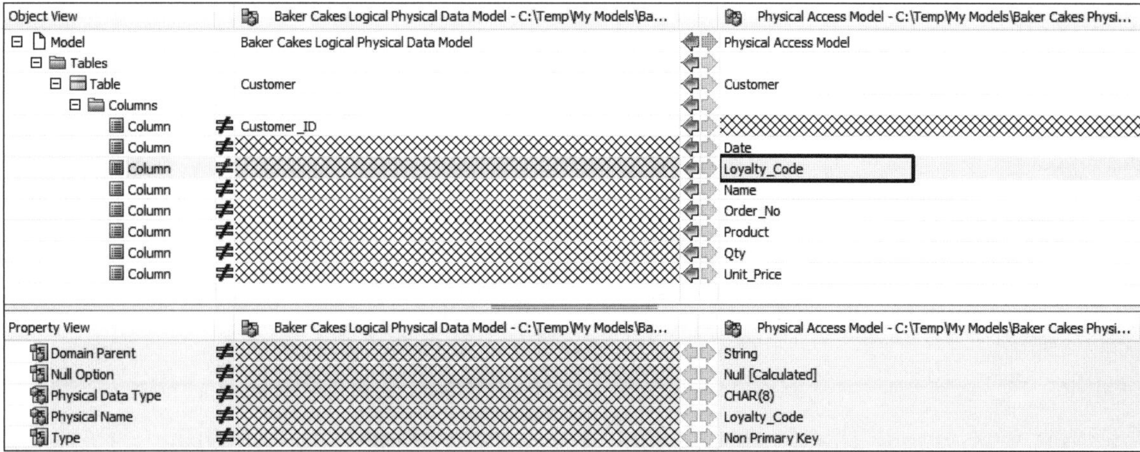

To move the column to the left model, select the left arrow button, and you'll see that the **Loyalty_Code** column disappears from the right model listing, as shown in Figure 19.39. Does this mean that we've removed it from that model? No, it's still there, don't worry. Remember that this dialog shows the differences between models—it is not a complete listing of the model objects. So now that both the left and right model both contain the **Loyalty_Code** column, it is no longer listed as a difference. Also, remember that we set the right model to be read-only, so that we're certain not to change it in any way.

Figure 19.39 Resolve of Column Merge in Complete Compare

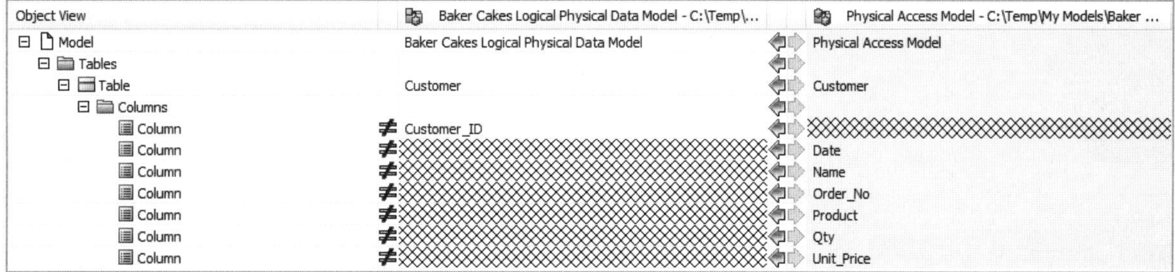

Although we understand why the **Loyalty_Code** column is no longer shown, it might be helpful to show it listed as being resolved, so that we can keep a running history of our changes. Select the **Show Resolved Items** button from the Standard Filters Toolbar, as shown in Figure 19.40.

Figure 19.40 Selecting the Show Resolved Items Toolbar Button

You'll now see the **Loyalty_Code** shown in both the left and right models, as shown in Figure 19.41.

Figure 19.41 Showing Resolved Differences in Complete Compare

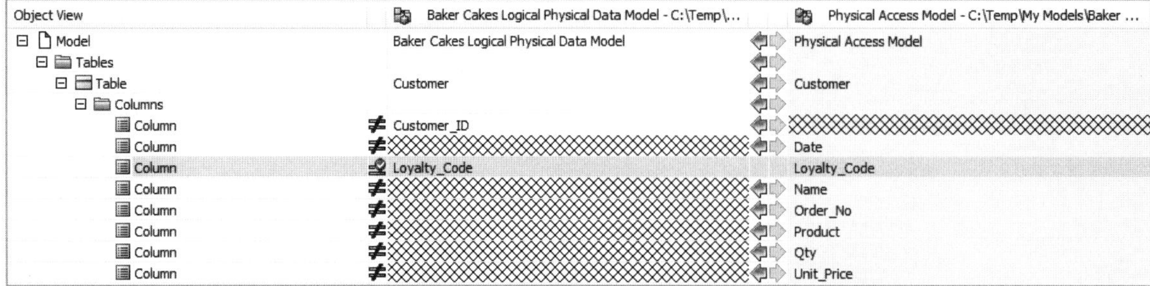

Now that we've made the necessary changes, so select **Finish** and you'll be returned to the Complete Compare dialog. Note that if you're using the Community Edition, the **Finish** button will be disabled, as the Complete Compare functionality is read-only in this edition. If you'd like to continue with the example, you may want to add the **Loyalty Code** manually for now.

Select **Close** to view our final models with the changes we've made. (You'll be asked if you'd like to close the models—select **Cancel**, since we'd like to see the changes first.) In the modified models, you'll see that the physical model we created now has the **Loyalty_Code** column correctly listed in the **Customer** table, as shown in Figure 19.42.

Figure 19.42 Baker Cakes Relational PDM with Loyalty_Code Column Added

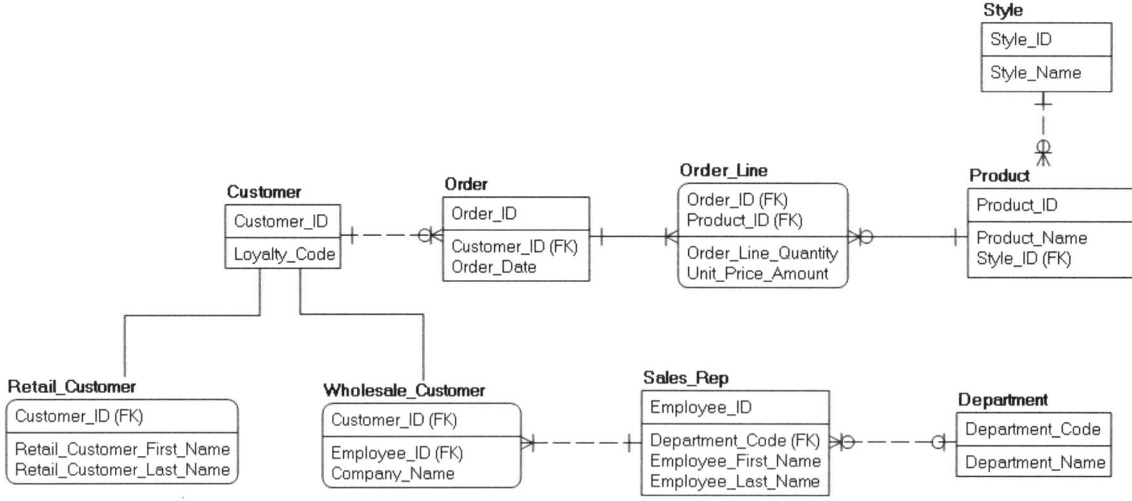

Switch to the logical model, and you'll see that it has also been automatically created as an attribute, as shown in Figure 19.43. Since we're using a combined logical/physical model, changes to one model are automatically synched with the other, unless we explicitly turn off this behavior (using logical only or physical only objects). Note that you'll need to manually remove the underscore for the **Loyalty_Code** in the logical model (i.e. **Loyalty Code**), since we did not implement physical-to-logical naming standards in this example, only logical-to-physical rules.

Figure 19.43 Baker Cakes LDM with Loyalty Code Attribute Added

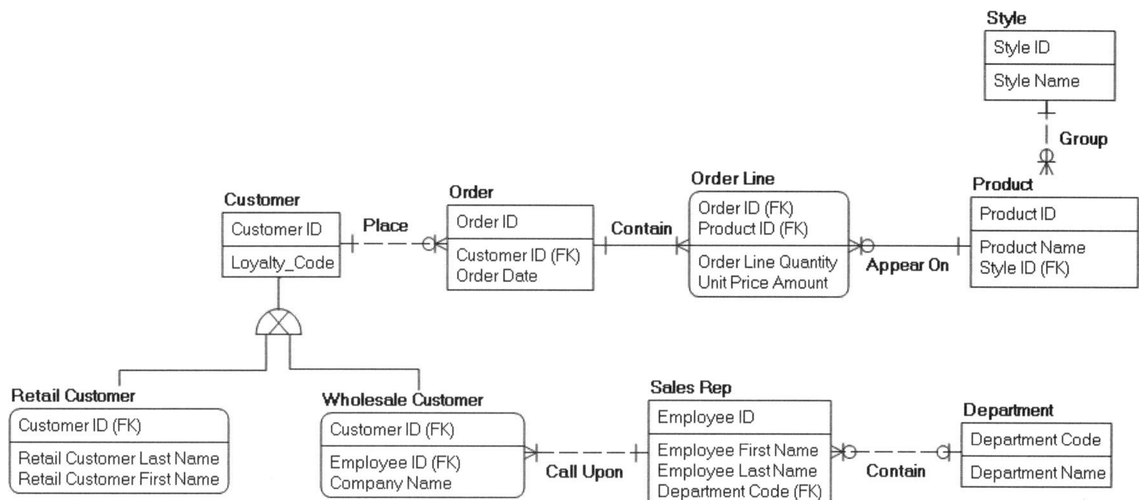

Let's take a look at the Access data model to ensure that it has remained unchanged. Yes, as shown in Figure 19.44, this model is exactly the same as it was before the Complete Compare operation, which is what we intended.

Figure 19.44 Access PDM Unchanged After Complete Compare

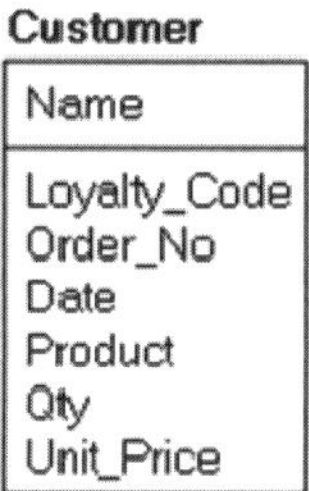

Now that we've made sure that we have all the necessary information in the model through both our 'top down' and 'bottom up' analysis, we're ready to refine the physical data model for performance and query optimization.

SUBTYPING RESOLUTION

One refinement we'll need to make is to resolve the supertype/subtype relationship for the **Customer** entity. Since relational databases do not support the concept of subtyping, we need to resolve this in our physical data model. Recall from our earlier discussion that there are three ways of resolving subtyping in the physical model: identity, rolling down, and rolling up. In this case, we'll choose the rolling down method to preserve two distinct entities: **Retail Customer** and **Wholesale Customer**. Since in the original design, the intern neglected to include wholesale customers, two separate applications had been built: one to manage retail customers and one for wholesale customers. Although this is not an ideal situation, we are unable to rewrite the applications themselves, and provide a solution that matches the real world implementation, in this case. These types of 'work-arounds' are common in 'real world' implementations. Another 'work-around' is that since we're using a combined logical and physical data model, denormalization changes will be applied to both the logical and physical models simultaneously. Ideally, we'll want to keep our logical models (business) and physical models (technical implementation) distinct, which would require us to use separate logical and physical data models and use the **Derive** functionality. Refer to Table 18.5 for a summary of the pros and cons of using a combined logical/physical model vs. separate logical and physical models.

Recall our subtype relationship for customer in the logical model, shown in Figure 19.45.

Figure 19.45 Subtype Relationship for Customer

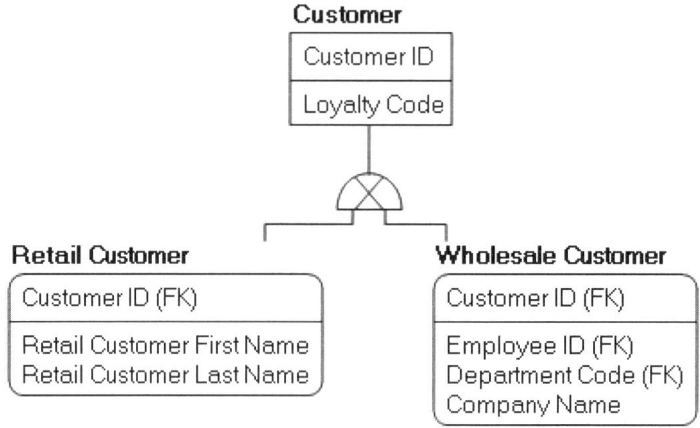

To resolve this subtype, first select the subtype symbol ⊗ on the diagram, as shown in Figure 19.46.

Figure 19.46 Selecting the Subtype Symbol

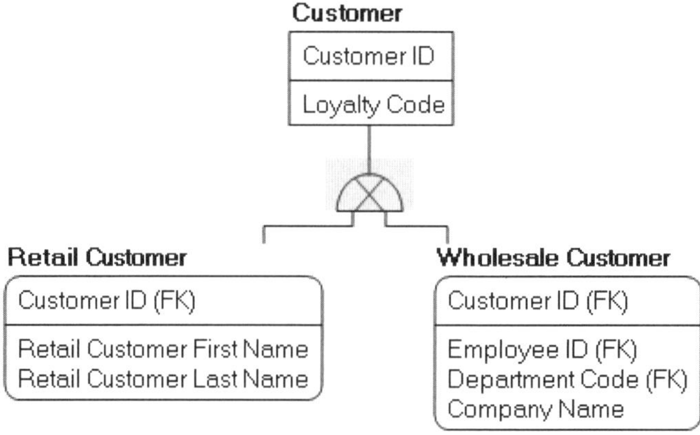

Next, select **Actions|Transformations|Supertype-Subtype RollDown** from the **Main Menu**. The Supertype Subtype Rolldown Wizard appears as shown in Figure 19.47.

Figure 19.47 Supertype Subtype Rolldown Wizard

Select **Next** to complete the action. A panel summarizing the changes appears, as shown in Figure 19.48, explaining that the **Customer** entity will roll down into the **Retail Customer** and **Wholesale Customer** entities, which is the action we want.

Figure 19.48 Completing the Supertype Subtype Wizard

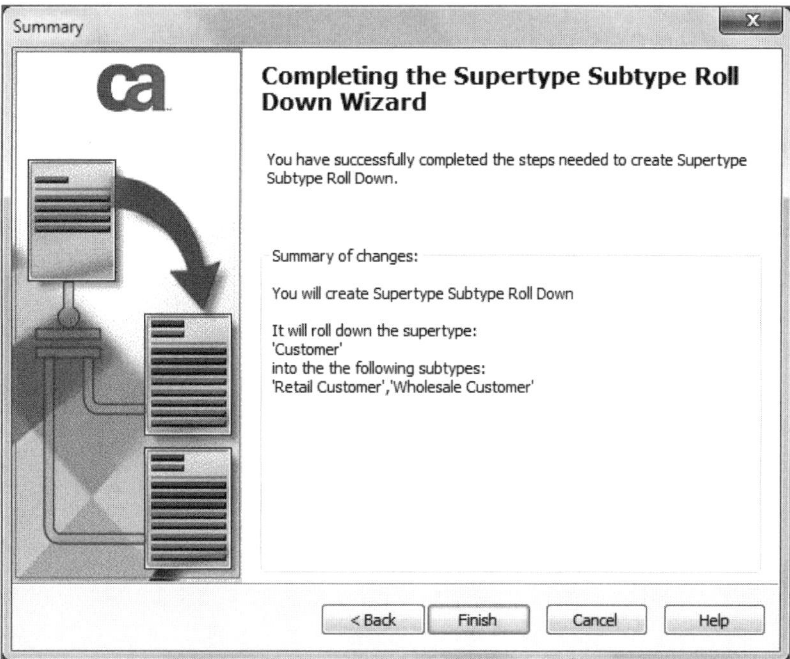

Select **Finish** and you will be returned to the diagram, shown in Figure 19.49. Note that you may need to reorganize the diagram slightly, since the entities and relationships have been modified.

Figure 19.49 Relational LDM for Baker Cakes with Subtyping Resolved via Rolling Down

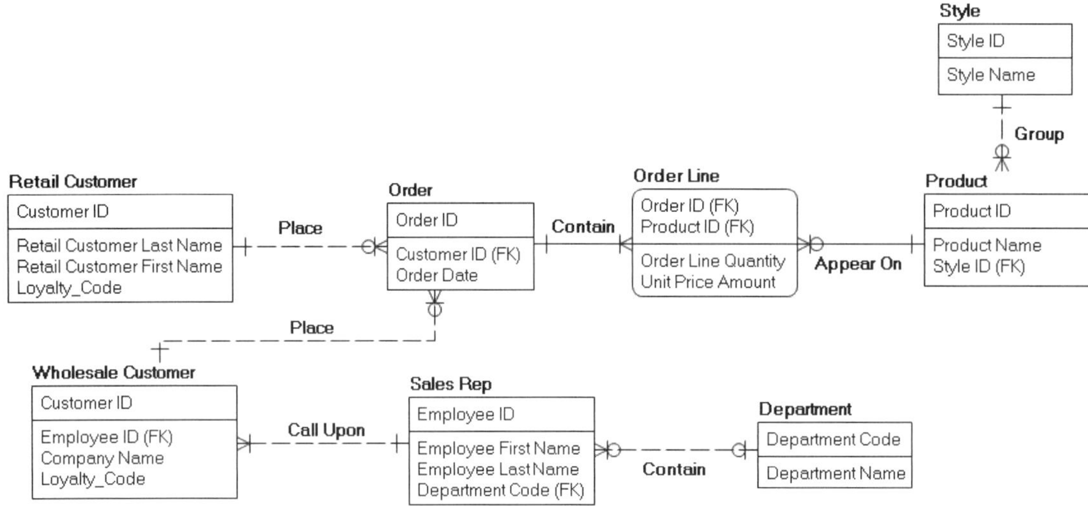

We've created some redundancy in our model, with the **Loyalty_Code** repeated in both the **Retail Customer** and **Wholesale Customer** tables, and a redundant relationship between **Retail Customer** and **Order** and **Wholesale Customer** and **Order**. But we've maintained readability of the model and, importantly, matched the implementation requirements of the organization.

One thing that seems strange, however, is that there is only one **Customer ID** attribute as a foreign key in the **Order** entity that refers to both **Retail Customers** and **Wholesale Customers**. While that's technically correct, since customer IDs are unique, it makes the model difficult to interpret. Remember our discussion of role names earlier in this chapter? This is a perfect use case for role naming—we'll create a separate role name for the **Customer ID** attribute in the **Retail Customer** and **Wholesale Customer** entities. To create a role name, open the Relationship Properties Editor for the relationship between **Retail Customer** and **Order**, and move to the **Role Name** tab, as shown in Figure 19.50. For more information on the Relationship Properties Editor, refer to Chapter 6.

Figure 19.50 Invoking the Relationship Properties Editor to Add a Role Name

Relationship 'R/4_1' Editor

Enter filter text

Name	Parent	Child	Logical Only
R/22	Product	Order Line	☐
R/4_1	Retail Customer	Order	☐
R/4_2	Wholesale Customer	Order	☐
R/6	Style	Product	☐

General | Definition | Role Name | RI Actions | Style | UDP | Notes

Migrated Key/Index

Key Group | XPKRetail Customer

Role Name Info

Migrated Attribute	Role Name
Customer ID	

Close | Cancel

Details...

In the **Role Name** field, enter our role name for the **Customer ID** attribute, in this case 'Retail Customer ID', as shown in Figure 19.51.

Figure 19.51 Adding a Role Name for a Foreign Key Attribute

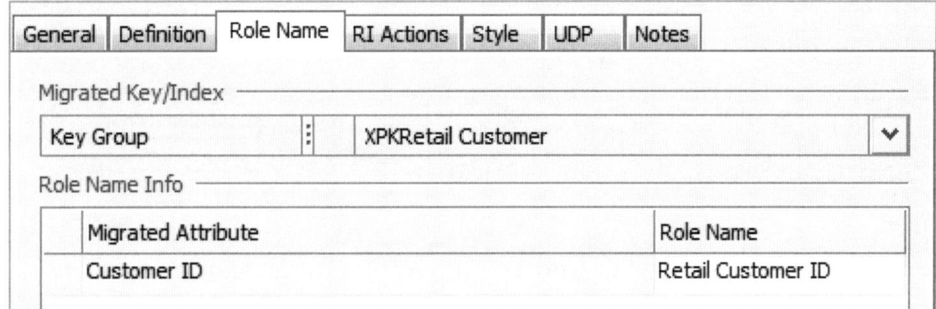

Select **Close**, and your model diagram should now look like Figure 19.52. Notice that the **Customer ID** attribute remains as-is in the **Retail Customer** entity, but is role named to **Retail Customer ID** in the **Order** table.

Figure 19.52 Role Name Added for Retail Customer ID

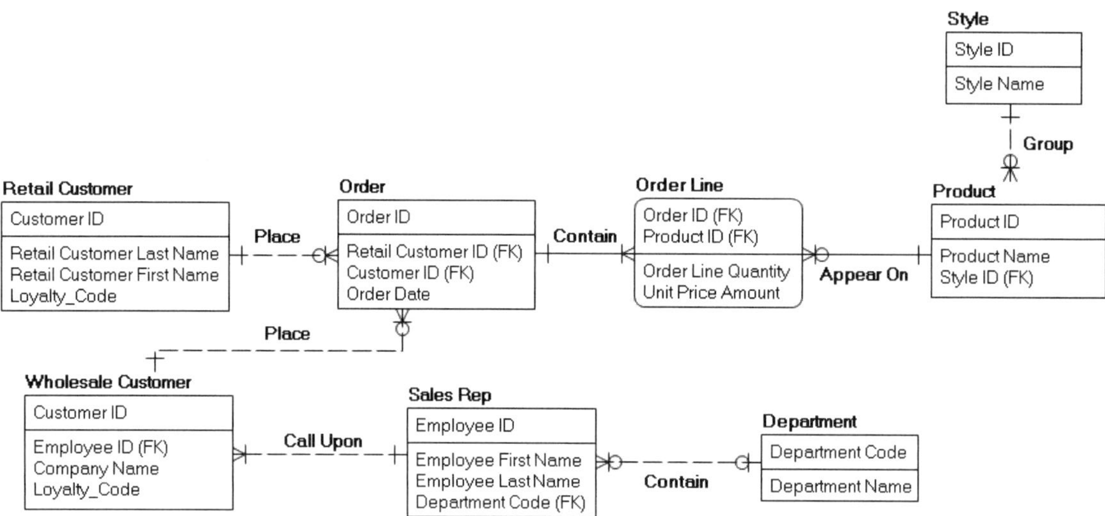

Create a role name called 'Wholesale Customer ID' for the **Customer ID** attribute in the **Wholesale Customer** entity. We won't walk you through this—use similar steps to those you used for the **Retail Customer ID** role name. When complete, your model should look similar to Figure 19.53.

Figure 19.53 Subtyping Resolved in LDM with Role Names Added

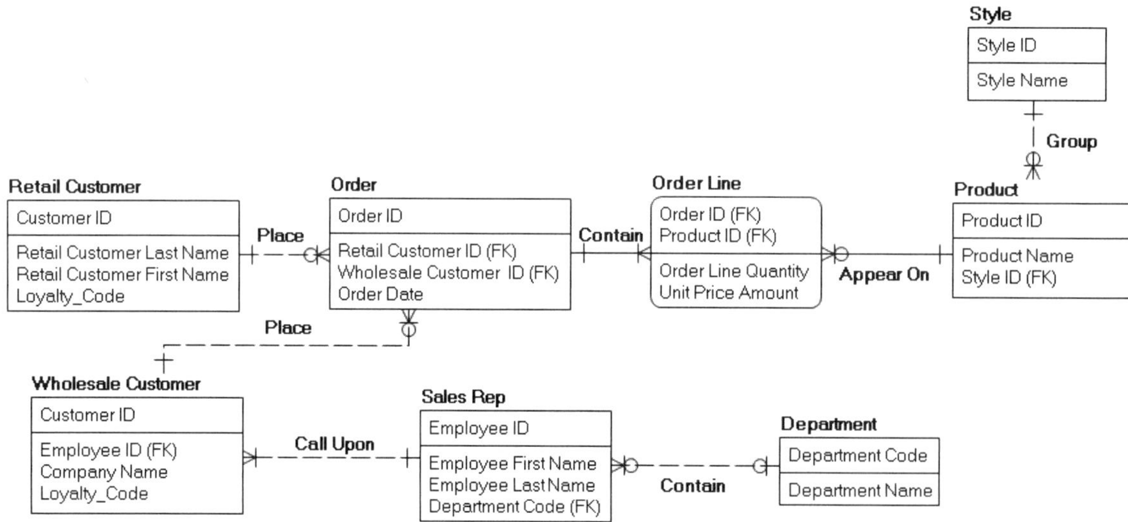

Switch to the physical data model, and you'll see a similar design, as shown in Figure 19.54.

Figure 19.54 Subtyping Resolved in PDM

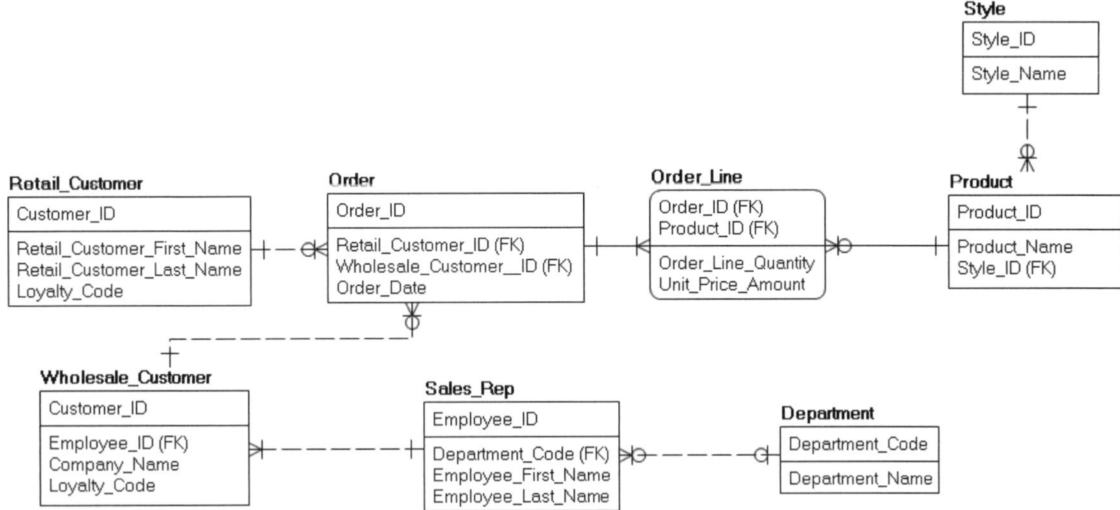

This is close to the design we need, but notice the relationships between **Order** and **Retail_Customer** and **Order** and **Wholesale Customer**. If you read these relationships, you'll see that an order must have a retail customer ***and*** a wholesale customer, which is not a correct business rule. To change this, select the relationship between **Order** and **Retail Customer** and open the Relationship Properties Editor. Then change the **Null Option** on the **General** tab to **Nulls Allowed**, as shown in Figure 19.55.

Figure 19.55 Changing the Null Option for a Relationship

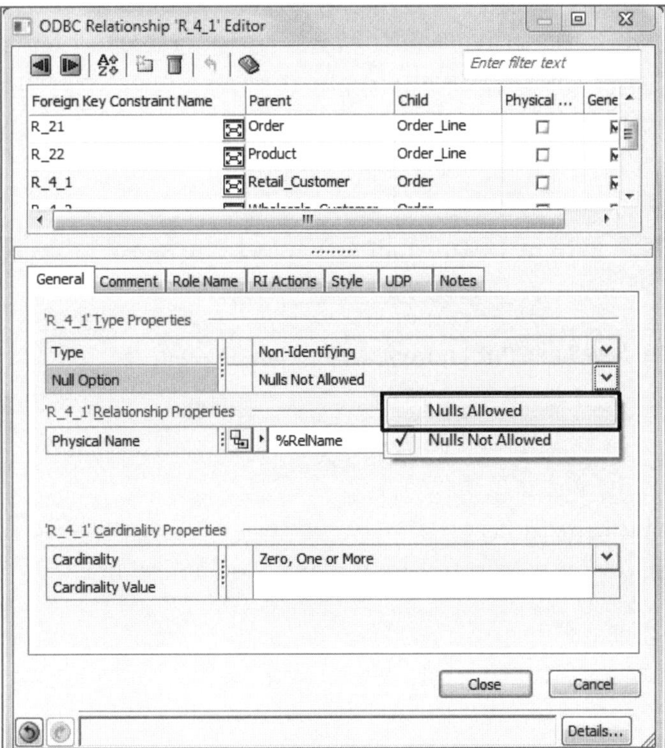

Follow similar steps for the relationship between **Wholesale Customer** and **Order**, and your model will look similar to Figure 19.56.

Figure 19.56 Subtyping Resolved in PDM – with Correct Cardinality

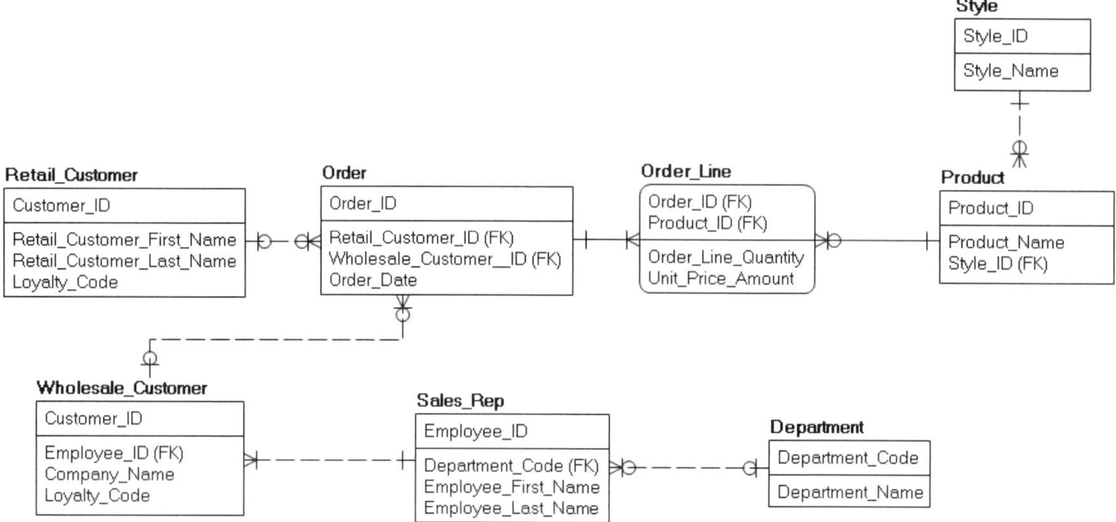

VIEWS

As we mentioned earlier, Baker Cakes has built a number of applications to access their customer data. We'll want to implement some views in our physical model to assist in the retrieval of data for these applications. Baker Cakes is running a marketing campaign to try to increase the number of retail customers in their loyalty program. They are sending out special promotions to those customers not yet enrolled in the program, and for those in the program, they are offering special features in their online ordering application. For the marketing application, we need to create a query that lists the names of all retail customers who are not yet enrolled in the loyalty program. For this, we'll want to use a view in our physical data model.

To create a view in CA ERwin Data Modeler, select the **View table** button from the Toolbox Toolbar, as shown in Figure 19.57.

Figure 19.57 Selecting the View Table Button from the Toolbox Toolbar

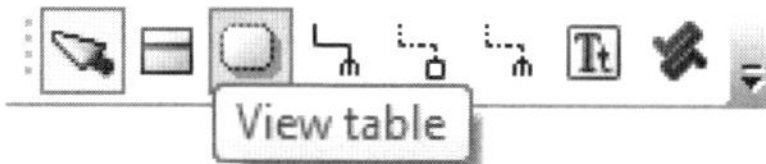

Next, click on the diagram to create a new view, as shown in Figure 19.58. A view is represented on the diagram by a rounded box with a dashed border.

Figure 19.58 Creating a New View in the Physical Data Model

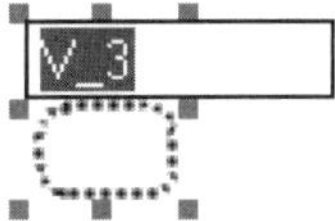

You'll notice that the view is automatically placed in the name edit mode, so you can name the view by simply typing in the highlighted area. Name this view **Customers_Not_Loyal**, as shown in Figure 19.59.

Figure 19.59 Naming a View

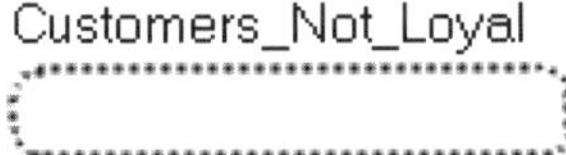

Next, we'll need to create the query that's embedded within the view, so that we can extract the list of customer names from the **Retail_Customer** table. To access this table for querying, we'll need to use a view relationship. Select the **View/Materialized relationship** button from the Toolbox Toolbar, as shown in Figure 19.60.

Figure 19.60 Selecting the View/Materialized Relationship Button from the Toolbox Toolbar

Next, click on the **Retail_Customer** table as the source object, then the **Customers_Not_Loyal** view as the target object, and a view relationship will be created between the two objects, as shown in Figure 19.61.

Figure 19.61 Creating a View Relationship Between a Table and a View

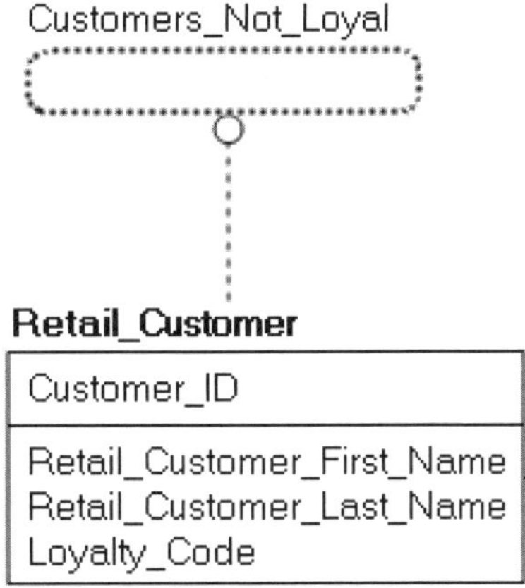

Now that we've established a relationship to the table to be queried, we have access to this table's column information and other key metadata from which we can create our

view query. To create the query, double-click on the **Customers_Not_Loyal** view to invoke the ODBC View Editor[18], as shown in Figure 19.62.

Figure 19.62 ODBC View Editor

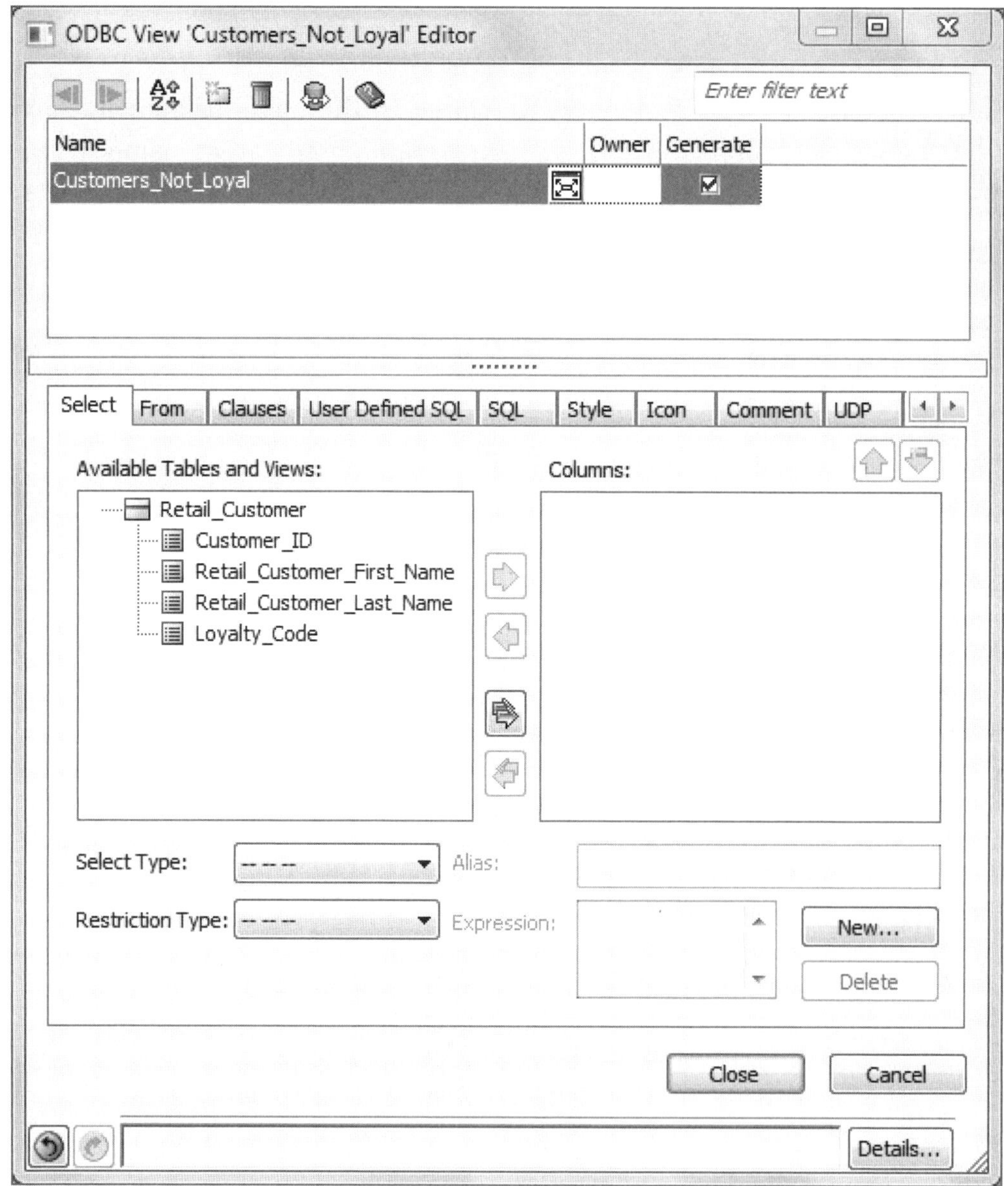

The first tab we encounter is the **Select** tab, which is where we define what columns we want to show in the query results. For example, we'll want to show the customer's name, as well as their customer ID in the report that we show to the marketing department. For this, we'll need to select the **Retail_Customer_First_Name**,

[18] Note that the type of View Editor invoked is determined by the target database type defined for the physical data model. For example, if we had chosen Oracle as our target database, the name of the editor would be Oracle View Editor.

Retail_Customer_Last_Name, and **Customer_ID** columns. To choose these columns, highlight each column in the **Available Tables and Views** box, and then use the right arrow button ⇨ to move it to the **Columns** box, as shown in Figure 19.63.

Figure 19.63 Selecting Columns to be Retrieved in a View Query

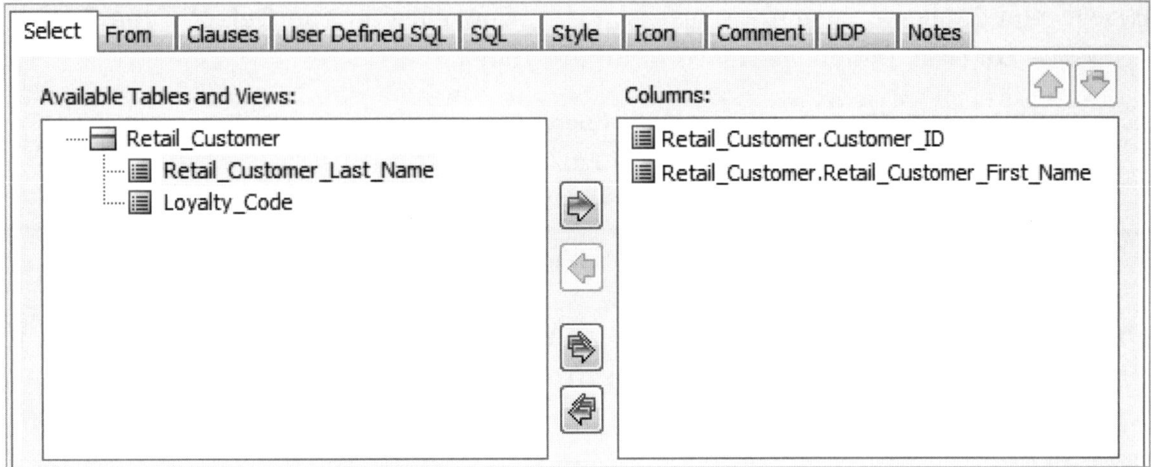

Once we have all of the columns we'd like to include, we'll want to make sure we have the correct order. In our case, we want to list first name, last name, followed by the customer ID. To change the default order, highlight the column to be moved, and use the down arrow button to move the order of the column, as shown in Figure 19.64.

Figure 19.64 Changing the Default Column Order in a View Query

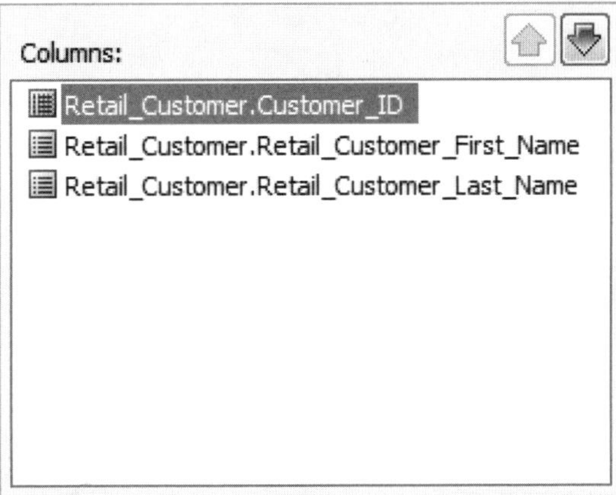

The **Customer_ID** column is now displayed last in the list, as shown in Figure 19.65.

Figure 19.65 Final Column Order for a View Query

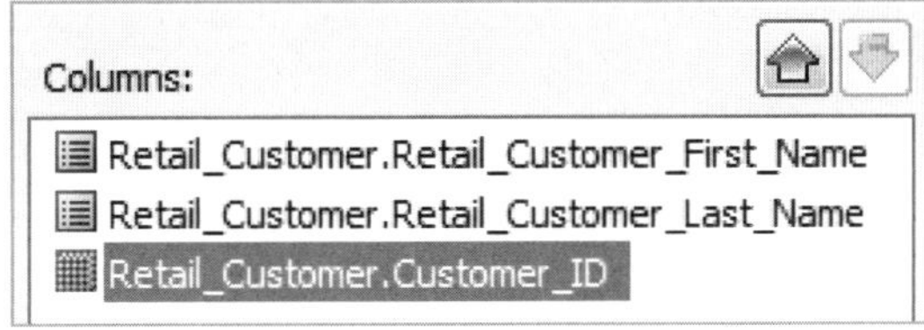

The next decision we'll need to make in our query selection is whether to include only unique customers. For example, if a customer is listed twice in the database, do you want to list their name multiple times, or only once? In this case, we only want a list of the unique customers. In fact, this list *should* be unique, since each customer should have a unique customer ID; but, it never hurts to be overly safe. To enforce that we only retrieve non-duplicate customers, use the drop-down list in the **Select Type** field to choose the **Distinct** option, as shown in Figure 19.66.

Figure 19.66 Enforcing the Distinct option in a View Query

Now that we've defined the columns we want to retrieve in our query, we'll need to specify where we'll retrieve these columns 'from'. For this, we'll move to the **From** tab, as shown in Figure 19.67.

Figure 19.67 From Tab in the View Query Editor

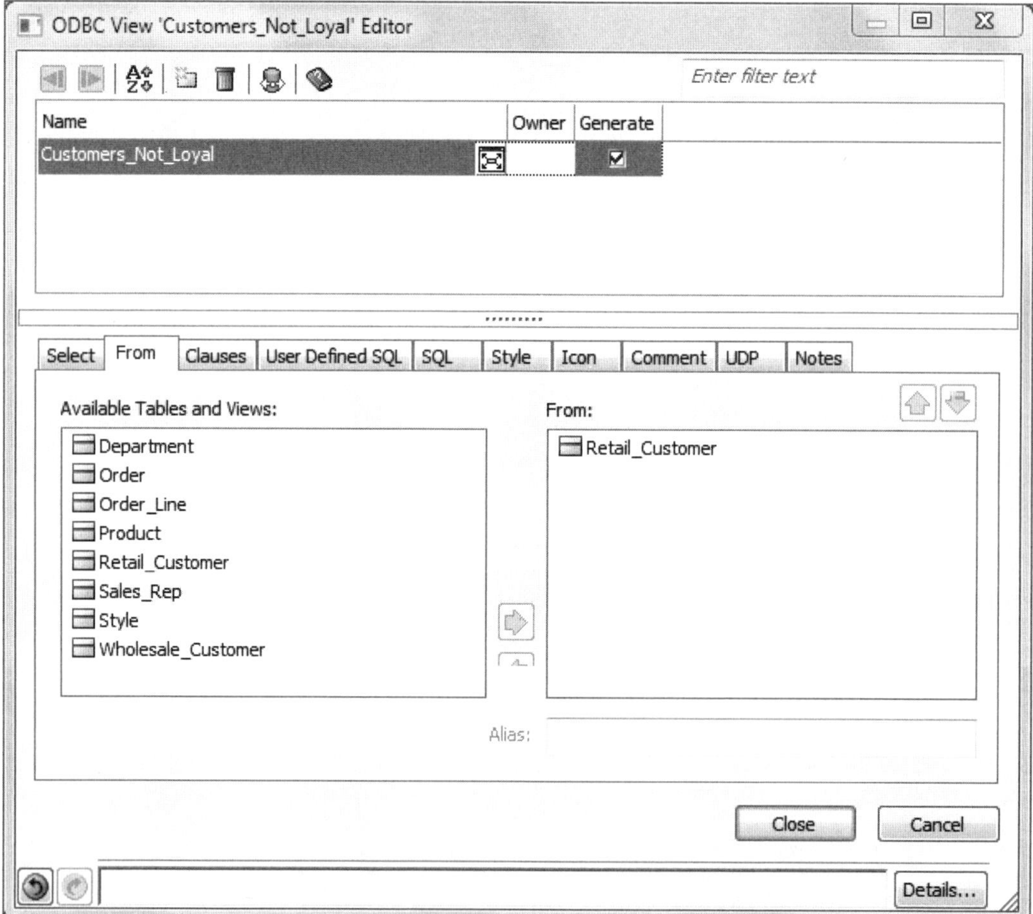

You'll see the default source table defined in the **From** box is the **Retail_Customer** table. Since **Retail_Customer** is the source of our view relationship, it is automatically populated for us. If we wanted to retrieve columns from multiple tables (or views) and join them together in a single query, we could select other tables from the **Available Tables and Views** box and simply move them using the arrow keys to the **From** box. But in this case, we're only interested in the **Retail_Customer** table, so we'll stay with the default.

Next, we'll want to define the restrictions on our query using the **Clauses** tab. In this tab, we can limit the scope of our query. For example, for our application, we only want to retrieve the customers who do not have a loyalty code assigned to them. In SQL, we can use the WHERE clause for this. In the **Where** box of the **Clauses** tab, type **`Loyalty_Code NOT NULL`**, as shown in Figure 19.68.

Figure 19.68 Defining a WHERE Clause for a SQL View

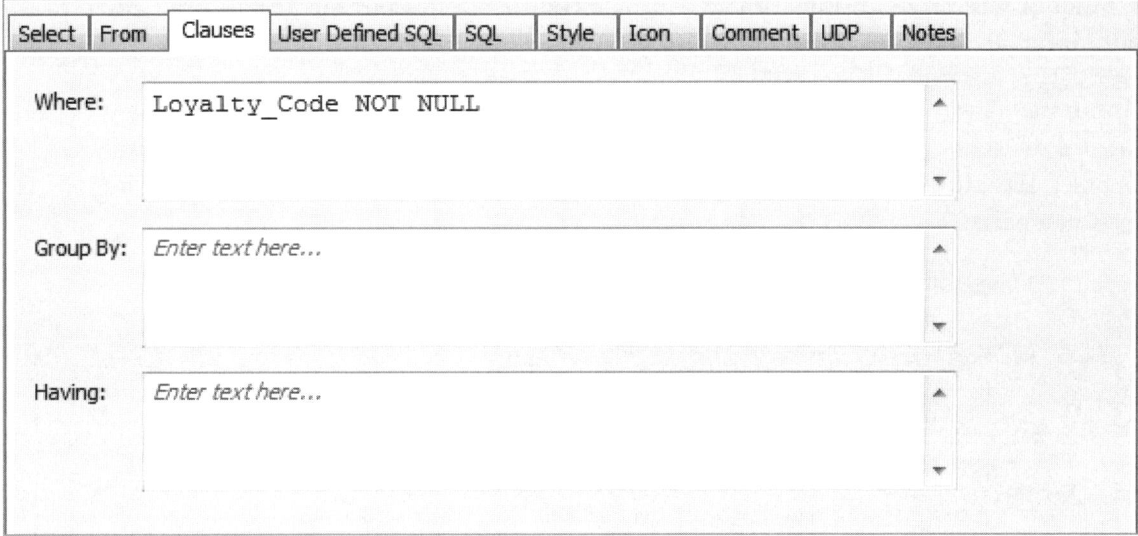

Now that we've defined which columns to retrieve (in the **Select** tab), where to retrieve the columns (in the **From** tab), and what criteria we want to use to limit the scope of our query (in the **Clauses** tab), we can see the full SQL statement created by moving to the **SQL** tab, as shown in Figure 19.69. We'll skip over the **User Defined SQL** tab. That tab is used if you'd like to hand-code your own SQL, which is beyond the scope of a 'Made Simple' book. In fact, using the wizard-driven approach in the View Query Editor as we just walked through is a helpful way to help you learn SQL syntax by example.

Figure 19.69 SQL Tab of View Query Editor Showing Completed SQL Statement

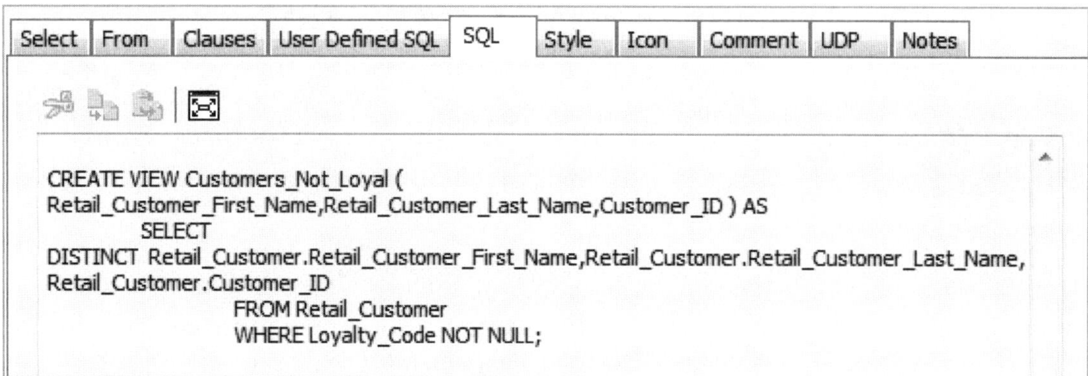

Congratulations! You've created your first SQL statement within a view to retrieve information from a table in your physical data model. But before we leave this editor, we'll want to document the purpose of this query so that the next person who looks at this model will have an idea of the original requirements behind the query. Move to the **Comment** tab, and enter the following summary, as shown in Figure 19.70.

Comment: This view query retrieves a list of all customers who do not have a loyalty code assigned to them. The information shown for each customer is first name, last name, and customer ID. This query was originally requested by the marketing department for their 'Get Loyal' campaign.

Figure 19.70 Documenting a View Query Using the Comment Tab for Good IT Citizenship

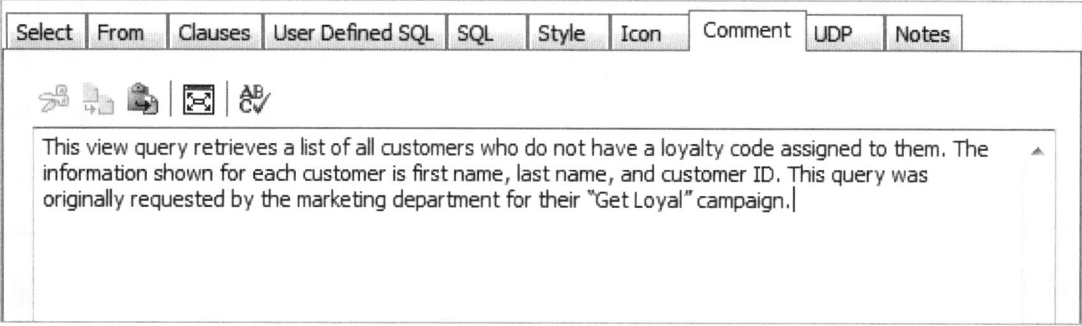

Now that we're finished defining the view, select **Close** to return to your model diagram. The completed view is shown in Figure 19.71.

Figure 19.71 Final Customer_Not_Loyal View

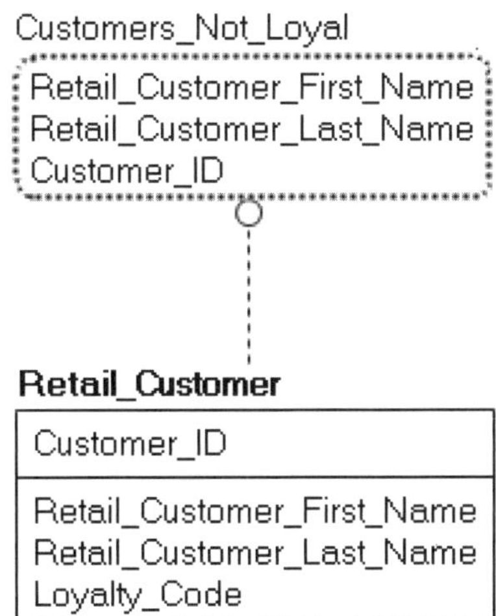

You'll see that the visual representation on the diagram provides a good deal of helpful information about the view. From the columns listed within the view, we can easily see what information is retrieved from this view, in this case **Retail_Customer_First_Name**, **Retail_Customer_Last_Name**, and **Customer_ID**. From the view relationship, we can easily see the source table(s) for this view, in this case **Retail_Customer**. As in many areas, a data model diagram provides an intuitive visual summary of key information without having to read SQL or DDL scripts.

PHYSICAL NAMING STANDARDS

One thing you may have noticed in working with our physical data model is that some of the object names are rather long and unwieldy. For example, typing **Retail_Customer_First_Name** into a SQL query can be cumbersome. For this reason, and to help manage object names on the DBMS platform, many data modelers choose to abbreviate the object names on the physical model. This is where the naming standards that we learned about in Chapter 12 come into play. Since we covered naming standards in detail in Chapter 12, we won't give a step-by-step walkthrough here.

To convert the business-friendly logical names to shortened, more efficient physical names, we'll use a naming standards file. Create a **`Baker Cakes Naming.nsm`** file with the following Glossary information, shown in Figure 19.72. A **`Baker Cakes Glosary.csv`** file with these values is available on www.erwin.com/datamodelingmadesimple if you'd like to import them that way.

Figure 19.72 Naming Standards Glossary for Baker Cakes

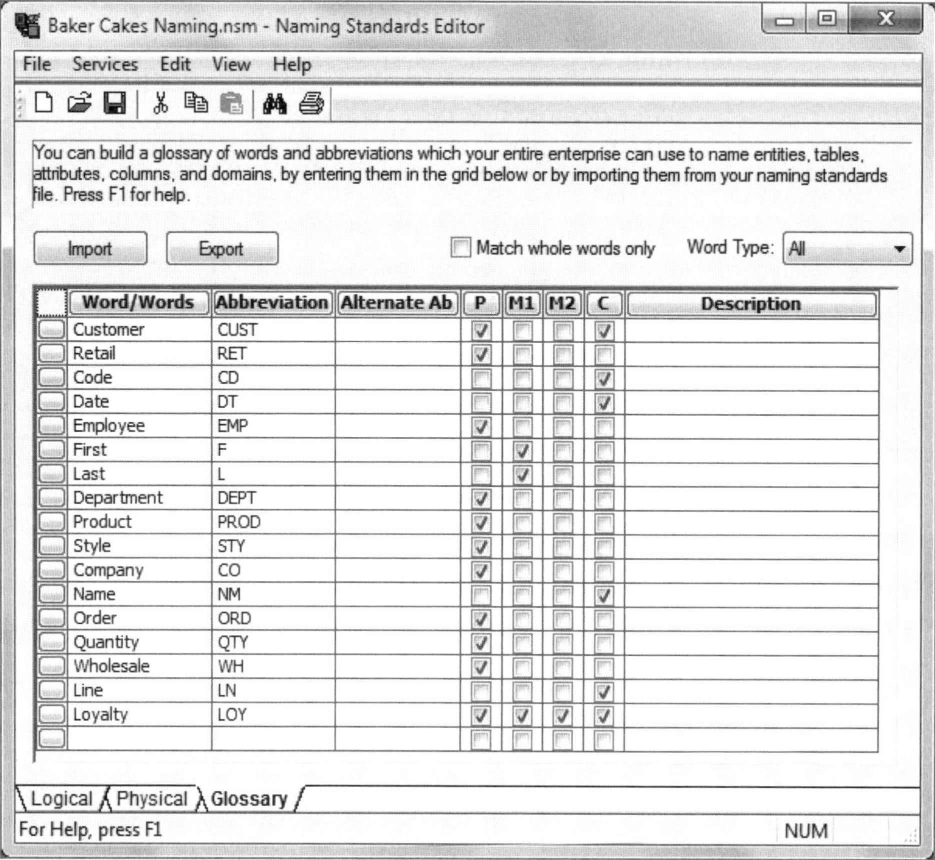

For the **Physical** mapping tab, enter the information shown in Figure 19.73.

Figure 19.73 Physical Mapping Tab for Baker Cakes Naming Standards

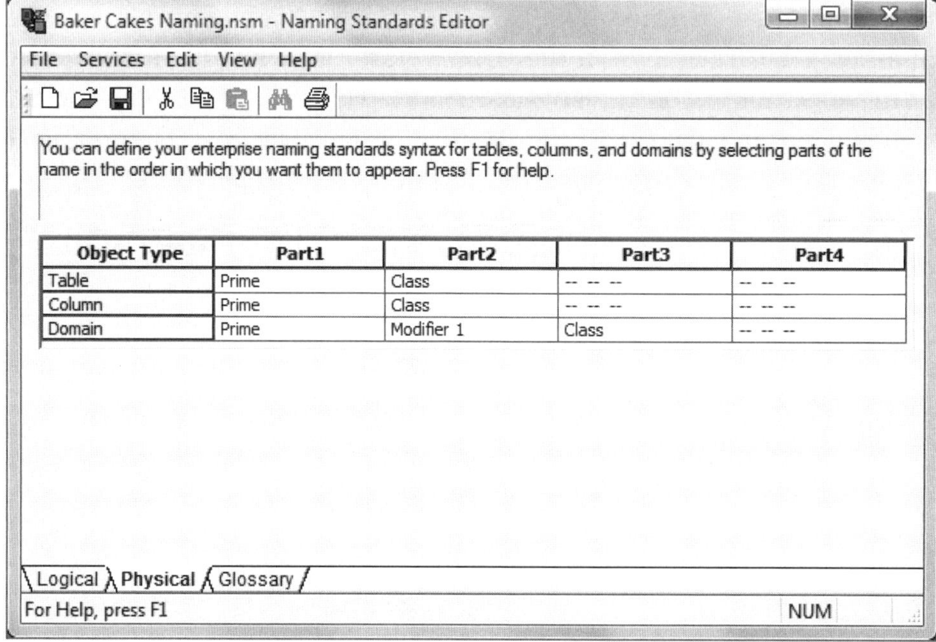

Next, we'll need to specify that the model use this naming standards file to perform the logical to physical name translation. Select **Actions|Model Naming Options** from the **Main Menu**, and the **Model Naming Options** dialog appears, as shown in Figure 19.74.

Figure 19.74 Model Naming Options Dialog

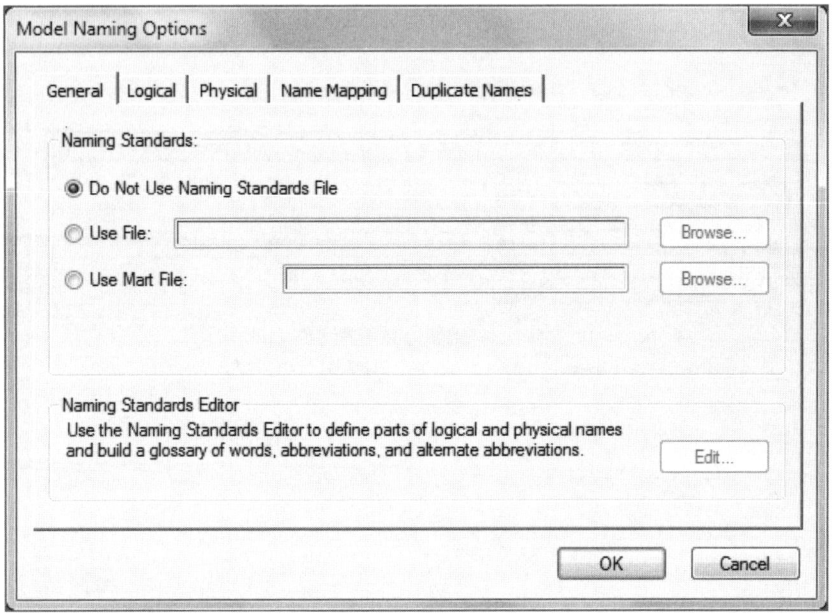

You'll see that the default is to not use a naming standards file. We'll want to specify our new naming standards file we created as the default. Select the **Use File** radio button and select the location for your **`Baker Cakes Naming.nsm`**, as shown in Figure 19.75. You can also download this file at www.erwin.com/datamodelingmadesimple.

Figure 19.75 Specifying a Naming Standards File for a Model

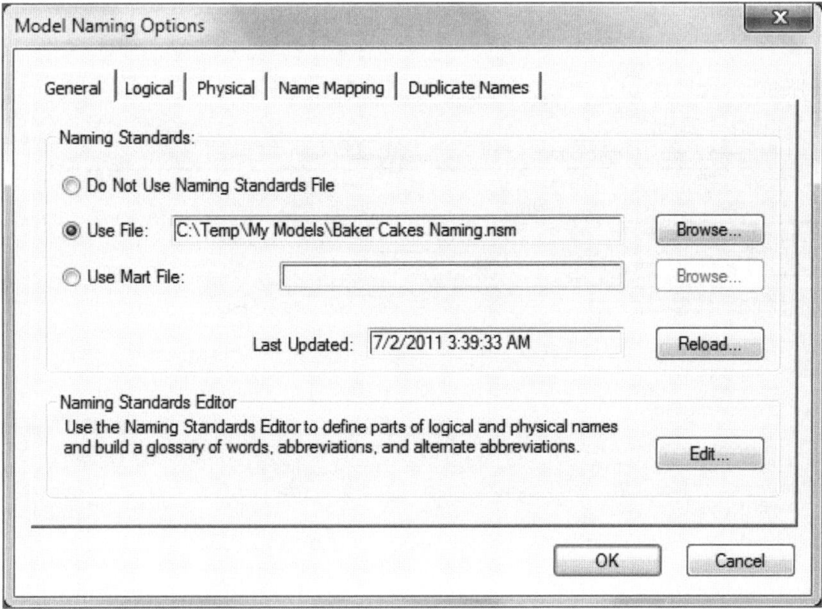

We'd also like all of the physical objects to be listed in uppercase. Move to the **Physical** tab and change the **Case** field to **UPPER**, using the drop-down menu, as shown in Figure 19.76.

Figure 19.76 Changing Physical Model Objects to Uppercase

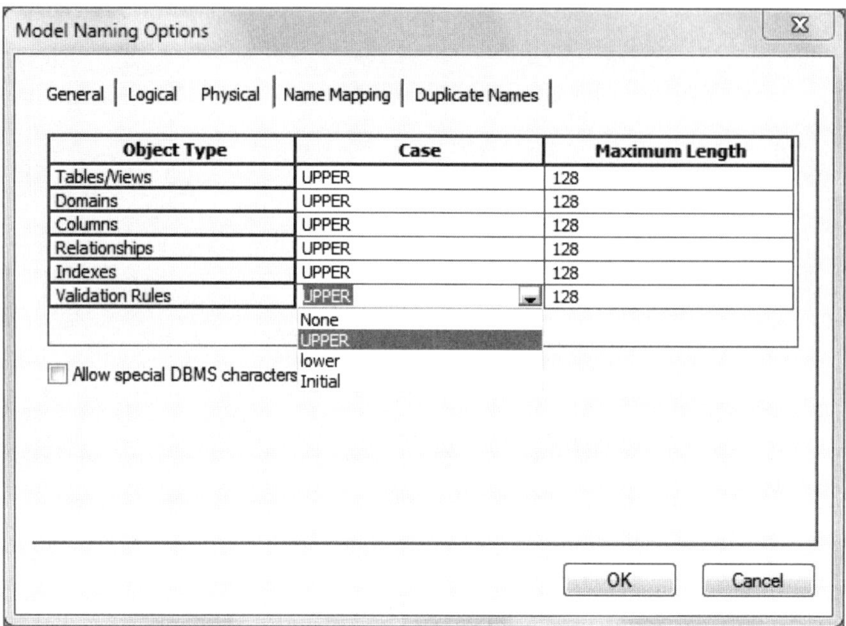

To indicate which object names to translate from the logical to physical layer, move to the **Name Mapping** tab, and choose to use the Glossary abbreviations to translate table and column names by checking **Use Glossary** for the **Entity to Table** and **Attribute to Column** selections, as shown in Figure 19.77.

Figure 19.77 Name Mapping Tab of the Model Naming Options Dialog

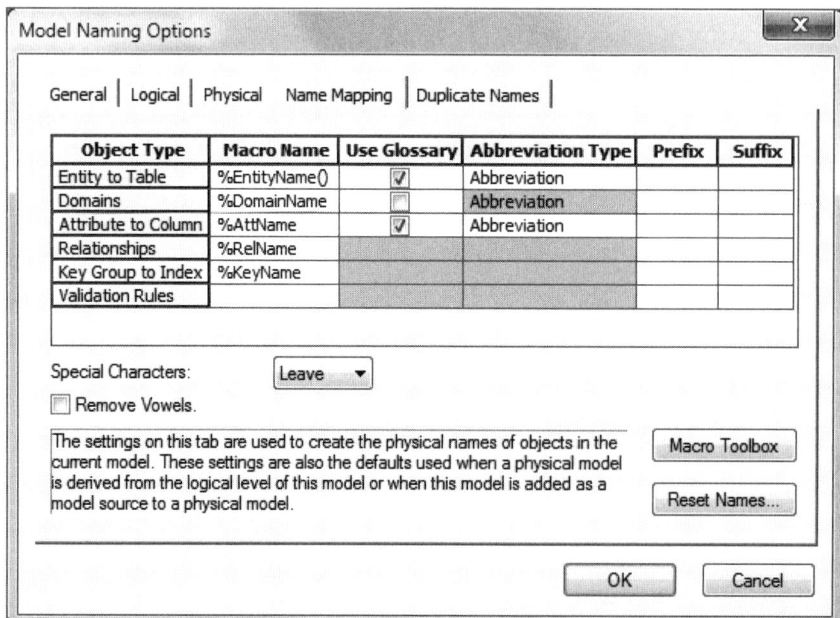

Before we leave this tab, select the **Reset Names** button and click **OK** when asked whether you'd like to globally reset all physical names. While not always necessary, it's a good best practice safeguard to make sure that all of your new names are set across the model. Select **OK** to return to your model diagram and you'll see that the new names reflect the abbreviations we specified in the naming standards glossary, as shown in Figure 19.78.

Figure 19.78 Relational PDM for Baker Cakes with Naming Standards Applied

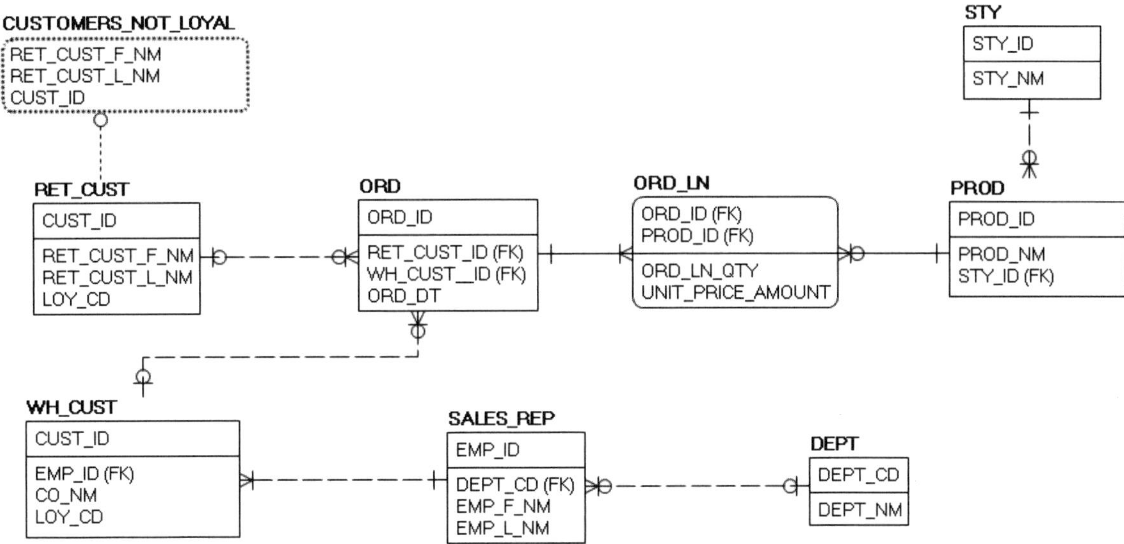

FORWARD ENGINEER

Now that we've finalized our physical data model, we'll want to create a physical database from it through forward engineering. Before we generate any code, however, we'll want to validate our model to make sure that it will generate valid SQL structures for the database. CA ERwin Data Modeler has a process called **Check Model** which allows us to do a validation of the physical model before we reverse engineer. To run this validation, select **Actions|Forward Engineer|Check Model** from the **Main Menu**. A model validation report will be generated, as shown in Figure 19.79, which alerts you to any design errors in the model that will affect forward engineering[19].

[19] Note: There is a separate product in the CA ERwin Data Modeler family that runs a full diagnostic evaluation of the model for normalization errors and analyzes data structures, keys, indexes, columns and relationships for violations of relational database design rules.

Figure 19.79 Model Validation Report

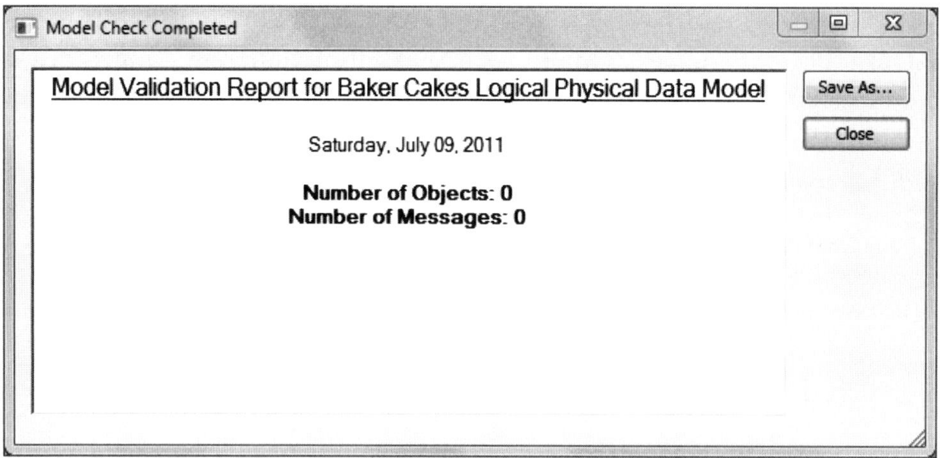

Our validation showed no errors (we're such good modelers!), so we're ready to move ahead to the forward engineering process to create a physical database. Select **Actions|Forward Engineer|Schema** from the **Main Menu**, and the Forward Engineer Schema Generation Editor appears, as shown in Figure 19.80. Note that since we're creating a new database structure, we'll use the **Schema** generation menu item. If we were looking to modify an existing database structure, we'd select the **Alter Script** menu item.

Figure 19.80 Forward Engineer Schema Generation Editor

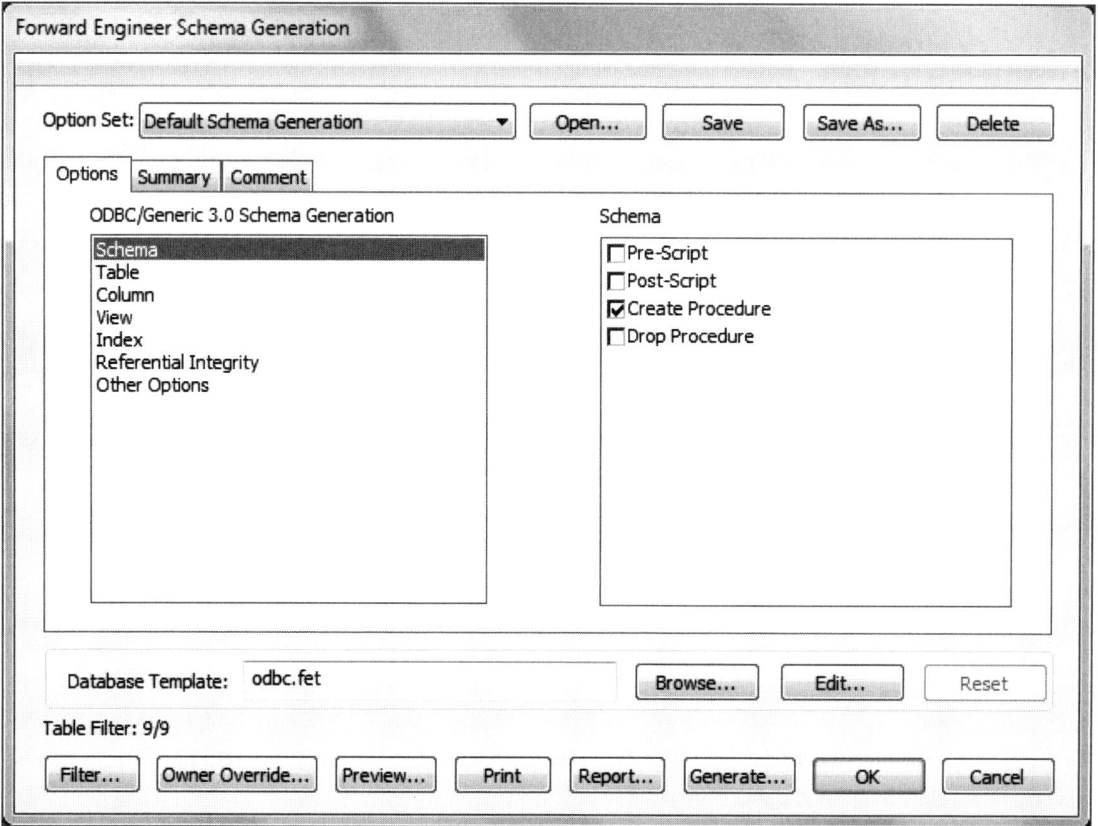

The first thing we'll need to define in the Forward Engineer Schema Generation Editor is the types of objects we want included in our final schema .DDL file. Like the majority of the editors within CA ERwin Data Modeler, you can save your selections as an option set, so that you can reuse them in the future. In our case, we'll use the **Default Schema Generation** template, which defines the commonly used objects for database creation. The objects included in schema generation are customized for each target database platform, as defined in the **Database Template** file. Since we have chosen ODBC as our target platform, the `odbc.fet` database template is automatically selected, as shown in Figure 19.81. You can customize these templates or even create your own for database platforms not supported by CA ERwin Data Modeler, but this is beyond the scope of this book.

Figure 19.81 Database Templates Define Platform-Specific Object Types for Forward Engineering

The **Options** tab defines the object types and statements that will be created in the schema or DDL file generated. For example, highlight the **Table** object, as shown in Figure 19.82, and you'll see that our schema generation will create **CHECK** constraints, **CREATE TABLE** statements, and any necessary stored procedures.

Figure 19.82 Table-Related Objects Created in ODBC Schema Generation

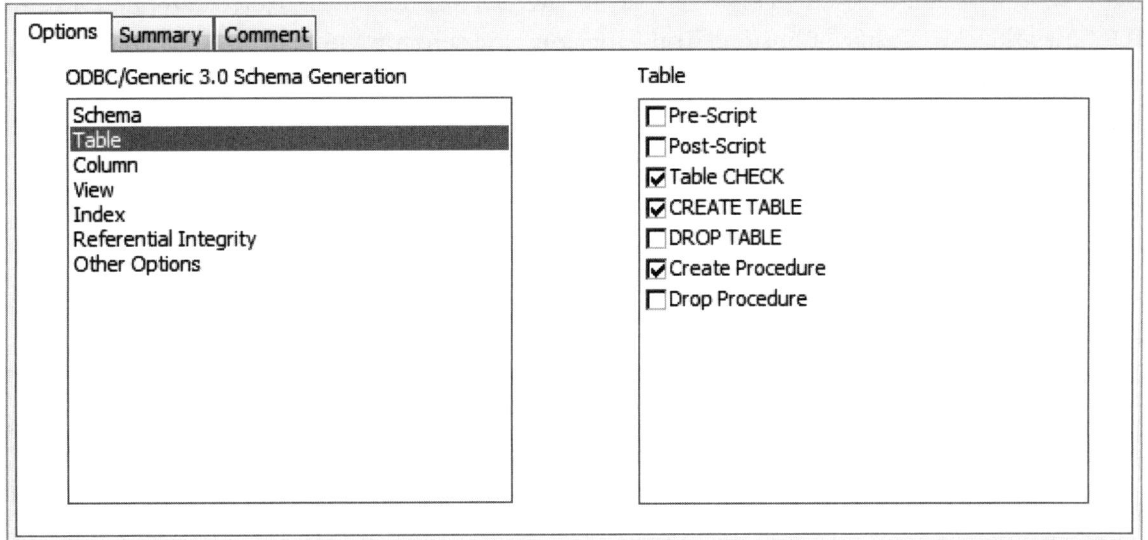

For a summary of all options selected shown in a single view, select the **Summary** tab, as shown in Figure 19.83.

Figure 19.83 Summary of Options Selected for ODBC Schema Generation

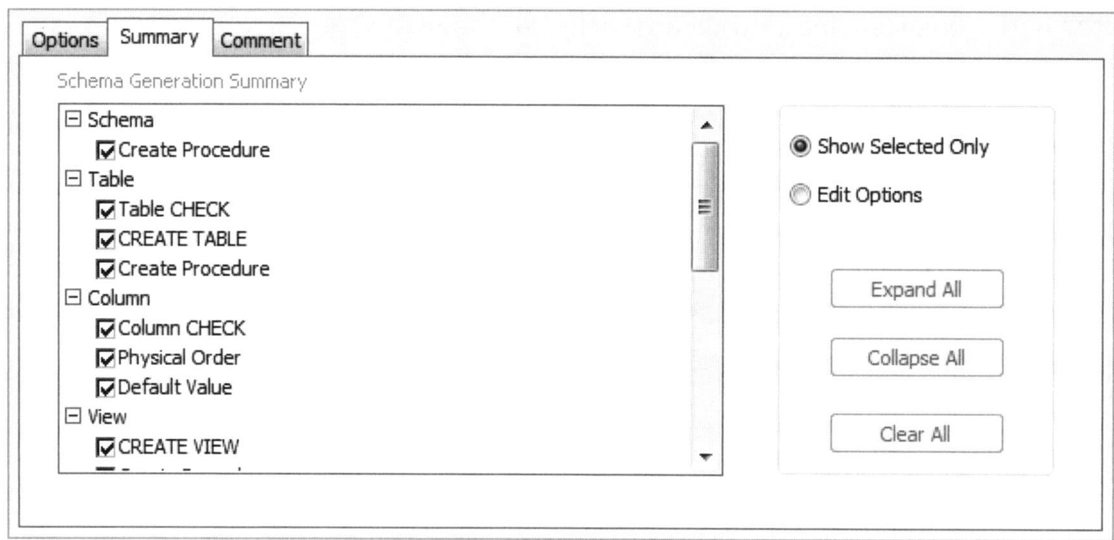

The **Comment** tab is used to provide a brief explanation of the option set you've created. For example "This option set creates tables and columns only" or "This option set creates views, but not tables." Since we're using the default option set in this example, we won't add a comment.

Now that we've defined and reviewed the options for schema generation, we're ready to generate the schema itself. The buttons at the bottom of the editor, shown in Figure 19.84, provide a number of options and functions for schema generation.

Figure 19.84 Schema Generation Buttons

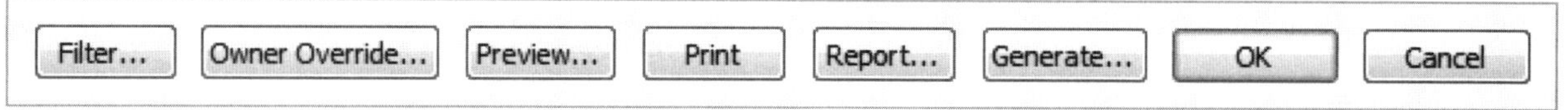

Table 19.6 provides an overview of the functionality of each of these buttons.

Table 19.6 Schema Generation Buttons

Button	Definition
Filter	The **Filter** button allows you to select a subset of tables to be generated in the physical database. The Table Filter Indicator, shown below, appears above the **Filter** button showing how many tables out of the total table list have been selected. In this example, of the 9 total tables available, 8 are included in schema generation. Table Filter: 8/9

Button	Definition
Owner Override	The **Owner Override** option allows you to override the default database owner for objects in the database. You have the option to override all object owners using the **Global Override** option, only table owners using the **Table** option, or only view owners, using the **View** option.
Preview	The **Preview** option opens a preview window in which you can view the schema DDL script that is created based on the options you've set. In addition to viewing the script in this window, you also have options to: • Save the DDL script as a separate file • Print the script • Search/replace key words • Edit the script, either directly in the editor, or with the help of cut/copy/paste buttons. • Generate a database directly into a physical DBMS
Print	The **Print** option automatically prints the DDL script to the default printer.
Report	The **Report** option saves a copy of the DDL script with a file extension of `.ddl`, `.ers`, or `.sql`.
Generate	The **Generate** option creates the database directly into the physical DBMS, without creating an interim file. Note that you need access rights to log into the target database for this option.
OK	Selecting **OK** saves changes to the editor and closes the editor window.
Cancel	Selecting **Cancel** saves changes to the editor and closes the editor window.

In our example, we'd like to generate an external `.DDL` file for our database schema. This gives us the option of checking the DDL script before loading into the database, and allows us to easily share the DDL script with others. In this case, for example, we don't have access to the DBMS, and will need to pass the DDL script to our database administrator (DBA) to load for us. We'll use the **Preview** option, since that gives us the option to preview the script and make any necessary edits before we save the file. Select the **Preview** button, and the Schema Generation Preview Editor opens, as shown in

Figure 19.85. Note that the order of the tables on your screen may be different from that presented here.

Figure 19.85 Schema Generation Preview Editor

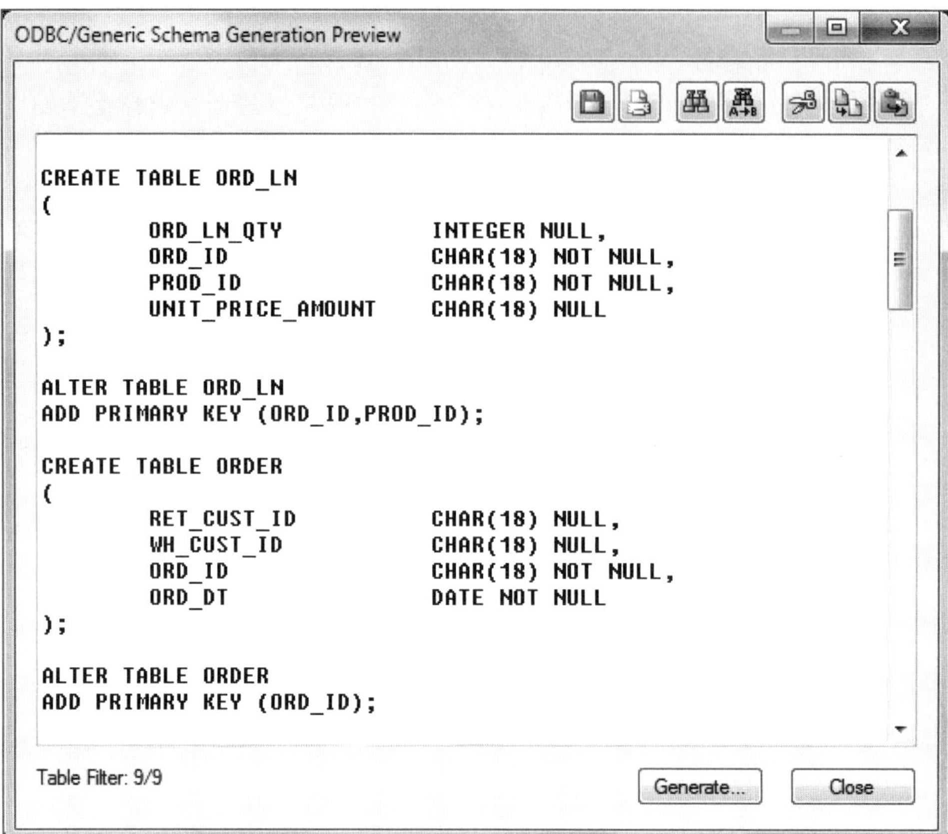

In this editor, we're able to see the DDL script for the database we're creating. Even if you're not familiar with DDL SQL, you should be able to get a sense of what's going on in this script. You'll see **`CREATE`** statements for the tables and columns we defined, as well as **`PRIMARY KEY`** definitions, for example. In this case, we don't need to make any modification to the default DDL, so we'll go ahead and save this file to share with the DBA. Select the **Save** button from the toolbar, and save this file as **`BakerCakes.DDL`**, as shown in Figure 19.86. This file is also available on www.erwin.com/datamodelingmadesimple for your reference.

Figure 19.86 Saving Database Generation Script as an External .DDL file

Congratulations! You've successfully created a conceptual, logical, and physical data model, and learned about data modeling theory along the way. Much of what you'll learn about data modeling will come from your experiences in the field, through interviewing your business sponsors and understanding their organization, and by working and experimenting with the CA ERwin Data Modeler tool. There are a wealth of resources to help you on www.erwin.com, with a broad community of experienced data modelers to help you. We look forward to 'seeing' you in the online community. Good luck on your data modeling journey, as it is a lifelong journey that can be very enjoyable and rewarding.

Key Points

- The physical data model builds upon the logical data model to produce a technical solution.
- Denormalization is the process of selectively violating normalization rules and reintroducing redundancy into the model.
- There are five denormalization techniques: standard, repeating groups, repeating data elements, FUBES, and summarization.
- A view is a virtual table.
- An index is a pointer to something that needs to be retrieved.
- Partitioning is breaking up a table into rows, columns or both. If a table is broken up into columns, the partitioning is vertical. If a table is broken into rows, the partitioning is horizontal.
- Reverse Engineering in CA ERwin Data Modeler creates a physical model from a physical database structure, either from a script file or by directly accessing the database.
- Transforms in CA ERwin Data Modeler assist with common denormalization techniques such as supertype-subtype rolldown.
- Complete Compare allows you to compare models against each other or against physical databases or scripts.
- Use Naming Standards in CA ERwin Data Modeler to translate business names in the logical model to technical names in the physical model (or vice-versa).
- Forward Engineering in CA ERwin Data Modeler creates a physical database structure from a physical data model, either from a script file, or by directly accessing the database.

Suggested Reading

Books

Adelman S., Moss L., Abai M. 2005. *Data Strategy*. Boston, MA: Addison-Wesley Publishing Company.

Blaha,M. 2010. *Patterns in Data Modeling*, Boca Raton, FL: CRC Press.

Chisholm, M. 2010. *Definitions in Information Management*, Orem, UT: Design Media Publishing.

DAMA International 2011. *The DAMA Dictionary of Data Management*, New Jersey: Technics Publications, LLC.

DAMA International 2009. *Data Management Body of Knowledge (DAMA-DMBOK)*, New Jersey: Technics Publications, LLC.

Hay, D. 2011. *Enterprise Model Patterns*. New Jersey: Technics Publications, LLC.

Hoberman, S. 2001. *The Data Modeler's Workbench*. New York: John Wiley & Sons, Inc.

Hoberman, S., Burbank, D., Bradley C. 2009. *Data Modeling for the Business*, New Jersey: Technics Publications, LLC.

Imhoff C., Galemmo, N., Geiger, J. 2003. *Mastering Data Warehouse Design: Relational and Dimensional Techniques*. New York: John Wiley & Sons, Inc.

Kimball R., Ross M., Thornthwaite W., Mundy J., Becker B. 2008. *The Data Warehouse Lifecycle Toolkit: Practical Techniques for Building Data Warehouse and Business Intelligence Systems*. Second Edition. New York: John Wiley & Sons, Inc.

Loshin, David. 2009. *Master Data Management*. San Francisco: Morgan Kaufmann Publishers.

Marco D., Jennings M. 2004. *Universal Metadata Models*. New York: John Wiley & Sons, Inc.

Maydanchik, A. 2007. *Data Quality Assessment*. New Jersey: Technics Publications, LLC.

Potts, C. 2008. *fruITion: Creating the Ultimate Corporate Strategy for Information Technology*. New Jersey: Technics Publications, LLC.

Potts, C. 2010. *recrEAtion: Realizing the Extraordinary Contribution of Your Enterprise Architects*. New Jersey: Technics Publications, LLC.

Silverston, L. 2001. *The Data Model Resource Book, Revised Edition, Volume 1, A Library of Universal Data Models For All Enterprises*. New York: John Wiley & Sons, Inc.

Silverston, L. 2001. *The Data Model Resource Book, Revised Edition, Volume 2, A Library of Universal Data Models For Industry Types.* New York: John Wiley & Sons, Inc.

Silverston, L. Agnew, P. 2009. *The Data Model Resource Book, Volume 3, Universal Patterns for Data Modeling.* New York: John Wiley & Sons, Inc.

Simsion, G. 2007. *Data Modeling Theory and Practice.* New Jersey: Technics Publications, LLC.

Simsion G., Witt G. 2005. *Data Modeling Essentials, Third Edition.* San Francisco: Morgan Kaufmann Publishers.

Web Sites

ERWIN-SPECIFIC RESOURCES

www.erwin.com – A single source for all things ERwin and data modeling related. White Papers, webcasts, videos, software downloads, User Community, and more

www.erwin.com/datamodelingmadesimple – Web site specifically for this book, sample models, answers to exercises, and more

CA ERwin on LinkedIn – CA ERwin Modeling group (group id = 2637898)

CA ERwin on Facebook – www.facebook.com/erwinmodeling

CA ERwin on Twitter – www.twitter.com/erwinmodeling

CA ERwin on YouTube – www.youtube.com/erwinmodeling

INDUSTRY SITES

www.dama.org – Conferences, chapter information, and articles

www.infoadvisors.com – Website dedicated to information technology processes, from industry expert Karen Lopez

www.information-management.com – Check out their Data Modeling Channel

www.metadata-standards.org/11179 – Formulation of data definition

www.stevehoberman.com – Add your email address to the Design Challenge list to receive modeling puzzles

www.tdan.com – In-depth quarterly newsletter. I visit this site very often to read the current newsletter or search the archives

www.technicspub.com – Practical and user-friendly business intelligence and data management books (like this one!)

APPENDIX A: CA ERwin Data Modeler Toolbars

The following is a list of the toolbars available in CA ERwin Data Modeler, and a brief overview of their functionality. A list of the available toolbars can be seen by invoking the **View | Toolbars** selection from the **Main Menu**, as shown in Figure A.1.

Figure A.1 List of Toolbars Available in CA ERwin Data Modeler

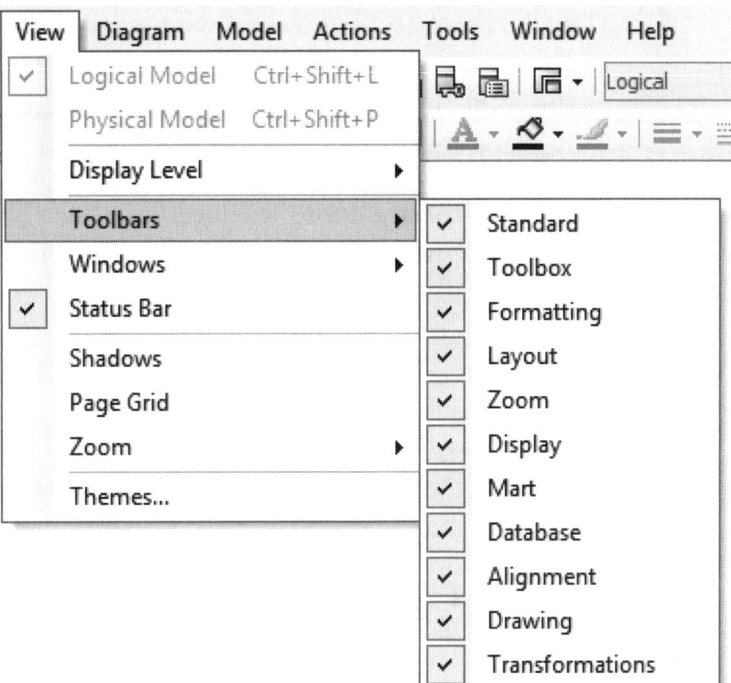

Standard Toolbar: The **Standard Toolbar**, shown in Figure A.2, contains shortcuts to common functions such as saving, printing, etc. A list of these functions and a description of their use is listed in Table A.1.

Figure A.2 Standard Toolbar

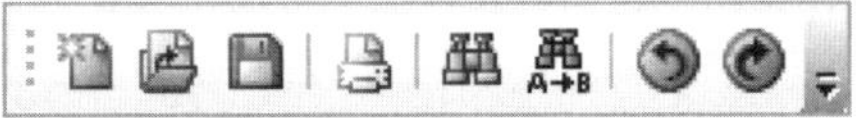

Table A.1 Standard Toolbar Buttons with Descriptions

Icon	Name	Description
	New Model	Creates a new CA ERwin Data Modeler model or template.
	Open Model	Opens an existing CA ERwin Data Modeler model or template.
	Save Model	Saves the current open model.

Icon	Name	Description
	Print	Invokes the **Print** dialog, where you can define whether to print the current diagram or all diagrams, specify the number of copies, define horizontal or vertical orientation, etc.
	Find	Invokes the **Find and Replace** dialog where you can run a text string search across the currently open model and optionally replace with the text specified. You can use features such as matching case, wild cards, and search direction. <u>**Note:**</u> The 'Replace' selection is not selected by default using the Find option, but you can easily invoke by selecting the Replace check box.
A→B	**Replace**	Invokes the Find and Replace dialog where you can run a text string search across the currently open model and replace with the text specified. You can use features such as matching case, wild cards, and search direction. Using this button, the **Replace** check box is automatically selected for you.
	Undo	Reverses the last (most recent) action from the Action Log. For more information on the **Action Log**, see Chapter 9.
	Redo	Recreates the first (most recent) undone transaction from the **Action Log**. For more information on the Action Log, see Chapter 9.

Toolbox Toolbar: The **Toolbox Toolbar** provides the 'tools of the trade' for the data modeler. It is this toolbar that contains the main objects that you will place on your model diagrams. The content of this toolbar is dependent upon the model level and notation you are working with—there are model objects that are unique to logical data modeling vs. physical data modeling, IDEF Notation vs. IE (Information Engineering) Notation, etc. The following is an overview of the model objects available in the **Toolbox Toolbar**.

The **Logical Model Toolbar** has two variations: one for the IDEF Notation, shown in Figure A.3, and another for the IE Notation, shown in Figure A.4. You'll notice that the main difference is in the relationship symbols, which are described in more detail in Chapter 6. Table A.2 provides a detailed description of the functionality of each of the toolbar buttons, which is similar for both notations.

Figure A.3 Toolbox Toolbar for Logical IDEF Notation

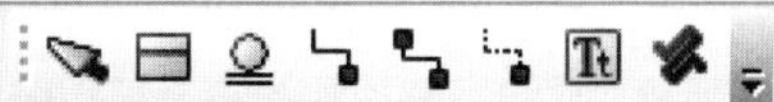

Figure A.4 Toolbox Toolbar for Logical IE Notation

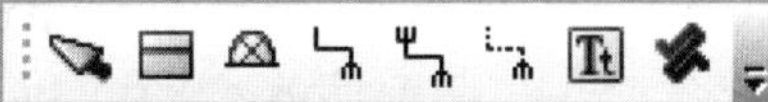

Table A.2 Toolbox Toolbar Buttons for Logical Model (IDEF and IE) with Descriptions

Icon for IDEF Notation	Icon for IE Notation	Name	Description
		Select Pointer	The **Select Pointer** allows you to select objects on the diagram. You'll notice that the mouse cursor changes shape depending on the object type and action to be taken. For example: a hand icon allows you to move the order of an attribute, a pointer icon selects an object for editing, a double arrow allows you to change the size of an object, etc.
		Entity	The **Entity** button allows you to create a new entity on the diagram. After selecting the button, click on the diagram to place the object in the desired location. An entity will be created with the name field in auto-entry mode, where you can simply type the name of the new entry and hit **Enter**. The default name is E/*n* where *n* is a consecutive number for each entity created in the model. **Note:** You can invoke the multi-drop feature by holding down the **Ctrl** key as you select the **Entity** button. This will allow you to drop multiple entities on the diagram without reselecting the toolbar button.

Icon for IDEF Notation	Icon for IE Notation	Name	Description
		Subcategory	The **Subcategory** button requires that you have at least three entities on the diagram in order to function properly. First, click the parent entity in the relationship, then click the first child entity. This will create the subtype relationship between the parent and child. To create the second child relationship, select the Subcategory icon on the toolbar, next click the symbol on the relationship, then click another child entity. To create additional child relationship, simply repeat the previous step for as many child relationships as exist. **Note:** You can invoke the multi-drop feature by holding down the **Ctrl** key as you select the **Entity** button. This will allow you to drop multiple entities on the diagram without reselecting the toolbar button.
		Identifying Relationship	The **Identifying Relationship** button allows you to create a relationship between two entities in which the child entity is identified through its association with a parent entity. To create the identifying relationship, click the parent entity, then click the child entity. Notice that the child entity's corners become rounded, indicating that it is a dependent entity. **Note**: Primary key attributes are automatically migrated from a parent entity to a child entity, so you do not need to enter any foreign keys in the child.
		Many-to-Many Relationship	The **Many-to-Many Relationship** button allows you to create a many-to-many relationship between two entities where instances in one entity have zero, one, or more related instances in the other entity. To create the relationship, first click on the parent entity, then select the child entity, and a solid relationship line will be created.

Icon for IDEF Notation	Icon for IE Notation	Name	Description
		Non-Identifying Relationship	The **Non-Identifying Relationship** button allows you to create a non-identifying relationship between two entities where the child entity is not dependent on the parent entity for its identity and can exist without it. In a non-identifying relationship, one instance of the parent entity is related to multiple instances of the child. To create the relationship, first click on the parent entity, then select the child entity, and a dashed relationship line will be created.
		Annotation	An **Annotation** allows you to add text-based comments and explanations to your model. Like other model objects, an annotation can have its own metadata defined, such as a definition or UDP. You can connect annotations to other model objects using the **Connector** object on the **Drawing Toolbar**. Unlike drawing objects (which also can contain text) annotations are persisted across the model, not just the diagram, and therefore can be included as members in multiple diagrams or subject areas. The downside of this reusability is that annotations require more memory than drawing objects.
		Line	The **Line** button allows you to create the line drawing object on the diagram. Note that the **Line** object is different from the **Connector** object on the **Drawing Toolbar**. Rather than connect various objects, its main purpose is to draw a graphic image. To draw a line, select the **Line** button, click on the diagram, and then drag the cursor to create a line of the desired length. A second click adds a bend point to the line, where you can continue to drag, click, and drag to create multiple bend points. Double-clicking finalizes the line creation.

The **Physical Model Toolbar** has three variations: one for the IDEF Notation, shown in Figure A.5, another for the IE Notation, shown in Figure A.6, and a third for dimensional (data warehousing), shown in Figure A.7. You'll notice that the main difference is in the relationship symbols, which are described in more detail in Chapter 6. Table A.3 provides a detailed description of the functionality of each of the toolbar buttons, which is similar for all three notations.

Figure A.5 Toolbox Toolbar for Physical IDEF Notation

Figure A.6 Toolbox Toolbar for Physical IE Notation

Figure A.7 Toolbox Toolbar for Physical Dimensional (Data Warehousing) Model

Table A.3 Toolbox Toolbar Buttons for Physical Model (IDEF,IE, Dimensional) with Descriptions

Icon for IDEF Notation	Icon for IE Notation	Icon for Dimensional Notation	Name	Description
			Select Pointer	The select pointer allows you to select objects on the diagram. You'll notice that the mouse cursor changes shape depending on the object type and action to be taken. For example: a hand icon allows you to move the order of a column, a pointer icon selects an object for editing, a double arrow allows you to change the size of an object, etc.
			Table	The **Table** button allows you to create a new physical database table on the diagram. After selecting the button, click on the diagram to place the object in the desired location. A table will be created with the name field in auto-entry mode, where you can simply type the name of the new entry and hit **Enter**. The default name is E/*n* where *n* is a consecutive number for each table created in the model. **Note:** You can invoke the multi-drop feature by holding down the **Ctrl** key as you select the **Table** button. This will allow you to drop multiple entities on the diagram without reselecting the toolbar icon.

Icon for IDEF Notation	Icon for IE Notation	Icon for Dimensional Notation	Name	Description
			Materialized View (Oracle) or Materialized Query Table (DB2)	This button only appears when the target database is set to Oracle or DB2 (LUW or z/OS). The **Materialized Query Table** button is used for DB2, and **Materialized View** is used for Oracle. Both terms refer to a database object that is used to hold the results of a query. You can define the parameters of this query within the object's property editor.
			View Table	The **View Table** button allows you to create a database view on a physical diagram. After selecting the button, click on the diagram to place the object in the desired location. A View is a virtual table containing the result set of a query. You can define the parameters of this query within the object's property editor.
			Identifying Relationship	The **Identifying Relationship** button allows you to create a relationship between two tables in which the child table is identified through its association with a parent table. To create the identifying relationship, click the parent table, then click the child table. Notice that the child table's corners become rounded, indicating that it is a dependent table.
			View/ Materialized Relationship	A **View/Materialized Relationship** creates a linkage between a view and the table to be queried in the view or materialized query (for DB2).

Icon for IDEF Notation	Icon for IE Notation	Icon for Dimensional Notation	Name	Description
			Non-Identifying Relationship	The **Non-Identifying Relationship** button allows you to create a non-identifying relationship between two tables where the child table is not dependent on the parent table for its identity and can exist without it. In a non-identifying relationship, one instance of the parent table is related to multiple instances of the child. To create the relationship, first click on the parent table, then select the child table, and a dashed relationship line will be created.
Tt	Tt	Tt	**Annotation**	An **Annotation** allows you to add text-based comments and explanations to your model. Like other model objects, an annotation can have its own metadata defined, such as a definition or UDP. You can connect annotations to other model objects using the **Connector** object on the **Drawing Toolbar**. Unlike drawing objects (which also can contain text) annotations are persisted across the model, and therefore can be included as members in multiple diagrams or subject areas. The downside of this reusability is that annotations require more memory than drawing objects.
			Line	The **Line** button allows you to create the line drawing object on the diagram. Note that the **Line** object is different from the **Connector** object on the **Drawing Toolbar**. Rather than connect various objects, its main purpose is to draw a graphic image. To draw a line, select the **Line** button, click on the diagram, and then drag the cursor to create a line of the desired length. A second click adds a bend point to the line, where you can continue to drag, click, and drag to create multiple bend points. Double-clicking finalizes the line creation.

Formatting Toolbar: The **Formatting Toolbar**, shown in Figure A.8, provides a number of options to change the display of the objects on your diagram, including font, color, and formatting settings. Table A.4 provides a detailed description of the functionality of each of the toolbar buttons.

Figure A.8 Formatting Toolbar

Table A.4 Formatting Toolbar Buttons with Descriptions

Icon	Name	Description
Microsoft Sans Serif	**Font Style**	Allows you to change the typeface style for selected text on the diagram, including object names, annotation boxes, etc. Over 290 default types styles are included.
10	**Font size**	Changes the point size of selected text on the current diagram using a drop-down list box. Sixteen default sizes are included in the drop-down list (8,9,19,12,14,16,18,20,24,26,2836,48,72), or you can enter your own custom size by simply typing directly into the text box and pressing **Enter**.
B	**Bold**	Changes selected text to **bold.**
I	**Italic**	Changes selected text to *italic.*
U	**Underline**	Places an underline under selected text.
S	**Strikethrough**	Marks a ~~strikethrough~~ line through selected text.
A	**Text Color**	Allows you to modify the color of selected text using the drop-down color palette shown below. The automatic option bases font color on the current Theme. Automatic Theme Colors Standard Colors More Colors...

Icon	Name	Description
	**Background Color**	Allows you to modify the background color of shaped objects (entities, tables, annotations, etc.) using the drop-down color palette shown below. The automatic option bases the background color on the current Theme. 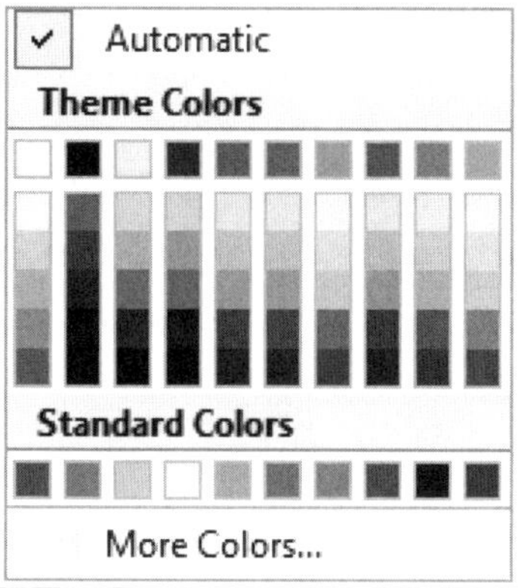 Automatic Theme Colors Standard Colors More Colors...
	**Line/Outline Color**	Allows you to modify the color of the border line for shaped objects (entities, tables, annotations, etc.) using the drop-down color palette shown below. The automatic option bases the outline color on the current Theme. 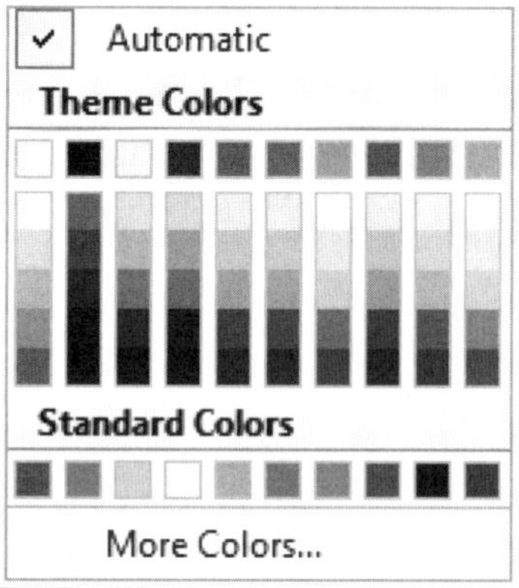 Automatic Theme Colors Standard Colors More Colors...
	**Line Weight**	Changes the thickness (or weight) of a selected line using the drop-down menu shown below. The automatic option bases the line color on the current Theme. 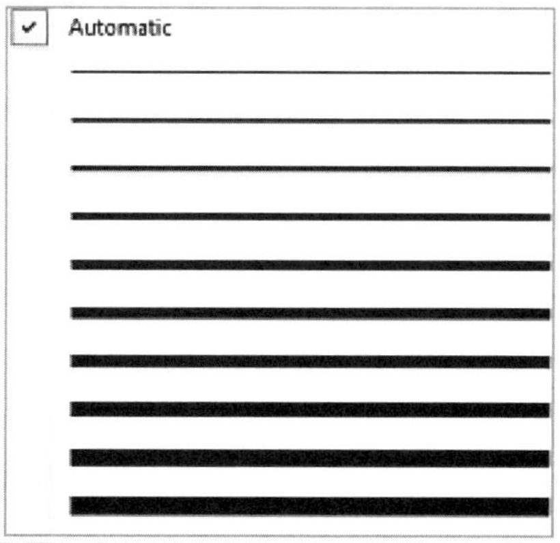 Automatic

Icon	Name	Description
	Line Pattern	Modifies the line pattern of a selected line shape, according to the drop-down menu options shown below. Note that this option is only active for drawing shapes, not relationship lines. The patterns for relationship lines are metadata-driven (e.g. dashed line for non-identifying relationship). The automatic option uses the line patterns from the current Theme. 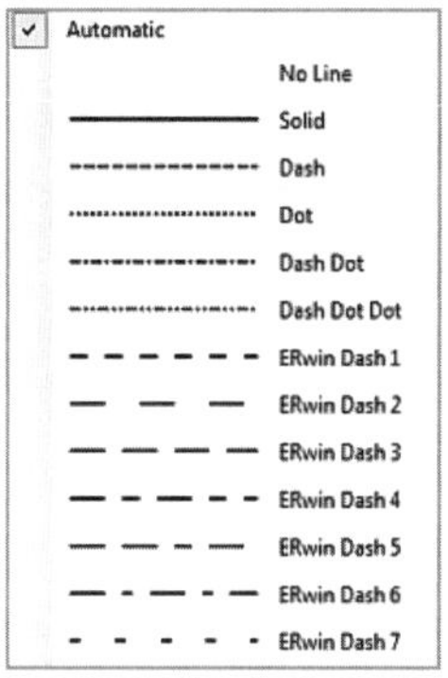 Automatic No Line Solid Dash Dot Dash Dot Dash Dot Dot ERwin Dash 1 ERwin Dash 2 ERwin Dash 3 ERwin Dash 4 ERwin Dash 5 ERwin Dash 6 ERwin Dash 7
	Line Ends	Customizes the beginning and end shape connectors for a selected line shape, according to the drop-down menu options shown below. Note that this option is only active for drawing shapes, not relationship lines. The patterns for relationship lines are metadata-driven (e.g. round connector for many relationships in IDEF notation). The automatic option uses the line patterns from the current Theme. 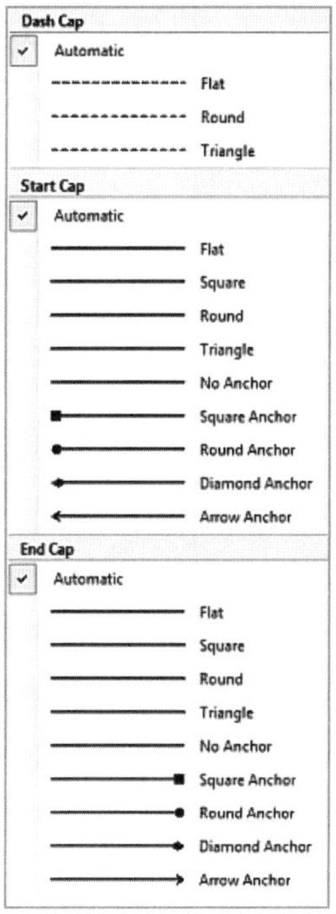 Dash Cap Automatic Flat Round Triangle Start Cap Automatic Flat Square Round Triangle No Anchor Square Anchor Round Anchor Diamond Anchor Arrow Anchor End Cap Automatic Flat Square Round Triangle No Anchor Square Anchor Round Anchor Diamond Anchor Arrow Anchor

Layout Toolbar: The **Layout Toolbar**, shown in Figure A.9, contains auto-layout options that will redraw your diagram layout in a single click. Table A.5 provides a detailed description of the functionality of each of the toolbar buttons.

Figure A.9 Layout Toolbar

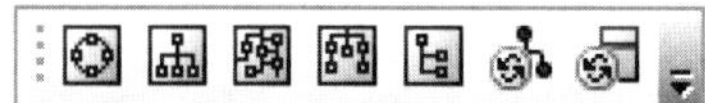

Table A.5 Layout Toolbar Buttons with Descriptions

Icon	Name	Description
	Circular Layout	A circular layout displays objects in a ring-like or circular pattern, as shown below. 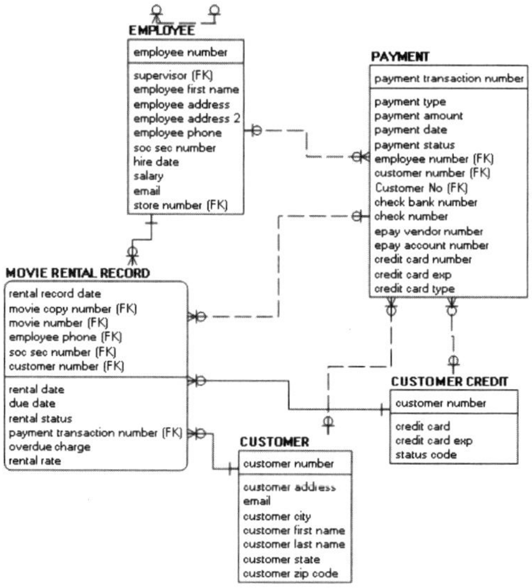
	Hierarchical Layout	A hierarchical layout displays model objects in a top-down, organization chart-style manner, as shown below. 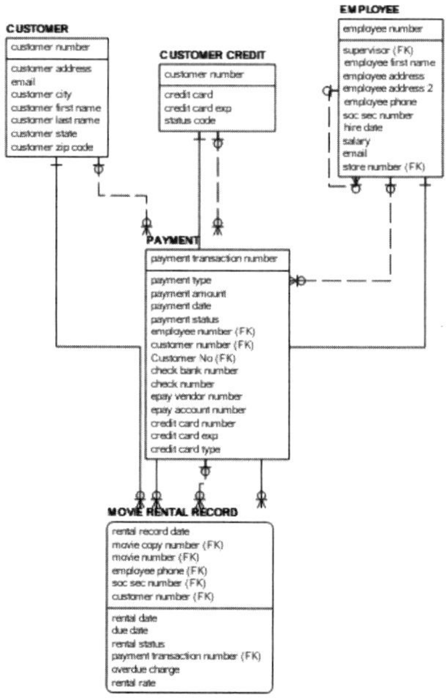

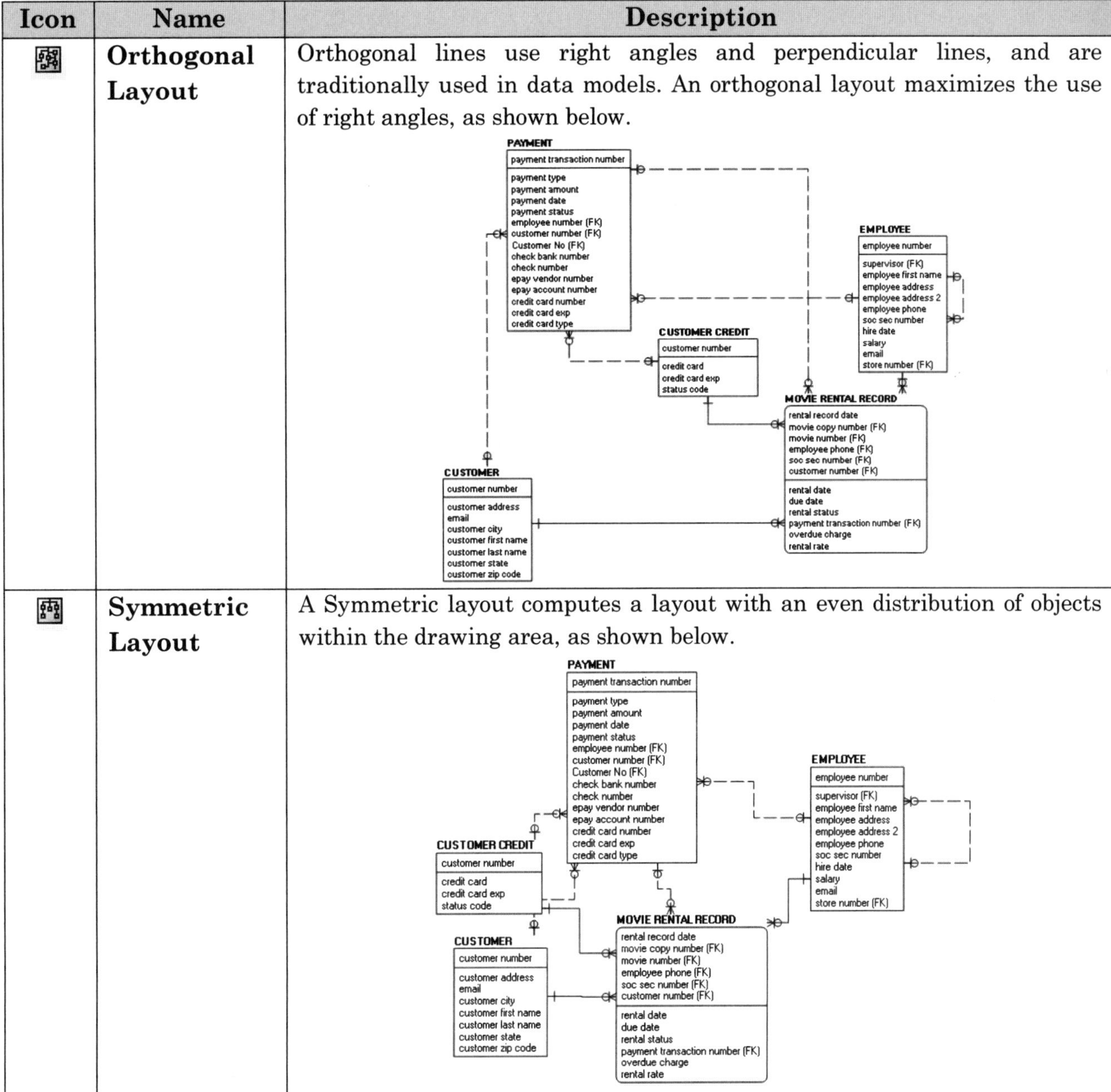

Icon	Name	Description
	Orthogonal Layout	Orthogonal lines use right angles and perpendicular lines, and are traditionally used in data models. An orthogonal layout maximizes the use of right angles, as shown below.
	Symmetric Layout	A Symmetric layout computes a layout with an even distribution of objects within the drawing area, as shown below.

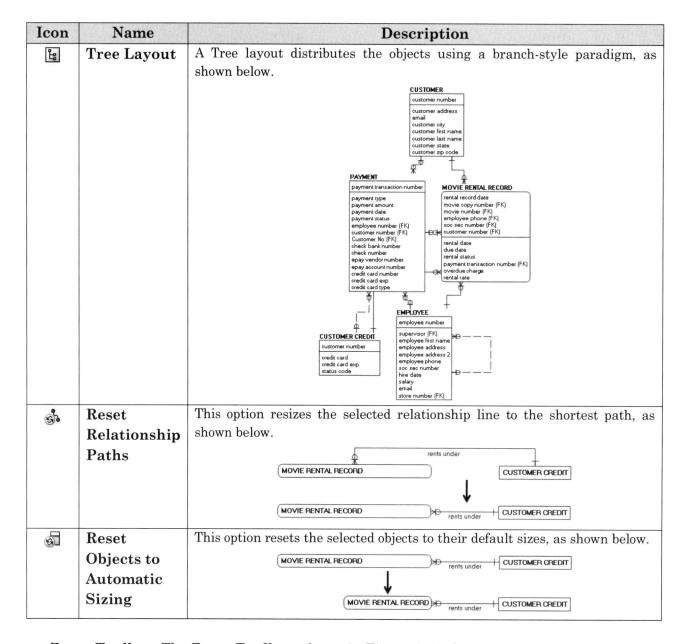

Icon	Name	Description
	Tree Layout	A Tree layout distributes the objects using a branch-style paradigm, as shown below.
	Reset Relationship Paths	This option resizes the selected relationship line to the shortest path, as shown below.
	Reset Objects to Automatic Sizing	This option resets the selected objects to their default sizes, as shown below.

Zoom Toolbar: The **Zoom Toolbar**, shown in Figure A.10, has a number of options to allow you to change the magnification level of the model diagram. Note that these settings affect the model diagram only, and do not apply to print settings. Table A.6 provides a detailed description of the functionality of each of the toolbar buttons.

Figure A.10 Zoom Toolbar

Table A.6 Zoom Toolbar Buttons with Descriptions

Icon	Name	Description
	Zoom Out	Clicking the **Zoom Out** button decreases the magnification of your model diagram (i.e. makes the diagram smaller). Each click decreases the magnification by 10% (i.e. from 50% to 40%).
	Zoom In	Clicking the **Zoom In** button increases the magnification of your model diagram (i.e. makes the diagram larger). Each click increases the magnification by 10% (i.e. from 50% to 60%).
	Zoom Normal	The **Zoom Normal** button resets the magnification to 100%, regardless of the previous setting.
	Zoom to Fit Model	The **Zoom to Fit Model** button automatically sets the magnification level so that the entire model diagram fits within the diagram window.
	Zoom to Fit Selection	The **Zoom to Fit Selection** button allows you to easily 'zoom in' on a particular area of your model diagram. Simply select the button, drag the magnifying glass cursor around objects that you want to view, and click the button again to apply the zoom level. The magnification level will be automatically adjusted so that the selected area fills the diagram window.

Display Toolbar: The **Display Toolbar**, shown in Figure A.11, allows you to change the display level settings for your model diagram or selected objects on the diagram. See Chapter 4 for more information on display levels. Table A.7 provides a detailed description of the functionality of each of the toolbar buttons.

Figure A.11 Display Toolbar

Table A.7 Display Toolbar Buttons with Descriptions

Icon	Name	Description
	Entity or Table Display Level	This option converts the open model to an entity-level or table-level display, where only entity names are shown, as displayed below: MOVIE_RENTAL_RECORD
	Primary Key Display Level	The **Primary Key Display Level** lists the entity or table with only the primary key attributes shown, as displayed below: MOVIE RENTAL RECORD rental record date DATE movie copy number INTEGER (FK) movie number INTEGER (FK) soc sec number INTEGER (FK) employee phone INTEGER (FK) customer number INTEGER (FK)
	Attribute or Column Display Level	Converts the open model to an attribute-level display, where attributes are shown inside of the entity box, as displayed below: MOVIE RENTAL RECORD rental record date DATE movie copy number INTEGER (FK) movie number INTEGER (FK) employee phone INTEGER (FK) soc sec number INTEGER (FK) customer number INTEGER (FK) rental date DATE due date DATE rental status VARCHAR(20) payment transaction number INTEGER (FK) overdue charge INTEGER rental rate INTEGER
	Keys Display Level	The **Keys Display Level** lists the entity or table with only all of the key attributes shown (e.g. primary keys and foreign keys), as displayed below: MOVIE RENTAL RECORD rental record date DATE movie copy number INTEGER (FK) movie number INTEGER (FK) employee phone INTEGER (FK) soc sec number INTEGER (FK) customer number INTEGER (FK) payment transaction number INTEGER (FK)

Icon	Name	Description
	Definition Level	This option shows the definition inside of the entity box instead of attributes, as displayed below: MOVIE RENTAL RECORD A MOVIE RENTAL RECORD is a record that is kept on every MOVIE in the STORE on who and when a MOVIE is rented
	Edit Subject Area	Allows you to toggle to a selected Subject Area or create a new subject area. Selecting the downward arrow ▾ invokes a drop-down list of Subject Areas to choose from, as displayed below: Logical <Model> Accounting Customer Employee Movie Selecting the Subject Area icon invokes the **Subject Area Properties Editor**, which is discussed in detail in Chapter 8. In this editor, you can create new Subject Areas, or edit existing ones.
Logical	**Design Layer Indicator**	Allows you to toggle between Design Layers, e.g. Logical/Physical, as displayed below: Logical Logical Physical

Mart Toolbar: The **Mart Toolbar**, shown in Figure A.12, contains common functions used for change management, versioning, and collaboration features found in the CA ERwin Data Modeler Workgroup Edition. Note that the Workgroup Edition is not covered in this book, but we provide a brief overview of these features as an initial guide to their usage. Table A.8 provides a detailed description of the functionality of each of the toolbar buttons.

Figure A.12 Mart Toolbar

Table A.8 Mart Toolbar Buttons with Descriptions

Icon	Name	Description
	Open Mart Model	This button opens a model stored in a mart associated with the CA ERwin Data Modeler Workgroup Edition.
	Save Mart Model	Invoking this button saves a model into a mart associated with the CA ERwin Data Modeler Workgroup Edition.
	Lock Mart Model	This option locks a model stored in a mart so that it cannot be modified by other users.
	Library Manager	This button invokes the Library Manager where you can manage libraries within a mart (create, rename, and delete), as well as rename or delete a model stored in a mart.
	Sub-Model Manager	This option invokes the Sub-Model Manager where you can manage sub-models within a mart (create, rename, and delete). You can create sub-models within a mart to focus on a specific business unit or process. When you save a CA ERwin Data Modeler data model that contains subject areas to a mart, each subject area automatically becomes a sub-model.
	Merge Mart Model	This option allows you to merge one or more models within a mart. For example, you may need to merge models when you need to: • Combine two models into one larger model • Migrate from a stand-alone model file (**`.erwin`**) to a mart
	Refresh Mart Model	The **Refresh Mart Model** button updates the current, open model in use with any changes made to the server version by you or by other users.
	Review Changes to Mart Model	This option invokes the Resolve Differences dialog, which displays a list of changes to the current model since you opened the model from the mart.
	Version Manager	This button opens the Version Manager, where you can see previous versions of a model. Each time changes are saved, a new version is created with a sequential version number.
	Connect to Mart	This option invokes the Connection Manager where you can connect/disconnect to/from a mart to access models and perform administrative functions.
	Security Manager	This button opens the Security manager, where you can create and assign custom security profiles.

Database Toolbar: The **Database Toolbar**, shown in Figure A.13, contains a number of functions related to database generation, reverse engineering, comparison, etc. Table A.9 provides a detailed description of the functionality of each of the toolbar buttons.

Figure A.13 Database Toolbar

Table A.9 Database Toolbar Buttons with Descriptions

Icon	Name	Description
	Forward Engineer Schema Generation	This option invokes the **Forward Engineer Schema Generation** dialog to create a database schema (DDL) from a physical data model. Forward engineering is covered in more detail in Chapter 19. (Active for physical models only).
	Reverse Engineer from Script or Database	This option invokes the **Reverse Engineer** dialog wizard to generate a physical only or logical/physical model from a database or script. Reverse engineering is covered in more detail in Chapter 19.
	Complete Compare	This button opens the **Complete Compare** wizard, which allows you to compare two models and merge differences between the models. **Complete Compare** is covered in more detail in Chapter 19.
	Target Database	This option allows you to change the target DBMS for a physical data model (e.g. from MS SQL Server to DB2).
	Forward Engineer Check Model	This option validates a physical data model for valid SQL syntax. Note that this is the same action as invoking the **Actions|Forward Engineer|Check Model** option from the **Main Menu**, which is covered in more detail in Chapter 19.

Alignment Toolbar: The **Alignment Toolbar**, shown in Figure A.14, followed by a description of each icon in Table A.10, contains a number of helpful features for laying out model objects on the diagram in an organized way.

Figure A.14 Alignment Toolbar

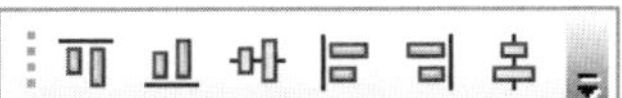

Table A.10 Alignment Toolbar Buttons with Descriptions

Icon	Name	Description
	Align Top	The **Align Top** option aligns objects along their topmost border. Alignment is based on the first item you select, i.e. all other objects will align to match the placement of this first object. In the example below, **Customer** was the first item selected, so the second item, **Product,** is moved down to align with the top of the **Customer** entity. 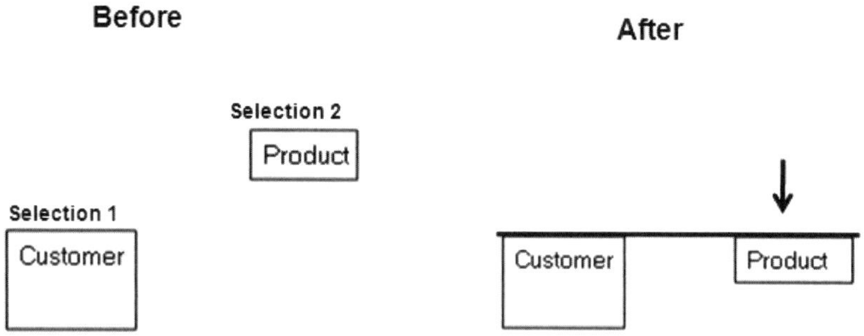 Before After Selection 2 Product Selection 1 Customer Customer Product
	Align Bottom	The **Align Bottom** option aligns objects along their bottommost border. Alignment is based on the first item you select, i.e. all other objects will align to match the placement of this first object. In the example below, **Customer** was the first item selected, so the second item, **Product,** is moved down to align with the bottom of the **Customer** entity. 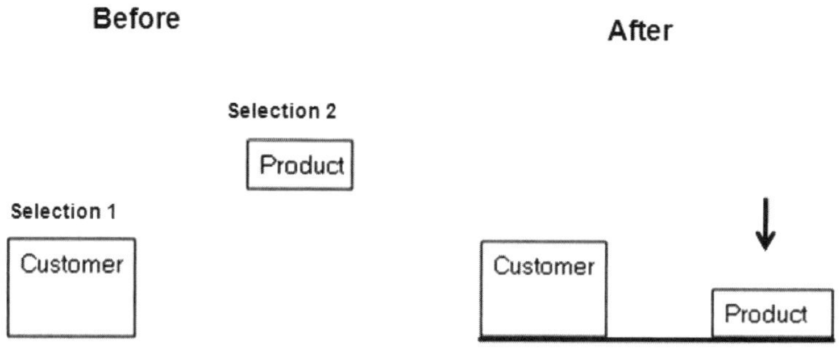 Before After Selection 2 Product Selection 1 Customer Customer Product
	Align Centers	The **Align Center** option aligns objects along their centers, using the horizontal axis. Alignment is based on the first item you select, i.e. all other objects will align to match the placement of this first object. In the example below, **Customer** was the first item selected, so the second item, **Product,** is moved down to align its horizontal center with the horizontal center of the **Customer** entity. 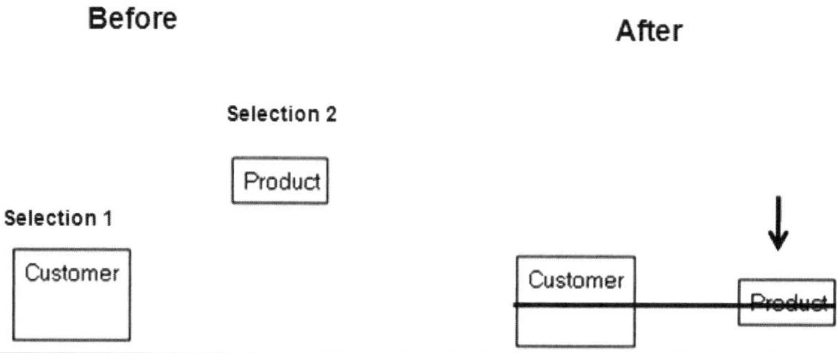 Before After Selection 2 Product Selection 1 Customer Customer Product

Icon	Name	Description
	Align Left	The **Align Left** option aligns objects along their leftmost border. Alignment is based on the first item you select, i.e. all other objects will align to match the placement of this first object. In the example below, **Customer** was the first item selected, so the second item, **Product,** is moved to the left to align its left side with the left side of the **Customer** entity.  Before After Selection 2 Product Selection 1 Customer Product Customer
	Align Right	The **Align Right** option aligns objects along their rightmost border. Alignment is based on the first item you select, i.e. all other objects will align to match the placement of this first object. In the example below, **Customer** was the first item selected, so the second item, **Product,** is moved to the left to align its right side with the right side of the **Customer** entity. 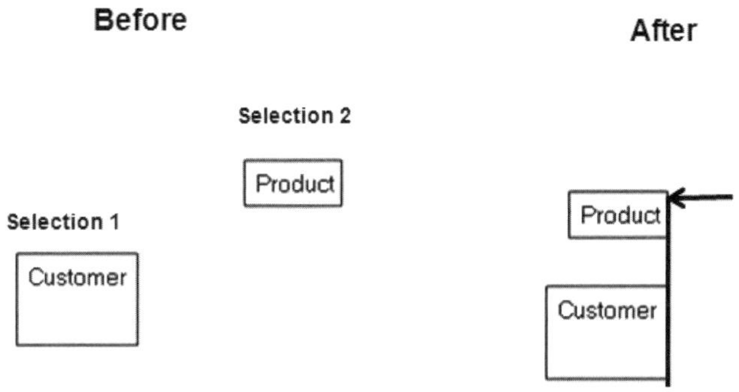 Before After Selection 2 Product Selection 1 Customer Product Customer
	Align Middle	The **Align Center** option aligns objects along their centers, using the vertical axis. Alignment is based on the first item you select, i.e. all other objects will align to match the placement of this first object. In the example below, **Customer** was the first item selected, so the second item, **Product,** is moved to the left to align its vertical center with the vertical center of the **Customer** entity.  Before After Selection 2 Product Selection 1 Customer Product Customer

Drawing Toolbar: The **Drawing Toolbar**, shown in Figure A.15, contains common drawing shapes which you can add to your diagram to add additional highlights to your model. The use of drawing shapes is covered in more detail in Chapter 8. Table A.11 provides a detailed description of the functionality of each of the toolbar buttons.

Figure A.15 Drawing Toolbar

Table A.11 Drawing Toolbar Buttons with Descriptions

Icon	Name	Description
	Rectangle	Draws a rectangle on the diagram, as shown below.
	Rounded Rectangle	Draws a rectangle with rounded corners on the diagram, as shown below.
	Ellipse	Draws an oval on the diagram, as shown below.
	Pentagon	Draws a pentagon on the diagram, as shown below.
	Hexagon	Draws a hexagon on the diagram, as shown below.
	Octagon	Draws an octagon on the diagram, as shown below.
	Triangle	Draws an upward-pointing triangle on the diagram, as shown below.

Icon	Name	Description
▽	**Down Triangle**	Draws a downward-pointing triangle on the diagram, as shown below. 
◁	**Left Triangle**	Draws a leftward-pointing triangle on the diagram, as shown below. 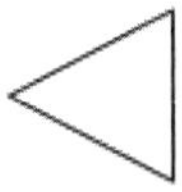
▷	**Right Triangle**	Draws a rightward-pointing triangle on the diagram, as shown below. 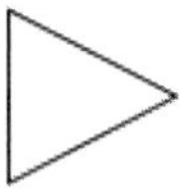
◇	**Diamond**	Draws a diamond on the diagram, as shown below. 
▱	**Parallelogram**	Draws a parallelogram on the diagram, as shown below. 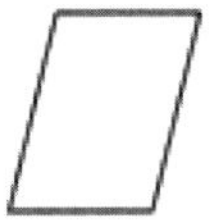
☆	**Star**	Draws a star on the diagram, as shown below. 
✚	**Cross**	Draws a cross on the diagram, as shown below. 

Icon	Name	Description
	Line	Draws a multi-bended line on the diagram, as shown below. To draw a line, select the line object from the toolbar and drag the cursor on the diagram to indicate the length of the desired line. To create a bend point, click the mouse to create a bend, drag the mouse to create another line segment, and click again to create an additional bend point. When you are finished drawing the line, double-click to complete the line drawing process.
	Connector	Draws a connector line on the diagram. Connector lines are different from drawing lines in that they link a source and target object, similar to a relationship. Unlike a drawing line, they cannot be drawn independently, but need a source and target for creation. An added benefit of using a drawing line is that they 'attach' and move in synch with their source/target objects, so that you don't need to redraw the line when you move the source/target objects. A common usage for a **Connector** is to associate an **Annotation** with a model object, as shown below. This table will be migrated to the DW. Customer customer_id customer_fname customer_lname

Transformations Toolbar: The **Transformations Toolbar**, shown in Figure A.16, contains common transformation objects for common denormalization and design layer tasks such as resolving many-to-many relationships, vertical partitions, etc. Denormalization is covered in more detail in Chapter 19. Table A.12 provides a detailed description of the functionality of each of the toolbar buttons.

Figure A.16 Transformations Toolbar

Table A.12 Transformations Toolbar Buttons with Descriptions

Icon	Name	Description
	Resolve Many-to-Many Relationship	This option automatically resolves a many-to-many relationship by creating an associative entity. Note: If you are using the Dimensional Modeling notation for your physical model, the associative table is a fact table. The example below shows a model before and after the many-to-many relationship is resolved. 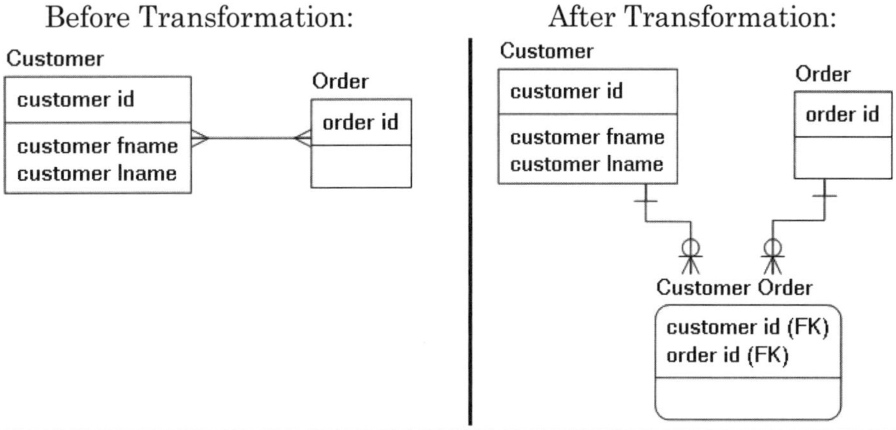 Before Transformation: Customer (customer id; customer fname, customer lname) — Order (order id) After Transformation: Customer (customer id; customer fname, customer lname); Order (order id); Customer Order (customer id (FK), order id (FK))
	Resolve to Supertype-Subtype Identity	This option resolves a supertype-subtype relationship using the identity method, where the subtyping symbol is replaced with a one-to-one relationship for each supertype/subtype combination, as shown below. 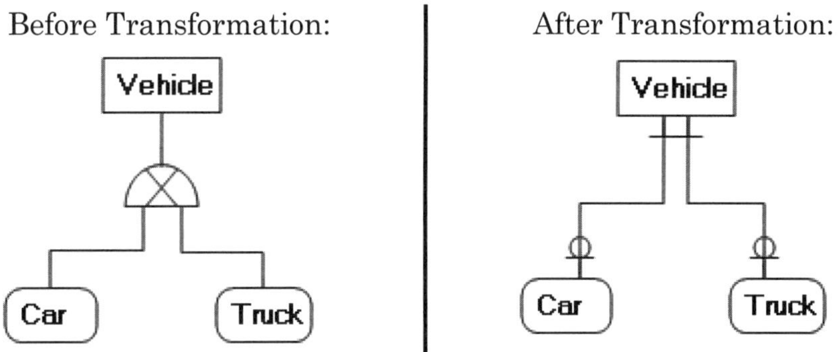 Before Transformation: Vehicle; Car; Truck After Transformation: Vehicle; Car; Truck

Icon	Name	Description
	Supertype-Subtype Rollup	This option resolves a supertype-subtype relationship using the Rolling Up method, where each subtype is 'rolled up' into the supertype, moving the data elements and relationships from each subtype up into the supertype, as shown below. Before Transformation: 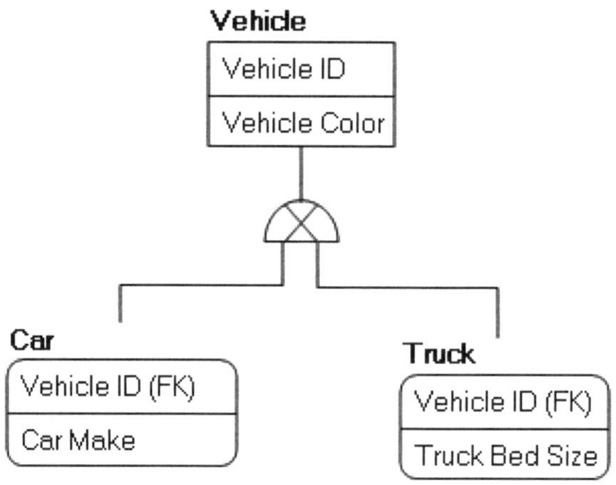 Vehicle: Vehicle ID / Vehicle Color Car: Vehicle ID (FK) / Car Make Truck: Vehicle ID (FK) / Truck Bed Size After Transformation: Vehicle: Vehicle ID / Vehicle Color, Car Make, Truck Bed Size 
	Supertype-Subtype Rolldown	This option resolves a supertype-subtype relationship using the Rolling Down method, where the supertype is 'rolled down' into each subtype, moving all of the data elements and relationships from the supertype into each subtype, then removing the supertype from the data model, as shown below. Before Transformation: 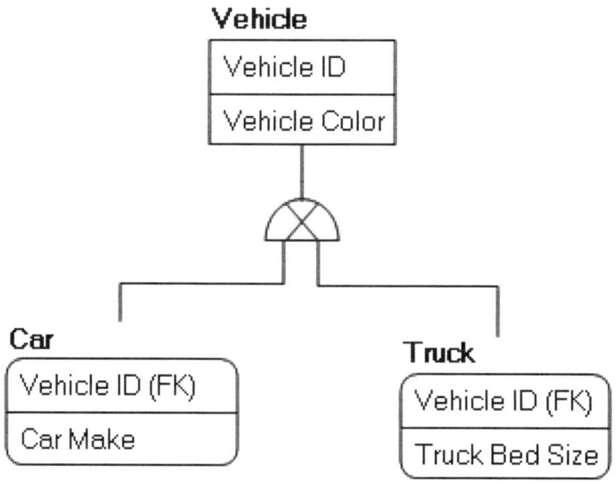 Vehicle: Vehicle ID / Vehicle Color Car: Vehicle ID (FK) / Car Make Truck: Vehicle ID (FK) / Truck Bed Size After Transformation: Car: Vehicle ID / Car Make Truck: Vehicle ID / Truck Bed Size, Vehicle Color 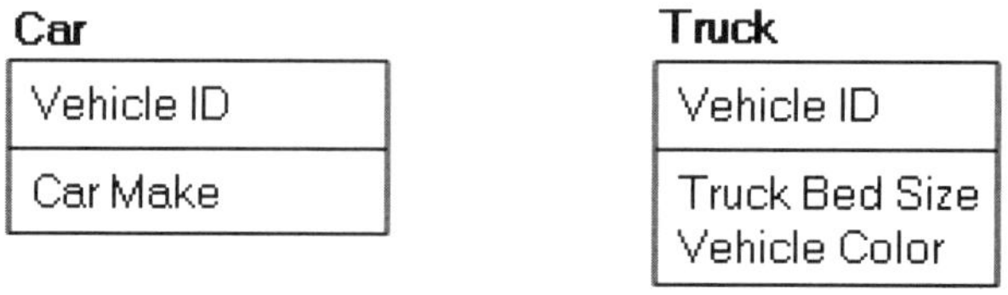

Icon	Name	Description
	Vertical Partition	This option creates a vertical partition for a table, which is the process of creating multiple tables from a single table by separating the columns (i.e. data elements) into separate tables, as shown below. 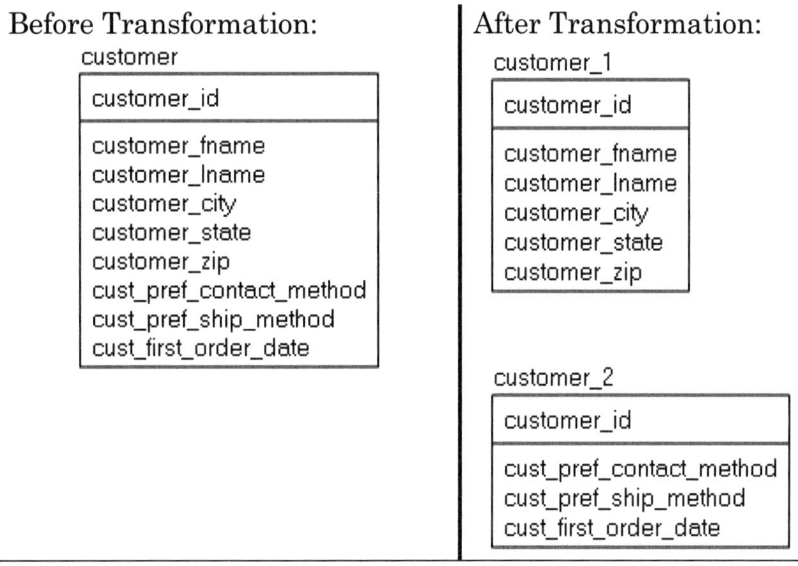 Before Transformation: customer customer_id customer_fname customer_lname customer_city customer_state customer_zip cust_pref_contact_method cust_pref_ship_method cust_first_order_date After Transformation: customer_1 customer_id customer_fname customer_lname customer_city customer_state customer_zip customer_2 customer_id cust_pref_contact_method cust_pref_ship_method cust_first_order_date
	Horizontal Partition	This option creates a horizontal partition for a table, which is the process of creating multiple tables from a single table by separating the rows (i.e. entity instances), as shown below. 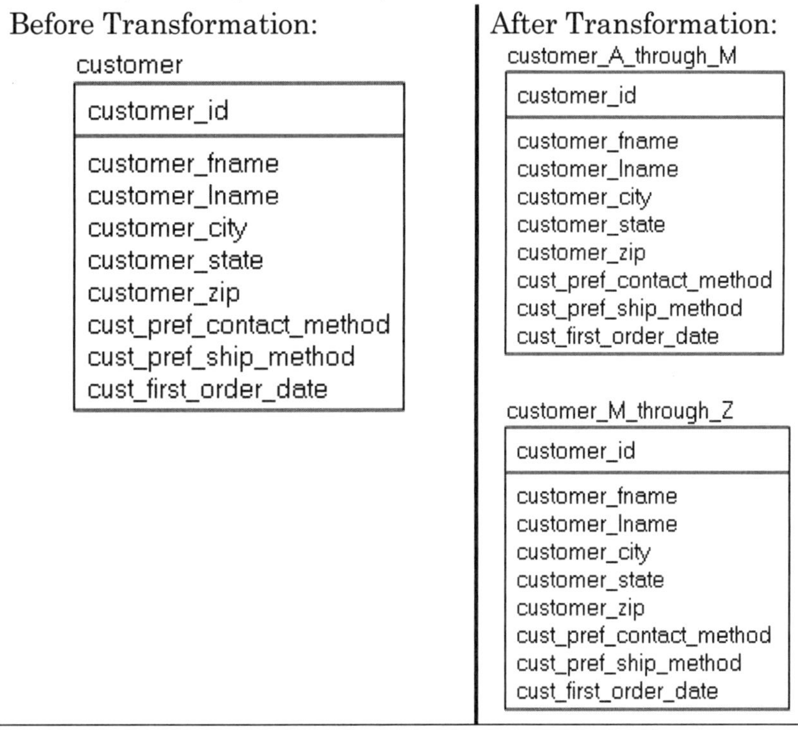 Before Transformation: customer customer_id customer_fname customer_lname customer_city customer_state customer_zip cust_pref_contact_method cust_pref_ship_method cust_first_order_date After Transformation: customer_A_through_M customer_id customer_fname customer_lname customer_city customer_state customer_zip cust_pref_contact_method cust_pref_ship_method cust_first_order_date customer_M_through_Z customer_id customer_fname customer_lname customer_city customer_state customer_zip cust_pref_contact_method cust_pref_ship_method cust_first_order_date

Icon	Name	Description
	Two Table RollDown	This option creates a rolldown denormalization of two tables, which is the process of creating a single table from two tables by combining the attributes/columns of the parent table into the child table, as shown below. Before Transformation: 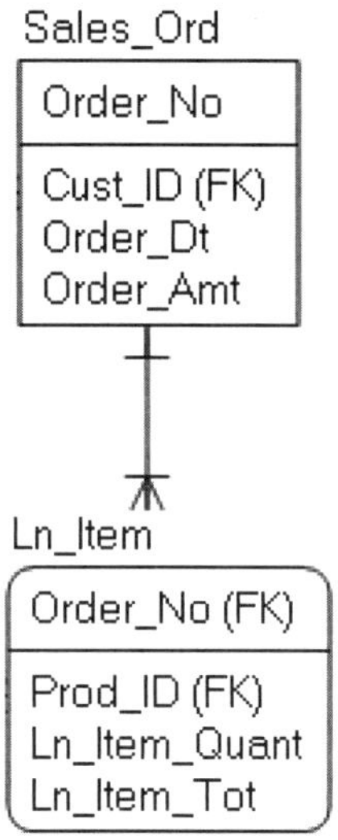 Sales_Ord: Order_No / Cust_ID (FK), Order_Dt, Order_Amt Ln_Item: Order_No (FK) / Prod_ID (FK), Ln_Item_Quant, Ln_Item_Tot After Transformation: Ln_Item: Order_No / Prod_ID (FK), Ln_Item_Quant, Ln_Item_Tot, Cust_ID (FK), Order_Dt, Order_Amt 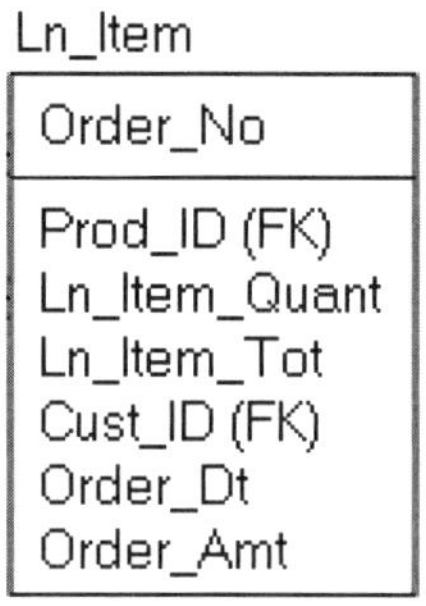

Icon	Name	Description
	Two Table RollUp	This option creates a rollup denormalization of two tables, which is the process of creating a single table from two tables by combining the attributes/columns of the child table into the parent table. In the Table Denormalization Roll Up Wizard, you will be asked to provide a number of records to be rolled-up into the parent table. For each record in the child table, a corresponding set of columns will be created in the parent table. An example is shown below. Before Transformation: Sales_Ord Order_No Cust_ID (FK) Order_Dt Order_Amt Ln_Item Order_No (FK) Prod_ID (FK) Ln_Item_Quant Ln_Item_Tot After Transformation (Number of records = 1): Sales_Ord Order_No Cust_ID (FK) Order_Dt Order_Amt Prod_ID (FK) Ln_Item_Quant Ln_Item_Tot After Transformation (Number of records = 2): Sales_Ord Order_No Cust_ID (FK) Order_Dt Order_Amt Prod_ID_1 (FK) Prod_ID_2 (FK) Ln_Item_Quant_1 Ln_Item_Quant_2 Ln_Item_Tot_1 Ln_Item_Tot_2
	Resolve All Transformations	This option automatically resolves all many-to-many and supertype/subtype relationship transformations on the model diagram.

APPENDIX B: Keyboard Navigations and Shortcuts

CA ERwin Data Modeler has a number of handy keyboard shortcuts for completing common tasks. This is especially helpful for those users who are unable to or have difficulty in using a mouse. The default key assignments are based on Windows standards, where applicable, and you can also customize your own keyboard shortcuts, which is covered in Chapter 9.

File Shortcuts

Command	Key Assignment(s)	Customizable?
New (Model)	`Ctrl + N`	Yes
Open (Model)	`Ctrl + O`	Yes
Print	`Ctrl + P`	Yes
Save	`Ctrl + S`	Yes

Edit Shortcuts

Command	Key Assignment(s)	Customizable?
Cut	`Ctrl + X` `Shift + Delete`	Yes
Copy	`Ctrl + C` `Ctrl + Insert`	Yes
Exit Edit Mode	`<Esc>` `<Ctrl> + Enter`	No
Find	`Ctrl + F`	Yes
Go To	`Ctrl + G`	Yes
Redo	`Ctrl + Y`	Yes
Rename an Object	`F2`	No
Replace	`Ctrl + H`	Yes
Select All	`CTRL + A`	No
Paste	`Ctrl + V` `Shift + Insert`	Yes
Undo	`Ctrl + Z` `Alt + Backspace`	Yes

Menu and Window Shortcuts

Command	Key Assignment(s)	Customizable?
Action Log	`CRTL + L`	No
Advisory Pane	`CRTL + D`	No
Bulk Editor	`CRTL + B`	
Model Explorer	`CRTL + E`	No
Overview Window	`CRTL + W`	No
Print Menu	`CRTL + P`	No

Object Movement and Navigation Shortcuts

Command	Key Assignment(s)	Customizable?
Move Attribute or Column between Key and Non-Key areas (i.e. above or below 'the line')	`Ctrl + Up/Down` `Ctrl + Shift + Up/Down`	No
Move Object	`Alt + Arrow Key`	No
Navigate one Page (up/down/left/right)	All Directions: `Shift + Arrow Key` Up: `Page Up` Down: `Page Down` Top Left: `Shift + End` Down to Right: `Shift + Page Down` Up to Left: `Shift + Home` Up to Right: `Shift + Page Up`	No
Navigate to Page Boundary/Rectangle Lines (up/down/left/right)	Move to Edge: `Ctrl + Arrow Key` Bottom Left of Rectangle: `Ctrl + End` Bottom Right of Rectangle: `Ctrl + Page Dn` Top Left of Rectangle: `Ctrl + Home` Top Right of Rectangle: `Ctrl + Page Up`	
Resize Object	`Alt+Shift+Arrow Key`	No

Model View Shortcuts

Command	Key Assignment(s)	Customizable?
Logical Model (Switch to)	`Ctrl + Shift + L`	Yes
Physical Model (Switch to)	`Ctrl + Shift + P`	Yes

alternate key An alternate key is a candidate key that although unique, was not chosen as the primary key, but still can be used to find specific entity instances.

architect In information technology, an experienced and skilled designer responsible for architecture supporting a broad scope of requirements over time beyond the scope of a single project. The term implies a higher level of professional experience and expertise than an analyst, designer, modeler, or developer. [20]

array An array is a repeating group that requires making the number of times something can occur static.

associative entity An entity or table that resolves a many-to-many relationship between two other related entities or tables.[20]

Basel II Basel II, published in 2002, contains recommendations on banking laws and regulations intended to create an international standard for banking regulation.

business analyst An IT or business professional responsible for understanding the business processes and the information needs of an organization, for serving as a liaison between IT and business units, and acting as a facilitator of organizational and cultural change.[20]

business intelligence A set of concepts, methods, and processes to improve business decision-making using any information from multiple sources that could affect the business, and applying experiences and assumptions to deliver accurate perspectives of business dynamics. (Brackett 2011).[20]

candidate key A candidate key is one or more data elements that uniquely identify an entity instance. Sometimes a single data element identifies an entity instance, such as ISBN for a book, or **Account Code** for an account. Sometimes it takes more than one data element to uniquely identify an entity instance. For example, both a **Promotion Code** and **Promotion Start Date** are necessary to identify a promotion.

[20] This definition is from the DAMA Dictionary of Data Management, 2nd Edition, DAMA International, Technics Publications 2011

cardinality Cardinality defines the number of instances of each entity that can participate in a relationship. It is represented by the symbols that appear on both ends of a relationship line.

CHAR A data type that contains fixed-length character data.

class word A class word is the last term in a data element name, such as Amount, Code, and Name. Class words allow for the assignment of common domains.

Conceptual data model (CDM) A conceptual data model is a set of symbols and text representing the key concepts and rules binding these key concepts for a specific business or application scope, for a particular audience, that fits neatly on one page.

CSV File CSV stands for Comma Separated Value, a common format for exchanging database information between programs. Each line in a CSV file corresponds to a row in a table. Within a line, fields are separated by commas, each field belonging to one table column.

data element A data element is a property of importance to the business whose values contribute to identifying, describing, or measuring instances of an entity.

data model A data model is a wayfinding tool for both business and IT professionals, which uses a set of symbols and text to precisely explain a subset of real information to improve communication within the organization and thereby lead to a more flexible and stable application environment.

data modeler A business systems analyst who identifies data requirements, defines data, and develops and maintains data models.*

data modeling Data modeling is the process of building a data model. More specifically, data modeling is the set of techniques and activities that enable us to capture the structure and operations of an organization, as well as the proposed information solution that will enable the organization to achieve its goals. The process requires many skills, such as listening ability, courage to ask lots of questions, and even patience.

database administrator (DBA) The IT professional role responsible for database administration, the function of managing the physical aspects of data resources, including database design and integrity, backup and recovery, performance and tuning.[20]

DDL Data Definition Language is made up of SQL commands that define the physical structures in a relational database.

denormalization Denormalization is the process of selectively violating normalization rules and reintroducing redundancy into the model (and therefore, the database). This extra redundancy can reduce data retrieval time, which is the primary reason for denormalizing. We can also denormalize to create a more user-friendly model.

dependent entity A child entity of another parent entity that cannot exist on its own and contains the parent entity key as a foreign key attribute.[20]

developer A person who designs, codes and/or tests software. Synonymous with software developer, systems developer, application developer, software engineer, and application engineer.[20]

diagram Diagrams in CA ERwin provide a way to create custom display formats for various audiences. Within each diagram, you can define display options for diagrams, entities, tables, relationships, definitions, and UDPs. Note: In previous versions of CA ERwin (r7.3 and earlier), diagrams were referred to as Stored Displays.

dimension A dimension is reference information whose purpose is to add meaning to the measures. All the different ways of filtering, sorting, and summing measures make use of dimensions. Dimensions are often, but not exclusively, hierarchies.

dimensional model A dimensional model focuses on capturing and aggregating the metrics from daily operations that enable the business to evaluate how well it is doing by manipulating the numbers. For example, examining the measure **Gross Sales Amount** at a day level and then, after getting the answer, looking at **Gross Sales Amount** at a month or year level, or at a product or brand level, or a city or country level. The dimensional model is all about playing with numbers.

domain A domain is the complete set of all possible values that a data element may be assigned. A domain is a set of validation criteria that can be applied to more than one data element.

entity An entity represents a collection of information about something that the business deems important and worthy of capture. A noun or noun phrase identifies a specific entity. It fits into one of several categories - who, what, when, where, why, or how.

entity instance Entity instances are the occurrences or values of a particular entity. Think of a spreadsheet as being an entity, with the column headings representing the pieces of information about the entity. Each spreadsheet row containing the actual values represents an entity instance.

ETL (Extract Transform Load) An approach to data integration from multiple source databases to integrated target databases (operational data stores, data warehouses or data marts).[20]

Extensible Markup Language (XML) Extensible Markup Language (XML) is a type of data model which displays information in a hierarchy format using human-readable tags, allowing both people and software applications to more easily exchange and share information.

foreign key A foreign key is a data element that provides a link to another entity. A foreign key allows a database management system to navigate from one entity to another. For example, we need to know who owns an Account, so we would want to include the identifier of the customer to whom it belongs in the entity. The Customer Id in Account is the primary key of that Customer in the Customer entity. Using this foreign key back to Customer enables the database management system to navigate from a particular account or accounts, to the customer or customers that own each account. Likewise, the database can navigate from a particular customer or customers, to find all of their accounts.

forward engineering Forward engineering is the process of moving from a high-level, logical, or implementation-independent design to the physical implementation through a process of data definition language (DDL) script generation.

HIPAA The Health Insurance Portability and Accountability Act (HIPAA) was enacted by the U.S. Congress in 1996, and requires the establishment of national standards for electronic health care transactions and national identifiers for providers, health insurance plans, and employers.

IDEF1X Notation A style of notation for **entity relationship diagrams** in **data models**, developed by Robert G. Brown in 1979 and extended by the U. S. Air Force in 1985.[20]

identifying relationship An identifying relationship is an association between two entities in which an instance of a child entity is identified through its association with a parent entity. The child entity is dependent on the parent entity for its identity and cannot exist without it.

IE (Information Engineering) Notation A systems development approach described by James Martin, integrating several best practices from the 1980s.[20]

index An index is a pointer to something that needs to be retrieved. The index points directly to the place on the disk where the data is stored, thus reducing retrieval time. Indexes work best on data elements whose values are requested frequently but rarely updated.

key There is often a need to find specific entity instances using one or more data elements. Those data element(s) that allow us to find specific entity instances are known as keys. The Library of Congress assigns an ISBN (International Standard Book Number) to every book.

logical data model (LDM) A logical data model (LDM) is a business solution to a business problem. It is how the data modeler captures the business requirements without complicating the model with implementation concerns such as software and hardware.

many-to-many relationship A many-to-many relationship is an association between two entities where instances in one entity have zero, one, or more related instances in the other entity.

materialized query table A materialized query table is a database object that contains the results of a query, and is often used for performance reasons. Materialized query tables are used in the DB2 DBMS.

materialized view A materialized view is a database object that contains the results of a query, and is often used for performance reasons. Materialized views are used in the Oracle DBMS.

measure A measure is a data element that may be manipulated in or is the result of a calculation (e.g., sum, count, average, minimum, maximum).

metadata Metadata is text, voice, or image that describes what the audience wants or needs to see or experience. The audience could be a person, group, or software program. Metadata is important because it aids in clarifying and finding the actual data. A particular context or usage can turn what we traditionally consider data into metadata. For example, search engines allow users to enter keywords to retrieve web pages. These keywords are traditionally data, but in the context of search engines they play the role of metadata.

natural key A natural key is what the business sees as the unique identifier for an entity.

non-identifying relationship A non-identifying relationship is an association between two entities where the child entity is not dependent on the parent entity for its identity and can exist without it.

normalization Normalization is the process of applying a set of rules with the goal of organizing *something*. With respect to data elements, normalization ensures that every data element is single-valued and provides a fact completely and only about its primary key. 'Single-valued' means a data element must contain only one piece of information. 'Provides a fact' means that a given primary key value will always return no more than one of every data element that is identified by this key. If a **Customer Identifier** value of '123' for example, returns three customer last names ('Smith', 'Jones', and 'Roberts'), this violates the dependency definition. 'Completely' means that the minimal set of data elements that uniquely identify an instance of the entity is present in the primary key. If, for example, there are two data elements in an entity's primary key, but only one is needed for uniqueness, the data element that is not needed for uniqueness should be removed from the primary key. 'Only' means that each data element must provide a fact about the primary key and nothing else. That is, there can be no hidden dependencies.

NULL NULL is a special element of the SQL language that is neither equal to nor unequal to any value in any data type. NULL is not zero, an empty string, or false. NULL returns UNKNOWN. Another way to view this is to consider NULL as a state, not a value, i.e. the state of having no value, similar to a Zen Koan.

ODBC Open Database Connectivity, a standard method for accessing database management systems (DBMS).

orthogonal line Orthogonal lines use right angles, and are traditional in relational data models. (Dimensional models traditionally use diagonal lines).

partition In general, a partition is a structure that divides or separates. Specific to the physical design, partitioning is used to break a table into rows, columns or both. There are two types of partitioning - vertical and horizontal. To understand the difference between these two types, visualize a physical entity in a spreadsheet format where the data elements are the columns in the spreadsheet and the entity instances are the rows. Vertical means up and down. So vertical partitioning means separating the columns (the data elements) into separate tables. Horizontal means side to side. So horizontal partitioning means separating rows (the entity instances) into separate tables.

physical data model (PDM) The physical data model (PDM) is the logical data model modified for a specific set of software or hardware. The PDM often gives up perfection for practicality, factoring in real concerns such as speed, space, and security.

primary key A primary key is a candidate key that has been chosen to be *the* unique identifier for an entity.

recursive relationship A relationship between instances of the same entity. For instance, one organization can report to another organization.*

referential integrity The assertion that the foreign key values in an instance of a child entity have corresponding values in a parent entity.

relational model A relational model captures how the business works and contains business rules, such as "A Customer must have at least one Account", or "A Product must have a **Product Short Name**."

relationship Rules are captured on our data model through relationships. A relationship is displayed as a line connecting two entities. If the two entities are Employee and Department, the relationship may capture the rules "Each Employee must work for one Department" and "Each Department may contain many Employees."

reverse engineering Reverse engineering is the process of generating a physical or logical data model by analyzing the physical structures and/or code definitions of a database, database definition script, or file.

role name A new name for a foreign key. A role name is used to indicate that the set of values of the foreign key is a subset of the set of values of the attribute in the parent, and performs a specific function (or role) in the entity.

Sarbanes-Oxley The Sarbanes–Oxley Act, passed in the U.S. in 2002, set new or enhanced governance standards for all U.S. public company boards, management, and public accounting firms.

schema The structure of a database. Usually refers to the DDL (data definition language) script file. DDL consists of CREATE TABLE, CREATE INDEX, and other statements.

slowly changing dimension (SCD) Reference entity instances will experience changes over time, such as a person moving to a new address, or product name changing, or an account description being updated. On dimensional models, there is a special term that describes how to handle changing values: Slowly Changing Dimension (SCD). An SCD of Type 1 means only the most current information will be stored. An SCD of Type 2 means the most current along with all history. And an SCD of Type 3 means the most current and some history will be stored.

snowflake A snowflake is when there are one or more tables for each dimension. Sometimes the snowflake structure is equivalent to the dimensional logical model, where each level in a dimension hierarchy exists as its own table. Sometimes in a snowflake there can be even more tables than exist on the dimensional logical model. This is because vertical partitioning is applied to the dimensional model.

spreadsheet A spreadsheet is a representation of a paper worksheet, containing a grid defined by rows and columns, where each cell in the grid can contain text or numbers.

SQL SQL stands for Structured Query Language, a database computer language designed for the retrieval and management of data in relational databases.

stakeholder A stakeholder is a person who has an interest in the successful completion of a project. Examples of stakeholders are project sponsors, business users, and team leads.

star schema A star schema is the most common dimensional physical data model structure. A star schema results when each set of tables that make up a dimension is flattened into a single table. The fact table is in the center of the model and each of the dimensions relate to the fact table at the lowest level of detail. A star schema is relatively easy to create and implement, and visually appears elegant and simplistic to both IT and the business.

subject matter expert (SME) A person with significant experience and knowledge of a given topic or function[20]

subtype A specialized subset of occurrences of a more general **entity** type, having one or more additional **attributes** or relationships not inherent to other occurrences of the entity.[20]

subtype discriminator A Subtype Discriminator is an attribute of the Supertype whose values determine the Subtype. For example, a supertype of **Employee** might have a subtype discriminator of **Employee Type** with values of 'H' for hourly and 'S' for salaried to indicate the subtypes of **Hourly Employee** and **Salaried Employee**.

surrogate key A surrogate key is a primary key that substitutes for a natural key, which is what the business sees as the unique identifier for an entity. It has no embedded intelligence and is used by IT (and not the business) for integration or performance reasons.

UDP User Defined Properties (UDPs) are custom properties created by the user to document logical and physical objects in CA ERwin Data Modeler.

UML (Unified Modeling Language)	The dominant modeling language for object-oriented analysis and design, Developed by Jacobsen, Booch, and Rumbaugh by consolidating several earlier object-oriented modeling standards.[20]
user	A person who enters information into an application or queries the application to answer business questions and produce reports.
validation rule	A validation rule helps enforce the business rules of your organization by defining a list of values, or a range of acceptable values to store in a table, column, entity, or attribute.
VARCHAR	A data type that contains variable-length character data.
view	A view is a virtual table. It is a dynamic "view" or window into one or more tables (or other views) where the actual data is stored. A view is defined by a query that specifies how to collate data from its underlying tables to form an object that looks and acts like a table but doesn't physically contain data. A query is a request that a user (or reporting tool) makes of the database, such as "Bring me back all **Customer Ids** where the Customer is 90 days or more behind in their bill payments." The difference between a qucry and a view, however, is that the instructions in a view are already prepared for the user (or reporting tool) and stored in the database as the definition of the view, whereas a query is not stored in the database and may need to be written each time a question is asked.
wayfinding	Wayfinding encompasses all of the techniques and tools used by people and animals to find their way from one site to another. If travelers navigate by the stars, for example, the stars are their wayfinding tools. Maps and compasses are also wayfinding tools. All models are wayfinding tools. A model is a set of symbols and text used to make a complex concept easier to grasp. The world around us is full of obstacles that can overwhelm our senses and make it very challenging to focus only on the relevant information needed to make intelligent decisions. A map helps a visitor navigate a city. An organization chart helps an employee understand reporting relationships. A blueprint helps an architect communicate building plans.

Index